Antique Trader®

Book
Collector's

PRICE GUIDE • 3rd Edition

W9-BOU-449

Published by

krause publications
A subsidiary of F+W Media, Inc.

700 East State Street • Iola, WI 54990-0001
715-445-2214 • 888-457-2873
www.krausebooks.com

Our toll-free number to place an order or obtain
a free catalog is (800) 258-0929.

Cover photography by Kris Kandler

Library of Congress Control Number: 2009923188

ISBN-13: 978-1-4402-0372-5
ISBN-10: 1-4402-0372-5

Books shown on the cover and what page more information on them can be found: Albert Goldman, *Ladies and Gentlemen: Lenny Bruce!!*, P. 84; A.A. Fair, *Up For Grabs*, P. 231; Blanche Grant, *Doña Lona: A Story of Old Taos and Santa Fé*, P. 24; Agatha Christie, *Sleeping Murder*, P. 226; John D. MacDonald, *The Girl in the Plain Brown Wrapper*, P. 246; Edgar Rice Burroughs, *Tarzan and the Jewels of Opar*, P. 137; William S. Burroughs, *Naked Lunch*, P. 57.

Designed by Katrina Newby
Edited by Kristine Manty

Printed in China

Antique Trader®

Book
Collector's

PRICE GUIDE • 3rd Edition

Richard Russell

DEDICATION

To Heather, Laurel and Scott

ACKNOWLEDGMENTS

The Author wishes to thank the following booksellers for their advice, knowledge and photos:

Richard Murain of Alcuin Books, Scottsdale, AZ

Melanie James of M. James, Bookseller, Hertford, NC

Barry Levin of Barry R. Levin Science Fiction and Fantasy Literature, Santa Monica, CA

Fran Durako of The Kelmscott Bookshop, Baltimore, MD

Kevin Johnson of Royal Books, Baltimore, MD

Tom Macaluso of Thomas Macaluso Rare Books in Kennett Square, PA

CONTENTS

Introduction. 6

Americana 10

Art and Illustrated Books. 32

Banned Books 56

Biographies 76

Children's Books 98

Fantasy, Horror and Science Fiction 130

Literature in Translation 162

Modern First Editions 184

Occult and Paranormal 270

Philosophy and Religion 294

Poetry and Belles Lettres. 316

Vanity and Small Press. 336

Vintage Fiction. 360

First Edition Identifier 384

    Method 1 385

    Method 2 386

    Method 3 390

    Method 4 393

    Method 5 395

    Method 6 395

    English Language Publishers Using
    Unique or Semi-Unique Methods. 396

Bookman's Glossary. 398

INTRODUCTION

When I started these books, as a guide for my daughter to go to garage sales, almost fifteen years ago, printed it at Kinko's and sold a couple thousand copies, the object of it all never really dawned on me. As I said in the introduction to the first edition of the series as it was picked up by Antique Trader, "I love to read and I hate to work." I've only understood in doing this third edition, that we, my readers and I, are deciders. Literature, as an art, is in our hands, or should I say in our collections. Who else?

The academics? Who spent half a century arguing whether the greatest novel in English was Bulwer-Lytton's *Pelham* or Disraeli's *Vivian Grey*? And I have, in my collection, the "literary" magazines where they argued it. They know how it's been done, not how it will be done; we will decide that. We will decide the "greatest novels," by collecting them.

The publishers? Who say, "You may have written the greatest book of the century. Now you need to search out a friend of ours who gets fifteen percent of everything you make and kicks back a few bucks to us?" What artist of any integrity would even agree to be published by them?

I was young in a world where literature was just beginning to take off in new and exciting directions. In America the Beats were doing new and wonderful things. In France they had a whole new form, nouveau roman. The barriers were being beaten down. Sexuality could be art. It looked like literature was ready to ride a rocket. God how it excited me. I waited for the next Claude Simon like it was the second coming. And what do our publishers hand us now? A little bat-faced girl with big breasts who is probably no better in bed than she is an actress to tell us how to make love "like a porn star." Stephen King, the century's Thomas Prest, pulp fiction in hard cover? Where is the literature? The great writers? Hell, a grocery list by F. Scott Fitzgerald or Arthur Machen would have been written better than ninety percent of what gets into hardback today. There isn't a single mystery published since 1961 that fooled me. No creativity, no art, just something as absurd as *If I Did It*, or something that makes a movie. Want to write a best seller? Write something that fools Oprah Winfrey.

The critics? With their degrees in journalism. Trained to disregard both the art of language and that of telling a story.

No, it's on us. We are the only people left who care. We need to read more, collect more, find the writers, because no one else is even looking. We need to buy some vanity press, small publications, and make them a larger part of the fourth edition of this book. Because that's the only way things will change. Shelley, Poe, they had to suck it up and pay, when literature got as bad then as it is now. And it's probably the only way you'll get something new, something without the stale lingering feeling that you read it before. Half the sci-fi authors today change the planet and the characters' names; read James D. MacDonald, if you can stomach a whole book of it.

Why not try *In a Garden of Eden* by Justin Vicari (Philadelphia: Plan B Press, 2004)? Out of print, it may cost, but it's worth it. Or *For Fuck's Sake* by Robert Lasner (Brooklyn, NY: Ig Publishing, 2002)? It's tickling $30, in first. That's the future, the only possible future, unless the future is the pablum of the major publishers and the mind candy of movies and TV.

I was born five thousand years behind in my reading. I've spent about fifty years trying to catch up. I haven't read a book by a major publisher since 1987 that I hadn't read before with different locales and characters with different names. Where are the books like *Recurrent Melody =: Passacaille: a Novel*

(Robert Pinget. London: Calder and Boyars, 1975)? A whodunit, whydunit, howdidit, ifdidit, huh? All at once, just fascinating.

I haven't fallen in love since Marguerite Duras introduced me to a lady with *Blue Eyes and Black Hair* (New York: Pantheon Books, 1987) and I fall in love so easily. Ayesha, *She* who must be obeyed (H. Rider Haggard. London: Longmans, Green, and Co., 1887), Dejah Thoris, *A Princess of Mars* (Edgar Rice Burroughs. Chicago: A. C. McClurg & Co., 1917), Renee, *La Vagabonde* (Collette. New York: Farrar, Straus and Young, 1955), *Zuleika Dobson* (Max Beerbohm. London: Wm. Heinemann, 1911), *Charmaine Lady Vibart* (Jeffrey Farnol. London: Sampson Low, Marston, 1932) are just a few of my former lovers; why isn't there someone my age, someone like Zuleika, to die for? My tastes are only for a woman created so artistically that I fall in love in spite of myself. Maybe, in my own way, I am *Cheri* (Collette. Paris: Artheme Fayard & Cie, 1920), fascinated with things older than I. Modern authors don't hold that fascination, just someone like Nora Roberts rewriting *Lady Charmaine*, badly. Romance writing has become plagiarism, or something perilously close to it. Where are the love letters like the one *O* (Pauline Reage. Paris: Olympia Press, 1954) wrote?

The point is that the only people who can change things are the people who buy this book, collectors and readers. In this edition I've tried to make it a bit easier and followed your suggestions as well as the space permits. I suppose the biggest change is the lack of detailed information on how to collect. The fact is that it doesn't fit. The first edition listings, the pseudonym dictionary, have both grown well beyond the limits of front matter. Perhaps at some time in the future I may try to make a separate book out of it all. That is if publishers want you to have the information. I rather suspect they don't. Ask one how they mark their editions. I asked a new company and was basically told, "Get outta here kid, you bother me." I suppose used books are competition,

and they'd rather not encourage that. Of course they could search out better books than the older ones, the next steps in Beat or nouveau roman, but apparently they'd rather not.

I have added the dimensions you've asked me for. I've added more points of issue, and designated them better. In a way, it's a little ironic. A point of issue is a mistake made by a publisher that identifies the first print run of a book. In point of actual fact, the collectible and valuable book is the flawed one. The better book, the corrected version, is readily available and hardly pricey. For example: F. Scott Fitzgerald's classic *The Great Gatsby* (New York: Scribners, 1925) has the following points of issue (ie: misprints) designating the most valuable First State: "chatter" p. 60 line 16, "northern" p. 119 line 22, "sick in tired" p. 205 lines 9-10, and "Union Street station" p. 211 lines 7-8. Perhaps that is why publishers are so sloppy and incompetent, we exalt their errors. In any case, I have added nearly a 1,000 such points, isn't it wonderful publishers are incompetent enough to make enough mistakes that we need to catalogue them?

Another thing you asked for was limited editions, and there are about 1,000 added. The caveat is that the ones I added are known limitations. Open-ended "limited" editions such as those of Easton and Franklin Library aren't covered and only the first editions are listed for them. Not all such limited editions are signed; however, I give you enough bibliographic data that it should be clear.

I've fielded a lot of questions about series books. This started with the first edition of the Antique Trader series, so I started collecting prices and tracking series books about five years ago. In this edition there are a tad over a hundred series, about 3,000 books. There are a few ground rules to this.

First, I left out "house name" series. Syndicates, various other writing groups and publishers have put out series that carry a single author's name, but are in actuality written by numerous authors for hire. Thus there are only isolated Carolyn Keenes or Victor Appletons. Just the Stratemeyer syndicate alone would produce several books the size I am contracted for. I have, however, included series that have several authors, such as *OZ* and *James Bond*.

Second, certain books in a series are PBO (paperback originals), if that is the case, the first edition is designated as the PBO and the first hardcover edition is also noted as the first hardcover edition, not the First Edition.

Third, the last book or two in a series may have been completed by another author, usually due to the original author's death. Also this posthumous collaborator may continue the series. In the first case the collaborator is noted as the author's name and the collaborator alphabetized by the original author. In the second case the book is alphabetized under the collaborator's name alone, without mention of the original author.

Fourth, if a significant amount of time has passed before a series is continued, the continuation will not be included unless it is by the original author. So what are basically pastiches of famous characters, such as Sherlock Holmes, Tarzan, Fu Manchu, and others are not included as a continuation of the series.

Including both Limited Editions and series books forces me to acknowledge that there are some books I cannot factually derive a price for. Every book has either a Near Fine-Fine (NF/F) price or a Good-Very Good (G/VG) price; however, I cannot, in a few cases, find enough books at retail to get a solid value. An example might be a relatively new limited edition for which all copies, or nearly all copies I can find, are Fine or Near Fine. Every price in the book is the average of a minimum of at least three books out of five currently for sale (or at least currently with my writing the book). If I cannot find enough books to make this determination, I note *Not Seen* where the price would be. My prices are derived by dropping the highest

and lowest prices I can verify and averaging the rest, with the average being a minimum of three books from which you can see I need a minimum of five books. The exceptions are the books included in the ten rarities, which are modified by auction figures and may be an average of as little as two prices.

I have added a section on Vanity Press and Small Press books. I think from dissatisfaction with major publishers and for the fact that they represent the best targets of opportunity currently available for the collector. I have grouped them together because they often crossover. Many small presses are or began as self-publishing for an author or group of authors and often the books they produce are with the financial participation of the author. Most of these books are superior to trade publications on several levels. They are much less likely to be ensemble productions as are many trade publications, edited into mush. As art they are honest expressions, not make a buck, get on Oprah shams. Unlike hack productions from major publishers, they are much more likely to be innovative and creative.

Literature, I believe, has turned the corner recently and the major trade houses can no longer be regarded as producing any of it. The major publishers have become the popular press, basically dime novels and penny dreadfuls in hardcover. Not that the popular press is bad, or not collectible, it is just not innovative, and rarely creative, though there is a certain amount of creativity in recasting old forms to a new use.

How bad is it? So bad that literature isn't even considered important to learn anymore. What is the big push in education? Math and science, math and science, like a mantra echoes through the corridors of every school in America. About all these disciplines ever created was the means to destroy a city using one bomb instead of several. Progress is made by dreamers. Even math and science, at least according to one of its major practitioners, Albert Einstein, rests on imagination. Who told man he could travel underwater, or build machines that fly, a scientist, or Francis Bacon in *The New Atlantis*, in 1626? The dream precedes the reality. After Bacon dreamed the future, it took scientists and mathematicians about three hundred years or so to catch up. Our publishers have become so bad at what they do that the dream, the starting place of all discovery, is disappearing from our society, and with it the rebellion that changes our conventions, improves society as a whole. We travel home in lines down freeways like ants to our bland, beige homes with mathematical precision, choking in the air that science has turned hazy on a planet that is gradually warming its way into oblivion. We used to have the tools to cure it. Art and literature, the starting points of the dream, the imagination that makes things better isn't even taught to our children, and the means of communicating it held captive by giant corporations who refuse to even read it.

Another factor I have looked into since the last edition is POD publishing. What should have been, if correctly handled, a reader's bonanza, cheap readable reprints of classic books and books that had run their retail course, has been turned into a massive and somewhat cruel confidence game. The unscrupulous vanity publisher finally has his dream; he has found a way to get money from writers, without even printing books. The old vanity/subsidy houses were so good that established writers used them. Look at the section on the vanity press. Evelyn Everett Green, a best selling English writer under her Cecil Adair pseudonym, used Dorrance to enter the American market, spurning the trade publishers. Similarly, Arthur W. Upfield used Dorrance to publish his first foray into the American market. Major sports figures chose Exposition or Vantage over the trade publishers, and the three largest vanity publishers carried the majority of minority and civil rights books through the fifties into the sixties. Why? Because they printed the books they were paid for. They didn't expect the author or his representative to sell blue sky to bookstores and readers. Quietly major publishers and others are buying in; Random House owns nearly half of Xlibris, Amazon owns Booksurge. All apparently, to be sure the better books don't reach the public and damage their market.

I had several talks with POD publishers, both phone and email, trying to get some sort of handle on some markings, some way to distinguish the first printings. They couldn't get rid of me fast enough. I have a few POD books that I bought. They take forever to deliver, the printing is deplorable, the design is pure amateur, and the real kicker is that the books themselves are as good or better than anything the major publishers have to offer. The concept of POD, apparently, is to keep better books off the market, by "publishing" them without printing a book. What a marvelous use of a new technology!

First Editions

Several people have asked for a shorthand version of first edition identification. Something you can memorize and use without resorting to a guidebook. While it is not the best option, and not comprehensive, there are a few rules of thumb.

The basic methods of designating a modern first edition are: a date on the title page that matches the copyright date, with no other printings listed on the verso (copyright page); the verso doesn't list any additional printings; "First Edition," "First Printing," "First Impression," "First Issue," or a variation of these appears on the title page or verso; "First Published (date)" or "Published (date)" is printed on the verso without additional printings; a colophon (Publisher's seal or logo) printed on the title page, verso or at the end of the text block; a printers code, basically a line of numbers or letters printed on the verso, showing a "1" or an A at one end or the other, with certain variations. If the book has an ISBN number, check this first.

AMERICANA

In the broadest sense, Americana is any book dealing with the United States or the area that is now the United States

It is also called Usiana, after the basic bibliography of the genre, Howes, Wright. Usiana 1750-1950. New York, R.R. Bowker, 1954, which, as a collectible itself, ranges from $70 to $100, depending on condition.

Early Americana deals with the explorations of the English, French and Spanish in the New World, and settles down to more specific works on geography, history, and culture by the eighteenth century.

The category allows for several sub genres, some of which are very well collected.

Beginning in the mid-1800s, the government began issuing books on exploration and the culture of various Indian groups.

Three prime examples are: Marcy, Randolph B. and George B. McClellan. *Exploration of the Red River of Louisiana in the Year 1952.* Washington: Beverly Tucker, Senate Printer, 1854 ($75-$200); Fremont, Captain John C. *Report of the Exploring Expedition to the Rocky Mountains in the Year 1852 and to Oregon and North California in the Years 1843-44*, House Document 166, Washington, D.C.: Gales and Seaton, 1845 ($1,000-$3,000); and Featherstonhaugh, G.W. *Report of a Geological Reconnaissance Made in 1835 From the Seat of Government, By the Way of Green Bay and the Wisconsin Territory to the Coteau De Prairie.* Washington, D.C.: Gales and Seaton, 1836 ($400-$850).

In 1879, Congress commissioned an annual report from the Bureau of American Ethnology (BAE), whose reports have become collectible.

Local history is another area. City, town, village, county and state histories ranging from the early nineteenth century to the present day. The American Guide Series, published under the Depression's Works Progress Administration's Federal Writer's project, also fits in here.

The last half of the nineteenth century saw a fascination with the American West that hasn't really dwindled away. Works on American Indians, cowboys and western personalities such as Bill Cody, Bill Hickok and the Earps, among others, remain solid sellers as new books and collectibles as used ones.

About the turn of the century, writers, photographers and artists began producing art books based on western themes. Frederic Remington and Charles Russell are two of the best known and were followed by the quintessential cowboy, Will James. This led to the 20th century development of small presses specializing in Americana, such as Arthur H. Clarke, Grabhorn and Caxton.

The Civil War has fostered an entire field of collectible and important books. In terms of sheer volume, it may be the single-largest category within the area of Americana.

From regimental histories to the photographs of early photographers such as Matthew Brady, the war between the states seems to hold an endless fascination for the book collector.

TEN CLASSIC RARITIES

Dobie, J. Frank. *Mustangs.*
Boston: Little, Brown, 1952. Bound in
cowhide and issued in a slipcase.
NF/F: $1,600   **G/VG: $500**

James, Will. *American Cowboy.*
New York: NY: Charles Scribner's
Sons, 1942. Profit by fulfilling a
childhood fancy.
NF/F: $1,250   **G/VG: $700**

**King, Jeff and Joseph Campbell
and Maud Oakes.** *Where the Two
Came To Their Father; A Navajo War
Ceremonial.*
New York; Pantheon, 1943. A
pamphlet in wraps.
NF/F: $3,200   **G/VG: $1,000**

Lea, Tom. *The Hands of Cantu.*
Boston; Little, Brown and Company,
1964. Limited Edition.
NF/F: $2,100   **G/VG: $700**

Remington, Frederic. *Done in the
Open.*
New York: R. H. Russell, Publisher,
1902. Signed, limited edition; with
an introduction and verses by Owen
Wister.
NF/F: $2,400   **G/VG: $750**

Roosevelt, Theodore. *The Rough
Riders.*
Charles Scribner's Sons, New York,
1899. The first edition is illustrated by
Frederic Remington and Charles Dana
Gibson. Be careful of "signed" editions
as it contains a facsimile signature.
NF/F: $1,200   **G/VG: $750**

Russell, Charles M, *Good Medicine.*
Garden City, NY: Doubleday, Doran
& Co., 1929. Limited Edition of 134
copies introduction by Will Rogers.
NF/F: $6,500   **G/VG: $1,650**

Schreyvogel, Charles. *My Bunkie
and Others. Pictures of Western
Frontier Life.*
New York: Moffat, Yard & Co., 1909.
Issued with a slipcase.
NF/F: $2,800   **G/VG: $800**

Siringo, Charles. *A Texas Cow Boy
or, Fifteen Years on the Hurricane
Deck of a Spanish Pony.*
Chicago: Rand McNally, 1886.
NF/F: $1,900   **G/VG: $1,000**

Wheat, Carl I. *The Maps of the
California Gold Region, 1848-1857.*
A Biblio-cartography of an Important
Decade. San Francisco: Grabhorn
Press, 1942.
NF/F: $2,000   **G/VG: $1,000**

J. Frank Dobie.

Theodore Roosevelt.

PRICE GUIDE

Andy Adams.

Ramon F. Adams.

SIX-GUNS
& SADDLE
LEATHER

A BIBLIOGRAPHY
of Books and Pamphlets on Western
Outlaws and Gunmen

RAMON F. ADAMS

Ramon F. Adams.

Abbott, Carl. *The Great Extravaganza; Portland and the Lewis and Clark Exposition.* First Edition: Portland, OR: Oregon Historical Society. 1981.
NF/F: $40   **G/VG: $18**

Adams, Andy. *Texas Matchmaker.* First Edition: Boston: Houghton, Mifflin, 1904.
NF/F: $185   **G/VG: $85**

_____. *Log of a Cowboy.* First Edition: Boston, Houghton, Mifflin, 1903.
NF/F: $375   **G/VG: $150**

_____. *The Outlet.* First Edition: Boston: Houghton, Mifflin and Company, 1905.
NF/F: $250   **G/VG: $100**

Adams, Ramon F. *Come an' Get It.* First Edition: Norman, OK: University of Oklahoma Press, 1952.
NF/F: $85   **G/VG: $25**

_____. *The Old Time Cowhand.* Limited Edition: New York: Macmillan, 1961 (350 copies).
NF/F: $300   **G/VG: Not Seen**
First Edition: New York: Macmillan, 1961.
NF/F: $195   **G/VG: $80**

_____. *The Rampaging Herd.* First Edition: Norman, OK: University of Oklahoma Press, 1959.
NF/F: $250   **G/VG: $100**

_____. *Six-Guns & Saddle Leather.* First Edition: Norman, OK: University of Oklahoma Press, 1959.
NF/F: $225   **G/VG: $100**

Aken, David. *Pioneers of the Black Hills.* First Edition: Milwaukee: Allied Printing, 1911.
NF/F: $350   **G/VG: $145**
Reprint: Milwaukee: Allied Printing, 1920.
NF/F: $125   **G/VG: $75**

Alexander, E. P. *Military Memoirs of a Confederate.* First Edition: New York: Charles Scribners, 1907. Points of Issue: Black cloth lettered in gilt in first issue.
NF/F: $350   **G/VG: $145**

Alexander, Hartley Burr. *The World's Rim: Great Mysteries of the North American Indians.* First Edition: Lincoln, NE: University of Nebraska Press, 1953.
NF/F: $65   **G/VG: $15**

_____. *The Mystery Of Life A Poetization of "The Hako" A Pawnee Ceremony.* First Edition: Chicago: Open Court Publishing, 1913
NF/F: $100   **G/VG: $35**

Allen, William A. *Adventures with Indians and Game or Twenty Years in the Rocky Mountains.* First Edition: Chicago: A. W. Bowen & Co. 1903.
NF/F: $550   **G/VG: $150**

Alter, J. Cecil. *Jim Bridger.* First Edition: Salt Lake City: Shepard Book Co. 1925.
NF/F: $85   **G/VG: $25**

_____. *Through the Heart of the Scenic West.* First Edition: Salt Lake City: Shepard Book Co. 1927.
NF/F: $150   **G/VG: $35**

Alvord, Clarence Walworth and Lee Bidgood. *The First Explorations of the Trans-Allegheny Region by the Virginians, 1650-1674.* First Edition: Cleveland, Arthur H. Clark Company, 1912.
NF/F: $425   **G/VG: $100**

Alvord, Clarence Walworth. *Kaskaskia Records, 1778-1790.* First Edition: Springfield, IL: Illinois State Historical Library, 1909.
NF/F: $125   **G/VG: $40**

Amsden, Charles. *Navaho Weaving.*
First Edition: Santa Ana, CA: Fine Arts
Press, 1934.
NF/F: $700   **G/VG: $175**

Andrews, Matthew Page. *Social
Planning By Frontier Thinkers.*
First Edition: New York: Richard R.
Smith, 1944.
NF/F: $35   **G/VG: $15**

Andrist, Ralph K. *The Long Death.*
First Edition: New York: Macmillian, 1964.
NF/F: $65   **G/VG: $25**

_____. *The American Heritage History
Of The Making Of The Nation, 1783-1860.*
First Edition: New York: American
Heritage Publishing Co., 1968.
NF/F: $35   **G/VG: $10**

Anthony, Irvin. *Down to the Sea in Ships.*
First Edition: Philadelphia: The Penn
Publishing Co., 1924.
Points of Issue: First Issue in black cloth
with gilt letters and decoration, blue and
white decoration.
NF/F: $125   **G/VG: $25**

_____. *Paddle Wheels and Pistols.*
First Edition: Philadelphia: Macrae
Smith Co., 1929.
NF/F: $150   **G/VG: $45**

Applegate, Frank G. *Indian Tales
from the Pueblos.*
First Edition: Philadelphia: J. B.
Lippincott, 1929.
NF/F: $150   **G/VG: $45**
Reprint as: *Indian Stories from the Pueblos.*
Points of Issue: Issued without a dust jacket.
First Edition: Glorieta, NM: Rio Grande
Press, 1971.
NF/F: $35   **G/VG: $15**

_____. *Native Tales from New
Mexico.*
First Edition: Philadelphia: J. B.
Lippincott, 1932.
NF/F: $125   **G/VG: $45**

Arbor, Marilyn. *Tools & Trades of
America's Past - the Mercer Collection.*
First Edition: Doylestown, PA: Bucks
County Historical Society, 1981.
NF/F: $50   **G/VG: $15**

Arnold, R. Ross. *Indian Wars of
Idaho.*
First Edition: Caldwell, Idaho Caxton
Printers, Ltd., 1932.
NF/F: $900   **G/VG: $400**

Arthur, John Preston. *Western North
Carolina.*
First Edition: Raleigh, N.C.: The
Edward Buncombe Chapter of the
Daughters of the American Revolution,
of Asheville, N.C., 1914.
NF/F: $275   **G/VG: $75**

Arthurs, Stanley. *The American
Historical Scene.*
Limited Edition: Philadelphia: University
of Pennsylvania Press, 1935 (100
copies). Points of Issue: Contains an
original water color by Stanley Arthurs.
NF/F: $1,250   **G/VG: Not Seen**
First Edition: Philadelphia: University
of Pennsylvania Press, 1935.
NF/F: $65   **G/VG: $25**

Asbury, Herbert. *The Barbary Coast.*
First Edition: New York: Alfred A
Knopf, 1933.
NF/F: $85   **G/VG: $20**

_____. *The French Quarter.*
First Edition: New York: Alfred A.
Knopf, 1936.
NF/F: $95   **G/VG: $35**

_____. *The Gangs of New York.*
First Edition: New York: Alfred A.
Knopf, 1928.
NF/F: $525   **G/VG: $275**

_____. *The Great Illusion.*
First Edition: Garden City, NY:
Doubleday, 1950.
NF/F: $85   **G/VG: $30**

Charles Amsden.

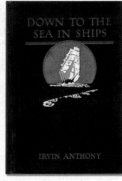
Irvin Anthony.

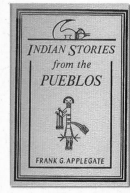
Frank G. Applegate.

Herbert Asbury.

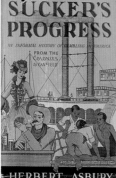

Robert G. Athearn.

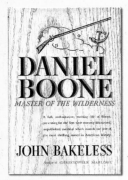

John Bakeless.

_____. *Sucker's Progress: An Informal History Of Gambling In America From The Colonies To Canfield.*
First Edition: New York: Dodd, Mead & Co., 1938.
NF/F: $375   **G/VG: $80**

Ashley, Clifford W. *The Yankee Whaler.*
First Edition: Boston: Houghton Mifflin, 1926.
NF/F: $200   **G/VG: $85**
Limited Edition: Boston: Houghton Mifflin, 1926 (1,625 copies).
NF/F: $800   **G/VG: $375**
Limited Edition: London: Martin Hopkinson and Co., 1926 (1,625 copies).
NF/F: $1000   **G/VG: Not Seen**

Athearn, Robert G. *Forts of the Upper Missouri.*
First Edition: Englewood Cliffs, NJ: Prentice Hall, 1967.
NF/F: $85   **G/VG: $25**

_____. *Rebel of the Rockies.*
First Edition: New Haven and London: Yale University Press, 1962.
NF/F: $80   **G/VG: $25**

_____. *William Tecumseh Sherman and the Settlement of the West.*
First Edition: Norman, OK: University of Oklahoma Press, 1956.
NF/F: $150   **G/VG: $45**

Atherton, Gertrude. *California: an Intimate History.*
First Edition: New York: Harper & Brothers, 1914. Points of Issue: First issue is red cloth lettered in gilt.
NF/F: $125   **G/VG: $25**

Ayers, James J. *Gold and Sunshine.*
First Edition: Boston: Richard G. Badger/Gorham Press, 1922.
NF/F: $125   **G/VG: $55**

Bakeless, John. *Daniel Boone.*
First Edition: New York: William Morrow, 1939.
NF/F: $110   **G/VG: $25**

_____. *The Eyes of Discovery.*
First Edition: Philadelphia: J. B. Lippincott, 1950.
NF/F: $60   **G/VG: $25**

_____. *Lewis & Clark.*
First Edition: William Morrow & Company, 1947.
NF/F: $75   **G/VG: $30**

_____. *Spies of the Confederacy.*
First Edition: Philadelphia J.B. Lippincott Co., 1970.
NF/F: $75   **G/VG: $25**

Baker, Hozial. *Overland Journey to Carson Valley, Utah.*
First Edition: San Francisco: The Book Club of California, 1973.
NF/F: $85   **G/VG: $30**

Ballantine, Betty. *The Art of Charles Wysocki.*
First Edition: New York: Greenwick Press/Workman Publishing, 1985.
NF/F: $70   **G/VG: $25**

Bancroft, Hubert Howe. *The Native Races Of The Pacific States (Five Volumes).*
First Edition: New York: D. Appleton And Company, 1875-1886.
NF/F: $625   **G/VG: $200**

_____. *Popular Tribunals (Two Volumes).*
First Edition: San Francisco: The History Company, 1887.
NF/F: $150   **G/VG: $40**

_____. *History of the Northwest Coast (Two Volumes).*
First Edition: San Francisco: A.L. Bancroft & Company, 1884.
NF/F: $275   **G/VG: $125**

Bandelier, Adolf F. *The Delight Makers.*
First Edition: New York: Dodd, Mead and Co., 1890.
NF/F: $135   **G/VG: $45**

Bandini, Joseph and Giorda, Joseph. *Smiimii Lu Tel Kaimintis Kolinzuten; Narrative from the Holy Scripture in Kalispell.*
First Edition: Montana: St. Ignatius Print, 1876.
NF/F: $675   **G/VG: $200**

_____. *A Dictionary of the Kalispel Or Flat-Head Indian Language, Compiled By the Missionaries of the Society of Jesus.* Part I: Kalispel-English. Part II: English-Kalispel.
First Edition: Montana: St. Ignatius Print, 1877-89.
NF/F: $2650   **G/VG: $1,200**

Banta, R.E. *The Ohio.*
First Edition: New York: Rinehart and Company, 1949.
NF/F: $100   **G/VG: $40**

_____. *Indiana Authors and Their Books 1816-1916.*
First Edition: Crawfordsville, Indiana: Wabash College, 1949.
NF/F: $165   **G/VG: $25**

Barnard, Evan G. *A Rider on the Cherokee Strip.*
First Edition: Boston: Houghton Mifflin, 1936.
NF/F: $120   **G/VG: $55**

Barnes, Will C. *Apaches and Longhorns.*
First Edition: Los Angeles Ward Ritchie Press, 1941.
NF/F: $165   **G/VG: $55**

_____. *Tales from the Bar X Horse Camp.*
First Edition: Chicago: Breeders' Gazette, 1920.
NF/F: $300   **G/VG: $130**

_____ **and William MacLeod Raine.** *Cattle.*
First Edition: New York: Doubleday Doran Co, 1930.
NF/F: $200   **G/VG: $65**

Barney, James. *Tales of Apache Warfare.*
First Edition: Phoenix, AZ: James Barney, 1933. Points of Issue: printed wraps.
NF/F: $300   **G/VG: $175**

_____. *A Historical Sketch of the Volunteer Fire Department of Phoenix, Arizona.*
First Edition: Phoenix, AZ: Phoenix Volunteer Fireman's Association, 1954.
NF/F: $20   **G/VG: $6**

Barry, Ada Loomis. *Yunini's Story of the Trail of Tears.*
First Edition: London: Fudge & Co., 1932.
NF/F: $300   **G/VG: $65**

Bates, Finis L. *Escape and Suicide of John Wilkes Booth.*
First Edition: Memphis, TN: Pilcher Printing Company, 1907.
NF/F: $225   **G/VG: $55**

Beard, Dan. *Hardly a Man is Now Alive.*
First Edition: Garden City, NY: Doubleday, Doran, 1939.
NF/F: $75   **G/VG: $35**

Beard, Dan. *Dan Beard's Animal Book and Camp-Fire Stories.*
First Edition: Chicago: Donohue, 1920.
NF/F: $200   **G/VG: $85**

Bechdolt, Frederick. *Giants of the Old West.*
First Edition: New York Century Co., 1930.
NF/F: $65   **G/VG: $25**

_____. *Tales of the Old Timers.*
First Edition: New York: The Century Co., 1924.
Points of Issue: Frontispiece by Frederic Remington.
NF/F: $75   **G/VG: $30**

_____. *Horse Thief Trail.*
First Edition: Garden City, NY: Doubleday, 1932.
NF/F: $100   **G/VG: $45**

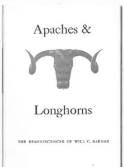

Will C. Barnes.

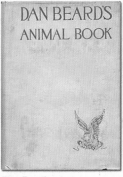

Dan Beard.

Frederick Bechdolt.

Henry C. Beck.

Lucius Beebe.

Carl P. Benedict.

Beck, Henry Charlton. *The Roads of Home - Lanes and Legends of New Jersey.* First Edition: New Brunswick, NJ: Rutgers Univ. Press, 1956 .

NF/F: $35   G/VG: $10

_____. *Jersey Genesis: The Story of the Mullica River.* First Edition: New Brunswick, NJ: Rutgers Univ. Press, 1945.

NF/F: $50   G/VG: $15

_____. *Forgotten Towns Of Southern New Jersey.* First Edition: New York: E. P. Dutton, 1936.

NF/F: $50   G/VG: $15

Beebe, Lucius. *The American West.* First Edition: New York: E.P. Dutton & Co., 1955.

NF/F: $85   G/VG: $20

_____. *Mr. Pullman's Palace Car.* First Edition: Garden City Doubleday & Co., 1961.

NF/F: $125   G/VG: $50

_____. *Mansions on Wheels.* First Edition: Berkeley: Howell-North, 1959.

NF/F: $200   G/VG: $85

_____ **and Charles Clegg.** *U.S. West: The Saga of Wells Fargo.* First Edition: New York: E. P. Dutton, 1949.

NF/F: $75   G/VG: $25

_____ **and Charles Clegg.** *Rio Grande; Mainline of the Rockies.* Limited Edition: Berkeley, CA: Howell-North, 1962 (1,250 copies).

NF/F: $75   G/VG: $25

Bell, Horace. *On the Old West Coast.* First Edition: New York, William Morrow, 1930 (limited 210 copies).

NF/F: $200   G/VG: $100

_____. *Reminiscences of a Ranger.* First Edition: Los Angeles: Yarness, Caystile & Mathes, 1881.

NF/F: $750   G/VG: $225

Benedict, Carl P. *A Tenderfoot Kid on Gyp Water.* Limited Edition: Austin, Texas: Texas Folklore Society, 1943 (550 copies).

NF/F: $450   G/VG: $200

Bennett, Estelline. *Old Deadwood Days.* First Edition: New York J.H. Sears & Co., 1928.

NF/F: $125   G/VG: $35

Bennett, George. *Early Architecture of Delaware.* First Edition: Wilmington, DE: Historical Press, 1932.

NF/F: $200   G/VG: $65

Benton, Frank. *Cowboy Life on the Side Track.* First Edition: Denver, Colorado: Western Stories Syndicate, 1903.

NF/F: $200   G/VG: $85

Berry, Don. *Majority of Scoundrels.* First Edition: New York: Harper & Brothers, 1961.

NF/F: $135   G/VG: $60

Bixby-Smith, Sarah. *Adobe Days.* First Edition: Cedar Rapids, IA: The Torch Press, 1925.

NF/F: $95   G/VG: $30

_____. *My Sagebrush Garden.* First Edition: Cedar Rapids, IA: The Torch Press, 1924.

NF/F: $55   G/VG: $20

Black, Glenn. *Angel Site.* First Edition: Indianapolis: Indiana Historical Society, 1967.

NF/F: $90   G/VG: $30

Blackford, W.W. *War Years with Jeb Stuart.* First Edition: New York: Charles Scribner's, 1945.

NF/F: $85   G/VG: $35

Boas, Franz. *Handbook of American Indian Languages (Two Volumes).*
First Edition: Washington DC: Smithsonian, 1911 & 1922.
NF/F: $300   G/VG: $125

Boatright, Mody. *Backwoods to Border.*
First Edition: Austin, TX: Texas Folklore Society, 1943.
NF/F: $50   G/VG: $20

_____. *From Hell to Breakfast.*
First Edition: Austin, TX: Texas Folklore Society, 1944.
NF/F: $75   G/VG: $30

_____. *Coyote Wisdom.*
First Edition: Austin, TX: Texas Folklore Society, 1938.
NF/F: $95   G/VG: $35

_____. *Tall Tales from Texas Cow Camps.*
First Edition: Dallas, TX: The Southwest Press, 1934.
NF/F: $275   G/VG: $85

_____ . *Folk Laughter on the American Frantier.*
First Edition: New York: Macmillan, 1949.
NF/F: $125   G/VG: $45

Bolton, Herbert Eugene. *Fray Juan Crespi - Missionary Explorer on the Pacific Coast 1769-1774.*
First Edition: Berkeley, CA: University of California, 1927.
NF/F: $275   G/VG: $125

_____. *Rim of Christendom.*
First Edition: New York: Macmillan, 1936.
NF/F: $150   G/VG: $45

Bolton, Reginald Pelham. *Indian Life of Long Ago in the City of New York.*
First Edition: New York: Joseph Graham Boltons Books, 1934.
NF/F: $125   G/VG: $45

Bordeux, William. *Custer's Conqueror.*
First Edition: np: Smith & Company, Publishers, 1952.
NF/F: $550   G/VG: $300

_____. *Conquering the Sioux.*
First Edition: Sioux Falls, SD: William J. Bordeaux, 1929.
NF/F: $250   G/VG: $100

Bowman, Elizabeth Skaggs. *Land of High Horizons.*
First Edition: Kingsport, TN: Southern Publishers, 1951.
NF/F: $75   G/VG: $35

Bowman, Isiah. *The Pioneer Fringe.*
First Edition: New York: American Geographical Society, 1931.
NF/F: $45   G/VG: $20

Brown, Dee. *Bury My Heart at Wounded Knee.*
First Edition: New York: Holt, Rinehart & Winston, 1970.
NF/F: $225   G/VG: $45

_____. *Wave High the Banner.*
First Edition: Philadelphia: Macrae Smith, 1942.
NF/F: $125   G/VG: $55

_____ **and Martin F. Schmitt.** *Trail Driving Days.*
First Edition: New York: Scribner's, 1952.
NF/F: $100   G/VG: $30

Brown, Mark. *Before Barbed Wire.*
First Edition: New York Henry Holt & Co., 1956.
NF/F: $175   G/VG: $55

Bryant, Billy. *Children of Ol' Man River.*
First Edition: New York: Lee Furman, Inc., 1936.
NF/F: $75   G/VG: $20

Burman, Ben Lucian. *Children Of Noah.*
First Edition: New York: Julian Messner, 1951.
NF/F: $25   G/VG: $10

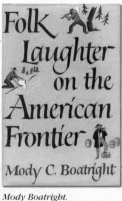

Mody Boatright.

Dee Brown.

Dee Brown.

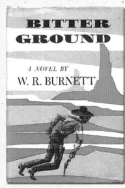

W. R. Burnett.

Bruce Catton.

Burman, Ben Lucian

_____. *It's a Big Country: America Off the Highways.*
First Edition: New York: Reynal and Co., 1956.
NF/F: $20   **G/VG: $8**

Burnett, W. R. *Adobe Walls.*
First Edition: New York: Alfred A. Knopf, 1953.
NF/F: $175   **G/VG: $55**

_____. *Bitter Ground.*
First Edition: New York: Alfred A. Knopf, 1957.
NF/F: $275   **G/VG: $45**

Burns, Walter Noble. *The Saga of Billy the Kid.*
First Edition: Garden City, NY: Doubleday, Page & Co., 1926.
NF/F: $100   **G/VG: $30**

_____. *Tombstone An Iliad of the Southwest.*
First Edition: Garden City, NY: Doubleday, Page & Co., 1926.
NF/F: $85   **G/VG: $35**

Carey, A Merwyn. *American Firearms Makers.*
First Edition: New York: Thomas Y. Crowell, 1953.
NF/F: $75   **G/VG: $30**

Carr, John. *Pioneer Days in California.* Historical and Personal Sketches.
First Edition: Eureka, CA: Times Publishing Company, 1891.
NF/F: $425   **G/VG: $95**

Carroll, H. Bailey. *The Texas Santa Fe Trail.*
First Edition: Canyon, TX: Panhandle-Plains Historical Society, 1951.
NF/F: $125   **G/VG: $55**

Carson, James H. *Recollections Of The California Mines.*
Limited Edition: Oakland, CA: Biobooks, 1950 (750 copies).
NF/F: $100   **G/VG: $55**

Carter, Captain Robert G. *The Old Sergeant's Story.*
First Edition: New York: Frederick H. Hitchcock, 1926.
NF/F: $650   **G/VG: $225**

Cartland, Fernando G. *Southern Heroes or the Friends in War Time.*
First Ed: Boston: Riverside Press, 1895.
NF/F: $125   **G/VG: $60**

Casler, John O. *Four Years In The Stonewall Brigade.*
First Edition: Guthrie, Oklahoma: State Capital Printing Company, 1893.
NF/F: $800   **G/VG: $225**

Castaneda, Carlos E. *Our Catholic Heritage in Texas.*
First Edition: Austin, TX: The Knights of Columbus of Texas, 1936 (seven volume set).
NF/F: $1,500   **G/VG: $700**

_____. *The Mexican Side of the Texas Revolution.*
First Edition: Dallas: P.L. Turner, 1928.
NF/F: $500   **G/VG: $175**

Catton, Bruce. Civil War Series:

_____. *Mr. Lincoln's Army.*
First Edition: Garden City, NY: Doubleday & Company, 1951.
N.Fine/Fine, $125   **G/VG: $45**

_____. *Glory Road.*
First Edition: Garden City, NY: Doubleday & Company, 1952.
NF/F: $65   **G/VG: $25**

_____. *A Stillness at Appomattox.*
First Edition: Garden City, NY: Doubleday & Company, 1953.
NF/F: $95   **G/VG: $35**

_____. *The Coming Fury.*
First Edition: Garden City, NY: Doubleday & Company, 1961.
NF/F: $115   **G/VG: $35**

_____. *Terrible Swift Sword.*
First Edition: Garden City, NY:
Doubleday & Company, 1963.
NF/F: $100   **G/VG: $30**

_____. *Never Call Retreat.*
First Edition: Garden City, NY:
Doubleday & Company, 1965.
NF/F: $95   **G/VG: $25**

_____. *Grant Takes Command.*
First Edition: Boston: Little, Brown &
Co., 1968.
NF/F: $75   **G/VG: $20**

_____. *Grant Moves South.*
First Edition: Boston: Little, Brown &
Co., 1960.
NF/F: $95   **G/VG: $30**

Chabot, Frederick C. *The Alamo :
Mission Fortress and Shrine.*
First Edition: San Antonio, TX: The
Leake Press, 1935.
NF/F: $40   **G/VG: $25**

_____. *The Alamo, Altar of
Texas Liberty.*
First Edition: San Antonio, TX: Naylor, 1935.
NF/F: $175   **G/VG: $95**

Chapman, Arthur. *The Pony Express.*
First Edition: New York: G.P. Putnams, 1932.
NF/F: $125   **G/VG: $40**

_____. *The Route of the Rio
Grande.*
First Edition: Denver: Denver and Rio
Grande, 1926.
NF/F: $125   **G/VG: $40**

Claiborne, John Herbert. *Seventy
Five Years in Old Virginia.*
First Edition: New York and
Washington: Neale Pub. Co., 1904.
NF/F: $225   **G/VG: $85**

Clark, Thomas D. *The Kentucky.*
First Edition: New York: Farrar &
Rinehart Inc., 1942.
NF/F: $95   **G/VG: $35**

_____. *Pills, Petticoats & Plows.*
First Edition: Indianapolis: The Bobbs-
Merrill Company, 1944.
NF/F: $40   **G/VG: $15**

Clark, W. P. *The Indian Sign
Language.*
First Edition: Philadelphia: L. R.
Hamersly, 1885.
NF/F: $350   **G/VG: $150**

Clay, John. *My Life on the Range.*
First Edition: Chicago: privately
printed, 1924.
NF/F: $650   **G/VG: $200**

Cleland, Robert Glass. *This Reckless
Breed of Men.*
First Edition: New York: Alfred A.
Knopf, 1950.
NF/F: $85   **G/VG: $35**

Clum, Woodworth. *Apache Agent.*
First Edition: Boston Houghton Mifflin,
1936.
NF/F: $345   **G/VG: $75**

Coates, Harold Wilson. *Stories of
Kentucky Feuds.* (Five volumes.)
First Edition: Knoxville, Holmes-Darst
Coal Corporation, 1942.
NF/F: $125   **G/VG: $25**

Coates, Robert M. *The Outlaw Years.*
First Edition: New York: The Macaulay
Company, 1930.
NF/F: $300   **G/VG: $125**

Cody, William F. *Story of the Wild
West and Camp-fire Chats.*
First Edition: Philadelphia: Historical
Publishing Company, 1888.
NF/F: $250   **G/VG: $100**

Arthur Chapman.

Arthur Chapman.

John Herbert Claiborne.

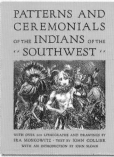

John Collier.

William E. Connelley &
Frank W. Root.

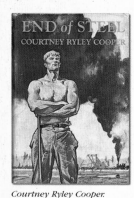

Courtney Ryley Cooper.

Cohn, David. *New Orleans and Its Living Past.*
First Edition: Boston: Houghton Mifflin, 1941 (limited to 1,030 copies).
NF/F: $1250   G/VG: $550

Cole, Faye Cooper. *Rediscovering Illinois.*
First Edition: Chicago: University of Chicago Press, 1937.
NF/F: $65   G/VG: $25

Collier, John. *Patterns and Ceremonials of the Indians of the Southwest (limited to 1,475 copies).*
First Edition: New York: E. P. Dutton, 1949.
NF/F: $250   G/VG: $100

Connelley, William E. *Quantrill and the Border Wars.*
First Edition: Cedar Rapids, IA: Torch Press, 1910.
NF/F: $500   G/VG: $150

_____. *War with Mexico, 1846-1847.*
First Edition: Topeka: By the Author, 1907.
NF/F: $350   G/VG: $150
First Trade Edition: Kansas City: Bryant & Douglas, 1907.
NF/F: $225   G/VG: $100

_____ **and Frank W Root.** *The Overland Stage to California.*
First Edition: Topeka, KS: by the authors, 1901.
NF/F: $1,500   G/VG: $950

Conover, Charlotte Reeve. *Builders in New Fields.*
First Edition: New York: G.P. Putnams, 1939.
NF/F: $55   G/VG: $15

Cook, James H. *Fifty Years Out on the Old Frontier.*
First Edition: New Haven: Yale University Press, 1923.
NF/F: $350   G/VG: $125

_____. *Longhorn Cowboy.*
First Edition: New York: G.P. Putnam's, 1942.
NF/F: $100   G/VG: $35

Coolidge, Dane and Mary. *The Navajo Indians.*
First Edition: Boston: Houghton Mifflin, 1930.
NF/F: $225   G/VG: $50

_____. *The Last of the Seris.*
First Edition: New York: E. P. Dutton, 1939.
NF/F: $95   G/VG: $25

Cooper, Courtney Ryley. *Annie Oakley--Woman At Arms.*
First Edition: New York: Duffield and Co., 1927.
NF/F: $155   G/VG: $55

_____. *End of Steel.*
First Edition: Boston: Little Brown, 1928.
NF/F: $125   G/VG: $45

_____. *Circus Day.*
First Edition: New York: Farrar, Rinehart, 1931.
NF/F: $115   G/VG: $40

_____. *The Golden Bubble.*
First Edition: New York: Farrar, Rinehart, 1931.
NF/F: $120   G/VG: $40

Cornplanter, Jesse J. *Legends of the Longhouse.*
First Edition: Philadelphia J.B. Lippincott Co., 1938.
NF/F: $150   G/VG: $45

Cossley-Batt, Jill L. *The Last of the California Rangers.*
First Edition: New York: Funk & Wagnalls, 1928.
NF/F: $125   G/VG: $55

Croy, Homer. *Jesse James was My Neighbor.*
First Edition: New York: Duell, Sloan & Pearce, 1949.
NF/F: $85   G/VG: $35

Cruse, Thomas. *Apache Days and After.*
First Edition: Caldwell ID: The Caxton Printers, Ltd., 1941.
NF/F: $375   **G/VG: $155**

Cunningham, Eugene. *Pistol Passport.*
First Edition: Boston: Houghton Mifflin Company, 1936.
NF/F: $250   **G/VG: $35**

_____. *Triggernometry: A Gallery of Gunfights.*
First Edition: New York: The Press of the Pioneers, 1934.
NF/F: $450   **G/VG: $100**

Custer, Elizabeth. *Boots and Saddles.*
First Edition: New York: Harper & Brothers, 1885.
NF/F: $400   **G/VG: $100**

Custer, George. *My Life on the Plains, or Personal Experiences with Indians.*
First Edition: New York: Sheldon and Company, 1874.
Points of Issue: Several binding variants all having a buffalo in common on front, no known precedence.
NF/F: $2,800   **G/VG: $775**

Cutter, Donald. *Malaspina in California (limited to 1,000 copies).*
First Edition: San Francisco: John Howell, 1960.
NF/F: $125   **G/VG: $55**

Dacus, J. A. *Life And Adventures Of Frank And Jesse James The Noted Western Outlaws.*
First Edition: St. Louis, MO: W.S. Bryan, 1880.
NF/F: $750   **G/VG: $300**

Dale E.E. *Cow Country.*
First Edition: Norman, OK: University of Oklahoma, 1942.
NF/F: $175   **G/VG: $45**

_____. *Indians of the Southwest.*
First Edition: Norman, OK: University of Oklahoma, 1949.
NF/F: $75   **G/VG: $30**

Dalton, Emmett. *When the Daltons Rode.*
First Edition: New York: Doubleday, Doran & Company, 1931.
NF/F: $625   **G/VG: $175**

Dane, G. Ezra. *Ghost Town.*
First Edition: New York: Alfred A. Knopf, 1941.
NF/F: $100   **G/VG: $30**

Davis, Mary Lee. *Uncle Sam's Attic Alaska.*
First Edition: Boston: W.A. Wilde Co., 1930.
NF/F: $125   **G/VG: $35**

_____. *Sourdough Gold.*
First Edition: Boston: W.A. Wilde Co., 1931.
NF/F: $85   **G/VG: $25**

DeVoto, Bernard. Historical Trilogy:

_____. *Year of Decision 1846.*
First Edition: Boston Little, Brown & Co., 1943.
NF/F: $85   **G/VG: $20**

_____. *Across the Wide Missouri.*
First Edition: Boston: Houghton Mifflin, 1947.
NF/F: $100   **G/VG: $35**

_____. *The Course of Empire.*
First Edition: Boston: Houghton Mifflin, 1952.
NF/F: $85   **G/VG: $25**

_____. *House of Sun-Goes-Down.*
First Edition: New York: Macmillan Company, 1928.
NF/F: $145   **G/VG: $35**

Dick, Everett. *The Sod-House Frontier 1854-1890.*
First Edition: New York: D. Appleton-Century, 1937.
NF/F: $100   **G/VG: $35**

Eugene Cunningham.

George Custer.

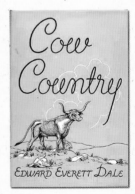
E.E. Dale.

Norman Feder.

Vardis Fisher.

Dobie, J. Frank. *Coronado's Children.*
First Edition: Dallas, TX: The Southwest Press, 1930. Points of Issue: First printing dedication is from "a cowman of the Texas soil."
NF/F: $395   **G/VG: $85**

_____. *Apache Gold and Yaqui Silver.*
First Edition (Limited): Boston: Little, Brown and Company, 1939.
NF/F: $1,200   **G/VG: $550**
First Edition (trade): Boston: Little, Brown and Company, 1939.
NF/F: $125   **G/VG: $45**

_____. *Mustangs.*
First Edition (Limited-Pinto Edition): Boston Little, Brown and Co., 1952.
NF/F: $3,600   **G/VG: $1,800**
First Edition (trade): Boston Little, Brown and Co., 1952.
NF/F: $100   **G/VG: $45**

_____. *Mustangs and Cow Horses.*
First Edition: Austin, TX: Texas Folklore Society, 1940. Points of Issue: The first printing is Teexas Folklore Society Publication Number XVI.
NF/F: $550   **G/VG: $150**

Drago, Harry S. *Great American Cattle Trails.*
First Edition: New York: Dodd Mead, 1965.
NF/F: $45   **G/VG: $15**

_____. *Great Range Wars.*
First Edition: New York: Dodd Mead, 1970.
NF/F: $45   **G/VG: $10**

_____. *Outlaws on Horseback.*
Limited Edition: New York: Dodd, Mead, 1964 (150 copies).
NF/F: $275   **G/VG: $100**
First Edition: New York: Dodd, Mead, 1964.
NF/F: $75   **G/VG: $30**

_____. *Red River Valley.*
First Edition: New York: Clarkson N. Potter, 1962.
NF/F: $65   **G/VG: $20**

Dunbar, Seymour. *A History of Travel in America.* (Four Volumes limited to 250 copies).
First Edition: Indianapolis: Bobbs-Merrill Co., 1915.
NF/F: $425   **G/VG: $150**

Earle, Alice Morse. *Colonial Days in Old New York.*
First Edition: New York: Charles Scribners, 1896.
NF/F: $135   **G/VG: $45**

Elman, Robert. *Great American Shooting Prints.*
Limited Edition: New York: Ridge Press/Alfred A. Knopf, 1972 (450 copies).
NF/F: $400   **G/VG: $250**
First Edition: New York: Alfred A. Knopf, 1972.
NF/F: $150   **G/VG: $45**

Evans, Bessie. *American Indian Dance Steps.*
First Edition: New York A. S. Barnes & Co., 1931.
NF/F: $250   **G/VG: $85**

Feder, Norman. *American Indian Art.*
First Edition: New York: Harry Abrams, 1965.
NF/F: $350   **G/VG: $100**

Fisher, Vardis. *Idaho Lore.*
First Edition: Caldwell, Idaho: Caxton Printers, 1939.
NF/F: $450   **G/VG: $150**

Fisher, Vardis (Director WPA). *Idaho A Guide.*
First Edition: Caldwell, Idaho: Caxton Printers, 1937.
NF/F: $650   **G/VG: $280**

Foreman, Grant. *Advancing the Frontier.*
First Edition: Norman, OK: Univ. of Oklahoma Press, 1933.
NF/F: $235   **G/VG: $100**

_____. *Muskogee and Eastern Oklahoma.*
First Edition: Muskogee, OK: Muskogee Chamber of Commerce, 1947.
NF/F: $155   **G/VG: $60**

Forrest, Earle R. *Missions and Pueblos of the Old Southwest.*
First Edition: Cleveland: The Arthur H. Clark Company, 1929.
NF/F: $200   **G/VG: $75**

_____ **and Edwin B. Hill.**
Lone War Trail Of Apache Kid.
Limited Edition: Pasadena, CA: Trail's End, 1947 (250 copies).
NF/F: $175   **G/VG: Not Seen**

Freeman, Douglas Southall. *Lee's Lieutenants (Three Volumes).*
First Edition: New York: Charles Scribners, 1942-1944.
NF/F: $1,250   **G/VG: $300**

Fulmore, Z.T. *History and Geography of Texas.* First Edition: Austin: E. L. Steck, 1915.
NF/F: $175   **G/VG: $65**

Fundaburk, Emma Lila, and Mary Douglass Foreman. *Sun Circles and Human Hands: The Southeastern Indians-Art and Industry.*
First Edition: Luverne, AL: Emma Lila Fundaburk, 1957.
NF/F: $150   **G/VG: $50**

Garavaglia, Louis A. *Firearms of the American West 1803-1865.*
First Edition: Albuquerque, NM: University of New Mexico Press, 1984.
NF/F: $200   **G/VG: $75**

_____. *Firearms of the American West 1866-1894.*
First Edition: Albuquerque, NM: University of New Mexico Press, 1984.
NF/F: $175   **G/VG: $75**

Gard, Wayne. *Sam Bass.*
First Edition: Boston: Houghton Mifflin, 1936.
NF/F: $165   **G/VG: $65**

_____. *The Chisholm Trail.*
First Edition: Norman, OK: University of Oklahoma Press, 1954.
NF/F: $70   **G/VG: $25**

_____. *Frontier Justice.*
First Edition: Norman, OK: University of Oklahoma Press, 1949.
NF/F: $100   **G/VG: $35**

Garland, Hamlin. *The Book of the American Indian.*
First Edition: New York: Harper & Brothers, 1923.
NF/F: $400   **G/VG: $100**

Gerhard, Peter. *Lower California Guidebook: A Descriptive Traveler's Guide.*
First Edition: Glendale, CA: Arthur H. Clarke Co., 1956.
NF/F: $85   **G/VG: $25**

_____. *Pirates on the West Coast of New Spain 1575-1742.*
First Edition: Glendale, CA: Arthur H. Clarke Co., 1960.
NF/F: $150   **G/VG: $45**

Ghent, W. J. *The Early Far West.*
First Edition: New York: Longmans, Green, 1931.
NF/F: $45   **G/VG: $15**

_____. *The Road to Oregon.*
First Edition: New York: Longmans, Green, 1929.
NF/F: $75   **G/VG: $20**

Earle R. Forrest & Edwin B. Hill.

Wayne Gard.

W.J. Ghent.

Blanche Grant..

Ben K. Green.

Zane Grey.

Gillett, James B. *Six Years with the Texas Rangers 1875-1881.*
First Edition: Austin, TX: Von Boeckmann-Jones Co., 1921.
NF/F: $850   **G/VG: $200**

Grant, Blanche. *Doña Lona: A Story of Old Taos and Santa Fé.*
First Edition: New York: Wilfred Funk, Inc., 1941.
NF/F: $75   **G/VG: $25**

_____. *When Old Trails Were New.*
First Edition: New York: Press of the Pioneers, 1934.
NF/F: $150   **G/VG: $35**

Green, Ben K. *A Thousand Miles of Mustangin'.*
Limited Edition (Slipcased): Flagstaff, AZ: Northland Press, 1972 (150 copies).
NF/F: $800   **G/VG: $300**
First Edition (trade): Flagstaff, AZ: Northland Press, 1972.
NF/F: $95   **G/VG: $35**

_____. *Village Horse Doctor West of the Pecos.*
Limited Edition: New York: Alfred A. Knopf, 1971 (250 copies).
NF/F: $300   **G/VG: $125**
First Edition: New York: Alfred A. Knopf, 1971.
NF/F: $100   **G/VG: $45**

_____. *Wild Cow Tales.*
Limited Edition: New York: Alfred A. Knopf, 1971 (300 copies).
NF/F: $675   **G/VG: $200**
First Edition: New York: Alfred A. Knopf, 1969.
NF/F: $120   **G/VG: $30**

Grey, Zane. *Wanderer of the Wasteland.*
First Edition: New York: Harper and Brothers, 1923. Points of Issue: The Harper code for the first issue is "L-W."
NF/F: $1,025   **G/VG: $400**

Gridley, Marion. *Indians of Yesterday.*
First Edition: Chicago: M.A. Donohue & Co., 1940.
NF/F: $125   **G/VG: $30**

_____ **and Chief Whirling Thunder.** *Indian Legends of American Scenes.*
First Edition: Chicago: M.A. Donohue & Co., 1939.
NF/F: $80   **G/VG: $30**

Griffin, James B (Editor). *Archeology of the Eastern United States.*
First Edition: Chicago: The University of Chicago, 1952.
NF/F: $250   **G/VG: $65**

Grinnell, George Bird. *The Fighting Cheyennes.*
First Edition: New York: Scribners, 1915.
NF/F: $450   **G/VG: $185**

_____. *American Duck Shooting.*
First Edition: New York: Forest and Stream Publishing Company, 1901.
NF/F: $250   **G/VG: $90**

_____. *American Big Game in its Haunts.*
First Edition: New York: Forest and Stream Publishing Company, 1904.
NF/F: $350   **G/VG: $75**

Hafen, Le Roy R. *The Overland Mail.*
First Edition: Cleveland, OH: Arthur H. Clark Co., 1926.
NF/F: $350   **G/VG: $100**

Hafen, LeRoy R. & Ghent, W. J. *Broken Hand.*
First Edition: Denver: The Old West Publishing Co., 1931.
NF/F: $400   **G/VG: $150**

Halbert, Henry S. *A Dictionary of the Chocktaw Language.*
First Edition: Washington, D. C.: U. S. Gov't. Printing Office, 1915.
NF/F: $85   **G/VG: $30**

Hale, Will T. *True Stories of Jamestown and Its Environs.*
First Edition: Nashville, TN: Smith & Lamar, 1907.
NF/F: $75   **G/VG: $35**

Hanley, J.Frank. *A Day in The Siskiyous an Oregon Extravaganza with fold out of Ashland Town.*
First Edition: Indianapolis, IN: Art Press, 1916.
NF/F: $95   **G/VG: $35**

Harte, Bret. *MLISS: An Idyl of Red Mountain.MLISS.* Pirate Edition: New York: Robert M. DeWitt, n.d (1863). Points of Issue: First appearance as a separate volume, story in The Luck of Roaring Camp and San Francisco periodicals.
NF/F: $550   **G/VG: $130**

Haven, Charles T. and Frank A. Belden. *A History of the Colt Revolver.*
First Edition (Limited/Slipcased): New York: William Morrow, 1940. Points of Issue: The limited edition is signed by both authors and the Secretary and a Vice-President of the Colt Arms Co.
NF/F: $475   **G/VG: Not Seen**
First Edition (trade): New York: William Morrow, 1940.
NF/F: $100   **G/VG: $35**

Havighurst, Walter. *Three Flags at the Straits The Forts of Mackinaw.*
First Edition: Englewood Cliffs, N.J.: Prentice-Hall, 1966.
NF/F: $55   **G/VG: $15**

Hebard, Grace R. *The Bozeman Trail (Two Volumes).*
First Edition: Cleveland, OH: Arthur H. Clark Co., 1922.
NF/F: $750   **G/VG: $275**

Henry, Alexander. *Travels and Adventures in Canada and the Indian Territories, Between the Years 1760 and 1776.*
First Edition: New York: I. Riley, 1809.
NF/F: $2,500   **G/VG: $750**

Hinkle, James F. *Early Days of a Cowboy On The Pecos.* Originally published as a pamphlet in 1937- Not Seen Limited Edition: Santa Fe, NM: Stagecoach Press, 1965 (50 copies for the Rogers Library at New Mexico Highlands University).
NF/F: $135   **G/VG: Not Seen**
Limited Edition: Santa Fe, NM: Stagecoach Press, 1965 (550 copies).
NF/F: $75   **G/VG: $25**

Hollister, Ovando J. *Mexico Bay.*
First Edition: New York: Farrar, Straus Giroux, 1982.
NF/F: $100   **G/VG: $25**

Horgan, Paul. *Boldly They Rode.*
First Edition: Lakewood, CO: Golden Press, 1949.
NF/F: $300   **G/VG: $125**

Hough, Alfred Lacey. *Soldier in the West.*
First Edition: Philadelphia: Univ. of Pennsylvania Press, 1957.
NF/F: $85   **G/VG: $35**

Howard, Helen Addison. *War Chief Joseph.*
First Edition: Caldwell, ID: The Caxton Printers, Ltd, 1941.
NF/F: $250   **G/VG: $50**

Hubbard, Harlan. *Shantyboat.*
First Edition: New York: Dodd, Mead, 1954.
NF/F: $75   **G/VG: $20**

Hughes, Langston. *A Pictorial History of the Negro in America.*
First Edition: New York: Crown, 1956.
NF/F: $250   **G/VG: $75**

Marion Gridley & Chief Whirling Thunder.

George Bird Grinnell.

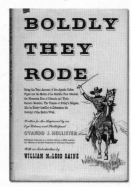
Paul Horgan.

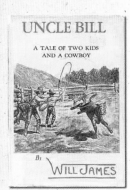

Will James.

Oliver LaFarge.

Tom Lea.

Hungerford, Edward. *Locomotives on Parade.*
First Edition: New York: Thomas Y. Crowell, 1940.
NF/F: $35   **G/VG: $10**

Hurston, Zora Neale. *Dust Tracks on the Road.*
First Edition: Philadelphia: J. B. Lippincott, 1942.
NF/F: $450   **G/VG: $65**

Inverarity, Bruce. *Art of the Northwest Coast Indians.*
First Edition: Berkeley, CA: University of California, 1950.
NF/F: $100   **G/VG: $30**

James, Marquis. *Cherokee Strip.*
First Edition: New York: Viking, 1945.
NF/F: $65   **G/VG: $20**

James, Will. *Uncle Bill. A Tale of Two Kids and a Cowboy.*
First Edition: New York: Charles Scribners, 1932.
NF/F: $375   **G/VG: $100**

_____. *Smoky.*
Points of Issue: First Issue has "Sand" as top title opposite title page.
First Edition: New York. Charles Scribners, 1929.
NF/F: $750   **G/VG: $300**

Johnson, Clifton. *Highways and Byways of the Mississippi Valley.*
First Edition: New York: Macmillan, 1906.
NF/F: $200   **G/VG: $45**

Johnson, Guion. *Ante-Bellum North Carolina.*
First Edition: Chapel Hill, NC: Univ. of North Carolina Press, 1937.
NF/F: $150   **G/VG: $55**

Kane, Harnett T. *Louisiana Hayride.*
First Edition: New York: William Morrow, 1940.
NF/F: $100   **G/VG: $35**

_____. *Gone Are the Days An Illustrated History of the Old South.*
First Edition: New York: E. P. Dutton, 1960.
NF/F: $60   **G/VG: $20**

Kelly, Charles. *The Outlaw Trail.*
First Edition: Salt Lake City, published by the author, 1938 (limited to 1,000 copies).
NF/F: $1500   **G/VG: $775**

King, Blanche Busey. *Under Your Feet.*
First Edition: New York: Dodd Mead, 1939.
NF/F: $85   **G/VG: $20**

Knox, Dudley W. *Naval Sketches of the War in California.*
Limited Edition: New York Random House 1939 (1,000 copies).
Points of Issue: Printed by Grabhorn Press.
NF/F: $345   **G/VG: $200**

LaFarge, Oliver. *The Mother Ditch.*
First Edition: Boston: Houghton Mifflin, 1954.
NF/F: $55   **G/VG: $15**

Lea, Tom. *George Catlin: Westward Bound a Hundred Years Ago.*
First Edition: El Paso, TX: Pass of the North, 1939.
NF/F: $2,600   **G/VG: $1,600**

_____. *The Wonderful Country.*
First Edition: Boston: Little, Brown, & Co., 1952.
NF/F: $95   **G/VG: $20**

Lummis, Charles F. *A Bronco Pegasus.*
First Edition: Boston Houghton Mifflin, 1928.
NF/F: $135   **G/VG: $45**

_____. *Spanish Pioneers.*
First Edition: Chicago: A.C. McClurg and Co, 1893.
NF/F: $155   **G/VG: $60**

_____. *Mesa, Canon and Pueblo.*
First Edition: New York: The Century
Co., 1925.
NF/F: $150   **G/VG: $30**

Mails, Thomas E. *Mystic Warriors of
the Plains.*
First Edition: Garden City, NY:
Doubleday & Company, 1972.
NF/F: $225   **G/VG: $65**

_____. *Dog Soldiers, Bear Men
and Buffalo Women.*
Limited Edition: Englewood Cliffs, NJ:
Prentice-Hall, 1973 (250 copies).
NF/F: $295   **G/VG: Not Seen**
First Edition: Englewood Cliffs, NJ:
Prentice-Hall, 1973.
NF/F: $175   **G/VG: $75**

McCracken, Harold. *The Frank
Tenney Johnson Book.*
Limited Edition: Garden City, NY:
Doubleday & Company, 1974 (350
copies).
NF/F: $650   **G/VG: $250**
First Edition: Garden City, NY:
Doubleday & Company, 1974.
NF/F: $225   **G/VG: $100**

_____. *The American Cowboy.*
Limited Edition: Garden City, NY:
Doubleday & Co, 1973 (300 copies).
NF/F: $250   **G/VG: $85**
First Edition (trade): Garden City, NY:
Doubleday & Co, 1973.
NF/F: $35   **G/VG: $15**

_____. *Portrait of the Old West.*
First Edition: New York: McGraw-Hill
Book Co., 1952
NF/F: $150   **G/VG: $45**

Miller, Joaquin. *Life Amongst the Modocs.*
First Edition: London: Richard Bentley
and Son, 1873.
NF/F: $950   **G/VG: $200**
First US Edition: Hartford, CT:
American Publishing Co., 1874.
NF/F: $250   **G/VG: $75**

Mitchell, John D. *Lost Mines of the
Great Southwest.*
First Edition: Mesa, AZ: M.F. Rose, 1933.
NF/F: $275   **G/VG: $150**
First Hardcover Edition: Phoenix, AZ:
The Journal Co., Inc., 1933.
NF/F: $110   **G/VG: $45**

Moorehead, Warren K. *A Report on
the Archaeology of Maine.*
First Edition: Andover, MA: Andover
Press, 1922 .
NF/F: $300   **G/VG: $125**

Muir, John. *Picturesque California
(Two Volumes).*
First Edition: New York and San
Francisco.: J. Dewing Publishing
Company, 1888.
NF/F: $2,650   **G/VG: $1,100**

_____. *The Yosemite.*
First Edition: New York: The Century
Co., 1912.
NF/F: $450   **G/VG: $175**

_____. *The Mountains of
California.*
First Edition: Boston: Houghton
Mifflin, 1915.
NF/F: $3,000   **G/VG: $1,275**

_____. *Travels in Alaska.*
First Edition: New York: The Century
Co., 1903.
NF/F: $800   **G/VG: $350**

Myers, John Myers. *Death of the Bravos.*
First Edition: Boston: Little, Brown &
Company, 1962.
NF/F: $95   **G/VG: $20**

_____. *Doc Holliday.*
First Edition: Boston: Little, Brown &
Company, 1955.
NF/F: $85   **G/VG: $20**

Harold McCracken.

Joaquin Miller.

John Muir.

Albert Bigelow Paine.

Allan Pinkerton.

William MacLeod Raine.

Neihardt, John G. *Black Elk Speaks: Being the Life Story of a Holy Man of the Oglala Sioux.*
First Edition: New York: William Morrow, 1932.
NF/F: $1250   G/VG: $650

Otero, Miguel. *The Real Billy the Kid.*
First Edition: New York, Rufus Rockwell Wilson Inc., 1936.
NF/F: $375   G/VG: $150

_____. *My Nine Years as Governor of the Territory of New Mexico: 1897-1906.*
First Edition: Albuquerque, NM: University of New Mexico Press, 1940.
NF/F: $225   G/VG: $95

Paine, Albert Bigelow. *Captain Bill McDonald, Texas Ranger. A Story of Frontier Reform.*
First Edition: New York: J. J. Little & Ives Co., 1909.
NF/F: $300   G/VG: $125

_____. *The Tent Dwellers.*
First Edition: New York: The Outing Publishing Co., 1908.
NF/F: $600   G/VG: $220

Pinkerton, Allan. *Strikers, Communists, Tramps and Detectives.*
First Edition: New York: G.W. Carleton & Co., 1878.
NF/F: $350   G/VG: $120

_____. *Claude Melnotte as a Detective.*
First Edition: Chicago: W. B. Keen, Cooke, 1875.
NF/F: $375   G/VG: $140

_____. *The Expressman and the Detective.*
First Edition: Chicago: W. B. Keen, Cooke, 1874.
NF/F: $350   G/VG: $135

Quaife, M. M. *Chicago's Highways Old & New: from Indian Trail to Motor Road.*
First Edition: Chicago: D.F. Keller & Company, 1923. Points of Issue: Two fold out maps tipped in.
NF/F: $100   G/VG: $30

_____. *"Yellowstone Kelly": The Memoirs of Luther S. Kelly.*
First Edition: New Haven, CT: Yale University Press, 1926.
NF/F: $200   G/VG: $85

Raine, William MacLeod. *Oh, You Tex!*
First Edition: Boston: Houghton Mifflin, 1920.
NF/F: $650   G/VG: $275

_____. *Rutledge Trails the Ace of Spades.*
First Edition: Garden City, NY: Doubleday, Doran, 1930.
NF/F: $450   G/VG: $185

_____. *The Vision Splendid.*
First Edition: New York: G. W. Dillingham, 1913.
NF/F: $250   G/VG: $75

Rascoe, Burton. *The Dalton Brothers.*
Originally published in wraps in 1892, Not Seen. First Hardcover Edition: New York: Frederick Fell, 1954.
NF/F: $75   G/VG: $15

Reichard, Gladys. *Navajo Shepherd and Weaver.*
First Edition: New York: J.J. Augustin, 1936.
NF/F: $250   G/VG: $75

Rhodes, Eugene Manlove. *The Trusty Knaves.*
First Edition: Boston: Houghton Mifflin, 1933.
NF/F: $300   G/VG: $115

Richman, Irving B. *Ioway to Iowa.*
First Edition: Iowa City, IA: State Hist.
Soc. of Iowa, 1931.
NF/F: $85   **G/VG: $30**

Ridings, Sam P. *The Chisholm Trail.*
First Edition: Guthrie, OK: Co-
Operative Publ. Co., 1936.
NF/F: $500   **G/VG: $175**

Rister, Carl Coke. *The Southwestern
Frontier, 1865-1881.*
First Edition: Cleveland, OH: Arthur H.
Clark Co., 1928.
NF/F: $375   **G/VG: $165**

_____. *Border Captives. The
Traffic in Prisoners by Southern
Plains Indians, 1835-1875.*
First Edition: Norman, OK: University
Of Oklahoma Press, 1940.
NF/F: $200   **G/VG: $75**

Roosevelt, Theodore. *Hunting Trips
of a Ranchman.*
First Edition: New York: G. P. Putnams,
1885. (Medora edition limited to 500
copies.)
NF/F: $2,800   **G/VG: $1,200**

_____. *Naval War of 1812.*
First Edition: New York: G. P. Putnams,
1882.
NF/F: $1,000   **G/VG: $400**

_____. *The Wilderness Hunter.*
Limited Edition: New York: G. P.
Putnams, 1893 (1,000 copies).
NF/F: $4,200   **G/VG: $1,850**
First Edition (trade): New York: G. P.
Putnams, 1893.
NF/F: $650   **G/VG: $200**

Russell, Don. *The Lives And Legends
Of Buffalo Bill.*
First Edition: Norman, OK: University
of Oklahoma Press, 1960.
NF/F: $75   **G/VG: $20**

Rynning, Thomas. *Gun Notches.*
First Edition: New York: Frederick A.
Stokes Company, 1931.
NF/F: $150   **G/VG: $55**

Sabin, Edwin L. *Kit Carson Days.*
First Edition: Chicago: A.C. McClurg,
1914.
NF/F: $450   **G/VG: $165**

_____. *Wild Men of the Wild West.*
First Edition: New York: Thomas Y.
Crowell, 1929.
NF/F: $100   **G/VG: $35**

_____. *Building the Pacific
Railway.*
First Edition: Philadelphia: Lippincott,
1919.
NF/F: $85   **G/VG: $30**

Sandoz, Mari. *Crazy Horse The
Strange Man of the Oglalas.*
First Edition: New York: Alfred A.
Knopf, 1942.
NF/F: $500   **G/VG: $200**

_____. *Old Jules.*
First Edition: Boston: Little Brown and
Company, 1935.
NF/F: $250   **G/VG: $100**

_____. *Son of the Gamblin' Man.*
First Edition: New York: Clarkson N.
Potter, 1960.
NF/F: $125   **G/VG: $40**

_____. *Apache Land.*
First Edition: New York: Scribners, 1947.
NF/F: $200   **G/VG: $85**

_____. *Lost Pony Tracks.*
First Edition: New York: Scribners, 1953.
NF/F: $125   **G/VG: $45**

Seton, Ernest Thompson. *Lives of
the Hunted.*
First Edition: New York: Charles
Scribners, 1901.
NF/F: $400   **G/VG: $100**

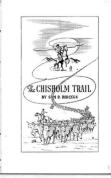
Sam P. Ridings.

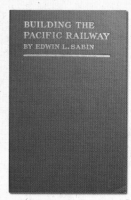
Edwin L. Sabin.

Ernest Thompson Seton.

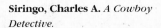

Charles A. Siringo.

Chief Standing Bear.

Stanley Vestal.

Siringo, Charles A. *A Cowboy Detective.*
First Edition: Chicago: W. B. Conkey Company, 1912.
NF/F: $450　　　　　**G/VG: $165**

_____. *A History of Billy the Kid.*
First Edition: Santa Fe, NM: published for the author, 1920.
NF/F: $2,200　　　　　**G/VG: $1,200**

_____. *Lone Star Cowboy.*
First Edition: Santa Fe, NM: published for the author, 1919.
NF/F: $250　　　　　**G/VG: $100**

_____. *Riata and Spurs.*
First Edition: Boston Houghton Mifflin Co. 1927. Points of Issue: Original edition was suppressed by Pinkerton, later printings lack Pinkerton material.
NF/F: $650　　　　　**G/VG: $200**

Sprague, Marshall. *Money Mountain.*
First Edition: Boston: Little, Brown and Company, 1953.
NF/F: $35　　　　　**G/VG: $15**

Spring, Agnes Wright. *The Cheyenne and Black Hills Stage and Express Routes.*
First Edition: Glendale, CA: Arthur H. Clark Co., 1949.
NF/F: $350　　　　　**G/VG: $125**

Standing Bear, Chief. *My People the Sioux.*
First Edition: Boston: Houghton Mifflin Co., 1928.
NF/F: $150　　　　　**G/VG: $45**

Stewart, Hilary. *Totem Poles.*
First Edition: Seattle, WA: University Of Washington Press, 1990.
NF/F: $65　　　　　**G/VG: $20**

Tarbell, Ida M. *The History of the Standard Oil Company.*
First Edition: New York: McClure, Phillips & Co., 1904.
NF/F: $2,000　　　　　**G/VG: $650**

Thompson, R.A. *Conquest of California--Capture of Sonoma by the Bear Flag Men, Raising the American Flag in Monterey.*
First Edition: Santa Rosa, CA: Sonoma Democrat Publishing, 1896.
NF/F: $150　　　　　**G/VG: $45**

Tourgee, Albion W. *An Appeal to Caesar.*
First Edition: New York: Fords, Howard, & Hulbert, 1884.
NF/F: $140　　　　　**G/VG: $45**

Underhill, Ruth. *Singing for Power: The Song Magic of the Papago Indians of Southern Arizona.*
First Edition: Berkeley, CA: University of California Press, 1938.
NF/F: $100　　　　　**G/VG: $35**

Vestal, Stanley. *Big Foot Wallace.*
First Edition: Boston: Houghton and Mifflin, 1942.
NF/F: $225　　　　　**G/VG: $100**

_____. *Happy Hunting Grounds.*
First Edition: Chicago: Lyons and Carnahan, 1928.
NF/F: $200　　　　　**G/VG: $75**

_____. *Warpath and Council Fire.*
First Edition: New York: Random House, 1948.
NF/F: $150　　　　　**G/VG: $60**

Walker, Tacetta. *Stories of Early Days in Wyoming.*
First Edition: Casper WY: Prairie Publishing Co., 1936.
NF/F: $250   **G/VG: $100**

Wall, Oscar Garrett. *Recollections Of The Sioux Massacre.*
First Edition: Lake City, MN: M. C. Russell, 1908.
NF/F: $225   **G/VG: $85**

Wallace, Ernest. *Commanches: Lords of the Plains.*
First Edition: Norman, OK: University of Oklahoma Press, 1952.
NF/F: $45   **G/VG: $15**

Walsh, Richard J. *Making of Buffalo Bill: A Study In Heroics.*
First Edition: Indianapolis, IN: Bobbs-Merrill, 1928.
NF/F: $175   **G/VG: $55**

Walters, Lorenzo D. *Tombstone's Yesterday.*
First Edition: Tucson: Acme Printing Company, 1928.
NF/F: $450   **G/VG: $150**

Washington, Booker T. *The Man Farthest Down.*
First Edition: Garden City, NY: Doubleday Page, 1912.
NF/F: $1,200   **G/VG: $450**

_____. *The Future of the American Negro.*
First Edition: Boston: Small, Maynard & Co., 1899.
NF/F: $950   **G/VG: $350**

Webb, Walter Prescott. *The Great Plains.*
First Edition: Boston: Ginn & Co. 1931.
NF/F: $250   **G/VG: $85**

_____. *Texas Rangers.*
Limited Edition: Boston: Houghton Mifflin Co., 1935 (250 copies).
NF/F: $1,650   **G/VG: $650**
First Edition: Boston: Houghton Mifflin Co., 1935.
NF/F: $350   **G/VG: $135**

White Horse Eagle, Big Chief. *We Indians.*
First Edition: New York: E.P. Dutton, 1931.
NF/F: $150   **G/VG: $45**

Willcox, R.N. *Reminiscences of California Life.*
First Edition: Avery, Ohio: Willcox Printing, 1897.
NF/F: $1,250   **G/VG: $450**

Wilson, Mitchell. *American Science and Invention.*
First Edition: New York: Simon and Schuster, 1954.
NF/F: $85   **G/VG: $25**

Wilstach, Paul. *Hudson River Landings.*
First Edition: Indianapolis, IN: Bobbs Merrill, 1933.
NF/F: $80   **G/VG: $35**

Wood, Frederic. *The Turnpikes of New England.*
First Edition: Boston: Marshall Jones Co, 1919.
NF/F: $145   **G/VG: $60**

Young, Harry. *Hard Knocks.*
First Edition: Portland, OR: Wells & Co., 1915.
NF/F: $325   **G/VG: $120**

Booker T.Washington.

Booker T.Washington.

Harry Young.

ART AND ILLUSTRATED BOOKS

Sometimes considered two separate and distinct categories, these two have a great deal in common, and overlap in many places. The straight "art" book, such as Philip R. St. Clair's *Frederic Remington, The American West*. New York: Bonanza Books, 1981, which sells between $25 and $50, depending on condition, is overshadowed by Henry Wadsworth Longfellow's *Song of Hiawatha. With illustrations from designs by Frederic Remington*. Boston: Houghton, Mifflin and Company, 1891, which sells in the $2,500 to $3,500 range, actually outdoing the first edition, Wadsworth's *Song of Hiawatha*. Boston: Ticknor and Fields, 1855, which goes in the $800 to $1,500 range.

There are many books, both classic and popular, where the artist or illustrator is the important factor to the collector. A few examples are Sidney Paget's illustrations of Sherlock Holmes, Joseph Clement Coll's drawings of Fu Manchu, and renderings of Tarzan by both J. Allen St. John and John Coleman Burroughs. So the illustrated book becomes collectible based on the illustrator.

Artists also produce books that are, in and of themselves, works of art.

Book illustration is hardly a new idea. The illuminated manuscripts of the Middle Ages were works of art as well as books. The more modern trend began with poet/designer William Morris and his famous Kelmscott Press. At Kelmscott, a book was produced as a piece of ensemble art, meshing together the artist, publisher, lithographer, typographer, printer and binder. If the book was a new piece, the writer as well became a part of the team, working hand in glove to create the book.

The books created by Kelmscott were wonders. Today, most are in museums and it takes a pretty hefty bankroll to own just one. Kelmscott had a major impact in France where the tradition created the "Livre d' Artiste," literally "book of the Artist," which were books created in the close collaboration pioneered by Kelmscott.

Amboise Vollard created fine art books in a similar fashion, choosing the best artists of his generation, Picasso, Matisse and Braque, among others. In the United States, an artist and writer named Howard Pyle changed book illustration on his own and then taught his technique to what has been called the Brandywine School, which included such artists as N.C. Wyeth, Frank Schoonover, Stanley Arthurs, Elizabeth Shippen Green and Maxfield Parrish.

Another group of American artists, the Ashcan School of Arthur B. Davies, Robert Henri, George Luks, William Glackens, John Sloan, Everett Shinn, Alfred Maurer, George Wesley Bellows, Edward Hopper and Guy Pène Du Bois, also had a profound effect on book illustration.

TEN CLASSIC RARITIES

Beardsley, Aubrey. *The Early Work;*
The Later Work; The Uncollected Work.
London, John Lane, Bodley Head, 1899-
1925. Three limited-edition volumes.
NF/F: $5,400   **G/VG: $2,200**

Chagall, Marc. *The Jerusalem*
Windows.
New York/Monte Carlo: George
Braziller & André Sauret, 1962. Issued
in a slipcase, text by Jean Leymarie.
NF/F: $3,000   **G/VG: $1,800**

Duchamp, Marcel & Andre Breton.
Le Surréalisme en 1947.
Paris: "Pierre ˆ Feu," Maeght Editeur,
1947. THE surrealist source, art by
Duchamp, Miro, Jean, Maria, Tanguy,
Tanning, Bellmer, Brignoni, Calder,
Capacci, Damme, de Diego, Donati,
Hare, Lamba, Matta, Sage, Tanguy
and Toyen: texts by Breton, Bataille,
Cesairek, Brun, Bellmer, Kiesler.
NF/F: $10,000   **G/VG: $6,200**

Dulac, Edmund. *Lyrics Pathetic &*
Humorous from A to Z.
London: Frederick Warne & Co., 1908.
Dulac's alphabet, the limited portfolio
issued concurrently brings auction
prices in the stratosphere.
NF/F: $4,000   **G/VG: $1,500**

Hassam, Childe. *The Etchings and Dry-*
Points of Childe Hassam.
New York: Charles Scribner's Sons, 1925.
In the First Edition, the initial etching "Cos
Cob" is signed.
NF/F: $2,750   **G/VG: $1,400**

Matisse, Henri. *Poèmes de Charles*
d'Orléans.
Manuscrits et illustrés par Henri
Matisse. Paris: Tériade, 1950. Beautiful
book, awesomely so.
NF/F: $7,600   **G/VG: $4,500**

Miro, Joan. *Joan Miro.* Lithographs.
Volumes I, II, & III. Vol. I: Tudor, 1972/
Vol. II: NY: Amiel, 1975/ Vol. III: Paris:
Maeght, 1977.
NF/F: $3,500   **G/VG: $1,600**

Picasso, Pablo. *Picasso, Le Gout Du*
Bonheur: a Suite of Happy, Playful,
and Erotic Drawings.
NY: Abrams, 1970. Issued in slipcase in
a limited edition of 666.
NF/F: $3,500   **G/VG: $1,400**

Rackham, Arthur. *The Arthur*
Rackham Fairy Book.
Edinburgh, Scotland: George G. Harrap
& Co., Ltd., 1933. Limited edition of
460/signed.
NF/F: $3,600   **G/VG: $1,600**

Warhol, Andy. *The Index Book.*
New York: Random House, 1967. Issued
with 1) colored pop-up castle 2) folding
page with paper accordion 3) "The
Chelsea Girls" paper disc.; 4) colored
pop-up airplane 5) mobile on a piece of
black string 6) flexi-disc of the Velvet
Underground illustrated with a portrait
of Lou Reed 7) folding illustration of a
nose 8) colored pop-up Hunt's Tomato
Paste Cans 9) Inflatable sponge 10)
balloon (almost never found, if present
the price would escalate dramatically)
11) tear-out postcard.
NF/F: $3,800   **G/VG: $1,800**

Arthur Rackman.

Andy Warhol.

PRICE GUIDE

Charles Addams.

Cecil Aldin.

Cecil Aldin.

Aalto, Alvar. *Sketches.*
First US Edition: Cambridge, MA: The MIT Press, 1978.
NF/F: $100   G/VG: $50

Addams, Charles. *Nightcrawlers.*
First Edition: New York: Simon and Schuster, 1957.
NF/F: $125   G/VG: $40

_____. *Addams and Evil.*
First Edition: New York: Random House, 1947.
NF/F: $150   G/VG: $45

Aldin, Cecil. *Mac.*
First Edition: London: Henry Frowde and Hodder & Stoughton, 1912.
NF/F: $1,200   G/VG: $550

_____. *White-ear & Peter - The Story of a Fox and a Fox Terrier.*
(Neils Heiberg).
First Edition: London: Macmillan, 1912.
NF/F: $350   G/VG: $125

_____. *Old Inns.*
Limited Edition: London: William Heinemann, 1921 (380 copies).
NF/F: $650   G/VG: Not Seen
London: William Heinemann, 1921.
NF/F: $275   G/VG: $85

Anderson, Anne. *Briar Rose Book of Old Fairy Tales.*
First Edition: London: T. C. & E. C. Jack, Ltd., 1930.
NF/F: $375   G/VG: $125

_____. *Sleeping Beauty.*
First Edition Thus: London & New York: Thomas Nelson & Sons, 1928.
NF/F: $300   G/VG: $125

Anderson, C.W. *Horse Show.*
First Edition: New York: Harper & Brothers, 1951.
NF/F: $150   G/VG: $40

_____. *Sketchbook: Horse Drawings.*
First Edition: New York: Macmillan, 1948.
NF/F: $250   G/VG: $100

Angelo, Valenti. *Valenti Angelo.*
Author. Illustrator. Printer.
First Edition: San Francisco: Book Club of California, 1976 (400 copies, unspecified number hand colored by Angelo).
NF/F: $900   G/VG: $500

_____. *Salome.* (Oscar Wilde).
First Edition Thus: San Francisco: Grabhorn Press, 1927 (195 copies).
NF/F: $350   G/VG: $100

_____. *The Long Christmas.*
(Ruth Sawyer.)
First Edition: New York: Viking, 1941.
NF/F: $150   G/VG: $45

_____. *A Sentimental Journey Through France & Italy.* (Laurence Sterne.)
First Edition Thus: New York: Dodd Mead, 1929.
NF/F: $125   G/VG: $40

Arthurs, Stanley. *"Posson Jone" and Père Raphaël.* (George Washington Cable.)
First Edition: New York: Charles Scribner's Sons, 1909.
NF/F: $125   **G/VG: $45**

_____. *Stanley Arthurs.*
First Edition: Wilmington, Delaware: Delaware Art Museum, May 3-June 16, 1974.
NF/F: $55   **G/VG: $25**

Artzybasheff, Boris. *Poor Shaydullah.*
First Edition: New York: Macmillan, 1931.
NF/F: $265   **G/VG: $70**

_____. *Orpheus; Myths of the World.* (Padraic Colum.)
Limited Edition: New York: Macmillan, 1930 (350 copies).
NF/F: $900   **G/VG: $400**
First Edition (trade): New York: Macmillan, 1930.
NF/F: $100   **G/VG: $30**

Austen, John. *Adventures of a Harlequin.* (Francis Bickley.)
First Edition: London: Selwyn and Blount Ltd, 1923.
NF/F: $150   **G/VG: $35**

Avery, Milton. *Milton Avery-Prints & Drawings.*
First Edition: Brooklyn. NY: Brooklyn Museum, 1966.
NF/F: $55   **G/VG: $20**

Beardsley, Aubrey. *Le Morte D'Arthur.* (Sir Thomas Mallory.)
Limited Edition: London: J M Dent and Sons Ltd, 1893-4. (300 Copies on Dutch hand made paper).
NF/F: $10,500   **G/VG: $8,500**
First Edition thus: London: J M Dent and Sons Ltd, 1893-4 (1,500 copies).
NF/F: $3,600   **G/VG: $1,200**

_____. *Salomé A Tragedy in One Act.* Translated from the French of Oscar Wilde [by Lord Alfred Douglas]: Pictured by Aubrey Beardsley.
First Edition in English: London: Elkin Matthews & John Lane, 1894.
NF/F: $5,200   **G/VG: $2,400**

Beerbohm, Max. *A Book of Caricatures.*
First Edition: London: Methuen & Co., 1907.
NF/F: $1,200   **G/VG: $350**

_____. *Observations.* London: William Heinemann, 1925.
NF/F: $400   **G/VG: $125**
Deluxe Edition: London: William Heinemann, 1926 (280 copies).
NF/F: $1,200   **G/VG: $400**

Bellows, George W. *George W. Bellows: His Lithographs.*
First Edition: New York and London: Alfred A. Knopf, 1927.
NF/F: $250   **G/VG: $75**

Betts, Ethel Franklin. *While The Heart Beats Young.* (James Whitcomb Riley.)
First Edition: Indianapolis: Bobbs Merrill, 1906.
NF/F: $300   **G/VG: $100**

_____. *Humpty Dumpty.* (Amma Alice Chapin.)
First Edition: New York: Dodd, Mead, 1905.
NF/F: $195   **G/VG: $75**

Valenti Angelo.

Stanley Arthurs.

Aubrey Beardsley.

Reginald B. Birch.

Reginald B. Birch.

Mahlon Blaine.

Birch, Reginald B. *Little Lord Fauntleroy.* (Francis Hodgeson Burnett.)
New York: Scribners, 1886. Points of Issue: First Issue has a Devinne Press seal P. 201 and "14" lower right margin on P. 209.
NF/F: $2,800   **G/VG: $950**
First UK Edition: London: Frederick Warne and Co., 1886.
NF/F: $550   **G/VG: $150**

_____. *The Vizier of the Two-Horned Alexander.* (Frank R. Stockton.)
First Edition: New York: The Century Company, 1899.
NF/F: $100   **G/VG: $25**

Blaine, Mahlon. *Hashish and Incense.* (Paul Verlaine.)
First Edition Thus: New York: Paul Verlaine Society, 1929 (500 copies).
NF/F: $400   **G/VG: $95**

_____. *Alraune.* (Hanns Heinz Ewers.)
First Edition Thus: New York: John Day, 1929.
NF/F: $450   **G/VG: $125**

_____. *The Monster Men.* (Edgar Rice Burroughs.)
First Edition Thus: New York Canaveral, 1962.
NF/F: $65   **G/VG: $25**

Boston, Peter. *Treasure of Green Knowe.*
First Edition: New York: Harcourt Brace & World, 1958.
NF/F: $80   **G/VG: $25**

Boylan, Grace and Ike Morgan. *Kids of Many Colors.*
Volume One First Edition: Chicago: Jamieson Higgins Co., 1901. Points of Issue: Jamieson imprint & colophon dated 1901.
NF/F: $225   **G/VG: $85**
Volume Two First Edition: New York: Hurst & Co., 1901.
NF/F: $300   **G/VG: $85**

Bradley, Will. *Fringilla or Tales in Verse.*
First Edition: Cleveland: Burrows Brothers, 1895 (600 copies).
NF/F: $1500   **G/VG: $600**

_____. *War is Kind.* (Stephen Crane.)
First Edition: New York: Frederick A. Stokes, 1899 (96 copies).
NF/F: $1,850   **G/VG: $550**

Brangwyn, Frank and Walter Shaw Sparrow. *The Book of Bridges.*
Limited Edition: London: John Lane/The Bodley Head, 1916 (75 copies).
NF/F: $1,200   **G/VG: $550**
First Edition: London: John Lane/The Bodley Head, 1916.
NF/F: $600   **G/VG: $175**
First US Edition: London and New York: John Lane The Bodley Head and John Lane Company, 1926.
NF/F: $450   **G/VG: $100**

Bransom, Paul. *The Wind in the Willows.* (Kenneth Graham.)
First Edition Thus: London: Methuen and Co, 1913.
NF/F: $950   **G/VG: $350**
First US Edition Thus: New York: Charles Scribners, 1913.
NF/F: $350   **G/VG: $100**

_____. *The Argosy of Fables.*
Limited Edition: New York: Frederick
A. Stokes, 1921 (365 copies).
NF/F: $2,300   **G/VG: $850**
First Edition (trade): New York:
Frederick A. Stokes, 1921.
NF/F: $300   **G/VG: $85**

Braque, Georges. *Ten Works.* With
a Discussion by the Artist: Braque
Speaks to Dora Vallier.
First Edition: New York: Harcourt,
Brace & World, 1963. (Limited. First
35 with original signed lithograph 330
copies).
NF/F: $5,000   **G/VG: $1,500**
(with litho)   **(without litho)**

_____. *Georges Braque.*
First Edition: New York: Museum of
Modern Art in collaboration with
Cleveland Museum of Art, 1949.
NF/F: $50   **G/VG: $15**

Bratby, John. *Breakdown.*
First Edition: London: Hutchinson,
1960.
NF/F: $175   **G/VG: $60**
First US Edition: New York: The World
Publishing Co, 1960.
NF/F: $85   **G/VG: $20**

Brock, H. M. *The Scarlet Pimpernel.*
(Baroness Orczy.)
First Edition Thus: London: Greening
& Co, 1906.
NF/F: $600   **G/VG: $175**

_____. *A Book of Old Ballads.*
(Beverly Nichols.)
Limited Edition: London: Hutchinson
& Co., Ltd., 1934.
NF/F: $1,200   **G/VG: $575**
First Edition: London: Hutchinson &
Co., Ltd., 1934.
NF/F: $225   **G/VG: $75**

_____. *Songs and Ballads.*
(William Makepeace Thackery.)
First Edition: London: Cassell and Co,
1896.
NF/F: $125   **G/VG: $45**

Brown, Ethel P. *Once Upon a Time
in Delaware.* (Katherine Pyle.)
First Edition: Delaware: Society of the
Colonial Dames of America, 1911.
NF/F: $35   **G/VG: $15**

Brundage, Francis. *Kidnapped.*
(Robert Lewis Stevenson.)
First Edition Thus: Akron, Ohio:
Saalfield Publishing Co., 1926.
NF/F: $25   **G/VG: $10**

Buffet, Bernard. *Bernard Buffet
Lithographs 1952-1966.*
Limited Edition: New York: Tudor
Publishing Company, 1968 (125 copies
on Velin d'Arches paper).
NF/F: $3,500   **G/VG: Not Seen**
First Edition: New York: Tudor
Publishing Company, 1968.
NF/F: $850   **G/VG: $500**

Burd, Clara. *A Child's Garden of
Verses.* (Robert Lewis Stevenson.)
First Edition: Akron, Ohio: Saalfield
Publishing Company, 1929.
NF/F: $185   **G/VG: $65**

Burroughs, John Coleman. *The
Deputy Sheriff of Comanche County.*
(Edgar Rice Burroughs.)
First Edition: Tarzana, CA: Burroughs,
1941.
NF/F: $3,000   **G/VG: $850**

John Bratby.

H. M. Brock.

Francis Brundage.

Floyd V. Campbell.

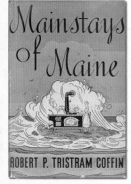

Marc Chagall.

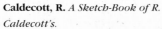

Robert P. Tristram Coffin.

Caldecott, R. *A Sketch-Book of R. Caldecott's.*
First Edition: London & New York: George Routledge, 1883.
NF/F: $250   **G/VG: $85**

Calder, Alexander. *Three Young Rats.*
First Edition: New York: Curt Valentin, 1944.
NF/F: $1500   **G/VG: $550**

Campbell, Floyd V. *The Roosevelt Bears Their Travels and Adventures.* (Seymour Eaton.)
First Edition: Philadelphia: Edward Stern & Company, Inc., 1906.
NF/F: $850   **G/VG: $275**

Cassatt, Mary. *Mary Cassatt: A Catalogue Raisonne of the Graphic Work.*
First Edition: Washington, D.C.: Smithsonian Institution Press, 1970.
NF/F: $950   **G/VG: $300**

Cezanne, Paul. *Cezanne's Portrait Drawings.*
First Edition: Cambridge, MA: MIT Press, 1970.
NF/F: $200   **G/VG: $65**

_____. *Cezanne's Composition.*
First Edition: Berkeley, CA: University of California Press, 1950.
NF/F: $75   **G/VG: $30**

Chagall, Marc. *Chagall's Posters.*
First Edition: New York: Crown, 1975.
NF/F: $300   **G/VG: $125**

_____. *Daphnis and Chloe.*
Limited Edition: Paris: Teriade Editeur, 1961 (250 copies).
NF/F: $46,000   **G/VG: Not Seen**
First Trade Edition: New York: George Braziller, 1977.
NF/F: $195   **G/VG: $85**

_____. *The World of Marc Chagall.*
First Edition: Garden City: Doubleday, 1968.
NF/F: $150   **G/VG: $45**

Christo. *Christo: Running Fence: Sonoma and Marin Counties, California, 1972-1976.*
Limited Edition: New York: Harry Abrams, 1978 (2,159 copies).
NF/F: $825   **G/VG: $300**
First Edition (trade/Softcover): New York: Harry Abrams, 1978.
NF/F: $45   **G/VG: $20**

Christy, Howard Chandler. *The American Girl.*
First Edition: New York: Moffat, Yard, 1906.
NF/F: $400   **G/VG: $125**

_____. *The Christy Girl.*
First Edition: Indianapolis: Bobbs-Merrill, 1906.
NF/F: $250   **G/VG: $85**

_____. *The Lion and the Unicorn.* (Richard Harding Davis.)
First Edition: New York: Scribners, 1899.
NF/F: $50   **G/VG: $20**

Coffin, Robert P. Tristram. *Mainstays of Maine.*
First Edition: New York: Macmillan, 1944.
NF/F: $75   **G/VG: $25**

_____. *Lost Paradise: a Boyhood on a Maine Coast Farm.*
First Edition: New York: Macmillan, 1934.
NF/F: $95   **G/VG: $40**

Coll, Joseph Clement. *Messiah of the Cylinder.* (Victor Rousseau.)
First Edition: Chicago: A. C. McClurg & Co., 1917.
NF/F: $950   **G/VG: $275**

_____. *King of the Khyber Rifles.* (Talbot Mundy.)
First Edition: Indianapolis IN: Bobbs-Merrill, 1916. Points of Issue: In the first state, the author's names is misspelled "Talbott" on the title page.
NF/F: $375   **G/VG: $125**

_____. *Fire Tongue.* (Sax Rohmer.).
First Edition: Garden City, NY: Doubleday Page, 1922.
NF/F: $125   **G/VG: $55**

Constable, John. *Constable and his Influence on Landscape Painting.* (C. J. Holmes.)
First Edition: London; Archibald Constable & Co., 1902 (50 copies).
NF/F: $475   **G/VG: $200**
Limited Edition: New York: E. P. Dutton, 1902 (350 copies).
NF/F: $250   **G/VG: $85**

Corbett, Bertha. *What We Saw at Madame World's Fair.* (Elizabeth Gordon.)
First Edition: San Francisco: Samuel Levinson, 1915.
NF/F: $95   **G/VG: $20**

Cox, Palmer. The Brownie Series

_____. *The Brownies, Their Book.*
First Edition: New York: The Century Co, 1887.
NF/F: $3,500   **G/VG: $1,800**

_____. *Another Brownie Book.*
First Edition: New York: The Century Co, 1890.
NF/F: $1,200   **G/VG: $200**

_____. *The Brownies At Home.*
First Edition: New York: The Century Co, 1893.
NF/F: $1,200   **G/VG: $200**

_____. *The Brownies Around the World.*
First Edition: New York: The Century Co, 1894.
NF/F: $1,150   **G/VG: $200**

_____. *The Brownies Through the Union.*
First Edition: New York: The Century Co, 1895.
NF/F: $1,600   **G/VG: $400**

_____. *The Brownie Yearbook.*
First Edition: New York: McLoughlin Brothers, 1895.
NF/F: $550   **G/VG: $225**

_____. *The Brownies in the Philippines.*
First Edition: New York: The Century Co, 1904. Points of Issue: De Vine Press colophon at foot of verso (copyright) page.
NF/F: $500   **G/VG: $145**

Joseph Clement Coll.

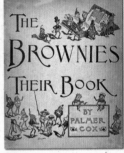
Palmer Cox.

Palmer Cox.

Walter Crane.

_____ **and Mary C. Judd.** *The Palmer Cox Brownie Primer.*
First Edition: New York: The Century Co, 1906.
NF/F: $100   **G/VG: $25**

_____. *Brownie Clown of Brownie Town.*
First Edition: New York: The Century Co, 1906.
NF/F: $300   **G/VG: $85**

_____. *The Brownies' Latest Adventures.*
First Edition: New York: The Century Co, 1910.
NF/F: $250   **G/VG: $85**

_____. *The Brownies Many More Nights.*
First Edition: New York: The Century Co, 1918.
NF/F: $200   **G/VG: $75**

_____. *The Brownies and Prince Florimel.*
First Edition: New York: The Century Co, 1918.
NF/F: $325   **G/VG: $85**

_____. *The Brownies in Fairyland.*
First Edition: New York: The Century Co, 1925.
NF/F: $325   **G/VG: $100**

Crane, Walter. *The Flower Wedding.*
First Edition: London: Cassell, 1905.
NF/F: $375   **G/VG: $150**

_____. *Goody Two Shoes Picture Book.*
First Edition: London: George Routledge, 1874.
NF/F: $1,375   **G/VG: $725**

_____. *Claims of Decorative Art.*
First Edition: London: Lawrence and Bullen, 1892.
NF/F: $350   **G/VG: $100**

Cruikshank, George. *Adventures of Oliver Twist; Or, The Parish Boy's Progress.* (Charles Dickens.)
First Edition Thus: London: Bradbury and Evans, 1846.
NF/F: $28,000   **G/VG: $14,000**

Dali, Salvador. *Conquest of the Irrational.*
First Edition in English: New York: Julien Levy, 1935 (1,000 copies).
NF/F: $700   **G/VG: $250**

_____. *Hidden Faces.*
First Edition in English: New York: Dial Press, 1944.
NF/F: $225   **G/VG: $85**
Limited Edition: London: Peter Owen, 1973 (100 copies).
NF/F: $3,500   **G/VG: Not Seen**

_____. *The Secret Life of Salvador Dali.*
First Edition: New York: Dial Press, 1942.
NF/F: $500   **G/VG: $125**

Salvador Dali.

Salvador Dali.

Davies, Arthur B. *The Etchings & Lithographs of Arthur B. Davies.*
First Edition: N.Y. & London: Mitchell Kennerley, 1929 (200 copies)
NF/F: $450   **G/VG: $225**

De Angeli, Marguerite. *The Door in the Wall.*
First Edition: Garden City, NY: Doubleday & Company, 1949.
NF/F: $275   **G/VG: $75**

De Kooning, Willem. *De Kooning.*
First Edition: New York: Harold Rosenberg, 1974 (100 copies).
NF/F: $2,800   **G/VG: $1,100**

_____. *Willem De Kooning Drawings.*
Limited Edition: Lausanne: Editions des Massons, 1972 (100 copies).
NF/F: $3,200   **G/VG: Not Seen**
First Edition: Greenwich, CT: Thomas B. Hess, 1972
NF/F: $1,450   **G/VG: $600**

Degas, Edgar. *Degas Dancers.*
First Edition: London: Faber and Faber, 1949.
NF/F: $300   **G/VG: $95**

_____. *Portraits by Degas.*
First Edition: Berkeley, CA: University of California, 1962.
NF/F: $155   **G/VG: $45**

Denslow, W.W. *An Arkansas Planter.*
(Opie Read).
First Edition: Chicago and New York: Rand, McNally & Company, 1896.
NF/F: $100   **G/VG: $35**

_____. *W.W. Denslow.*
First Edition: .np: Clarke Historical Library, Central Michigan University, 1976.
NF/F: $75   **G/VG: $25**

_____. *Denslow's Picture Book Treasury.*
First Edition: New York: Arcade/Little, Brown, 1990.
NF/F: $45   **G/VG: $20**

Detmold, E. *Fabre's Book Of Insects* (Fabre; Alexander Teixeira De Mattos' translation, retold by Mrs. R. Stawell).
First Edition: London: Hodder & Stoughton, 1920.
NF/F: $650   **G/VG: $225**

_____. *Hours of Gladness.*
(Maurice Maeterlinck).
First Edition: London: George Allen & Unwin Ltd, 1912.
NF/F: $895   **G/VG: $350**

_____. *The Book of Baby Birds.*
(Florence E. Dugdale).
First Edition: New York: Hodder & Stoughton, 1912.
$800   **G/VG: $300**

Dine, Jim. *The Poet Assassinated.*
(Guillaume Apollinaire translated by Ron Padgett).
Limited Edition: New York: Tanglewood Press, 1968 (250 copies).
NF/F: $6,000   **G/VG: Not Seen**
First Edition Thus: New York: Henry Holt, 1968.
NF/F: $275   **G/VG: $45**

Marguerite De Angeli.

E. Detmold.

Edmund Dulac.

Edmund Dulac.

Edmund Dulac.

_____. *Jim Dine: Painting What One Is (Contemporary Artists Series).* (David Shapiro).
First Edition: New York: Harry N. Abrams, 1981.
NF/F: $500   **G/VG: $175**

Duchamps, Marcel. *The Complete Works of Marcel Duchamps.*
First Edition: New York: Harry N. Abrams, 1969.
NF/F: $1,200   **G/VG: $300**
First U.K. Edition: London: Thames and Hudson, 1969.
NF/F: $1,100   **G/VG: $300**

_____. *Marcel Duchamp: The Box in a Valise.* (Ecke Bonk).
First Edition: New York: Rizzoli, 1989.
NF/F: $185   **G/VG: $85**

Dufy, Raoul. *Dufy.* (Dora Perez-Tibi).
First Edition: New York: Harry N. Abrams, Inc., 1989.
NF/F: $125   **G/VG: $45**

Dulac, Edmund. *Bells and Other Poems.* (Edgar Allen Poe).
First Edition Thus: London Hodder and Stoughton, 1912 (750 copies).
NF/F: $2,500   **G/VG: $900**

_____. *Edmund Dulac's Fairy-Book Fairy Tales of the Allied Nations.*
Limited Edition: London: Hodder & Stoughton, 1916 (350 copies).
NF/F: $3,000   **G/VG: $1,400**
First Trade Edition: London: Hodder & Stoughton, 1916.
NF/F: $650   **G/VG: $200**
First US Edition: New York: George H. Doran, 1924.
NF/F: $750   **G/VG: $200**

_____. *Sinbad the Sailor.*
First Edition: London: Hodder and Stoughton, 1914 (500 copies).
NF/F: $5,350   **G/VG: $2,600**
Limited Edition: Paris: H. Piazza L'Edition D'Art, 1919 (1,500 copies)
NF/F: $1,250   **G/VG: $600**

_____. *The Sleeping Beauty and Other Fairy Tales (1,001 copies).* (Arthur Quiller-Couch).
First Edition: London: Hodder and Stoughton, 1909.
NF/F: $5,000   **G/VG: $950**

Durer, Albrecht. *Jerome.* (Randall Jarrell).
First Edition: New York: Grossman, 1971.
NF/F: $85   **G/VG: $30**

Dwiggins, Clare Victor. *Only a Grain of Sand.* (Charles Maus Taylor).
First Edition: Philadelphia: John C. Winston Company, 1905.
NF/F: $65   **G/VG: $20**

Edwards, George Wharton. *Thus Think and Smoke Tobacco: A Rhyme (XVII Century).* (Ralph Erskine).
First Edition: New York: Frederick A. Stokes, 1891.
NF/F: $800   **G/VG: $200**

EMSH (Ed Emshsmiller). *Conan the Barbarian.* (Robert E. Howard).
First Edition: New York: Gnome Press, 1954.
NF/F: $450   **G/VG: $150**

_____. *Highways In Hiding.*
(George O. Smith).
First Edition: New York: Gnome Press,
1955.
NF/F: $75   **G/VG: $20**

Faberge, Karl. *The Art of Karl
Faberge.* (Marvin C. Ross).
First Edition: Norman: University of
Oklahoma Press, 1965.
NF/F: $475   **G/VG: $175**

Feiffer, Jules. *Sick Sick Sick.*
First Edition: London: Collins, 1959.
NF/F: $65   **G/VG: $20**

Fisher, Harrison. *American Girls in
Miniature.*
First Edition: New York: Scribner's,
1909.
NF/F: $1,400   **G/VG: $600**

_____. *Bachelor Belles.*
First Edition: New York: Dodd, Mead,
1908.
NF/F: $700   **G/VG: $200**

_____. *Cowardice Court.*
(George Barr McCutcheon).
First Edition: New York: Dodd, Mead &
Company, 1906.
Points of Issue: The spine in first issue
splits the word "Coward/Ice."
NF/F: $95   **G/VG: $35**

_____. *Maidens Fair.*
First Edition: New York: Dodd, Mead,
and Company, 1912.
NF/F: $1,400   **G/VG: $600**

Frazetta, Frank. *Fantastic Art of
Frank Frazetta Book 1.*
First Edition: New York: Scribners,
1975.
NF/F: $450   **G/VG: $175**

_____. *Tarzan At the Earth's
Core.* (Edgar Rice Burroughs).
First Edition: New York: Canaveral
Press, 1962.
NF/F: $85   **G/VG: $35**

Gag, Wanda. *The Funny Thing.*
First Edition: New York: Coward-
McCann, 1929.
NF/F: $550   **G/VG: $125**

Gauguin, Paul. *Gauguin: Watercolors
and Pastels.* (Jean Leymarie).
First Edition: New York: Abrams, 1962.
NF/F: $250   **G/VG: $65**

Gibson, Charles Dana. *Americans.*
First Edition: New York; R. H. Russell,
1900.
NF/F: $200   **G/VG: $65**

_____. *Drawings by Charles
Dana Gibson.*
First Edition: New York; R. H. Russell,
1894.
NF/F: $500   **G/VG: $200**

Glackens, William. *Santa Claus's
Partner.*
First Edition: New York: Charles
Scribner's Sons, 1899. (Thomas Nelson
Page).
First Edition: New York: Charles
Scribner's Sons, 1899.
NF/F: $65   **G/VG: $20**

Jules Feiffer.

Harrison Fisher.

Harrison Fisher.

Edward Gorey.

Milt Gross.

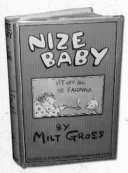

Elizabeth Shippen Green
(Josephine Preston Peabody).

_____. *A Traveler at Forty.*
(Theodore Dreiser).
First Edition: New York: The Century
Co., 1914.
NF/F: $145　　　　　　**G/VG: $65**

Goble. Warwick. *Green Willow and
Other Japanese Fairy Tales.* (Grace
James).
Limited Edition: London: Macmillan
and Co., 1910 (500 copies).
NF/F: $4,000　　　　　**G/VG: $1,350**
First Edition: London: Macmillan and
Co., 1910.
NF/F: $600　　　　　　**G/VG: $225**

Gorey, Edward. *Amphigorey Also.*
First Edition Limited: New York:
Congdon & Weed, 1983 (250 copies).
NF/F: $750　　　　　　**G/VG: $400**
First Edition Trade: New York:
Congdon & Weed, 1983.
NF/F: $150　　　　　　**G/VG: $50**

_____. *Dracula, A Toy Theater.*
First Edition: New York: Charles
Scribner's Sons, 1979.
NF/F: $500　　　　　　**G/VG: $200**

_____. *The Listing Attic.*
First Edition: New York: Duell, Sloan
and Pearce, 1954.
NF/F: $400　　　　　　**G/VG: $125**

Goya. *Goya: Engravings and
Lithographs.*
First Edition: London: Bruno Cassirer,
1964.
NF/F: $1,050　　　　　**G/VG: $525**

Green, Elizabeth Shippen. *An
Alliterative Alphabet Aimed at Adult
Abecedarians.* (Huger Elliot).
First Edition: Philadelphia: David
McKay Company, 1947.
NF/F: $250　　　　　　**G/VG: $55**

_____. *The Book of the Little
Past.* (Josephine Preston Peabody).
First Edition: Boston: Houghton Mifflin
Co., 1908.
NF/F: $175　　　　　　**G/VG: $45**

Greenaway, Kate. *Greenaway's
Babies.*
First Edition: Akron, OH: Saalfield,
1907.
NF/F: $135　　　　　　**G/VG: $45**

_____. *Mother Goose or Old
Nursery Rhymes.*
First Edition: London George
Routledge, 1881. Points of Issue: Last
line of P. 18 ending in "bush," page
number 38 printed upside down and
P. 47 last line ending in "boy" in the
first state.
NF/F: $2,200　　　　　**G/VG: $550**

Gross, Milt. *Nize Baby.*
First Edition: New York: George H.
Doran Company, 1926.
NF/F: $175　　　　　　**G/VG: $45**

_____. *Famous Fimmales Witt
Odder Ewents From Heestory.*
First Edition: Garden City, NY:
Doubleday, Doran, 1928.
NF/F: $100　　　　　　**G/VG: $30**

_____. *De Night in de Front
From Chreesmas.*
First Edition: New York: George H.
Doran Company, 1927.
NF/F: $85　　　　　　**G/VG: $25**

Grosz, George. *1001 Afternoons in
New York.* (Ben Hecht).
First Edition: New York: Viking Press,
1941.
NF/F: $250　　　　　　**G/VG: $65**

_____. *Ecce Homo.*
First Edition: Berlin: Malik-Verlag, 1923.
NF/F: $3,900   **G/VG: $850**
First US Edition: New York: Jack
Brussel, 1965 (1,000 copies).
NF/F: $1,000   **G/VG: $450**

Gruelle, Johnny. *Raggedy Ann's
Magical Wishes.*
First Edition: Chicago: Donohue, 1928.
Points of Issue: Volland editions are
reprints, Donohue is the original publisher.
NF/F: $400   **G/VG: $125**

Hader, Berta & Elmer. *The Picture
Book of Travel.*
First Edition: New York: Macmillan, 1929.
NF/F: $75   **G/VG: $20**

_____. *Sonny Elephant.* (Madge
A, Bigham).
First Edition: Boston: Little, Brown and
Company, 1930.
NF/F: $225   **G/VG: $85**

Henri, Robert. *Robert Henri, His Life
and Works.*
First Edition: New York: Boni and
Liveright, 1921 (990 copies).
NF/F: $175   **G/VG: $45**

Hockney, David. *The Erotic Arts.*
(Peter Webb).
Limited Edition: London: Secker &
Warburg, 1975 (100 copies).
NF/F: $6,000   **G/VG: $2,400**
First Edition: London: Secker &
Warburg, 1975.
NF/F: $50   **G/VG: $20**

_____. *Cameraworks.*
First Edition: London: Thames &
Hudson, 1984.
NF/F: $300   **G/VG: $125**
First US Edition: New York: Alfred A
Knopf, 1984.
NF/F: $650   **G/VG: $185**

Holling, Holling C. *The Road In
Storyland.* (Wally Piper).
First Edition: New York: Platt & Munk,
1932.
NF/F: $175   **G/VG: $65**

_____. *Tree in the Trail.*
First Edition: Boston, Houghton
Mifflin, 1942.
NF/F: $75   **G/VG: $30**

_____**and Lucille.** *The Magic
Story Tree.*
First Edition: New York: Platt & Munk,
1964.
NF/F: $95   **G/VG: $25**

Homer, Winslow. *Winslow Homer.*
(John Wilmerding).
First Edition: New York: Praeger, 1972.
NF/F: $125   **G/VG: $35**

Hopper, Edward. *Edward Hopper.*
The Complete Prints. (Gail Levin).
First Edition: New York: W.W. Norton,
1979.
NF/F: $85   **G/VG: $35**

Humphrey, Maud. *Children of the
Revolution.*
First Edition: New York: Frederick A.
Stokes, 1900.
NF/F: $1,100   **G/VG: $350**

_____. *Little Heroes and
Heroines.*
First Edition: New York: Frederick A.
Stokes, 1899.
NF/F: $600   **G/VG: $200**

_____. *Favorite Rhymes from
Mother Goose.*
First Edition: New York: Frederick A.
Stokes, 1891.
NF/F: $800   **G/VG: $325**

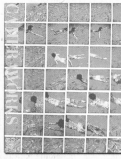

David Hockney.

Holling C. Holling.

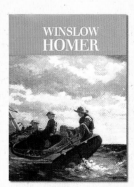

Winslow Homer.

Louis Icart.

Jasper Johns.

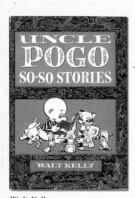

Walt Kelly.

Icart, Louis. *The Complete Etchings of Louis Icart.*
First Edition: Exton, PA: Schiffer Publishing Ltd, 1982.
NF/F: $275   **G/VG: $100**

_____. *Icart.*
First Edition: New York: Clarkson N. Potter, 1976.
NF/F: $85   **G/VG: $30**

Johns, Jasper. *Jasper Johns: Paintings, Drawings and Sculpture 1954 - 1964.* (Alan R. Solomon, John Cage).
First Edition: London: Whitechapel Gallery, 1964.
NF/F: $75   **G/VG: $45**

_____. *Jasper Johns.* (Michael Crichton).
First Edition: New York: Harry N. Abrams. Whitney Museum of American Art, 1977.
NF/F: $350   **G/VG: $125**

Kane, Paul. *Paul Kane's Frontier.*
First Edition: Toronto: University of Toronto Press, 1971 (100 copies).
NF/F: $800   **G/VG: $275**

_____. *Wanderings of an Artist Among the Indians of North America.*
First Edition: London: Longman, Brown, Green, Longmans, and Roberts, 1859.
NF/F: $12,000   **G/VG: $2,500**

Kay, Gertrude. *Tommy Tingle Tangle.* (Sarah Addington).
First Edition: New York: P. F. Volland, 1927.
NF/F: $325   **G/VG: $135**

_____. *Through the Cloud Mountain.* (Florence Scott Bernard).
First Edition: Philadelphia: J. B. Lippincott, 1922.
NF/F: $300   **G/VG: $85**

Kelly, Ellsworth. *Ellsworth Kelly: Drawings, Collages, Prints.*
First Edition: Greenwich, CT: New York Graphic Society, 1971.
NF/F: $775   **G/VG: $250**

Kelly, Walt. *I Go Pogo.*
First Edition: New York: Simon & Schuster, 1952.
NF/F: $300   **G/VG: $95**

_____. *Uncle Pogo So-So Stories.*
First Edition: New York: Simon & Schuster, 1953.
NF/F: $250   **G/VG: $85**

Kent, Rockwell. *Moby Dick, or, The Whale.* (Three Volumes). (Herman Melville).
First Edition Thus Limited: Chicago: The Lakeside Press, 1930 (1,000 copies).
NF/F: $11,500   **G/VG: $4,500**

_____. *City Child.* (Selma Robinson).
Limited Edition: New York: The Colophon Ltd., 1931 (300 copies).
NF/F: $400   **G/VG: $175**
First Edition (trade): New York: Farrar & Rinehart, 1931.
NF/F: $125   **G/VG: $40**

_____. *Salamina.*
First Edition: New York: Harcourt, Brace, 1935.
NF/F: $600   **G/VG: $200**

Kirk, Maria. *Bimbi: Stories for Children.* (Louisa De La Rame).
First Edition Thus: Philadelphia: J. B. Lippincott Company, 1910. Points of Issue: The first US (Lippincott, 1900) was issued in green cloth. Illustrated by Edmund H. Garrett. This edition is in red cloth.
NF/F: $85   **G/VG: $20**

Klee, Paul. *The Thinking Eye.*
First Edition: New York: George
Wittenborn Inc., 1961.
NF/F: $750   **G/VG: $300**

Lathrop, Dorothy P. *Down-Adown-Derry*
A Book of Fairy Poems. (Walter De la Mare).
Limited Edition: London: Constable
and Co., 1922 (325 copies).
NF/F: $350   **G/VG: $100**
First Edition: London: Constable and
Co., 1922.
NF/F: $150   **G/VG: $55**

_____. *Fairy Circus.*
First Edition: New York: The
Macmillan Co., 1931.
NF/F: $600   **G/VG: $250**

Lawson, Robert. *Rabbit Hill.*
First Edition: New York: Viking Press, 1944.
NF/F: $300   **G/VG: $95**

_____. *The Tough Winter.*
First Edition: New York: Viking Press,
1954.
NF/F: $150   **G/VG: $35**

Le Mair, H. Willebeek. *Old Dutch*
Nursery Rhymes.
First Edition: Philadelphia: David
McKay, 1917.
NF/F: $1,425   **G/VG: $350**
First UK Edition: London: Augener
Ltd., 1917.
NF/F: $1,250   **G/VG: $225**

Lenski, Lois. *Prairie School.*
First Edition: Philadelphia: J.B.
Lippincott Co., 1951.
NF/F: $200   **G/VG: $45**

_____. *The Little Engine that*
Could. (Watty Piper).
First Edition: New York: Platt and
Munk, 1930.
NF/F: $500   **G/VG: $125**

Lentz, Harold. *Jack The Giant Killer*
and Other Tales With "Pop-Up"
Illustrations.
First Edition Thus: New York: Blue
Ribbon Books, 1932.
NF/F: $925   **G/VG: $350**

Lichtenstein, Roy. *Roy Lichtenstein*
1970-1980.
First Edition: New York: Hudson Hills
Press, Inc., 1981.
NF/F: $150   **G/VG: $65**

Low, Loretta. *Timothy Toddlekin.*
(Harriet Eunice Hawley).
First Edition: New York: Cupples and
Leon, 1914.
NF/F: $95   **G/VG: $25**

Luks, George. *George Luks: 1866-*
1933: An Exhibition of Paintings and
Drawings Dating from 1889 to 1931.
First Edition: Utica, NY: Museum
of Art, Munson-Williams-Proctor
Institute, 1973 (3,000 copies).
NF/F: $25   **G/VG: $10**

Manet, Edouard. *Manet By Himself:*
Paintings, Pastels, Prints And
Drawings.
First Edition: London: Macdonald,
1991.
NF/F: $85   **G/VG: $35**

_____. *Edouard Manet: Graphic*
Works; A Definitive Catalogue
Raisonné.
First Edition: New York: Collectors
Editions, 1970.
NF/F: $450   **G/VG: $185**

Marsh, Reginald. *Reginald Marsh.*
First Edition: New York: Harry N.
Abrams, Inc, 1972.
NF/F: $425   **G/VG: $165**

Robert Lawson.

H. Le Mair.

Lois Lenski.

Thomas Maybank.

Louis Moe.

Ike Morgan.

Matisse, Henri. *Etchings by Matisse.*
First Edition: New York: The Museum
of Modern Art, 1954.
NF/F: $25　　　　　　　**G/VG: $10**

_____. *Matisse: His Works and
His Public.*
First Edition: New York: The Museum
of Modern Art, 1951.
NF/F: $575　　　　　　**G/VG: $150**

Maybank, Thomas. *The Goblin
Scouts.* (Harry Golding).
First Ed: London: Ward, Lock, no date.
NF/F: $65　　　　　　　**G/VG: $15**

Meteyard, Sidney N. *The Golden
Legend.* (Henry Wadsworth
Longfellow).
First Edition Thus: London & New
York.: Hodder and Stoughton &
George H. Doran, 1910.
NF/F: $275　　　　　　**G/VG: $95**

Miro, Joan. *Miro Engravings 1928-
1975.* (Four Volumes). First US Edition
Thus: New York: Rizzoli, 1989.
NF/F: $1,500　　　　　**G/VG: $600**

_____. *Miro, Life and Work.*
First US Edition: New York: Harry N.
Abrams, 1962.
NF/F: $250　　　　　　**G/VG: $75**

_____. *The Captured Imagination
Drawings by Joan Miro.* First US
Edition: New York: The American
Federation of Arts, 1987.
NF/F: $275　　　　　　**G/VG: $85**

Modigliani, Amedeo. *Forty-Five
Drawings By Modigliani.*
Limited Edition: New York: Grove
Press, 1959 (1,000 copies).
NF/F: $800　　　　　　**G/VG: $300**

Moe, Louis. *The Life and Adventures
of Peter Croak.*
First Edition Thus: London: Thomas de
la Rue, n.d.
NF/F: $345　　　　　　**G/VG: $125**

Monet, Claude. *Monet: Catalogue
Raisonne.*
First Edition: Lausanne & Paris: La
Bibliotheque des Arts, 1970-9. (Three
Volumes).
NF/F: $3,500　　　　　**G/VG: $1,100**
First US Edition: New York: Taschen
America, LLC, 1996.
NF/F: $450　　　　　　**G/VG: $150**

Moore, Henry. *As the Eye Moves...A
Sculpture.*
First Edition: New York. Harry N.
Abrams, 1970.
NF/F: $155　　　　　　**G/VG: $40**

_____. *Mother And Child
Etchings.*
Limited Edition: Much Hadham:
Raymond Spencer Company Limited,
1988 (750 copies).
NF/F: $175　　　　　　**G/VG: $65**
Limited Edition: New York: Raymond
Spencer Company Limited, 1988
(3,000 copies).
NF/F: $35　　　　　　　**G/VG: $15**

Moreau, Gustave. *Gustave Moreau
with a catalogue of the finished
paintings, watercolors and drawings.*
First Edition: Boston: New York
Graphic Society, 1976.
NF/F: $450　　　　　　**G/VG: $112**

Morgan, Ike. *Young Folks' Uncle
Tom's Cabin.* (Harriet Beecher Stowe
& Grace Duffie Boylan).
First Edition: Chicago: Jamieson
Higgins, 1901.
NF/F: $145　　　　　　**G/VG: $25**

Moses, Anna Mary Robertson.
Grandma Moses: American Primitive.
First Edition: Garden City, NY: Doubleday & Company, 1947.
NF/F: $100   **G/VG: $35**

Motherwell, Robert. *The Dada Painters and Poets.*
First Edition: New York: Wittenborn, Schultz, Inc., 1951.
NF/F: $425   **G/VG: $150**

Mucha, Alphonse. *Alphonse Maria Mucha: His Life and Art.*
First Edition: New York: Rizzoli, 1989.
NF/F: $125   **G/VG: $45**
First UK Edition: London: Academy Editions, 1989.
NF/F: $150   **G/VG: $55**

Neill, John R. *The Curious Cruise of Captain Santa.* (Ruth Plumly Thompson).
First Edition: Chicago: Reilly & Lee, 1926.
NF/F: $750   **G/VG: $250**

Nelson, Emile A. *The Magic Airplane.*
First Edition: Chicago: Reilly & Lee, 1911.
NF/F: $275   **G/VG: $95**

Newell, Peter. *Ghosts I Have Met.* (John Kendrick Bangs).
First Edition: New York Harper & Brothers, 1898.
NF/F: $95   **G/VG: $35**

Neilson, Kay. *East of the Sun and West of the Moon.*
First Edition: London: Hodder & Stoughton, 1914.
NF/F: $14,000   **G/VG: $4,500**

O'Keeffe, Georgia. *Georgia O'Keeffe.*
First Edition: New York: Viking Press, 1976. Points of Issue: First Issue is an elephant folio (14" x 23").
NF/F: $350   **G/VG: $145**

_____. *Georgia O'Keeffe: The New York Years.*
First Edition: New York: Alfred A. Knopf, 1991.
NF/F: $125   **G/VG: $45**

Olitski, Jules. *Jules Olitski.*
First Edition Thus: Boston: New York Graphic Society, 1973.
NF/F: $200   **G/VG: $85**

Pape, Frank C. *The Revolt of the Angels.* (Anatole France).
First Edition: New York: Dodd Mead, 1924.
NF/F: $125   **G/VG: $35**

_____. *The Silver Stallion.* (James Branch Cabell).
First Edition: New York: Robert M. McBride, 1926.
NF/F: $150   **G/VG: $45**

Parker, Agnes Miller and H. E. Bates. *Down the River.*
First Edition: London: Victor Gollancz, 1937.
NF/F: $250   **G/VG: $85**

Parrish, Maxfield. *The Maxfield Parrish Poster Book.*
First Edition: New York: Harmony, 1974.
NF/F: $700   **G/VG: $300**

_____. *The Knave of Hearts.* (Louise Saunders).
First Edition: New York: Charles Scribners, 1925.
NF/F: $4,800   **G/VG: $1,750**

Georgia O'Keeffe.

Agnes Miller Parker & H. E. Bates.

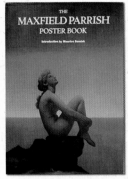
Maxfield Parrish.

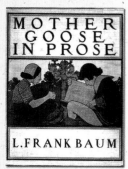

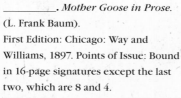

Maxfield Parrish.
(L. Frank Baum).

_____. *Mother Goose in Prose.* (L. Frank Baum).
First Edition: Chicago: Way and Williams, 1897. Points of Issue: Bound in 16-page signatures except the last two, which are 8 and 4.
NF/F: $6,500   **G/VG: $3,000**

Peat, Fern Bisel. *Round The Mulberry Bush* (Marion L. McNeil).
First Edition: Akron, OH: Saalfield Publishing, 1933.
NF/F: $165   **G/VG: $50**

Picasso, Pablo. *The Cubist Years 1907-1916.*
First Edition: London: Thames and Hudson, 1979.
NF/F: $375   **G/VG: $100**

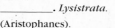

_____. *Lysistrata.* (Aristophanes).
First Edition: New York: Limited Editions Club, 1934.
NF/F: $10,000   **G/VG: $5,800**

_____. *Picasso and the Human Comedy.*
First Edition: New York: Harcourt Brace, 1954.
NF/F: $1,600   **G/VG: $550**

Willy Pogany.

_____. *Picasso's Posters.*
First Edition: New York: Random House, 1970/1971.
NF/F: $275   **G/VG: $85**

Pogany, Willy. *Rubáiyát of Omar Khayyám.*
First Edition Thus: London: George G. Harrap, 1909.
NF/F: $1,600   **G/VG: $675**

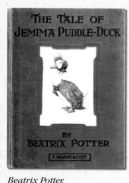

Beatrix Potter.

_____. *The King of Ireland's Son.* (Padraic Colum).
First Edition: New York: Henry Holt, 1916.
NF/F: $400   **G/VG: $175**

_____. *Casanova Jones.* (Joseph Anthony).
First Edition: New York, The Century Co., 1930.
NF/F: $165   **G/VG: $45**

Pollack, Jackson. *Jackson Pollack.*
First Edition: New York: Museum of Modern Art, 1967.
NF/F: $25   **G/VG: $10**

Potter, Beatrix. *Tale of Jemima Puddle-Duck.*
First Edition: London: Frederick Warne and Co., 1908.
NF/F: $3,100   **G/VG: $1,000**

Pyle, Howard. *The Ruby of Kishmoor.*
First Edition: New York: Harper and Brothers, 1908.
NF/F: $250   **G/VG: $95**

_____. *Men of Iron.*
First Edition: New York: Harper and Brothers, 1892.
NF/F: $350   **G/VG: $100**

_____. *The First Christmas Tree.* (Henry Van Dyke).
First Edition: New York: Scribners, 1897.
NF/F: $100   **G/VG: $25**

Rackham, Arthur. *Grimm's Fairy Tales.*
Limited Edition: London: Constable, 1909 (750 copies).
NF/F: $16,250   G/VG: $8,600
First Edition Thus: London: Constable, 1909.
NF/F: $2,950   G/VG: $1,600
First US Edition Thus: Garden City, NY: Doubleday, Page, 1912.
NF/F: $225   G/VG: $85

_____. *The Book of Betty Barber.* (Maggie Brown).
First Edition: London, Duckworth & Co., 1910.
NF/F: $2,500   G/VG: $1,050

_____. *The Chimes.* (Charles Dickens).
First Edition Thus: London: Limited Editions Club, 1931 (1,500 copies).
NF/F: $1,600   G/VG: $700

_____. *A Christmas Carol.* (Charles Dickens).
Limited Edition: London: William Heinemann, 1915 (525 copies).
NF/F: $8,500   G/VG: $3,400
First Edition Thus: London: William Heinemann, 1915.
NF/F: $1,250   G/VG: $550

_____. *Peter Pan in Kensington Gardens.* (James M. Barrie).
Limited Edition: London: Hodder and Stoughton, 1906 (500 copies).
NF/F: $6,800   G/VG: $2,850
First Edition: London: Hodder and Stoughton, 1906.
NF/F: $2,100   G/VG: $850

Rae, John. *Granny Goose.*
First Edition: Joliet, IL: Volland, 1926.
NF/F: $225   G/VG: $75

Rauschenberg, Robert. *Rauschenberg.*
First Edition: West Islip, N.Y., ULAE Inc., 1982.
NF/F: $200   G/VG: $80

Remington, Frederic. *An Apache Princess.* (Charles King).
First Edition: New York: The Hobart Co., 1903.
NF/F: $90   G/VG: $30

_____. *Crooked Trails.*
First Edition: New York: Harper & Brothers, 1898.
NF/F: $525   G/VG: $200

_____. *Remington's Frontier Sketches.*
First Edition: Chicago: The Werner Company, 1898.
NF/F: $2,500   G/VG: $900

_____. *Sundown Leflare.*
First Edition: New York: Harpers & Brothers, 1899.
NF/F: $300   G/VG: $125

Rivera, Diego. *The Frescoes of Diego Rivera.*
First Edition: New York: Harcourt, Brace, 1929.
NF/F: $1,500   G/VG: $675

Robinson, Charles. *The Four Gardens.* (Handasyde).
First Edition: London: William Heinemann, 1912.
NF/F: $325   G/VG: $120

_____. *The Farm Book.* (Walter Copeland).
First Edition: London & New York: J. M. Dent, E. P. Dutton, 1901.
NF/F: $225   G/VG: $85

Arthur Rackham.

Arthur Rackham.

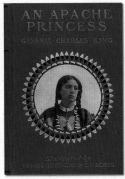
Frederic Remington.

John Rombola.

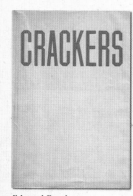

Edward Ruscha.

Robinson, W. Heath. *The Book of Goblins.*
First Edition: London: Hutchinson, 1934.
NF/F: $700   **G/VG: $300**

Rockwell, Norman. *Norman Rockwell: Artist and Illustrator.*
First Edition: New York: Harry N. Abrams, 1970.
NF/F: $300   **G/VG: $100**

_____. *The Secret Play.* (Ralph Henry Barbour).
First Edition: New York: D. Appleton, 1915.
NF/F: $525   **G/VG: $155**

Rodin, Auguste. *Rodin: Drawings and Watercolors.*
First Edition: London & New York: Thames and Hudson, 1983.
NF/F: $155   **G/VG: $65**

Rombola, John. *Rombola by Rombola.*
First Edition: New York & London: A.S. Barnes And Co. & Thomas Yoseloff Ltd., 1965.
NF/F: $50   **G/VG: $20**

Ross, Penny. *Loraine and the Little People.* (Elizabeth Gordon).
First Edition: Chicago: Rand McNally & Co, 1915.
NF/F: $165   **G/VG: $75**

Rouault, Georges. *Georges Rouault.*
First Edition: New York: Harry N. Abrams, 1961.
NF/F: $200   **G/VG: $70**

Rowlandson, Thomas. *The Watercolor Drawings of Thomas Rowlandson. From the Albert H. Wiggin Collection.*
First Edition: New York: Watson Guptil, 1947.
NF/F: $85   **G/VG: $35**

Ruscha, Edward. *Crackers.*
First Edition: Hollywood, CA: Heavy Industry Publications, 1969.
NF/F: $850   **G/VG: $300.**

Russell Charles M. *The Charles M. Russell Book.*
First Edition: Garden City, NY: Doubleday & Company, 1957.
NF/F: $95   **G/VG: $30**

_____. *Studies of Western Life.*
First Edition: Cascade: The Albertype Co., 1890.
NF/F: $4,500   **G/VG: $1,400**

Samaras. Lucas. *Samaras Album.*
First Edition: New York: Whitney Museum of American Art/Pace Editions, 1971.
NF/F: $750   **G/VG: $250**

Sargent, John Singer. *John Singer Sargent.*
First Edition: New York: Harper & Row, 1970.
NF/F: $200   **G/VG: $75**

Schaeffer, Mead. *Wings of Morning.* (Louis Tracy).
First Edition: Chicago: John C. Winston, 1924.
NF/F: $100   **G/VG: $35**

_____. *Wreck of the Grosvenor.* (W. Clark Russell).
First Edition: New York: Dodd, Mead, nd.
NF/F: $85   **G/VG: $25**

Schoonover, Frank. *Frank E. Schoonover. Painter-Illustrator. A Bibliography.* (John F, Apgar).
First Edition: np: John F. Apgar, 1969.
NF/F: $350   **G/VG: $185**

_____. *Yankee Ships in Pirate Waters.* (Rupert Holland).
First Edition: Philadelphia: Macrae Smith Company, 1931.
NF/F: $85   **G/VG: $30**

Seuss, Dr. *You're Only Old Once.*
First Edition: New York: Random House, 1986.
NF/F: $40   **G/VG: $15**

Shahn, Ben. *Ecclesiastes.*
Limited Edition : Paris: Trianon Press, 1967 (200 copies).
NF/F: $750   **G/VG: $275**
Limited Edition : New York: Spiral Press, 1965 (285 copies).
NF/F: $650   **G/VG: $200**
First Edition (trade): New York/Paris: Grossman/Trianon, 1971.
NF/F: $75   **G/VG: $30**

Shepard, Ernest H. *When We Were Very Young.* (A.A. Milne).
Limited Edition: New York: E. P. Dutton, 1924 (100 copies).
NF/F: $5,000   **G/VG: Not Seen**
First Edition: London: Methuen & Co., 1924. Points of Issue: Page six is not numbered in the first issue.
NF/F: $800   **G/VG: $300**
First US Edition: New York: E. P. Dutton, 1924.
NF/F: $275   **G/VG: $85**

Shin, Everett. *A Christmas Carol.* (Charles Dickens).
First Edition: Chicago: John C. Winston, 1938.
NF/F: $450   **G/VG: $100**

Sloan, John. *John Sloan's Prints.*
Limited Edition: New Haven, CT: Yale University Press, 1969 (150 copies).
NF/F: $2,950   **G/VG: Not Seen**
First Edition: New Haven, CT: Yale University Press, 1969.
NF/F: $250   **G/VG: $95**

Smith, Jessie Willcox. *Boys and Girls of Bookland.* (Nora Archibald Smith).
First Edition: New York: Cosmopolitan Book Corporation, 1923.
NF/F: $265   **G/VG: $85**

_____. *Dream Blocks.* (Aileen Cleveland Higgins).
First Edition: New York: Duffield, 1908.
NF/F: $400   **G/VG: $100**

_____. *In the Closed Room.* (Frances Hodgson Burnett).
First Edition: New York: McClure, Phillips & Co., 1904.
NF/F: $225   **G/VG: $55**

Soyer Raphael. *Lost In America.* (I. B. Singer).
Limited Edition: Garden City, NY: Doubleday & Company, 1981 (500 copies).
NF/F: $600   **G/VG: $150**
First Edition (trade): Garden City, NY: Doubleday & Company, 1981.
NF/F: $25   **G/VG: $10**

Steele, Frederic Dorr. *The Scarlet Car.* (Richard Harding Davis).
First Edition: New York Charles Scribner's Sons, 1907.
NF/F: $125   **G/VG: $55**

Strothman, F. *Over The Nonsense Road.* (Lucile Gulliver).
First Edition: New York: D. Appleton, 1910.
NF/F: $85   **G/VG: $35**

Frank Schoonover.

Dr. Seuss.

Henri de Toulouse-Lautrec.

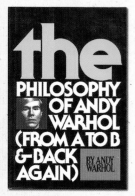

Andy Warhol.

Stuart, Gilbert. *Gilbert Stuart's Portraits of George Washington.*
First Edition: Philadelphia: Privately printed, 1923.
NF/F: $275   **G/VG: $100**

Szyk, Arthur. *The New Order.*
First Edition: New York: G.P. Putnams, 1941.
NF/F: $275   **G/VG: $95**

Tenggren, Gustaf. *The Red Fairy Book.* (Andrew Lang).
First Edition Thus: Philadelphia: David McKay, 1924.
NF/F: $450   **G/VG: $135**

_____. *Stories of the Magic World.* (Elizabeth Woodruff).
First Edition: Springfield, MA: McLoughlin Bros., 1938.
NF/F: $650   **G/VG: $225**

Toulouse-Lautrec, Henri De. *The Circus.*
First Edition Thus: New York: Paris Book Center, 1952.
NF/F: $550   **G/VG: $300**

_____. *Toulouse-Lautrec.*
First Edition: New York: Harry Abrams, 1966.
NF/F: $85   **G/VG: $30**

Tudor, Tasha. *Alexander the Gander.*
First Edition: New York: Oxford University Press, 1939.
NF/F: $850   **G/VG: $325**

Van Gogh, Vincent. *Van Gogh in Arles.*
First Edition: New York: Metropolitan Museum of Art, 1984.
NF/F: $100   **G/VG: $35**

_____. *The Works of Vincent Van Gogh.*
First Edition: New York: Reynal & Co., 1970.
NF/F: $300   **G/VG: $100**

Varga, Alberto. *Varga: The Esquire Years - A Catalogue Raisonne.*
First Edition: New York: Alfred Van Der Marck, 1987.
NF/F: $300   **G/VG: $100**

Wagstaff, Dorothy. *Stories of Little Brown Koko.* (Blanche Seale Hunt).
First Edition: Chicago and New York: American Colortype Company, 1940.
NF/F: $225   **G/VG: $85**

Wain, Louis. *Cat's Cradle A Picture-Book for Little Folk.*
First Edition: London: Blackie and Son, 1908.
NF/F: $1,250   **G/VG: $500**

Ward, Lynd. *The Cat Who Went to Heaven.* (Elizabeth Coatsworth).
First Edition: New York: Macmillan, 1931.
NF/F: $750   **G/VG: $225**

_____. *Impassioned Clay.* (Llewellyn Powys).
First Edition: New York & London: Longmans, Green, 1931.
NF/F: $75   **G/VG: $25**

Warhol, Andy. *The Philosophy of Andy Warhol (From A to B & Back Again).*
First Edition: New York: Harcourt, Brace Jovanovich, 1975.
NF/F: $245   **G/VG: $95**

_____. *Wild Raspberries.*
First Edition: Boston: Bulfinch/Little, Brown, 1997.
NF/F: $75   **G/VG: $20**

Whistler, James McNeil. *Whistler Lithographs.*
First Edition: London: Jupiter Books, 1975.
NF/F: $35   **G/VG: $10**

Williams, Garth. *Miss Bianca.* (Margery Sharp).
First Edition: Boston: Little Brown, 1962.
NF/F: $100   **G/VG: $30**

Wright, Alan. *Queen Victoria's Dolls.*
First Edition: London: George Newnes, 1894.
NF/F: $300   **G/VG: $100**

Wright, Frank Lloyd. *An American Architecture.*
First Edition: New York: Horizon Press, 1955.
NF/F: $300   **G/VG: $120**

_____. *The Living City.*
First Edition: New York: Horizon Press, 1958.
NF/F: $175   **G/VG: $55**

Wulfing, Sulamith. *The Fantastic Art of Sulamith Wulfing.*
First Edition: New York: Peacock Press/Bantam Books, 1978.
NF/F: $85   **G/VG: $30**

Wyeth, Andrew. *Christina's World.*
Limited Edition: Boston: Houghton Mifflin, 1982. (Two Volumes 200 copies).
NF/F: $2,800   **G/VG: $1,150**
First Edition: Boston: Houghton Mifflin, 1982.
NF/F: $195   **G/VG: $65**

_____. *Wyeth at Kuerners.*
First Edition: Boston: Houghton Mifflin, 1976.
NF/F: $250   **G/VG: $65**

Wyeth, N.C. *Beth Norvell.* (Randall Parrish).
First Edition: Chicago, IL: A. C. McClurg, 1907.
NF/F: $120   **G/VG: $55**

_____. *Captain Blood.* (Rafael Sabatini).
First Edition Thus: Boston: Houghton Mifflin, 1922.
NF/F: $375   **G/VG: $100**

_____. *The Deerslayer.* (James Fenimore Cooper).
First Edition Thus: New York: Charles Scribners, 1925.
NF/F: $250   **G/VG: $80**

_____. *The Mysterious Stranger.* (Mark Twain).
First Edition: New York: Harper & Brothers, 1916.
NF/F: $350   **G/VG: $125**

_____. *The Yearling.* (Marjorie Kinnan Rawlings).
Limited Edition: New York: Charles Scribner's Sons, 1939 (770 copies).
NF/F: $3,000   **G/VG: $1,100**

Andrew Wyeth.

Andrew Wyeth.

BANNED BOOKS

Ever since man invented written communication, there has been someone, somewhere who didn't want THAT communicated.

The writer and the censor have walked hand in hand through human history. There has never been a government that has successfully resisted the sick and destructive urge to control the reading matter available to its citizens.

Even the United States, which enshrined freedom of the press in its Constitution, is not immune from the cancer of censorship. In fact, more books have been burned under the aegis of the United States government than under any other political power that has ever existed.

This leaves an extremely large and varied field for the collector, as well a lucrative one. In a very general way, banned books can be broken down into four major categories: religious, political, societal and sexual, though it should be admitted that sexual is a sub-category of societal. There are fertile fields for collectors in very small and specialized areas of it. I have helped collectors build collections of early Christian heresies, as well as collections of sex manuals and porn books.

In any society, part of the artist's role is to challenge the givens. Literary art often takes the lead. And literary artists often pay the highest prices for their anti-social stands.

The Emperor Augustus personally banished Ovid, and his nasty little book, *Ars Amatoria*, from the Imperial city. The Pope himself decreed the execution of Giordano Bruno and burning of his heretical work, *On the Infinite Universe and Worlds*.

Because of bans and burnings, collectible, rare copies are a rule rather than an exception. And where else in the world do you have the opportunity to snub a Pope, flip the bird at an Emperor or give the razzberry to your local Puritan?

A note on rebinding

From the 1920s through the 1960s, Parisian book binders carried on a special sideline, rebinding banned books to allow the purchaser to slip them through customs in the United States or United Kingdom.

Rebinds of Henry Miller's *Tropics* are somewhat common and have served to preserve what would have become fragile paperbacks. Often the title was changed. I have seen several copies of the *Kama Sutra* in black buckram, titled *The Sacred Principles of the Brahmans*, apparently a specialty of a certain bookbinder.

One of the more interesting specimens to pass through my hands was a rebind of Maurice Giorodias' first reprint of Frank Harris' *My Life and Loves*, four paperback volumes bound together in half leather in a custom-made slipcase emblazoned with the title: *Birds of the Mediterranean* (obviously done in the late 1950s or early '60s, given the double entendre).

I know and have dealt with several collectors who specialize in collecting these rebindings.

TEN CLASSIC RARITIES

Bannerman, Helen. *The Story of Little Black Sambo.*
London: Grant Richards, 1899. Find this and forsake politically correct behavior forever.
NF/F: $14,000　　　**G/VG: $6,500**

Burroughs, William S. *Naked Lunch.*
Paris: Olympia Press, 1959. A green paperback No. 79 in the Traveler's Companion Series. No dust jacket (added a month after publication). A green border on the title page.
NF/F: $9,000　　　**G/VG: $1,800**

Faulkner, William. *As I Lay Dying.*
New York: Jonathan Cape/Harrison Smith, 1930 Initial "I" on page 11 misaligned hardcover in dust jacket.
NF/F: $12,000　　　**G/VG: $5,000**

Ginsberg, Allen. *Howl and Other Poems.*
San Francisco: City Lights, 1956. Pocket Poets Series: Number Four. Stapled black wrappers with white wraparound pastedown. Rear cover is priced at 75 cents (printed in blue), and the rear label contains twenty lines of publisher's text and a misprint of a period instead of comma on line 18.
NF/F: $6,500　　　**G/VG: $2,800**

Golding, William. *Lord of the Flies.*
London: Faber & Faber, 1954. Red cloth, white titles to spine, hardcover in dust jacket.
NF/F: $12,500　　　**G/VG: $3,500**

Huxley, Aldous. *Brave New World.*
London: Chatto & Windus, 1932. Blue cloth hardback in blue dust jacket. It will be a new world for you if you pick this up.
NF/F: $8,500　　　**G/VG: $3,000**

Kerouac, Jack. *Mexico City Blues.*
New York: Grove Press, Inc., 1959. Gray cloth, white pictorial dust-jacket, printed in black, design by Roy Kuhlman, author's photograph to rear panel, by William Eichel. Finding this a cure for the blues anywhere.
NF/F: $3,750　　　**G/VG: $2,000**

Miller, Henry. *Tropic of Capricorn.*
Paris: Obelisk Press, 1939. Errata slip, and price (60 francs) stamped on back, in red wrappers lettered in black. Find this and study the Tropics from Club Med.
NF/F: $3,200　　　**G/VG: $1,000**

Nabokov, Vladimir. *Lolita.*
Paris: Olympia Press, 1955. Two volumes, a green paperback issue #66 in Olympia's Traveller's Companion Series. Find it and you can join Chevalier in singing "Thank Heaven for Little Girls."
NF/F: $11,000　　　**G/VG: $4,000**

Helen Bannerman.

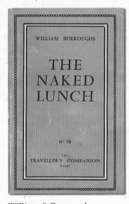

William S. Burroughs.

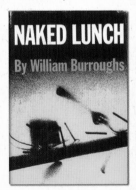

William S. Burroughs.

Isabel Allende.

Anonymous.

PRICE GUIDE

Ableman, Paul. *I Hear Voices.*
First Edition: Paris: Olympia Press, 1957.
NF/F: $65   **G/VG: $20**

Allard, Harry. *Bumps in the Night.*
First Edition: New York: Doubleday, 1979.
NF/F: $50   **G/VG: $15**

Allende, Isabel. *The House of Spirits.*
First American Edition: New York: Alfred A. Knopf, 1985.
NF/F: $250   **G/VG: $55**
First U.K. Edition: London: Jonathan Cape, 1985.
NF/F: $200   **G/VG: $45**

Angelique, Pierre (Georges Bataille). *The Naked Beast at Heaven's Gate.*
First Edition in English: Paris: Olympia Press, 1956.
NF/F: $700   **G/VG: $250**

_____. *A Tale of Satisfied Desire.*
First Edition in English: Paris: Olympia Press, 1953.
NF/F: $700   **G/VG: $200**

Angelou, Maya. *I Know Why the Caged Bird Sings.*
First Edition: New York: Random House, 1969. Points of Issue: The topstain in first issue is magenta.
NF/F: $450   **G/VG: $175**

Anonymous. *Go Ask Alice.*
First Edition: Englewood Cliffs, NJ: Prentice-Hall, 1971.
NF/F: $195   **G/VG: $100**

_____ **(Marie-Therese Cointre).** *I'm for Hire.*
First Edition: Paris: Olympia Press, 1955.
NF/F: $350   **G/VG: $100**

First U.S. Edition: as by Marie Therese. North Hollywood: Brandon House, 1966.
NF/F: $50   **G/VG: $15**

_____ **(Diane Bataille).** *The Whip Angels.*
First Edition: Paris Olympia, 1955.
NF/F: $300   **G/VG: $75**
First U.S. Edition: as by Selena Warfield. New York: Olympia Book Society, 1968.
NF/F: $45   **G/VG: $20**

_____. *The Illustrated Presidential Report of the Commission on Obscenity and Pornography.*
First Edition: San Diego: Greenleaf, 1970.
NF/F: $295   **G/VG: $150**

Anaya, Rudolfo. *Bless Me, Ultima.*
First Edition: Berkeley: Quinto Sol, 1972.
NF/F: $600   **G/VG: $200**

Apollinaire, Guillaume. *Amorous Exploits of a Young Rakehell.*
First Edition in English: Paris: Olympia Press, 1953. Original French publication in 1907.
NF/F: $185   **G/VG: $50**

_____. *The Debauched Hospodar.*
First Edition in English: Paris: Olympia Press, 1953. Original French publication in 1906.
NF/F: $165   **G/VG: $35**

Arsan, Emmanuelle. *Emmanuelle.*
First Edition in English: New York: Grove Press, 1971.
NF/F: $75   **G/VG: $25**

_____. *Emmanuelle II.*
First Edition in English: New York: Grove Press, 1974.
NF/F: $95   **G/VG: $45**

Emmanuelle Arsan.

Ash, Sholem. *The God of Vengeance.*
First Edition in English: Boston: The
Stratford Co., 1918.
NF/F: $250   **G/VG: $115**

Atwood, Margaret. *The Handmaid's Tale.*
First Edition: Toronto: McClelland &
Stewart, 1985.
NF/F: $150   **G/VG: $35**

Baldwin, James. *Another Country.*
First Edition: New York: The Dial
Press, 1962.
NF/F: $250   **G/VG: $100**
First U.K. Edition: London: Michael
Joseph, 1963.
NF/F: $65   **G/VG: $30**

Baron, Willy (Baird Bryant). *Play
My Love.*
First Edition: Paris: Olympia Press,
1960.
NF/F: $35   **G/VG: $10**

Baudelaire, Charles. *Les Fleurs du mal.*
First Edition: Paris: Poulet-Malassis et
de Broise, 1857.
NF/F: $22,500   **G/VG: $10,000**

Beardsley, Aubrey & John Glasco.
Under the Hill.
Limited Edition: Paris: Olympia Press,
1959 (3,000 copies).
NF/F: $125   **G/VG: $55**

Beckett, Samuel. *Molloy.*
First Edition: Paris: Olympia Press,
1955. Points of Issue: First issue has no
price on rear flap.
NF/F: $950   **G/VG: $250**

_____. *Molloy, Malone Dies, The
Unnamable.*
First Edition: Paris: Olympia Press, 1959.
NF/F: $400   **G/VG: $125**

Blanche, Jean. *The Return of Angela.*
First Edition: New York: Castle Books,
1956.
NF/F: $30   **G/VG: $10**

Blume, Judy. *Are You There, God? It's
Me, Margaret.*
First Edition: Englewood Cliffs, NJ:
Bradbury, 1970.
NF/F: $50   **G/VG: $15**

_____. *Blubber.*
First Edition: Scarsdale, NY: Bradbury,
1974.
NF/F: $65   **G/VG: $20**

_____. *Tiger Eyes.*
First Edition: Scarsdale, NY: Bradbury
Press, 1981.
NF/F: $100   **G/VG: $35**

Boff, Leonardo. *Church: Charism
and Power: Liberation Theology and
the Institutional Church.*
First Edition in English: New York:
Crossroads, 1985.
NF/F: $60   **G/VG: $20**

Boyer, Pamela. *Blonde Flames.*
First Edition: New York: Key
Publishing, 1957.
NF/F: $35   **G/VG: $10**

Bradbury, Ray. *Fahrenheit 451.*
Limited Edition: New York: Ballantine,
1953 (200 copies bound in Asbestos).
NF/F: $18,500   **G/VG: Not Seen**
First Edition: New York: Ballantine,
1953. Points of Issue: Contains two
short stories, "The Playground" and
"And the Rock Cried" (paperbound).
NF/F: $600   **G/VG: $300**
First Hardcover Trade Edition: New
York: Ballantine, 1953.
NF/F: $1,800   **G/VG: $650**

Margaret Atwood.

Samuel Beckett.

Jean Blanche.

Anthony Burgess.

William S. Burroughs.

A. R. Butz.

Broughton, James. *Almanac for Amorists.*
First Edition: Paris: Collections Merlin in collaboration with the Olympia Press, 1955.
NF/F: $95   **G/VG: $25**

Brown, Claude. *Manchild in the Promised Land.*
First Edition: New York: Macmillan, 1965.
NF/F: $200   **G/VG: $65**

Burgess, Anthony. *A Clockwork Orange.*
First Edition: London: Heinemann, 1962.
NF/F: $6,500   **G/VG: $3,000**
First US Edition: New York: W.W. Norton, 1963.
NF/F: $500   **G/VG: $150**

Burns, R. Bernard. *The Ordeal of the Rod.*
First Edition: Paris: Ophelia/Olympia Press, 1958.
NF/F: $85   **G/VG: $25**

Burroughs, William S. *Naked Lunch.*
First U.S. Edition-New York: Grove Press, 1959. Points of Issue: First issue dust jacket lacks publisher's zip code on rear panel.
NF/F: $1,200   **G/VG: $450**
First U.K. Edition- London: John Calder, 1959.
NF/F: $650   **G/VG: $250**

_____. *The Soft Machine.*
First Edition: Paris: Olympia Press, 1961.
NF/F: $550   **G/VG: $100**
First U.S. Edition: New York: Grove Press, 1966.
NF/F: $175   **G/VG: $65**
First U.K. Edition: London: Calder & Boyars, 1968.
NF/F: $150   **G/VG: $70**

_____. *The Ticket that Exploded.*
First Edition: Paris: Olympia Press, 1961.
NF/F: $1,200   **G/VG: $350**
First U.S. Edition: New York: Grove Press, 1967.
NF/F: $150   **G/VG: $45**

Butz, A.R. *The Hoax of the Twentieth Century.*
First Edition: Richmond, Surrey: Historical Review Press, 1976.
NF/F: $160   **G/VG: $55**
First U.S. Edition: Los Angeles: Noontide Press, 1977.
NF/F: $115   **G/VG: $45**

Cabell, James Branch. *Jurgen.*
Limited Edition: London: Golden Cockerel Press, 1949 (500 copies).
NF/F: $650   **G/VG: $300**
First Edition: New York: Robert M. McBride & Co, 1919.
NF/F: $2,300   **G/VG: $850**

Cadivec, Edith. *Eros: The Meaning of My Life.*
First Edition: New York: Grove Press, 1969.
NF/F: $35   **G/VG: $15**

Carroll, Jock. *Bottoms Up.*
First Edition: Paris: Olympia Press, 1961.
NF/F: $75   **G/VG: $25**

Casement, Roger. *The Black Diaries.*
Limited Edition: Paris: Olympia Press, 1959 (1,500 copies).
NF/F: $600   **G/VG: $185**

Caughey, John W., John Hope Franklin and Ernest R. May. *Land of the Free.*
First Edition: New York: Benziger Brothers, Inc, 1965.
NF/F: $55   **G/VG: $20**

Childress, Alice. *A Hero Ain't Nothin' but a Sandwich.*
First Edition: New York: Cowand-McCann, 1973.
NF/F: $75   **G/VG: $25**

Cleaver, Eldridge. *Soul on Ice.*
First Edition: New York: McGraw-Hill/Ramparts, 1968.
NF/F: $250   **G/VG: $85**

Cohen, Daniel. *Curses, Hexes and Spells.*
First Edition: Philadelphia: Lippincott/Williams & Wilkins, 1974.
NF/F: $100   **G/VG: $30**
First U.K. Edition: London: J.M. Dent, 1977.
NF/F: $85   **G/VG: $25**

Cole, Babette. *Mommy Laid An Egg.*
First Edition: San Francisco, CA: Chronicle Books, 1993.
NF/F: $45   **G/VG: $15**

Cole, Joanna. *Asking About Sex and Growing Up.*
First Edition: New York.: Morrow Junior Books, 1988.
NF/F: $40   **G/VG: $10**

Conly, Jane Leslie. *Crazy Lady.*
First Edition: New York: HarperCollins Children's Book Group, 1993.
NF/F: $55   **G/VG: $20**

Cooney, Caroline B. *The Face on the Milk Carton.*
First Edition: New York: Bantam, 1990.
NF/F: $45   **G/VG: $10**

Cormier, Robert. *The Chocolate War.*
First Edition: New York: Pantheon, 1974.
Points of Issue: First issue is brown boards with gilt lettering on spine.
NF/F: $145   **G/VG: $50**
First U.K. Edition: London: Victor Gollancz, 1974.
NF/F: $45   **G/VG: $10**

_____. *Fade.*
First Edition: New York: Delacorte Press, 1988.
NF/F: $65   **G/VG: $25**
First U.K. Edition: London: Victor Gollancz Ltd, 1988.
NF/F: $15   **G/VG: $6**

_____. *I Am the Cheese.*
First Edition: New York: Pantheon, 1977.
NF/F: $75   **G/VG: $25**

Corso, Gregory. *The American Express.* First Edition: Paris: Olympia Press, 1961.
NF/F: $450   **G/VG: $85**

Cousins, Sheila (Graham Greene and Ronald Matthews). *To Beg I Am Ashamed.*
First Edition: London: Roultedge, 1938.
NF/F: $26,000   **G/VG: $10,000**
Paris Editon: Paris: Obelisk Press, 1938.
NF/F: $350   **G/VG: $100**
First American Edition: New York: The Vanguard Press, 1938.
NF/F: $500   **G/VG: $125**

Crannach, Henry (Marilyn Meeske). *Flesh and Bone.*
First Edition: Paris: Olympia Press, 1957.
NF/F: $45   **G/VG: $20**

Crutcher, Chris. *Athletic Shorts.*
First Edition: New York : Greenwillow Books, 1989.
NF/F: $70   **G/VG: $20**

Jane Leslie Conly.

Robert Cormier.

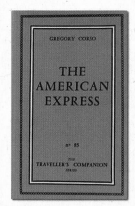

Gregory Corso.

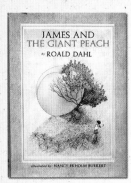
Roald Dahl.

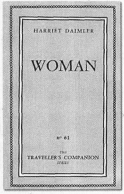
*Harriet Daimler.
(Iris Owens).*

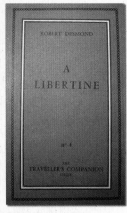
Robert Desmond.

Dahl, Roald. *James and the Giant Peach.*
First Edition: New York: Alfred A. Knopf, 1961. Points of Issue: First issue is dark red boards, yellow/peach-colored head, Knopf logo on rear boards, blind stamped head surrounded by wreath on front boards and gilt lettering on the spine, green endpapers, and the most important point to the first printing which is a five-line colophon that includes the statement, 'BOUND BY H. WOLFF, NEW YORK.' Original price on dust-wrapper $3.95 - back panel of dust-wrapper has no numbers printed at the bottom edge.
NF/F: $5,000   **G/VG: $2,000**
First U.K. Edition: London: George Allen & Unwin, 1967.
NF/F: $1,000   **G/VG: $300**

Daimler, Harriet (Iris Owens). *Darling.*
First Edition: Paris: Olympia Press, 1956.
NF/F: $75   **G/VG: $40**

_____. *Innocence.* First Editon: Paris: Olympia Press, 1956.
NF/F: $45   **G/VG: $20**

_____. *The Organization.*
First Edition: Paris: Olympia Press, 1957.
NF/F: $85   **G/VG: $30**

_____. *The Woman Thing.*
First Edition: Paris: Olympia Press, 1958.
NF/F: $65   **G/VG: $25**

Daimler, Harriet and Henry Crannach (Iris Owens and Marilyn Meeske). *The Pleasure Thieves.*
First Edition: Paris: Olympia Press, 1958.
NF/F: $65   **G/VG: $25**

Darwin, Charles. *On the Origin of Species.*
First Edition: London: John Murray, 1859.
NF/F: $170,000   **G/VG: $50,000**

de Farniente, Beauregard (J.C. Gervaise de Latouche). *The Adventures of Father Silas.*
First Edition: Paris: Ophelia/Olympia Press, 1958.
NF/F: $85   **G/VG: $30**

De Leeuw, Hendrik. *Fallen Angels.*
First Edition: London: Arco Publishers, 1954.
NF/F: $50   **G/VG: $20**

Del Piombo, Akbar (Norman Rubington). *The Boiler Maker.*
First Edition: Paris: Olympia Press, 1961.
NF/F: $65   **G/VG: $25**

_____. *Cosimo's Wife.* First Editon: Paris: Olympia Press, 1957.
NF/F: $85   **G/VG: $25**

Desmond, Robert. *An Adult's Story.*
First Edition: Paris: Olympia Press, 1954.
NF/F: $35   **G/VG: $15**

_____. *Heaven, Hell and the Whore.*
First Edition: Paris: Olympia Press, 1956.
NF/F: $30   **G/VG: $15**

_____. *Iniquity.*
First Edition: Paris: Ophelia/Olympia Press, 1958.
NF/F: $55   **G/VG: $20**

_____. *A Libertine.*
First Edition: Paris: Olympia Press, 1955.
NF/F: $75   **G/VG: $25**

_____. *Professional Charmer.*
First Edition: Paris: Olympia Press, 1961.
NF/F: $45   **G/VG: $20**

_____. *The Sweetest Fruit.*
First Edition: Paris: Ophir/Olympia Press, 1951.
NF/F: $95   **G/VG: $35**

Devlin, Barry. *Acapulco Nocturne.*
First Edition: New York: Vixen Press, 1952.
NF/F: $35   **G/VG: $10**

_____. *Chains of Silk.*
First Edition: New York: Vixen Press, 1954.
NF/F: $35   **G/VG: $15**

_____. *Moon-Kissed.*
First Edition: New York: Vixen Press, 1953.
NF/F: $45   **G/VG: $12**

_____. *No Holds Barred.*
First Edition: New York: Vixen Press, 1954.
NF/F: $20   **G/VG: $8**

d'Musset, Alfred. *Passion's Evil.*
First Edition: Paris: Olympia Press, 1953.
NF/F: $35   **G/VG: $15**

Donleavy, J.P. *The Ginger Man.*
First Edition: Paris: Olympia Press, 1955. Points of Issue: #7 in Traveler's Companion Series. Price on rear cover is "Francs 1,500."
NF/F: $1,200   **G/VG: $600**
First U.S. Edition: New York: McDowell, Obolensky, 1958.
NF/F: $300   **G/VG: $95**
First U.K. Edition: London: Neville Spearman, 1956.
NF/F: $265   **G/VG: $90**

Drake, Hamilton (Mason Hoffenberg). *Sin for Breakfast.*
First Edition: Paris: Olympia Press, 1957.
NF/F: $70   **G/VG: $20**

Dreiser, Theodore. *An American Tragedy.*
First Edition: New York: Boni and Liveright, 1925.
NF/F: $2,200   **G/VG: $950**

_____. *The Genius.*
First Edition: New York: John Lane, 1915.
NF/F: $400   **G/VG: $135**

Duncan, Lois. *Killing Mr. Griffin.*
First Edition: Boston: Little, Brown and Company, 1978.
NF/F: $30   **G/VG: $10**

Duras, Marguerite and Alain Resnais. *Hiroshima Mon Amour.*
First Edition: Paris: Gallimard, 1960.
NF/F: $85   **G/VG: $30**
First US Edition: New York: Grove Press, 1961.
NF/F: $55   **G/VG: $20**

Durrell, Lawrence. *The Black Book.*
First Edition: Paris: The Obelisk Press, 1938.
NF/F: $3,000   **G/VG: $700**
First U.S. Edition: New York: E. P. Dutton, 1960. Points of Issue: First state dust jacket reads, "Lawrence Durrel's Black Book" not "T. S. Eliot said…"
NF/F: $175   **G/VG: $65**

Edward, Brett. *The Passion of Youth.*
First Edition: Paris: Ophelia/Olympia Press, 1960.
NF/F: $65   **G/VG: $25**

Barry Devlin.

J.P. Donleavy.

Lawrence Durrell.

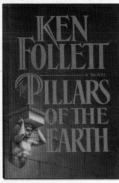

Ken Follett.

Jean Craighead George.

Günther Grass.

Ellis, Bret Easton. *American Psycho.*
First Edition: New York: Vintage, 1991.
NF/F: $165   **G/VG: $40**
First U.K. Edition: London: Picador,
1991.
NF/F: $350   **G/VG: $90**

El Saadawi, Nawal. *The Hidden Face
of Eve: Women in the Arab World.*
First U.K. Edition: London: Zed Press,
1980.
NF/F: $135   **G/VG: $50**

Faulkner, William. *Sanctuary.*
First Edition: New York: Jonathan
Cape & Harrison Smith, 1931. Points
of Issue: First issue endpapers are gray
printed in magenta.
NF/F: $18,000   **G/VG: $5,800**

Feral, Rex. *Hit Man: A Technical
Manual for Independent Contractors.*
First Edition: Denver: Paladin Press,
1983.
NF/F: $300   **G/VG: $95**

Follett, Ken. *Pillars of the Earth.*
First Edition: New York: Wm. Morrow
& Co., 1989.
NF/F: $195   **G/VG: $45**

Foster, Gerald. *Lust.*
First Edition: New York: Balzac Press,
1949.
NF/F: $35   **G/VG: $15**

Frank, Anne. *Anne Frank: The Diary
of a Young Girl.*
First Edition in English: New York:
Doubleday, 1952.
NF/F: $450   **G/VG: $165**
First U.K. Edition: London:
Constellation Books, 1952.
NF/F: $100   **G/VG: $45**

Freedman, Nancy. *The Prima
Donna.*
First Edition: New York: William
Morrow, 1981.
NF/F: $40   **G/VG: $10**

Friday, Nancy. *Women on Top: How
Real Life Has Changed Women's
Sexual Fantasies.*
First Edition: New York: Simon &
Schuster, 1991
NF/F: $35   **G/VG: $10**

Garden, Nancy. *Annie on My Mind.*
First Edition: New York: Farrar, Straus,
Giroux, 1982.
NF/F: $50   **G/VG: $15**

George, Jean Craighead. *Julie of the
Wolves.*
First Edition: New York: Harper and
Row, 1972.
NF/F: $275   **G/VG: $95**

Ginzberg, Ralph (ed.). *Eros
Magazine.* Quarterly Magazine issued
in 1962 (4 issues).
NF/F: $165   **G/VG: $60**

Gordimer, Nadine. *Burger's
Daughter.*
First Edition: London: Jonathon Cape,
1979.
NF/F: $125   **G/VG: $35**
First U.S. Edition: New York: Viking
Press, 1979.
NF/F: $95   **G/VG: $25**

Grass, Günther. *The Tin Drum.*
First Edition in English: London:
Secker & Warburg, 1959.
NF/F: $95   **G/VG: $30**
First American Edition: New York:
Pantheon, 1959.
NF/F: $350   **G/VG: $85**

Greene, Bette. *The Drowning of Stephan Jones.*
First Edition: New York: Bantam, 1991.
NF/F: $75   G/VG: $20

_____. *The Summer of My German Soldier.*
First Edition: New York: The Dial Press, 1973.
NF/F: $65   G/VG: $20

Griffin, John Howard. *Black Like Me.*
First Edition: Boston: Houghton Mifflin, 1961.
NF/F: $500   G/VG: $175

Guest, Judith. *Ordinary People.*
First Edition: New York: Viking Press, 1976.
NF/F: $200   G/VG: $55

Guterson, David. *Snow Falling on Cedars.*
First Edition: New York: Harcourt Brace, 1994.
NF/F: $250   G/VG: $90

Hall, Radcliffe. *The Well of Loneliness.*
First Edition: New York: Covici-Friede, 1928.
NF/F: $200   G/VG: $85

Hamilton, David. *The Age Of Innocence.*
First Edition: London: Aurum Press, 1995.
NF/F: $250   G/VG: $100

Hammer, Stephen (John Coleman). *The Itch.*
First Edition: Paris: Olympia Press, 1956.
NF/F: $40   G/VG: $15

Hardy, Thomas. *Jude the Obscure.*
Limited Edition: London: Macmillan, 1919-20 (Mellstock Edition 500 copies.)
NF/F: $10,000   G/VG: Not Seen
First Edition: New York: Harper and Brothers, 1895.
NF/F: $650   G/VG: $150
First U.K. Edition: London: Osgood, McIlvaine & Co, 1896.
NF/F: $5,000   G/VG: $1,800

Harris, Frank. *My Life and Loves.*
First Edition: Paris and Nice: Privately Printed for the Author, 1922-27.
Note: Harris privately printed his memoirs in bits and pieces over a five-year period, a complete collection of these fragments is worth about $8,000. The fragments run, according to size and condition, from $100 to $500.
First Trade Edition: Paris: Obelisk, 1933.
NF/F: $850   G/VG: $300

_____. **(Alexander Trocchi).** *My Life and Loves* Volume 5.
First Edition: Paris: Olympia Press, 1954.
NF/F: $40   G/VG: $15

Harris, Robie, H. *It's Perfectly Normal.*
First Edition: Cambridge, MA: Candlewick Press, 1994.
NF/F: $45   G/VG: $15

Hawthorne, Nathaniel. *The Scarlet Letter.*
First Edition: Boston: Ticknor, Reed & Fields, 1850.
Points of Issue: First State has a misprint "reduplicate" for "repudiate" at line 20 on page 21.
NF/F: $13,500   G/VG: $5,500

David Guterson.

Radcliffe Hall.

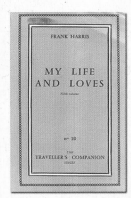

Frank Harris.

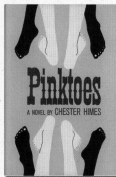

Chester Himes.

S. E. Hinton.

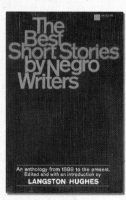

Langston Hughes.

Heckstall-Smith, Anthony. *The Consort.*
First Edition: London: Anthony Blond, 1962.
NF/F: $135　　　**G/VG: $50**
First US Edition: New York: Grove Press, 1965. Points of Issue: Issued with two dust jackets, one clothed one nude.
NF/F: $95　　　**G/VG: $35**

Helper, Hinton Rowan. *The Impending Crisis in the South - How to Meet It.*
First Edition: New York: Burdick Brothers, 1857.
NF/F: $365　　　**G/VG: $125**

Himes, Chester. *Pinktoes.*
First Edition: Paris: Olympia Press, 1961.
NF/F: $800　　　**G/VG: $250**
First U.S. Edition: New York: Putnam/Stein & Day, 1965.
NF/F: $325　　　**G/VG: $75**

Hinton, S.E. *The Outsiders.*
First Edition: New York: Viking Press, 1967.
NF/F: $650　　　**G/VG: $225**

_____. *That Was Then, This is Now.*
First Edition: New York: The Viking Press, 1971.
NF/F: $75　　　**G/VG: $20**

Hitler, Adolf. *Mein Kampf.*
First Edition: Munich: Eher Verlag, 1925.
NF/F: $21,000　　　**G/VG: $5,000**

Homer and Associates (Michel Gall). *A Bedside Odyssey.*
First Edition: Paris: Olympia Press, 1962.
NF/F: $85　　　**G/VG: $30**

Hughes, Langston (ed.). *The Best Short Stories by Negro Writers.*
First Edition: Boston: Little, Brown & Company, 1967.
NF/F: $80　　　**G/VG: $30**

Humphrey, Derek. *Final Exit.*
First Edition: Eugene, Oregon: The Hemlock Society, 1991.
NF/F: $25　　　**G/VG: $10**

Huxley, Aldous. *Brave New World.*
First Edition: London: Chatto & Windus, 1932.
NF/F: $8,500　　　**G/VG: $4,500**
Limited Edition: London: Chatto & Windus, 1932 (324 copies).
NF/F: $6,000　　　**G/VG: Not Seen**
Limited Edition: Garden City, N.Y.: Doubleday, Doran, 1932 (250 copies).
NF/F: $5,000　　　**G/VG: $2,100**
First U.S. Edition: Garden City, N.Y.: Doubleday, Doran, 1932 (trade).
NF/F: $500　　　**G/VG: $150**

Huysmans, J(oris), K(arl). *A Rebours.*
First Editon: Paris: Bibliotheque Charpentier, 1892.
NF/F: $1,400　　　**G/VG: $500**
First U.S. Edition: New York: Lieber & Lewis, 1922.
NF/F: $500　　　**G/VG: $185**

_____. *La Bas.*
First Editon: Paris: Tresse & Stock, 1891.
NF/F: $2,500　　　**G/VG: $800**
First Edition in English: New York: Albert & Charles Boni, 1924.
NF/F: $350　　　**G/VG: $145**

Jones, Henry (John Coleman). *The Enormous Bed.*
First Edition: Paris: Olympia Press, 1955.
NF/F: $75　　　**G/VG: $30**

Joyce, James. *Ulysses.*
First Editon: Paris: Shakespeare & Co.,
1922. Points of issue: First state issued
in turquoise (blue/green) wraps.
NF/F: $60,000   G/VG: $45,000

Justice, Jean. *Murder vs. Murder.*
First Edition: Paris: Olympia Press,
1964.
NF/F: $50   G/VG: $20

Kantor, MacKinlay. *Andersonville.*
Limited Edition: Cleveland, OH: World
Publishing Company, 1955 (1,000
copies).
NF/F: $650   G/VG: $275
First Edition: Cleveland, OH: World
Publishing Company, 1955.
NF/F: $200   G/VG: $85

Kazantzakis, Nikos. *The Last
Temptation of Christ.*
First Edition in English: New York:
Simon & Schuster, 1960.
NF/F: $125   G/VG: $35

**Kenton, Maxwell. (Terry Southern
and Mason Hoffenberg).** *Candy.*
First Edition: Paris: Olympia Press,
1958. Points of Issue: Both volumes
printed: "Printed October 1958 by
S.I.P. Montreuil, France."
NF/F: $650   G/VG: $125
First U.S. Edition: New York: G.P.
Putnam's Sons, 1964.
NF/F: $200   G/VG: $50
First U.K. Edition: London: Bernard
Geis, 1968.
NF/F: $100   G/VG: $35

Kesey, Ken. *One Flew Over the
Cuckoo's Nest.*
First Edition: New York: Viking Press,
1962. Points of Issue: "that fool Red
Cross woman" on page 9, lines 12-13.
NF/F: $10,000   G/VG: $7,500

Keyes, Daniel. *Flowers for Algernon.*
First Edition: New York: Harcourt
Brace & World, 1966.
NF/F: $2,000   G/VG: $500

King, Stephen. *Carrie.*
First Edition: Garden City, N.Y.:
Doubleday & Co., Inc., 1974. Points
of Issue: P. 6 printed in gutter of page
199.
NF/F: $2,000   G/VG: $800

_____. *Christine.*
Limited Edition: Hampton Falls, NH:
M. Donald Grant, 1983 (1,000 copies).
NF/F: $1,800   G/VG: Not Seen
First Edition: New York: Viking
Penguin, 1983.
NF/F: $15   G/VG: $5

_____. *Cujo.*
Limited Edition: New York: Mysterious
Press, 1981 (750 copies).
NF/F: $1,100   G/VG: Not Seen
First Edition: New York: Viking Press,
1981. Points of Issue: First state dust
jacket is priced $13.95.
NF/F: $10   G/VG: $5

_____. *The Dead Zone.*
First Edition: New York: The Viking
Press, 1979.
NF/F: $75   G/VG: $30

Kung, Hans. *Infallible? An Inquiry.*
First U.S. Edition: Garden City, NY:
Doubleday and Company, 1971.
NF/F: $35   G/VG: $15

LaFarge, Oliver. *Laughing Boy.*
First Edition: Boston: Houghton Mifflin
Company, 1929.
NF/F: $150   G/VG: $35

Landshot, Gustav. *How To Do It.*
First Edition: Paris: Olympia Press, 1956.
NF/F: $35   G/VG: $10

Daniel Keyes.

Stephen King.

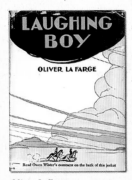

Oliver LaFarge.

William J. Lederer &
Eugene Burdick.

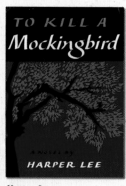

Harper Lee.

Bernard Malamud.

Lawrence, D. H. *Women in Love.*
Limited Edition: New York: Privately
Printed, 1920 (1,250 copies).
NF/F: $2,850   **G/VG: $1,250**

**Lederer, William J. & Eugene
Burdick.** *The Ugly American.*
First Edition: New York: W.W. Norton,
1958.
NF/F: $275   **G/VG: $65**

Lee, Harper. *To Kill a Mockingbird.*
(Caution: This book brings a premium
signed, be sure signed copies have
a verified signature.) First Edition:
Philadelphia and New York: J.B.
Lippincott Company, 1960.
NF/F: $15,000   **G/VG: $3,500**

**Lengel, Frances (Alexander
Trocchi).** *The Carnal Days of Helen
Seferis.*
First Edition: Paris: Olympia Press,
1954.
NF/F: $35   **G/VG: $15**

_____. *Helen and Desire.*
First Edition: Paris: Olympia Press,
1954.
NF/F: $55   **G/VG: $15**

L'Engle, Madeleine. *A Wrinkle in
Time.*
First Edition: New York: Farrar, Straus
& Giroux, 1962.
NF/F: $45   **G/VG: $15**

Lesse, Ruth. *Lash.*
First Edition: Paris: Olympia Press:
1962.
NF/F: $55   **G/VG: $15**

**Lincoln, James & Christopher
Collier.** *Jump Ship to Freedom.*
First Edition: New York: Delacorte,
1981.
NF/F: $25   **G/VG: $8**

_____. *My Brother Sam is Dead.*
First Edition: New York: Four Winds,
1974.
NF/F: $50   **G/VG: $15**

Lowry, Lois. *The Giver.*
First Edition: Boston: Houghton Mifflin
Company, 1993.
NF/F: $200   **G/VG: $75**

Madonna. *Sex.*
First Edition: New York: Warner
Books, 1992.
NF/F: $700   **G/VG: $250**

Malamud, Bernard. *The Fixer.*
First Edition: New York: Farrar, Straus
& Giroux, 1966.
NF/F: $250   **G/VG: $100**

Mardaan, Attaullah. *Deva-Dasi.*
First Edition: Paris: Olympia Press,
1957.
NF/F: $35   **G/VG: $15**
First U.S. Edition: New York: The
Macaulay Company, 1959.
NF/F: $25   **G/VG: $12**

Mathabane, Mark. *Kaffir Boy.*
First Edition: New York: Macmillan
Publishing Co., 1986.
NF/F: $85   **G/VG: $25**

Matthiesen, Peter. *In the Spirit of
Crazy Horse.*
First Edition: New York: Viking Press,
1983.
NF/F: $150   **G/VG: $65**

McCarthy, Mary. *The Group.*
First Edition: New York: Harcourt
Brace & World, 1963.
NF/F: $145   **G/VG: $55**

Meng, Wu Wu (Sinclair Beiles).
Houses of Joy.
First Edition: Paris: Olympia Press, 1958.
NF/F: $65 **G/VG: $25**

Merriam, Eve. *Halloween ABC.*
First Edition: New York Macmillan Publishing Co., 1987.
NF/F: $45 **G/VG: $15**

Metalious, Grace. *Peyton Place.*
First Edition: New York: Julian Messner, 1956.
NF/F: $250 **G/VG: $95**

_____. *Return to Peyton Place.*
First Edition: New York: Julian Messner, 1959.
NF/F: $65 **G/VG: $20**

Miller, Henry. The Rosy Crucifixion Series:

_____. *Nexus.*
First Edition: Paris: Corrêa, 1960 (in French).
NF/F: $400 **G/VG: $145**
First Edition in English: Paris: Obelisk Press, 1960.
NF/F: $250 **G/VG: $85**
First U.S. Edition: NY: Grove Press, 1965.
NF/F: $150 **G/VG: $30**
First U.K. Edition: London: Weidenfeld & Nicolson, 1964.
NF/F: $175 **G/VG: $45**

_____. *Sexus.*
First Edition: Paris: Obelisk Press, 1949.
NF/F: $750 **G/VG: $300**

_____. *Plexus.*
First Edition: Paris: Correa, 1952.
NF/F: $650 **G/VG: $155**
First Edition in English: Paris: Olympia Press, 1953 (2,000 copies).
NF/F: $400 **G/VG: $145**

_____. *Quiet Days in Clichy.*
First Edition: Paris: Olympia Press, 1956.
NF/F: $2,400 **G/VG: $900**

_____. *Tropic of Cancer.*
First Edition: Paris: The Obelisk Press, 1934. Points of Issue: Wrap around band "First Published September 1934" present for first issue.
$4,500 **G/VG: $1,500**
Limited Edition: New York: Grove Press, 1961 (100 copies).
NF/F: $5,000 **G/VG: $3,500**

_____. *Tropic of Capricorn.*
First Edition: Paris: The Obelisk Press, 1939. Points of Issue: Errata slip included in first issue.
NF/F: $2,000 **G/VG: $700**

_____. *The World of Sex.*
Limited Edition: Printed by J.H.N. for Friends of Henry Miller. [Chicago: Ben Abramson, 1941]. (250 copies.)
NF/F: $400 **G/VG: $250**

Moravia, Alberto. *The Wayward Wife.*
First US Edition: New York: Farrar, Straus and Cudahy, 1960.
NF/F: $45 **G/VG: $20**

_____. *Two- A Phallic Novel.* First US Edition: New York: Farrar Straus Giroux, 1972.
NF/F: $40 **G/VG: $15**

Morris, Desmond. *The Naked Ape.*
First Edition: London: Jonathan Cape, 1967.
NF/F: $75 **G/VG: $25**

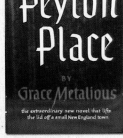
Grace Metalious.

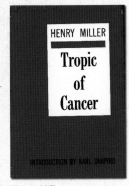
Henry Miller.

Alberto Moravia.

Toni Morrison.

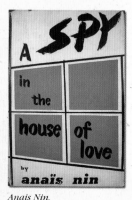

Anaïs Nin.

SEDUCTION
of the MINOTAUR

the new novel by
anaïs nin

Anaïs Nin.

Morrison, Toni. *Beloved.*
First Edition: New York: Alfred A.
Knopf, 1987.
NF/F: $500   G/VG: $175
First U.K. Edition: London: Chatto &
Windus, 1987.
NF/F: $150   G/VG: $55

_____. *The Bluest Eye.*
First Edition: New York: Holt, Rinehart
& Winston, 1970.
NF/F: $7,500   G/VG: $3,000
First U.K. Edition: London: Chatto and
Windus, 1970.
NF/F: $650   G/VG: $250

_____. *The Song of Solomon.*
First Edition: New York: Alfred A
Knopf, 1977.
NF/F: $300   G/VG: $125
First U.K. Edition: London: Chatto and
Windus, 1970.
NF/F: $100   G/VG: $50

Nesbit, Malcom (Alfred Chester).
Chariot of Flesh.
First Edition: Paris: Olympia Press, 1955.
NF/F: $45   G/VG: $15

Newman, Leslea. *Heather Has Two
Mommies.*
First Edition: Los Angeles: Alyson
Wonderland, 1989.
NF/F: $65   G/VG: $20

Nin, Anais. Cities of the Interior
Series:

_____. *Ladders to Fire.*
First Edition: New York: E. P. Dutton,
1946.
NF/F: $350   G/VG: $145

_____. *Children of the Albatross.*
First Edition: New York: E. P. Dutton,
1947.
NF/F: $450   G/VG: $200

_____. *The Four-Chambered
Heart.*
First Edition: New York: Duell, Sloan
and Pearce, 1950.
NF/F: $200   G/VG: $85

_____. *A Spy in the House of Love.*
First Edition: New York: British Book
Centre, 1954.
NF/F: $250   G/VG: $100

_____. *Seduction of the Minotaur.*
First Edition: Denver: Alan Swallow,
1961.
NF/F: $150   G/VG: $55

_____. *Nearer the Moon.*
First Edition: New York and San Diego:
Harcourt Brace, 1996.
NF/F: $25   G/VG: $15

O'Hara, John. *Appointment in
Samarra.*
First Edition: New York. Harcourt,
Brace and Co., 1934. Points of Issue:
Errata slip tipped it to first issue.
NF/F: $6,000   G/VG: $2,500

O'Neill, Peter. *The Corpse Wore Grey.*
First Edition: Paris: Othello/Olympia
Press, 1962.
NF/F: $35   G/VG: $15

_____. *Hell is Filling Up.*
First Edition: Paris: Ophir/Olympia
Press, 1961.
NF/F: $75   G/VG: $20

Orwell, George. *Animal Farm.*
First Edition: London, Secker &
Warburg, 1945.
NF/F: $4,100   G/VG: $1,100
First U.S. Edition: New York: Harcourt,
Brace and Co., 1946. Points of Issue:
First issue dust jacket lacks "Published
in the U.S.A." on rear flap.
NF/F: $700   G/VG: $275

_____. *1984.*
First Edition: London: Secker &
Warburg, 1949.
NF/F: $2,250   **G/VG: $900**
First U.S. Edition: New York: Harcourt
Brace & Co., 1949.
NF/F: $950   **G/VG: $300**

Parkinson, J. Hume. *Sextet.*
First Edition: Paris: Olympia Press,
1965.
NF/F: $45   **G/VG: $20**

Pasternak, Boris. *Doctor Zhivago.*
First U.S. Edition: New York: Pantheon
Books, 1958.
NF/F: $95   **G/VG: $25**
First U.K. Edition: London: Collins &
Harvill, 1958.
NF/F: $900   **G/VG: $325**

Paterson, Katherine. *Bridge to
Terabithia.*
First Edition: New York: Thomas Y.
Crowell, 1977.
NF/F: $75   **G/VG: $25**

_____. *The Great Gilly Hopkins.*
First Edition: New York: Thomas Y.
Crowell, 1978.
NF/F: $125   **G/VG: $40**

Peck, Robert Newton. *A Day No Pigs
Would Die.*
First Edition: New York: Alfred A
Knopf, 1972.
NF/F: $85   **G/VG: $20**

Peters, Solimon. *Business as Usual.*
First Edition: Paris: Olympia Press,
1958.
NF/F: $35   **G/VG: $15**

Plath, Sylvia. *The Bell Jar.*
First Edition: As by Victoria Lucas.
London: Heinemann, 1963.
NF/F: $6,500   **G/VG: $2,225**
First US Edition: New York: Harper &
Row, 1971.
NF/F: $350   **G/VG: $95**

Pomeroy, Wardell B. *Boys and Sex.*
First Edition: New York: Delacorte
Press, 1968.
NF/F: $45   **G/VG: $15**

_____. *Girls and Sex.*
First Edition: New York: Delacorte
Press, 1981.
NF/F: $35   **G/VG: $10**

Pond, Lily & Richard Russo. *Yellow
Silk.*
First Edition: New York: Harmony,
1990.
NF/F: $35   **G/VG: $12**

Powell, William. *The Anarchist
Cookbook.*
First Edition: New York: Lyle Stuart,
Inc., 1971.
NF/F: $600   **G/VG: $175**

Queneau, Raymond. *Zazi Dans le
Metro.*
First Edition: Paris: Olympia Press,
1959.
NF/F: $75   **G/VG: $35**

Reage, Pauline (Dominique Aury).
The Story of O.
First Edition: Simultaneous in French
and in English: Paris: Olympia Press,
1954.
NF/F: $680   **G/VG: $425**

George Orwell.

Boris Pasternak.

Sylvia Plath.

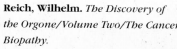

George Revelli.

Reich, Wilhelm. *The Discovery of the Orgone/Volume Two/The Cancer Biopathy.*
First Edition: New York: Orgone Institute Press, 1948.
NF/F: $235   **G/VG: $100**

Remarque, Erich Maria. *All Quiet on the Western Front.*
First U.S. Edition: Boston: Little, Brown and Co., 1929.
NF/F: $850   **G/VG: $225**

Revelli, George. *Commander Amanda Nightingale.*
First U.S. Edition: New York: Grove Press, 1968.
NF/F: $65   **G/VG: $20**

Rodriguez, Luis J. *Always Running La Vida Loca: Gang Days in L.A.*
First Edition: Willimantic, CT: Curbstone Press, 1993.
NF/F: $65   **G/VG: $20**

Rowling, J. K. Harry Potter Series:

_____. *Harry Potter and the Philosopher's Stone.*
London: Bloomsbury, 1997.
Points of Issue: The first state was issued without a dust jacket and the copyright credits "Joanne Rowling."
First Edition:
NF/F: $30,000   **G/VG: $20,000**

_____. *Harry Potter and the Chamber of Secrets.*
London: Bloomsbury, 1998. Points of Issue: The first state was issued without a dust jacket.
First Edition:
NF/F: $6,000   **G/VG: $2,250**

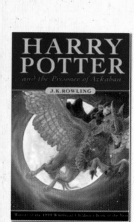

J. K. Rowling.

J. K. Rowling.

_____. *Harry Potter and the Prisoner of Azkaban.*
London: Bloomsbury, 1999. Points of Issue: The first state shows 'Copyright Joanne Rowling' on the copyright page. Clays Ltd is listed as the printer. The first page of text (page 7) has a misaligned dropped text block "burnt/so much." The second state has "J K Rowling" listed as copyright holder. Clays Ltd is also still noted as the printer. The dropped text on page 7 has been corrected. The third state lists J K Rowling as the copyright holder, and has the corrected text on page 7. It also has an added 2 pages of black and white advertisements for the first 2 books at the back of the book. And it lacks the Clays Ltd imprint, and lists no firm as the printer. (Price is first state).
First Edition:
NF/F: $5,200   **G/VG: $2,450**

_____. *Harry Potter and the Goblet of Fire.*
London: Bloomsbury, 2000.
First Edition:
NF/F: $1,500   **G/VG: $500**

_____. *Harry Potter and the Order of the Phoenix.*
London: Bloomsbury, 2003. Points of Issue: On page 7 "The only person left outside was a teenage bo." Probably first state, but the publisher doesn't admit a priority, price considers it first state.
First Edition:
NF/F: $500   **G/VG: Not Seen**

Rushdie, Salmon. *The Satanic Verses.*
First Edition: London: Viking Press, 1988.
NF/F: $150   **G/VG: $55**

Sachar, Louis. *The Boy Who Lost His Face.*
First Edition: New York: Alfred A. Knopf, 1989.
NF/F: $40　　　　　　**G/VG: $10**

Salinger, J. D. *The Catcher in the Rye.*
First Edition: Boston, Little, Brown & Co., 1951.
NF/F: $19,000　　　　**G/VG: $12,000**
Points of Issue: First state dust jacket carries a photo of Salinger.
First U.K. Edition: London: Hamish Hamilton, 1951.
NF/F: $2200　　　　　**G/VG: $850**

Savage, Kim. *Bent to Evil.*
First Edition: New York: Vixen, 1952.
NF/F: $45　　　　　　**G/VG: $25**

_____. *Hellion.*
First Edition: New York: Vixen, 1951.
NF/F: $45　　　　　　**G/VG: $25**

Schwartz, Alvin. *Cross Your Fingers, Spit in Your Hat.*
First Edition: New York & Philadelphia: Lippincott, 1974.
NF/F: $125　　　　　**G/VG: $55**

Selby, Hubert, Jr. *Last Exit to Brooklyn.*
First Edition: New York: Grove Press, 1964.
NF/F: $325　　　　　**G/VG: $125**
First U.K. Edition: London: Calder and Boyars, 1966.
NF/F: $300　　　　　**G/VG: $95**
U.K. Post Trial Edition: London: Calder and Boyars, 1968.
NF/F: $85　　　　　　**G/VG: $25**

Sendak, Maurice. *In the Night Kitchen.*
First Edition: New York: Harper & Row, 1970.
NF/F: $850　　　　　**G/VG: $325**

Shaw, (George) Bernard. *Plays Pleasant and Unpleasant: The First Volume, Containing the Three Unpleasant Plays.*
First Edition: London, Grant Richards, 1898.
NF/F: $500　　　　　**G/VG: $175**
First US Edition: New York: Brentano's, 1905.
NF/F: $45　　　　　　**G/VG: $15**

Silverstein, Charles and Felice Picano. *The New Joy of Gay Sex.*
First Edition: New York: HarperCollins, 1992.
NF/F: $45　　　　　　**G/VG: $15**

Silverstein, Shel. *A Light in the Attic.*
First Edition: New York: Harper & Row, 1981.
NF/F: $125　　　　　**G/VG: $45**

Sjoman, Vilgot. *I Am Curious (Yellow).*
First US Edition: New York: Grove, 1960.
NF/F: $85　　　　　　**G/VG: $25**

Snepp, Frank. *Decent Interval.*
First Edition: New York: Random House, 1977.
NF/F: $400　　　　　**G/VG: $175**

Solzhenitsyn, Aleksandr I. *The Gulag Archipelago.*
First English Language Edition: New York, Evanston, San Francisco and London: Harper & Row Publishers, 1973.
NF/F: $175　　　　　**G/VG: $65**

Steinbeck, John. *The Grapes of Wrath.*
First Edition: New York: Viking Press, 1939. Points of Issue: The first issue dust jacket has "First Edition" in the lower inner corner.
NF/F: $18,000　　　　**G/VG: $6,500**

J. D. Salinger.

Kim Savage.

Shel Silverstein.

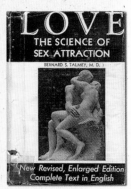
Bernard Talmey.

Henrik Tjele.

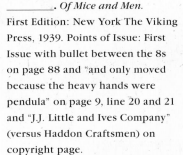

_____. *Of Mice and Men.*
First Edition: New York The Viking Press, 1939. Points of Issue: First Issue with bullet between the 8s on page 88 and "and only moved because the heavy hands were pendula" on page 9, line 20 and 21 and "J.J. Little and Ives Company" (versus Haddon Craftsmen) on copyright page.
NF/F: $10,000   **G/VG: $3,800**

Stern, Howard. *Private Parts.*
First Edition: New York: Simon & Schuster, 1993.
NF/F: $40   **G/VG: $10**

Stone, Scott. *Blaze.*
First Edition: New York: Vixen Press, 1954.
NF/F: $35   **G/VG: $15**

Stowe, Harriet Beecher. *Uncle Tom's Cabin.*
First Edition: Boston and Cleveland: Jewett, Proctor & Worthington, 1852.
NF/F: $24,000   **G/VG: $11,500**

Sturges, Jock. *Radiant Identities.*
New York: Aperture, 1994.
NF/F: $300   **G/VG: $95**

Talmey, Bernard. *Love.*
First Edition: New York: Practitioners' Publishing Co, 1916.
NF/F: $95   **G/VG: $35**

Tjele, Henrik. *Two and Two.*
First Edition: New York: Grove Press, 1970.
NF/F: $30   **G/VG: $10**

Thomas, Piri. *Down These Mean Streets.*
First Edition: New York: Alfred A. Knopf, 1967.
NF/F: $150   **G/VG: $45**

Trumbo, Dalton. *Johnny Got His Gun.*
First Edition: Philadelphia: J. B. Lippincott, 1939.
NF/F: $2,200   **G/VG: $700**

Twain, Mark (Samuel L. Clemens).
The Adventures of Huckleberry Finn.
First Edition: London: Chatto and Windus, 1884.
NF/F: $10,000   **G/VG: $4,500**
First U.S. Edition: New York: Charles L. Webster and Co., 1885. Points of Issue: At p. 13 the erroneous page reference 88 was changed to 87; at p. 57 the misprint with the was was corrected to "with the saw"; and at p. 9 the misprint Decided was corrected to "Decides" in later editions.
NF/F: $28,000   **G/VG: $12,000**

_____. *The Adventures of Tom Sawyer.*
First Edition: London: Chatto and Windus, 1884.
NF/F: $32,000   **G/VG: $15,000**
First U.S. Edition: American Publishing Co.: Hartford, Chicago, Cincinnati, 1876.
NF/F: $36,000   **G/VG: $16,000**

Dalton Trumbo.

Tynan, Kenneth. *Oh! Calcutta!*
First Editon: New York: Grove Press, 1969.
NF/F: $250   **G/VG: $85**
United States Vietnam Relations 1945-1967 (The Pentagon Papers).
First Edition: Washington, D.C.: United States Government Printing Office, 1971.
NF/F: $1,050   **G/VG: $300**

Vonnegut, Kurt. *Slaughterhouse-Five; or The Children's Crusade.*
First Edition: New York: Delecorte Press, 1969.
NF/F: $2,500   **G/VG: $1,200**

Walker, Alice. *The Color Purple.*
First Edition: New York: Harcourt Brace Jovanovich, 1982.
NF/F: $1,100   **G/VG: $250**

Willhoite, Michael. *Daddy's Roommate.*
First Edition: Boston: Alyson Wonderland, 1990.
NF/F: $60   **G/VG: $20**

Whitman, Walt. *Leaves of Grass.*
First Edition: Brooklyn, NY: Privately Printed, July 1855.
NF/F: $165,000   **G/VG: $75,000**
Whitman continued to add and revise the book so there are several "firsts" of different revisions up to the "Deathbed" edition: David McKay, Philadelphia, 1891-2.
NF/F: $600   **G/VG: $275**

Wilson, Edmund. *Memoirs of Hecate County.*
First Edition: Garden City, NY: Doubleday & Co. Inc., 1946.
NF/F: $400   **G/VG: $150**

Winsor, Kathleen. *Forever Amber.*
First Edition: New York: Macmillan Company, 1944.
NF/F: $600   **G/VG: $225**

Woodford, Jack. *White Heat.* First US Edition: New York: Woodford, 1947.
NF/F: $30   **G/VG: $10**

Wright, Peter. *Spycatcher.*
First Edition: Melbourne: William Heinneman, 1987.
NF/F: $225   **G/VG: $70**
First U.S. Edition: New York: Viking Press, 1987.
NF/F: $35   **G/VG: $15**

Wright, Richard. *Black Boy.*
First Edition: New York and London: Harper & Brothers, 1945. Points of Issue: Stated First Edition with code M-T Dust Jacket- $250 price, "5760" on front flap, "5761" on back flap, and "No. 2209" on back cover of jacket.
NF/F: $775   **G/VG: $350**

_____. *Native Son.*
First Edition: New York: Harper & Brothers, 1940.
Points of Issue: First state dust jacket is yellow and green.
NF/F: $2,500   **G/VG: $750**

Zindel, Paul. *The Pigman.*
First Edition: New York: Harper & Row, 1968.
NF/F: $85   **G/VG: $30**

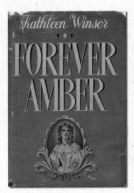

Alice Walker.

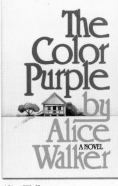

Kathleen Winsor.

Richard Wright.

BIOGRAPHIES

Let's face it, there is a little of the voyeur in all of us. Peeks inside the private world of other people are a source of endless fascination. If the person is prominent, a celebrity, well so much the better.

This fascination has carried us through history, we love the gossip, the facts and the rumors about those we admire.

We are also enamored of clay feet, deriving a simple, if satisfying, pleasure from reading about scandals or even small private vices in those our society seeks to venerate. So, for the last few thousand years, we've been writing it all down.

Biographies also present a personalized view of history. In many cases, the individual view of world events is more accessible to the average reader than the academic exercises that we call history.

The impact of history is seen much more clearly in biographies, memoirs and autobiographies. Many collections of biographies center on a particular era in history for this reason.

Other collections I have seen are built around a particular profession or pursuit.

Politics, literature and art are major focal points, but by no means the only focus of biographical collections.

One client I have worked with for many years has a collection of movie star biographies centered on medicine, exploration, philosophy, counter-culture, and even one based on eccentricity.

Biography also expands the collector's base for signatures. A biography can be signed by either or both the writer and the subject. The value of such signed editions tends to favor the subject, though occasionally, the author might be favored based on his relative status in regard to the subject.

A modern trend in biography bases the form on that of a novel. Sometimes a stretch, it provides a readable and enjoyable story for those who aren't enamored of biography per se.

Plot devices in such books makes them border on fiction, might be called "faction" but they seem to sell well and the trend can probably be counted on to continue.

TEN CLASSIC RARITIES

Blixen, Karen. *Out Of Africa.*
London: Putnam, 1937. Maroon cloth boards stamped in gilt at spine, scarce First of a common book.
NF/F $2,800   **G/VG $1,050**

Churchill, Winston S. Marlborough.
His Life and Times.
London: George G. Harrap & Co. Ltd., 1934-38, 4 vols. Nice value without the blood sweat or tears.
NF/F $4,500   **G/VG $2,200**

(Clay, John) as by: His Eldest Son. *John Clay: A Scottish Farmer.*
Chicago: Privately Printed, 1906. The founder of a large ranch and cattle company profiles his pioneer father.
NF/F $5,800   **G/VG $2,800**

Darrow, Clarence. *The Story of My Life.*
New York: Charles Scribner's Sons, 1932. A limited edition of 294 numbered and signed copies with some unnumbered and signed copies apparently slipping by.
NF/F $3,100   **G/VG $1,200**

Graves, Robert. *Good-Bye To All That: An Autobiography.*
London: Jonathan Cape.
First Edition, 1929. The First state carries a poem by Sassoon P. 341-343.
NF/F $3,500   **G/VG $1,400**

Lewis, Wyndham. *Hitler.*
London: Chatto & Windus, 1931. One of the First denunciations of the Nazis, Goebbels pulped or burned every copy he got a hold of.
NF/F $3,200   **G/VG $1,000**

Nesbit, Evelyn. *Prodigal Days the Untold Story.*
New York: Julian Messner, Inc., 1934. Some light on an old scandal.
NF/F $4,200   **G/VG $2,000**

Vasari, Giorgio & Gaston du C.
de Vere, Lives of the Most Eminent Painters, Sculptors & Architects: in ten volumes.
London: Macmillan and Co. & The Medici Society, 1912. THE source for this type of biography.
NF/F $2,500   **G/VG $1,000**

Washington, Booker T. *Up From Slavery.*
New York: Doubleday, Page & Company, 1901. A best seller in its day, should be findable.
NF/F $2,400   **G/VG $1,100**

Yeats, William Butler. *The Trembling of the Veil.*
London: T. Werner Laurie, 1922. There are 1,000 copies, signed and numbered only about half of which can be found.
NF/F $2,600   **G/VG $1,200**

GOOD-BYE TO ALL THAT
AN AUTOBIOGRAPHY BY
ROBERT GRAVES

Robert Graves.

PRICE GUIDE

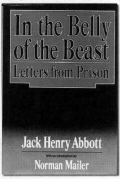

Jack Henry Abbott.

Abbott, Jack Henry. *In the Belly of the Beast: Letters from Prison.* First Edition: New York: Random House, 1981.
NF/F: $70   **G/VG: $25**

Ackerley, J. R. *My Father and Myself.* First Edition: New York: Coward-McCann, 1969. Points of Issue: First Issue has a wrap around band with a Capote quote.
NF/F: $60   **G/VG: $20**

Adams, Henry. *The Education of Henry Adams.* Limited Edition: New York: Limited Editions Club, 1942 (1,500 copies).
NF/F: $400   **G/VG: $150**
First Edition: Boston: Houghton Mifflin, 1918.
NF/F: $250   **G/VG: $100**

Adams, Samuel Hopkins. *Alexander Woolcott: His Life and His World.* First Edition: New York: Reynal & Hitchcock, 1945
NF/F: $25   **G/VG: $$8**
First Edition: New York: Hamish Hamilton, 1946.
NF/F: $20   **G/VG: $7**

Agee, James. *Letters of James Agee to Father Flye.* First Edition: New York: George Braziller, 1962.
NF/F: $95   **G/VG: $35**

Amburn, Ellis. *Dark Star: The Roy Orbison Story.* First Edition: Secaucus, NJ: Carol Publishing Group, 1990.
NF/F: $55   **G/VG: $20**

_____. *Subterranean Kerouac: The Hidden Life of Jack Kerouac.* First Edition: New York: St. Martin's Press, 1998.
NF/F: $35   **G/VG: $10**

_____. *Pearl; the Obsessions and Passions of Janis Joplin.* First Edition: New York: Warner Books, 1992.
NF/F: $25   **G/VG: $8**

Anderson, Loni, with Warren, Larkin. *My Life in High Heels.* First Edition: New York: William Morrow & Company Inc., 1995.
NF/F: $12   **G/VG: $5**

Anderson, Sherwood. *Tar: A Midwest Childhood.* Limited Edition: New York: Boni and Liveright, 1926 (350 copies).
NF/F: $375   **G/VG: Not Seen**
First Edition: New York: Boni and Liveright, 1926.
NF/F: $225   **G/VG: $65**

Ashe, Arthur. *Days of Grace: A Memoir.* First Edition: New York: Alfred A. Knopf, 1993.
NF/F $35   **G/VG: $10**

Asimov, Isaac. *In Memory Yet Green the Autobiography of Isaac Asimov, 1920-1954.* First Edition: Garden City, New York: Doubleday, 1979.
NF/F: $45   **G/VG: $15**

_____. *In Joy Still Felt: The Autobiography of Isaac Asimov, 1964-1978.* First Edition: Garden City, NY: Doubleday & Company, 1980.
NF/F: $50   **G/VG: $15**

Auster, Paul. *Hand To Mouth: A Chronicle Of Early Failure.* First Editon: New York: Henry Holt, 1997.
NF/F: $45   **G/VG: $20**

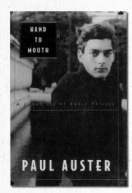

Ellis Amburn.

Paul Auster.

Austin, Gene. *Gene Austin's Ol' Buddy.*
First Edition: Phoenix, AZ: Augury
Press, 1984.
NF/F: $35   **G/VG: $15**

Bacall, Lauren. *Lauren Bacall By Myself.*
First Edition: New York: Alfred A
Knopf, 1978.
NF/F: $45   **G/VG: $15**

Bach, Steven. *Marlene Dietrich: Life
and Legend.*
First Edition: New York: William
Morrow, 1992.
NF/F: $25   **G/VG: $12**
First U.K. Edition: London: Harper
Collins, 1992.
NF/F: $20   **G/VG: $10**

Baez, Joan. *Daybreak.*
First Edition: New York: Dial Press, 1968.
NF/F: $40   **G/VG: $15**

Bailey, F. Lee. *The Defense Never Rests.*
First Edition: New York: Stein and Day, 1971.
NF/F: $25   **G/VG: $10**

Bair, Deirdre. *Simone De Beauvoir: A
Biography.*
First Edition: New York: Summit
Books, 1990.
NF/F: $35   **G/VG: $10**

_____. *Anais Nin: A Biography.*
First Edition: New York: Putnam, 1995.
NF/F: $45   **G/VG: $15**

_____. *Samuel Beckett: A
Biography.*
First Edition: New York: Harcourt
Brace Jovanovich, 1978.
NF/F: $65   **G/VG: $25**

Baker, Russell. *Growing Up.*
First Edition: New York: Congdon &
Weed, Inc., 1982.
NF/F: $25   **G/VG: $10**

Ball, Lucille. *Love Lucy.*
First Edition: New York: G. P. Putnam,
1996.
NF/F: $35   **G/VG: $10**

**Barrows, Sydney Biddle with
William Novak.** *Mayflower Madam.*
First Edition: New York: Arbor House,
1986.
NF/F: $20   **G/VG: $6.**

Bate, W. Jackson. *Samuel Johnson.*
First Edition: New York: Harcourt
Brace Jovanovich, 1977.
NF/F: $35   **G/VG: $10**

Behrman, S.N. *Portrait of Max:
An Intimate Memoir of Sir Max
Beerbohm.*
First Edition: New York: Random
House, 1960.
NF/F: $30   **G/VG: $10**

Benchley, Robert. *Chips Off the Old
Benchley.*
First Edition: New York: Harper &
Brothers, 1949.
NF/F: $45   **G/VG: $15**

Birmingham, Stephen. *The Late
John Marquand: A Biography.*
First Edition: Philadelphia: J.B.
Lippincott Co., 1972.
NF/F: $25   **G/VG: $10**

_____. *Duchess: The Story of
Wallis Warfield Windsor.*
First Edition: Boston: Little, Brown and
Company, 1981.
NF/F: $35   **G/VG: $10**

Blair, Gwenda. *Almost Golden:
Jessica Savitch and the Selling of
Television News.*
First Edition: New York: Simon &
Schuster, 1988.
NF/F: $25   **G/VG: $8**

Gene Austin.

Robert Benchley.

Gwenda Blair.

John Malcolm Brinnin.

George Burns.

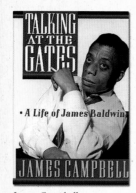

James Campbell.

Bloom Claire. *Leaving A Doll's House.*
First Edition: Boston: Little Brown, 1996.
NF/F: $35   G/VG: $10

Bok, Edward. *The Americanization of Edward Bok.*
Limited Edition: New York Charles Scribner's Sons, 1922 (1,250 copies).
NF/F: $200   G/VG: $85
First Edition: New York Charles Scribner's Sons, 1922.
NF/F: $65   G/VG: $20

Bowen, Catherine Drinker. *Yankee from Olympus: Justice Holmes and His Family.*
First Edition: Boston: Little, Brown & Company, 1944.
NF/F: $25   G/VG: $10

Brando, Marlon with Robert Lindsey. *Brando: Songs My Mother Taught Me.*
First Edition: New York: Random House, 1994.
NF/F: $20   G/VG: $8

Bresler, Fenton. *The Mystery of Georges Simenon: A Biography.*
First Edition: London: William Heinemann/Quixote Press, 1983.
NF/F: $35   G/VG: $15
First U.S. Edition: New York, Beaufort, 1983.
NF/F: $25   G/VG: $10

Brightman, Carol. *Writing Dangerously: Mary McCarthy And Her World.*
First Edition: New York: Clarkson Potter, 1992.
NF/F: $25   G/VG: $10

Brinnin, John Malcolm. *The Third Rose: Gertrude Stein and Her World .*
First Edition: Boston: Little, Brown, 1959.
NF/F: $45   G/VG: $20

_____. *Dylan Thomas in America: An Intimate Journal.*
First Edition: Boston: Little, Brown and Company, 1955.
NF/F: $45   G/VG: $20

Brite, Poppy Z. *Courtney Love: The Real Story.*
First Edition: New York: Simon & Schuster, 1997.
NF/F: $20   G/VG: $8

Brome, Vincent. *Frank Harris: the Life and Loves of a Scoundrel.*
First Edition: New York: Thomas Yoseloff, 1959.
NF/F: $40   G/VG: $15

Brown, Larry. *On Fire.*
First Edition: Chapel Hill, North Carolina: Algonquin Books, 1994.
NF/F: $40   G/VG: $10

Brownstein, Rachel M. *Tragic Muse: Rachel of the Comedie-Francaise.*
First Edition: New York: Alfred A. Knopf, 1993.
NF/F: $30   G/VG: $10

Burgess, Anthony. *Flame into Being; the Life and Work of D.H. Lawrence.*
First Edition: London: Heinemann, 1985.
NF/F: $40   G/VG: $20
First Edition: New York: Arbor House, 1985.
NF/F: $30   G/VG: $10

Burns, George. *Gracie: A Love Story.*
First Edition: New York: G.P. Putnam's, 1988.
NF/F: $25   G/VG: $10

Campbell, James. *Talking at the Gates: A Life of James Baldwin.*
First Edition: New York: Viking, 1991.
NF/F: $25   G/VG: $10

Canby, Henry Seidel. *Walt Whitman, An American.*
First Edition: Boston: Houghton, Mifflin, 1943.
NF/F: $40   G/VG: $10

Carr, John Dickson. *The Life Of Sir Arthur Conan Doyle.*
First Edition: London: John Murray, 1949.
NF/F: $95   G/VG: $35
First Edition: New York: Harper and Brothers, 1949.
NF/F: $75   G/VG: $25

Cate, Curtis. *George Sand.*
First Edition: Boston: Houghton Mifflin, 1975.
NF/F: $35   G/VG: $10

Cerf, Bennett. *At Random: The Reminiscences of Bennett Cerf.*
First Edition: New York: Random House, 1977.
NF/F: $40   G/VG: $10

Charters, Ann. *Kerouac: A Biography.*
First Editon: San Francisco: Straight Arrow Press, 1973.
NF/F: $70   G/VG: $30

Charles Chaplin. *My Autobiography.*
First Edition: New York: Simon & Schuster, 1964.
NF/F: $40   G/VG: $15

Cheever, John. *The Journals Of John Cheever.*
Limited Edition: as Atlantic Crossing: Cottondale: AL Ex Ophidia, 1986 (90 copies).
NF/F: $1,250   G/VG: Not Seen
First Edition: New York: Alfred A. Knopf, 1991.
NF/F: $40   G/VG: $10

Cheever, Susan. *Home Before Dark: a Biographical Memoir of John Cheever By His Daughter.*
First Edition: Boston: Houghton Mifflin, 1984.
NF/F: $35   G/VG: $10

Christie, Agatha. *An Autobiography.*
First Edition: London: Collins, 1977.
NF/F: $40   G/VG: $15
First U.S. Edition: New York: Dodd Mead, 1977.
NF/F: $25   G/VG: $10

Clark, Ronald W. *Einstein. The Life and Times.*
First Edition: New York, World Publishing, 1971.
NF/F: $50   G/VG: $10

Clarke, Gerald. *Capote: A Biography.*
First Edition: New York: Simon & Schuster, 1988.
NF/F: $35   G/VG: $10

Cobb, Irvin S. *Exit Laughing.*
First Editon: Indianapolis: Bobbs-Merrill, 1941.
NF/F: $65   G/VG: $20

Cohen, Mickey. *In My Own Words.*
First Edition: Englewood Cliffs, New Jersey: Prentice-Hall, 1975.
NF/F: $85   G/VG: $30

Colson, Charles W. *Born Again: What Really Happened to the White House Hatchet Man.*
First Edition: Old Tappan, NJ: Fleming H. Revell (Chosen Books), 1976.
NF/F: $25   G/VG: $8

Connell, Evan S. *Son of the Morning Star.*
First Edition: San Francisco: North Point Press, 1984.
NF/F: $200   G/VG: $95

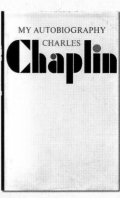

Charles Chaplin.

Agatha Christie.

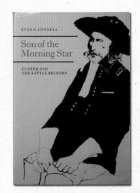

Evan S. Connell.

Walter Cronkite.

John Dean.

Margaret Drabble.

Coward, Noel. *Present Indicative.*
First Edition: London: William Heinemann Ltd., 1937. Points of Issue: First issue has a wrap around band indicating a "Book Society Choice."
NF/F: $85   **G/VG: $25**
First Edition: New York: Doubleday, Doran & Co., Inc., 1937.
NF/F: $35   **G/VG: $10**

Cowley, Malcolm. *Exile's Return.*
First Edition: New York: Norton, 1934.
NF/F: $550   **G/VG: $250**
First U.K. Edition: London: Jonathon Cape, 1935.
NF/F: $600   **G/VG: $150**
Limited Edition: New York: Limited Editions Club, 1981 (2,000 copies).
NF/F: $400   **G/VG: $200**

Craven, Margaret. *Again Calls The Owl.*
First Edition: New York: Putnam, 1980.
NF/F: $25   **G/VG: $10**

Cronkite, Walter. *A Reporter's Life.*
First Edition: New York: Alfred A Knopf, 1996.
NF/F: $55   **G/VG: $20**

Day, Donald. *Will Rogers: A Biography.*
First Edition: New York: David McKay, 1962.
NF/F: $35   **G/VG: $15**

Dean, John. *Blind Ambition: The White House Years.*
First Edition: New York: Simon & Schuster, 1976.
NF/F: $20   **G/VG: $8**

Dillard, Annie. *An American Childhood.*
First Edition: New York: Harper & Row, 1987.
NF/F: $40   **G/VG: $15**

_____. *The Writing Life.*
First Edition: New York: Harper & Row, 1989.
NF/F: $35   **G/VG: $10**

Dillon, Millicent, ed. *Out in the World: Selected Letters of Jane Bowles 1935-1970.*
First Edition (Signed & Limited): Santa Barbara: Black Sparrow, 1985 (200 copies).
NF/F: $100   **G/VG: Not Seen**

_____. *A Little Original Sin: The Life and Work of Jane Bowles.*
First Edition: New York: Holt, Rinehart and Winston, 1981.
NF/F: $40   **G/VG: $10**

Donald, David H. *Look Homeward: A Life of Thomas Wolfe.*
First Editon: Boston: Little, Brown and Co., 1987.
NF/F: $25   **G/VG: $10**

Donaldson, Scott. *John Cheever: A Biography.*
First Edition: New York: Random House, 1988.
NF/F: $25   **G/VG: $10**

_____. *Archibald MacLeish: An American Life.*
First Edition: Boston: Houghton Mifflin Co., 1992.
NF/F: $30   **G/VG: $10**

Douglas, Kirk. *The Ragman's Son.*
First Edition: New York: Simon & Schuster, 1988.
NF/F: $30   **G/VG: $10**

Drabble, Margaret. *Angus Wilson: A Biography.*
First Edition: London: Secker & Warburg, 1995.
NF/F: $35   **G/VG: $10**

Dunaway, David King. *Huxley in Hollywood.*
First Edition: New York: Harper & Row, 1989.
NF/F: $30   **G/VG: $10**

Duras, Marguerite. *Duras by Duras.*
First Edition: San Francisco: City Lights
Books, 1987.
NF/F: $25   **G/VG: $10**

Edwards, Anne. *Sonya The Life of
Countess Tolstoy.*
First Edition: New York: Simon and
Schuster, 1981.
NF/F: $30   **G/VG: $10**

Elledge, Scott. *E.B.White: A
Biography.*
First Edition: New York: W. W. Norton
& Company, 1984.
NF/F: $35   **G/VG: $15**

Ellmann Richard. *Oscar Wilde.*
First Edition: London: Hamish
Hamilton, 1987.
NF/F: $95   **G/VG: $40**
First U.S. Edition: New York: Knopf:
Distributed by Random House, 1988.
NF/F: $45   **G/VG: $15**

_____. *James Joyce.*
First Edition: New York: Oxford
University Press, 1959.
NF/F: $65   **G/VG: $25**

Epstein, Edward Jay. *Legend: The
Secret World of Lee Harvey Oswald.*
First Edition: New York: McGraw Hill,
1978.
NF/F: $35   **G/VG: $10**
First U.K. Edition: London: Hutchinson, 1978
NF/F: $50   **G/VG: $15**

Fast, Howard. *Being Red: A Memoir.*
First Edition: Boston: Houghton Mifflin
Co., 1990.
NF/F: $20   **G/VG: $8**

Field, Andrew. *Nabokov: His Life in Art.*
First Edition: Boston: Little, Brown,
1967.
NF/F: $45   **G/VG: $15**

Gabler, Neal. *Winchell, Gossip, Power
and the Culture of Celebrity.*
First Edition: New York: Alfred A.
Knopf, 1994.
NF/F: $25   **G/VG: $10**
First U.K. Edition: London: Picador, 1995.
NF/F: $25   **G/VG: $10**

Galbraith, John Kenneth. *A Life in
Our Times.*
Limited Edition: Boston: Houghton Mifflin
Co., 1981 (350 copies). Points of Issue:
Issued in slipcase with no dust jacket.
NF/F: $330   **G/VG: $125**
First Edition: Boston: Houghton Mifflin
Co., 1981.
NF/F: $40   **G/VG: $10**

_____. *Ambassador's Journal: A
Personal Account of the Kennedy Years.*
First Edition: Boston: Houghton
Mifflin, 1969.
NF/F: $25   **G/VG: $10**

Gide, Andre. *The Journals of Andre
Gide.* (Four volumes.)
First Editon: London: Secker &
Warburg, 1947-1949.
NF/F: $175   **G/VG: $60**
First Editon: New York. Alfred A.
Knopf, 1947-1951.
NF/F: $125   **G/VG: $55**

Gifford, Barry and Lawrence Lee. *Jack's
Book: An Oral Biography of Jack Kerouac.*
First Edition: New York: St Martin's, 1978.
NF/F: $45   **G/VG: $15**

Gifford, Frank. *The Whole Ten Yards.*
First Edition: New York: Random
House, 1993.
NF/F: $25   **G/VG: $10**

Gill, Brendan. *Here At The New Yorker.*
First Edition: New York: Random
House, 1975.
NF/F: $50   **G/VG: $15**

Scott Elledge.

Richard Ellmann.

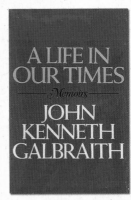
John Kenneth Galbraith.

Victoria Glendinning.

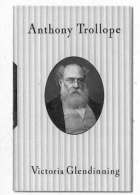

Victoria Glendinning.

Albert Goldman.

Girodias, Maurice. *The Frog Prince: An Autobiography.*
First Edition: New York: Crown, 1980.
NF/F: $30　　　　　　**G/VG: $10**

Glendinning, Victoria. *Rebecca West: A Life.*
First Edition: London: Weidenfeld & Nicolson, 1987.
NF/F: $40　　　　　　**G/VG: $15**
First Edition: New York: Alfred A. Knopf, 1987.
NF/F: $25　　　　　　**G/VG: $10**

_____. *Vita - A Biography of Vita Sackville-West.*
First Edition: London: Weidenfeld & Nicolson, 1983.
NF/F: $35　　　　　　**G/VG: $15**
First Edition: New York: Alfred A. Knopf, 1983.
NF/F: $30　　　　　　**G/VG: $10**

_____. *Trollope.*
First Edition: London: Hutchinson, 1992.
NF/F: $35　　　　　　**G/VG: $10**
First U.S. Edition as Anthony Trollope: New York: Alfred A. Knopf, 1992.
NF/F: $20　　　　　　**G/VG: $8**

Goldman, Albert. *The Lives Of John Lennon.*
First Edition: New York: William Morrow, 1988.
NF/F: $40　　　　　　**G/VG: $15**

_____. *Ladies and Gentlemen: Lenny Bruce!!* First Edition: New York: Random House, 1974.
NF/F: $40　　　　　　**G/VG: $15**

Gray, Francine du Plessix. *Rage and Fire a Life of Louise Colet Pioneer Feminist, Literary Star, Flaubert's Muse.*
First Edition: New York: Simon & Schuster, 1994.
NF/F: $35　　　　　　**G/VG: $10**

Greene, Graham. Autobiography:

_____. *A Sort of Life.*
First U.K. Edition: London: The Bodley Head, 1971. Points of Issue: The First state has "Sir John Barrie" page 177, line 4.
NF/F: $135　　　　　　**G/VG: $25**
First U.S. Edition: New York: Simon & Shuster, 1971.
NF/F: $65　　　　　　**G/VG: $20**

_____. *Ways of Escape.*
Limited Edition: Toronto: Lester & Orpen Dennys, 1980 (150 copies).
NF/F: $550　　　　　　**Not Seen**
First Edition: London: The Bodley Head, 1980.
NF/F: $75　　　　　　**G/VG: $20**
First U.S. Edition: New York: Simon & Shuster, 1980.
NF/F: $65　　　　　　**G/VG: $20**

_____. *Getting to Know the General.*
First U.K. Edition: London: The Bodley Head, 1984.
NF/F: $50　　　　　　**G/VG: $15**
First U.S. Edition: New York: Simon & Shuster, 1984.
NF/F: $45　　　　　　**G/VG: $10**

_____. *A World of My Own: A Dream Diary.*
First Edition: London: Reinhardt/Viking, 1992.
NF/F: $25　　　　　　**G/VG: $10**
First U.S. Edition: New York: Viking, 1992.
NF/F: $25　　　　　　**G/VG: $10**

Griffin, Peter. *Along With Youth: Hemingway, The Early Years.*
First Edition: New York: Oxford University Press, 1985.
NF/F: $50　　　　　　**G/VG: $20**

_____. *Less Than a Treason: Hemingway in Paris.*
First Edition: New York: Oxford University Press, 1990.
NF/F: $40   **G/VG: $15**

Hale, Janet Campbell. *Bloodlines: Odyssey of A Native Daughter.*
First Edition: New York: Random House, 1993.
NF/F: $30   **G/VG: $10**

Hall, Susan. *Gentleman of Leisure A Year in the Life of A Pimp.*
First Edition: New York: New American Library/Prarie Press, 1972.
NF/F: $75   **G/VG: $30**

Hamill, Pete. *A Drinking Life.*
First Edition: Boston: Little, Brown, 1994.
NF/F: $25   **G/VG: $10**

Hammarskjold, Dag. *Markings.*
First Edition in English: New York: Alfred A Knopf, 1964.
NF/F: $45   **G/VG: $20**

Hamilton, Ian. *Robert Lowell.*
First Edition: New York: Random House, 1982.
NF/F: $30   **G/VG: $12**

Harrer, Heinrich. *Seven Years in Tibet.*
Limited Edition: New York: Limited Editions Club, 1993 (300 copies).
NF/F: $4,500   **G/VG: Not Seen**
First Edition in English: London: Rupert Hart-Davis, 1953.
NF/F: $125   **G/VG: $55**
First U.S. Edition: New York E.P. Dutton, 1954.
NF/F: $95   **G/VG: $40**

Harris, Frank. *Bernard Shaw. An Unauthorized Biography Based on Firsthand Information. With a Postscript by Mr Shaw.*
First Edition: London: Victor Gollancz Ltd, 1931.
NF/F: $155   **G/VG: $65**
First U.S. Edition: New York: Simon and Schuster, 1931.
NF/F: $85   **G/VG: $30**

_____. *Oscar Wilde His Life and Confessions* (2 volumes).
First Edition: New York: Frank Harris, 1918.
NF/F: $950   **G/VG: $400**

_____. *New Preface To "The Life and Confessions of Oscar Wilde."*
First Edition: London: The Fortune Press, 1925.
NF/F: $95   **G/VG: $35**
First U.S. Edition (as-*Oscar Wilde;* including the hitherto unpublished Full and final confession by Lord Alfred Douglas and My memories of Oscar Wilde by George Bernard Shaw.: New York: Covici. Friede, 1930.
NF/F: $125   **G/VG: $50**

Hart, Moss. *Act One: An Autobiography.*
First Edition: New York: Random House, 1959.
NF/F: $55   **G/VG: $20**

Hathaway, Katharine Butler. *The Little Locksmith.*
First Edition: New York: Coward-McCann, 1943.
NF/F: $35   **G/VG: $10**

Hellman, Lillian. *Scoundrel Time.*
First Edition: Boston: Little, Brown, 1976.
NF/F: $65   **G/VG: $25**

_____. *An Unfinished Woman.*
First Edition: Boston: Little Brown, 1969.
NF/F: $50   **G/VG: $20**

Susan Hall.

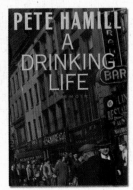
Pete Hamill.

Lillian Hellman.

Ernest Hemingway.

C. David Heyman.

Charles Highman.

_____. *Pentimento: A Book of Portraits.*
First Edition: Boston: Little, Brown, 1973.
NF/F: $45　　　　　**G/VG: $15**

Hemingway, Ernest. *A Moveable Feast: Sketches of the Author's Life in Paris in the Twenties.*
First Edition: New York: Scribners, 1964.
NF/F: $425　　　　　**G/VG: $150**

_____. *The Dangerous Summer.*
First Edition: New York: Scribners, 1985.
NF/F: $175　　　　　**G/VG: $45**

_____. *The Green Hills of Africa.*
First Edition: New York: Scribner's, 1935.
NF/F: $3,200　　　　　**G/VG: $1,200**

Hemingway, Gregory H. *Papa - A Personal Memoir.*
First Edition: Boston: Houghton Mifflin, 1976.
NF/F: $30　　　　　**G/VG: $10**

Hemingway, Jack. *Misadventures of a Fly Fisherman: My Life With & Without Papa.*
First Edition: Lanham, MD: Taylor Publishing Company, 1986.
NF/F: $85　　　　　**G/VG: $25**

Hemingway, Mary Welsh. *How It Was.*
First Edition: New York: Alfred A. Knopf, 1976.
NF/F: $40　　　　　**G/VG: $15**

Herrmann, Dorothy. *S.J. Perelman A Life.*
First Edition: New York: G.P. Putnam's Sons, 1986.
NF/F: $25　　　　　**G/VG: $10**

Heymann, C. David. *Poor Little Rich Girl.*
First Edition: New York: Random House, 1983.
NF/F: $40　　　　　**G/VG: $15**

_____. *A Woman Named Jackie.*
First Edition: Secaucus, NJ: Carol Publishing Group, 1989.
NF/F: $30　　　　　**G/VG: $10**

_____. *Liz: An Intimate Biography of Elizabeth Taylor.*
First Edition: New York: Birch Lane Press, 1995.
NF/F: $20　　　　　**G/VG: $8**

Higham, Charles. *Errol Flynn: The Untold Story.*
First Edition: New York, NY, U.S.A.: Doubleday, 1980.
NF/F: $30　　　　　**G/VG: $10**

_____. *Lucy: The Real Life of Lucille Ball.*
First Edition: New York: St. Martin's Press, 1986.
NF/F: $25　　　　　**G/VG: $10**

_____. *The Adventures of Conan Doyle: The Life of Creator of Sherlock Holmes.*
First Edition: New York: W.W. Norton, 1976.
NF/F: $25　　　　　**G/VG: $10**

Hobson, Laura Z. *Laura Z. A Life.*
First Edition: New York: Arbor House, 1983.
NF/F: $20　　　　　**G/VG: $10**

Holmes, Charles S. *The Clocks of Columbus. The Literary Career of James Thurber.*
First Edition: New York: Atheneum, 1972.
NF/F: $25　　　　　**G/VG: $10**

Holmes Jr., Oliver Wendell. *Touched with Fire Civil War Letters and Diary.*
First Edition: Cambridge, MA: Harvard University Press, 1946.
NF/F: $35　　　　　**G/VG: $20**

Holroyd, Michael. *Lytton Strachey: A Critical Biography* (two volumes). First Edition: New York: Holt, Rinehart & Winston, 1967.
NF/F: $100　　　　　**G/VG: $35**

_____. *Augustus John - A Biography* (two volumes). First Edition: Chatham, Kent: Printed by W. & J. Mackay for William Heinemann, 1974-1975.
NF/F: $475　　　　　**G/VG: $200**

_____. *Bernard Shaw; A Biography* (five volumes). First Edition: London: Chatto & Windus, 1988-1992.
NF/F: $140　　　　　**G/VG: $65**

Hotchner, A. E. *Papa Hemingway.* First Edition: New York: Random House, 1966.
NF/F: $60　　　　　**G/VG: $15**

Howard, John Tasker. *Stephen Foster: America's Troubador.* First Editon: New York: Thomas Y. Crowell, 1934.
NF/F: $50　　　　　**G/VG: $15**

Howe, Irving. *A Margin of Hope: An Intellectual Autobiography.* First Edition: New York: Harcourt Brace Jovanovich, 1982.
NF/F: $30　　　　　**G/VG: $10**

Huffington, Arianna Stassinopoulos. *Picasso: Creator and Destroyer.* First Trade Edition: New York: Simon and Schuster, 1988.
NF/F: $15　　　　　**G/VG: $6.**

Huntley, Chet. *The Generous Years Remembrances of a Frontier Boyhood.* First Edition: New York: Random House, 1968.
NF/F: $20　　　　　**G/VG: $8**

Huxley, Elspeth. *The Flame Trees of Thika: Memories of an African Childhood.* First Edition: London: Chatto & Windus, 1959.
NF/F: $65　　　　　**G/VG: $25**
First U.S. Edition: New York: William Morrow and Co., 1959.
NF/F: $30　　　　　**G/VG: $10**

Huxley, Laura Archera. *This Timeless Moment: A Personal View of Aldous Huxley.* First Edition: New York: Farrar, Straus & Giroux, 1968.
NF/F: $70　　　　　**G/VG: $25**
First U.K. Edition: London: Chatto & Windus, 1969.
NF/F: $25　　　　　**G/VG: $10**

Iacocca, Lee (w/William Novak). *Iacocca An Autobiography.* First Edition: New York: Bantam Books, 1984.
NF/F: $15　　　　　**G/VG: $6**

Jackson, Shirley. *Life Among the Savages.* First Edition: .New York: Farrar, Straus, & Young, 1953.
NF/F: $135　　　　　**G/VG: $65**

Johnson, Diane. *Dashiell Hammett: A Life.* First Edition: New York: Random House, 1983.
NF/F: $45　　　　　**G/VG: $15**

Johnson, Edgar. *Charles Dickens: His Tragedy and Triumph* (two volumes). First Edition: Boston: Little, Brown and Co., 1952.
NF/F: $85　　　　　**G/VG: $25**

Johnson, Lyndon B. *The Vantage Point: Perspectives of the Presidency, 1963-1969.* First Edition: New York: Holt, Rinehart and Winston, 1971.
NF/F: $50　　　　　**G/VG: $20**

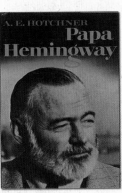
A. E. Hotcher.

Laura Archera Huxley.

Shirley Jackson.

John Keats.

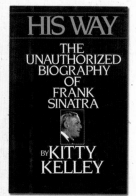

Kitty Kelley.

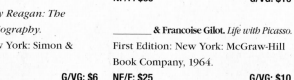

Sir Walter Ralegh
by Robert Lacey

Robert Lacey.

Kalb, Marvin & Benard Kalb. *Kissinger.*
First Edition: Boston: Little, Brown and
Company, 1974.
NF/F: $30   **G/VG: $10**

Kanin, Garson. *Tracy and Hepburn
an Intimate Memoir.*
First Edition: New York: Viking Press, 1971.
NF/F: $35   **G/VG: $10**

Kaplan, Justin. *Mr. Clemens and
Mark Twain: A Biography.*
First Edition: New York: Simon and
Schuster, 1966.
NF/F: $75   **G/VG: $25**

_____. *Walt Whitman: A Life.*
First Edition: New York: Simon and
Schuster, 1980.
NF/F: $35   **G/VG: $10**

Karr, Mary. *The Liar's Club.*
First Edition: New York: Viking, 1995.
NF/F: $75   **G/VG: $25**

Kazin, Alfred. *New York Jew.*
First Edition: New York: Alfred A.
Knopf, 1978.
NF/F: $55   **G/VG: $20**

Keats, John. *You Might As Well Live
The Life and Times of Dorothy Parker.*
First Edition: New York: Simon and
Schuster, 1970.
NF/F: $45   **G/VG: $15**

Kelley, Kitty. *His Way: The Unauthorized
Biography of Frank Sinatra.*
First Edition: New York: Bantam
Books, 1986.
NF/F: $30   **G/VG: $10**

_____. *Nancy Reagan: The
Unauthorized Biography.*
First Edition: New York: Simon &
Schuster, 1991.
NF/F: $15   **G/VG: $6**

Kennedy, John F. *Profiles in Courage.*
First Edition: New York: Harper &
Brothers, 1956.
NF/F: $800   **G/VG: $250**

Kincaid, Jamaica. *My Brother.*
First Edition: New York: Farrar Straus
Giroux, 1997.
NF/F: $45   **G/VG: $15**

Kreyling, Michael. *Author and Agent
Eudora Welty and Diarmuid Russell.*
First Edition: New York: Farrar Straus
Giroux, 1991.
NF/F: $40   **G/VG: $15**

Krutch, Joseph Wood. *Samuel Johnson.*
First Edition: New York: Henry Holt
and Company, 1944.
NF/F: $35   **G/VG: $10**

Kuralt, Charles. *A Life on the Road.*
First Edition: New York: G.P. Putnam, 1990.
NF/F: $25   **G/VG: $8**

L'Amour, Louis. *Education of a Wandering Man.*
First Edition: New York: Bantam
Books, 1989.
NF/F: $35   **G/VG: $10**

Lacey, Robert. *Sir Walter Ralegh.*
First Edition: New York: Atheneum, 1974.
NF/F: $25   **G/VG: $10**

_____. *Ford: The Men and the Machine.*
First Edition: Boston: Little, Brown and
Company, 1986.
NF/F: $35   **G/VG: $10**

Lake, Carlton. *In Quest Of Dali.*
First Edition: New York: G.P. Putnam's, 1969.
NF/F: $35   **G/VG: $10**

_____ **& Francoise Gilot.** *Life with Picasso.*
First Edition: New York: McGraw-Hill
Book Company, 1964.
NF/F: $25   **G/VG: $10**

Lash, Joseph P. *Eleanor: The Years Alone.*
First Edition: New York: W. W. Norton, 1972.
NF/F: $45   **G/VG: $15**

Leamer, Laurence. *King of The Night: Life of Johnny Carson.*
First Edition: New York: Morrow & Co., 1989.
NF/F: $35   **G/VG: $10**

Lee, Lawrence and Barry Gifford. *Saroyan: A Biography.*
First Edition: New York: Harper & Row, 1984.
NF/F: $$20   **G/VG: $8**

Leggett, John. *Ross & Tom Two American Tragedies.*
First Edition: New York: Simon and Schuster, 1974.
NF/F: $35   **G/VG: $10**

Levin, Harry. *James Joyce. A Critical Introduction.*
First Edition: Norfolk, CT.: New Directions Books, 1941.
NF/F: $45   **G/VG: $20**

Lewis, C. S. *Surprised By Joy: The Shape of My Early Life.*
First Edition: London: Geoffrey Bles, 1955.
NF/F: $185   **G/VG: $65**
First U.S. Edition: New York: Harcourt, Brace and Co, 1956.
NF/F: $85   **G/VG: $30**

Lewis, Joe E. *The Joker is Wild.*
First Edition: New York: Random House, 1955.
NF/F: $75   **G/VG: $20**

Lofts, Nora. *Emma Hamilton.*
First Edition: New York: Coward, McCann, & Geoghegan, 1978.
NF/F: $15   **G/VG: $8**

Lovell, Mary S. *Straight On Till Morning; The Biography of Beryl Markham.*
First Edition: New York: St. Martins, 1987.
NF/F: $30   **G/VG: $10**

_____. *The Sound of Wings: The Life of Amelia Earhart.*
First Edition: New York: St. Martin's Press, 1989.
NF/F: $25   **G/VG: $10**

MacArthur, Douglas. *Reminiscences.*
Limited Edition: New York: McGraw-Hill, 1964 (1,750 copies).
NF/F: $1,225   **G/VG: $450**
First Trade Edition: New York: McGraw-Hill, 1964.
NF/F: $55   **G/VG: $25**

Malraux, Andre. *Anti-Memoirs.*
First Edition in English: New York: Holt, Rinehart, Winston, 1968.
NF/F: $35   **G/VG: $15**

Manchester, William. *American Caesar -- Douglas MacArthur 1880-1964.*
First Edition: Boston: Little Brown, 1978.
NF/F: $35   **G/VG: $10**

Manso, Peter. *Mailer His Life and Times.*
First Edition: New York: Simon & Schuster, 1985.
NF/F: $25   **G/VG: $10**

Maquet, Albert. *Albert Camus: The Invincible Summer.*
First Edition in English: New York: George Braziller, 1958.
NF/F: $35   **G/VG: $10**

Markham, Beryl. *West With the Night.*
First Edition: Boston: Houghton, Mifflin and Company, 1942.
NF/F: $750   **G/VG: $300**

Marnham Patrick. *The Man Who Wasn't Maigret a Portrait of Georges Simenon.*
First Edition: London: Bloomsbury, 1992.
NF/F: $35   **G/VG: $10**
First U.S. Edition: New York: Farrar Straus Giroux, 1993.
NF/F: $25   **G/VG: $10**

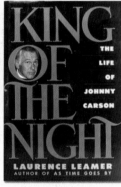
Joseph P. Lash.

Laurence Leamer.

Albert Maquet.

Billy Martin with
Phil Pepe.

Groucho Marx.

Eugene McCarthy.

Martin, Billy. With Phil Pepe.
Billyball.
First Edition: Garden City, NY:
Doubleday Inc., 1987.
NF/F: $20   **G/VG: $10**

Martin, Ralph G. *Jennie: The Life of Lady Randolph Churchill 2 Volumes--Vol.1 The Romantic Years 1854-1895 & Vol.2 The Dramatic Years 1895-1921.*
First Edition: Englewood Cliffs NJ:
Prentice Hall, 1969-1971.
NF/F: $65   **G/VG: $25**

_____. *The Woman He Loved the Story of the Duke & Duchess of Windsor.*
First Edition: New York: Simon and Shuster, 1974.
NF/F: $20   **G/VG: $10**

Marx, Groucho. *Memoirs of a Mangy Lover.*
First Edition: New York: Bernard Geis Associates, 1963.
NF/F: $85   **G/VG: $25**

Robert K. Massie. *Nicholas and Alexandra.*
First Edition: New York: Atheneum, 1967.
NF/F: $35   **G/VG: $10**

Maugham, W. Somerset. *The Summing Up.*
Limited Edition: Garden City, NY:
Doubleday & Company, 1954 (375 copies).
NF/F: $1,000   **G/VG: $425**
First Edition: London: William Heinemann, LTD., 1938.
NF/F: $85   **G/VG: $30**
First Edition: New York: Doubleday, Doran, 1938.
NF/F: $55   **G/VG: $20**

Maurois, Andre. *Disraeli: A Picture of the Victorian Age.*
First Edition: New York: D. Appleton & Company, 1928.
NF/F: $95   **G/VG: $30**
First U.K. Edition: London: John Lane the Bodley Head, 1929.
NF/F: $65   **G/VG: $25**

Mayfield, Sara. *The Constant Circle. H.L. Mencken and His Friends.*
First Edition: New York: Delacorte Press, 1968.
NF/F: $40   **G/VG: $15**

Maynard, Joyce. *At Home in the World: A Memoir.*
First Edition: New York: Picador, 1998.
NF/F: $25   **G/VG: $10**

Mayle, Peter. *A Year in Provence.*
First Edition: London: Hamish Hamilton, 1989.
NF/F: $45   **G/VG: $20**
First U.S. Edition: New York: Alfred A. Knopf, 1990.
NF/F: $40   **G/VG: $10**

McCall, Nathan. *Makes Me Wanna Holler: A Young Black Man in America.*
First Edition: New York: Random House, 1994.
NF/F: $25   **G/VG: $10**

McCarthy, Eugene. *Up 'til Now: A Memoir.*
First Edition: San Diego: Harcourt Brace Jovanovich, 1987.
NF/F: $20   **G/VG: $10**

McCarthy, Mary. *How I Grew.*
First Edition: New York: Harcourt Brace Jovanovich, 1987.
NF/F: $25   **G/VG: $10**

McCourt, Malachy. *A Monk Swimming.*
First Edition: New York: Hyperion, 1998.
NF/F: $30   **G/VG: $10**

McGinniss, Joe. *The Last Brother.*
First Edition: New York: Simon &
Schuster, 1993.
NF/F: $25   **G/VG: $10**

Mead, Margaret. *Blackberry Winter:
My Earlier Years.*
First Edition: New York: William
Morrow & Co., 1972.
NF/F: $25   **G/VG: $10**
First U.K. Edition: London: Angus &
Robertson, 1973.
NF/F: $20   **G/VG: $8**

Mellow, James R. *Invented Lives: The
Marriage of F. Scott & Zelda Fitzgerald.*
First Edition: Boston & New York:
Houghton Mifflin Company, 1984.
NF/F: $45   **G/VG: $20**

_____. *Charmed Circle: Gertrude
Stein & Company.*
First Edition: New York: Praeger
Publishers, 1974.
NF/F: $30   **G/VG: $10**

_____. *Nathaniel Hawthorne and
His Times.*
First Edition: Boston: Houghton
Mifflin, 1980.
NF/F: $25   **G/VG: $10**

Middlebrook, Diane Wood. *Anne
Sexton.*
First Edition: Boston: Houghton
Mifflin, 1991.
NF/F: $25   **G/VG: $12.**

Miles, Barry. *Ginsberg.*
First Edition: New York: Simon and
Schuster, 1989.
NF/F: $40   **G/VG: $15**

Milford, Nancy. *Zelda.*
First Edition: New York: Harper and
Row, 1970.
NF/F: $55   **G/VG: $15**

Miller, Arthur. *Timebends, A Life.*
First Edition: Franklin Center, PA:
Franklin Library, 1987.
NF/F: $275   **G/VG: Not Seen**
First Trade Edition: New York: Grove
Press, 1987.
NF/F: $35   **G/VG: $10**

Miller, Donald L. *Lewis Mumford, A Life.*
First Editon: New York: Weidenfeld &
Nicolson, 1989.
NF/F: $20   **G/VG: $8**

Miller, Merle. *Plain Speaking: An
Oral Biography of Harry S. Truman.*
First Edition: New York NY: Berkley, 1974.
NF/F: $35   **G/VG: $15**

Monti, Carlotta (w/Cy Rice).
W.C. Fields & Me.
First Edition: Englewood Cliffs, NJ:
Prentice-Hall, Inc., 1971.
NF/F: $20   **G/VG: $10**

Mowat, Farley. *Woman in the Mist:
The Story of Dianne Fossey and the
Mountain Gorillas of Africa.*
First Edition: New York: Warner
Books, 1987.
NF/F: $25   **G/VG: $10**

Nabokov, Vladimir. *Speak, Memory.*
First Edition: London: Victor Gollancz Ltd., 1951.
NF/F: $275   **G/VG: $120**

Nin, Anais. *The Diary of Anais Nin
Volumes 1 & 2.*
First U.S. Editions: The Swallow Press,
and Harcourt Brace & World, Inc.,
1964-1966.
NF/F: $35   **G/VG: $15**

_____. *The Diary of Anais Nin.*
Volumes 3-7.
First U.S. Editions: San Diego & New
York, Harcourt Brace etal, 1969-1980.
NF/F: $20   **G/VG: $10**

Carlotta Monti.

Anais Nin.

Anais Nin.

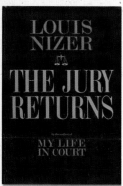

Louis Nizer.

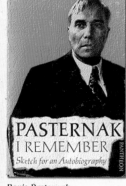

Boris Pasternak.

The first eyewitness account of how the world's most secretive man lived and died in his own bizarre asylum—as revealed by two of his personal aides

HOWARD HUGHES: THE HIDDEN YEARS

James Phelan

James Phelon.

_____. *Incest.*
First Edition: New York: Harcourt, Brace Jovanovich, 1992.
NF/F: $35   **G/VG: $15**

_____. *Henry and June.*
First Edition: San Diego and New York: Harcourt Brace Jovanovich, 1986.
NF/F: $40   **G/VG: $20**

Niven, David. *The Moon's a Balloon.*
First Edition: New York: G. P. Putnam, 1972.
NF/F: $15   **G/VG: $8**

_____. *Bring on the Empty Horses.*
First Edition: New York: G. P. Putnam, 1975.
NF/F: $15   **G/VG: $8**
First U.K. Edition: London: Hamish Hamilton, 1976.
NF/F: $15   **G/VG: $8**

Nizer, Louis. *The Jury Returns.*
First Edition: Garden City, NY: Doubleday & Co., 1966.
NF/F: $20   **G/VG: $10**

Nolan, Christopher. *Under the Eye of the Clock: The Life Story of Christopher Nolan.*
First Edition: London: Weidenfield & Nicholson, 1987.
NF/F: $45   **G/VG: $20**
First U.S. Edition: New York: St. Martin's Press, 1987.
NF/F: $25   **G/VG: $10**

North, Sterling. *Rascal: A Memoir of a Better Era.*
First Edition: New York: E. P. Dutton, 1963.
NF/F: $50   **G/VG: $15**

Nowell, Elizabeth. *Thomas Wolfe: A Biography.*
First Edition: Garden City, N.Y.: Doubleday & Company, 1960.
NF/F: $35   **G/VG: $10**

Pasternak, Boris. *I Remember: Sketch for an Autobiography.*
First Edition: New York: Pantheon, 1959.
NF/F: $30   **G/VG: $10**

Paulsen, Gary. *Eastern Sun Winter Moon An Autobiographical Odyssey.*
First Editon: New York: Harcourt Brace Jovanovich, 1993.
NF/F: $20   **G/VG: $8**

Payne, Robert. *The Life and Death of Adolf Hitler.*
First Edition: New York: Praeger, 1972.
NF/F: $45   **G/VG: $20**

_____. *The Rise and Fall of Stalin.*
First Edition: New York: Simon & Schuster, 1965.
NF/F: $25   **G/VG: $8**

Peacock, Molly. *Paradise, Piece By Piece.*
First Edition: New York: Riverhead Books, Penguin Putnam Inc, 1998.
NF/F: $25   **G/VG: $10**

Phelan, James. *Howard Hughes: The Hidden Years.*
First Edition: New York: Random House, 1976.
NF/F: $25   **G/VG: $10**

Phillips, Julia. *You'll Never Eat Lunch in This Town Again.*
First Edition: New York; Random House; 1991.
NF/F: $20   **G/VG: $8**

Plimpton, George. *Truman Capote: In Which Various Friends, Enemies, Acquaintances, and Detractors Recall His Turbulent Career.*
First Edition: New York: Doubleday, 1997.
NF/F: $25   **G/VG: $10**
First U.K. Edition: London: Picador, 1997.
NF/F: $25   **G/VG: $10**

Pohl, Frederik. *Frederik Pohl: The Way the Future Was - A Memoir.*
First Edition: New York: Del Rey, 1978.
NF/F: $25   **G/VG: $10**

Presley, Priscilla Beaulieu. *Elvis and Me.*
First Edition: New York: Putnam, 1985.
NF/F: $25   **G/VG: $8**

Price, Reynolds. *Clear Pictures: First Loves, First Guides.*
First Edition: New York: Atheneum, 1989.
NF/F: $35   **G/VG: $15**

Pyle, Ernie. *Home Country.*
First Edition: New York: William Sloane Associates, 1947.
NF/F: $25   **G/VG: $10**

Ramsland, Katherine. *Prism of the Night: A Biography of Anne Rice.*
First Edition: New York: E. P. Dutton, 1991.
NF/F: $15   **G/VG: $8**

Rawlings, Marjorie Kinnan. *Cross Creek.*
First Edition: New York: Charles Scribner's Sons, 1942.
NF/F: $400   **G/VG: $150**
First Edition: London: William Heinemann, 1942.
NF/F: $225   **G/VG: $100**

Ray, Gordon N. *H.G. Wells & Rebecca West.*
First Edition: New Haven: Yale University Press, 1974.
NF/F: $25   **G/VG: $10**
First U.K. Ed: London: Macmillan, 1974.
NF/F: $20   **G/VG: $8**

Roth, Philip. *The Facts: A Novelist's Autobiography.*
Limited Edition: New York: Farrar, Straus & Giroux, 1988 (250 copies).
NF/F: $250   **G/VG: $95**
First Edition: New York: Farrar, Straus & Giroux, 1988.
NF/F: $50   **G/VG: $15**

Russell, Bertrand. *The Autobiography of Bertrand Russell* (3 volumes).
First Edition: London: George Allen & Unwin, 1967.
NF/F: $125   **G/VG: $60**

Salter, James. *Burning The Days.*
First Edition: New York: Random House, 1997.
NF/F: $80   **G/VG: $25**

Sartre, Jean-Paul. *The Words: The Autobiography of Jean-Paul Sartre.*
First U.S. Edition: New York: George Braziller, 1964.
NF/F: $85   **G/VG: $30**

_____. *Saint Genet.*
First Edition in English: New York: George Braziller, 1963.
NF/F: $55   **G/VG: $20**

Sassoon, Siegfried. *Memoirs of a Fox-Hunting Man.*
Limited Edition: London: Faber & Gwyer Limited, 1928 (260 copies).
NF/F: $4,100   **G/VG: Not Seen**
First Trade Edition: London: Faber & Gwyer Limited, 1928.
NF/F: $600   **G/VG: $250**

_____. *Memoirs of an Infantry Officer.*
Limited Editon: London: Faber & Faber, 1931 (320 copies).
NF/F: $2,500   **G/VG: $950**
First Trade Editon: London: Faber & Faber, 1930.
NF/F: $350   **G/VG: $150**

Sawyer-Laucanno, Christopher. *An Invisible Spectator: A Biography of Paul Bowles.*
First Edition: New York: Weidenfeld and Nicolson, 1989.
NF/F: $25   **G/VG: $10**

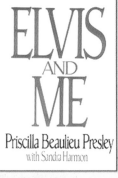
Priscilla Beaulieu Presley.

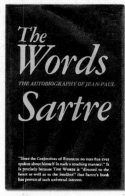
Jean-Paul Sartre.

Jean-Paul Sartre.

H. Allen Smith.

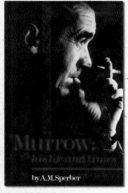

Ann M. Sperber.

Schorer, Mark. *Sinclair Lewis an American Life.*
First Edition: New York: McGraw-Hill, 1961.
NF/F: $35   **G/VG: $10**

Seaman, Barbara. *Lovely Me; The Life of Jacqueline Susan.*
First Edition: New York: William Morrow & Co., 1987.
NF/F: $25   **G/VG: $10**

See, Carolyn. *Dreaming: Hard Luck and Good Times in America.*
First Edition: New York: Random House, 1995.
NF/F: $20   **G/VG: $8**

Shelden, Michael. *Friends of Promise: Cyril Connolly and the World of Horizon.*
First Edition: New York: Harper & Row, 1989.
NF/F: $25   **G/VG: $10**

Shiber, Etta. *Paris-Underground.*
First Edition: New York: Charles Scribner's Sons, 1944.
NF/F: $35   **G/VG: $10**

Silverman, Willa Z. *The Notorious Life of Gyp: Right-Wing Anarchist in Fin-de-Siecle France.*
First Edition: New York: Oxford University Press, 1995.
NF/F: $25   **G/VG: $10**

Simon, Linda. *The Biography of Alice B. Toklas.*
First Edition: Garden City, NY: Doubleday & Co., 1977.
NF/F: $25   **G/VG: $8**

Sitwell, Edith. *Taken Care Of, An Autobiography.*
First Edition: London: Hutchinson, 1965.
NF/F: $35   **G/VG: $10**

Sitwell, Osbert. Autobiography:

_____. *Left Hand, Right Hand! An Autobiography.* Vol. I: *The Cruel Month.* (II) *The Scarlet Tree: Being the Second Volume of Left Hand, Right Hand! An Autobiography.* (III) *Great Morning: Being the Third Volume of Left Hand, Right Hand! An Autobiography.* (IV) *Laughter in the Next Room: Being the Fourth Volume of Left Hand, Right Hand! An Autobiography.* (V) *Noble Essences or Courteous Revelations: Being a Book of Characters and the Fifth and Last Volume of Left Hand, Right Hand! An Autobiography.*
First Edition: London: Macmillan, 1945-1950.
NF/F: $400   **G/VG: $85**

Skinner, Cornelia Otis. *Madame Sarah.*
First Edition: Boston: Houghton Mifflin, 1967.
NF/F: $30   **G/VG: $10**

Smith, Gene. *When The Cheering Stopped.*
First Edition: New York: William Morrow, 1964.
NF/F: $25   **G/VG: $10**

Smith, H. Allen. *Lo, the Former Egyptian!* First Edition: Garden City, NY: Doubleday, 1947.
NF/F: $25   **G/VG: $10**

Sonnenberg, Ben. *Lost Property: Memoirs & Confessions of a Bad Boy.*
First Edition: New York: Summit Books, 1991.
NF/F: $15   **G/VG: $8**
First U.K. Edition: London: Faber & Faber, 1991.
NF/F: $15   **G/VG: $6**

Souhami, Diana. *Gertrude & Alice.*
First Edition: London: Pandora Press, 1991.
NF/F: $30   **G/VG: $10**

Spender, Stephen. *World Within World. The Autobiography of Stephen Spender.*
First Edition: London: Hamish Hamilton, 1951.
NF/F: $75　　　　**G/VG: $30**
First U.S. Edition: New York: Harcourt Brace and Company, 1951.
NF/F: $40　　　　**G/VG: $15**

Sperber, Ann M. *Murrow: His Life and Times.*
First Edition: New York: Freundlich Books, 1986.
NF/F: $15　　　　**G/VG: $6**

Starkie, Enid. *Arthur Rimbaud.*
First Edition: New York: New Directions, 1961.
NF/F: $60　　　　**G/VG: $20**

Stein, Gertrude. *The Autobiography of Alice B. Toklas.*
First Edition: New York: Harcourt, Brace and Company, 1933. Points of Issue: The First state dust jacket is unpriced.
NF/F: $750　　　　**G/VG: $300**
First U.K. Edition: London: John Lane The Bodley Head, 1933.
NF/F: $150　　　　**G/VG: $60**

_____. *Picasso.*
First Edition: Paris: Librairie Floury, 1938.
NF/F: $750　　　　**G/VG: $300**
First Edition in English: London: B. T. Batsford, 1946.
NF/F: $150　　　　**G/VG: $85**

_____. *Wars I Have Seen.*
First Edition: London: Batsford, 1945.
NF/F: $125　　　　**G/VG: $50**
First U.S. Edition: New York: Random House, 1945.
NF/F: $85　　　　**G/VG: $40**

Steinbeck, John. *Travels with Charley in Search of America.*
First Edition: New York: The Viking Press, 1962. Points of Issue: The First state dust jacket carries no mention of the Nobel Prize.
NF/F: $320　　　　**G/VG: $100**

Strouse, Jean. *Alice James - A Biography.*
First Edition: Boston: Houghton Mifflin, 1980.
NF/F: $30　　　　**G/VG: $10**
First U.K. Edition: London: Johnathan Cape, 1981.
NF/F: $25　　　　**G/VG: $8**

Stuart, Jesse. *The Thread That Runs So True.*
First Edition: New York: Charles Scribner's Sons, 1949.
NF/F: $125　　　　**G/VG: $50**

Swanberg, W.A. *Luce and His Empire.*
First Edition: New York: Charles Scribners, 1972.
NF/F: $25　　　　**G/VG: $8**

Swanson, Gloria. *Swanson on Swanson.*
First Edition: New York: Random House, 1980.
NF/F: $45　　　　**G/VG: $15**

Sykes, Christopher. *Evelyn Waugh: A Biography.*
First Editon: London: Collins, 1975.
NF/F: $25　　　　**G/VG: $10**
First U.S. Edition: Boston: Little, Brown and Co., 1975.
NF/F: $25　　　　**G/VG: $10**

Teichmann, Howard. *George S. Kaufman.*
First Edition: New York: Atheneum, 1972.
NF/F: $15　　　　**G/VG: $5**

Gertrude Stein.

Gertrude Stein.

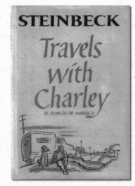
John Steinbeck.

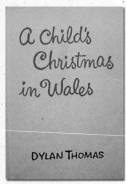

Dylan Thomas.

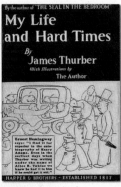

James Thurber.

Calvin Tomkins.

Thomas, D. M. *Alexander Solzhenitsyn: A Century in His Life.*
First Edition: New York: St. Martin's Press, 1998.
NF/F: $25   **G/VG: $10**

Thomas, Dylan. *A Child's Christmas in Wales.*
First Edition: Norfolk, CT: New Directions, 1954.
NF/F: $185   **G/VG: $65**

Thurber, James. *My Life and Hard Times.*
First Edition: New York: Harper & Brothers, 1933.
NF/F: $200   **G/VG: $95**

Thurman, Judith. *Isak Dinesen. The Life of a Storyteller.*
First Edition: New York: St. Martin's Press, 1982.
NF/F: $30   **G/VG: $10**

Toklas, Alice B. *What Is Remembered.*
First Edition: London: Michael Joseph, 1963.
NF/F: $120   **G/VG: $45**
First U.S. Edition: New York: Holt, Rinehart and Winston, 1963.
NF/F: $95   **G/VG: $35**

Tolson, Jay. *Pilgrim in the Ruins: A Life of Walker Percy.*
First Edition: New York: Simon and Schuster, 1992.
NF/F: $30   **G/VG: $10**

Tomkins, Calvin. *Living Well is the Best Revenge.*
First Edition: New York: Viking Press, 1971.
NF/F: $45   **G/VG: $15**

Treglown, Jeremy. *Roald Dahl: A Biography.*
First Edition: London: Faber & Faber, 1994.
NF/F: $35   **G/VG: $10**

Turnbull, Andrew. *Scott Fitzgerald.*
First Edition: New York: Scribner's, 1962.
NF/F: $50   **G/VG: $15**
First U.K. Edition: London: Bodley Head, 1962.
NF/F: $45   **G/VG: $15**

Twain, Mark. *Life on the Mississippi.*
First Editon: London: Chatto & Windus, 1883.
NF/F: $2,100   **G/VG: $700**
First U.S. Edition: Boston: James R. Osgood And Co., 1883. Points of Issue: Page 411 tail-piece with urn, flames and head of Twain; page 443 caption reads "The St. Louis Hotel."
NF/F: $3,200   **G/VG: $1,500**

_____. *Roughing It.*
First Edition: Hartford: American Publishing Company, 1872. Points of Issue: Page xi, line "My perfect," page 242, lines 20-21 "premises-said he/was occupying his..." in First issue.
NF/F: $1,500   **G/VG: $600**

_____. *A Tramp Abroad.*
First Edition: Hartford: American Publishing Company, 1880.
NF/F: $3,200   **G/VG: $1,000**
Points of Issue: Cover blind stamped border and the frontispiece is labeled "Moses."
First U.K. Edition: London: Chatto & Windus, 1880.
NF/F: $2,100   **G/VG: $800**

Tytell, John. *Ezra Pound. The Solitary Volcano.*
First Edition: New York: Anchor Press/ Doubleday, 1987.
NF/F: $35   **G/VG: $15**

Ustinov, Peter. *Dear Me.*
First Edition: London: Heinemann,
1977.
NF/F: $25   **G/VG: $8**
First Edition: Boston: Little, Brown &
Company, 1977.
NF/F: $15   **G/VG: $6.**

Vonnegut Kurt. *Palm Sunday An
Autobiographical Collage.*
Limited Edition: New York: Delacorte
Press, 1981 (500 copies).
NF/F: $325   **G/VG: $135**
First Edition (trade): New York:
Delacorte Press, 1981.
NF/F: $65   **G/VG: $15**

Waugh, Evelyn. *A Little Learning.*
First Edition: London: Chapman &
Hall, 1964.
NF/F: $95   **G/VG: $40**
First U.S. Edition: Boston: Little, Brown
and Company, 1964.
NF/F: $35   **G/VG: $15**

Welty, Eudora. *One Writer's
Beginnings.*
First Edition: Cambridge and London:
Harvard University Press, 1984.
NF/F: $200   **G/VG: $75**

Weintraub, Stanley. *Beardsley.*
First Edition: London: W.H. Allen,
1967.
NF/F: $65   **G/VG: $25**
First Edition: New York: George
Braziller, 1967.
NF/F: $35   **G/VG: $15**

White, Edmund. *Genet: A Biography.*
First Edition: London: Chatto &
Windus, 1993.
NF/F: $45   **G/VG: $15**
First Edition: New York: Alfred A.
Knopf, 1993.
NF/F: $35   **G/VG: $10**

White, William Allen. *The
Autobiography of William Allen White.*
First Edition: New York: Macmillan,
1946.
NF/F: $50   **G/VG: $20**

Williams, William Carlos. *Yes, Mrs.
Williams: A Personal Record of My
Mother.*
First Edition: New York: McDowell,
Oblensky Inc., 1959.
NF/F: $55   **G/VG: $20**

Wineapple, Brenda. *Sister Brother:
Gertrude and Leo Stein.*
First Edition: New York: G. P.
Putnam's, 1996.
NF/F: $25   **G/VG: $8**

Wolff, Geoffrey. *The Duke of
Deception: Memories of My Father.*
First Edition: New York: Random
House, 1979.
NF/F: $25   **G/VG: $10**

Wolff, Tobias. *This Boy's Life: A Memoir.*
First Edition: New York: Grove/
Atlantic, 1989.
NF/F: $115   **G/VG: $35**

Zierold, Norman. *Garbo.*
First Edition: New York: Stein & Day,
1969.
NF/F: $20   **G/VG: $8**

Zweig, Stefan. *Balzac.*
First Edition: New York: The Viking
Press, 1946.
NF/F: $45   **G/VG: $20**

Geoffrey Wolff.

Tobias Wolff.

Norman Zierold.

CHILDREN'S BOOKS

Children's books have become as wide a field almost as books themselves since John Newberry began publishing books for children back in the 1770s. Nearly every area of collecting in adult books is replicated in the collection of children's books.

Like all books, a certain importance is attached to the idea of a "first edition"; however, in children's books there are other considerations.

A great many collectors build a collection to pass on to younger generations in which the object is to find the books they owned as children. Adult collections of various types also contain children's books.

Art book collectors find that many prominent artists such as Maxfield Parrish were prominent children's book illustrators. One of the most visible banned books is Helen Bannerman's *Little Black Sambo*. And many major science fiction/fantasy writers have turned in children's books and series, such as C. S. Lewis' *Narnia* series and Isaac Asimov's *Lucky Starr*.

Series play a large part in collecting children's books, both from thematic and format points of view. One of the better collected formats for children's books is the Little Golden Book. This guide won't cover Little Golden Books, as KP Books has an excellent guide to them, Steve Santi's *Collecting Little Golden Books* (0873496264). Little Big books are also prized collectibles in the area of format, published by Whitman of Racine, Wisconsin.

Thematic and series books are also a major focus of collections. Beginning with the genius of L. Frank Baum, the Oz series has seen books created by 70 other authors.

The Stratemeyer Syndicate founded by Edward Stratemeyer (1862-1930) produced several series under various pseudonyms. Beginning with Stratemeyer's work, then farmed out to freelancers, such as Weldon J. Cobb (1849-1922), and Howard R. Garis (1873-1962), some series, such as the Rover Boys and Nancy Drew, are still being expanded upon today. To get an idea of the influence of the Stratemeyer Syndicate, just take a look at the author's pseudonyms and the number of writers who wrote under Stratemeyer pseudonyms such as Victor Appleton.

Vintage children's books are a further focus of some collections. Publishers such as Lothrop, the McLoughlin Brothers and Raphael Tuck, are creating unique and interesting variations such as shaped (die-cut) books and books printed on linen and other fabrics.

Many of these children's books were the pioneer stage of such printing techniques as chromo-litho.

Everyone wants to experience the fountain of youth. Many collectors of children's books have found it in a collection that they can peruse from time to time to travel back to the day when they first learned of the existence of the *Wonderful Wizard of Oz*, and their first trip "over the rainbow."

TEN CLASSIC RARITIES

Alger, Horatio, Jr. *Ragged Dick; Or, Street Life in New York With the Boot-Blacks.* Boston: Loring, 1868. First state with "Fame and Fortune" announced for December and Dick alone on the decorative title page.
NF/F: $6,500   **G/VG: $3,800**

Baum, L. Frank. *The Wonderful Wizard of Oz.*
Chicago and New York: Geo M. Hill, 1900. There are three states of the first edition. The true first is determined by a blank title page verso, two dark blotches on the moon in plate facing p. 34 and a red horizon/background in plate facing p. 92.
NF/F: $37,000   **G/VG: $12,000**
(Series in Children)

Carroll, Lewis (Charles Dodgson). *Alice's Adventures in Wonderland.* London: Macmillan & Co., 1866. Red cloth binding with gilt titles to spine, circular gilt decoration to boards, powder blue endpapers, all edges gilt.
NF/F: $52,000   **G/VG: $30,000**

Cox, Palmer. *Brownies: Their Book.* New York: Century, 1887. Very early example of a dust jacket which must be present for a complete first edition.
NF/F: $3,500   **G/VG: $1,800**
(See series in Art)

Dixon, Franklin W. *The Tower Treasure.* New York: Grosset & Dunlap, 1927. First Hardy Boys book. Ads in back starting with "This Isn't All!," Tom Swift Series 29 titles ending with Airline Express, Don Sturdy 7 titles ending Among Gorillas, Radio Boys Series, Garry Grayson Football Series, Ending with Western Stories For Boys with 5 titles Round-Up Being Last Title, in red cloth.
NF/F: $1,000   **G/VG: $600**
(Note: This title has been updated several times, be sure you check points of issue.)

Grahame, Kenneth. *Wind in the Willows.*
London: Methuen and Co., 1908. Blue cloth pictorially stamped and lettered in gilt within a single gilt rule border on front cover and pictorially stamped and lettered in gilt on spine. Top edge gilt, others uncut.
NF/F: $14,000   **G/VG: $5,800**

Keene, Carolyn. *The Secret of Shadow Ranch.*
Grosset and Dunlap: New York, 1931. First issue has copyright page listing to this title and front flap of dust jacket listing to The Secret of Red Gate Farm.
NF/F: $1,400   **G/VG: $650**
(Note: This title has been updated several times, be sure you check points of issue.)

Nesbit, E. *The Railway Children.*
London: Wells Gardner, Darton & Co. Ltd., 1906. First edition has gilt pictorial burgundy covers.
NF/F: $1,800   **G/VG: $1,000**

Potter, Beatrix. *The Tale of Peter Rabbit.*
London: Privately printed for the author by Strangeways, London, 1901. The first print run was 250 copies designated by the 1901 date, the second run was 1902.
NF/F: $85,000   **G/VG: $45,000**

Rackham, Arthur. *Mother Goose.*
London: William Heinemann, 1913. A limited edition of 1,130 signed and numbered copies.
NF/F: $5,600   **G/VG: $2,400**

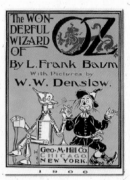
Frank L. Baum.

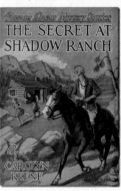
Carolyn Keene.

PRICE GUIDE

Louisa May Alcott.

Anonymous.

Anonymous.

Adams, Harrison. *The Pioneer Boys of Kansas, or: a Prairie Home in Buffalo Land.* First Edition: Boston: L. C. Page & Company, 1928.
NF/F: $125   G/VG: $45

Akers, Floyd (L. Frank Baum). The Boy Fortune Hunters Series:

Fitzgerald, Captain Hugh. *Sam Steele's Adventures on Land and Sea.* Chicago: Reilly & Britton, 1906.
NF/F: $1,550   G/VG: $600
Republished as **Akers, Floyd (L. Frank Baum).** *The Boy Fortune Hunters in Alaska.*
First Edition: Chicago: Reilly and Britton, 1908. Points of Issue: First issue page 271 ends "…unvarying food fortune and The End."
NF/F: $265   G/VG: $125

Fitzgerald, Captain Hugh. *Sam Steele's Adventures in Panama.* Chicago: Reilly & Britton, 1907.
NF/F: $1,800   G/VG: $750
Republished as **Akers, Floyd (L. Frank Baum).** *The Boy Fortune Hunters in Panama.*
First Edition: Chicago: Reilly and Britton, 1908. Points of Issue: Open book device above imprint on the title page is first issue.
NF/F: $1,000   G/VG: $425

_____ **(L. Frank Baum).** *The Boy Fortune Hunters in Egypt.*
First Edition: Chicago: Reilly and Britton, 1908.
Points of Issue: Open book device above imprint on the title page is first issue.
NF/F: $750   G/VG: $325

_____ **(L. Frank Baum).** *The Boy Fortune Hunters in China.*
First Edition: Chicago: Reilly and Britton, 1909.
NF/F: $950   G/VG: $375

_____ **(L. Frank Baum).** *The Boy Fortune Hunters in the Yucatan.*
First Edition: Chicago: Reilly and Britton, 1911.
NF/F: $650   G/VG: $300

_____ **(L. Frank Baum).** *The Boy Fortune Hunters in the South Seas.*
First Edition: Chicago: Reilly and Britton, 1911.
Points of Issue: Ads list "The Darling Twins," "Annabel," and the first six Aunt Jane's Nieces titles.
NF/F: $650   G/VG: $300

Alcott, Louisa May. *Flower Fables.* First Edition: Boston: George W. Briggs & Co., 1855.
NF/F: $3,500   G/VG: $1,000

Allen, Captain Quincy. *The Outdoor Chums on the Lake or Lively Adventures on Wildcat Island.*
First Edition: Cleveland, OH: The Goldsmith Publishing Co., 1911.
NF/F: $25   G/VG: $10

Allen, Betsy. *The Silver Secret.* Points of Issue: Titles on jacket list to *The Ruby Queens.*
First Edition: New York: Grosset & Dunlap, 1956.
NF/F: $95   G/VG: $45

Anonymous. *Little Mother Goose.* First Edition: New York: McLoughlin Bros., 1901.
NF/F: $85   G/VG: $35

_____ **(Charles Perrault).** *The Ideal Fairy Tales.*
First Edition: New York: McLoughlin Bros., 1897.
NF/F: $200   G/VG: $85

_____. *Mother Goose's Melodies With Music Old and New.*
First Edition: Springfield, Massachusetts: McLoughlin Bros., 1920.
NF/F: $500   **G/VG: $200**

_____. *Lil Bo Peep.*
Little Dot Series Edition: New York: McLoughlin Bros., 1890.
NF/F: $35   **G/VG: $15**

_____. *Jack The Giant Killer.*
First Edition: New York: McLoughlin Bros., 1898.
NF/F: $200   **G/VG: $95**

_____. *Jolly Animal A B C.*
First Edition: New York: McLoughlin Bros., 1890.
NF/F: $65   **G/VG: $20**

_____. *Jolly Animal A B C (Linen edition).*
First Edition: New York: McLoughlin Bros., 1890.
NF/F: $95   **G/VG: $60**

_____. *Aladdin or The Wonderful Lamp.*
First Edition Wonder Story Series: New York: McLoughlin Bros., 1889.
NF/F: $85   **G/VG: $35**

_____. *A B C Jingles.*
First Edition: Syracuse, New York: C. C. Hanford, 1911.
NF/F: $25   **G/VG: $15**

_____. *My Bunny.*
First Edition: New York: Sam Gabriel and Sons, 1927.
NF/F: $35   **G/VG: $15**

_____. *Four Doll Mammas.*
First Edition: Boston: D. Lothrop, 1877.
NF/F: $45   **G/VG: $25**

_____. *Little Sunshine.*
First Edition: Boston: De Wolfe, Fiske, 1900.
NF/F: $45   **G/VG: $12**

_____. *Brave Deeds of Our Naval Heroes.*
First Edition: Boston: De Wolfe, Fiske, 1900.
NF/F: $65   **G/VG: $25**

_____. *Little A B C Book.* (Linen Edition).
First Edition: New York: McLoughlin Bros., 1884.
NF/F: $65   **G/VG: $30**

_____ **(L. Frank Baum).** *The Last Egyptian.*
First Edition: Philadelphia: Edward Stern, 1908. Points of Issue: The verso carries no imprint and states "Published May 1, 1908."
NF/F: $180   **G/VG: $65**

_____ **(Louise A. Field)**. *Peter Rabbit and His Ma.*
First Edition: Chicago: Saalfield Publishing Co., 1917.
NF/F: $120   **G/VG: $45**

Anthony, Lotta Rowe. *Anne Thornton, Wetamoo.*
First Edition: Philadelphia: Penn Publishing Company, 1922.
NF/F: $25   **G/VG: $10**

Appleton, Victor. *Tom Swift And His Giant Magnet (or: Bringing Up the Lost Submarine).*
First Edition: New York: Grosset & Dunlap, 1932.
NF/F: $350   **G/VG: $130**

Arnold, Orn. *Jim Starr of the Border Patrol.* Points of Issue: Big Little #1428.
First Edition: Racine, WI: Whitman, 1937.
NF/F: $275   **G/VG: $125**

Anonymous.

Anonymous.

Anonymous (Louise A. Field).

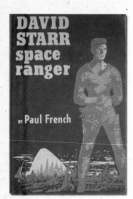

*Isaac Asimov
(as by Paul French).*

*Isaac Asimov
(as by Paul French).*

Arthur Scott Bailey.

Asimov, Isaac (as by Paul French).
Lucky Starr Series:

_____. *David Starr, Space Ranger.*
First Edition: Garden City, NY:
Doubleday & Company, Inc., 1952.
NF/F: $450   **G/VG: $150**

_____. *Lucky Starr and the Pirates
of the Asteroids.*
First Edition: Garden City, NY:
Doubleday & Company, Inc., 1953.
NF/F: $600   **G/VG: $225**

_____. *Lucky Starr and the Oceans
of Venus.*
First Edition: Garden City, NY:
Doubleday & Company, Inc., 1954.
NF/F: $650   **G/VG: $200**

_____. *Lucky Starr and the Big
Sun of Mercury.*
First Edition: Garden City, NY:
Doubleday & Company, Inc., 1956.
NF/F: $450   **G/VG: $175**

_____. *Lucky Starr and the Moons
of Jupiter.*
First Edition: Garden City, NY:
Doubleday & Company, Inc., 1957.
NF/F: $250   **G/VG: $100**

_____. *Lucky Starr and the Rings
of Saturn.*
First Edition: Garden City, NY:
Doubleday & Company, Inc., 1958.
NF/F: $300   **G/VG: $100**

Atwater, Richard and Florence. *Mr.
Popper's Penguins.*
First Edition: Boston: Little Brown, 1938.
NF/F: $125   **G/VG: $55**

Aunt Hattie. *The Golden Rule.*
First Edition: Boston: Henry A. Young
& Co., 1867.
NF/F: $85   **G/VG: $35**

Bailey, Arthur Scott. *The Tale of
Buster Bumblebee.*
First Edition: New York: Grosset &
Dunlap, 1918.
NF/F: $45   **G/VG: $10**

Baldwin, Faith. *Divine Corners
Series:*

_____. *Judy : A Story of Divine
Corners.*
First Edition: New York: Dodd Mead &
Co, 1930.
NF/F: $65   **G/VG: $25**

_____. *Babs : A Story of Divine
Corners.*
First Edition: New York: Dodd Mead &
Co, 1931.
NF/F: $55   **G/VG: $15**

_____. *Mary Lou : A Story of
Divine Corners.*
First Edition: New York: Dodd Mead &
Co, 1931.
NF/F: $35   **G/VG: $15**

_____. *Myra : A Story of Divine
Corners.*
First Edition: New York: Dodd Mead &
Co, 1932.
NF/F: $35   **G/VG: $15**

Bancroft, Laura (L. Frank Baum).
Babes in Birdland.
First Edition: Chicago: Reilly and
Britton, 1911.
Points of Issue: a revision of Policeman
Blue Jay.
NF/F: $325   **G/VG: $100**

_____ **(L. Frank Baum).**
Policeman Blue Jay.
First Edition: Chicago: Reilly and
Britton, 1907.
NF/F: $1,500   **G/VG: $700**

Bardwell, Harrison. *The Airplane Girl and the Mystery of Seal Island.*
First Edition: Cleveland, OH: World Syndicate, 1931.
NF/F: $35　　　　　　**G/VG: $10**

Barnes, Elmer Tracey. *The Moving Picture Comrades in African Jungles.*
First Edition: Chicago: The Saalfield Publishing Company, 1917.
NF/F: $25　　　　　　**G/VG: $12**

Barnum, Vance. *Joe Strong and His Wings of Steel.*
First Edition: New York: George Sully & Company, 1916.
NF/F: $150　　　　　　**G/VG: $80**

Bartlett, Philip A. *The Mystery of the Circle of Fire : A Roy Stover Mystery Story.*
First Edition: New York: Grosset & Dunlap, 1934.
NF/F: $65　　　　　　**G/VG: $30**

Barton, May Hollis. *Plain Jane and Pretty Betty.*
First Edition: New York: Cupples & Leon, 1926.
NF/F: $55　　　　　　**G/VG: $20**

Baum, L. Frank. *Father Goose His Book.*
First Edition: Chicago: Geo. M. Hill, 1899.
NF/F: $1,150　　　　　　**G/VG: $400**

_____. *Mother Goose in Prose.*
First Edition: Chicago: Way and Williams, 1897.
Points of Issue: In the first state the signatures are 16 pages, the last two are eight and four, ending on page 268
NF/F: $6,500　　　　　　**G/VG: $3,000**

_____. *Sea Fairies.*
First Edition: Chicago: Reilly and Britton, 1911.
Points of Issue: Lines transposed on Pages 95 and 105
NF/F: $450　　　　　　**G/VG: $175**

_____. The Oz Series:

_____. *The Wonderful Wizard of Oz* .
First Edition: Chicago: George M. Hill, 1900.
(See in Ten Classic)

_____. *The Marvelous Land of Oz.*
First Edition: Chicago: Reilly and Britton, 1904.
Points of Issue: The cover title is printed in blue in first issue.
NF/F: $7,500　　　　　　**G/VG: $3,000**

_____. *Ozma of Oz.*
First Edition: Chicago: Reilly and Britton, 1907.
Points of Issue: First state is believed to be missing an "O" in the author's note.
NF/F: $3,600　　　　　　**G/VG: $1,000**

_____. *Dorothy and the Wizard in Oz.*
First Edition: Chicago: Reilly and Britton, 1908.
NF/F: $1,800　　　　　　**G/VG: $800**

_____. *The Road to Oz.*
First Edition: Chicago: Reilly and Britton, 1909.
Points of Issue: First State has perfect type on pages 34 & 121 (broken in later states) with a number and caption in page 129.
NF/F: $2,200　　　　　　**G/VG: $850**

_____. *The Emerald City of Oz.*
First Edition: Chicago: Reilly and Britton, 1910.
NF/F: $2,500　　　　　　**G/VG: $1,100**

_____. *The Patchwork Girl of Oz.*
First Edition: Chicago: Reilly and Britton, 1913.
Points of Issue: In the first state the "C" in "Chapter Three" is partially on page 35.
NF/F: $3,000　　　　　　**G/VG: $1,400**

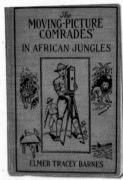
Elmer Tracey Barnes.

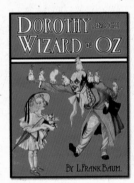
L. Frank Baum.

L. Frank Baum.

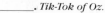_____. *Tik-Tok of Oz.*
First Edition: Chicago: Reilly and
Britton, 1914.
Points of Issue: Ads on verso of half title
end with The Patchwork Girl of Oz.
NF/F: $300   **G/VG: $125**

_____. *The Scarecrow of Oz.*
First Edition: Chicago: Reilly and
Britton, 1915.
Points of Issue: Ads on verso of half
title end with The Scarecrow of Oz.
NF/F: $800   **G/VG: $275**

L. Frank Baum.

_____. *Rinkitink in Oz.*
First Edition: Chicago: Reilly and Britton, 1916.
Points of Issue: No ads in first issue.
NF/F: $400   **G/VG: $125**

_____. *The Lost Princess of Oz.*
First Edition: Chicago: Reilly and
Britton, 1904.
Points of Issue: Ads on verso of half
title end with The Lost Princess of Oz.
NF/F: $400   **G/VG: $125**

Amy E. Blanchard.

_____. *The Tin Woodsman of Oz.*
First Edition: Chicago: Reilly and
Britton, 1918.
Points of Issue: Ads on verso of half title
end with The Tin Woodsman of Oz.
NF/F: $450   **G/VG: $150**

_____. *The Magic of Oz.*
First Edition: Chicago: Reilly and
Britton, 1919.
Points of Issue: Ads on verso of half title
end with The Tin Woodsman of Oz.
NF/F: $1,800   **G/VG: $850**

Clair Blank.

_____. *Glinda of Oz.*
First Edition: Chicago: Reilly and Lee, 1920.
NF/F: $3,000   **G/VG: $1,250**
(See Also: Ruth Plumly Thompson,
John R. Neill, Jack Snow, Rachel R.
Cosgrove, and Eloise Jarvis McGraw
and Lauren Lynn Mc Graw.)

Baum, Roger S. *Dorothy of Oz.*
First Edition: New York: Books of
Wonder/William Morrow and Co., Inc.
1989.
NF/F: $65   **G/VG: $25**

Beach, Charles Amory. *Air Service
Boys Over the Enemy's Lines.*
First Edition: New York: Charles Sully, 1918.
NF/F: $35   **G/VG: $12**

Becker, Eve. *Abracadabra: The Magic
Mix Up.*
First Edition: New York: Bantam
Books, 1989.
NF/F: $10   **G/VG: $5**

Berends, Polly. *Ozma and the
Wayward Wand.*
First Edition: New York: Random
House, 1985.
NF/F: $15   **G/VG: $6**

Blaine, John. *The Blue Ghost
Mystery. A Rick Brant Science
Adventure Story.*
First Edition: New York: Grosset and
Dunlap, 1960.
NF/F: $150   **G/VG: $65**

Blanchard, Amy E. *My Own Dolly.*
First Edition: New York: E.P. Dutton,
1882.
NF/F: $350   **G/VG: $150**
First U.K. Edition: London: Griffith and
Farran, 1886.
NF/F: $150   **G/VG: $50**

Blank, Clair. *Beverly Gray at the
World's Fair.*
First Edition: New York & Chicago: A.
L. Burt Company, 1935.
Points of Issue: The front flap lists The
Arden Blake Mystery Series by Cleo
F. Garis. Back flap lists The Mary Lou
Series by Edith Lovell.
NF/F: $1,050   **G/VG: $425**

Bonehill, Captain Ralph. *For the Liberty of Texas.*
First Edition: Boston: Dana Estes & Company, 1900.
NF/F: $165　　　　**G/VG: $65**

_____. *With Taylor on the Rio Grande.*
First Edition: Boston: Dana Estes & Company, 1901.
NF/F: $140　　　　**G/VG: $60**

Breckenridge, Gerald. *The Radio Boys On The Mexican Border.*
First Edition: New York: A. L. Burt Company, 1922.
NF/F: $35　　　　**G/VG: $12**

Brink, Carol Ryrie. *Magical Melons More Stories About Caddie Woodlawn.*
First Edition: New York: Macmillan, 1944.
NF/F: $65　　　　**G/VG: $20**

Brooks, Amy. *Dorothy Dainty's New Friends.*
First Edition: Boston: Lothrop, Lee & Shepard, 1916.
NF/F: $35　　　　**G/VG: $10**

Broughall, Helen K. *Barbara Winthrop at Camp.*
First Edition: Boston: L. C. Page & Company, 1926.
NF/F: $35　　　　**G/VG: $10**

Burgess, Gelett. *The Burgess Nonsense Book.*
First Edition: New York: Frederick A. Stokes, 1901.
NF/F: $125　　　　**G/VG: $45**

Burgess, Thornton W. *The Adventures of Paddy the Beaver.*
First Edition: Boston, MA: Little Brown & Co. 1917.
NF/F: $175　　　　**G/VG: $75**

_____. *The Adventures of Grandfather Frog.*
First Edition: Boston, MA: Little Brown & Co., 1944.
NF/F: $85　　　　**G/VG: $35**

Burnett, Carolyn Judson. *The Blue Grass Seminary Girls on the Water.*
First Edition: New York: A.L. Burt Company, 1916.
NF/F: $50　　　　**G/VG: $20**

Burnett, Frances Hodgson. *The Secret Garden.*
First Edition: London: William Heinemann, 1911.
Points of Issue: First variation in Green cloth with frontispiece and three plates tipped in.
NF/F: $4,000　　　　**G/VG: $2,100**
First Edition: London: William Heinemann, 1911.
Points of Issue: Second variation in Blue cloth with no illustrations.
NF/F: $3,200　　　　**G/VG: $1,200**
First U.S. Edition: New York: Frederick Stokes, 1911.
NF/F: $650　　　　**G/VG: $200**

Cady, Harrison. *A Great Feast on Butternut Hill.*
First Edition: Racine, WI: Whitman Publishing Co., 1929.
NF/F: $150　　　　**G/VG: $80**

Caniff, Milton. *Terry and the Pirates in Shipwrecked: Pop-Up.*
First Edition: Chicago: Pleasure Books, Inc: Blue Ribbon Press Book, 1935.
NF/F: $400　　　　**G/VG: $175**

Gerald Breckenridge.

Amy Brooks.

Frances Hodgson Burnett.

Lester Chadwick.

Allen Chapman.

John R. Cooper.

Carr, Annie Roe. *Nan Sherwood at Rose Ranch.*
First Edition: New York: George Sully, 1919.
Points of Issue: (A difficult title, George Sully is the first, Goldsmith is a reprint, a number of spurious facsimiles and reprints are being hawked at prices up to the $130s, check carefully).
NF/F: $25   G/VG: $8

Carson, Captain James. *The Saddle Boys At Circle Ranch.*
First Edition: New York: Cupples & Leon, 1913.
NF/F: $40   G/VG: $12

Cavanna, Betty. *The Surfer and the City Girl.*
First Edition: Philadelphia: Westminster Press, 1981.
NF/F: $120   G/VG: $55

Chadwick, Lester. *Baseball Joe Captain of the Team.*
First Edition: New York: Cupples & Leon, 1924.
Points of Issue: First is gray cloth with blue lettering.
NF/F: $260   G/VG: $85

_____. *Baseball Joe Pitching Wizard.*
First Edition: New York: Cupples & Leon, 1928.
Points of Issue: First is gray cloth with blue lettering.
NF/F: $275   G/VG: $100

Champney, Elizabeth W. *Three Vassar Girls in South America.*
First Edition: Boston: Estes & Lauriat, 1885.
NF/F: $700   G/VG: $300

Chapman, Allen. *Frank Roscoe's Secret- The Darewell Chums in the Woods.*
First Edition: Chicago: Goldsmith Publishing, 1908.
NF/F: $25   G/VG: $10

Childs, L. M. *The Young Artist.*
First Edition: Boston: D. Lothrop, nd (1878).
NF/F: $55   G/VG: $20

Cleary, Beverly. *Ramona Quimby, Age 8.*
First Edition: New York: Morrow/Avon, 1981.
NF/F: $85   G/VG: $30

Colver, Alice Ross. *Babs.*
First Edition: Philadelphia: Penn Publishing, 1917.
NF/F: $365   G/VG: $200

_____. *Babs at Home.*
First Edition: Philadelphia: Penn Publishing, 1921.
NF/F: $150   G/VG: $60

Cooke, John Estes (L. Frank Baum). *Tamawaca Folks.*
First Edition: np: Tamawaca Press, 1907.
NF/F: $1,750   G/VG: $800

Cooper, John R. *The Southpaw's Secret.*
First Edition: New York: Cupples & Leon, 1947.
NF/F: $65   G/VG: $25

Cosgrove, Rachel R. Oz Series:

_____. *The Hidden Valley of Oz.*
First Edition: Chicago: Reilly and Lee, 1951.
NF/F: $300   G/VG: $75
(See Also: L. Frank Baum, Ruth Plumly Thompson, John R. Neill, Jack Snow, and Eloise Jarvis McGraw and Lauren Lynn Mc Graw.)

Coville, Bruce and Katherine.
Sarah's Unicorn.
First Edition: New York: Harper & Row
Publishers, 1985.
NF/F: $85   **G/VG: $50**

Crane, Laura Dent. *The Automobile
Girls Along the Hudson.*
First Edition: Philadelphia: Henry
Altemus Co., 1910.
NF/F: $45   **G/VG: $15**

Crowley, Maude. *Azor.*
First Edition: New York: Oxford, 1948.
NF/F: $85   **G/VG: $30**

Cummings, E.E. *Fairy Tales.*
First Edition: New York: Harcourt
Brace, 1965.
NF/F: $95   **G/VG: $30**

Curry, Jane Louise. *The Sleepers.*
First Edition: London: Dennis
Dobson, 1968.
NF/F: $70   **G/VG: $25**
First U.S. Edition: New York: Harcourt
Brace and World, 1968.
NF/F: $50   **G/VG: $20**

Curtis, Alice Turner. *A Little Maid of
Massachusetts Colony.*
First Edition: Philadelphia: Penn Pub,
1914.
NF/F: $100   **G/VG: $35**

_____. *A Yankee Girl at
Richmond.*
First Edition: Philadelphia: Penn Pub,
1930.
NF/F: $225   **G/VG: $85**

Davenport, Spencer. *The Rushton
Boys at Treasure Cove.*
First Edition: New York: George Sully
& Company, 1916.
NF/F: $30   **G/VG: $10**

Davis, G. A. *Robin Hood.*
First Edition: Springfield, MA:
McLoughlin Bros., 1929.
Points of Issue: First Edition is diecut
and Springfield, MA not New York.
NF/F: $45   **G/VG: $20**

Dawson, Elmer A. *Garry Grayson At
Stanley Prep.*
First Edition: New York: Grosset and
Dunlap, 1927.
NF/F: $35   **G/VG: $10**

De Barthe, Penn. *Betty and Teddy #3*
First Edition: Rochester, NY: Stecher
Litho. Co., 1916.
NF/F: $55   **G/VG: $20**

Dean, Graham. *Daring Wings.*
First Edition: Chicago: Goldsmith,
1931.
NF/F: $45   **G/VG: $15**

Denslow, W. W. *When I Grow Up.*
First Edition: New York: The Century
Co., 1909.
NF/F: $650   **G/VG: $200**

DeVries, Julianne. *The Campfire
Girls at Holly House.*
First Edition: Cleveland, OH: The
World Syndicate, 1933.
NF/F: $30   **G/VG: $10**

Disney Studios. *Who's Afraid of the
Big Bad Wolf: Three Little Pigs.*
First Edition: Philadelphia: David
McKay, 1933.
NF/F: $300   **G/VG: $125**

Dixon, Franklin W. *Through the Air
to Alaska.*
First Edition: New York: Grossett &
Dunlap, 1930.
NF/F: $100   **G/VG: $45**

E. E. Cummings.

G. A. Davis.

Disney Studios.

Amanda M. Douglas.

Edward Eager.

Douglas, Amanda M. *Helen Grant in College.*
First Edition: Boston : Lothrop, Lee & Shepard, 1906.
NF/F: $75   **G/VG: $30**

_____. *The Mistress of Sherburne.*
First Edition: New York: Dodd Mead, 1896.
NF/F: $65   **G/VG: $20**

Dreany, E. Joseph. *Cowboys in Pop-Up Action Pictures.*
First Edition: London: Publicity Products Ltd., 1951.
NF/F: $65   **G/VG: $30**

du Bois, William Pene. *Otto At Sea.*
First Edition: New York: Viking, 1936.
NF/F: $400   **G/VG: $125**

Duncan, Julia K. *Doris Force at Locked Gates.*
First Edition: Philadelphia: Henry Altemus, 1931.
NF/F: $25   **G/VG: $9**

Eager, Edward. *The Time Garden.*
First Edition: New York: Harcourt Brace and Company, 1958.
NF/F: $350   **G/VG: $125**

Emerson, Alice B. *Ruth Fielding and Her Greatest Triumph or Saving Her Company from Disaster.*
First Edition: New York: Cupples and Leon, 1933.
NF/F: $150   **G/VG: $60**

_____. *Betty Gordon in Mexican Wilds or the Secret of the Mountains.*
First Edition: New York: Cupples and Leon, 1926.
NF/F: $55   **G/VG: $20**

_____. *Betty Gordon at Ocean Park.*
First Edition: New York: Cupples and Leon, 1923.
NF/F: $45   **G/VG: $15**

Endicott, Ruth Belmore. *Carolyn Of The Sunny Heart.*
First Edition: New York: Dodd, Mead & Company, 1919.
NF/F: $15   **G/VG: $8**

Estes, Eleanor. *The Moffat Museum.*
First Edition: New York: Harcourt Brace Jovanovich, 1983.
NF/F: $55   **G/VG: $20**

Farley, Walter. The Black Stallion Series:

_____. *The Black Stallion.*
First Edition: New York: Random House, 1941.
NF/F: $200   **G/VG: $85**

_____. *The Black Stallion Returns.*
First Edition: New York: Random House, 1945.
NF/F: $185   **G/VG: $120**

_____. *Son of the Black Stallion.*
First Edition: New York: Random House, 1947.
NF/F: $100   **G/VG: $60**

_____. *The Island Stallion.*
First Edition: New York: Random House, 1948.
NF/F: $185   **G/VG: $85**

_____. *The Black Stallion and Satan.*
First Edition: New York: Random House, 1949.
NF/F: $125   **G/VG: $95**

_____. *The Black Stallion's Blood Bay Colt.*
First Edition: New York: Random House, 1951.
NF/F: $145   **G/VG: $60**

_____. *The Island Stallion's Fury.*
First Edition: New York: Random House, 1951.
NF/F: $175   **G/VG: $75**

_____.*The Black Stallion's Filly.*
First Edition: New York: Random House, 1952.
NF/F: $200   **G/VG: $90**

_____. *Black Stallion Revolts.*
First Edition: New York: Random House, 1953.
NF/F: $100   **G/VG: $40**

_____.*The Black Stallion's Sulky Colt.*
First Edition: New York: Random House, 1954.
NF/F: $165   **G/VG: $80**

_____. *The Island Stallion Races.*
First Edition: New York: Random House, 1955.
NF/F: $185   **G/VG: $110**

_____. *Black Stallion's Courage.*
First Edition: New York: Random House, 1956.
NF/F: $100   **G/VG: $45**

_____. *The Black Stallion Mystery.*
First Edition: New York: Random House, 1957.
NF/F: $155   **G/VG: $70**

_____. *The Horse Tamer.*
First Edition: New York: Random House, 1958.
NF/F: $125   **G/VG: $55**

_____. *The Black Stallion and Flame.*
First Edition: New York: Random House, 1960.
NF/F: $100   **G/VG: $40**

_____. *The Black Stallion Challenged.*
First Edition: New York: Random House, 1964.
NF/F: $95   **G/VG: $35**

_____. *The Black Stallion's Ghost.*
First Edition: New York: Random House, 1969.
NF/F: $85   **G/VG: $35**

_____. *The Black Stallion and the Girl.*
First Edition: New York: Random House, 1971.
NF/F: $100   **G/VG: $45**

_____. *The Black Stallion Legend.*
First Edition: New York: Random House, 1983.
NF/F: $75   **G/VG: $25**

_____ **and Steven Farley.** *The Young Black Stallion.*
First Edition: New York: Random House, 1989.
NF/F: $65   **G/VG: $20**

Father Tuck. *Little Bo Peep.* (Dolly Dear Edition).
First Edition: New York, London, Paris: Raphael Tuck, nd (1898).
NF/F: $25   **G/VG: $10**

_____. *Little Bo Peep.* (Linen Little Pets Edition).
First Edition: New York, London, Paris: Raphael Tuck, nd (1901).
NF/F: $45   **G/VG: $20**

Walter Farley.

Walter Farley.

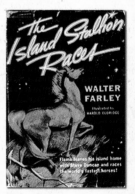

Walter Farley.

Eugene Field.

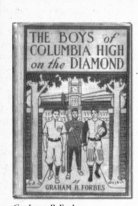

Percy K. Fitzhugh.

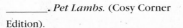

THE BOYS of COLUMBIA HIGH on the DIAMOND

Graham B. Forbes.

_____. *Pet Lambs.* (Cosy Corner Edition).
First Edition New York, London, Paris: Raphael Tuck, nd (1896).
NF/F: $25   **G/VG: $10**

Fayerweather, Margaret Doane. Anne Series:

_____. *Anne Alive! A Year in the Life of a Girl of New York State.*
First Edition: New York: Robert McBride, 1933.
NF/F: $75   **G/VG: $40**

_____. *Anne at Large.*
First Edition: New York: Robert McBride, 1934.
NF/F: $35   **G/VG: $15**

_____. *Anne at Work.*
First Edition: New York: Robert McBride, 1935.
NF/F: $45   **G/VG: $20**

Ferris, James Cody. *The X Bar X Boys in the Haunted Gully.*
First Edition: New York: Grosset & Dunlap, 1940.
NF/F: $120   **G/VG: $40**

Field, Eugene. *Poems of Childhood.*
First Edition: New York: Charles Scribner's, 1904.
NF/F: $750   **G/VG: $275**

Finley, Jean. *The Blue Domers and the Hidden Shanty.*
First Edition: New York: A. L. Burt, 1930.
NF/F: $35   **G/VG: $15**

Fisher, Paul R. *The Ash Staff.*
First Edition: New York: Atheneum, 1979.
NF/F: $35   **G/VG: $10**

Fitzgerald, Captain Hugh (L. Frank Baum). *Sam Steel Series* (See also Akers, Floyd):

_____ **(L. Frank Baum).** *Sam Steele's Adventures on Land and Sea.*
Chicago: Reilly & Britton, 1906.
NF/F: $1,550   **G/VG: $600**

_____ **(L. Frank Baum).** *Sam Steele's Adventures in Panama.*
Chicago: Reilly & Britton, 1907.
NF/F: $1,800   **G/VG: $750**

Fitzhugh, Percy K. *Along the Mohawk Trail or Boy Scouts on Lake Champlain.*
First Edition: New York: Thomas Crowell, 1912.
NF/F: $45   **G/VG: $15**

Flower, Jessie Graham. *Grace Harlowe's Plebe Year at Oakdale High School.*
First Edition: Philadelphia: Altemus, 1910.
NF/F: $35   **G/VG: $10**

Forbes, Graham B. *The Boys of Columbia High on the Diamond.*
First Edition: New York: Grosset & Dunlap, 1911.
NF/F: $30   **G/VG: $10**

Gardner, John. *In the Suicide Mountains.*
First Edition: New York: Alfred A. Knopf, 1977.
NF/F: $150   **G/VG: $65**

Garis, Cleo F. *The Mystery of Jockey Hollow.*
First Edition: New York: A. L. Burt Company, 1934.
NF/F: $40   **G/VG: $10**

Garis, Howard R. *The Second Adventures of Uncle Wiggily.*
First Edition: Newark, N. J.: Charles E., Graham & Co., 1925.
NF/F: $250　　　　**G/VG: $90**

_____. *Mystery Boys at Round Lake.*
First Edition: Springfield, Il: Martin Bradley, 1931.
NF/F: $225　　　　**G/VG: $75**

_____. *Charlie And Arabella Chick.*
First Edition: New York: R. F. Fenno & Company, 1914.
NF/F: $100　　　　**G/VG: $35**

Giff, Patricia Reilly. *Lily's Crossing.*
First Edition: New York: Delacorte, 1997.
NF/F: $45　　　　**G/VG: $15**

Ginther, Mary Pemberton. *Beth Anne's New Cousin.*
First Edition: Philadelphia, PA: Penn Pub Co, 1917.
NF/F: $85　　　　**G/VG: $35**

Gordon, Elizabeth. *The Butterfly Babies' Book.*
First Edition: Chicago: Rand McNally & Company, 1914.
NF/F: $225　　　　**G/VG: $100**

Gordon, Frederick. *Fairview Boys at Lighthouse Cove.*
First Edition: New York: Graham, 1914.
NF/F: $55　　　　**G/VG: $15**

Gray, Harold. *Little Orphan Annie and Jumbo, the Circus Elephant.*
First Edition: Chicago: Pleasure Books Inc., 1935.
NF/F: $500　　　　**G/VG: $200**

Greenaway, Kate. *Marigold Garden.*
First Edition: London & New York: George Routledge, 1885.
Points of Issue: Front and rear illustrations match in the first issue.
NF/F: $600　　　　**G/VG: $175**

Greene, Constance C. *A Girl Called Al.*
First Edition: New York: Viking Press, 1969.
NF/F: $30　　　　**G/VG: $10**

_____. *Isabelle The Itch.*
First Edition: New York: Viking Press, 1972.
NF/F: $45　　　　**G/VG: $20**

Grosby, Ruth. *The Stolen Blueprints.*
First Edition: New York: Grosset & Dunlap, 1939.
NF/F: $40　　　　**G/VG: $10**

Gruelle, Johnny. *Marcella A Raggedy Anne Story.*
First Edition: Chicago and New York: M.A. Donohue & Company, 1929.
NF/F: $250　　　　**G/VG: $95**

_____. *Raggedy Ann and Betsy Bonnet String.*
First Edition: New York: Johnny Gruelle Co., 1943.
NF/F: $150　　　　**G/VG: $65**

Hardy, Alice Dale. *The Flyaways and Little Red Riding Hood.*
First Edition: New York: Grosset & Dunlap, 1925.
NF/F: $35　　　　**G/VG: $15**

Haywood, Carolyn. *Snowbound With Betsy.*
First Edition: New York: William Morrow and Company, 1962.
NF/F: $150　　　　**G/VG: $65**

Elizabeth Gordon.

Kate Greenaway.

Johnny Gruelle.

Grace Brooks Hill.

Frances K. Judd.

Henderley, Brooks. *The Y.M.C.A. Boys Of Cliffwood Or the Struggle for the Holwell Prize.*
First Edition: New York: Cupples & Leon, 1916.
NF/F: $45   G/VG: $15

Hill, Mabel Betsy. *Along Comes Judy Jo.*
First Edition: New York: Frederick A. Stokes, 1943.
NF/F: $70   G/VG: $25

Hill, Grace Brooks. *The Corner House Girls.*
First Edition: New York: Barse & Hopkins, 1915.
NF/F: $135   G/VG: $50

Hope, Laura Lee. *The Bobbsey Twins.*
First Edition: New York: Grosset & Dunlap, 1904.
NF/F: $200   G/VG: $100

_____. *The Outdoor Girls in Desert Valley.*
First Edition: New York: Grosset & Dunlap, 1933.
NF/F: $100   G/VG: $45

_____. *The Blythe Girls: Rose's Hidden Talent.*
First Edition: New York: Grosset & Dunlap, 1931.
NF/F: $100   G/VG: $55

Jacques, Brian. *The Pearls of Lutra.*
First Edition: London: Hutchinson, 1996.
NF/F: $55   G/VG: $20
First U.S. Edition: New York: Philomel Books, 1996.
NF/F: $45   G/VG: $15

Johnson, Martha. *Ann Bartlett Returns to the Philippines.*
First Edition: New York: Thomas Y. Crowell & Company, 1945.
NF/F: $250   G/VG: $100

Johnston, Annie Fellows. The Little Colonel Series:

_____. *The Little Colonel.*
First Edition: Boston: L. C. Page and Company, 1895.
NF/F: $100   G/VG: $35
Photoplay Edition: New York: A. L. Burt, nd (1935).
NF/F: $350   G/VG: $125

_____. *The Giant Scissors.*
First Edition: Boston: L. C. Page and Company, 1898.
NF/F: $75   G/VG: $25

_____. *Two Little Knights of Kentucky.*
First Edition: Boston: L. C. Page and Company, 1899.
NF/F: $85   G/VG: $35

_____. *The Little Colonel's House Party.*
First Edition: Boston: L. C. Page and Company, 1900.
NF/F: $150   G/VG: $45

_____. *The Little Colonel's Holidays.*
First Edition: Boston: L. C. Page and Company, 1901.
NF/F: $125   G/VG: $45

_____. *The Little Colonel's Hero.*
First Edition: Boston: L. C. Page and Company, 1902.
NF/F: $165   G/VG: $70

_____. *The Little Colonel at Boarding School.*
First Edition: Boston: L. C. Page and Company, 1903.
NF/F: $65   G/VG: $25

_____. *The Little Colonel in Arizona.*
First Edition: Boston: L. C. Page and Company, 1904.
NF/F: $80   G/VG: $25

_____. *The Little Colonel's Christmas Vacation.*
First Edition: Boston: L. C. Page and Company, 1905.
NF/F: $55   **G/VG: $20**

_____. *The Little Colonel, Maid of Honor.*
First Edition: Boston: L. C. Page and Company, 1906.
NF/F: $95   **G/VG: $40**

_____. *The Little Colonel's Knight Comes Riding.*
First Edition: Boston: L. C. Page and Company, 1907.
NF/F: $65   **G/VG: $30**

_____. *Mary Ware, The Little Colonel's Chum.*
First Edition: Boston: L. C. Page and Company, 1908.
NF/F: $90   **G/VG: $40**

_____. *Mary Ware in Texas.*
First Edition: Boston: L. C. Page and Company, 1910.
NF/F: $85   **G/VG: $30**

_____. *Mary Ware's Promised Land.*
First Edition: Boston: L. C. Page and Company, 1912.
NF/F: $125   **G/VG: $55**

Jones, Buck. *Buck Jones in The Fighting Rangers.*
First Edition: Racine, WI: Whitman, 1936.
Points of Issue: Big Little #1188.
NF/F: $45   **G/VG: $25**

Jones, Raymond F. *Stories of Great Physicians.*
First Edition: Racine, WI: Whitman, 1963.
NF/F: $20   **G/VG: $8**

Judd, Frances K. *The Lone Footprint (Kay Tracey Mystery Stories #15).*
First Edition: New York: Cupples & Leon Co., 1941.
NF/F: $45   **G/VG: $20**

Juster, Norton. *Phantom Tollbooth.*
First Edition: New York: Epstein & Carroll, 1961.
NF/F: $375   **G/VG: $100**

Kalman, Maira. *Ooh-La-La.* (Max In Love).
First Edition: New York: Viking Books, 1991.
NF/F: $85   **G/VG: $30**

Keene, Carolyn. *A Three Cornered Mystery.* (Dana Girls Series).
First Edition: New York: Grosset & Dunlap, 1935.
NF/F: $250   **G/VG: $100**

Keith, Brandon. *The Affair of the Gentle Saboteur (Series: Man From U.N.C.L.E.).*
First Edition: Racine, WI: Whitman Publishing Co., 1966.
NF/F: $15   **G/VG: $8**

Kenny, Kathryn. *Trixie Belden and the Happy Valley Mystery.*
First Edition: Racine, WI: Whitman, 1962.
NF/F: $30   **G/VG: $12**

_____. *Trixie Belden and The Pet Show Mystery.*
First Edition: Racine, WI: Whitman, 1985.
NF/F: $40   **G/VG: $18**

Maira Kalman.

Brandon Keith.

Kathryn Kenny.

Frederick Kohner.

Frederick Kohner.

Kohner, Frederick. Gidget Series:

_____. *Gidget.*
First Edition: New York: G.P. Putnam's Sons, 1957.
NF/F: $800　　　　　**G/VG: $275**
First U.K. Edition: London: Michael Joseph, 1958.
NF/F: $250　　　　　**G/VG: $100**

_____. *Cher Papa.*
First Edition: New York: G.P. Putnam's Sons, 1960.
NF/F: $50　　　　　**G/VG: $20**

_____. *The Affairs of Gidget.*
First Edition: New York: Bantam, 1963.
NF/F: $20　　　　　**G/VG: $10**

_____. *Gidget in Love.*
First Edition: New York: Dell, 1965.
NF/F: $35　　　　　**G/VG: $15**

_____. *Gidget Goes Parisienne.*
First Edition: New York: Dell, 1966.
NF/F: $15　　　　　**G/VG: $5**

_____. *Gidget Goes New York.*
First Edition: New York: Dell, 1968.
NF/F: $25　　　　　**G/VG: $15**

_____. *Gidget Goes Hawaiian.*
First Edition: New York: Bantam, 1961.
NF/F: $20　　　　　**G/VG: $8**

_____. *Gidget Goes to Rome.*
First Edition: New York: Bantam, 1963.
NF/F: $20　　　　　**G/VG: $8**

Knerr. *The Katzenjammer Kids, an Animated Novelty Book.*
First Edition: Kenosha, WI: John Martin's House, Inc., 1948.
NF/F: $360　　　　　**G/VG: $95**

Krensky, Stephen. *Woodland Crossings.*
First Edition: New York: Atheneum, 1977.
NF/F: $65　　　　　**G/VG: $20**

Lambert, Janet. *Candy Kane.*
First Edition: New York: E. P. Dutton & Co., 1947.
NF/F: $85　　　　　**G/VG: $25**

Lancer, Jack. *Trial By Fury.*
First Edition: New York: Grosset & Dunlap, 1969.
Points of Issue: Christopher Cool/Teen Agent #6.
NF/F: $40　　　　　**G/VG: $10**

Lathrop, Gilbert A. *Whispering Rails.*
First Edition: Chicago: Goldsmith, 1936.
NF/F: $35　　　　　**G/VG: $10**

Lawlor, Laurie. *Second-Grade Dog.*
First Edition: Niles, IL: Albert Whitman & Company, 1990.
NF/F: $55　　　　　**G/VG: $20**

Lawrence, Josephine. *Man in the Moon Stories Told Over the Radio-Phone.*
First Edition: New York: Cupples & Leon Company, 1922.
NF/F: $350　　　　　**G/VG: $150**

Lewis, C. S. The Chronicles of Narnia:

_____. *The Lion, the Witch, and the Wardrobe.*
First Edition: London: Geoffrey Bles, 1950.
NF/F: $15,000　　　　　**G/VG: $7,500**

_____. *Prince Caspian.*
First Edition: London: Geoffrey Bles, 1951.
NF/F: $5,000　　　　　**G/VG: $1,800**

_____. *Voyage of the Dawn Treader.*
First Edition: London: Geoffrey Bles, 1952.
NF/F: $5,000   **G/VG: $1,800**

_____. *The Silver Chair.*
First Edition: London: Geoffrey Bles, 1953.
NF/F: $4,600   **G/VG: $2,000**

_____. *The Horse and his Boy.*
First Edition: London: Geoffrey Bles, 1954.
NF/F: $2,800   **G/VG: $950**

_____. *The Magician's Nephew.*
First Edition: London: Bodley Head,
1955.
NF/F: $4,500   **G/VG: $2,150**

_____. *The Last Battle.*
First Edition: London: Bodley Head,
1956.
NF/F: $3,200   **G/VG: $1,450**

Lindgren, Astrid. Pippi Longstocking
Series:

_____. *Pippi Longstocking.*
First U.S. Edition: New York: Viking
Press, 1950.
Points of Issue: "Published by the
Viking Press in October 1950, stated
1st edition, 1st printing."
NF/F: $650   **G/VG: $225**

_____. *Pippi Goes on Board.*
First U.S. Edition: New York: Viking
Press, 1957.
NF/F: $85   **G/VG: $35**

_____. *Pippi in the South Seas.*
First U.K. Edition: Oxford: Oxford
University Press, 1957.
NF/F: $150   **G/VG: $65**

Lindquist, Jennie D. *Little Silver House.*
First Edition: New York: Harper &
Brothers, 1959.
NF/F: $160   **G/VG: $60**

Locke, Clinton W. *Who Closed the Door.*
First Edition: Philadelphia: Henry
Altemus Co., 1931.
NF/F: $50   **G/VG: $15**

Long, Helen Beecher. *The Mission of Janice Day.*
First Edition: New York: George Sully
and Company, 1917.
NF/F: $40   **G/VG: $15**

Lovelace, Maud Hart. Betsy-Tacy
Series:

_____. *Betsy-Tacy.*
First Edition: New York: Thomas Y.
Crowell Company, 1940.
NF/F: $650   **G/VG: $300**

_____. *Betsy-Tacy and Tib.*
First Edition: New York: Thomas Y.
Crowell Company, 1941.
NF/F: $500   **G/VG: $200**

_____. *Betsy and Tacy Go Over the Big Hill.*
First Edition: New York: Thomas Y.
Crowell Company, 1942.
NF/F: $525   **G/VG: $200**

_____. *Betsy and Tacy Go Downtown.*
First Edition: New York: Thomas Y.
Crowell Company, 1943.
NF/F: $500   **G/VG: $250**

_____. *Heaven to Betsy.*
First Edition: New York: Thomas Y.
Crowell Company, 1945.
NF/F: $450   **G/VG: $250**

_____. *Betsy in Spite of Herself.*
First Edition: New York: Thomas Y.
Crowell Company, 1946.
NF/F: $550   **G/VG: $300**

Gilbert A. Lathrop.

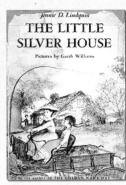

Jennie D. Lindquist.

Lovelace, Maud Hart

Eloise Jarvis McGraw and Lauren McGraw.

A.A. Milne.

_____. *Betsy was a Junior.*
First Edition: New York: Thomas Y. Crowell Company, 1947.
NF/F: $300   **G/VG: $125**

_____. *Betsy and Joe.*
First Edition: New York: Thomas Y. Crowell Company, 1948.
NF/F: $300   **G/VG: $150**

_____. *Betsy and the Great World.*
First Edition: New York: Thomas Y. Crowell Company, 1952.
NF/F: $400   **G/VG: $175**

_____. *Betsy's Wedding.*
First Edition: New York: Thomas Y. Crowell Company, 1955.
NF/F: $350   **G/VG: $100**

Lowry, Lois. *Anastasia Krupnik.*
First Edition: Boston: Houghton Mifflin Company, 1979.
NF/F: $55   **G/VG: $15**

Marlowe, Amy Bell. *When Oriole Came To Harbor Light.*
First Edition: New York: Grosset & Dunlap, 1920.
NF/F: $35   **G/VG: $15**

Martin, Marcia. *Donna Parker on Her Own.*
First Edition: Racine, Wisconsin: Whitman Publishing, 1963.
NF/F: $35   **G/VG: $12**

Mathews, Joanna H. *Belle's Pink Boots.*
First Edition: New York: E. P. Dutton and Co., 1881.
Points of Issue: First Edition has 16 chromolithos, 15 in text and frontispiece.
NF/F: $170   **G/VG: $75**

Matthiessen, Peter. *Seal Pool.*
First Edition: Garden City, NY: Doubleday, 1972.
NF/F: $300   **G/VG: $130**

McGraw, Eloise Jarvis and McGraw, Lauren. Oz Series *:

_____. *Merry Go Round in Oz.*
First Edition: Chicago: Reilly and Lee, 1963.
NF/F: $500   **G/VG: $125**
(See Also: L. Frank Baum, Ruth Plumly Thompson, John R. Neill, Rachel R. Cosgrove, and Jack Snow.)

Metcalf, Susan (L. Frank Baum). *Annabel.*
First Edition: Chicago: Reilly and Britton, 1906.
NF/F: $550   **G/VG: $225**

Meyers Barlow. *Walt Disney's Annette Mystery at Medicine Wheel.*
First Edition: Racine, Wisconsin: Whitman Publishing Company, 1962.
Points of Issue: Whitman B0007FDKUU.
NF/F: $25   **G/VG: $8**

Milne, A. A. *Winnie The Pooh.*
Limited Edition: London: Methuen & Co., 1926 (350 copies).
NF/F: $20,000   **G/VG: Not Seen**
Limited Edition: London: Methuen & Co., 1926 (200 copies).
NF/F: $12,000   **G/VG: Not Seen**
First Edition: London: Methuen & Co., 1926.
NF/F: $11,000   **G/VG: $5000**

Montgomery, L. M. Anne of Green Gables Series:

_____. *Anne of Green Gables.*
First Edition: Boston: L. C. Page & Co., 1908.
NF/F: $9,000   **G/VG: $4,700**

_____. *Anne of Avonlea.*
First Edition: Boston: L. C. Page & Co., 1909.
NF/F: $3,200   **G/VG: $1,400**

_____. *Anne of the Island.*
First Edition: Boston: L. C. Page & Co., 1915.
NF/F: $2,650   **G/VG: $1,100**

_____. *Anne's House of Dreams.*
First Edition: Toronto: McClelland, Goodchild, Stewart, 1917.
NF/F: $200   **G/VG: $75**

_____. *Rainbow Valley.*
First Edition: New York: Frederick A. Stokes Company, 1919.
NF/F: $500   **G/VG: $200**

_____. *Rilla of Ingleside.*
First Edition: New York: Frederick A. Stokes Company, 1921.
NF/F: $175   **G/VG: $55**

_____. *Anne of Windy Poplars.*
First Edition: Toronto: McClelland and Stewart, 1936.
NF/F: $500   **G/VG: $200**
First U.K. Edition as *Anne of Windy Willows*: London: Heinemann, 1936.
NF/F: $250   **G/VG: $85**

_____. *Anne of Ingleside.*
First Edition: Toronto: McClelland and Stewart, 1939.
NF/F: $200   **G/VG: $75**

Moore, Fenworth. *Cast Away in the Land of Snow.*
First Edition: New York: Cupples & Leon, 1931.
NF/F: $50   **G/VG: $15**

Morrison, Gertrude W. *The Girls of Central High on Track and Field.*
First Edition: New York: Grossett & Dunlap, 1914.
NF/F: $45   **G/VG: $20**

Mullins, Isla May. *The Blossom Shop: A Story of the South.*
First Edition: Boston: L.C. Page & Co., 1913.
NF/F: $35   **G/VG: $10**

Naylor, Phyllis Reynolds. *Witch Herself.*
First Edition: New York: Atheneum, 1978.
NF/F: $350   **G/VG: $125**

Neill, John R. *The Adventures of a Brownie.* (Red Book Edition).
First Edition Chicago: Reilly and Britton, 1908.
NF/F: $125   **G/VG: $55**

_____. Oz Series:

_____. *The Wonder City of Oz.*
First Edition: Chicago: Reilly and Lee, 1940.
NF/F: $800   **G/VG: $350**

_____. *The Scalawagons of Oz.*
First Edition: Chicago: Reilly and Lee, 1941.
NF/F: $600   **G/VG: $200**

_____. *Lucky Bucky in Oz.*
First Edition: Chicago: Reilly and Lee, 1942.
NF/F: $1,000   **G/VG: $400**
(See Also: L. Frank Baum, Ruth Plumly Thompson, Jack Snow, Rachel R. Cosgrove, and Eloise Jarvis McGraw and Lauren Lynn Mc Graw.)

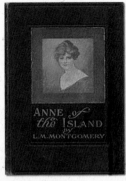
L.M. Montgomery.

John R. Neill.

John R. Neill.

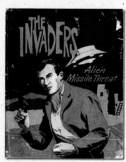

Paul S. Newman.

Grace May North.

The Magic Bed-Knob

Mary Norton.

Newman, Paul S. *The Invaders: Alien Missile Threat.*
First Edition: Racine, WI: Whitman, 1967.
Points of Issue: Big Little No. 2012.
NF/F: $20   **G/VG: $8**

Newman, Robert. *The Case Of The Baker Street Irregular.*
First Edition: New York: Atheneum, 1978.
NF/F: $50   **G/VG: $15**

North, Grace May. *Adele Doring at Vineyard Valley.*
First Edition: Boston: Lothrop, Lee & Shepard Co, 1923.
NF/F: $55   **G/VG: $15**

Norton, Mary. *The Magic Bed-Knob or, How to Become a Witch in Ten Easy Lessons.*
First Edition: New York: Hyperion, 1943.
NF/F: $450   **G/VG: $185**

Optic, Oliver. *A Victorious Union: The Blue and the Gray Afloat.*
First Edition: Boston: Lothrop, Lee & Shepard Co., 1893.
NF/F: $450   **G/VG: $150**

Pansy. *The Prince of Peace; or The Beautiful Life of Jesus.*
First Edition: Philadelphia, PA: John Y. Huber, 1890.
NF/F: $200   **G/VG: $55**

_____. *The Fortunate Calamity.*
First Edition: Philadelphia, PA: Lippincott, 1927.
NF/F: $100   **G/VG: $45**

Patchin, Frank Gee. *The Pony Rider Boys in Alaska.*
First Edition: Philadelphia, PA: Altemus, 1924.
NF/F: $35   **G/VG: $15**

Peat, Fern Bisel. *Mother Goose.*
First Edition: Akron, OH: Saalfield, 1932.
NF/F: $85   **G/VG: $35**

Peattie, Elia W. *Azalea: the Story of a Girl in the Blue Ridge Mountains.*
First Edition: Chicago: The Reilly & Britton Co., 1912.
NF/F: $95   **G/VG: $35**

Penrose, Margaret. *The Radio Girls of Roselawn.*
First Edition: New York: Cupples & Leon, 1922.
NF/F: $85   **G/VG: $35**

Place, Marion T. *Retreat to the Bear Paw. The Story of the Nez Perce.*
First Edition: New York: Four Winds Press, 1969.
NF/F: $25   **G/VG: $10**

Rendina, Laura Cooper. *Summer for Two.*
First Edition: Boston: Little, Brown, 1952.
NF/F: $95   **G/VG: $35**

Rey, Margaret & H.A. *Curious George Goes To The Hospital.*
First Edition: Boston: Houghton Mifflin Company, 1966.
NF/F: $475   **G/VG: $200**

Richards, Laura E. *The Silver Crown: Another Book of Fables.*
First Edition: Boston: Little, Brown, 1906.
NF/F: $200   **G/VG: $65**

Rock, Gail. *A Dream For Addie.*
First Edition: New York: Alfred A. Knopf, 1975.
NF/F: $100   **G/VG: $30**

Rockwell, Carey. Tom Corbett Series:

_____. *Tom Corbett: Stand By for Mars.*
First Edition: New York: Grosset & Dunlap, 1952.
NF/F: $95   **G/VG: $35**

_____. *Tom Corbett, Space Cadet: Danger in Deep Space.*
First Edition: New York: Grosset & Dunlap, 1953.
NF/F: $125   **G/VG: $55**

_____. *On the Trail of the Space Pirates.*
First Edition: New York: Grosset & Dunlap, 1953.
NF/F: $85   **G/VG: $25**

_____. *The Space Pioneers.*
First Edition: New York: Grosset & Dunlap, 1953.
NF/F: $100   **G/VG: $35**

_____. *Revolt on Venus.*
First Edition: New York: Grosset & Dunlap, 1954.
NF/F: $55   **G/VG: $12**

_____. *Treachery in Outer Space.*
First Edition: New York: Grosset & Dunlap, 1954.
NF/F: $80   **G/VG: $30**

_____. *Sabotage in Space.*
First Edition: New York: Grosset & Dunlap, 1955.
NF/F: $65   **G/VG: $20**

_____. *The Robot Rocket.*
First Edition: New York: Grosset & Dunlap, 1956.
NF/F: $75   **G/VG: $30**

Rockwood, Roy. *By Air Express to Venus.*
First Edition: New York: Cupples & Leon, 1929.
NF/F: $150   **G/VG: $60**

_____. *Bomba the Jungle Boy in the Steaming Grotto.*
First Edition: New York: Cupples & Leon, 1935.
NF/F: $95   **G/VG: $35**

Roe, Harry Mason. *Lanky Lawson and His Trained Zebra.*
First Edition: New York: Barse & Co., 1930.
NF/F: $25   **G/VG: $8**

Roy, Lillian Elizabeth. *The Prince of Atlantis.*
First Edition: New York: The Educational Press, 1929.
NF/F: $75   **G/VG: $30**

Sachs, Marilyn. *Matt's Mitt.*
First Edition: Garden City, NY: Doubleday, 1975.
NF/F: $85   **G/VG: $30**

Saint-Exupery, Antoine de. *The Little Prince.*
Limited Edition: New York: Reynal & Hitchcock, 1943 (525 copies).
NF/F: $18,500   **G/VG: $10,000**
Trade First Edition: New York: Reynal & Hitchcock, 1943.
NF/F: $1,500   **G/VG: $800**

Salten, Felix. *Bambi: A Life in the Woods.*
First Edition in English: New York: Simon & Schuster, 1928.
NF/F: $4,200   **G/VG: $1,850**

Carey Rockwell.

Roy Rockwood.

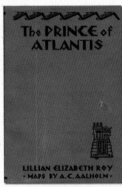
Lillian Elizabeth Roy.

Felix Salten.

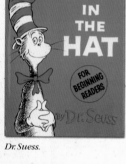

Dr. Suess.

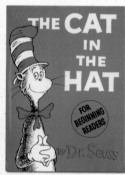

Charles M. Schultz.

_____. *Perri.*
First Edition in English: Indianapolis, IN: Bobbs-Merrill Co., 1938.
NF/F: $75   **G/VG: $30**

Schroeder, Doris. *Walt Disney's Annette and the Mystery at Moonstone Bay.*
First Edition: Racine, Wisconsin: Whitman Publishing Company, 1962.
NF/F: $30   **G/VG: $12**

Selden, George. *The Dog That Could Swim Under Water: Memoirs Of A Springer Spaniel.*
First Edition: New York: The Viking Press, 1956.
NF/F: $155   **G/VG: $50**

Sendak, Maurice. *In the Night Kitchen.*
First Edition: New York: Harper and Row, 1970.
NF/F: $450   **G/VG: $165**

Seuss, Dr. *The Cat In The Hat.*
First Edition: New York: Random House, 1957.
Points of Issue: The first state has matte boards.
NF/F: $14,000   **G/VG: $6,000**

_____. *Thidwick the Big-Hearted Moose.*
First Edition: New York: Random House, 1948.
NF/F: $2,400   **G/VG: $850**

Schultz, Charles M. *It's The Great Pumpkin, Charlie Brown.*
First Edition: Cleveland & New York: World Publishing, 1967.
NF/F: $65   **G/VG: $35**

_____. *He's Your Dog, Charlie Brown.*
First Edition: Cleveland & New York: World Publishing, 1968.
NF/F: $55   **G/VG: $15**

Sheldon, Ann. *Phantom of Dark Oaks.* (Linda Craig Adventures No. 10).
First Edition: New York: Wanderer/ Simon and Schuster, 1984.
NF/F: $55   **G/VG: $20**

Sidney, Margaret. Five Little Peppers Series:

_____. *Five Little Peppers and How They Grew.*
First Edition: Boston: D. Lothrop & Company, 1880.
Points of Issue: In first issue the caption on page 231 is "said Polly."
NF/F: $850   **G/VG: $325**

_____. *Five Little Peppers Midway.*
First Edition: Boston: D. Lothrop & Company, 1890.
NF/F: $125   **G/VG: $65**

_____. *Five Little Peppers Grown Up.*
First Edition: Boston: D. Lothrop & Company, 1892.
NF/F: $275   **G/VG: $125**

_____. *Five Little Peppers: Phronsie Pepper.*
First Edition: Boston: D. Lothrop & Company, 1897.
NF/F: $250   **G/VG: $125**

_____. *Five Little Peppers: Stories Polly Pepper Told.*
First Edition: Boston: D. Lothrop & Company, 1899.
NF/F: $100   **G/VG: $45**

_____. *Five Little Peppers: The Adventures of Joe Pepper.*
First Edition: Boston: D. Lothrop & Company, 1900.
NF/F: $150　　　　　　**G/VG: $60**

_____. *Five Little Peppers Abroad.*
First Edition: Boston: Lothrop, Lee and Shepard Co., 1902.
NF/F: $120　　　　　　**G/VG: $45**

_____. *Five Little Peppers At School.*
First Edition: Boston: Lothrop, Lee and Shepard Co., 1903.
NF/F: $100　　　　　　**G/VG: $35**

_____. *Five Little Peppers and Their Friends.*
First Edition: Boston: Lothrop, Lee and Shepard Co., 1904.
NF/F: $250　　　　　　**G/VG: $100**

_____. *Five Little Peppers: Ben Pepper.*
First Edition: Boston: Lothrop, Lee and Shepard Co., 1905.
NF/F: $200　　　　　　**G/VG: $85**

_____. *Five Little Peppers in the Brown House.*
First Edition: Boston: Lothrop, Lee and Shepard Co., 1907.
NF/F: $150　　　　　　**G/VG: $50**

_____. *Five Little Peppers: Our Davie Pepper.*
First Edition: Boston: D. Lothrop & Company, 1916.
NF/F: $250　　　　　　**G/VG: $100**

Silvers, Earl Reed. *Jackson Of Hillsdale High.*
First Edition: New York: D. Appleton Company, 1923.
NF/F: $45　　　　　　**G/VG: $15**

Smith, Carl W. *Red Ryder and the Secret of the Lucky Mine.*
First Edition: Racine WI.: Whitman Pub. Co, 1943.
NF/F: $25　　　　　　**G/VG: $10**

Smith, Harriet Lummis. *Pollyanna of the Orange Blossoms.*
First Edition: Boston: L.C. Page, 1924.
NF/F: $75　　　　　　**G/VG: $30**

Smith, Mary P. Wells. *The Boy Captive in Canada.*
First Edition: Boston: Little, Brown and Company, 1905.
NF/F: $120　　　　　　**G/VG: $50**

Snell, Roy J. *Air Fighters of America.*
First Edition: Racine, WI: Whitman Publishing Co., 1941.
Points of issue: Little Big Book 1448.
NF/F: $65　　　　　　**G/VG: $25**

Snow, Dorothea J. *Roy Rogers' Favorite Western Stories.*
First Edition: Racine, WI: Whitman Publishing Co., 1956.
NF/F: $75　　　　　　**G/VG: $40**

Snow, Jack. Oz Series*:

_____. *The Magical Mimics in Oz.*
First Edition: Chicago: Reilly and Lee, 1946.
NF/F: $350　　　　　　**G/VG: $100**

_____. *The Shaggy Man of Oz.*
First Edition: Chicago: Reilly and Lee, 1949.
NF/F: $350　　　　　　**G/VG: $100**
(See Also: L. Frank Baum, Ruth Plumly Thompson, John R. Neill, Rachel R. Cosgrove, and Eloise Jarvis McGraw and Lauren Lynn Mc Graw.)

Speed, Eric. *Dead Heat at Le Mans.*
First Edition: New York: Grosset & Dunlap, 1977.
NF/F: $40　　　　　　**G/VG: $10**

Carl W. Smith.

Harriet Lummis Smith.

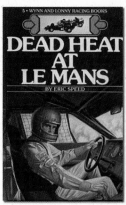

Eric Speed.

Julie Tatham.

Julie Tatham.

Julie Tatham.

Staunton, Schuyler (L. Frank Baum).
Daughters of Destiny.
First Edition: Chicago: Reilly and
Britton, 1906.
NF/F: $400   G/VG: $100

_____. *The Fate of a Crown.*
First Edition: Chicago: Reilly and
Britton, 1905.
NF/F: $300   G/VG: $100

Stone, Raymond. *Tommy Tiptop And
His Baseball Nine.*
First Edition: New York: Graham &
Matlack, 1912.
NF/F: $75   G/VG: $30

Sumner, Cid Ricketts. *Tammy Tell Me True.*
First Edition: New York: Bobbs-Merrill
Company, 1959.
NF/F: $95   G/VG: $45

Tatham, Julie. Cherry Ames Series:

_____. *Cherry Ames At Spencer.*
First Edition: New York: Grosset &
Dunlap, 1949.
NF/F: $90   G/VG: $35

_____. *Cherry Ames Night
Supervisor.*
First Edition: New York: Grosset &
Dunlap, 1950.
NF/F: $50   G/VG: $20

_____. *Cherry Ames Mountaineer
Nurse.*
First Edition: New York: Grosset &
Dunlap, 1951.
NF/F: $50   G/VG: $20

_____. *Cherry Ames Clinic Nurse.*
First Edition: New York: Grosset &
Dunlap, 1952.
NF/F: $50   G/VG: $20

_____. *Cherry Ames Dude Ranch
Nurse.*
First Edition: New York: Grosset &
Dunlap, 1953.
NF/F: $50   G/VG: $20

_____. *Cherry Ames Rest Home
Nurse.*
First Edition: New York: Grosset &
Dunlap, 1954.
NF/F: $50   G/VG: $20

_____. *Cherry Ames Country
Doctor's Nurse.*
First Edition: New York: Grosset &
Dunlap, 1955.
NF/F: $50   G/VG: $20

_____. *Cherry Ames Boarding
School Nurse.*
First Edition: New York: Grosset &
Dunlap, 1955.
NF/F: $50   G/VG: $20

_____. *Cherry Ames Department
Store Nurse.*
First Edition: New York: Grosset &
Dunlap, 1956.
NF/F: $50   G/VG: $20
(See: Wells, Helen)

_____. Vicki Barr Series:

_____. *The Clue of the Broken Blossom.*
New York: Grosset & Dunlap, 1950.
NF/F: $45   G/VG: $15

_____. *Behind the White Veil.* New
York: Grosset & Dunlap, 1951.
NF/F: $40   G/VG: $15

_____. *The Mystery at Hartwood
House.* New York: Grosset & Dunlap,
1952.
NF/F: $20   G/VG: $8
(See: Wells, Helen)

Taggart, Marion Ames. *Pussy-Cat Town.*
First Edition: Boston: L. C. Page and Co., 1906.
NF/F: $200   **G/VG: $100**

Taylor, Sydney. *All-Of-A-Kind Family Downtown.*
First Edition: Chicago, IL: Follett, 1972.
NF/F: $120   **G/VG: $40**

Terhune, Albert Payson. *Real Tales of Real Dogs.*
First Edition: Akron, Ohio: Saalfield, 1935.
NF/F: $165   **G/VG: $55**

Thompson, Mary Wolfe. *Two in the Wilderness: Before Vermont Had a Name.*
First Edition: New York: David McKay, 1967.
NF/F: $85   **G/VG: $25**

Thompson, Ruth Plumly. The Oz Series*:

_____. *The Royal Book of Oz.*
First Edition: Chicago: Reilly and Lee, 1921.
Points of Issue: First state has a typo "scarecorws" on page 255.
NF/F: $800   **G/VG: $250**

_____. *Kabumpo in Oz.*
First Edition: Chicago: Reilly and Lee, 1922.
NF/F: $400   **G/VG: $175**

_____. *The Cowardly Lion of Oz.*
First Edition: Chicago: Reilly and Lee, 1923.
NF/F: $400   **G/VG: $175**

_____. *Grampa in Oz.*
First Edition: Chicago: Reilly and Lee, 1924.
First state has perfect type on pages 171 and 189
NF/F: $500   **G/VG: $200**

_____. *The Lost King of Oz.*
First Edition: Chicago: Reilly and Lee, 1925.
Points of Issue: Serif is unbroken on the k in line 4 on page 193 of the first issue.
NF/F: $500   **G/VG: $200**

_____. *The Hungry Tiger of Oz.*
First Edition: Chicago: Reilly and Lee, 1926.
First state has a hyphen on the last line of page 21 and the word "two" in perfect type on the last line of page 252.
NF/F: $400   **G/VG: $175**

_____. *The Gnome King of Oz.*
First Edition: Chicago: Reilly and Lee, 1927.
NF/F: $600   **G/VG: $225**

_____. *The Giant Horse of Oz.*
First Edition: Chicago: Reilly and Lee, 1928.
Points of Issue: A damaged 'r' in 'morning' on p. 116 line 1 and frontispiece misprint 'Oniberon' for 'Quiberon' in first issue.
NF/F: $500   **G/VG: $175**

_____. *Jack Pumpkinhead of Oz.*
First Edition: Chicago: Reilly and Lee, 1929.
NF/F: $300   **G/VG: $100**

_____. *The Yellow Knight of Oz.*
First Edition: Chicago: Reilly and Lee, 1930.
NF/F: $300   **G/VG: $100**

_____. *Pirates in Oz.*
First Edition: Chicago: Reilly and Lee, 1931.
NF/F: $450   **G/VG: $175**

Albert Payson Terhune.

Ruth Plumly Thompson.

Ruth Plumly Thompson.

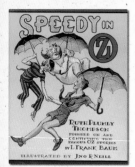

Ruth Plumly Thompson.

Ruth Plumly Thompson.

Helen Louise Thorndyke.

_____. *The Purple Prince of Oz.*
First Edition: Chicago: Reilly and Lee, 1932.
NF/F: $450   **G/VG: $175**

_____. *Ojo in Oz.*
First Edition: Chicago: Reilly and Lee, 1933.
NF/F: $400   **G/VG: $175**

_____. *Speedy in Oz.*
First Edition: Chicago: Reilly and Lee, 1934.
NF/F: $800   **G/VG: $325**

_____. *The Wishing Horse of Oz.*
First Edition: Chicago: Reilly and Lee, 1935. First edition was the last Oz book to have colored plates of which there are 12.
NF/F: $800   **G/VG: $350**

_____. *Captain Salt in Oz.*
First Edition: Chicago: Reilly and Lee, 1936.
NF/F: $300   **G/VG: $100**

_____. *Handy Mandy in Oz.*
First Edition: Chicago: Reilly and Lee, 1937.
NF/F: $600   **G/VG: $250**

_____. *The Silver Princess in Oz.*
First Edition: Chicago: Reilly and Lee, 1938.
NF/F: $600   **G/VG: $250**

_____. *Ozoplaning with the Wizard of Oz.*
First Edition: Chicago: Reilly and Lee, 1939.
NF/F: $800   **G/VG: $350**
(See Also: L. Frank Baum, John R. Neill, Jack Snow, Rachel R. Cosgrove, and Eloise Jarvis McGraw and Lauren Lynn Mc Graw.)

Thorndyke, Helen Louise. *Her First Trip to a Lighthouse.* (Honey Bunch -28).
First Edition: New York: Grosset and Dunlap, 1949.
NF/F: $85   **G/VG: $35**

Trent, Margaret. *Hollywood Ho.*
First Edition: New York & Chicago: A. L. Burt, 1932.
NF/F: $65   **G/VG: $15**

Tudor, Tasha. *Dorcas Porkus.*
First Edition: New York: Oxford University Press, 1942.
NF/F: $800   **G/VG: $350**

Van Allsburg, Chris. *The Sweetest Fig.*
First Edition: Boston: Houghton Mifflin Company, 1993.
NF/F: $65   **G/VG: $20**

_____. *Jumanji.*
First Edition: Boston: Houghton Mifflin Company, 1981.
NF/F: $700   **G/VG: $325**

Van Dyne, Edith (L. Frank Baum). *Mary Louise Solves a Mystery.*
First Edition: Chicago: Reilly and Britton, 1917.
NF/F: $65   **G/VG: $35**

_____. Aunt Jane's Nieces Series:

_____. *Aunt Jane's Nieces.*
First Edition: Chicago: Reilly and Britton, 1906.
NF/F: $400   **G/VG: $175**

_____. *Aunt Jane's Nieces Abroad.*
First Edition: Chicago: Reilly and Britton, 1907.
Points of Issue: Top stain is green in first issue.
NF/F: $275   **G/VG: $120**

_____. *Aunt Jane's Nieces at Millville.*
First Edition: Chicago: Reilly and Britton, 1908.
NF/F: $225   **G/VG: $95**

_____. *Aunt Jane's Nieces at Work.*
First Edition: Chicago: Reilly and Britton, 1909.
NF/F: $245   **G/VG: $95**

_____. *Aunt Jane's Nieces in Society.*
First Edition: Chicago: Reilly and Britton, 1910.
NF/F: $225   **G/VG: $100**

_____. *Aunt Jane's Nieces and Uncle John.*
First Edition: Chicago: Reilly and Britton, 1911.
NF/F: $200   **G/VG: $85**

_____. *Aunt Jane's Nieces on Vacation.*
First Edition: Chicago: Reilly and Britton, 1912.
NF/F: $235   **G/VG: $90**

_____. *Aunt Jane's Nieces on the Ranch.*
First Edition: Chicago: Reilly and Britton, 1913.
NF/F: $300   **G/VG: $125**

_____. *Aunt Jane's Nieces Out West.*
First Edition: Chicago: Reilly and Britton, 1914.
NF/F: $125   **G/VG: $50**

_____. *Aunt Jane's Nieces in the Red Cross.*
First Edition: Chicago: Reilly and Britton, 1915.
NF/F: $125   **G/VG: $45**

Warde, Margaret. *Nancy Lee's Lookout.*
First Edition: Philadelphia: Penn Publishing, 1915.
NF/F: $75   **G/VG: $25**

_____. *Betty Wales Decides.*
First Edition: Philadelphia: Penn Publishing, 1911.
NF/F: $40   **G/VG: $20**

Warner, Frank A. *Bobby Blake at Snowtop Camp.*
First Edition: New York: Barse & Hopkins, 1916.
NF/F: $50   **G/VG: $20**

Warner, Gertrude Chandler. *The Boxcar Children.*
First Edition: Chicago: Scott, Foresman, 1950.
NF/F: $165   **G/VG: $70**

Wayne, Dorothy. *Dorothy Dixon and the Mystery Plane.*
First Edition: Chicago: Goldsmith Publishing Company, 1933.
NF/F: $55   **G/VG: $15**

Weber, Lenora Mattingly. *Beany Malone.*
First Edition: New York: Thomas Y. Crowell, 1948.
NF/F: $200   **G/VG: $120**

Margaret Warde.

Dorothy Wayne.

Lenora Mattingly Weber.

Helen Wells.

Helen Wells.

Helen Wells.

Wells, Helen. Cherry Ames Series:

_____. *Cherry Ames Student Nurse.*
First Edition: New York: Grosset & Dunlap, 1943.
NF/F: $150   **G/VG: $65**

_____. *Cherry Ames Senior Nurse.*
First Edition: New York: Grosset & Dunlap, 1944.
NF/F: $100   **G/VG: $45**

_____. *Cherry Ames Army Nurse.*
First Edition: New York: Grosset & Dunlap, 1944.
NF/F: $135   **G/VG: $40**

_____. *Cherry Ames Chief Nurse.*
First Edition: New York: Grosset & Dunlap, 1944.
NF/F: $150   **G/VG: $65**

_____. *Cherry Ames Flight Nurse.*
First Edition: New York: Grosset & Dunlap, 1945.
NF/F: $75   **G/VG: $35**

_____. *Cherry Ames Veteran's Nurse.*
First Edition: New York: Grosset & Dunlap, 1946.
NF/F: $65   **G/VG: $25**

_____. *Cherry Ames Private Duty Nurse.*
First Edition: New York: Grosset & Dunlap, 1946.
NF/F: $100   **G/VG: $55**

_____. *Cherry Ames Visiting Nurse.*
First Edition: New York: Grosset & Dunlap, 1947.
NF/F: $125   **G/VG: $55**

_____. *Cherry Ames Cruise Nurse.*
First Edition: New York: Grosset & Dunlap, 1948.
NF/F: $65   **G/VG: $25**

_____. *Cherry Ames, Camp Nurse: The Clue of the Faceless Criminal.*
First Edition: New York: Grosset & Dunlap, 1957.
NF/F: $65   **G/VG: $25**

_____. *Cherry Ames, At Hilton Hospital: The Case of the Forgetful Patient.*
First Edition: New York: Grosset & Dunlap, 1959.
NF/F: $50   **G/VG: $15**

_____. *Cherry Ames' Book of First Aid and Home Nursing.*
First Edition: New York: Grosset & Dunlap, 1959.
NF/F: $200   **G/VG: $85**

_____. *Cherry Ames, Island Nurse: Mystery of Rogue's Cave.*
First Edition: New York: Grosset & Dunlap, 1960.
NF/F: $100   **G/VG: $35**

_____. *Cherry Ames, Rural Nurse: The Case of the Dangerous Remedy.*
First Edition: New York: Grosset & Dunlap, 1961.
NF/F: $350   **G/VG: $165**

_____. *Cherry Ames Staff Nurse.*
First Edition: New York: Grosset & Dunlap, 1962.
NF/F: $275   **G/VG: $135**

_____. *Cherry Ames, Companion Nurse.*
First Edition: New York: Grosset & Dunlap, 1964.
NF/F: $75   **G/VG: $25**

_____. *Cherry Ames, Jungle Nurse.*
First Edition: New York: Grosset &
Dunlap, 1965.
NF/F: $150   **G/VG: $65**

_____ **and Julie Tatham.**
*Cherry Ames, The Mystery in the
Doctor's Office.*
First Edition: New York: Grosset &
Dunlap, 1966.
NF/F: $250   **G/VG: $100**

_____. *Ski Nurse Mystery - A
Cherry Ames Nurse Story.*
First Edition: New York: Grosset &
Dunlap, 1968.
NF/F: $450   **G/VG: $200**
(See: Tatham, Julie)

_____. Vicki Barr Series:

_____. *Silver Wings for Vicki.* New
York: Grosset & Dunlap, 1947.
NF/F: $65   **G/VG: $25**

_____. *Vicki Finds the Answer.*
New York: Grosset & Dunlap, 1947.
NF/F: $75   **G/VG: $20**

_____. *The Hidden Valley Mystery.*
New York: Grosset & Dunlap, 1948.
NF/F: $80   **G/VG: $25**

_____. *The Secret of Magnolia
Manor.* New York: Grosset & Dunlap,
1949.
NF/F: $115   **G/VG: $45**

_____. *Peril Over the Airport.* New
York: Grosset & Dunlap, 1953.
NF/F: $30   **G/VG: $10**

_____. *The Mystery of the
Vanishing Lady.* New York: Grosset &
Dunlap, 1954.
NF/F: $40   **G/VG: $15**

_____. *The Search for the Missing
Twin.* New York: Grosset & Dunlap,
1954.
NF/F: $40   **G/VG: $15**

_____. *The Ghost at the Waterfall.*
New York: Grosset & Dunlap, 1956.
NF/F: $65   **G/VG: $20**

_____. *The Clue of the Gold Coin.*
New York: Grosset & Dunlap, 1958.
NF/F: $80   **G/VG: $35**

_____. *The Silver Ring Mystery.*
New York: Grosset & Dunlap, 1960.
NF/F: $75   **G/VG: $30**

_____. *The Clue of the Carved
Ruby.*
New York: Grosset & Dunlap, 1961.
NF/F: $100   **G/VG: $40**

_____. *The Mystery of Flight 908.*
New York: Grosset & Dunlap, 1962.
NF/F: $150   **G/VG: $65**

_____. *The Brass Idol Mystery.*
New York: Grosset & Dunlap, 1964.
NF/F: $100   **G/VG: $35**
(See: Tathem, Julie)

West, Jerry. *The Happy Hollisters
and the Mystery of the Golden
Witch.*
First Edition: Garden City, NY:
Doubleday & Company, 1966.
NF/F: $100   **G/VG: $30**

Helen Wells.

Helen Wells.

THE HAPPY HOLLISTERS
AND THE **MYSTERY OF THE
GOLDEN
WITCH**

Jerry West.

E. B. White.

Laura Ingalls Wilder.

Laura Ingalls Wilder.

Wheeler, Janet D. *Billie Bradley at Three-Towers Hall.*
First Edition: New York: George Sully & Company, 1920.
NF/F: $140   **G/VG: $45**

White, E. B. *Charlotte's Web.*
First Edition: New York: Harper & Brothers, 1952.
NF/F: $2,500   **G/VG: $900**

_____. *Stuart Little.*
First Edition: New York: Harper & Brothers, 1945.
NF/F: $2,000   **G/VG: $825**

White, Ramy Allison. *Sunny Boy in the Big City.*
First Edition: New York: Barse & Hopkins, 1920.
NF/F: $40   **G/VG: $15**

Wilder, Laura Ingalls. Little House Series:

_____. *Little House in the Big Woods.*
First Edition: New York: New York: Harper & Brothers, 1932.
NF/F: $1,200   **G/VG: $575**

_____. *Farmer Boy.*
First Edition: New York: New York: Harper & Brothers, 1933.
NF/F: $1,000   **G/VG: $400**

_____. *Little House on the Prairie.*
First Edition: New York: New York: Harper & Brothers, 1935.
Point of Issue: Code E-K on Verso.
NF/F: $1,400   **G/VG: $600**

_____. *On the Banks of Plum Creek.*
First Edition: New York: New York: Harper & Brothers, 1937.
NF/F: $1,000   **G/VG: $400**

_____. *By The Shores of Silver Lake.*
First Edition: New York: New York: Harper & Brothers, 1939.
NF/F: $1,500   **G/VG: $650**

_____. *The Long Winter.*
First Edition: New York: New York: Harper & Brothers, 1940.
NF/F: $1,100   **G/VG: $400**

_____. *Little Town on the Prairie.*
First Edition: New York: New York: Harper & Brothers, 1941.
NF/F: $1,600   **G/VG: $700**

_____. *These Happy Golden Years.*
First Edition: New York: New York: Harper & Brothers, 1943.
NF/F: $1,200   **G/VG: $525**

_____. *Fairy Poems.*
First Edition: New York: Bantam Books - Doubleday - Dell, 1998.
NF/F: $100   **G/VG: $45**

Williams, Margery. *The Velveteen Rabbit.*
First Edition: London: William Heinemann, 1922.
NF/F: $16,000   **G/VG: $6,000**

Winfield, Arthur M. *The Rover Boys on the Great Lakes.*
First Edition: Rockaway, NY: Mershon Co., 1901.
NF/F: $175   **G/VG: $65**

Winterbotham, Russel R. *Tom Beatty Ace of the Secret Service Scores Again.*
First Edition: Racine, WI: Whitman Publishing Company, 1937.
NF/F: $75 **G/VG: $35**

Wirt, Mildred A. *Pirate Brig.*
First Edition: New York: Charles Scribner's Sons, 1950.
NF/F: $300 **G/VG: $90**

_____. *Courageous Wings.*
First Edition: Philadelphia: Penn Publishing Company, 1937.
NF/F: $255 **G/VG: $105**

_____. *The Mystery of the Laughing Mask.*
First Edition: New York: Cupples & Leon, 1940.
NF/F: $300 **G/VG: $125**

Wollheim, Donald A. Mike Mars Series*:

_____. *Mike Mars Astronaut.*
First Edition: Garden City, NY: Doubleday & Company, Inc., 1964.
NF/F: $70 **G/VG: $15**

_____. *Mike Mars Flys the X-15.*
First Edition: Garden City, NY: Doubleday & Company, Inc., 1964.
NF/F: $85 **G/VG: $20**

_____. *Mike Mars at Cape Canaveral.*
First Edition: Garden City, NY: Doubleday & Company, Inc., 1964.
NF/F: $50 **G/VG: $15**

_____. *Mike Mars in Orbit.*
First Edition: Garden City, NY: Doubleday & Company, Inc., 1964.
NF/F: $85 **G/VG: $25**

_____. *Mike Mars Flies the Dyna-Soar.*
First Edition: Garden City, NY: Doubleday & Company, Inc., 1964.
NF/F: $75 **G/VG: $30**

_____. *Mike Mars South Pole Spaceman.*
First Edition: Garden City, NY: Doubleday & Company, Inc., 1964.
NF/F: $75 **G/VG: $20**

_____. *Mike Mars and the Mystery Satellite.*
First Edition: Garden City, NY: Doubleday & Company, Inc., 1964.
NF/F: $85 **G/VG: $20**

_____. *Mike Mars Around the Moon.*
First Edition: Garden City, NY: Doubleday & Company, Inc., 1964.
NF/F: $95 **G/VG: $25**

Young, Clarence. *The Motor Boys on the Firing Line.*
First Edition: New York: Cupples and Leon, 1919.
NF/F: $100 **G/VG: $35**

Mildred A. Wirt.

Mildred A. Wirt.

Clarence Young.

FANTASY, HORROR AND SCIENCE FICTION

The capacity to create worlds beyond our own in our dreams and in our imagination forms what might be called the literature of the fantastic.

The realm is a wide one, ranging from the pure invention of an entirely new universe, to a minor alteration in invention. As a literary form it has been around as long as man has been able to dream, and to write.

Man touched the moon with his feet for the first time in 1968, but in his mind he has been roaming its surface for centuries. The wind rustling the branches of trees in the night conjures up phantoms of the supernatural. Beyond the hills we know there may lie worlds of magic and mystery. The automobile changed forever the face of our civilization; what other invention might alter the world of tomorrow? All this is the stuff of the literature of the fantastic.

Roughly, it can be broken down into three broad areas. The first, science fiction, involves a forecasting of the future. Strictly, given the name, it should involve rather rigid guidelines, a possible future, one that conforms to scientific principles, but this is not necessarily the case.

Works classed as science fiction can consist of an entirely new civilization on a far planet where science, as we know it, does not exist. It has been written by high school dropouts and scientists with a wall full of degrees.

The second, horror, is the addition of the supernatural to reality. Within it the primal fears of things that go bump in the night are exploited to frighten us, thrill us and entertain us.

The last, fantasy, is an exercise in being a God. It is the literary equivalent of saying "... let there be light." It is the creation of a new universe, with new rules and new laws. The realm of fairies, ogres, trolls and sorcerers. All three are an exercise in dreaming, and imagining.

Fantastic literature, for the collector, ranges wide. There are collections based solely on going to the moon or to Mars. Collections of a mythos developed by a single author and explored by others such as Lovecraft's *Cluthlu* or Andre Norton's *Witch World*.

Collections based on publishers such as Fantasy Press, Shasta Publications, Gnome Press or Arkham House. Like the field of literature it is, the field of collecting it has spawned is nearly as limitless as time, and extends beyond the farthest star.

TEN CLASSIC RARITIES

Asimov, Isaac. *Pebble In The Sky.*
Garden City, NY: Doubleday & Co.,
1950. Needle in a haystack, pebble in
the sky, hard to find but the pebble is
more rewarding.
NF/F: $2,800   **G/VG: $1,500**

Bradbury, Ray. *Dark Carnival.*
Arkham House Sauk City, 1947. Issued
without a dust jacket. Finding one of
the eighty copies of Dark Carnival can
shed a lot of light on your finances.
NF/F: $6,500   **G/VG: $2,000**

Burroughs, Edgar Rice. *The Outlaw
of Torn.*
Chicago: A.C. McClurg & Company,
1927. Issued with dust jacket. Find this
and make out like a bandit.
NF/F: $6,000   **G/VG: $2,000**

Dick, Philip K. *A Handful of
Darkness.*
London: Rich & Cowen, 1955. No
listing of "World of Chance" on rear
panel. Covert this to a handful of
money.
NF/F: $2,000   **G/VG: $900**

Heinlein, Robert A. *Stranger in a
Strange Land.*
New York: G. P. Putnam's, 1961. The
first printing has a code C22 on page
408. Find it and be as strange as you
like.
NF/F: $4,400   **G/VG: $1,800**

Herbert, Frank. *Dune.*
Philadelphia: Chilton Books, 1965.
Blue binding dust jacket price of $595.
Great way to start a vacation would be
to find this.
NF/F: $10,500   **G/VG: $4,000**

Lovecraft, H. P. *The Shadow Over
Innsmouth.*
Everett, Pennsylvania: Visionary
Publishing Co., 1936. Find it and cast
some light in your own shadow.
NF/F: $7,500   **G/VG: $3,500**

Machen, Arthur. *The Cosy Room.*
London: Rich & Cowan, 1936. Finding
this could certainly make things cosier
around your room.
NF/F: $2,200   **G/VG: $850**

Tolkien, J.R.R. *The Hobbit or There
and Back Again.*
London: George Allen & Unwin, 1937.
"Dodgeson" (should be Dodgson) on
rear dust jacket flap. Go there, back
again or anywhere at all if you find
this.
NF/F: $35,000   **G/VG: $20,000**

Wells, H.G. *The Time Machine.*
London: William Heinemann, 1895.
First Edition. Gray stamped in purple
with 16 pages of ads. Time will be on
your side with this.
NF/F: $5,000   **G/VG: $2,300**

Ray Bradbury.

J.R.R. Tolkien.

PRICE GUIDE

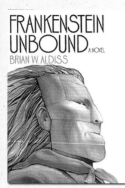

Brian W. Aldiss.

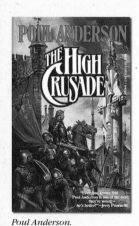

N. Amosoff.

Abe, Kobo. *Inter Ice Age 4.*
First U.S. Edition: New York: Alfred A. Knopf, 1970.
NF/F: $45   **G/VG: $15**

Aldiss, Brian W. *Barefoot in the Head.*
First Edition: London: Faber and Faber, 1969.
NF/F: $85   **G/VG: $25**
First U.S. Edition: New York: Doubleday, 1970.
NF/F: $45   **G/VG: $15**

_____. *Frankenstein Unbound.*
First Edition: London: Jonathan Cape, 1973.
NF/F: $95   **G/VG: $35**
First U.S. Edition: New York: Random House, 1973.
NF/F: $45   **G/VG: $15**

Aldrich, Thomas Bailey. *The Queen of Sheba.*
First Edition: London: George Routledge, 1877.
NF/F: $95   **G/VG: $35**
First U.S. Edition: Boston, James R. Osgood, 1877.
NF/F: $75   **G/VG: $30**

Allingham, Garry. *Verwoerd: The End: A Look-back from the Future.*
First Edition: Cape Town, S.A.: Purnell & Sons, 1961.
NF/F: $30   **G/VG: $10**
First U.K. Edition: London, Boardman, 1961.
NF/F: $20   **G/VG: $8**

Amosoff, N. *Notes from the Future.*
First U.S. Edition: New York: Simon & Schuster, 1970.
NF/F: $25   **G/VG: $10**

Anderson, Olof W. *The Treasure Vault of Atlantis.*
First Edition: 511 Masonic Temple, MN: Midland Publishing Co., 1925.
NF/F: $125   **G/VG: $40**

Anderson, Poul. *The High Crusade.*
First Edition: Garden City, NY: Doubleday, 1960.
NF/F: $200   **G/VG: $65**

_____. *Harvest the Fire.*
First Edition: New York: Tom Doherty Associates, 1995.
NF/F: $25   **G/VG: $8**

Anthony, Piers. Incarnations of Immortality:

_____. *On a Pale Horse.*
First Edition: New York: Ballantine Books, 1983.
NF/F: $65   **G/VG: $20**

_____. *Bearing an Hourglass.*
First Edition: New York: Ballantine Books, 1984.
NF/F: $45   **G/VG: $10**

_____. *With a Tangled Skein.*
First Edition: New York: Ballantine Books, 1985.
NF/F: $45   **G/VG: $10**

_____. *Wielding a Red Sword.*
First Edition: New York: Ballantine Books, 1986.
NF/F: $35   **G/VG: $10**

_____. *Being a Green Mother.*
First Edition: New York: Ballantine Books, 1987.
NF/F: $25   **G/VG: $8**

_____. *For Love of Evil.*
First Edition: New York: William Morrow & Co, 1988.
NF/F: $35   **G/VG: $12**

Poul Anderson.

_____. *And Eternity.*
First Edition: New York: William
Morrow & Co, 1990.
NF/F: $25   **G/VG: $10**

_____. *Under a Velvet Cloak.*
Limited Edition: np: Mundania Press LLC, 2007.
Points of Issue: Two series numbered 1-250 and
lettered A-Z all signed by the author. Not Seen.
POD: np: Mundania Press LLC, 2007.
Points of Issue: Publisher does not disclose
his markings or corrections so as a
collectible this issue is essentially worthless.
NF/F: $5   **G/VG: $1**

_____. *Harpy Thyme.*
First Edition: New York: Tor Books, 1994.
NF/F: $15   **G/VG: $8**

Asimov, Isaac. *I, Robot.*
First Edition: New York: Gnome Press, 1950.
NF/F: $5,500   **G/VG: $1,200**

_____. *The Gods Themselves.*
First Edition: New York: Doubleday &
Company, 1972.
NF/F: $250   **G/VG: $40**

_____. Foundation Series*:

_____. *Foundation.*
First Edition: New York: Gnome Press, 1951.
NF/F: $2,500   **G/VG: $1,100**

_____. *Foundation and Empire.*
First Edition: New York: Gnome Press, 1952.
NF/F: $1,500   **G/VG: $600**

_____. *Second Foundation.*
First Edition: New York: Doubleday &
Company, 1953.
NF/F: $500   **G/VG: $100**

_____. *Foundation's Edge.*
First Edition: New York: Doubleday &
Company, 1982.
NF/F: $100   **G/VG: $35**

_____. *Foundation and Earth.*
First Edition: New York: Doubleday &
Company, 1986.
NF/F: $75   **G/VG: $15**

_____. *Prelude to Foundation.*
First Edition: New York: Doubleday &
Company, 1988.
NF/F: $25   **G/VG: $10**

_____. *Forward the Foundation.*
First Edition: New York: Doubleday &
Company, 1993.
NF/F: $25   **G/VG: $10**

Bahnson Jr, Agnew H. *The Stars Are
Too High.*
First Edition: New York: Random
House, 1959.
NF/F: $25   **G/VG: $10**

Ballard, J.G. *The Crystal World.*
First Edition: London: Jonathon Cape,
1966.
NF/F: $325   **G/VG: $100**
First U.S. Edition: New York: Farrar,
Straus & Giroux, 1966.
NF/F: $145   **G/VG: $45**

_____. *The Day of Creation.*
Limited Edition: London: Victor
Gollancz, 1987 (100 copies).
NF/F: $300   **G/VG: Not Seen**
First Edition: London: Victor Gollancz,
1987.
NF/F: $65   **G/VG: $15**
First U.S. Edition: New York: Farrar,
Straus & Giroux, 1987.
NF/F: $35   **G/VG: $10**

Balmer, Edwin and Philip Wylie.
Worlds Collide Series:

_____. *When Worlds Collide.*
First Edition: New York: Frederick A
Stokes, 1933.
NF/F: $150   **G/VG: $65**

J.G. Ballard.

J.G. Ballard.

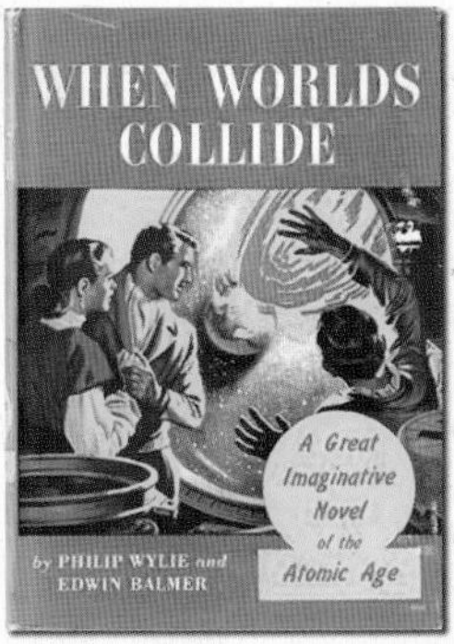

*Edwin Balmer and Philip
Wylie.*

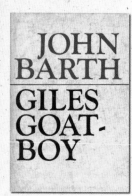

John Barth.

Margot Bennett.

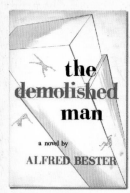

Alfred Bester.

_____. *After Worlds Collide.*
First Edition: New York: Frederick Stokes, 1934.
NF/F: $150   **G/VG: $65**

Barker, Clive. *Weaveworld.*
Limited Edition: London: Collins, 1987 (526 copies).
NF/F: $250   **G/VG: $100**
First Edition (trade): London: Collins, 1987.
NF/F: $55   **G/VG: $20**
Limited Edition: NY: Poseidon Press, 1987 (552 copies).
NF/F: $200   **G/VG: $100**
First U.S. Edition (trade): NY: Poseidon Press, 1987.
NF/F: $25   **G/VG: $10**

Barjavel, Rene. *The Ice People.*
First U.K. Edition: London: Rupert Hart-Davis, 1970.
NF/F: $25   **G/VG: $10**
First U.S. Edition: New York; William Morrow and Co., 1971.
NF/F: $30   **G/VG: $10**

Barnes, Arthur. *Interplanetary Hunter.*
First Edition: New York: Gnome Press, 1956.
NF/F: $65   **G/VG: $25**

Barth, John. *Giles Goat-Boy or, The Revised New Syllabus.*
Limited Edition: Garden City, NY: Doubleday & Co., 1966 (250 copies).
NF/F: $400   **G/VG: $175**
First Edition: Garden City, NY: Doubleday & Co., 1966.
Points of Issue: First state has "H18" at the bottom of the last page and lacks a "First Edition" notice on the verso.
NF/F: $75   **G/VG: $25**
First U.K. Edition: London: Secker & Warburg, 1967.
NF/F: $45   **G/VG: $15**

Beagle, Peter S. *The Last Unicorn.*
First Edition: New York: Viking Press, 1968.
NF/F: $500   **G/VG: $165**

_____. *The Innkeeper's Song.*
First Edition: New York: Roc Books, 1993.
NF/F: $45   **G/VG: $15**

Benford, Gregory. *Timescape.*
First Edition: New York: Simon and Schuster, 1980.
NF/F: $95   **G/VG: $25**

_____. *Against Infinity.*
First Edition: New York: Timescape, 1983.
NF/F: $25   **G/VG: $8**

Bennett, Margot. *The Long Way Back.*
First Edition: London: The Bodley Head, 1954.
NF/F: $65   **G/VG: $25**
First U.S. Edition: New York Coward-McCann, 1955.
NF/F: $50   **G/VG: $15**

Best, Herbert. *The Twenty-Fifth Hour.*
First Edition: New York: Random House, 1940.
NF/F: $95   **G/VG: $30**

Bester, Alfred. *The Demolished Man.*
First Edition: Chicago: Shasta Publishers, 1953.
NF/F: $850   **G/VG: $350**

Binder, Eando. *Lords of Creation.*
Limited Edition: Philadelphia: Prime
Press, 1949 (112 copies).
NF/F: $180   **G/VG: $85**
First Edition: Philadelphia: Prime
Press, 1949.
NF/F: $55   **G/VG: $20**

Blackwood, Algernon. *John Silence.*
First Edition: London: Eveleigh Nash,
1908.
NF/F: $375   **G/VG: $150**
First U.S. Edition: John W. Luce &
Company, 1909.
NF/F: $225   **G/VG: $75**

Blish, James. *Jack of Eagles.*
First Edition: New York: Greenberg:
Publisher, 1952.
NF/F: $150   **G/VG: $40**

_____. *The Star Trek Reader.*
First Edition: New York: E.P. Dutton,
1976.
NF/F: $25   **G/VG: $10**

Bloch, Robert. *Psycho.*
First Edition: New York: Simon and
Schuster, 1959.
NF/F: $1,900   **G/VG: $700**

_____. *King of Terrors.*
Limited Edition: New York: Mysterious
Press, 1977 (250 copies).
NF/F: $125   **G/VG: $55**
First Edition (trade): New York:
Mysterious Press, 1977.
NF/F: $35   **G/VG: $15**

Boulle, Pierre. *Garden on the Moon.*
First U.K. Edition: London: Secker &
Warburg, 1965.
NF/F: $85   **G/VG: $20**
First U.S. Edition: New York: Vanguard
Press, 1965.
NF/F: $30   **G/VG: $10**

_____. *Planet of the Apes.*
First U.K. Edition as *Monkey Planet*:
London: Seker & Warburg, 1963.
NF/F: $1,450   **G/VG: $500**
First U.S. Edition: New York: Vanguard
Press, 1963.
NF/F: $950   **G/VG: $350**

Bouve, Edward T. *Centuries Apart.*
First Edition: Boston: Little, Brown and
Co., 1894.
NF/F: $125   **G/VG: $65**

Bowen, John. *After the Rain.*
First Edition: London: Faber and Faber,
1958.
NF/F: $75   **G/VG: $25**
First U.S. Edition: New York: Random
House, 1967.
NF/F: $35   **G/VG: $10**

Boyd, John. *The Last Starship From
Earth.*
First Edition: New York: Weybright
and Talley, 1968.
NF/F: $60   **G/VG: $20**
First U.K. Edition: London: Gollancz,
1969.
NF/F: $10   **G/VG: $5**

Brackett, Leigh. *The Starmen.*
First Edition: New York: Gnome Press,
1952.
NF/F: $250   **G/VG: $95**

Bradbury, Ray. *The Golden Apples Of
The Sun.*
First Edition: Doubleday & Co., Inc.
Garden City, 1953.
NF/F: $950   **G/VG: $400**

_____. *A Medicine for
Melancholy.*
First Edition: Doubleday & Co., Inc.
Garden City, 1959.
NF/F: $400   **G/VG: $100**

Eando Binder.

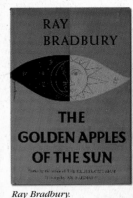

Pierre Boulle.

Ray Bradbury.

Terry Brooks.

Terry Brooks.

John Brunner.

_____. *Graveyard For Lunatics.*
First Edition: NY: Alfred Knopf, 1990.
NF/F: $20   **G/VG: $10**

Bradshaw, William R. *The Goddess of Atvatabar.*
First Edition: New York: J. F. Douthitt, 1892.
NF/F: $375   **G/VG: $150**

Bradley, Marion Zimmer. Avalon Series:

_____. *The Forest House.*
First Edition: New York: Viking, 1993.
NF/F: $35   **G/VG: $10**

Bradley, Marion Zimmer (with Diana L. Paxson). *Lady of Avalon.*
First Edition: London: Michael Joseph, 1997.
NF/F: $45   **G/VG: $15**

_____. *Priestess of Avalon.*
First Edition: London: Harper Collins, 2000.
NF/F: $30   **G/VG: $10**
First U.S. Edition: New York: Viking, 2001.
NF/F: $35   **G/VG: $10**

_____. *Ancestors of Avalon.*
First Edition: London: Voyager, 2004.
NF/F: $35   **G/VG: $10**
First U.S. Edition: New York: Viking, 2004.
NF/F: $35   **G/VG: $10**
(See: Paxson, Diana L.)

Brooks, Terry. *The Sword of Shannara.*
First Edition: New York: Random House, 1977.
NF/F: $950   **G/VG: $300**

_____. *Running With The Demon.*
First Edition: New York: Ballantine Books/Del Rey, 1997.
NF/F: $20   **G/VG: $8**

_____. Magic Kingdom of Landover Series:

_____. *Magic Kingdom For Sale -Sold!*
First Edition: New York: Ballantine Books/Del Rey, 1986.
NF/F: $65   **G/VG: $15**

_____. *The Black Unicorn.*
First Edition: New York: Ballantine Books/Del Rey, 1987.
NF/F: $45   **G/VG: $10**

_____. *Wizard at Large.*
First Edition: New York: Ballantine Books/Del Rey, 1988.
NF/F: $55   **G/VG: $10**

_____. *The Tangle Box.*
First Edition: New York: Ballantine Books/Del Rey, 1994.
NF/F: $45   **G/VG: $10**

_____. *Witches' Brew.*
First Edition: New York: Ballantine Books/Del Rey, 1995.
NF/F: $25   **G/VG: $8**

Brown, Fredric. *Angels and Spaceships.*
First Edition: New York: Dutton, 1954.
NF/F: $400   **G/VG: $125**

Brunner, John. *The Sheep Look Up.*
First Edition: New York: Harper & Row, 1972.
NF/F: $195   **G/VG: $70**
First U.K. Edition: London: J. M. Dent & Sons Ltd., 1974.
NF/F: $30   **G/VG: $10**

_____. *Stand on Zanzibar.*
First Edition: Garden City, NY:
Doubleday, 1968.
NF/F: $300   **G/VG: $100**
First U.K. Edition: London: Macdonald
& Co., 1969.
NF/F: $145   **G/VG: $65**

_____. *Quicksand.*
First Edition: Garden City, NY:
Doubleday, 1967.
NF/F: $45   **G/VG: $15**
First U.K. Edition: London: Sidgwick &
Jackson, 1969.
NF/F: $25   **G/VG: $10**

Brunngraber, Rudolf. *Radium.*
First Edition: New York: Random
House, 1937.
NF/F: $50   **G/VG: $20**

Burgess, Anthony. *A Clockwork
Orange.*
First Edition: London: Heinemann,
1962.
Points of Issue: First Issue is black
boards with silver lettering, the first
state dust jacket carries an ad for
Burgess' Devil of a State on rear panel.
NF/F: $5,500   **G/VG: $2,000**
First U.S. Edition: New York: W. W.
Norton & Company Inc., 1963.
NF/F: $325   **G/VG: $100**

Burgess, Gelett. *The White Cat.*
First Edition: Indianapolis: Bobbs,
Merrill, 1907.
NF/F: $65   **G/VG: $25**

Burroughs, Edgar Rice. *The Land
That Time Forgot.*
First Edition: Chicago: A. C. McClurg
& Co., 1924.
NF/F: $450   **G/VG: $250**

_____. The Tarzan Series:

_____. *Tarzan of the Apes,*
First Edition: Chicago: A. C. McClurg
& Co., 1914.
Points of Issue: First state has an acorn
stamped between the A. and C. on the
spine.
NF/F: $24,000   **G/VG: $4,000**

_____. *The Return of Tarzan.*
First Edition: Chicago: A. C. McClurg
& Co., 1915.
Points of Issue: First Printing has W.F.
Hall imprint on the copyright page.
NF/F: $850   **G/VG: $300**

_____. *The Beasts of Tarzan.*
First Edition: Chicago: A. C. McClurg
& Co., 1916.
NF/F: $1,200   **G/VG: $500**

_____. *The Son of Tarzan.*
First Edition: Chicago: A. C. McClurg
& Co., 1917.
NF/F: $500   **G/VG: $175**

_____. *Tarzan and the Jewels of
Opar.*
First Edition: Chicago: A. C. McClurg
& Co., 1918.
NF/F: $1,500   **G/VG: $650**

_____. *Jungle Tales of Tarzan.*
First Edition: Chicago: A. C. McClurg
& Co., 1919.
Points of Issue: First issue is bound in
orange, subsequent issues in green.
NF/F: $1,750   **G/VG: $525**

_____. *Tarzan the Untamed.*
First Edition: Chicago: A. C. McClurg
& Co., 1920.
NF/F: $1,650   **G/VG: $600**

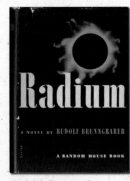

Rudolph Brunngraber.

Anthony Burgess.

Edgar Rice Burroughs.

Edgar Rice Burroughs.

Edgar Rice Burroughs.

_____. *Tarzan the Terrible.*
First Edition: Chicago: A. C. McClurg & Co., 1921.
NF/F: $1,800   **G/VG: $650**

_____. *Tarzan and the Golden Lion.*
First Edition: Chicago: A. C. McClurg & Co., 1923.
NF/F: $1,725   **G/VG: $800**

_____. *Tarzan and the Ant Men.*
First Edition: Chicago: A. C. McClurg & Co., 1924.
NF/F: $900   **G/VG: $350**

_____. *The Tarzan Twins.*
First Edition: Joliet, Il: P. F. Volland, 1927.
NF/F: $725   **G/VG: $250**

_____. *Tarzan, Lord of the Jungle.*
First Edition: Chicago: A. C. McClurg & Co., 1928.
NF/F: $2,250   **G/VG: $700**

_____. *Tarzan and the Lost Empire.*
First Edition: New York: Metropolitan, 1929.
NF/F: $1,000   **G/VG: $350**

_____. *Tarzan at the Earth's Core.*
First Edition: New York: Metropolitan, 1930.
NF/F: $550   **G/VG: $200**

_____. *Tarzan the Invincible.*
First Edition: Tarzana, CA: Burroughs, 1931.
NF/F: $900   **G/VG: $325**

_____. *Tarzan Triumphant.*
First Edition: Tarzana, CA: Burroughs, 1932.
NF/F: $1,500   **G/VG: $500**

_____. *Tarzan and the City of Gold.*
First Edition: Tarzana, CA: Burroughs, 1933.
NF/F: $600   **G/VG: $150**

_____. *Tarzan and the Lion Man.*
First Edition: Tarzana, CA: Burroughs, 1934.
NF/F: $950   **G/VG: $225**

_____. *Tarzan and the Leopard Men.*
First Edition: Tarzana, CA: Burroughs, 1935.
NF/F: $500   **G/VG: $150**

_____. *Tarzan's Quest.*
First Edition: Tarzana, CA: Burroughs, 1936.
NF/F: $450   **G/VG: $125**

_____. *Tarzan and the Forbidden City.*
First Edition: Tarzana, CA: Burroughs, 1938.
NF/F: $625   **G/VG: $275**

_____. *Tarzan the Magnificent.*
First Edition: Tarzana, CA: Burroughs, 1939.
NF/F: $700   **G/VG: $250**

_____. *Tarzan and the Foreign Legion.*
First Edition: Tarzana, CA: Burroughs, 1947.
NF/F: $300   **G/VG: $95**

_____. *Tarzan and the Madman.*
First Edition: New York: Canaveral Press, 1964.
NF/F: $325   **G/VG: $85**

_____. *Tarzan and the Castaways.*
First Edition: New York: Canaveral Press, 1965.
NF/F: $225   **G/VG: $65**

_____. The Pellucidar Series:

_____. *At the Earth's Core.*
First Edition: Chicago: A. C. McClurg & Co. 1922.
NF/F: $900   **G/VG: $350**

_____. *Pellucidar.*
First Edition: Chicago: A. C. McClurg & Co., 1923.
NF/F: $1,000   **G/VG: $300**

_____. *Tanar of Pellucidar.*
First Edition: New York: Metropolitan Books, 1930.
NF/F: $450   **G/VG: $150**

_____. *Back to the Stone Age.*
First Edition: Tarzana, CA: Burroughs, 1937.
NF/F: $650   **G/VG: $150**

_____. *Land of Terror.*
First Edition: Tarzana, CA: Burroughs, 1944.
NF/F: $475   **G/VG: $100**

_____. *Savage Pellucidar.*
First Edition: New York: Canaveral Press, 1963.
NF/F: $150   **G/VG: $45**

_____. The Venus Series:

_____. *Pirates of Venus.*
First Edition: Tarzana, CA: Burroughs, 1934.
NF/F: $450   **G/VG: $150**

_____. *Lost on Venus.*
First Edition: Tarzana, CA: Burroughs, 1935.
NF/F: $700   **G/VG: $250**

_____. *Carson of Venus.*
First Edition: Tarzana, CA: Burroughs, 1939.
NF/F: $500   **G/VG: $200**

_____. *Escape on Venus.*
First Edition: Tarzana, CA: Burroughs, 1946.
NF/F: $300   **G/VG: $85**

_____. *Tales of Three Planets.*
First Edition: New York: Canaveral Press, 1964.
NF/F: $225   **G/VG: $50**

_____. *The Mars Series:*

_____. *A Princess of Mars.*
First Edition: Chicago: A. C. McClurg & Co., 1917.
NF/F: $1,200   **G/VG: $400**

_____. *The Gods of Mars.*
First Edition: Chicago: A. C. McClurg & Co., 1918. First Printing has W.F. Hall imprint on the copyright page.
NF/F: $1,250   **G/VG: $500**

_____. *The Warlord of Mars.*
First Edition: Chicago: A. C. McClurg & Co., 1919.
NF/F: $600   **G/VG: $200**

_____. *Thuvia, Maid of Mars.*
First Edition: Chicago: A. C. McClurg & Co., 1920.
NF/F: $1,000   **G/VG: $350**

_____. *The Chessmen of Mars.*
First Edition: Chicago: A. C. McClurg & Co., 1922.
NF/F: $2,100   **G/VG: $450**

_____. *The Mastermind of Mars.*
First Edition: Chicago: A. C. McClurg & Co., 1928.
NF/F: $250   **G/VG: $95**

_____. *A Fighting Man of Mars.*
First Edition: New York: Metropolitan, 1931.
NF/F: $500   **G/VG: $150**

_____. *Swords of Mars.*
First Edition: Tarzana, CA: Burroughs, 1936.
NF/F: $1,800   **G/VG: $650**

Edgar Rice Burroughs.

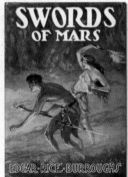
Edgar Rice Burroughs.

Edgar Rice Burroughs.

Hortense Calisher.

John W. Campbell Jr.

_____. *Synthetic Men of Mars.*
First Edition: Tarzana, CA: Burroughs, 1940.
NF/F: $725   **G/VG: $80**

_____. *Llana of Gathol.*
First Edition: Tarzana, CA: Burroughs, 1948.
NF/F: $400   **G/VG: $150**

_____. *John Carter of Mars.*
First Edition: New York: Canaveral Press, 1964.
NF/F: $225   **G/VG: $50**

Burroughs, William S. *Nova Express.*
First Edition: New York: Grove Press, Inc., 1964.
NF/F: $250   **G/VG: $65**

_____. *The Wild Boys.*
First Edition: New York: Grove Press, Inc., 1971.
NF/F: $200   **G/VG: $65**
First U.K. Edition: London: Calder & Boyars, 1972.
NF/F: $225   **G/VG: $85**

Butler, Samuel. *Erewhon or Over the Range.*
First Edition: London: Trubner & Co., 1872.
NF/F: $750   **G/VG: $200**

_____. *Erewhon Revisited.*
First Edition: London: Grant Richards, 1901.
NF/F: $250   **G/VG: $125**

Caidin, Martin. *Cyborg.*
First Edition: New York: Arbor House, 1972.
NF/F: $85   **G/VG: $30**

_____. *The God Machine.*
First Edition: New York: E.P. Dutton, 1968.
NF/F: $30   **G/VG: $10**

Calisher, Hortense. *Journal from Ellipsia.*
First Edition: Boston: Little, Brown, 1965.
NF/F: $45   **G/VG: $15**

Calvino, Italo. *Cosmicomics.*
First U.S. Edition: New York: Harcourt Brace & World, Inc., 1968.
NF/F: $350   **G/VG: $155**
First U.K. Edition: London: Jonathan Cape, 1969.
NF/F: $450   **G/VG: $200**

Cameron, John. *The Astrologer.*
First Edition: New York: Random House, 1972.
NF/F: $20   **G/VG: $8**

Campbell, John W. Jr. *The Black Star Passes.*
Limited Edition: Reading, Pennsylvania: Fantasy Press, 1953 (500 copies).
NF/F: $400   **G/VG: $185**
First Edition: Reading, Pennsylvania: Fantasy Press.
NF/F: $175   **G/VG: $60**

_____. *Islands of Space.*
Limited Edition: Reading, Pennsylvania: Fantasy Press, 1956 (500 copies, 50 signed).
NF/F: $1,100   **G/VG: Not Seen**
Limited Edition: Reading, Pennsylvania: Fantasy Press, 1956 (450 copies, unsigned).
NF/F: $700   **G/VG: $350**
First Edition: Reading, Pennsylvania: Fantasy Press, 1956.
NF/F: $300   **G/VG: $135**

_____. *Invaders From The Infinite.*
Limited Edition (signed): Reading, Pennsylvania: Fantasy Press, 1956 (2,888 copies, 112 signed).
NF/F: $1250   **G/VG: Not Seen**
Limited Edition (unsigned): Reading, Pennsylvania: Fantasy Press, 1956 (2,888 copies, unsigned).
NF/F: $600   **G/VG: $150**
First Edition: New York: Gnome Press, 1961.
NF/F: $85   **G/VG: $25**

_____. *The Mightiest Machine.*
First Edition: Providence, RI: Hadley
Publishing Company, 1947
NF/F: $300   **G/VG: $85**

_____. *Who goes There?*
First Edition: Chicago: Shasta
Publishers, 1948.
Points of Issue: Colophon Page with
unstated limitation marks the first
issue.
NF/F: $750   **G/VG: $350**

Campbell, Ramsey. *Hungry Moon.*
First Edition: New York: Macmillan,
1986.
NF/F: $35   **G/VG: $10**
First U.K. Edition: London, Century/
Hutchinson Ltd., 1987.
NF/F: $20   **G/VG: $8**

_____. *Demons by Daylight.*
First Edition: Sauk City, Wisconsin:
Arkham House, 1973.
NF/F: $65   **G/VG: $20**

Capon, Paul. *The Other Side of the
Sun.*
First Edition: London: Heinemann,
1950.
NF/F: $50   **G/VG: $15**

Capek, Karel. *The Absolute at
Large.* First U.S. Edition: New York:
Macmillan, 1927.
NF/F: $150   **G/VG: $60**

_____. *War with the Newts.*
First U.K. Edition: London: Allen &
Unwin, 1937.
NF/F: $525   **G/VG: $200**
First U.S. Edition: New York: G. P.
Putnam's Sons, 1937.
NF/F: $400   **G/VG: $175**

_____. *R.U.R.:* Rossom's Universal
Robots - A Fantastic Melodrama.
First U.S. Edition: Garden City, NY
Doubleday, Page & Co. 1923.
NF/F: $200   **G/VG: $65**

Card, Orson Scott. *Lost Boys.*
First Edition: New York: Harper
Collins, 1992.
NF/F: $25   **G/VG: $8**

Carr, Robert Spencer. *Beyond
Infinity.*
Limited Edition: Reading, PA: Fantasy
Press, 1951.
NF/F: $625   **G/VG: $185**
First Edition (Trade): Reading, PA:
Fantasy Press, 1951.
NF/F: $50   **G/VG: $20**

Carter, Angela. *The Magic Toyshop.*
First Edition: New York: Simon and
Schuster, 1967.
NF/F: $125   **G/VG: $35**

_____. *Nights at the Circus.*
First Edition: London: Chatto and
Windus, 1984.
NF/F: $85   **G/VG: $25**
First U.S. Edition: New York: Viking,
1985.
NF/F: $50   **G/VG: $20**

Ramsey Campbell.

Paul Capon.

Karel Capek.

Arthur C. Clarke.

Arthur C. Clarke.

Hal Clement.

Chambers, Robert W. *The King In Yellow.*
First Edition: Chicago: F. Tennyson Neely, 1895.
Points of Issue: First state is green cloth with no frontispiece.
NF/F: $1,650   G/VG: $750
Points of Issue: Later states with 1895 on Title page.
NF/F: $350   G/VG: $125

_____. *The Green Mouse.*
First Edition: New York: Appleton, 1910.
NF/F: $65   G/VG: $20

Chandler, A. Bertram. *The Rim of Space.*
First Edition: New York: Avalon Books, 1961.
NF/F: $65   G/VG: $35

Chester, George Randolph. *The Jingo.*
First Edition: Indianapolis, IN: Bobbs-Merrill Co., 1912.
NF/F: $50   G/VG: $20

Clarke, Arthur C. *Childhood's End.*
First Edition: New York: Ballantine, 1953.
NF/F: $1,200   G/VG: $800
First U.K. Edition: London: Sidgwick and Jackson, 1954.
NF/F: $800   G/VG: $250

_____. *Rendezvous With Rama.*
First Edition: London: Victor Gollancz, 1973.
NF/F: $350   G/VG: $100
First U.S. Edition: New York: Harcourt Brace Jovanovich, 1973.
NF/F: $55   G/VG: $25

_____. *2061: Odyssey Three.*
Limited Edition: Hastings-On-Hudson: Ultramarine Press, 1988 (26 lettered, 124 numbered copies).
NF/F: $300   G/VG: Not Seen
First Edition: New York: Del Rey/Ballantine, 1988.
NF/F: $20   G/VG: $10
First U.K. Edition: London: Grafton Books, 1988.
NF/F: $20   G/VG: $8

Clarke, Arthur C. and Gentry Lee. *Cradle.*
First Edition: New York: Warner Books, 1988.
NF/F: $15   G/VG: $10
First U.K. Edition: London: Victor Gollancz Ltd., 1988.
NF/F: $10   G/VG: $6

Clement, Hal. *Needle.*
First Edition: Garden City, NY: Doubleday & Co., 1950.
NF/F: $165   G/VG: $75

_____. *Mission of Gravity.*
First Edition: Garden City, NY: Doubleday & Co., 1952.
NF/F: $850   G/VG: $350
First U.K. Edition: London: Robert Hale Publishers, 1955.
NF/F: $1,200   G/VG: $600

Clifton, Mark. *Eight Keys to Eden.*
First Edition: Garden City, NY: Doubleday & Co., 1960.
NF/F: $40   G/VG: $20

Coblentz, Stanton A. *Hidden World.*
First Edition: New York: Avalon, 1957.
NF/F: $60   G/VG: $20

_____. *The Sunken World.*
First Edition: Los Angeles: Fantasy Publishing Co., 1948.
NF/F: $75   G/VG: $25

Cole, Everett B. *The Philosophical Corps.*
First Edition: Hicksville, New York:
Gnome Press, Inc., 1961.
NF/F: $45   **G/VG: $15**

Collier, John. *Tom's A-Cold.* A Tale.
First Edition: London: Macmillan, 1933.
NF/F: $500   **G/VG: $130**
First U.S. Edition as Full Circle: New
York: D. Appleton, 1933.
NF/F: $300   **G/VG: $125**

Copper, Basil. *The House of the Wolf.*
First Edition: Sauk City, Wisconsin:
Arkham House, 1983.
NF/F: $35   **G/VG: $10**

Corelli, Marie. *The Mighty Atom.*
First Edition: London: Hutchinson, 1896.
NF/F: $75   **G/VG: $30**
First U.S. Edition: Philadelphia:
Lippincott, 1896.
NF/F: $50   **G/VG: $20**

Crichton, Michael. *The Andromeda Strain.*
First Edition: New York: Alfred A.
Knopf, Inc, 1969.
NF/F: $300   **G/VG: $75**

_____. *Jurassic Park.*
First Edition: New York: Alfred A.
Knopf, Inc, 1990.
NF/F: $60   **G/VG: $15**

Cummings, Ray. *Brigands of the Moon.*
First Edition: Chicago. A.C. McClurg, 1931.
NF/F: $95   **G/VG: $30**

_____. *The Girl in The Golden Atom.*
New York: Harper & Brothers
Publishers, 1923.
Points of Issue: First state is dark
yellow stamped in black.
NF/F: $500   **G/VG: $150**
Points of Issue: Second state is blue
stamped in yellow.
NF/F: $100   **G/VG: $30**

Cummins, Harle Oren. *Welsh
Rarebit Tales.*
First Edition: Boston: Mutual Book Co., 1902.
NF/F: $95   **G/VG: $35**

DeCamp, L. Sprague. *The Rogue Queen.*
First Edition: New York: Doubleday
and Co., 1951.
NF/F: $55   **G/VG: $15**

De La Mare, Walter. *Henry Brocken.*
Limited Edition: London, Collins nd
[1924]. (250 copies).
NF/F: $425   **G/VG: $200**
First Edition: London, Collins nd [1924].
NF/F: $50   **G/VG: $25**
First U.S. Edition: New York: Alfred A.
Knopf, 1924.
NF/F: $45   **G/VG: $20**

del Rey, Lester. *Marooned on Mars.*
First Edition: Philadelphia: The John C.
Winston Company, 1952.
NF/F: $125   **G/VG: $40**

DeMille, James. *A Strange Manuscript
Found in a Copper Cylinder.*
First Edition: New York: Harper &
Brothers, 1888.
NF/F: $135   **G/VG: $40**

Delany, Samuel R. *Stars in my Pocket
Like Grains of Sand.*
First Edition: New York: Bantam, 1984.
NF/F: $35   **G/VG: $10**

Derleth, August, *Dwellers in
Darkness.*
First Edition: Sauk City, Wisconsin:
Arkham, 1976.
NF/F: $65   **G/VG: $30**

Derleth, August and H. P. Lovecraft.
The Watchers Out of Time and Others.
First Edition: Sauk City, Wisconsin:
Arkham, 1974.
NF/F: $95   **G/VG: $40**

Ray Cummings.

August Derleth.

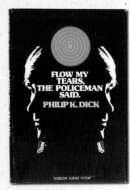

Philip K. Dick.

Philip K. Dick.

Arthur Conan Doyle.

Dick, Philip K. *Flow My Tears the Policeman Said.*
First Edition: New York: Doubleday, 1974.
Points of Issue: Code O50 on page 231.
NF/F: $650   G/VG: $150

_____. *The Divine Invasion.*
First Edition: NY: Timescape Books, 1981.
NF/F: $55   G/VG: $20

Disch, Thomas. *On Wings of Song.*
First Edition: London, Victor Gollancz Ltd, 1979.
NF/F: $45   G/VG: $20
First U.S. Edition: New York: St. Martin's, 1979.
NF/F: $25   G/VG: $10

Dixon, Thomas. *The Fall of a Nation - a Sequel to "The Birth of a Nation."*
First Edition: New York: D. Appleton & Co., 1916.
NF/F: $185   G/VG: $65

Donnelly, Ignatius. (as by Edmund Boisgilbert, M.D.). *Doctor Huguet. A Novel.*
First Edition: Chicago: Schulte, (1891).
NF/F: $100   G/VG: $75

Donnelly, Ignatius. *The Golden Bottle.*
First Edition: New York and St. Paul MN: D.D. Merrill Co., 1892.
NF/F: $185   G/VG: $85

Doyle, Arthur Conan. *The Maracot Deep and Other Stories.*
First Edition: London: John Murray, 1929.
NF/F: $1,800   G/VG: $650
First U.S. Edition: New York: Doubleday, Doran, 1929.
NF/F: $650   G/VG: $250

_____. Professor Challenger Series:

_____. *The Lost World.*
First Edition: London: Hodder & Stoughton, 1912, (two volumes).
NF/F: $900   G/VG: $400
First U.S. Edition: NY: Hodder & Stoughton and George H. Doran, 1912.
NF/F: $450   G/VG: $175

_____. *The Poison Belt.* Being an Account of Another Amazing Adventure of Professor Challenger.
First Edition: London: Hodder and Stoughton, 1913.
NF/F: $650   G/VG: $275
First U.S. Edition: New York: George H. Doran, 1913.
NF/F: $300   G/VG: $100

_____. *The Land of Mist.*
First Edition: London, Hutchinson, 1926.
NF/F: $850   G/VG: $300
First U.S. Edition: New York: George H. Doran, 1926.
NF/F: $700   G/VG: $250

Dunsany, Lord. *The Charwoman's Shadow.*
First Edition: London & New York: G.P. Putnam's Sons, 1926.
NF/F: $500   G/VG: $250

_____. *The King of Elfland's Daughter.*
Limited Edition: London & New York: G.P. Putnam's Sons, 1924 (250 copies).
NF/F: $1850   G/VG: Not Seen
First Edition: London & New York: G.P. Putnam's Sons, 1924.
NF/F: $180   G/VG: $85

_____. *Dreamer's Tales.*
First Edition: London: George Allen &
Sons, 1910.
NF/F: $350   **G/VG: $165**
First U.S. Edition: Boston: John W.
Luce, 1916.
NF/F: $250   **G/VG: $100**

Eddings, David. *The King of Murgos.*
First Edition: New York: A Del Rey
Book/Ballantine Books, 1988.
NF/F: $35   **G/VG: $15**

_____. *The Ruby Knight.*
First Edition: New York: A Del Rey
Book/Ballantine Books, 1989.
NF/F: $30   **G/VG: $15**

Eddison, E.R. The Zimiamvia Trilogy*:

_____. *Mistress of Mistresses.*
First Edition: London: Faber & Faber, 1935.
NF/F: $2,500   **G/VG: $1,150**
First U.S. Edition: New York: E.P.
Dutton & Co. Inc, 1935.
NF/F: $100   **G/VG: $40**

_____. *A Fish Dinner in Memison.*
First Edition: New York: E.P. Dutton
& Co. Inc, 1941. Limited to 998
numbered copies.
NF/F: $650   **G/VG: $175**

_____. *The Mezentian Gate.*
First Edition: London: Curwen Press,
1958.
NF/F: $450   **G/VG: $150**

_____. *The Worm Ouroboros.*
First Edition: London: Jonathan Cape,
1922.
Points of Issue: The first issue has a
windmill blinstamped on the back cover.
NF/F: $650   **G/VG: $200**
First U.S. Edition: New York: Albert &
Charles Boni, 1926.
NF/F: $200   **G/VG: $65**

_____. *Styrbiorn The Strong.*
First Edition: London: Jonathan Cape,
1926.
NF/F: $600   **G/VG: $200**
First U.S. Edition: New York: Albert &
Charles Boni, 1926.
NF/F: $400   **G/VG: $125**

Ellison, Harlan. *Deathbird Stories.*
First Edition: New York: Harper &
Row, 1975.
NF/F: $85   **G/VG: $30**

England, George Allen. *The Flying
Legion.*
First Edition: Chicago: A. C. McClurg,
1920.
NF/F: $45   **G/VG: $20**

_____. Darkness and Dawn Series:

_____. *The Vacant World.*
First Edition: New York: Avalon, 1967.
NF/F: $70   **G/VG: $25**

_____. *Beyond The Great
Oblivion.*
First Edition: New York: Avalon, 1967.
NF/F: $70   **G/VG: $25**

_____. *The Afterglow.*
First Edition: New York: Avalon, 1967.
NF/F: $40   **G/VG: $15**

_____. *Darkness and Dawn.*
(Omnibus of above three titles).
First Edition: Boston: Small, Maynard &
Company, 1914.
NF/F: $500   **G/VG: $225**

_____. *The People of the Abyss.*
First Edition: New York: Avalon, 1966.
NF/F: $35   **G/VG: $15**

E.R. Eddison.

E.R. Eddison.

Harlan Ellison.

_____. *Out of the Abyss.*
First Edition: New York: Avalon, 1967.
NF/F: $35   **G/VG: $15**

Ewers, Hans Heinz. *Alraune.*
First Edition: München (Munich),
Georg Müller Verlag, 1916.
NF/F: $2,500   **G/VG: $1,500**
First U.S. Edition: New York: John Day,
1929.
NF/F: $200   **G/VG: $75**

Farley, Ralph Milne. *The Radio Man.*
First Edition: Los Angeles: Fantasy
Publishing Co., 1948.
NF/F: $75   **G/VG: $25**

Farmer, Philip Jose. *Lord Tyger.*
First Edition: Garden City: Doubleday,
1970.
NF/F: $150   **G/VG: $85**

_____. Riverworld Series:

_____. *To Your Scattered Bodies Go.*
First Edition: New York: Putnam's,
1972.
NF/F: $1,500   **G/VG: $675**

_____. *The Fabulous Riverboat.*
First Edition: New York: Putnam's,
1971.
NF/F: $750   **G/VG: $275**

_____. *The Dark Design.*
First Edition: New York: Berkeley/
Putnam, 1977.
NF/F: $100   **G/VG: $35**

_____. *The Magic Labyrinth.*
Limited Edition: New York: Phantasia,
1980 (500 copies).
NF/F: $100   **G/VG: $65**
First Edition: New York: Berkeley/
Putnam, 1980.
NF/F: $75   **G/VG: $25**

_____. *Gods of Riverworld.*
Limited Edition: Huntington Woods,
MI: Phantasia, 1980 (650 copies).
NF/F: $95   **G/VG: $60**
First Edition: New York: Berkeley/
Putnam, 1980.
NF/F: $25   **G/VG: $10**

_____. *River of Eternity.*
First Edition: Huntington Woods, MI:
Phantasia, 1983.
NF/F: $125   **G/VG: $35**

_____. World of Tiers Series:

_____. *The Maker of Universes.*
Limited Edition: Huntington Woods,
MI: Phantasia, 1980 (200 copies).
NF/F: $150   **G/VG: $60**
First Edition: New York: Ace Books, 1965.
Points of Issue: Ace F-367
NF/F: $15   **G/VG: $6**
First Hardcover Edition: NY & London:
Garland Publishing, 1975.
NF/F: $55   **G/VG: $20**

_____. *The Gates of Creation.*
Limited Edition: Huntington Woods,
MI: Phantasia, 1981 (200 copies).
NF/F: $250   **G/VG: $85**
First Edition: New York: Ace Books,
1966.
Points of Issue: Ace F-412
NF/F: $20   **G/VG: $8**

_____. *A Private Cosmos.*
Limited Edition: Huntington Woods,
MI: Phantasia, 1981 (250 copies)
NF/F: $200   **G/VG: Not Seen**
First Edition: New York: Ace Books,
1968.
Points of Issue: Ace G-724
NF/F: $20   **G/VG: $8**

_____. *Behind the Walls of Terra.*
Limited Edition: Huntington Woods,
MI: Phantasia, 1981 (250 copies).
NF/F: $150   **G/VG: Not Seen**
First Edition: New York: Ace Books,
1968.
Points of Issue: Ace 47420-9
NF/F: $20   **G/VG: $8**

_____. *The Lavalite World.*
First Edition: New York: Ace Books,
1968. Points of Issue: Ace 05360.
NF/F: $20   **G/VG: $9**

_____. *Red Orc's Rage.*
First Edition: New York: Tom Doherty
Associates, 1991.
NF/F: $20   **G/VG: $8**

_____. *More Than Fire.*
First Edition: New York: TOR, 1993.
NF/F: $65   **G/VG: $15**

Farris, John. *The Fury.*
First Edition: Chicago: Playboy Press,
1976.
NF/F: $55   **G/VG: $20**

_____. *All Heads Turn as the
Hunt Goes By.*
First Edition: Chicago: Playboy Press,
1977.
NF/F: $30   **G/VG: $10**

Finney, Jack. *The Woodrow Wilson
Dime.*
First Edition: New York: Simon &
Schuster, 1968.
NF/F: $155   **G/VG: $75**

Fuller, Alvarado M. *A.D. 2000.*
First Edition: Chicago: Laird & Lee,
1890. Points of Issue: Title page is
dated 1890.
NF/F: $475   **G/VG: $150**

Futrelle, Jacques. *The Diamond
Master.*
First Edition: Indianapolis, IN: Bobbs
Merrill, 1909.
NF/F: $125   **G/VG: $55**

Ganpat (Gompertz, M. L. A.). *Mirror
Of Dreams.*
First Edition: Garden City, NY:
Doubleday, Doran & Company, 1928.
NF/F: $85   **G/VG: $35**

Gardner, John. *Grendel.*
First Edition: New York: Alfred A.
Knopf, 1971.
NF/F: $700   **G/VG: $275**

Gernsback, Hugo. *Ralph 124C 41+ A
Romance of the Year 2660.*
First Edition: Boston: The Stratford
Company, 1925.
NF/F: $950   **G/VG: $350**

Gibbons, Floyd. *The Red Napoleon.*
First Edition: New York: Jonathan Cape
and Harrison Smith, 1929.
NF/F: $400   **G/VG: $125**

Godfrey, Hollis. *The Man Who Ended
War.*
First Edition: Boston: Little, Brown &
Company, 1908.
NF/F: $165   **G/VG: $50**

John Farris.

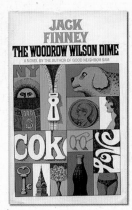

Jack Finney.

Hugo Gernsback.

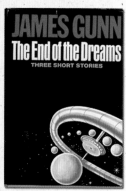

James Gunn.

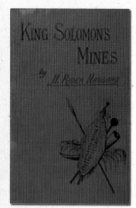

H. Rider Haggard.

H. Rider Haggard.

Gunn, James. *This Fortress World.*
First Edition: Hicksville, NY: Gnome
Press, 1955.
NF/F: $75   **G/VG: $25**

_____. *The End of the Dreams.*
First Edition: New York: Charles
Scribner's Sons, 1975.
NF/F: $35   **G/VG: $15**

Haggard, H. Rider. Allan Quatermain
Series:

_____. *King Solomon's Mines.*
First Edition: London: Cassell & Co., 1885.
Points of Issue: First Issue has 16 pages of
ads at the rear dated 5 G.885 and 5 B 885;
page 10 has the misprint Bamamgwato;
page 122 has "to let twins to live"; page 307
has "until the new wrod supplants the old."
NF/F: $8,000   **G/VG: $3,100**
Second Issue: London: Cassell & Co., 1887.
NF/F: $250   **G/VG: $55**

_____. *Allan Quatermain.*
First Edition: London: Longmans,
Green & Co, 1887.
Points of Issue: In the first state
"Qaurtermain" is misspelled on
page 78.
NF/F: $1,200   **G/VG: $400**
Limited Large Paper Edition of 112
numbered copies.
NF/F: $4,000   **G/VG: $1500**

_____. *Allan's Wife.*
First Edition: London: Spencer
Blackett, 1889.
NF/F: $500   **G/VG: $150**

_____. *Maiwa's Revenge.*
First Edition: London: Longmans,
Green & Co, 1888.
NF/F: $300   **G/VG: $100**
First U.S. Edition: New York: Harper &
Brothers, 1888.
NF/F: $400   **G/VG: $125**

_____. *Marie.*
First Edition: London: Cassell & Co,
1912.
NF/F: $150   **G/VG: $60**

_____. *Child of Storm.*
First Edition: London: Cassell & Co,
1913.
NF/F: $300   **G/VG: $125**

_____. *The Holy Flower.*
First Edition: London: Ward Locke,
1915.
NF/F: $150   **G/VG: $55**

_____. *The Ivory Child.*
First Edition: London: Hutchinson,
1916.
NF/F: $1,500   **G/VG: $500**

_____. *Finished.*
First Edition: London: Ward Locke,
1917.
NF/F: $150   **G/VG: $60**

_____. *The Ancient Allan.*
First Edition: London: Cassell & Co,
1920.
NF/F: $1,600   **G/VG: $750**

_____. *She and Allan.*
First Edition: London: Hutchinson,
1920.
NF/F: $1,800   **G/VG: $800**

_____. *Heu-Heu.*
First Edition: London: Hutchinson,
1924.
NF/F: $350   **G/VG: $100**

_____. *The Treasure of the Lake.*
First Edition: London: Hutchinson,
1926.
NF/F: $475   **G/VG: $135**

_____. *Allan and the Ice Gods.*
First Edition: London: Hutchinson,
1927.
NF/F: $1,200   **G/VG: $450**

_____. She Who Must Be Obeyed
Series:

_____. *She A History of*
Adventure.
First Edition: London: Longmans,
Green, and Co., 1887.
Points of Issue: The first issue has
the following errors; 'geneleman' for
'genelman' p. 59, line 22, 'had' for
'have' p. 126, line 26, 'it compared'
for 'if compared' p. 258, line 37 and
'godness me' p. 269, line 38.
NF/F: $2,600   **G/VG: $1,100**

_____. *Ayesha, The Return of She.*
First Edition: London: Ward Locke,
1905.
NF/F: $1,000   **G/VG: $350**

_____. *She and Allan.*
First Edition: London: Hutchinson,
1920.
NF/F: $1,800   **G/VG: $800**

_____. *Wisdom's Daughter.*
First Edition: London: Hutchinson,
1923.
NF/F: $800   **G/VG: $250**

Hamilton, Edmond. *The Haunted*
Stars.
First Edition: New York: Dodd, Mead &
Company, 1960.
NF/F: $85   **G/VG: $20**

_____. *The Star Kings.*
First Edition: New York: Frederick Fell,
1949.
NF/F: $185   **G/VG: $50**

Harper, Vincent. *The Mortgage on*
the Brain.
First Edition: New York: Harper &
Brothers Publishers, 1905.
NF/F: $95   **G/VG: $30**

Harrison, Harry. *The Stainless Steel*
Rat.
First Edition: New York: Bantam
Books, 1987.
NF/F: $25   **G/VG: $8**

Hastings, Milo. *The City of Endless*
Night.
First Edition: NY: Dodd, Mead, 1920.
NF/F: $450   **G/VG: $125**

Hatfield, Richard. *Geyserland:*
Empiricisms in Social Reform.
First Edition: Washington, D.C: Printed
for Richard Hatfield, 1907.
NF/F: $165   **G/VG: $45**

Heinlein, Robert A. *The Puppet*
Masters.
First Edition: Garden City, NY:
Doubleday, 1951.
NF/F: $400   **G/VG: $150**

_____. *The Green Hills of Earth.*
First Edition: Chicago: Shasta, 1951.
NF/F: $500   **G/VG: $175**

_____. *Job: A Comedy of Justice.*
Limited Edition: New York: Del Rey/
Ballantine, 1984 (26 lettered copies).
NF/F: $1,200   **G/VG: Not Seen**
First Edition: New York: Del Rey/
Ballantine, 1984.
NF/F: $40   **G/VG: $15**

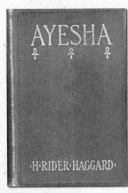
H. Rider Haggard.

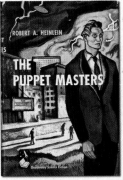
Edmond Hamilton.

Robert A. Heinlein.

Frank Herbert.

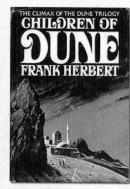

Frank Herbert.

L. Ron Hubbard.

Herbert, Frank. Dune Series*:

_____. *Dune.*
First Edition: Philadelphia & New York: Chilton, 1965.
NF/F: $1,400   **G/VG: $575**

_____. *Dune Messiah.*
First Edition: New York: G. P. Putnams' Sons, 1969.
NF/F: $900   **G/VG: $375**

_____. *Children of Dune.*
First Edition: New York: G. P. Putnams' Sons, 1976.
NF/F: $300   **G/VG: $75**

_____. *God Emperor of Dune.*
First Edition: New York: G. P. Putnams' Sons, 1981.
NF/F: $100   **G/VG: $25**

_____. *Heretics of Dune.*
First Edition: New York: G. P. Putnams' Sons, 1984.
NF/F: $150   **G/VG: $25**

_____. *Chapterhouse: Dune.*
First Edition: New York: G. P. Putnams' Sons, 1969.
NF/F: $65   **G/VG: $15**

_____. *Dragon in the Sea.*
First Edition: Garden City: Doubleday & Company Inc., 1956.
NF/F: $300   **G/VG: $135**

Howard, Robert E. *The Coming of Conan.*
First Edition: New York, Gnome Press, 1953.
NF/F: $400   **G/VG: $150**

_____. *Conan the Conqueror.*
First Edition: New York, Gnome Press, 1950.
NF/F: $400   **G/VG: $175**
First U.K. Edition: London: T. V. Boardman, 1954.
NF/F: $300   **G/VG: $125**

Howells, W.D. The Altrurian Trilogy:

_____. *A Traveler from Altruria.*
First Edition: New York: Harper & Brothers Publishers, 1894.
NF/F: $175   **G/VG: $65**

_____. *Letters of an Altrurian Traveler.*
First Edition: New York: Harper & Brothers Publishers, 1904.
NF/F: $85   **G/VG: $30**

_____. *Through the Eye of the Needle.*
First Edition: New York: Harper & Brothers Publishers, 1907.
NF/F: $65   **G/VG: $25**

Hoyle, Fred. *The Black Cloud.*
First Edition: London: Heinemann, 1957.
NF/F: $65   **G/VG: $20**
First U.S. Edition: New York: Harper & Brothers, 1957.
NF/F: $35   **G/VG: $10**

Hoyne, Thomas Temple. *Intrigue on the Upper Level.*
First Edition: Chicago: Reilly and Lee, 1934.
NF/F: $125   **G/VG: $40**

Hubbard, L. Ron. *Battlefield Earth.*
First Edition: New York: St. Martin's Press, 1982.
NF/F: $200   **G/VG: $65**

_____. *Typewriter in the Sky.*
First Edition: New York: Gnome Press, 1951.
NF/F: $300   **G/VG: $95**

Hudson, W. H. *A Crystal Age.*
First Edition: London: T. Fisher Unwin, 1887.
Points of Issue: Author's name missing from the title page in the first issue.
NF/F: $650   **G/VG: $200**
First U.S. Edition: New York: E. P. Dutton and Company, 1906.
NF/F: $50   **G/VG: $20**

Huxley, Aldous. *Brave New World.*
Limited Edition: London; Chatto & Windus; 1932 (324 copies).
NF/F: $8,500   **G/VG: $3,900**
First Edition: London; Chatto & Windus, 1932.
Points of Issue: First issue is blue boards with gilt title on the spine and a blue topstain.
NF/F: $4,600   **G/VG: $1,400**
First U.S. Edition: Garden City, NY: Doubleday, 1932.
NF/F: $95   **G/VG: $35**

James, M. R. *Ghost Stories of an Antiquary.*
First Edition: London: Edward Arnold, 1904.
NF/F: $1,850   **G/VG: $625**

Johnson, Owen. *The Coming of the Amazons.*
First Edition: New York: Longmans, Green, & Co., 1931.
NF/F: $125   **G/VG: $45**

Jones, Raymond. *This Island Earth.*
First Edition: Chicago: Shasta, 1952.
NF/F: $650   **G/VG: $200**
First U.K. Edition: London, T.V. Boardman & Co. Ltd., 1955.
NF/F: $145   **G/VG: $50**

Jordan, Robert. Wheel of Time Series:

_____. *The Eye of the World.*
First Edition: New York: Tor, 1990.
NF/F: $750   **G/VG: $300**

_____. *The Great Hunt.*
First Edition: New York: Tor, 1990.
NF/F: $650   **G/VG: $300**

_____. *The Dragon Reborn.*
First Edition: New York: Tor, 1991.
NF/F: $150   **G/VG: $55**

_____. *The Shadow Rising.*
First Edition: New York: Tor, 1992.
NF/F: $120   **G/VG: $55**

_____. *The Fires of Heaven.*
First Edition: New York: Tor, 1993.
NF/F: $65   **G/VG: $30**

_____. *Lord of Chaos.*
First Edition: New York: Tor, 1994.
NF/F: $45   **G/VG: $20**

_____. *A Crown of Swords.*
First Edition: New York: Tor, 1996.
NF/F: $55   **G/VG: $20**

_____. *The Path of Daggers.*
First Edition: New York: Tor, 1998.
NF/F: $40   **G/VG: $15**

_____. *Winter's Heart.*
First Edition: New York: Tor, 2000.
NF/F: $25   **G/VG: $10**

_____. *Knife of Dreams.*
First Edition: New York: Tor, 2003.
NF/F: $20   **G/VG: $8**

_____. *Knife of Dreams.*
First Edition: New York: Tor, 2005.
NF/F: $20   **G/VG: $8**

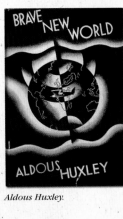

Aldous Huxley.

Owen Johnson.

Robert Jordan.

Stephen King.

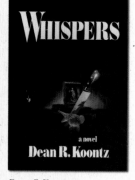

Otis Adelbert Kline.

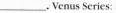

WHISPERS

a novel

Dean R. Koontz

Dean R. Koontz.

Kersh, Gerald. *Men Without Bones.*
First Edition: London, William
Heinemann, 1955.
NF/F: $185   **G/VG: $70**

Keyes, Daniel. *Flowers for Algernon.*
First Edition: New York; Harcourt,
Brace & World, 1966.
NF/F: $650   **G/VG: $200**

King, Stephen. *Carrie.*
First Edition: New York: Doubleday &
Co., 1974. Points of Issue: A Code "P6"
follows the text block.
NF/F: $1,800   **G/VG: $800**

_____. *Pet Sematary.*
First Edition: New York: Doubleday &
Co., 1983.
NF/F: $95   **G/VG: $25**

_____. *Insomnia.*
First Edition: New York: Viking
Publishers, 1994.
NF/F: $10   **G/VG: $5**

Kline, Otis Adelbert. *Maza of the Moon.*
First Edition: Chicago: A.C. McClurg,
1930.
NF/F: $250   **G/VG: $100**

_____. Venus Series:

_____. *The Planet of Peril.*
First Edition: Chicago: A. C. McClurg
& Co., 1929.
NF/F: $650   **G/VG: $260**

_____. *The Prince of Peril.*
First Edition: Chicago: A. C. McClurg
& Co., 1930.
NF/F: $350   **G/VG: $125**

_____. *The Port of Peril.*
First Edition: Providence, RI: The
Grandon Company, 1949.
NF/F: $200   **G/VG: $85**

Koontz, Dean R. *Strangers.*
First Edition: New York: G.P. Putnam's
Sons, 1986.
NF/F: $65   **G/VG: $15**

_____. *Whispers.*
First Edition: New York: G.P. Putmam's
Sons, 1980.
NF/F: $600   **G/VG: $250**

_____. *Watchers.*
First Edition: New York: G.P. Putnam's
Sons, 1987.
NF/F: $65   **G/VG: $30**

_____. *Mr. Murder.*
First Edition: New York: G.P. Putnam's
Sons, 1993.
NF/F: $25   **G/VG: $8**

Kornbluth, C.M. *The Mindworm.*
First Edition: London: Michael Joseph,
1955.
NF/F: $75   **G/VG: $25**

Kuttner, Henry. *Ahead of Time.*
First Edition: New York, Ballantine
Books, 1953.
NF/F: $155   **G/VG: $65**
First U.K. Edition: London: Weidenfeld
& Nicolson, 1954.
NF/F: $30   **G/VG: $10**

Large, E.C. *Sugar in the Air.*
First Edition: London: Jonathon Cape,
1937.
NF/F: $300   **G/VG: $95**
First U.S. Edition: New York: Charles
Scribner's Sons, 1937.
NF/F: $65   **G/VG: $20**

LeGuin, Ursula. *The Lathe of Heaven.*
First Edition: New York: Scribner's, 1971.
NF/F: $350   **G/VG: $155**
First U.K. Edition: London: Victor
Gollancz, 1972.
NF/F: $75   **G/VG: $20**

_____. Earthsea Series:

_____. *A Wizard of Earthsea.*
First Edition: Berkeley: Parnassus Press,
1968. Points of Issue: Embossed cover
with a smudge printed on the title page.
First State DJ had two prices, an "$395"
in the upper right hand corner of the
front flap and "Library Edition $390."
NF/F: $650   G/VG: $400

_____. *The Tombs of Atuan.*
First Edition: New York: Atheneum, 1971.
NF/F: $200   G/VG: $85

_____. *The Farthest Shore.*
First Edition: West Hanover, MA:
Atheneum, 1972.
NF/F: $60   G/VG: $20

_____. *Tehanu: The Last Book of
Earthsea.*
First Edition: New York: Atheneum,
1990.
NF/F: $35   G/VG: $15

_____. *Tales from Earthsea.*
First Edition: New York: Harcourt
Brace, 2001.
NF/F: $20   G/VG: $8

_____. *The Other Wind.*
First Edition: New York: Harcourt
Brace, 2001.
NF/F: $20   G/VG: $8

Leiber, Fritz. *The Green Millenium.*
First Edition: New York, Abelard Press,
1953.
NF/F: $125   G/VG: $45

Leinster, Murray. *The Last Space
Ship.*
First Edition: New York: Frederick Fell,
Inc., 1949.
NF/F: $125   G/VG: $45

Lem, Stanislaw. *Memoirs Found in a
Bathtub.*
First U.K. Edition: London: Andre
Deutsch, 1992.
NF/F: $55   G/VG: $15
First U.S. Edition: New York: Seabury
Press, 1973.
NF/F: $45   G/VG: $10

Lewis, C. S. The Space Trilogy:

_____. *Out of the Silent Planet.*
First Edition: London: John Lane The
Bodley Head, 1938.
NF/F: $950   G/VG: $400
First U.S. Edition: The Macmillan
Company, 1943.
NF/F: $700   G/VG: $200

_____. *Perelandra.*
First Edition: London: John Lane The
Bodley Head, 1943.
NF/F: $650   G/VG: $220
First U.S. Edition: The Macmillan
Company, 1944.
NF/F: $325   G/VG: $100

_____. *The Hideous Strength.*
First Edition: London: John Lane The
Bodley Head, 1945.
NF/F: $850   G/VG: $200
First U.S. Edition: The Macmillan
Company, 1946.
NF/F: $175   G/VG: $50

Lewis, Sinclair. *It Can't Happen Here.*
First Edition: Garden City, NY:
Doubleday, Doran & Co., 1935.
NF/F: $165   G/VG: $50

Lightner, A.M. *Star Dog.*
First Edition: New York: McGraw Hill,
1973.
NF/F: $75   G/VG: $35

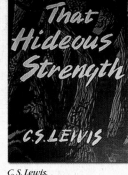

C. S. Lewis.

C. S. Lewis.

A. M. Lightner.

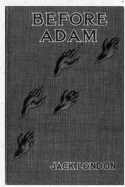

Jack London.

Jack London.

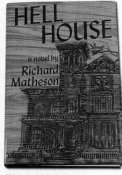

Richard Matheson.

London, Jack. *Before Adam.*
First Edition: New York: Macmillan, 1907.
NF/F: $300   **G/VG: $100**

_____. *The Iron Heel.*
First Edition: New York: The
Macmillan Company, 1908.
NF/F: $375   **G/VG: $95**

Lovecraft, H.P. *The Dunwich Horror
And Others.*
First Edition: Sauk City, WI: Arkham
House, 1963.
NF/F: $185   **G/VG: $65**

_____. *At the Mountains of
Madness.*
First Edition: Sauk City, WI; Arkham
House, 1964.
NF/F: $250   **G/VG: $75**

Machen, Arthur. *Three Imposters, or
The Transmutations.*
First Edition: London: John Lane, 1895.
NF/F: $550   **G/VG: $200**
First U.S. Edition: Boston: Roberts
Brothers, 1895.
NF/F: $450   **G/VG: $200**
Reprint First Thus: NY: Alfred A.
Knopf, 1923.
NF/F: $75   **G/VG: $25**

_____. *The Shining Pyramid.*
Limited Edition: Chicago: Covici-
McGee, 1923 (875 copies).
NF/F: $350   **G/VG: $175**
First Edition: Chicago: Covici-McGee,
1923.
NF/F: $175   **G/VG: $75**
Limited Edition U.K. (differs from
original): London: Martin Secker, 1925
(250 copies).
NF/F: $600   **G/VG: $250**
First Edition U.K. (differs from
original): London: Martin Secker, 1925.
NF/F: $100   **G/VG: $50**

First U.S. Edition (differs from original,
reprints U.K. first): New York: Alfred
A. Knopf, 1925.
NF/F: $75   **G/VG: $25**

Matheson, Richard. *Hell House.*
First Edition: New York: Viking, 1971.
NF/F: $325   **G/VG: $145**

McCaffrey, Anne. *Moreta:
Dragonlady of Pern.*
First Edition: New York: Ballantine
Books/Del Rey, 1983.
NF/F: $25   **G/VG: $8**

McKenna, Richard. *Casey Agonistes
and Other Science Fiction and
Fantasy Stories.*
First Edition: New York: Harper and
Row, 1973.
NF/F: $50   **G/VG: $20**

Merritt, A. *The Face in the Abyss.*
First Edition: New York: Horace
Liveright, 1931.
NF/F: $450   **G/VG: $95**

_____. *The Ship of Ishtar.*
First Edition: New York: G.P. Putnam's
Sons, 1926.
NF/F: $400   **G/VG: $95**
Reprint Edition (illustrated by
Virgil Finlay): Los Angeles: Borden
Publishing Company, 1949.
NF/F: $150   **G/VG: $45**

Miller, Walter. *A Canticle For
Leibowitz.*
First Edition: Philadelphia: Lippincott,
1960.
NF/F: $2,500   **G/VG: $650**

Moorcock, Michael. *Stormbringer.*
First Edition: London: Herbert Jenkins,
1965.
NF/F: $350   **G/VG: $150**

Moore, C.L. *Judgment Night.*
First Edition: New York: Gnome Press,
1952.
NF/F: $500   **G/VG: $145**

Mundy, Talbot. *Jimgrim.*
First Edition: New York & London: The
Century Co., 1931.
NF/F: $225   **G/VG: $85**

Niven, Larry. *Ringworld.*
First Edition: New York: Holt, Rinehart
and Winston, 1977.
NF/F: $150   **G/VG: $55**

Norton, Andre. *Star Man's Son: 2250
A.D.*
First Edition: New York: Harcourt
Brace & Company, 1952.
NF/F: $750   **G/VG: $300**

_____. *Mirror of Destiny.*
First Edition: New York: Morrow/Avon,
1995.
NF/F: $25   **G/VG: $10**

Orwell, George. *1984.*
First Edition: London: Secker &
Warburg, 1949. Points of Issue: First
Issue is green cloth with red lettering.
There are two dust jackets, green and
red, no known priority both priced
10s. net.
NF/F: $2,000   **G/VG: $1,000**
First U.S. Edition: New York: Harcourt
Brace, 1949. Points of Issue: First Issue
is gray boards red and black lettering.
The dust jacket is priced "$3.00" with
no book club slug.
NF/F: $1,000   **G/VG: $350**

Paine, Albert Bigelow. *The Mystery
of Evelin Delorme.*
First Edition: Boston: Arena Publishing
Co., 1894.
NF/F: $250   **G/VG: $65**

Pallen, Conde B. *Crucible Island:
a Romance, an Adventure and an
Experiment.*
First Edition: New York: The
Manhattanville Press, 1919.
NF/F: $75   **G/VG: $25**

Parry, David M. *The Scarlet Empire.*
First Edition: Indianapolis, Bobbs-
Merrill, 1906.
NF/F: $100   **G/VG: $40**

Paxson, Diana L. Avalon Series:

_____. *Ravens of Avalon.*
First Edition: New York: Viking, 2007.
NF/F: $25   **G/VG: $7**
(See: Bradley, Marion Zimmer)

Percy, Walker. *Love in the Ruins.*
First Edition: New York: Farrar Straus
Giroux, 1971.
NF/F: $185   **G/VG: $65**

Powys, T.F. *Mr. Weston's Good Wine.*
Limited Edition: London Chatto &
Windus, 1927 (660 copies).
NF/F: $400   **G/VG: $100**
First Edition: London Chatto &
Windus, 1927.
NF/F: $175   **G/VG: $55**
First U.S. Edition: New York: The
Viking Press, 1928.
NF/F: $85   **G/VG: $30**

_____. *Unclay.*
First Edition: London Chatto &
Windus, 1931.
NF/F: $200   **G/VG: $75**
First U.S. Edition: New York: The
Viking Press, 1932.
NF/F: $125   **G/VG: $45**

C. L. Moore.

Albert Bigelow Paine.

Walker Percy.

Akkad Pseudoman.

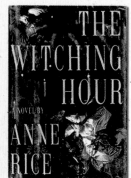

Anne Rice.

John Saul.

Pseudoman, Akkad. *Zero to Eighty.*
First Edition: Princeton, New Jersey:
Scientific Publishing Company, 1937.
NF/F: $125   **G/VG: $40**

Read, Herbert. *The Green Child.*
First Edition: London: William
Heinemann Ltd., 1935.
NF/F: $350   **G/VG: $90**

Reeve, Arthur B. *The Poisoned Pen.*
First Edition: New York: Harper &
Bros, 1911.
NF/F: $70   **G/VG: $30**

Reynolds, Mack. *The Case of the
Little Green Men.*
First Edition: New York: Phoenix
Press, 1951.
NF/F: $135   **G/VG: $55**

Rice, Anne. *Interview with a
Vampire.*
First Edition: New York: Alfred A.
Knopf, 1976.
NF/F: $650   **G/VG: $150**

_____. *The Vampire Armand.*
Limited Edition: New York: Alfred A.
Knopf, 1998 (250 copies).
NF/F: $675   **G/VG: Not Seen**
First Edition: New York: Alfred A.
Knopf, 1998.
NF/F: $25   **G/VG: $10**

_____. The Mayfair Witches
Series:

_____. *The Witching Hour.*
First Edition: New York: Alfred A.
Knopf, 1990.
NF/F: $65   **G/VG: $15**

_____. *Lasher.*
First Edition: New York: Alfred A.
Knopf, 1993.
NF/F: $20   **G/VG: $10**

_____. *Taltos.*
Limited Edition: New Orleans: B. E.
Trice, 1994 (500 copies).
NF/F: $475   **G/VG: None Seen**
First Trade Edition: New York: Alfred
A. Knopf, 1994.
NF/F: $15   **G/VG: $7**

Roberts, Keith. *The Chalk Giants.*
First Edition: London: Hutchinson,
London, 1974.
NF/F: $150   **G/VG: $55**
First U.S. Edition: New York: G.P.
Putnam's Sons, 1975.
NF/F: $85   **G/VG: $25**

Robinson, C. H. *Longhead: the Story
of the First Fire.*
First Edition: Boston: L.C. Page, 1913.
NF/F: $100   **G/VG: $45**

Rohmer, Sax. *Grey Face.*
First Edition: Garden City: Doubleday,
Page & Company, 1924.
NF/F: $650   **G/VG: $250**
First U.K. Edition: London: Cassell, 1924.
NF/F: $450   **G/VG: $100**

Rousseau, Victor. *The Messiah of the
Cylinder.*
First Edition: Chicago: A.C. McClurg &
Co., 1917. Points of Issue: Illustrated by
Joseph Clement Coll.
NF/F: $275   **G/VG: $100**

Saul, John. *Creature.*
First Edition: New York: Bantam Books,
1989.
NF/F: $25   **G/VG: $7**

_____. *Black Lightning.*
First Edition: New York: Fawcett
Columbine, 1995.
NF/F: $20   **G/VG: $5**

Serviss, Garrett P. *The Columbus of Space.*
First Edition: New York: D. Appleton & Co., 1911.
NF/F: $400　　　　　**G/VG: $150**

_____. *The Moon Metal.*
First Edition: New York and London: Harper & Brothers, 1900.
NF/F: $300　　　　　**G/VG: $95**

Shiel, M.P. *Purple Cloud.*
First Edition: London: Chatto & Windus, 1901.
NF/F: $1,750　　　　　**G/VG: $950**
First U.S. Edition: New York: Vanguard, 1930.
NF/F: $95　　　　　**G/VG: $35**

Silverberg, Robert. *The Book of Skulls.*
First Edition: New York: Charles Scribner's Sons, 1972.
NF/F: $40　　　　　**G/VG: $15**

_____. *Majipoor Series:*

_____. *Lord Valentine's Castle.*
First Edition: New York.: Harper and Row, 1980.
NF/F: $165　　　　　**G/VG: $60**

_____. *Majipoor Chronicles.*
First Edition: New York: Arbor House, 1982.
NF/F: $45　　　　　**G/VG: $15**

_____. *Valentine Pontifex.*
First Edition: New York: Arbor House, 1983.
NF/F: $45　　　　　**G/VG: $20**

_____. *The Mountains of Majipoor.*
First Edition: New York: Spectra, 1995.
NF/F: $20　　　　　**G/VG: $8**

_____. *Sorcerers of Majipoor.*
First Edition: New York: HarperPrism, 1997.
NF/F: $25　　　　　**G/VG: $10**

_____. *Lord Prestimion.*
First Edition: New York: Harper Collins, 1999.
NF/F: $25　　　　　**G/VG: $10**

_____. *The King of Dreams.*
First Edition: New York: Eos, 2001.
NF/F: $25　　　　　**G/VG: $10**

Simak, Clifford D. *Cosmic Engineers.*
First Edition: New York: Gnome Press, 1950.
NF/F: $165　　　　　**G/VG: $75**

Siodmak, Curt. *Donovan's Brain.*
First Edition: New York: Alfred A. Knopf, 1943.
NF/F: $700　　　　　**G/VG: $200**

Smith, Clark Ashton. *Genius Loci and Other Tales.*
First Edition: Sauk City, Wisconsin: Arkham, 1948.
NF/F: $675　　　　　**G/VG: $200**

Smith, E.E. *Spacehounds of IPC.*
Limited Edition: Reading, PA: Fantasy Press, 1947 (300 copies).
NF/F: $600　　　　　**G/VG: $200**
First Edition Trade: Reading, PA: Fantasy Press, 1947.
NF/F: $85　　　　　**G/VG: $20**

_____. *Skylark of Valeron.*
First Edition: Reading, PA: Fantasy Press, 1949.
NF/F: $250　　　　　**G/VG: $95**

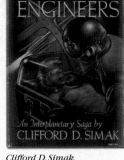

Garrett P. Serviss.

Clifford D. Simak.

E.E. Smith.

_____. The Lensmen Series:

_____. *Triplanetary.*
Limited Edition: Reading, PA: Fantasy Press, 1948 (500 copies).
NF/F: $450   **G/VG: $250**
First Edition Trade: Reading, PA: Fantasy Press, 1948.
NF/F: $225   **G/VG: $100**

_____. *First Lensman.*
Limited Edition: Reading, PA: Fantasy Press, 1951 (500 copies).
NF/F: $450   **G/VG: $250**
First Edition Trade: Reading, PA: Fantasy Press, 1950.
NF/F: $200   **G/VG: $85**

_____. *Galactic Patrol.*
Limited Edition: Reading, PA.: Fantasy Press, 1950 (500 copies).
NF/F: $450   **G/VG: $250**
First Edition Trade: Reading, PA: Fantasy Press, 1951.
NF/F: $250   **G/VG: $125**

_____. *Grey Lensman.*
Limited Edition: Reading, PA: Fantasy Press, 1951 (500 copies).
NF/F: $450   **G/VG: $275**
First Edition Trade: Reading, PA: Fantasy Press, 1951.
NF/F: $175   **G/VG: $75**
(Note: The Gnome Press edition was printed with the Fantasy Press plates and states "First Edition," it is not.)

_____. *Second Stage Lensmen.*
Limited Edition: Reading, PA: Fantasy Press, 1953 (500 copies).
NF/F: $500   **G/VG: $250**
First Edition Trade: Reading, PA: Fantasy Press, 1953.
NF/F: $150   **G/VG: $65**

_____. *Children of the Lens.*
Limited Edition: Reading, PA: Fantasy Press, 1954 (500 copies).
NF/F: $500   **G/VG: $225**
First Edition Trade: Reading, PA: Fantasy Press, 1954.
NF/F: $200   **G/VG: $85**

_____. *The History of Civilization.*
(Set of all Lensman Books). Limited Edition: Reading, PA.: Fantasy Press, 1955 (75 copies).
NF/F: $11,000   **G/VG: Not Seen**

Snell, Edmund. *Kontrol.*
First Edition: Philadelphia: J.B. Lippincott, 1928.
NF/F: $50   **G/VG: $20**

Spinrad, Norman. *Bug Jack Barron.*
First Edition: New York: Walker and Company, 1969.
NF/F: $85   **G/VG: $25**

Stapledon, Olaf. *Star Maker.*
First Edition: London: Methuen, 1932.
NF/F: $1,050   **G/VG: $450**

_____. *Odd John.*
First Edition: London: Methuen, 1937.
NF/F: $1,500   **G/VG: $600**

Stark, Harriett. *The Bacillus of Beauty.*
First Edition: New York: Frederick A. Stokes & Co., 1900.
NF/F: $225   **G/VG: $85**

Stewart, George R. *The Earth Abides.*
First Edition: New York: Random House, 1949.
NF/F: $650   **G/VG: $225**

Stockton, Frank R. *Great Stone of Sardis.*
First Edition: New York: Harper & Brothers, 1899.
NF/F: $125   **G/VG: $35**

Sturgeon, Theodore. *More Than Human.*
First Edition: New York: Farrar, Straus and Young, 1953.
NF/F: $375   **G/VG: $145**
First U.K. Edition: London: Victor Gollancz, 1954.
NF/F: $85   **G/VG: $25**

Taine, John. *The Crystal Horde.*
First Edition: Reading, PA: Fantasy Press, 1952.
NF/F: $125   **G/VG: $35**

_____. *Forbidden Garden.*
Limited Edition: Reading, PA: Fantasy Press, 1947 (500 copies).
NF/F: $650   **G/VG: $275**
First Edition: Reading, PA: Fantasy Press, 1947.
NF/F: $100   **G/VG: $45**

Thomas, Chauncey. *The Crystal Button.*
First Edition: Boston: Houghton Mifflin, 1891.
NF/F: $95   **G/VG: $35**

Thompson, Vance. *Green Ray.*
First Edition: Indianapolis, IN: Bobbs-Merrill Co., 1924.
NF/F: $65   **G/VG: $20**

Tolkien, J. R. R. *The Fellowship of the Ring.*
First Edition: London: Allen & Unwin, 1954.
NF/F: $7,500   **G/VG: $4,000**
First U.S. Edition: Boston: Houghton Mifflin Company, 1954.
NF/F: $2,000   **G/VG: $650**

_____. *The Two Towers.*
First Edition: London: Allen & Unwin, 1954.
NF/F: $6,500   **G/VG: $2,900**
First U.S. Edition: Boston: Houghton Mifflin Company, 1954.
NF/F: $1,800   **G/VG: $550**

_____. *The Return of the King.*
First Edition: London: Allen & Unwin, 1954.
NF/F: $6,500   **G/VG: $3,000**
First U.S. Edition: Boston: Houghton Mifflin Company, 1954.
NF/F: $2,000   **G/VG: $750**

_____. *The Return of the Shadow.*
First Edition: London: Allen & Unwin, 1988.
NF/F: $150   **G/VG: $85**
First U.S. Edition: Boston: Houghton Mifflin Company, 1988.
NF/F: $50   **G/VG: $35**

Train, Arthur, and Robert Williams Wood. *The Man Who Rocked the Earth.*
First Edition: New York: Doubleday, Page & Co., 1915. Points of Issue: "O" italicized on spine.
NF/F: $185   **G/VG: $60**

Van Vogt, A.E. *The Book of Ptath.*
First Edition: Reading, PA: Fantasy Press, 1947.
NF/F: $250   **G/VG: $70**

Waterloo, Stanley. *Armageddon.*
First Edition: Chicago: Rand, McNally, 1898.
NF/F: $150   **G/VG: $55**

_____. *The Story of Ab. A Tale of The Time of the Cave Man.*
First Edition: Chicago: Way & William, 1897.
NF/F: $250   **G/VG: $120**

Weinbaum, Stanley G. *The Black Flame.*
Limited Edition: Reading, PA: Fantasy Press, 1948 (500 copies).
NF/F: $150   **G/VG: $50**
First Edition: Reading, PA: Fantasy Press, 1948.
NF/F: $125   **G/VG: $45**

A.E. Van Vogt.

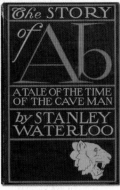
Stanley Waterloo.

Stanley G. Weinbaum.

Jack Williamson.

Gene Wolfe.

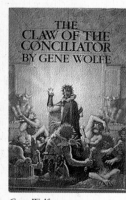

Gene Wolfe.

Wells, H.G. *The Island of Doctor Moreau.*
First Edition: London, William
Heinemann, 1896.
Points of Issue: The first issue has 32
pages of ads at the end.
NF/F: $1,800   **G/VG: $600**
First U.S. Edition: New York: Stone &
Kimball, 1896.
NF/F: $375   **G/VG: $165**

_____. *The Invisible Man.*
First Edition: London: C. Arthur Pearson,
1897. Points of Issue: Page 1 labeled 2.
NF/F: $4,800   **G/VG: $1,500**
First U.S. Edition: New York: Edward
Arnold, 1897.
NF/F: $700   **G/VG: $275**

_____. *The War of the Worlds.*
First Edition: London, William
Heinemann, 1898. Points of Issue: 16
pp of advertisements at end.
NF/F: $3,600   **G/VG: $1,500**
First U.S. Edition: New York; Harper &
Brothers, 1898.
NF/F: $750   **G/VG: $300**

_____. *The First Men in the Moon.*
First Edition: Indianapolis: Bowen-
Merrill Company, 1901.
NF/F: $450   **G/VG: $150**
First U.K. Edition: London: George
Newnes, 1901. Points of Issue: Original
issue is dark blue cloth stamped in gilt.
NF/F: $650   **G/VG: $200**
(Note: Strand Magazine 1900-01 (four
volumes), first appearances of First Men
in the Moon and A.C. Doyle's *The Hound
of the Baskervilles*, in the Strand Bindings
are worth about $2,500 in fine condition,
$1,000 in Very Good condition.)

White, Stewart Edward. *The Sign at Six.*
First Edition: Indianapolis: The Bobbs-
Merrill Company, 1912.
NF/F: $85   **G/VG: $30**

Wicks, Mark. *To Mars Via The Moon.*
First Edition: London: Seeley & Co., 1911.
NF/F: $435   **G/VG: $150**
First U.S. Edition: Philadelphia: J.B.
Lippincott Company, 1911.
NF/F: $365   **G/VG: $100**

Williams, Charles. *Descent into Hell.*
First Edition: London: Faber and Faber, 1937.
NF/F: $300   **G/VG: $125**
First U.S. Edition: New York: Pelligrini
& Cudahy, 1949.
NF/F: $70   **G/VG: $25**

Williamson, Jack. *The Legion of Time.*
First Edition: Reading, PA: Fantasy Press, 1952.
NF/F: $65   **G/VG: $25**

_____. *Darker Than You Think.*
Limited Edition: Reading, PA: Fantasy
Press, 1948 (350 copies).
NF/F: $250   **G/VG: $125**
First Edition (Trade): Reading, PA:
Fantasy Press, 1948.
NF/F: $50   **G/VG: $20**

Wilson, Colin. *The Philosopher's Stone.*
First Edition: London: Arthur Barker, 1969.
NF/F: $165   **G/VG: $70**
First U.S. Edition: New York: Crown, 1969.
NF/F: $55   **G/VG: $20**

Wolfe, Gene. *The Fifth Head of Cerberus.*
First Edition: New York: Scribners, 1972.
NF/F: $85   **G/VG: $30**

_____. *New Sun Series:*

_____. *The Shadow of the Torturer.*
First Edition: New York: Timescape
Books/Simon and Schuster, 1980.
NF/F: $175   **G/VG: $45**

_____. *The Claw of the Conciliator.*
First Edition: New York: Timescape
Books/Simon and Schuster, 1981.
NF/F: $75   **G/VG: $20**

_____. *The Sword of the Lictor.*
First Edition: New York: Timescape
Books/Simon and Schuster, 1982.
NF/F: $85   **G/VG: $25**

_____. *The Citadel of the Autarch.*
First Edition: New York: Timescape
Books/Simon and Schuster, 1981.
NF/F: $70   **G/VG: $15**

_____. *The Urth of the New Sun.*
First Edition: New York: TOR, 1987.
NF/F: $50   **G/VG: $10**

Wright, S. *Fowler.* Deluge.
First Edition: New York: Cosmopolitan,
1928.
NF/F: $100   **G/VG: $35**

Wyndham, John. *The Day of the
Triffids.*
First Edition: London: Michael Joseph,
1951.
Points of Issue: First Issue has
an advertising band stating
"The Daily Graphic Book Find
of the Month."
NF/F: $1,250   **G/VG: $500**
First U.S. Edition: Garden City:
Doubleday & Company, 1951.
NF/F: $475   **G/VG: $200**

_____. *The Midwich Cuckoos.*
First Edition: London: Michael Joseph,
1957.
NF/F: $225   **G/VG: $95**
First U.S. Edition: New York:
Ballantine, 1957.
NF/F: $85   **G/VG: $30**

Yarbo, Chelsea Quinn. *The Palace.*
First Edition: New York: St. Martins,
1978.
NF/F: $15   **G/VG: $6**

Zelazny, Roger. Chronicles of Amber:

_____. *Nine Princes in Amber.*
First Edition: Garden City: Doubleday, 1970.
NF/F: $3,800   **G/VG: $1,000**

_____. *The Guns of Avalon.*
First Edition: Garden City: Doubleday, 1972.
NF/F: $650   **G/VG: $200**

_____. *Sign of the Unicorn.*
First Edition: Garden City: Doubleday,
1975.
NF/F: $200   **G/VG: $80**

_____. *The Hand of Oberon.*
First Edition: Garden City: Doubleday,
1976.
NF/F: $175   **G/VG: $65**

_____. *The Courts of Chaos.*
First Edition: Garden City: Doubleday,
1978.
NF/F: $75   **G/VG: $30**

_____. *Trumps of Doom.*
First Edition: New York: Arbor House,
1985.
NF/F: $45   **G/VG: $15**

_____. *Blood of Amber.*
Limited Edition: Los Angeles:
Underwood-Miller, 1986.
NF/F: $100   **G/VG: $40**
First Edition: New York: Arbor House,
1986.
NF/F: $20   **G/VG: $8**

_____. *Knight of Shadows.*
First Edition: New York: William
Morrow, 1989.
NF/F: $30   **G/VG: $10**

_____. *Prince of Chaos.*
First Edition: New York: William
Morrow, 1991.
NF/F: $35   **G/VG: $15**

John Wyndham.

Roger Zelazny.

Roger Zelazny.

LITERATURE IN TRANSLATION

Much as the information may prove shocking, the greatest literary artists in the world have not all written in English. In point of fact, very few of them have.

As a language, English is a relative newcomer and due to its major fracture along the relative coasts of the Atlantic, fairly loose in its rules and constructions.

An example I have always found amusing is "knocking up." On the Eastern coast of the Atlantic it refers to a wake-up call. On the West coast, its meaning is somewhat different. Which is why I was so confused when I registered in a little inn in Wales and was asked if I would like to be "knocked up."

Older languages have explored further than English, establishing new and rather unique areas of literature. One example is what the French call "nouveau romàn" or literally "new novel." Essentially plotless and lacking an omniscient narrator, it reads like a slice of real life.

Pioneered by such writers as Alain Robbe-Grillet, Michel Butor, Marguerite Duras, Robert Pinget, Nathalie Sarrault, Nobel Prize winner Claude Simon and others, it is currently one of the hottest trends in American book collecting.

During the 1990s, nouveau roman books crept out of the dollar bins and have begun a steady rise to the $20 to $30 level in their first translated editions.

Classics such as Simon, Claude, *Flanders Road*, New York: George Braziller, 1961, flirt with the $100 level in trade edition, and limiteds like Robbe-Grillet, Alain, *The Voyeur*, New York: Grove, 1958, break the $500 level.

As modern American fiction has become more derivative and predictable, collectors, most of whom are essentially readers, are embracing more and more translated and unique works in literature.

Nor are the French the only innovators; Spanish, fractured like English by the Atlantic, has produced highly collectible works on both continents. Germans, Scandinavians and eastern Europeans produce as many Nobel Prize winners as those who write in English.

An interesting development within the 20th century was the appearance of oriental authors in book collections. China, Japan and Korea have what is perhaps the oldest continuing literary traditions in the world. Some of the work of Oriental literary artists, combining this tradition with the Western forms, has produced very interesting and enjoyable works, which are beginning to find room in American collections.

The largest single area of collecting translated works is collecting Nobel Prize winners. Such a collection is so full of translated works that books in English seem like interlopers on the shelves with them.

I have used an asterisk to identify the Nobel Prize winners in this chapter.

TEN CLASSIC RARITIES

Broch, Hermann. *The Death of Virgil.*
NY: Pantheon, 1945. Curious, as this is also the true first preceding the German version.
NF/F: $1,650   G/VG: $700

Brunhoff, Jean de. *The Travels of Babar.*
New York: Harrison Smith & Robert Haas, 1934.
NF/F: $2,600   G/VG: $950

Collodi, Carlo. *Story of a Puppet or The Adventures of Pinocchio.*
London: T. Fisher Unwin, 1892. And you thought it was Disney.
NF/F: $9,200   G/VG: $3,850

Dumas, Alexandre. *Celebrated Crimes.*
George Barrie & Son Pub, Philadelphia, 1895. Eight-volume set limited to 50 copies.
NF/F: $3,600   G/VG: $1,600

Ernst, Max and Paul Eluard. *Misfortunes of the Immortals.*
New York: Black Sun Press, 1943. One of 110 copies.
NF/F: $3,000   G/VG: $800

*Mann, Thomas. *Buddenbrooks.*
New York: Knopf, 1924. Two volumes.
NF/F: $2,500   G/VG: $1,200

*Marquez, Gabriel Garcia. *One Hundred Years of Solitude.*
New York: Harper and Row, 1970. The first state of the dust jacket has a "!" at the end of the first paragraph on the front flap.
NF/F: $5,500   G/VG: $2,400

Rimbaud Arthur. *A Season in Hell.*
New York: Limited Editions Club, 1986. A limited edition of 1,000 illustrated by Robert Mapplethorp.
NF/F: $2,400   G/VG: $1,200

Salten, Felix. *Bambi: A Life in the Woods.*
New York: Simon & Schuster, 1928. First Edition numbered 1,000 copies.
NF/F: $4,200   G/VG: $1,850

Sand, George. *The Masterpieces of George Sand.*
Philadelphia: George Barrie and Sons, 1900-1902. Printed in a limited set of 20 volumes for subscribers.
NF/F: $10,000   G/VG: $5,000

Hermann Broch.

Gabriel Garcia Marquez.

Felix Salten.

PRICE GUIDE

IN THE HEART OF THE SEAS

A novel by
the winner of the
Nobel Prize
for Literature
1966

S.Y. AGNON

Shmuel Yosef Agnon.

Isabel Allende.

Revolt in Aspromonte
Corrado Alvaro

A New Directions Paperbook

Corrado Alvaro.

Abell, Kjeld. *Three from Minikoi.*
First Edition in English: London: Seker
and Warburg, 1960.
NF/F: $25   G/VG: $10

*Agnon, Shmuel Yosef. *In the Heart
of the Seas.*
First U.S. Edition: New York: Schocken
Books, 1947.
NF/F: $85   G/VG: $25

_____. *Days of Awe.*
First U.S. Edition: New York: Schocken
Books, 1948.
NF/F: $75   G/VG: $20

_____. *A Book That Was Lost:
And Other Stories.*
First U.S. Edition: New York: Schocken
Books, 1995.
NF/F: $50   G/VG: $15

Ahad, Ha-'Am. *Selected Essays.*
First Edition: Philadelphia: Jewish
Publication Society, 1912.
NF/F: $35   G/VG: $10

Ahlin, Lars. *Cinnamon Candy.*
First U.S. Edition: New York: Garland
Publishing, 1990.
NF/F: $55   G/VG: $20

_____. *Destruction or Love.*
First Edition in English: Santa Cruz,
CA: Green Horse Three, 1976.
NF/F: $65   G/VG: $25

_____. *World Alone.*
First U.S. Edition: Great Barrington,
MA: Penmaen Press, 1982.
NF/F: $85   G/VG: $35

Allende, Isabel. *Of Love and Shadows.*
First U.S. Edition: New York: Alfred A.
Knopf, 1987.
NF/F: $85   G/VG: $25

_____. *The Stories of Eva Luna.*
First U.S. Edition: New York: Atheneum, 1991.
NF/F: $35   G/VG: $10

Alvaro, Corrado. *Man Is Strong.*
First U.S. Edition: New York: Alfred A.
Knopf, 1948.
NF/F: $65   G/VG: $20

_____. *Revolt in Aspromonte.*
First U.S. Edition: New Haven, CT:
New Directions, 1962.
NF/F: $60   G/VG: $20

Andersch, Alfred. *My Disappearance
in Providence & Other Stories.*
First Edition in English: Garden City,
NY: Doubleday and Co., 1978.
NF/F: $45   G/VG: $15

*Andric, Ivo. *The Bridge on the Drina.*
First Edition in English: London: Allen
& Unwin, 1959.
NF/F: $325   G/VG: $135

_____. *Bosnian Story.*
First Edition in English: London:
Lincolns-Prager, 1960.
NF/F: $75   G/VG: $35

Andrzejewski, Jerzy. *The Appeal.*
First Edition in English: London:
Weidenfeld and Nicolson, 1971.
NF/F: $45   G/VG: $20

Apollinaire, Guillaume. *Zone.*
First Edition of Translation by Samuel
Beckett: Dublin/London: The Dolmen
Press/Calder & Boyars, 1972.
NF/F: $1,500   G/VG: $600

*Asturias, Miguel Angel. *The Banana Republic Trilogy:*

_____. *The Green Pope.*
First Edition in English: New York: Delacorte, 1971.
NF/F: $125   G/VG: $40

_____. *Strong Wind.*
First Edition in English: New York: Delacorte, 1968.
NF/F: $160   G/VG: $45

_____. *The Eyes of the Interred.*
First Edition in English: New York: Delacorte, 1968.
NF/F: $125   G/VG: $45

Ayme, Marcel. *The Proverb and Other Stories.*
First U.S. Edition: New York: Antheneum, 1961.
NF/F: $125   G/VG: $35

_____. *Conscience of Love.*
First Edition in English: New York: Antheneum, 1961.
NF/F: $65   G/VG: $20
First U.K. Edition: London: The Bodley Head, 1962.
NF/F: $50   G/VG: $15

Barash, Asher. *Pictures from a Brewery.*
First U.S. Edition: Indianapolis: Bobbs-Merrill, 1971.
NF/F: $30   G/VG: $10

Bataille, Georges. *L'Abbe C.*
First U.K. Edition: London: Marion Boyars, 1983.
NF/F: $85   G/VG: $30

_____. *My Mother, Madame Edwarda, The Dead Man.*
First U.K. Edition: London: Marion Boyars, 1989.
NF/F: $45   G/VG: $15

Benda, Julien. *The Great Betrayal.*
First Edition in English: London: George Routledge, 1928.
NF/F: $85   G/VG: $40

Benjamin, Walter. *The Arcades Project.*
First U.S. Edition: Cambridge, MA: Harvard University Press, 1999.
NF/F: $100   G/VG: $30

*Bergson, Henri. *Time & Free Will.*
First Edition in English: London: Swan Sonnenschein, 1910.
NF/F: $275   G/VG: $85

_____. *Laughter: An Essay On the Meaning of the Comic.*
First Edition in English: London & New York: Macmillan, 1911.
NF/F: $185   G/VG: $50

Bernanos, Georges. *Mouchette.*
First Edition in English: New York: Holt, Rinehart and Winston, 1966.
NF/F: $60   G/VG: $20

Billetdoux, Francois. *A Man and His Master.*
First U.K. Edition: London: Secker & Warburg, 1963.
NF/F: $50   G/VG: $20

Billetdoux, Raphaele. *Night Without Day.*
First U.S. Edition: New York: Viking, 1987.
NF/F: $45   G/VG: $15

*Boll, Heinrich. *Billiards At Half-Past Nine.*
First Edition of Paul Bowles Translation: London: Weidenfeld and Nicolson, 1961.
NF/F: $185   G/VG: $60

Marcel Ayme.

Georges Bataille.

Francois Billetdoux.

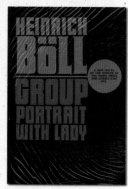

Henrich Boll.

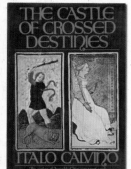

Michel Butor.

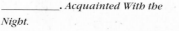

_____. *Acquainted With the Night.*
First U.S. Edition: New York: Henry Holt & Co, 1954.
NF/F: $99   **G/VG: $35**

_____. *Group Portrait with Lady.*
First Edition in English: London: Secker and Warburg, 1973.
NF/F: $55   **G/VG: $20**
First U.S. Edition: New York: McGraw-Hill, 1973.
NF/F: $45   **G/VG: $15**

. *The Clown.*
First U.S. Edition: New York: McGraw Hill Book Co., 1965.
NF/F: $75   **G/VG: $25**
First U.K. Edition: London: Weidenfeld & Nicolson, 1965.
NF/F: $75   **G/VG: $30**

Boulle, Pierre. *The Bridge on the River Kwai.*
First U.K. Edition: London: Secker & Warburg, 1954.
NF/F: $1,200   **G/VG: $400**

_____. *Sophia.*
First Edition: New York: Vanguard Press, Inc., 1959.
NF/F: $45   **G/VG: $20**

Breton, Andre. *Young Cherry Trees Secured Against Hares.*
First Edition in English: New York: View Editions, 1946.
NF/F: $750   **G/VG: $300**

*****Bunin, Ivan.** *Dark Avenues.*
First Edition in English: London: John Lehmann, 1949.
NF/F: $225   **G/VG: $85**

_____. *Grammar of Love.*
First U.S. Edition: New York: Harrison Smith and Robert Haas, 1934.
NF/F: $75   **G/VG: $30**

_____. *The Well of Days.*
First U.S. Edition: New York: Alfred A. Knopf, 1934.
NF/F: $115   **G/VG: $35**

Butor, Michel. *Degrees.*
First Edition in English: New York: Simon and Schuster, 1961.
NF/F: $85   **G/VG: $30**
First U.K. Edition: London: Methuen & Co., 1962.
NF/F: $50   **G/VG: $15**

. *Second Thoughts.*
First U.K. Edition: London: Faber and Faber, 1958.
NF/F: $135   **G/VG: $50**

Buzzati, Dino. *The Bears' Famous Invasion of Italy.*
First U.S. Edition: New York: Pantheon, 1947.
NF/F: $350   **G/VG: $125**

Calvino, Italo. *The Castle Of Crossed Destinies.*
First U.S. Edition: New York: Harcourt Brace Jovanovich, 1977.
NF/F: $145   **G/VG: $40**

_____. *Path to the Nest of Spiders.*
First Edition in English: London: Collins, 1956.
NF/F: $1,000   **G/VG: $325**
First U.S. Edition: Boston: Beacon Press, 1957.
NF/F: $350   **G/VG: $100**

Italo Calvino.

*Camus, Albert. *The Outsider.*
First Edition in English: London:
Hamish Hamilton, 1946.
Points of Issue: Original dust jacket
price is 6s. net.
NF/F: $1,200   G/VG: $350

_____. *The Fall.*
Limited Edition of O'Brien Translation:
Kentfield, CA: Allen Press, 1966 (140
copies).
NF/F: $850   G/VG: $400
First Edition in English: London:
Hamish Hamilton, 1957.
NF/F: $225   G/VG: $75
First U.S. Edition: New York: Alfred A.
Knopf, 1957.
NF/F: $100   G/VG: $25

_____. *The Exile and the Kingdom.*
First Edition in English: London:
Hamish Hamilton, 1958.
NF/F: $165   G/VG: $50
First U.S. Edition: New York: Alfred A.
Knopf, 1958.
NF/F: $150   G/VG: $30

_____. *Resistance, Rebellion, and Death.*
First Edition in English: London:
Hamish Hamilton, 1961.
NF/F: $125   G/VG: $35
First U.S. Edition: New York: Alfred A.
Knopf, 1961.
Points of Issue: The first state dust
jacket lacks a Rolo quote on the front
flap.
NF/F: $95   G/VG: $25

Capek, Karl. *Krakatit.*
First U.S. Edition: New York:
Macmillan, 1925.
NF/F: $75   G/VG: $30

*Carducci, Giosue. *Odi Barbare.*
First Edition in English: New York:
Vanni, 1950.
NF/F: $65   G/VG: $20

Castro, Ferreira de. *Jungle: a Tale of the Amazon Rubber-Tappers.*
First U.S. Edition: New York: Viking
Press, 1935.
Points of Issue: The Viking Edition is
bound British sheets and the Knopf,
also 1935 is sometimes considered
the First U.S. Edition as it was printed
here. The Knopf price is roughly
analogous, both are translations by
Charles Duff.
NF/F: $135   G/VG: $55

Cayrol, Jean. *All in a Night.*
First Edition in English: London: Faber
& Faber, 1956.
NF/F: $45   G/VG: $15

*Cela, Camilo José. *Pascual Duarte's Family.*
First Edition in English: London: Eyre
& Spottiswoode, 1946.
NF/F: $600   G/VG: $185
First U.S. Edition as *The Family of
Pascual Duarte*: Boston: Atlantic-Little
Brown, 1964.
NF/F: $125   G/VG: $35

_____. *The Hive.*
First U.S. Edition: New York: Farrar,
Straus & Young, 1953.
NF/F: $125   G/VG: $40
First U.K. Edition: London: Gollancz,
1953.
NF/F: $85   G/VG: $20

Cernuda, Luis. *The Poetry of Luis Cernuda.*
First Edition: New York: New York
University Press, 1971.
NF/F: $50   G/VG: $20

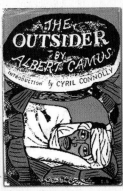
Albert Camus.

Albert Camus.

Camilo José Cela.

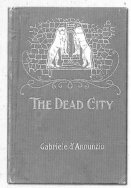

Gabriele D'Annunzio.

Isak Dinesen.

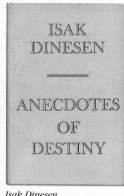

Isak Dinesen.

Char, René. *Hypnos Waking.*
First U.S. Edition: New York: Random
House, 1956.
NF/F: $65   **G/VG: $20**

_____. *The Dog of Hearts.*
First U.S. Edition: Santa Cruz, CA:
Green Horse, 1973.
NF/F: $35   **G/VG: $15**

Cocteau, Jean. *Opium The Diary of
an Addict.*
First U.K. Edition: London: Longmans,
Green, 1932.
NF/F: $750   **G/VG: $225**

_____. *The Imposter.*
First Edition Thus: New York: D.
Appleton, 1925.
NF/F: $150   **G/VG: $45**

_____. *Thomas the Imposter.*
First U.S. Edition: New York: The
Noonsday Press, 1957.
NF/F: $225   **G/VG: $75**

_____. *The Eagle Has Two Heads.*
First U.S. Edition: New York: Funk &
Wagnalls, 1948.
NF/F: $65   **G/VG: $20**

Colette. *Mitsou, or, How Girls Grow
Wise.*
First U.S. Edition: New York: Albert &
Charles Boni, 1930.
NF/F: $365   **G/VG: $125**

Colette and Willy. *The Indulgent
Husband.*
First U.S. Edition: New York: Farrar &
Rinehart, 1935.
NF/F: $225   **G/VG: $75**

_____. *The Innocent Wife.*
First U.S. Edition: New York: Farrar &
Rinehart, 1934.
NF/F: $200   **G/VG: $55**

Curtis, Jean-Louis. *Baccarat.*
First Edition: London: Thames &
Hudson, 1992.
NF/F: $185   **G/VG: $75**

D'Annunzio, Gabriele. *The Dead
City.*
First U.S. Edition: Chicago: Laird &
Lee, 1902.
NF/F: $400   **G/VG: $150**

_____. *The Triumph of Death.*
First U.S. Edition: New York: George
H. Richmond, 1896.
NF/F: $140   **G/VG: $55**

Dery, Tibor. *Niki: The Story of a Dog.*
First U.K. Edition: London: Secker &
Warburg, 1958.
NF/F: $45   **G/VG: $15**

_____. *The Portuguese Princess.*
First U.K. Edition: London: Calder &
Boyars, 1966.
NF/F: $45   **G/VG: $15**

Dinesen, Isak. *Seven Gothic Tales.*
First Edition: New York: Harrison
Smith & Robert Haas, 1934.
NF/F: $1,150   **G/VG: $375**

_____. *Anecdotes of Destiny
- Five Stories: The Diver, Babette's
Feast, Tempests, The Immortal Story,
The Ring.*
First Edition: London: Michael Joseph,
1958.
NF/F: $200   **G/VG: $65**

_____. *Last Tales.*
First U.S. Edition: New York: Random
House, 1957.
NF/F: $175   **G/VG: $65**
First U.K. Edition: London: Putnam,
1957.
NF/F: $325   **G/VG: $125**

Drieu La Rochelle, Pierre. *The Fire Within.*
First U.S. Edition: New York: Alfred A.
Knopf, 1965.
NF/F: $45   **G/VG: $15**

_____. *Will o' the Wisp.*
First U.K. Edition: London: Calder and
Boyars, 1963.
NF/F: $35   **G/VG: $15**

Druon, Maurice. *The Poisoned Crown.*
First U.S. Edition: New York: Scribners, 1957.
NF/F: $150   **G/VG: $65**

*Du Gard, Roger Martin.** *The Thibaults.*
First U.S. Edition: New York: Boni and
Liveright, 1926.
NF/F: $135   **G/VG: $45**

_____. *The Postman.*
First Edition in English: London: Andre
Deutsch, 1954.
NF/F: $125   **G/VG: $35**
First U.S. Edition: New York: Viking,
1955.
NF/F: $45   **G/VG: $15**

_____. *Jean Barois.*
First U.S. Edition: New York: Viking,
1949.
NF/F: $100   **G/VG: $30**

Duras, Marguerite. *Blue Eyes, Black
Hair.*
First Edition in English: New York:
Pantheon, 1987.
NF/F: $65   **G/VG: $25**
First U.K. Edition: London: Collins, 1988.
NF/F: $35   **G/VG: $10**

_____. *Summer Rain.*
First U.S. Edition: New York: Scribners,
1992.
NF/F: $35   **G/VG: $15**
First U.K. Edition: London:
HarperCollins, 1992.
NF/F: $25   **G/VG: $10**

_____. *War: a Memoir.*
First U.S. Edition: New York: Pantheon,
1986.
NF/F: $65   **G/VG: $20**

*Echegaray, Jose.** *The Son of Don
Juan.*
First Edition Thus: Boston: Roberts
Brothers, 1895.
NF/F: $60   **G/VG: $20**

*Elytis, Odysseus.** *Maria Nephele: A
Poem in Two Voices.*
First U.S. Edition: Boston: Houghton
Mifflin, 1981.
NF/F: $45   **G/VG: $15**

_____. *The Sovereign Sun.*
First Edition: Philadelphia: Temple
University, 1974.
NF/F: $35   **G/VG: $15**

Estang, Luc. *The Better Song.*
First U.S. Edition: New York: Pantheon,
1963.
NF/F: $35   **G/VG: $15**
First U.K. Edition: London: Hodder &
Stoughton, 1964.
NF/F: $20   **G/VG: $10**

Faure, Elie. *The Dance Over Fire and
Water.*
First Edition: New York: Harper &
Brothers, 1926.
NF/F: $55   **G/VG: $15**

Feuchtwanger, Lion. *Jew Suss A
Historical Romance.*
Limited Edition: London: Martin
Secker, 1926 (275 copies).
NF/F: $275   **G/VG: $125**
First U.K. Edition (trade): London:
Martin Secker, 1926.
NF/F: $100   **G/VG: $35**

Marguerite Duras.

Marguerite Duras.

Marguerite Duras.

Dario Fo.

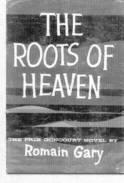

Romain Gary.

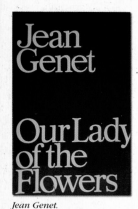

Jean Genet.

_____. *Success.*
First U.K. Edition: London: Martin Secker, 1930.
NF/F: $195   **G/VG: $60**
First U.S. Edition: New York: Viking, 1930.
NF/F: $45   **G/VG: $20**

*Fo, Dario. *We Can't Pay? We Won't Pay!*
First U.K. Edition: London: Pluto Press, 1982.
NF/F: $75   **G/VG: $20**

Fort, Paul. *Selected Poems and Ballads of Paul Fort.*
First U.S. Edition: New York: Duffield and Company, 1921.
NF/F: $45   **G/VG: $15**

*France, Anatole. *The Crime Of Sylvestre Bonnard.*
First Edition of Lafcadio Hearn Translation: New York: Harper & Brothers, 1890.
NF/F: $325   **G/VG: $135**

_____. *Bee the Princess of the Dwarfs.*
First U.K. Edition: London: J. M. Dent, 1912.
NF/F: $450   **G/VG: $200**

_____. *The Aspirations of Jean Servien.*
First U.K. Edition: London: John Lane The Bodley Head, 1912.
NF/F: $75   **G/VG: $25**

Frisch, Max. *I'm Not Stiller.*
First U.K. Edition: London: Abelard-Schuman, 1958.
NF/F: $165   **G/VG: $75**

Fussenegger, Gertrud. *Noah's Ark.*
First U.S. Edition: Philadelphia: J. B. Lippincott, 1982.
NF/F: $35   **G/VG: $15**

Fust, Milan. *The Story of My Wife.*
First Edition in English: New York: Paj Publications, 1987.
NF/F: $40   **G/VG: $15**

Gadda, Carlo Emilio. *Acquainted with Grief.*
First U.S. Edition: New York: George Braziller, 1969.
NF/F: $85   **G/VG: $20**

Gary, Romain. *The Roots of Heaven.*
First U.S. Edition: New York: Simon & Schuster, 1958.
NF/F: $75   **G/VG: $25**

_____. *The Ski Bum.*
First U.S. Edition: New York: Harper and Row, 1965.
NF/F: $45   **G/VG: $15**

Genet, Jean. *Our Lady of Flowers.*
Limited First Edition in English: Paris: Morihien, 1949 (500 copies).
NF/F: $250   **G/VG: $115**
First U.S. Edition: New York: Grove Press, 1963.
NF/F: $55   **G/VG: $20**
First U.K. Edition: London: Anthony Blond, 1964.
NF/F: $65   **G/VG: $20**

Gide, Andre. *Oscar Wilde. A Study.*
First Edition in English: London: The Holywell Press, 1905.
NF/F: $300   **G/VG: $125**

_____. *Two Symphonies.*
First U.S. Edition: New York: Alfred A. Knopf, 1931.
NF/F: $80   **G/VG: $20**
First U.K. Edition: London: Cassell, 1931.
NF/F: $100   **G/VG: $30**

_____. *Urien's Voyage.*
First U.S. Edition: New York:
Philosophical Library, 1964.
NF/F: $65   **G/VG: $20**
First U.K. Edition: London: Peter Owen, 1964.
NF/F: $50   **G/VG: $20**

Giono, Jean. *The Malediction.*
First U.S. Edition: New York: Criterion
Books, 1955.
NF/F: $155   **G/VG: $65**

Girandoux, Jean. *Tiger at the Gates.*
First Edition: New York: Oxford, 1955.
NF/F: $45   **G/VG: $15**

Gombrowicz, Witold. *Ferdydurke.*
First U.K. Edition: London: Macgibbon
and Kee, 1961.
NF/F: $250   **G/VG: $100**

_____. *Pornografia.*
First U.S. Edition: New York: Grove
Press, 1966.
NF/F: $85   **G/VG: $20**

Gomez de la Serna, Ramon. *Movieland.*
First Edition: New York: Macaulay, 1930.
NF/F: $195   **G/VG: $90**

Gorky, Maxim. *The Judge.*
First Edition: New York: McBride, 1924.
NF/F: $95   **G/VG: $30**

Gracq, Julien. *A Dark Stranger.*
First Edition: New York: New
Directions, 1951.
NF/F: $60   **G/VG: $25**

*Grass, Gunther. *The Flounder.*
Limited Edition: New York: Limited
Editions Club, 1985 (1,000 copies of
three volumes).
NF/F: $575   **G/VG: Not Seen**
First U.S. Edition: New York: Harcourt
Brace Jovanovich, 1977.
NF/F: $130   **G/VG: $40**

_____. *Show Your Tongue.*
First U.K. Edition: London: Secker
Warburg, 1989.
NF/F: $25   **G/VG: $10**

_____. *The Call of the Toad.*
First U.S. Edition: New York: Harcourt
Brace Jovanovich, 1992.
NF/F: $35   **G/VG: $10**

Green, Julien. *The Distant Lands.*
First U.S. Edition: New York: M.
Boyars, Distributed By Rizzoli
International Publications, 1991.
NF/F: $65   **G/VG: $20**

Gyllensten, Lars. *The Testament of
Cain.*
First Edition: London: Calder & Boyars,
1967.
NF/F: $55   **G/VG: $15**

*Hamsun, Knut. *Benoni.*
First U.S. Edition: New York: Alfred A,
Knopf, 1925.
NF/F: $275   **G/VG: $125**

_____. *Hunger.*
First Edition in English: London:
Leonard Smithers, 1899.
Points of Issue: First printing
announces Smither's "List of
Publications" for Spring 1899.
NF/F: $1,100   **G/VG: $375**
First U.S. Edition: New York: Alfred A
Knopf, 1920.
NF/F: $300   **G/VG: $125**

_____. *Dreamers.*
First U.S. Edition: New York: Alfred A
Knopf, 1921.
NF/F: $375   **G/VG: $165**

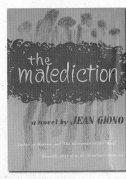
Jean Giono.

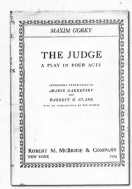
Maxim Gorky.

Knut Hamsun.

Hermann Hesse.

Hermann Hesse.

Kazuo Ishiguro.

*Hauptmann, Gerhart. *Phantom.*
First U.S. Edition: New York: B.W.
Huebsch, 1922.
NF/F: $175   **G/VG: $75**
First U.K. Edition: London: Martin
Secker, 1923.
NF/F: $225   **G/VG: $85**

_____. *The Heretic of Soana.*
First Edition in English: New York:
B.W. Huebsch, 1923.
NF/F: $100   **G/VG: $25**

_____. *The Fool In Christ.*
First Edition: New York: B.W. Huebsch, 1911.
NF/F: $65   **G/VG: $25**

*Hesse, Hermann. *Siddhartha.*
First U.S. Edition: New York: New
Directions, 1951.
NF/F: $1,650   **G/VG: $600**

_____. *Steppenwolf.*
First U.S. Edition: New York: Henry
Holt, 1929.
NF/F: $550   **G/VG: $175**

_____. *Beneath the Wheel.*
First U.S. Edition: New York: Farrar,
Strauss, Giroux, 1968.
NF/F: $90   **G/VG: $25**

Huysmans, Joris-Karl. *Down Stream
and Other Works.*
First U.S. Edition: Chicago: Pascal
Covici, 1927.
NF/F: $100   **G/VG: $35**

_____. *En Route.*
First U.S. Edition: New York: E. P.
Dutton, 1920.
NF/F: $110   **G/VG: $40**

Ishiguro, Kazuo. *A Pale View Of Hills.*
First U.K. Edition: London: Faber &
Faber, 1982.
NF/F: $1,950   **G/VG: $750**

Jacob, Max. *The Story of King Kabul
the First and Gawain the Kitchen-Boy.*
First U.S. Edition: Lincoln, NE:
University of Nebraska, 1994.
NF/F: $45   **G/VG: $20**

Jens, Walter. *The Blind Man.*
First U.K. Edition: London: Andre
Deutsch, 1954.
NF/F: $50   **G/VG: $15**

*Jensen, Johannes V. *The Long
Journey.* (Three Volumes).
First U.K. Edition: London: Gyldendal,
1922-1924.
NF/F: $300   **G/VG: $95**

*Jimenez, Juan Ramon. *Platero and I.*
First U.S. Edition: Austin, TX:
University of Texas, 1957.
NF/F: $85   **G/VG: $25**

_____. *Stories of Life and Death.*
First U.S. Edition: New York: Paragon
House, 1985.
NF/F: $45   **G/VG: $15**

*Johnson, Eyvind. *The Days of His
Grace.*
First U.K. Edition: London: Chatto and
Windus, 1968.
NF/F: $35   **G/VG: $10**

Junger, Ernst. *Copse 125.*
First U.K. Edition: London: Chatto and
Windus, 1930.
NF/F: $325   **G/VG: $125**

_____. *The Storm of Steel.*
First U.K. Edition: London: Chatto &
Windus, 1929.
NF/F: $300   **G/VG: $120**

Kaleb, Vjekoslav. *Glorious Dust.*
First Edition: London: Lincolns-Prager,
1960.
NF/F: $30   **G/VG: $10**

*Kawabata, Yasunari. *House of the Sleeping Beauties.*
First Edition in English: Palo Alto, CA: Kodansha, 1969.
NF/F: $250　　　　**G/VG: $95**

Kazantzakis Nikos. *Zorba The Greek.*
First Edition: London: John Lehmann, 1952.
NF/F: $475　　　　**G/VG: $145**
First U.S. Edition: New York: Simon and Schuster, 1953.
NF/F: $250　　　　**G/VG: $100**

*Lagerkvist, Par. *The Sibyl.*
First U.S. Edition: New York: Random House, 1958.
NF/F: $195　　　　**G/VG: $90**

_____. *The Dwarf.*
First U.S. Edition: New York: L. B. Fischer, 1954.
NF/F: $165　　　　**G/VG: $55**

_____. *Pilgrim at Sea.*
First Edition in English: London: Chatto & Windus, 1964.
NF/F: $100　　　　**G/VG: $35**
First U.S. Edition: New York: Random House, 1964.
NF/F: $75　　　　**G/VG: $20**

*Lagerlof, Selma. *General's Ring.*
First U.S. Edition: Garden City, NY: Doubleday, Doran, 1928.
NF/F: $65　　　　**G/VG: $20**

_____. *Outcast.*
First Edition in English: London: Gyldendal, 1922.
NF/F: $160　　　　**G/VG: $65**
First U.S. Edition: Garden City, NY: Doubleday, Page, 1922.
NF/F: $175　　　　**G/VG: $60**

_____. *The Wonderful Adventures of Nils.*
First U.K. Edition: London: Arthur F. Bird, 1925.
NF/F: $85　　　　**G/VG: $35**

*Laxness, Halldor. *Paradise Reclaimed.*
First U.S. Edition: New York: Thomas Y. Crowell, 1962.
NF/F: $200　　　　**G/VG: $85**

_____. *Fish Can Sing.*
First Edition: London: Methuen, 1966.
NF/F: $250　　　　**G/VG: $95**

_____. *The Happy Warriors.*
First U.K. Edition: London: Methuen, 1958.
NF/F: $265　　　　**G/VG: $120**

Levi, Primo. *Other People's Trades.*
First U.S. Edition: New York: Summit, 1985.
NF/F: $65　　　　**G/VG: $25**

_____. *If This Is a Man.*
First U.S. Edition: New York: Orion Press, 1959.
NF/F: $200　　　　**G/VG: $85**

Lind, Jakov. *Travels to Enu: Story of a Shipwreck.*
First U.K. Edition: London: Eyre Methuen, 1982.
NF/F: $125　　　　**G/VG: $45**
First U.S. Edition: New York: St. Martin's, 1982.
NF/F: $60　　　　**G/VG: $20**

Linna, Vaino. *The Unknown Soldier.*
First Edition: London: Collins, 1957.
NF/F: $70　　　　**G/VG: $25**

Lorca, Federico Garcia. *The Poet in New York and Other Poems of Federico Garcia Lorca.*
First Edition: New York: W.W. Norton, 1940.
NF/F: $1,600　　　　**G/VG: $650**

Yasunari Kawabata.

Par Lagerkvist.

Selma Lagerlof.

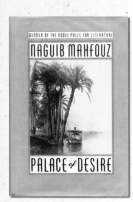

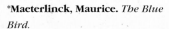

Naguib Mahfouz.

Heinrich Mann.

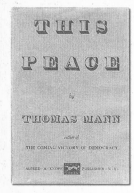

Thomas Mann.

*Maeterlinck, Maurice. *The Blue Bird.*
First U.S. Edition: New York: Dodd Mead & Co., 1909.
NF/F: $325   **G/VG: $130**

_____. *The Life of the Ant.*
First U.S. Edition Thus: New York: John Day, 1930.
NF/F: $45   **G/VG: $15**

_____. *The Life of The Bee.*
First U.S. Edition: New York: Dodd, Mead, 1901.
NF/F: $275   **G/VG: $95**

*Mahfouz, Naguib. Cairo trilogy:

_____. *Palace Walk.*
First U.S. Edition: Garden City, NY: Doubleday, 1990.
NF/F: $95   **G/VG: $30**

_____. *Palace of Desire.*
First U.S. Edition: Garden City, NY: Doubleday, 1991.
NF/F: $75   **G/VG: $35**

_____. *Sugar Street.*
First U.S. Edition: Garden City, NY: Doubleday, 1992.
NF/F: $100   **G/VG: $30**

_____. *Respected Sir.*
First U.K. Edition: London: Quartet, 1986.
NF/F: $75   **G/VG: $30**

Malaparte, Curzio. *The Skin.*
First U.S. Edition: Boston: Houghton Mifflin, 1952.
NF/F: $155   **G/VG: $45**

Mallet-Joris, Francoise. *The Witches: Three Tales of Sorcery.*
First U.S. Edition: New York: Farrar Strauss & Giroux, 1969.
NF/F: $50   **G/VG: $15**

Malroux, Andre. *Days of Wrath.*
First Edition: New York: Random House, 1936.
NF/F: $25   **G/VG: $10**

Mann, Heinrich. *In the Land of Cockaigne.*
First U.S. Edition: New York: Macaulay, 1929.
NF/F: $275   **G/VG: $120**

*Mann, Thomas. *This Peace.*
First U.S. Edition: New York: Alfred A. Knopf, 1938.
NF/F: $325   **G/VG: $100**

_____. *Joseph and His Brothers.*
First U.S. Edition: New York: Alfred A. Knopf, 1934.
NF/F: $750   **G/VG: $300**

_____. *Death in Venice and Other Stories.*
First U.S. Edition: New York: Alfred A. Knopf, 1925.
NF/F: $550   **G/VG: $200**

Marceau, Felicien. *The Flesh in the Mirror.*
First U.K. Edition: London: Vision Press, 1957.
NF/F: $75   **G/VG: $35**

Marnau, Fred. *The Death of the Cardinal.*
First Edition: London: Grey Walls, 1946.
NF/F: $85   **G/VG: $30**

*Marquez, Gabriel Garcia. *No One Writes to the Colonel and Other Stories.*
First U.S. Edition: New York: Harper & Row, 1968.
NF/F: $1,500   **G/VG: $600**
First U.K. Edition: London: Cape, 1971.
NF/F: $750   **G/VG: $250**

_____. *In Evil Hour.*
First U.S. Edition: New York: Harper & Row, 1979.
NF/F: $225   **G/VG: $85**

_____. *Love in the Time of Cholera.*
Limited Edition: New York: Alfred A. Knopf, 1988 (350 copies).
NF/F: $3,200   **G/VG: Not Seen**
First Edition: New York: Alfred A. Knopf, 1988.
NF/F: $275   **G/VG: $125**

*Martinson, Harry. *The Road.*
First U.K. Edition: London: Jonathan Cape, 1955.
NF/F: $675   **G/VG: $300**

_____. *Aniara: a Review of Man in Time and Space.*
First U.S. Edition: New York: Alfred A. Knopf, 1963.
NF/F: $75   **G/VG: $25**

_____. *Wild Bouquet.*
First U.S. Edition: Kansas City, Mo.: BKMK Press, 1985.
NF/F: $55   **G/VG: $20**

Matute, Ana Maria. *The Lost Children.*
First U.S. Edition: New York: Macmillan, 1965.
NF/F: $25   **G/VG: $10**

Mauriac, Francois. *The Frontenac Mystery.*
First Edition: London: Eyre & Spottiswoode, 1951.
NF/F: $85   **G/VG: $25**

Maurois, Andre. *Mape: The World of Illusion.*
First U.S. Edition: New York: D. Appleton & Company, 1926.
NF/F: $95   **G/VG: $30**

_____. *The Weigher of Souls.*
First U.S. Edition: New York: D. Appleton & Company, 1931.
NF/F: $100   **G/VG: $35**

Meyrink, Gustav. *The Golem.*
First U.S. Edition: Boston: Houghton Mifflin, 1928.
NF/F: $400   **G/VG: $125**

Mikhalov, Sergei. *Jolly Hares.*
First Edition in English: Moscow: Progress Publishers, 1969.
NF/F: $25   **G/VG: $10**

*Milosz, Czeslaw. *Bells In Winter.*
First U.S. Edition: New York: The Ecco Press, 1978.
NF/F: $125   **G/VG: $30**

_____. *Beginning With My Streets.*
First U.S. Edition: New York; Farrar Straus & Giroux, 1991.
NF/F: $100   **G/VG: $25**

_____. *The Usurpers.*
First Edition in English: London: Faber & Faber, 1955.
NF/F: $185   **G/VG: $80**

Mirbeau, Octave. *Torture Garden.*
First Edition: New York: Claude Kendall, 1931.
NF/F: $135   **G/VG: $55**

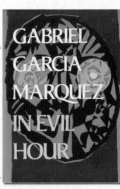
Gabriel Garcia Marquez.

Gustav Meyrink.

Octave Mirbeau.

Slawomir Mrozek.

Martin Andersen Nexo.

Kenzaburo Oe.

_____. *Celestine: Being the Diary of a Chambermaid.*
First Edition: New York: William Faro, 1932.
NF/F: $85　　　　　**G/VG: $30**

*****Mistral, Frederic.** *Anglore: The Song of the Rhone.*
Limited First U.S. Edition: Claremont, CA: Saunders Studio Press, 1937 (415 Copies).
NF/F: $100　　　　　**G/VG: $30**

*****Mistral, Gabriela.** *Crickets And Frogs.*
First U.S. Edition: New York: Atheneum, 1972.
NF/F: $75　　　　　**G/VG: $30**

Moravia, Alberto. *Wheel Of Fortune.*
First U.S. Edition: New York: Viking, 1937.
NF/F: $100　　　　　**G/VG: $35**

*****Montale, Eugenio.** *Satura: Poems 1962-1970.*
First U.S. Edition: New York: W.W. Norton, 1998.
NF/F: $175　　　　　**G/VG: $60**

_____. *The Butterfly of Dinard.*
First U.S. Edition: Lexington, KY: University Press of Kentucky, 1971.
NF/F: $85　　　　　**G/VG: $30**

Mrozek, Slawomir. *The Elephant.*
First U.S. Edition: New York: Grove Press, 1962.
NF/F: $55　　　　　**G/VG: $15**

*****Neruda, Pablo.** *Splendor And Death Of Joaquin Murieta.*
First U.S. Edition: New York: Farrar Straus & Giroux, 1972.
NF/F: $130　　　　　**G/VG: $45**

_____. *The Heights of Macchu Picchu.*
Limited Edition: New York: Limited Editions Club, 1998 (300 copies).
NF/F: $3,000　　　　　**G/VG: $1,600**
First U.S. Edition: New York: Farrar Straus & Giroux, 1967.
NF/F: $100　　　　　**G/VG: $35**

_____. *Residence On Earth.*
First U.S. Edition: Norfolk, CT: New Directions, 1946.
NF/F: $225　　　　　**G/VG: $95**

Nexo, Martin Andersen. *Days in the Sun.*
First U.S. Edition: New York: Coward-McCann, 1929.
NF/F: $100　　　　　**G/VG: $30**

Nossack, Hans Erich. *The Impossible Proof.*
First Edition: New York: Farrar, Straus & Giroux, 1968.
NF/F: $65　　　　　**G/VG: $20**

Odojewski, Wlodzimierz. *The Dying Day.*
First U.S. Edition: New York: Harcourt, Brace & World, 1959.
NF/F: $25　　　　　**G/VG: $10**

*****Oe, Kenzaburo.** *A Personal Matter.*
First U.S. Edition: New York: Grove Press, 1968.
NF/F: $200　　　　　**G/VG: $85**

_____. *Silent Cry.*
First Edition in English: Tokyo: Kodansha International, 1974.
NF/F: $100　　　　　**G/VG: $35**

Ortega Y Gasset, Jose. *Man and Crisis.*
First U.S. Edition: New York: W.W. Norton, 1958.
NF/F: $70　　　　　**G/VG: $20**

Otero, Blas De. *Twenty Poems.*
First Edition: Madison, MN: Sixties
Press, 1964.
NF/F: $65   **G/VG: $25**

Pasternak, Boris. *Doctor Zhivago.*
First U.K. Edition: London: Collins and
Harvill Press, 1958.
NF/F: $725   **G/VG: $250**
First U.S. Edition: New York: Pantheon, 1958.
NF/F: $175   **G/VG: $65**

_____. *Sister My Life, Summer, 1917.*
First U.S. Edition: New York:
Washington Square Press, 1967.
NF/F: $75   **G/VG: $25**

_____. *Selected Poems.*
First Edition: London: Lindsay
Drummond, 1946.
NF/F: $85   **G/VG: $35**

Paz, Octavio. *The Siren and the Seashell.*
First U.S. Edition: Austin, TX:
University of Texas Press, 1976.
NF/F: $125   **G/VG: $40**

_____. *The Labyrinth of Solitude.*
First U.S. Edition: New York: Grove
Press, 1961.
NF/F: $195   **G/VG: $85**
First U.K. Edition: London: Allen Lane/
Penguin Press, 1967.
$145   **G/VG: $55**

_____. *Alternating Current.*
First U.S. Edition: New York: Viking
Press, 1973.
NF/F: $200   **G/VG: $80**

Perse, St. John. *Anabasis.*
Limited Edition: London: Faber &
Faber, 1930 (350 copies).
NF/F: $3,500   **G/VG: $750**
First U.K. Edition: London: Faber &
Faber, 1930.
NF/F: $350   **G/VG: $125**

_____. *Birds.*
First Edition Thus: New York:
Bollingen Foundation, 1966.
NF/F: $145   **G/VG: $55**

_____. *Seamarks.*
First Edition: New York: Pantheon
Books, 1958.
NF/F: $100   **G/VG: $35**

Petersen, Nis. *Whistlers in the Night.*
First U.S. Edition: Philadelphia: Nordic
Books, 1983.
NF/F: $35   **G/VG: $10**

Peyre, Joseph. *Glittering Death.*
First Edition: New York: Random
House, 1937.
NF/F: $80   **G/VG: $30**

_____. *Rehearsal in Oviedo.*
First Edition: New York: Knight
Publishers, 1937.
NF/F: $65   **G/VG: $25**

Pinget, Robert. *The Inquisitory.*
First U.K. Edition: London: Calder and
Boyars, 1966.
NF/F: $65   **G/VG: $30**
First U.S. Edition: New York: Grove
Press, 1966.
NF/F: $95   **G/VG: $30**

_____. *Recurrent Memory
(Passacaille).*
First U.K. Edition: London: Calder &
Boyars, 1975.
NF/F: $55   **G/VG: $15**

Pirandello, Luigi. *Horse in the
Moon: Twelve Short Stories.*
First U.S. Edition: New York: E. P.
Dutton, 1932.
NF/F: $350   **G/VG: $155**

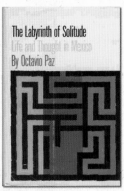
Octavio Paz.

St. John Perse.

Joseph Peyre.

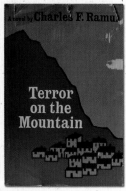

Charles F. Ramuz.

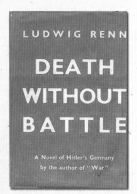

Ludwig Renn.

_____. *One, None and a Hundred Thousand.*
First U.S. Edition: New York: E. P. Dutton, 1933.
NF/F: $100   **G/VG: $35**

_____. *The Naked Truth.*
First U.S. Edition: New York: E. P. Dutton, 1935.
NF/F: $100   **G/VG: $30**

Proust, Marcel. *Jean Santeuil.*
First U.K. Edition: London: Weidenfeld and Nicholson, 1955.
NF/F: $65   **G/VG: $25**

_____. *In Search of Lost Time (Remembrance of Things Past):*

_____. *Swann's Way.*
First U.S. Edition: New York: Henry Holt & Co., 1922.
NF/F: $325   **G/VG: $125**

_____. *Within a Budding Grove.*
First U.S. Edition: New York: Thomas Seltzer, 1924.
NF/F: $125   **G/VG: $50**

_____. *The Guermantes Way.*
First U.K. Edition: London: Chatto and Windus, 1925.
NF/F: $185   **G/VG: $75**
First U.S. Edition: New York: Thomas Seltzer, 1925.
NF/F: $145   **G/VG: $65**

_____. *Cities of the Plain.* (Two Volumes).
First U.S. Edition: New York: Albert and Charles Boni, 1927.
NF/F: $275   **G/VG: $95**

_____. *The Captive.*
First U.S. Edition: New York: Albert and Charles Boni, 1929.
NF/F: $125   **G/VG: $50**

_____. *The Sweet Cheat Gone.*
First U.S. Edition: New York: Albert and Charles Boni, 1930.
NF/F: $125   **G/VG: $50**

_____. *The Past Recaptured.*
First U.S. Edition: New York: Albert and Charles Boni, 1932.
NF/F: $100   **G/VG: $35**

***Quasimodo, Salvatore.** *To Give and To Have and Other Poems.*
First U.S. Edition: Chicago: Henry Regnery, 1969.
NF/F: $85   **G/VG: $30**

_____. *The Tall Schooner: A Poem.*
First U.S. Edition: New York: Red Ozier Press, 1980.
NF/F: $75   **G/VG: $40**

_____. *The Poet and the Politician and other Essays.*
First Edition: Carbondale, IL: Southern Illinois University Press, 1964.
NF/F: $35   **G/VG: $15**

Ramuz, Charles F. *Terror On the Mountain.*
First U.S. Edition: New York: Harcourt, Brace & World, 1967.
NF/F: $60   **G/VG: $20**

Raynal, Paul. *The Unknown Warrior.*
First U.K. Edition: London: Methuen, 1928.
NF/F: $75   **G/VG: $35**

Remarque, Erich Maria. *The Road Back.*
First U.K. Edition: London: Putnams, 1931.
NF/F: $500   **G/VG: $185**
First U.S. Edition: Boston: Little, Brown, 1931.
NF/F: $525   **G/VG: $200**

_____. *Three Comrades.*
First U.S. Edition: Boston: Little, Brown & Co., 1937.
NF/F: $185   **G/VG: $70**

Renn, Ludwig. *Death Without Battle.*
First U.K. Edition: London: Martin Secker, 1937.
NF/F: $150   **G/VG: $45**

Ribeiro, Aquilino. *When the Wolves Howl.*
First U.S. Edition: New York: Macmillan, 1963.
NF/F: $45   **G/VG: $20**

Robbe-Grillet, Alain. *Jealousy.*
First U.K. Edition: London: John Calder, 1959.
NF/F: $165   **G/VG: $50**
First U.S. Edition: New York: Grove Press, 1959.
NF/F: $55   **G/VG: $20**

_____. *La Maison De Rendezvous.*
First U.S. Edition: New York: Grove Press, 1966.
NF/F: $65   **G/VG: $25**

Rolland, Romain. *Annette and Sylvie.*
Limited Edition: New York: Henry Holt, 1925 (515 copies of two volumes).
NF/F: $150   **G/VG: $80**
First U.S. Edition: New York: Henry Holt, 1925.
NF/F: $60   **G/VG: $15**

_____. *The Game of Love and Death.*
First U.S. Edition: New York: Henry Holt, 1926.
NF/F: $100   **G/VG: $45**

Romains, Jules. *Verdun.*
First Edition: New York: Alfred A. Knopf, 1939.
NF/F: $95   **G/VG: $35**

Roy, Jules. *The Navigator.*
First Edition: New York: Alfred A. Knopf, 1955.
NF/F: $55   **G/VG: $25**

Sabato, Ernesto. *The Outsider.*
First U.S. Edition: New York: Alfred A. Knopf, 1950.
NF/F: $385   **G/VG: $175**

_____. *The Angel of Darkness.*
First U.K. Edition: London: Jonathan Cape, 1991.
NF/F: $95   **G/VG: $30**
First U.S. Edition: New York: Ballantine Books, 1991.
NF/F: $75   **G/VG: $25**

*****Sachs, Nelly.** *O The Chimneys.*
First U.S. Edition: New York: Farrar, Straus and Giroux, 1967.
NF/F: $100   **G/VG: $35**

_____. *The Seeker and Other Poems.*
First U.S. Edition: New York: Farrar Straus Giroux, 1970.
NF/F: $65   **G/VG: $20**

Sagan, Francoise. *The Wonderful Clouds.*
First U.S. Edition: New York: E.P. Dutton, 1962.
NF/F: $75   **G/VG: $30**

Alain Robbe-Grillet.

Romain Rolland.

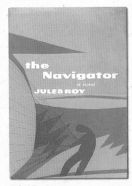

Jules Roy.

Jose Saramago.

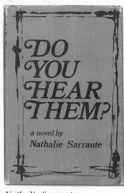

Nathalie Sarraute.

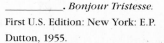

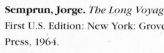

_____. *Bonjour Tristesse.*
First U.S. Edition: New York: E.P. Dutton, 1955.
NF/F: $125   **G/VG: $55**

Saramago, Jose. The Gospel According to Jesus Christ.
First U.S. Edition: New York: Harcourt Brace, 1994
NF/F: $95   **G/VG: $35**

_____. *Blindness.*
First U.S. Edition: New York: Harcourt Brace Jovanovich, 1997.
NF/F: $85   **G/VG: $30**

_____. *The Stone Raft.*
First U.S. Edition: New York: Harcourt Brace, 1995.
NF/F: $85   **G/VG: $25**

Sarraute, Nathalie. *Portrait of a Man Unknown.*
First U.S. Edition: New York: George Braziller, 1958.
NF/F: $125   **G/VG: $45**

_____. *Do You Hear Them?*
First U.S. Edition: New York: George Braziller, 1973.
NF/F: $65   **G/VG: $20**

Sartre, Jean-Paul. In The Mesh.
First U.K. Edition: London: Andrew Dakers, 1954.
NF/F: $185   **G/VG: $90**

_____. *The Diary Of Antoine Roquentin.*
First U.K. Edition: London: John Lehmann, 1949.
NF/F: $125   **G/VG: $70**
First U.S. Edition as *Nausea*: Norfolk, CT: New Directions, 1949.
NF/F: $115   **G/VG: $45**

_____. *The Chips are Down.*
First Edition in English: New York: Lear, 1948.
NF/F: $225   **G/VG: $110**
First U. K. Edition: London: Rider and Company, 1951.
NF/F: $200   **G/VG: $95**

Seferis, George. Three Secret Poems.
First Edition: Cambridge, MA: Harvard University Press, 1969.
NF/F: $65   **G/VG: $20**

_____. *The King of Asine.*
First Edition: London: John Lehmann, 1948.
NF/F: $150   **G/VG: $65**

Seifert, Jaroslav. Selected Poetry of Jaroslav Seifert.
First Edition: London: Andre Deutsch, 1986.
NF/F: $40   **G/VG: $15**
First U.S. Edition: New York: Macmillan, 1986.
NF/F: $25   **G/VG: $10**

Semprun, Jorge. *The Long Voyage.*
First U.S. Edition: New York: Grove Press, 1964.
NF/F: $95   **G/VG: $30**

Sholokhov, Mikhail. And Quiet Flows The Don.
First U.S. Edition: New York: Alfred A. Knopf, 1934.
NF/F: $65   **G/VG: $30**

_____. *Seeds of Tomorrow.*
First U.S. Edition: New York: Alfred A. Knopf, 1935.
NF/F: $70   **G/VG: $30**

_____. *Harvest on The Don.*
First U.K. Edition: London: G.P.
Putnams, 1960.
NF/F: $35　　　　　**G/VG: $20**
First U.S. Edition: New York: Alfred A.
Knopf, 1961.
NF/F: $35　　　　　**G/VG: $15**

*Sienkiewicz, Henryk. *Yanko the Musician and Other Stories.*
First U.S. Edition: Boston: Little Brown, 1893.
NF/F: $300　　　　　**G/VG: $100**

_____. *Quo Vadis?*
First U.S. Edition: Boston: Little Brown, 1896.
NF/F: $225　　　　　**G/VG: $95**

_____. *On The Bright Shore.*
First U.S. Edition: Boston: Little Brown, 1898.
NF/F: $50　　　　　**G/VG: $20**

*Sillanpaa, Frans Eemil. *Mid Silja: The History of the Last Offshoot of an Old Family Tree.*
First U.S. Edition: New York:
Macmillan, 1933.
NF/F: $45　　　　　**G/VG: $15**

_____. *People In the Summer Night. An Epic Suite.*
First U.S. Edition: Madison, WI: The
University of Wisconsin Press, 1966.
NF/F: $85　　　　　**G/VG: $25**

*Simon, Claude. *The Wind.*
First U.S. Edition: New York: George
Braziller, 1959.
NF/F: $70　　　　　**G/VG: $30**

_____. *The Palace.*
First U.S. Edition: New York: George
Braziller, 1963.
NF/F: $65　　　　　**G/VG: $20**

_____. *Triptych.*
First U.S. Edition: New York: Viking, 1976.
NF/F: $90　　　　　**G/VG: $30**

Sollers, Phillipe. *A Strange Solitude.*
First U.S. Edition: New York: Grove
Press Inc., 1959.
NF/F: $40　　　　　**G/VG: $15**

*Solzhenitsyn, Aleksandr I. *The Gulag Archipelago.*
First U.S. Edition: New York: Harper &
Row, 1974.
NF/F: $185　　　　　**G/VG: $75**

_____. *One Day In The Life Of Ivan Denisovich.*
First Edition in English: London: Victor
Gollancz, 1963.
NF/F: $300　　　　　**G/VG: $125**
First U.S. Edition: New York: Praeger, 1963.
NF/F: $200　　　　　**G/VG: $85**

_____. *Cancer Ward.* (Two
Volumes).
First U.K. Edition: London: Bodley
Head, 1968-69.
NF/F: $100　　　　　**G/VG: $35**

*Spitteler, Carl. *Selected Poems.*
First Edition: New York: Macmillan,
1928.
NF/F: $45　　　　　**G/VG: $15**

*Szymborska, Wislawa. *View with a Grain of Sand.*
First U.S. Edition: New York: Harcourt
Brace, 1995.
NF/F: $65　　　　　**G/VG: $25**

_____. *Poems New and Collected, 1957-1997.*
First Edition: New York: Harcourt
Brace & Company, 1998.
NF/F: $65　　　　　**G/VG: $20**

Taibo, Paco. *Leonardo's Bicycle.*
First U.S. Edition: New York:
Mysterious Press, 1995.
NF/F: $35　　　　　**G/VG: $15**

Claude Simon.

Wislawa Szymborska.

Paco Taibo.

Count Alexei Tolstoy.

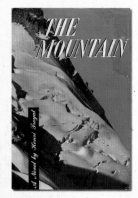

Henri Troyat.

Boris Vian.

_____. *An Easy Thing.*
First Edition: New York: Viking, 1990.
NF/F: $50   G/VG: $20

Teirlinck, Herman. *The Man in the Mirror.*
First Edition: London: Sythoff Leyden/
Heinemann, 1963.
NF/F: $30   G/VG: $10

Theotokas, George. *Leonis.*
First Edition: Minneapolis, MN: Nostos
Books, 1985.
NF/F: $25   G/VG: $10

Toller, Ernst. *Letters from Prison.*
First Edition in English: London John
Lane/The Bodley Head, 1936.
NF/F: $125   G/VG: $50

_____. *Pastor Hall: A Play In
Three Acts.*
First Edition of Stephen Spender
Translation: London: John Lane/The
Bodley Head, 1938.
NF/F: $150   G/VG: $55

Tolstoy, Count Alexei. *Tsar Fyodor
Ivanovitch.*
First U.S. Edition: New York:
Brentano's, 1922.
NF/F: $85   G/VG: $25

Troyat, Henri. *The Mountain.*
First U.S. Edition: New York: Simon &
Schuster, 1953.
NF/F: $65   G/VG: $20

**Tucholsky, Kurt (as by John
Heartfield).** *Deutschland,
Deutschland, Ÿber alles.*
First Edition in English: Amherst, MA:
University of Massachusetts Press,
1972.
NF/F: $145   G/VG: $65

*****Undset, Sigrid.** *Happy Times in
Norway.*
First U.S. Edition: New York: Alfred A.
Knopf, 1942.
NF/F: $65   G/VG: $25

_____. *The Faithful Wife.*
First U.S. Edition: New York: Alfred A.
Knopf, 1937.
NF/F: $95   G/VG: $30

_____. *The Bridal Wreath.*
First U.S. Edition: New York: Alfred A.
Knopf, 1929.
NF/F: $100   G/VG: $35

Vailland, Roger. *The Law.*
First U.K. Edition: London: Jonathan
Cape, 1958.
NF/F: $85   G/VG: $25

Valery, Paul. *The Graveyard by the
Sea.*
Limited Edition: London: Seker and
Warburg, 1946 (500 copies).
NF/F: $675   G/VG: $350
First U.S. Edition: Philadelphia, PA:
The Centaur Press, 1932.
NF/F: $325   G/VG: $100

Vian, Boris. *Heartsnatcher.*
First U.K. Edition: London: Rapp &
Whiting, 1968.
NF/F: $85   G/VG: $30

Vidale, Albert. *Moonlight Jewelers.*
First U.S. Edition: New York: Farrar,
Straus and Cudahy, 1958.
NF/F: $25   G/VG: $10

*Von Heidenstam, Verner. *The Charles Men.*
First U.K. Edition: London: Jonathan Cape, 1933.
NF/F: $100   **G/VG: $25**
First U.S. Edition: Boston: Merrymount Press, 1920.
NF/F: $85   **G/VG: $20**

_____. *The Tree of the Folkungs.*
First U.S. Edition: New York: Alfred A. Knopf, 1925.
NF/F: $80   **G/VG: $30**

Waltari, Mika. *The Egyptian.*
First U.S. Edition: New York: G.P. Putnams, 1949.
NF/F: $185   **G/VG: $65**

_____. *The Etruscan.*
First U.S. Edition: New York: G.P. Putnams, 1956.
NF/F: $85   **G/VG: $25**

Wasserman, Jacob. *Kerkhoven's Third Existence.*
First Edition: New York: Liveright Publishing Corp., 1934.
NF/F: $125   **G/VG: $40**

Weiss, Peter. *Bodies and Shadows.*
First U.S. Edition: New York: Delacorte Press A Seymour Lawrence Book, 1969.
NF/F: $45   **G/VG: $20**

Werfel, Franz. *The Song of Bernadette.*
First Edition: New York: Viking, 1942.
NF/F: $100   **G/VG: $35**

*Xingjian, Gao. *Soul Mountain.*
First Edition: New York: Harper Collins, 2000.
NF/F: $85   **G/VG: $30**

Yevtushenko, Yevgeny. *Stolen Apples.*
First U.S. Edition: New York: Doubleday & Company, 1971.
NF/F: $95   **G/VG: $35**

_____. *Wild Berries.* A Novel.
First U.S. Edition: New York: William Morrow, 1984.
NF/F: $45   **G/VG: $15**

Zweig, Arnold. *The Case of Sergeant Grischa.*
First U.S. Edition: New York: Viking Press, 1928.
NF/F: $95   **G/VG: $30**

Zweig, Stefan. *The Buried Candelabrum.*
First U.S. Edition: New York: Viking Press, 1937.
NF/F: $100   **G/VG: $35**

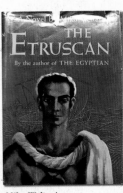

Mika Waltari.

Yevgeny Yevtushenko.

MODERN FIRST EDITIONS

Modern first editions are, perhaps, the largest category of book collecting. A general definition for the area is the first appearance of a work by a contemporary author.

Several dealers currently divide the field by centuries, a modern first having been published in the twentieth and now twenty-first century.

Authors who began publishing in the nineteenth may also be included if the bulk of their work was published in the twentieth. For example, James M. Barrie, H. G. Wells, and Arthur Conan Doyle all began their careers in the late nineteenth century, but continued well into the twentieth. The book might be a novel, a volume of poetry, a collection of essays, a short story omnibus, or even a play.

The field is basically collected by author, though I have seen some collections that cross over into other genres of collecting. Newer genres, such as fantasy or mystery, might be confined to modern firsts, and older genres such as religion or philosophy might be confined to the current century, though this is not very common.

Condition is of great importance to the collector of modern first editions. Small faults that might be overlooked in other areas of collecting are not tolerated by collectors of modern firsts. Even faults that might serve to enhance the value of a book in other areas, such as notes in the text by a prominent owner, devalue modern firsts.

Dust jackets are also very important as the vast majority of books published in the 20th century were originally issued with them.

The state comes into play as well with a greater emphasis than in other areas of collecting.

Later states are worth correspondingly less as they become further removed from the original state.

There are specialized areas to be dealt with in collecting modern firsts. A great many modern firsts were preceded by an advance reading copy, either as a corrected or uncorrected proof.

Some collectors prefer these as they are, in actuality, the first appearance of a work.

TEN CLASSIC RARITIES

Anderson, Sherwood. *Winesburg, Ohio. A Group of Tales of Ohio Small Town Life.*
New York: B.W. Huebsch, 1919.
First Edition, first issue, with line 5 of p. 86 reading "lay" and with broken type in "the" in line 3 of p. 251. Top edge stained yellow; map on front pastedown.
NF/F: $12,000   **G/VG: $3,000**

Bowles, Paul. *The Sheltering Sky.*
London: John Lehmann, 1949. Find this and more than sky will shelter you.
NF/F: $8,000   **G/VG: $3,500**

Buck Pearl S. *The Good Earth.*
New York: John Day Company, 1931. With "flees" for "fleas" on page 100.
NF/F: $6,000   **G/VG: $1,500**

Conrad, Joseph. *Lord Jim.*
Edinburgh and London: Blackwood, 1900. Originally issued in green card covers with thistle gilt on spine. First Issue, "anyrate" in line 5 of p. 77; 7 lines from the bottom of p. 226, there is no "keep" after "can"; also in the seventh line from the bottom of p. 226, it is "cure" instead of "cured"; in the last line of p. 319, "his" is out of alignment.
NF/F: $6,000   **G/VG: $2,200**

Durrell, Lawrence. *Pied Piper of Lovers.*
London: Cassell, 1935. Spine misprints title as 'Pied Pipers of Lovers.'
NF/F: $3,500   **G/VG: $1,200**

Faulkner, William. *The Sound and the Fury.*
New York: Jonathan Cape & Harrison Smith, 1929. Humanity Uprooted is priced at $300 on first state dust jacket.
NF/F: $45,000   **G/VG: $20,000**

Fitzgerald, F. Scott. *Tales of the Jazz Age.*
NY: Charles Scribner's Sons, 1922. "Published September, 1922 and Scribner's Seal" on the copyright page, with "and" for "an" on p. 232, line 6.
NF/F: $16,000   **G/VG: $7,000**

Mitchell, Margaret. *Gone with the Wind.*
New York: The Macmillan Company, 1936. Has "first published, May, 1936" on copyright page.
NF/F: $12,500   **G/VG: $7,000**

Steinbeck, John. *The Grapes of Wrath.*
NY: Viking, 1939. "First Edition" on lower corner of front dust jacket flap.
NF/F: $15,000   **G/VG: $6,500**

Wodehouse P.G. *The Pothunters.*
London: Adam and Charles Black, 1902. There are no advertisements in the first state.
NF/F: $5,000   **G/VG: $1,850**

William Faulkner.

F Scott Fitzgerald.

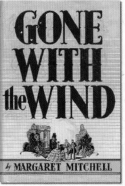

Margaret Mitchell.

PRICE GUIDE

Edward Abbey.

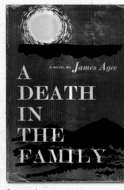

James Agee.

Nelson Algren.

Abbey, Edward. *The Monkey Wrench Gang.*
Limited Edition: Salt Lake City, UT: Dream Garden Press, 1985 (250 copies).
NF/F: $1,500   **G/VG: $725**
First Edition: Philadelphia, PA: J.B. Lippincott, 1975.
NF/F: $750   **G/VG: $200**

Abdullah, Achmed. *Steel and Jade.*
First Edition: New York: George H. Doran, 1927.
NF/F: $600   **G/VG: $150**

Acton, Harold. *Humdrum.*
First Edition: London: Chatto & Windus, 1928.
NF/F: $600   **G/VG: $250**

Ade, George. *The Old-Time Saloon.*
First Edition: New York: Ray Long & Richard R. Smith, 1931.
NF/F: $125   **G/VG: $45**

AE. *Voices of the Stones.*
First Edition: London: Macmillan, 1925.
NF/F: $100   **G/VG: $35**

Agee, James. *A Death in the Family.*
First Edition: New York: McDowell, Obolensky, 1957. Points of Issue: The title page is printed in blue and the first word on Page is "walking."
NF/F: $500   **G/VG: $200**

Aiken, Conrad. *King Coffin.*
First Edition: New York: Charles Scribner's Sons, 1935.
NF/F: $200   **G/VG: $65**

Albee, Edward. *All Over.*
First Edition: New York: Atheneum, 1971.
NF/F: $135   **G/VG: $50**

Aldrich, Bess Streeter. *Spring Came On Forever.*
First Edition: New York: D. Appleton, 1935.
NF/F: $75   **G/VG: $25**

Algren, Nelson. *The Man with the Golden Arm.*
First Edition: Garden City, NY: Doubleday, 1949. Points of Issue: The National Book Award sticker indicates a later issue.
NF/F: $800   **G/VG: $235**

Allen, Hervey. *Anthony Adverse.*
First Edition: New York: Farrar and Rinehart, 1933. Points of Issue: Page 352, line 6 "Zavier," page 397, line 22 "found found," page 1,086, line 18 "ship."
NF/F: $400   **G/VG: $150**

Amis, Kingsley. *Lucky Jim.*
First Edition: London: Victor Gollancz, 1953.
NF/F: $4,600   **G/VG: $1,800**

Anderson, Maxwell. *Winterset.*
First Edition: Washington: Anderson House, 1935.
NF/F: $125   **G/VG: $35**

Antin, Mary. *The Promised Land.*
First Edition: Boston: Houghton Mifflin, 1912.
NF/F: $135   **G/VG: $55**

Appel, Benjamin. *The Power House.*
First Edition: New York: E. P. Dutton, 1939.
NF/F: $650   **G/VG: $250**

Arlen, Michael J. *Man's Mortality.*
First Edition: London: William Heinemann, 1933.
NF/F: $275   **G/VG: $125**

Atherton, Gertrude. *Dido Queen of Hearts.*
First Edition: New York: Horace Liveright, 1929.
NF/F: $150   **G/VG: $65**

Auchincloss, Louis. *Portrait In Brownstone.*
First Edition: Boston: Houghton Mifflin, 1962.
NF/F: $125   **G/VG: $45**

Auden, W.H. *Collected Shorter Poems 1927-1957.*
First Edition: New York: Random House, 1966.
NF/F: $225   **G/VG: $80**

Auslander, Joseph. *Hell in Harness.*
First Edition: Garden City, NY: Doubleday Doran, 1929.
NF/F: $125   **G/VG: $45**

Austin, Mary. *The Land Of Journey's Ending.*
First Edition: New York: The Century Co., 1924.
NF/F: $400   **G/VG: $125**

Bacheller, Irving. *Uncle Peel.*
First Edition: New York: Fredrick Stokes, 1933.
NF/F: $95   **G/VG: $25**

Bacon, Leonard. *Guinea-Fowl and Other Poultry.*
First Edition: New York: Harper & Brothers, 1927.
NF/F: $100   **G/VG: $35**

Baker, Dorothy. *Young Man With A Horn..*
First Edition: Boston: Houghton Mifflin, 1938.
NF/F: $450   **G/VG: $165**

Baldwin, Faith. *Thresholds.*
First Edition: Boston: Small, Maynard, 1923.
NF/F: $350   **G/VG: $95**

Baldwin, James. *Just Above My Head.*
Limited Edition: New York: Dial Press, 1979 (500 copies).
NF/F: $400   **G/VG: $275**
First Edition: New York: Dial Press, 1979.
NF/F: $225   **G/VG: $95**

Bangs, John Kendrick. *The Foothills of Parnassus.*
First Edition: New York: Macmillan, 1914.
NF/F: $150   **G/VG: $55**

Barnes, Djuna. *Nightwood.*
First Edition: London: Faber and Faber, 1936.
NF/F: $800   **G/VG: $265**

Barth, John. *The Floating Opera.*
First Edition: New York: Appleton-Century Crofts, 1956.
NF/F: $450   **G/VG: $125**

Basso, Hamilton. *Beauregard: The Great Creole.*
First Edition: New York: Scribners, 1933.
NF/F: $250   **G/VG: $100**

Beach, Rex. *Flowing Gold.*
First Edition: New York & London: Harper & Brothers, 1922.
NF/F: $100   **G/VG: $40**

Behan, Brendan. *Borstal Boy.*
First Edition: London Hutchinson, 1958.
NF/F: $275   **G/VG: $95**

Joseph Auslander.

John Barth.

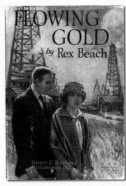

Rex Beach.

Maxwell Bodenheim.

Roark Bradford.

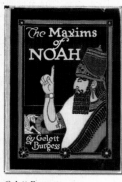

Gelett Burgess.

Belasco, David. *The Theatre Through Its Stage Door.*
First Edition: New York: Harper & Brothers, 1919.
NF/F: $150　　　　　**G/VG: $40**

Bellow, Saul. *Dangling Man.*
First Edition: New York: Vanguard, 1947.
NF/F: $3,100　　　　**G/VG: $1,400**

Bemelmans, Ludwig. *The Castle Number Nine.*
First Edition: New York: Viking Press, 1937.
NF/F: $225　　　　　**G/VG: $60**

Benchley, Robert. *No Poems. Or Around the World Backwards and Sideways.*
First Edition: New York: Harper & Brothers, 1932.
NF/F: $450　　　　　**G/VG: $150**

Benet, Stephen Vincent. *Young People's Pride.*
First Edition: New York: Henry Holt, 1922.
NF/F: $135　　　　　**G/VG: $50**

Bennett, Arnold. *Elsie and the Child: A Tale of Riceyman Steps and Other Stories.*
First Edition: London: Cassell and Company, 1924.
NF/F: $285　　　　　**G/VG: $100**

Bodenheim, Maxwell. *Ninth Avenue.*
First Edition: New York: Horace Liveright, 1926.
NF/F: $250　　　　　**G/VG: $85**

Boyle, Kay. *Primer for Combat.*
First Edition: New York: Simon and Schuster, 1942.
NF/F: $200　　　　　**G/VG: $75**

Bradford, Gamaliel. *Darwin.*
First Edition: Boston: Houghton Mifflin, 1926.
NF/F: $85　　　　　**G/VG: $30**

Bradford, Roark. *This Side of Jordan.*
First Edition: New York: Harper and Brothers, 1929.
NF/F: $350　　　　　**G/VG: $125**

Brautigan, Richard. *A Confederate General From Big Sur.*
First Edition: New York: Grove Press, 1964. Points of Issue: First state lacks Grove Presses usual "First Printing" on the verso.
NF/F: $600　　　　　**G/VG: $225**

Bromfield, Louis. *It Takes All Kinds.*
First Edition: New York: Harper & Brothers, 1939.
NF/F: $100　　　　　**G/VG: $40**

Broun, Heywood. *Gandle Follows His Nose.*
First Edition: New York: Boni & Liveright, 1926.
NF/F: $100　　　　　**G/VG: $35**

Buck, Pearl S. *The Promise.*
First Edition: New York: John Day, 1943.
NF/F: $75　　　　　**G/VG: $25**

Burgess, Gelett. *The Maxims of Noah. Derived from His Experience with Women Both Before and After the Flood as Given in Counsel to his Son Japhet.*
First Edition: New York: Frederick A. Stokes, 1913.
NF/F: $75　　　　　**G/VG: $35**

Byrne, Donn. *Destiny Bay.*
Limited Edition: Boston: Little, Brown,
1928 (365 copies).
NF/F: $400   **G/VG: $150**
First Edition: Boston: Little, Brown,
1928.
NF/F: $80   **G/VG: $15**

Cabell, Branch. *Smirt: An Urban
Nightmare.*
Limited Edition: New York: Robert
McBride, 1934 (153 copies).
NF/F: $250   **G/VG: Not Seen**
First Edition: New York: Robert
McBride, 1934.
NF/F: $135   **G/VG: $45**

Cable, George Washington. *Bylow
Hill.*
First Edition: New York: Scribners,
1902.
NF/F: $55   **G/VG: $20**

Caldwell, Erskine. *Kneel to the
Rising Sun.*
First Edition: New York: Viking Press,
1935.
NF/F: $300   **G/VG: $110**

Caldwell, Taylor. *The Final Hour.*
First Edition: New York: Scribners,
1944.
NF/F: $125   **G/VG: $45**

Canfield, Dorothy. *The Home-Maker.*
First Edition: New York: Harcourt,
Brace, 1924.
NF/F: $100   **G/VG: $30**

Capote, Truman. *Other Voices, Other
Rooms.*
First Edition: New York: Random
House, 1948.
NF/F: $1,600   **G/VG: $500**

Carver, Raymond. *Will You Please Be
Quiet, Please?*
First Edition: New York: McGraw-Hill
Book Co., 1976.
NF/F: $2,800   **G/VG: $1,000**

Cary, Joyce. *The Horse's Mouth.*
First Edition: London: Michael Joseph,
1944. Points of Issue: First state dust
jacket had "No. 7768" on front flap;
"No. 7769" on the back flap, and "No.
3170" on the back panel.
NF/F: $450   **G/VG: $185**

Cather, Willa. *Death Comes for the
Archbishop.* Limited Edition: New
York: Alfred A. Knopf, 1927 (175
copies).
NF/F: $3,550   **G/VG: $1,200**

Catton, Bruce. *Michigan: A
Bicentennial History.*
First Edition: New York: W.W. Norton
& Company, 1976.
NF/F: $50   **G/VG: $15**

Chambers, Robert W. *The Laughing
Girl.*
First Edition: New York: D. Appleton,
1918.
NF/F: $225   **G/VG: $85**

Chayefsky, Paddy. *The Tenth Man.*
First Edition: New York: Random
House, 1959.
NF/F: $95   **G/VG: $25**

Cheever, John. *The Way Some People
Live.*
First Edition: New York: Random
House, 1943.
NF/F: $1,700   **G/VG: $600**

Chesterton, G. K. *The Poet And The
Lunatics.*
First Edition: London: Cassell, 1929.
NF/F: $2,000   **G/VG: $800**

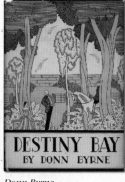

Donn Byrne.

Branch Cabell.

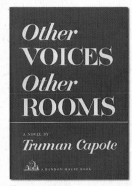

Truman Capote.

James Clavell.

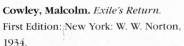

Evan S. Connell.

Harry Crews.

Ciardi, John. *Lives of X.*
First Edition: New Brunswick, NJ:
Rutgers University Press, 1971.
NF/F: $50   **G/VG: $15**

Clavell, James. *King Rat.*
First Edition: Boston: Little, Brown,
1962.
NF/F: $1,250   **G/VG: $400**

Cobb, Irvin S. *Faith, Hope, and Charity.*
First Edition: Indianapolis, IN: Bobbs
Merrill, 1934.
NF/F: $400   **G/VG: $125**

Connell, Evan S. *Mrs. Bridge.*
First Edition: New York.: Viking Press,
1959.
NF/F: $350   **G/VG: $125**

Connelly, Marc. *The Green Pastures.*
First Edition: New York: Farrar &
Rinehart, 1929.
NF/F: $350   **G/VG: $100**

Conrad, Joseph. *The Rover.*
Limited Edition: Garden City, New
York, Doubleday, Page, 1923 (377
copies).
NF/F: $1,500   **G/VG: Not Seen**
First Edition: Garden City, New York,
Doubleday, Page, 1923.
NF/F: $700   **G/VG: $225**

Cowley, Malcolm. *Exile's Return.*
First Edition: New York: W. W. Norton,
1934.
NF/F: $950   **G/VG: $300**

Cozzens, James Gould. *Ask Me Tomorrow.*
First Edition: New York: Harcourt,
Brace and Company, 1940.
NF/F: $150   **G/VG: $55**

Crane, Nathalia. *Venus Invisible and Other Poems.*
First Edition: New York: Coward-
McCann, 1928.
NF/F: $75   **G/VG: $15**

Crews, Harry. *The Gospel Singer.*
First Edition: New York: William
Morrow & Company, 1968.
NF/F: $1,250   **G/VG: $350**

Curwood, James Oliver. *The Flaming Forest.*
First Edition: New York: Cosmopolitan,
1921.
NF/F: $175   **G/VG: $65**

Dahl, Roald. *My Uncle Oswald.*
First Edition: London: Michael Joseph,
1979.
NF/F: $150   **G/VG: $65**

Dahlberg, Edward. *Do These Bones Live.*
First Edition: New York: Harcourt,
Brace, 1941.
NF/F: $225   **G/VG: $75**

Davies, W.H. *The Autobiography of a Super-Tramp.*
First Edition: London: A.C. Fifield,
1908.
NF/F: $400   **G/VG: $150**

Davis, Clyde Brion. *The Great American Novel.*
First Edition: New York: Farrar &
Rinehart, 1938.
NF/F: $95   **G/VG: $20**

Davis, H. L. *Honey in the Horn.*
First Edition: New York: Harper and
Brothers, 1935. Points of issue: Has
Harper date code "M – I."
NF/F: $600   **G/VG: $200**

Davis, Richard Harding. *With the Allies.*
First Edition: New York: Charles Scribner's Sons, 1914.
NF/F: $95   **G/VG: $35**

Day, Clarence. *This Simian World.*
First Edition: New York: Alfred A. Knopf, 1920.
NF/F: $100   **G/VG: $30**

Day-Lewis, Cecil. *The Magnetic Mountain.*
Limited Edition: London: Leonard and Virginia Woolf at the Hogarth Press, 1933 (100 copies).
NF/F: $850   **G/VG: $325**

De La Mare, Walter. *Memoirs of a Midget.*
First Edition: London: Collins, 1921.
NF/F: $250   **G/VG: $100**

De La Roche, Mazo. *The Building of Jalna.*
First Edition: Boston: Atlantic Little Brown, 1944.
NF/F: $75   **G/VG: $30**

Dell, Floyd. *King Arthur's Socks And Other Village Plays.*
First Edition: New York: Alfred A. Knopf, 1922.
NF/F: $85   **G/VG: $30**

Derleth, August. *Sac Prairie People.*
First Edition: Sauk City, WI: Stanton & Lee, 1948.
NF/F: $200   **G/VG: $85**

DeVries, Peter. *But Who Wakes The Bugler?*
First Edition: Boston: Houghton Mifflin, 1940.
NF/F: $825   **G/VG: $350**

Dickey, James. *Deliverance.*
First Edition: Boston: Houghton Mifflin, 1970. Points of Issue: First state of dust Jacket carries 6-84530 on rear flap.
NF/F: $425   **G/VG: $100**

Di Donato, Pietro. *Christ in Concrete.*
First Edition: Chicago: Esquire, 1937.
NF/F: $160   **G/VG: $40**

Dixon, Thomas. *Companions.*
First Edition: New York: Otis Publishing Corporation, 1931.
NF/F: $185   **G/VG: $55**

Donleavy, J. P. *A Singular Man.*
First Edition: London: Bodley Head, 1964.
NF/F: $165   **G/VG: $50**

Doolittle, Hilda (as by H.D.). *Palimpsest.*
Limited Edition: Boston: Houghton Mifflin, 1926 (700 copies).
NF/F: $675   **G/VG: $150**
First Edition: Boston: Houghton Mifflin, 1926.
NF/F: $400   **G/VG: $100**

Dos Passos, John. The U. S. A. Trilogy:

_____. *The 42nd Parallel.*
First Edition: New York: Harcourt, Brace, 1930.
NF/F: $1,600   **G/VG: $550**

_____. *1919.*
First Edition: New York: Harcourt, Brace, 1932.
NF/F: $500   **G/VG: $200**

_____. *Big Money.*
First Edition: New York: Harcourt, Brace, 1936.
NF/F: $250   **G/VG: $80**

Walter De La Mare.

Peter DeVries.

James Dickey.

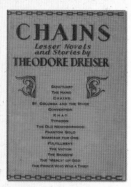

Theodore Dreiser.

Allen Drury.

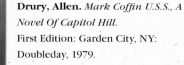

Daphne Du Maurier.

Douglas, Keith. *Alamein to Zem Zem - with Poems and Drawings.*
First Edition: London: Editions Poetry, 1946.
NF/F: $300   **G/VG: $105**

Douglas, Lloyd C. *The Robe.*
First Edition: Boston: Houghton Mifflin, 1942.
NF/F: $550   **G/VG: $180**

Dreiser, Theodore. *Chains Lesser Novels and Stories.*
First Edition: New York: Boni & Liveright, 1927.
NF/F: $400   **G/VG: $135**

Drury, Allen. *Mark Coffin U.S.S., A Novel Of Capitol Hill.*
First Edition: Garden City, NY: Doubleday, 1979.
NF/F: $55   **G/VG: $15**

Du Maurier, Daphne. *Rebecca.*
First Edition: London: Victor Gollancz, 1938.
NF/F: $4,200   **G/VG: $1,100**

Durrell, Lawrence. *A Private Country.*
First Edition: London: Faber & Faber, 1943.
NF/F: $400   **G/VG: $140**

_____. Alexandria Quartet:

_____. *Justine.*
First Edition: London: Faber & Faber, 1957.
Points of Issue: First state dust jacket lacks review by Gerald Sykes on front flap.
NF/F: $1,250   **G/VG: $575**

_____. *Balthazar.*
First Edition: London: Faber & Faber, 1958.
NF/F: $550   **G/VG: $200**

_____. *Mountolive.*
First Edition: London: Faber & Faber, 1958.
NF/F: $550   **G/VG: $250**

_____. *Clea.*
First Edition: London: Faber & Faber, 1960.
NF/F: $225   **G/VG: $100**

_____. Avignon Quintet:

_____. *Monsieur: or, The Prince of Darkness.*
First Edition: London: Faber & Faber, 1974.
NF/F: $200   **G/VG: $75**

_____. *Livia: or Buried Alive.*
First Edition: London: Faber & Faber, 1978.
NF/F: $350   **G/VG: $150**

_____. *Constance: or, Solitary Practices.*
First Edition: London: Faber & Faber, 1982.
NF/F: $85   **G/VG: $35**

_____. *Sebastian: or, Ruling Passions.*
First Edition: London: Faber & Faber, 1983.
NF/F: $75   **G/VG: $25**

_____. *Quinx: or, The Ripper's Tale.*
First Edition: London: Faber & Faber, 1985.
NF/F: $50   **G/VG: $20**

Eastlake, William. *Go In Beauty.*
First Edition: New York: Harper &
Brothers, 1956.
NF/F: $600   **G/VG: $135**

Edmonds, Walter D. *Chad Hanna.*
First Edition: Boston: Little Brown,
1940.
NF/F: $85   **G/VG: $25**

Eliot, T. S. *Old Possum's Book of
Practical Cats.*
First Edition: London: Faber and Faber,
1939.
NF/F: $3,500   **G/VG: $1,500**

Ellison, Ralph. *Shadow & Act.*
First Edition: New York : Random
House, 1964.
NF/F: $300   **G/VG: $95**

Farrell, James T. *Tommy Gallagher's
Crusade.*
First Edition: New York: Vanguard
Press, 1939.
NF/F: $165   **G/VG: $65**

Faulkner, William. *Go Down Moses.*
Limited Edition: New York: Random
House, 1942 (100 copies).
NF/F: $26,500   **G/VG: Not Seen**
First Edition: New York: Random
House, 1942.
Points of Issue: First state is black cloth
with a red topstain.
NF/F: $6,800   **G/VG: $2,400**

Ferber, Edna. *The Saratoga Trunk.*
First Edition: Garden City: Doubleday
Doran, 1941.
NF/F: $250   **G/VG: $65**

Fergusson, Harvey. *The Conquest of
Don Pedro.*
First Edition: New York: William
Morrow, 1954.
NF/F: $100   **G/VG: $30**

Ferlinghetti, Lawrence. *A Far
Rockaway of the Heart.*
First Edition: New York: New
Directions, 1997.
NF/F: $80   **G/VG: $25**

Firbank, Ronald. *Valmouth.*
First Edition: London: Grant Richards,
1919.
NF/F: $1,000   **G/VG: $275**

Fisher, Vardis. *Sonnets to an
Imaginary Madonna.*
First Edition: New York: Harold Vinal,
1927.
NF/F: $550   **G/VG: $185**

Fitzgerald, F. Scott. *Taps At Reveille.*
First Edition: New York: Scribners,
1935. Points of Issue: Page 51, lines 29-
30 "Oh, catch it – oh, catch it."
NF/F: $6,300   **G/VG: $2,800**

Forster, E.M. *A Room with a View.*
First Edition: London: Edwin Arnold,
1908.
NF/F: $600   **G/VG: $185**

Fowles, John. *The Collector.*
First Edition: London: Jonathan Cape,
1963. Points of Issue: The first state
dust jacket carries no reviews on the
front flap.
NF/F: $1,600   **G/VG: $600**

Frank, Waldo. *The Bridegroom
Cometh.*
First Edition: Garden City, NY:
Doubleday, 1939.
NF/F: $85   **G/VG: $25**

Freeman, Mary E. Wilkins. *The
Debtor.*
First Edition: New York: Harper &
Brothers, 1905.
NF/F: $375   **G/VG: $100**

William Eastlake.

T. S. Eliot.

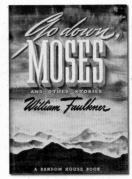

William Faulkner.

Zona Gale.

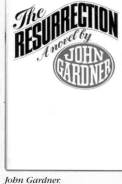

John Gardner.

Paul Goodman.

Gale, Zona. *Borgia.*
First Edition: New York: Alfred A.
Knopf, 1929.
NF/F: $125   G/VG: $65

Gardner, John. *The Resurrection.*
First Edition: New York: New
American Library, 1966.
NF/F: $1,400   G/VG: $600

Glasgow, Ellen. *The Builders.*
First Edition: Garden City, NY:
Doubleday, Page, 1919.
NF/F: $550   G/VG: $150

Gold, Herbert. *Birth Of A Hero.*
First Edition: New York: Viking, 1951.
NF/F: $100   G/VG: $35

Golding, William. *The Brass Butterfly.*
First Edition: London: Faber & Faber,
1958.
NF/F: $350   G/VG: $145

Goldman, William. *Tinsel.*
First Edition: New York: Delacorte,
1978.
NF/F: $35   G/VG: $10

Goodman, Paul. *The Empire City.*
First Edition: Indianapolis: Bobbs-
Merrill, 1959.
NF/F: $135   G/VG: $40

Goyen, William. *Come, the Restorer.*
First Edition: Garden City, NY:
Doubleday, 1974.
NF/F: $75   G/VG: $30

Grau, Shirley Ann. *The Keepers of the House.*
First Edition: New York: Alfred A.
Knopf, 1964.
NF/F: $145   G/VG: $40

Guthrie, A. B. *The Big Sky.*
First Edition: Boston: Houghton
Mifflin, 1947.
NF/F: $750   G/VG: $245

Haggard, H. Rider. *Belshazzar.*
First Edition: London: Stanley Paul,
1930.
NF/F: $1,800   G/VG: $600

Halper, Albert. *The Golden Watch.*
First Edition: New York: Henry Holt,
1953.
NF/F: $40   G/VG: $15

Harris, Mark. *The Southpaw.*
First Edition: Indianapolis: Bobbs
Merrill, 1953.
NF/F: $375   G/VG: $135

Harris, Thomas. *Red Dragon.*
First Edition: New York: Putnam, 1981.
NF/F: $300   G/VG: $95

Heller, Joseph. *Catch 22.*
First Edition: New York: Simon and
Schuster, 1961. Points of Issue: First
state dust jacket carries no reviews on
the back panel.
NF/F: $5,400   G/VG: $1,400

Hellman, Lillian. *Watch On The Rhine.*
Limited Edition: New York: Privately
Printed, 1942 (349 copies).
Points of Issue: Foreword by Dorothy
Parker.
NF/F: $2,500   G/VG: $450
First Edition: New York: Random
House, 1941.
NF/F: $300   G/VG: $85

Hemingway, Ernest. *The Torrents of Spring.*
First Edition: New York: Scribners,
1926.
NF/F: $9,200   G/VG: $2,800

Henry, O. *Postscripts.*
First Edition: New York: Harper &
Brothers, 1923. Points of Issue: The
first state is red cloth stamped in gilt.
NF/F: $400   **G/VG: $115**

Hergesheimer, Joseph. *The
Limestone Tree.*
First Edition: New York: Alfred A.
Knopf, 1931.
NF/F: $140   **G/VG: $40**

Hersey, John. *Antonietta.*
First Edition: New York: Alfred A.
Knopf, 1991.
NF/F: $95   **G/VG: $25**

Hilton, James. *Nothing So Strange.*
First Edition: Boston: Little, Brown,
1947.
NF/F: $150   **G/VG: $35**

Hough, Emerson. *Mother of Gold.*
First Edition: New York: D. Appleton,
1924.
NF/F: $95   **G/VG: $30**

Howells, W. D. *Between the Dark
and the Daylight: Romances.*
First Edition: New York: Harper &
Brothers, 1907. Points of Issue: First
state is green cloth stamped in gilt.
NF/F: $175   **G/VG: $55**

Hughes, Langston. *Fine Clothes To
The Jew.*
First Edition: New York: Alfred A.
Knopf, 1927.
NF/F: $2,500   **G/VG: $950**

Hughes, Rupert. *Within These Walls.*
First Edition: New York: Harper &
Brothers, 1923.
NF/F: $125   **G/VG: $35**

Huneker, James. *Ivory Apes And
Peacocks.*
First Edition: New York: Scribners,
1915.
NF/F: $85   **G/VG: $25**

Hunter, Evan. *The Blackboard
Jungle.*
First Edition: New York: Simon &
Schuster, 1954.
NF/F: $350   **G/VG: $85**

Hurst, Fannie. *Great Laughter.*
First Edition: New York: Harper
& Brothers, 1936. Points of Issue:
Harper's date code is "I – L."
NF/F: $500   **G/VG: $130**

Hurston, Zora Neale. *Jonah's Gourd
Vine.*
First Edition: Philadelphia: J.B.
Lippincott, 1934.
NF/F: $2,500   **G/VG: $500**

Huxley, Aldous. *Ape and Essence.*
First Edition: London: Chatto &
Windus, 1949.
NF/F: $125   **G/VG: $35**

Irving, John. *The Water-Method Man.*
First Edition: New York: Random
House, 1972.
NF/F: $945   **G/VG: $210**

Isherwood, Christopher. *Sally
Bowles.*
First Edition: London: The Hogarth
Press, 1937.
NF/F: $1,400   **G/VG: $450**

Jackson, Charles. *The Lost Weekend.*
First Edition: New York: Farrar &
Rinehart, 1944.
NF/F: $675   **G/VG: $160**

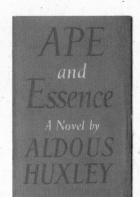
Emerson Hough.

Aldous Huxley.

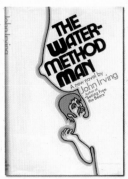
John Irving.

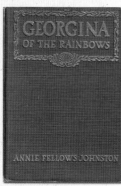

Annie Fellows Johnston.

Garson Kanin.

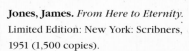

William Kennedy.

Jackson. Shirley. *The Road through the Wall.*
First Edition: New York: Farrar, Straus, 1948.
NF/F: $1,050   **G/VG: $275**

Janvier, Thomas. *Santa Fe's Partner.*
First Edition: New York: Harper & Brothers, 1907.
NF/F: $65   **G/VG: $25**

Jarrell, Randall. *Blood for a Stranger.*
First Edition: New York: Harcourt, Brace, 1942.
NF/F: $1,000   **G/VG: $285**

Jeffers, Robinson. *Solstice and Other Poems.*
First Edition: New York: Random House, 1935.
NF/F: $550   **G/VG: $200**

Johnston, Annie Fellows. *Georgina of the Rainbows.*
First Edition: New York: Britton Publishing, 1916.
NF/F: $150   **G/VG: $50**

Johnston, Mary. *The Exile.*
First Edition: Boston: Little, Brown, 1927.
NF/F: $135   **G/VG: $35**

Jones, James. *From Here to Eternity.*
Limited Edition: New York: Scribners, 1951 (1,500 copies).
NF/F: $1,500   **G/VG: $700**
First Edition: New York: Scribners, 1951.
Points of Issue: The first state dust jacket has a photo of Jones on the back panel.
NF/F: $800   **G/VG: $150**

Kanin, Garson. *Do Re Mi.*
First Edition: Boston: Little, Brown, 1955.
NF/F: $125   **G/VG: $35**

Kantor, MacKinlay. *God and My Country.*
First Edition: Cleveland, OH: World Publishing, 1954.
NF/F: $120   **G/VG: $35**

Kazan, Elia. *America America.*
First Edition: New York: Stein and Day, 1962.
NF/F: $65   **G/VG: $20**

Kelland, Clarence Buddington. *The Sinister Strangers.*
First Edition: New York: Dodd, Mead, 1961.
NF/F: $55   **G/VG: $15**

Kennedy, William. The Albany Cycle:

_____. *Legs.*
First Edition: New York: Viking, 1975.
NF/F: $275   **G/VG: $100**

_____. *Billy Phelan's Greatest Game.*
First Edition: New York: Viking, 1978.
NF/F: $250   **G/VG: $85**

_____. *Ironweed.*
First Edition: New York: Viking, 1983.
NF/F: $500   **G/VG: $140**

Kerouac, Jack. *On the Road.*
First Edition: New York: Viking, 1957.
Points of Issue: The first state dust jacket has a photo of Kerouac on the back panel.
NF/F: $18,000   **G/VG: $6,000**

Kesey, Ken. *One Flew Over the Cuckoo's Nest.*
First Edition: New York: Viking, 1962.
NF/F: $9,000   **G/VG: $2,700**

Kerr, Jean. *The Snake Has All The Lines.*
First Edition: Garden City, NY: Doubleday, 1960.
NF/F: $50   **G/VG: $15**

Kipling, Rudyard. *Puck of Pook's Hill.*
First Edition: London: Macmillan & Co., 1906.
NF/F: $1,200   **G/VG: $400**

Knowles, John. *A Separate Peace.*
First Edition: London: Secker & Warburg, 1959.
NF/F: $1,600   **G/VG: $500**

Kotzwinkle, William. *The Fan Man.*
First Edition: New York: Harmony Books, 1974.
NF/F: $100   **G/VG: $30**

Kyne, Peter B. *Cappy Ricks Retires.*
First Edition: New York: Cosmopolitan, 1922.
NF/F: $150   **G/VG: $35**

La Farge, Oliver. *The Enemy Gods.*
First Edition: Boston: Houghton Mifflin Company, 1937.
NF/F: $125   **G/VG: $35**

Lardner, Ring. *Lose With A Smile.*
First Edition: New York: Scribner's, 1933.
NF/F: $450   **G/VG: $125**

Lawrence, D. H. *Fantasia of the Unconscious.*
First Edition: New York: Thomas Seltzer, 1922.
NF/F: $1,400   **G/VG: $325**

Leacock, Stephen. *Winsome Winnie and Other New Nonsense Novels.*
First Edition: New York: John Lane, 1920.
NF/F: $225   **G/VG: $50**

Le Gallienne, Richard. *There Was a Ship.*
First Edition: Garden City, NY: Doubleday Doran, 1930. Points of Issue: Dust jacket and frontispiece by Erte.
NF/F: $75   **G/VG: $25**

Lessing, Doris. *The Grass is Singing.*
First Edition: London, Michael Joseph, 1950. Points of Issue: First issue had a band over the dust jacket advertising that the book was a Daily Graphic pick of the month.
NF/F: $500   **G/VG: $100**

Levertov, Denise as by Denise Levertoff. *The Double Image.*
First Edition: London: The Cresset Press, 1946.
NF/F: $425   **G/VG: $150**

Levin, Meyer. *Citizens.*
First Edition: New York: Viking, 1940.
NF/F: $180   **G/VG: $30**

Lewis, Sinclair. *Elmer Gantry.*
Points of Issue: The spine of the first state substitutes a "C" for the "G" in "Gantry."
First Edition: New York: Harcourt Brace, 1927.
NF/F: $4,200   **G/VG: $950**

Lewis, Wyndham. *The Apes of God.*
First Edition: London: Arthur Press, 1930 (750 copies).
NF/F: $1,000   **G/VG: $400**
First Trade Edition: London: Nash & Grayson, 1931.
NF/F: $350   **G/VG: $95**

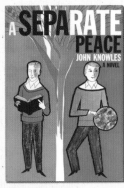
John Knowles.

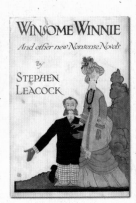
Stephen Leacock.

Sinclair Lewis.

Ludwig Lewisohn.

Ik Marvel.

Harold MacGrath.

Lewisohn, Ludwig. *Israel.*
First Edition: New York: Boni &
Liveright, 1925.
NF/F: $100   **G/VG: $35**

Liebling, A. J. *The Telephone Booth
Indian.*
First Edition: Garden City, NY:
Doubleday Doran, 1942.
NF/F: $300   **G/VG: $95**

Lockridge, Ross. *Raintree County.*
First Edition: Boston: Houghton
Mifflin, 1948.
NF/F: $350   **G/VG: $55**

Loos, Anita. *Gentlemen Prefer
Blondes.*
First Edition: New York: Boni and
Liveright, 1925.
NF/F: $1,250   **G/VG: $300**

Marvel, Ik. *Reveries of a Bachelor.*
First Edition: Indianapolis, IN: Bobbs
Merrill, 1906.
NF/F: $115   **G/VG: $30**

McCarthy, Mary. *The Company She
Keeps.*
First Edition: New York: Simon and
Schuster, 1942.
NF/F: $325   **G/VG: $65**

Machen, Arthur. *The Hill of Dreams.*
First Edition: London: Grant Richards,
1907.
NF/F: $950   **G/VG: $400**

McCullers, Carson. *The Heart is a
Lonely Hunter.*
First Edition: Boston: Houghton
Mifflin, 1940.
NF/F: $3,500   **G/VG: $850**

McCutcheon, George Barr. Graustark
Series:

_____. *Graustark: The Story of
a Love Behind a Throne.*
First Edition: Chicago: Herbert S. Stone
and Company, 1901. Points of Issue:
Page 150, line 6 reads "Noble's."
NF/F: $300   **G/VG: $55**

_____. *Beverly of Graustark.*
First Edition: New York: Dodd, Mead, 1904.
Points of Issue: Title page reads "Harris N Fisher."
NF/F: $325   **G/VG: $125**

_____. *Truxton King: A Story of
Graustark.*
First Ed: New York: Dodd, Mead, 1909.
NF/F: $175   **G/VG: $85**

_____. *The Prince of Graustark.*
Limited Edition: New York: Dodd,
Mead, 1914 (40 copies).
NF/F: $850   **G/VG: $400**
First Edition: New York: Dodd, Mead, 1914.
NF/F: $200   **G/VG: $85**

_____. *East of the Setting Sun.*
First Edition: New York: Dodd, Mead, 1924.
NF/F: $95   **G/VG: $30**

_____. *The Inn of the Hawk
and Raven.*
First Edition: New York: Dodd, Mead, 1927.
NF/F: $135   **G/VG: $55**

McFee, William. *Command.*
First Edition: Garden City, NY:
Doubleday Page, 1922. Points of Issue:
Page 185, line 31 reads "through thim"
in first state.
NF/F: $100   **G/VG: $25**

MacGrath, Harold. *The Goose Girl.*
First Edition: Indianapolis, IN: Bobbs-
Merrill, 1909.
NF/F: $350   **G/VG: $75**

McKenney, Ruth. *Mirage.*
First Edition: New York: Farrar, Strauss
and Cudahy, 1956.
NF/F: $50   **G/VG: $15**

Mailer, Norman. *The Naked and the
Dead.*
First Edition: New York: Rinehart,
1948.
NF/F: $3,500   **G/VG: $600**

Malamud, Bernard. *The Natural.*
First Edition: New York: Harcourt,
Brace, 1952. Points of Issue: First Issue
is considered either red or blue cloth
with gray second state.
NF/F: $5,200   **G/VG: $1100**

Marquand, John P. *Repent in Haste.*
First Edition: Boston: Little Brown,
1945.
NF/F: $95   **G/VG: $25**

Marquis, Don. *Chapters for the
Orthodox.*
First Edition: Garden City, NY:
Doubleday Doran, 1934.
NF/F: $120   **G/VG: $25**

Matthiessen, Peter. *Race Rock.*
First Edition: New York: Harper &
Brothers, 1954.
NF/F: $700   **G/VG: $185**

Maugham, W. Somerset. *The Narrow
Corner.*
First Edition: London: Heinemann,
1932.
NF/F: $450   **G/VG: $125**

Mencken, H. L. *Making a President/
A Footnote to the Saga of Democracy.*
First Edition: New York: Alfred A.
Knopf, 1932.
NF/F: $525   **G/VG: $150**

Michener, James. *The Fires of Spring.*
First Edition: New York: Random
House, 1949.
NF/F: $1,800   **G/VG: $400**

Milne, A. A. *The Ivory Door.*
First Edition: London: Chatto &
Windus, 1929.
NF/F: $300   **G/VG: $95**

Morley, Christopher. *Seacoast of
Bohemia.*
Limited Edition: Garden City, NY:
Doubleday Doran for the Old Realto
Theater, 1929 (50 copies). Points of
Issue: Contains a postcard signed by
Morley.
NF/F: $400   **G/VG: $165**
First Edition: Garden City, NY:
Doubleday Doran, 1929. Points of
Issue: Page 20, line 19 reads "rarely" in
first state.
NF/F: $100   **G/VG: $25**

Morrison, Toni. *Sula.*
First Edition: New York: Alfred A.
Knopf, 1974.
NF/F: $1,050   **G/VG: $225**

Morris, Wright. *My Uncle Dudley.*
First Edition: New York: Harcourt
Brace, 1942.
NF/F: $1400   **G/VG: $350**

Mowatt, Farley. *Sibir.*
First Edition: Toronto: McClelland &
Stewart, 1970.
NF/F: $65   **G/VG: $15**

Murdoch, Iris. *The Flight from the
Enchanter.*
First Edition: London: Chatto &
Windus, 1956.
NF/F: $1,500   **G/VG: $450**

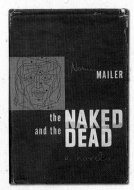

Norman Mailer.

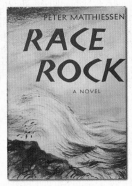

Peter Matthiessen.

H. L. Mencken.

Flannery O'Connor.

John O'Hara.

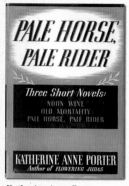

Katherine Anne Porter.

Nabokov, Vladimir. *Bend Sinister.* First Edition: New York: Henry Holt, 1947.
NF/F: $450   **G/VG: $125**

Naipaul, Shiva. *Fireflies.* First Edition: London: Andre Deutsch, 1970.
NF/F: $250   **G/VG: $75**

Nathan, George Jean. *Monks Are Monks: A Diagnostic Scherzo.* First Edition: New York: Alfred A. Knopf, 1929.
NF/F: $80   **G/VG: $20**

Nathan, Robert. *Portrait of Jennie.* First Edition: New York: Alfred A. Knopf, 1940. Points of Issue: First state has "Stuart" page 29, line 5 and "onght" page 171, line 14.
NF/F: $275   **G/VG: $90**

Nemerov, Harold. *The Homecoming Game.* First Edition: New York: Simon and Schuster, 1957.
NF/F: $95   **G/VG: $25**

O'Casey, Sean. *The Green Crow.* First Editon: New York: George Braziller, 1956.
NF/F: $65   **G/VG: $20**

O'Connor, Flannery. *Wise Blood.* First Edition: New York: Harcourt, Brace, 1952.
NF/F: $9,200   **G/VG: $2,600**

Odets, Clifford. *The Country Girl.* First Edition: New York: Viking, 1951.
NF/F: $125   **G/VG: $35**

O'Hara, John. *Butterfield 8.* First Edition: New York: Harcourt Brace, 1935.
NF/F: $2,400   **G/VG: $400**

Orwell, George. *Animal Farm.* First Edition: London, Secker & Warburg, 1945.
NF/F: $4,100   **G/VG: $1,100**

Parker, Dorothy. *Enough Rope.* First Edition: New York: Boni & Liveright, 1926.
NF/F: $775   **G/VG: $250**

Parrish, Anne. *The Methodist Faun.* First Edition: New York: Harper & Brothers, 1929.
NF/F: $100   **G/VG: $30**

Percy, Walker. *Early Architecture of Delaware.* First Edition: New York: Farrar, Straus & Giroux, 1966.
NF/F: $500   **G/VG: $125**

Perelman, S. J. *The Road to Miltown or Under the Spreading Atrophy.* First Edition: New York: Simon & Schuster, 1957.
NF/F: $120   **G/VG: $20**

Peterkin, Julia. *Black April.* First Edition: Indianapolis: Bobbs Merrill, 1927.
NF/F: $500   **G/VG: $165**

Porter, Katherine Anne. *Pale Horse, Pale Rider.* First Edition: New York: Harcourt Brace, 1939.
NF/F: $400   **G/VG: $85**

Powys, John Cowper. *Visions and Revisions.* First Edition: London & New York: William Rider and G. Arnold Shaw, 1915.
NF/F: $175   **G/VG: $45**

Powys, Llewelyn. *Ebony and Ivory.*
First Edition: London: Grant Richards,
1923.
NF/F: $185   **G/VG: $50**

Powys, T. F. *Unclay.*
Limited Edition: London: Chatto &
Windus, 1931 (160 copies).
NF/F: $725   **G/VG: $250**
First Edition: London: Chatto &
Windus, 1931.
NF/F: $225   **G/VG: $65**

Purdy, James. *The Color of Darkness.*
First Edition: Norfolk, CT: New
Directions, 1957.
NF/F: $95   **G/VG: $25**

Pyle, Ernie. *Home Country.*
First Edition: New York: William
Sloane, 1947.
NF/F: $45   **G/VG: $10**

Rand, Ayn. *We the Living.*
First Edition: London Cassell, 1936.
NF/F: $6,500   **G/VG: $1,800**

Rawlings, Marjorie Kinnan. *Golden
Apples.*
First Edition: New York: Scribner's, 1935.
NF/F: $650   **G/VG: $135**

Read, Opie. *The New Mr. Howerson.*
First Edition: Chicago: Reilly & Britton,
1914.
NF/F: $65   **G/VG: $15**

Richter, Conrad. The Awakening
Land Series:

_____. *The Trees.*
First Edition: New York: Random
House, 1940.
NF/F: $200   **G/VG: $50**

Limited Edition: New York: Alfred A.
Knopf, 1940 (255 copies).
NF/F: $150   **G/VG: $55**

_____. *The Fields.*
First Edition: New York: Alfred A.
Knopf, 1946.
NF/F: $85   **G/VG: $20**

_____. *The Town.*
First Edition: New York: Alfred A.
Knopf, 1946.
NF/F: $300   **G/VG: $95**

Rives, Amelie. *World's End.*
First Edition: New York: Frederick A.
Stokes, 1914.
NF/F: $45   **G/VG: $15**

Robbins, Harold. *A Stone for Danny
Fisher.*
First Edition: New York: Alfred A.
Knopf, 1952.
NF/F: $400   **G/VG: $130**

Roberts, Kenneth. *Rabble In Arms.*
First Edition: Garden City, NY:
Doubleday Doran, 1933.
NF/F: $145   **G/VG: $35**

Rosten, Leo, as by Leonard Q. Ross.
Education of Hyman Kaplan.
First Edition: New York: Harcourt
Brace, 1937.
NF/F: $135   **G/VG: $25**

Roth, Philip. *Goodbye, Columbus
And Five Short Stories.*
First Edition: Boston: Houghton
Mifflin, 1959.
NF/F: $1000   **G/VG: $250**

Ruark, Robert. *Something of Value.*
First Edition: Garden City, NY:
Doubleday, 1955.
NF/F: $225   **G/VG: $55**

James Purdy

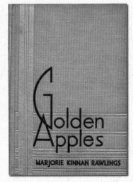
Marjorie Kinnan Rawlings.

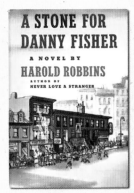
Harold Robbins.

William Saroyan.

Budd Schulberg.

Irwin Shaw.

Runyon, Damon. *Take It Easy.*
First Edition: New York: Frederick
Stokes, 1938.
NF/F: $850   G/VG: $265

Salinger, J. D. *Franny and Zooey.*
First Edition: Boston: Little Brown,
1961.
NF/F: $1,000   G/VG: $250

Saltus, Edgar. *Purple and Fine
Women.*
First Edition: New York: Ainslee
Publishing, 1903.
NF/F: $350   G/VG: $110

Santayana, George. *The Last Puritan.*
First Edition: New York: Scribners,
1936.
NF/F: $350   G/VG: $75

Saroyan, William. *Daring Young
Man on the Flying Trapeze and Other
Stories.*
First Edition: New York: Random
House, 1934.
NF/F: $725   G/VG: $270

Sarton, May. *The Single Hound.*
First Edition: Boston: Houghton
Mifflin, 1938.
NF/F: $625   G/VG: $140

Schulberg, Budd. *The Harder They
Fall.*
First Edition: New York: Random
House, 1947.
NF/F: $350   G/VG: $95

Scott, Paul. The Raj Quartet:

_____. *The Jewel in the Crown.*
First Edition: London: Heinemann, 1966.
NF/F: $150   G/VG: $45

_____. *The Day of the Scorpion.*
First Edition: London: Heinemann, 1968.
NF/F: $130   G/VG: $45

_____. *The Towers of Silence.*
First Edition: London: Heinemann, 1971.
NF/F: $100   G/VG: $30

_____. *A Division of the Spoils.*
First Edition: London: Heinemann, 1975.
NF/F: $120   G/VG: $35

Seton, Anya. *The Winthrop Woman.*
First Edition: Boston: Houghton
Mifflin, 1958.
NF/F: $120   G/VG: $35

Sexton, Anne. *To Bedlam and Part
Way Back.*
First Edition: Cambridge, MA:
Riverside Press, 1960.
NF/F: $500   G/VG: $125

Shaw, Irwin. *The Young Lions.*
First Edition: New York: Random
House, 1948.
NF/F: $425   G/VG: $115

Sillitoe, Alan. *Saturday Night and
Sunday Morning.*
First Edition: London: W. H. Allen, 1958.
NF/F: $400   G/VG: $125

Sinclair, Upton. *The Jungle.*
First Edition: New York: The Jungle
Publishing Company, 1906.
Point of Issue: "Sustainer's Edition" is
tipped into the first issue.
NF/F: $1,400   G/VG: $600

Skinner, Cornelia Otis. *Excuse It,
Please.*
First Edition: New York: Dodd Mead,
1936.
NF/F: $55   G/VG: $12

Smith, Thorne. *Skin and Bones.*
First Edition: Garden City, NY:
Doubleday Doran, 1933.
NF/F: $450   **G/VG: $150**

Spark, Muriel. *The Prime of Miss Jean Brodie.*
First Edition: London: Macmillan, 1961.
NF/F: $400   **G/VG: $135**

Stratton-Porter, Gene. *The White Flag.*
First Edition: Garden City, NY:
Doubleday Page, 1923.
NF/F: $350   **G/VG: $95**

Stein, Gertrude. *Three Lives.*
First Edition: New York: Grafton Press, 1909.
NF/F: $1,500   **G/VG: $350**

Steinbeck, John. *Cup of Gold.*
First Edition: New York: Robert M.
McBride, 1929.
NF/F: $32,000   **G/VG: $18,000**

_____. *The Moon is Down.*
First Edition: New York: Viking, 1942.
Points of Issue: In first issue, Page 112
line 11 has an extra period, "talk. this"
and lacks a mention of the printer
(Haddon in later printings).
NF/F: $6,500   **G/VG: $2,700**

Stone, Irving. *Depths of Glory.*
First Edition: Franklin Centre, PA: The
Franklin Library, 1985.
NF/F: $75   **G/VG: $25**

Stribling, T. S. *These Bars of Flesh.*
First Edition: Garden City, NY:
Doubleday Doran, 1938.
NF/F: $150   **G/VG: $35**

Styron, William. *Lie Down In Darkness.*
First Edition: Indianapolis, IN: Bobbs-Merrill, 1951.
NF/F: $1,200   **G/VG: $300**

Tarkington, Booth. *The Magnificent Ambersons.*
First Edition: Garden City, NY:
Doubleday Page, 1918.
NF/F: $850   **G/VG: $175**

Terhune, Albert Payson. *A Dog Named Chips.*
First Edition: New York: Harper &
Brothers, 1931.
NF/F: $450   **G/VG: $140**

Thomas, D. M. *The White Hotel.*
First Edition: London: Victor Gollancz, 1981.
NF/F: $200   **G/VG: $65**

Thurber, James. *The Great Quillow.*
First Edition: New York: Harcourt
Brace, 1944.
NF/F: $350   **G/VG: $150**

Toole, John Kennedy. *A Confederacy of Dunces.*
First Edition: Baton Rouge:
Louisiana State University Press,
1980. Points of Issue: The first state
dust jacket lacks a review in strip
above wall.
NF/F: $7,800   **G/VG: $2,800**

Totheroh, Dan. *Men Call Me Fool.*
First Edition: Garden City, N.Y:
Doubleday, Doran, 1929.
NF/F: $100   **G/VG: $35**

John Steinbeck.

William Styron.

John Kennedy Toole.

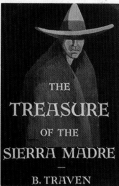

B. Traven.

Traven, B. *The Treasure Of The Sierra Madre.*
First Edition: London: Chatto &
Windus, 1934.
NF/F: $8,000   **G/VG: $2,100**
First U.S. Edition (Revised): New York:
Alfred A. Knopf, 1935.
NF/F: $9,500   **G/VG: $2,000**

Tyler, Anne. *If Morning Ever Comes.*
First Edition: New York: Alfred A. Knopf,
1964. Points of Issue: "than" in quote on
front flap of first issue dust jacket.
NF/F: $3,200   **G/VG: $800**

Updike, John. Rabbit Series:

_____. *Rabbit, Run.*
First Edition: New York: Alfred A.
Knopf, 1960.
NF/F: $1,250   **G/VG: $500**

_____. *Rabbit Redux.*
Limited Editon: New York: Alfred A.
Knopf, 1971 (350 copies).
NF/F: $450   **G/VG: Not Seen**
First Edition: New York: Alfred A.
Knopf, 1971.
NF/F: $150   **G/VG: $55**

_____. *Rabbit Is Rich.*
Limited Editon: New York: Alfred A.
Knopf, 1981 (350 copies).
NF/F: $500   **G/VG: Not Seen**
First Edition: New York: Alfred A.
Knopf, 1981.
NF/F: $85   **G/VG: $25**

_____. *Rabbit At Rest.*
First Edition: New York: Alfred A.
Knopf, 1990.
NF/F: $100   **G/VG: $35**

_____. *Licks of Love: Short Stories
and a Sequel, "Rabbit Remembered."*
First Edition: New York: Alfred A.
Knopf, 2000.
NF/F: $25   **G/VG: $10**

Gore Vidal.

Evelyn Waugh.

Van Vechten, Carl. *Nigger Heaven.*
First Edition: New York: Alfred A.
Knopf, 1927.
NF/F: $300   **G/VG: $95**

Vidal, Gore. *In A Yellow Wood.*
First Edition: New York: E. P. Dutton &
Co., 1947.
NF/F: $500   **G/VG: $100**

Vonnegut Jr., Kurt. *Player Piano.*
First Edition: New York: Scribners,
1952. Points of Issue: First state has
both Scribner's "A" and colophon on
the verso.
NF/F: $2,400   **G/VG: $650**

Walker, Alice. *The Color Purple.*
First Edition: New York: Harcourt
Brace Jovanovich, 1982.
NF/F: $1,100   **G/VG: $250**

Warren, Robert Penn. *Band Of
Angels.*
First Edition: New York: Random
House, 1955.
NF/F: $200   **G/VG: $50**

Watts, Mary. *The Rise of Jennie
Cushing.*
First Edition: New York: The
Macmillan Company, 1914.
NF/F: $35   **G/VG: $10**

Waugh, Alec. *Going Their Own Ways.*
First Edition: London: Cassell, 1938.
NF/F: $95   **G/VG: $25**

Waugh, Evelyn. *Brideshead
Revisited. The Sacred & Profane
Memories of Captain Charles Ryder.*
First Edition: London: Chapman & Hall
Ltd, 1945.
NF/F: $3,500   **G/VG: $1,000**

Welty, Eudora. *A Curtain of Green.*
First Edition: Garden City, NY:
Doubleday Doran, 1941.
NF/F: $1,200   **G/VG: $400**

West, Jessamyn. *The Friendly Persuasion.*
First Edition: New York: Harcourt, Brace, 1945.
NF/F: $300   **G/VG: $85**

West, Nathaniel. *The Day of the Locust.*
First Edition: New York: Random House, 1939.
NF/F: $3,500   **G/VG: $1,000**

White, Stewart Edward. *Gold.*
First Edition: Garden City, NY:
Doubleday Page, 1913.
Points of Issue: First Issue is bound in yellow.
NF/F: $275   **G/VG: $105**

White, T. H. The Once and Future King:

_____. *The Sword in the Stone.*
First Edition: London: Collins, 1938.
NF/F: $2,500   **G/VG: $775**

_____. *The Witch in the Wood.*
First Edition: New York: G. P. Putnam, 1939.
NF/F: $750   **G/VG: $250**

_____. *The Ill-Made Knight.*
First Edition: New York: G. P. Putnam, 1940.
NF/F: $850   **G/VG: $275**

_____. *The Candle in the Wind.*
First Edition: London: Collins, 1941.
NF/F: $1,000   **G/VG: $350**

_____. *The Book of Merlin.*
First Edition: Austin & London: The University Of Texas Press, 1977.
NF/F: $75   **G/VG: $25**

Wilder, Thornton. *Bridge of San Luis Rey.*
First Edition: New York: Albert and Charles Boni, 1927.
NF/F: $1,500   **G/VG: $400**

Williams, Ben Ames. *Splendor.*
First Edition: New York: E. P. Dutton, 1927.
NF/F: $150   **G/VG: $35**

Williams, Tennessee. *A Streetcar Named Desire.*
First Edition: New York: New Directions, 1947.
NF/F: $6,500   **G/VG: $1,200**

Wilson, Harry Leon. *Merton of the Movies.*
First Edition: Garden City, NY:
Doubleday Page, 1922.
NF/F: $350   **G/VG: $85**

Wister, Owen. *When West Was West.*
First Edition: New York: Macmillan, 1928.
NF/F: $165   **G/VG: $35**

Wodehouse, P. G. *Louder and Funnier.*
First Edition: London: Faber and Faber, 1932. Points of Issue: First Issue is red cloth with black lettering, copyright date in roman numerals.
NF/F: $950   **G/VG: $300**

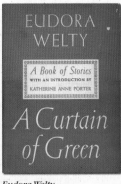

Eudora Welty.

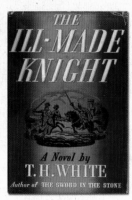

T. H. White.

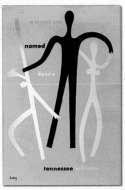

Tennessee Williams.

_____. Jeeves Series:

_____. *The Man with Two Left Feet.*
First Edition: London: Methuen, 1917.
Points of Issue: First Issue is gold/
yellow cloth with gold lettering.
NF/F: $1,550   **G/VG: $600**

_____. *My Man Jeeves.*
First Edition: London: George Newnes,
1919. Points of Issue: First Issue is red
cloth with black lettering.
NF/F: $3,250   **G/VG: $1,400**

_____. *The Inimitable Jeeves.*
First Edition: London: Herbert Jenkins,
1923. Points of Issue: First issue has
13 titles of Jenkins books ending with
"The Coming of Bill."
NF/F: $1,500   **G/VG: $500**

_____. *Carry On Jeeves.*
First Edition: London: Herbert Jenkins,
1925. Points of Issue: First Issue is
green cloth with black lettering with
title page dated in roman numerals.
NF/F: $1,500   **G/VG: $500**

_____. *Very Good Jeeves.*
First Edition: Garden City, NY:
Doubleday Doran, 1930.
NF/F: $950   **G/VG: $300**
First U.K. Edition: London: Herbert
Jenkins, 1930.
Points of Issue: First Issue is orange
cloth with black lettering.
NF/F: $1,500   **G/VG: $500**

_____. *Thank You, Jeeves.*
First Edition: London: Herbert Jenkins,
1934. Points of Issue: First Issue is gray
cloth with red lettering.
NF/F: $1,250   **G/VG: $450**

_____. *Right Ho, Jeeves.*
First Edition: London: Herbert Jenkins,
1934.
NF/F: $1,400   **G/VG: $400**
Points of Issue: First Issue is gray cloth
with red lettering, title page date is in
roman numerals.
First U.S. Edition as Brinkley Manor:
Boston: Little Brown, 1934.
NF/F: $725   **G/VG: $250**

_____. *The Code of the
Woosters.*
First Edition: London: Herbert Jenkins,
1938. Points of Issue: First Issue is
green cloth with black lettering and
decorations.
NF/F: $1,000   **G/VG: $400**

_____. *Joy in the Morning as
Jeeves in the Morning.*
First Edition: Garden City, NY:
Doubleday, 1946.
NF/F: $350   **G/VG: $125**
First U.K. Edition as Joy in the
Morning: London: Herbert Jenkins,
1947.
Points of Issue: First Issue is orange
cloth with black lettering.
NF/F: $350   **G/VG: $135**

_____. *The Mating Season.*
First Edition: London: Herbert Jenkins,
1949. Points of Issue: First Issue is
orange cloth with black lettering.
NF/F: $900   **G/VG: $375**

_____. *Ring for Jeeves.*
First Edition: London: Herbert Jenkins,
1953.
NF/F: $450   **G/VG: $150**
Points of Issue: First Issue is red cloth
with black lettering.
First U.S. Edition as *The Return of
Jeeves*: New York: Simon & Schuster,
1954.
NF/F: $250   **G/VG: $85**

_____. *Jeeves and the Feudal Spirit*.
First Edition: London: Herbert Jenkins, 1954.
Points of Issue: First Issue is red cloth with black lettering.
NF/F: $350   **G/VG: $125**
First U.S. Edition as *Bertie Wooster Sees It Through*: New York: Simon & Schuster, 1955.
NF/F: $225   **G/VG: $75**

_____. *A Few Quick Ones*.
First Edition: New York: Simon & Schuster, 1959.
NF/F: $100   **G/VG: $35**
First U.K. Edition: London: Herbert Jenkins, 1959.
Points of Issue: First Issue is red cloth with black lettering.
NF/F: $150   **G/VG: $65**

_____. *Jeeves in the Offing as Right You Are Jeeves*.
First Edition: New York: Simon & Schuster, 1960.
NF/F: $150   **G/VG: $55**
First U.K. Edition as *Jeeves in the Offing*: London: Herbert Jenkins, 1960.
Points of Issue: First Issue is red cloth with gold lettering.
NF/F: $250   **G/VG: $100**

_____. *Stiff Upper Lip, Jeeves*.
First Edition: New York: Simon & Schuster, 1963.
NF/F: $200   **G/VG: $85**
First U.K. Edition: London: Herbert Jenkins, 1963.
Points of Issue: First Issue is red buckram with gold lettering.
NF/F: $175   **G/VG: $85**

_____. *Plum Pie*.
First Edition: London: Herbert Jenkins, 1966.
Points of Issue: First Issue is purple cloth with silver lettering.
NF/F: $250   **G/VG: $120**

First U.S. Edition: New York: Simon & Schuster, 1966.
NF/F: $150   **G/VG: $65**

_____. *Much Obliged, Jeeves*.
First Edition: London: Barrie & Jenkins, 1971.
Points of Issue: First Issue is blue cloth with gold lettering.
NF/F: $125   **G/VG: $50**
First Edition (Concurrent Issue) as *Jeeves and the Tie that Binds*: New York: Simon & Schuster, 1971.
NF/F: $200   **G/VG: $95**

_____*Aunts Aren't Gentlemen*.
First Edition: London: Barrie & Jenkins, 1974.
Points of Issue: First Issue is blue cloth with gold lettering and decorations.
NF/F: $200   **G/VG: $80**
First U.S. Edition as *The Cat-nappers*: New York: Simon & Schuster, 1975.
NF/F: $135   **G/VG: $50**

Wolfe, Thomas. *Look Homeward, Angel*.
First Edition: New York: Charles Scribner's Sons, 1929. Points of Issue: dust jacket carries a picture of Wolfe and the verso has a Scribner's colophon in first issue.
NF/F: $5,200   **G/VG: $750**

Woolf, Virginia. *Granite & Rainbow*.
First Edition: London: The Hogarth Press, 1958.
NF/F: $500   **G/VG: $125**

Wright, Harold Bell. *The Mine with the Iron Door*.
First Edition: New York: D. Appleton, 1923.
NF/F: $200   **G/VG: $95**

P.G. Wodehouse.

P.G. Wodehouse.

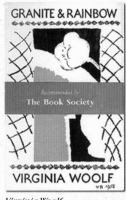

Virginia Woolf.

MYSTERY

The mystery genre is not new, the Chinese puzzle story borders on a millennium of existence and entertainment. In the modern, Western world, however, we can point to two definite events that ushered in the mystery genre as one of our most popular literary diversions.

The first was April Fool's Day in 1841. It was April 1st in 1841 when the fiction editor of *Graham's Magazine* published a little story called "The Murders in the Rue Morgue." That editor was Edgar Allen Poe, and the story created the genre we now know as mystery. C. Auguste Dupin, Poe's detective, would find a "Purloined Letter," solve the "Murder of Marie Roget," and confront a "Gold Bug," but the genre itself had to wait for a second event to find its way into the hearts of the public.

In the initial number of his new magazine, *The Strand*, George Newnes wrote of the street his offices were located on: "Of violent incident it has seen but little..." A statement that remained true for six months, before becoming one of the greatest ironies ever printed. In July of 1891, *The Strand* published "A Scandal in Bohemia," the first adventure of Sherlock Holmes. While Holmes had seen print earlier, it was this story that broke open the floodgates and ushered in the mystery genre. *The Strand*, thus, became the origin, the starting point for rivers of fictional blood, murder, robbery and mayhem.

There are older "crime" novels. Charles Dickens' *Oliver Twist*, for example, was primarily a crime novel suggested to the author by the well-publicized trial of a fence, Ikey Solomon. One of the most chilling of these early crime novels was Edward Bulwer Lytton's *Lucretia: Or, The Children of the Night*, suggested by the careers of two serial prisoners. These novels, however, bear little relation to the modern mystery genre of crime and detection.

As literary genres go, at least in the modern sense, mystery is still young. Outside of a couple volumes of *Graham's*, it can be contained in a collection beginning in 1891, just over a century. Almost since its appearance as a genre, mystery has fascinated the collector. Perhaps because of the hunt, the chase.

A good many collections within the mystery genre are built around a single classification or profession. The nosy old lady does her bit in Agatha Christie's Miss Jane Marple stories, or as Hildegarde Withers, by Stuart Palmer. Lawyers like Arthur Train's Ephram Tutt or Erle Stanley Gardner's Perry Mason solved crimes detectives couldn't. Clergymen from G. K. Chesterton's Father Brown to Harry Kemelman's Rabbi David Small used everything from scholastic to talmudic logic to expose the criminal. The rich and the bored amused themselves ferreting out the miscreants in S. S. Van Dines' Philo Vance books or Dorothy Sayers' Lord Peter Winsey series. Historical figures such as Dr. Samuel Johnson, in Lillian De La Torre's books, solved the crimes of their era. Even a boat bum, John D. MacDonald's Travis McGee, gets in the act.

Whether the clues are buried in the stacks of a bookstore, or out on the mean streets, one hunt is akin to the other. Whether it is the criminal that is exposed, or the first edition that is found, the detective and the book collector seem to have an affinity for each other.

TEN CLASSIC RARITIES

Cain, James M. *The Postman Always Rings Twice.*
New York: Alfred A, Knopf, 1934. And you only have to find this once.
NF/F: $7,500   **G/VG: $3,500**

Chandler, Raymond. *The Big Sleep.*
New York: Alfred A, Knopf, 1939. Finding this is a ticket to sleeping well.
NF/F: $21,500   **G/VG: $7,500**

Christie, Agatha. *Ten Little Niggers.*
London: Collins Crime Club, 1939. Issued in the U.S. as *And Then There Were None* then as *Ten Little Indians.*
NF/F: $15,000   **G/VG: $4,000**

Fleming, Ian. *Casino Royale.*
London: Jonathan Cape, 1953. Find this and avoid casinos, or buy one.
NF/F: $28,500   **G/VG: $9,500**

Gardner, Erle Stanley. *The Case of the Stuttering Bishop.*
New York: Morrow, 1936. Known to cause stuttering and other signs of surprise.
NF/F: $2,500   **G/VG: $1,000**

Hammett, Dashiell. *The Maltese Falcon.*
NY: Alfred Knopf, 1930. Probably better than finding the object of the book is finding a first edition in the unfindable dust jacket.
NF/F: $25,000   **G/VG: $10,000**

Queen, Ellery. *The Siamese Twin Mystery.*
New York: Fredrick A. Stokes, 1933. You only need one to make things a bit brighter.
NF/F: $2,000   **G/VG: $850**

Sayers, Dorothy L. *Hangman's Holiday.*
Victor Gollancz London, 1933. Have your own holiday after finding this.
NF/F: $4,500   **G/VG: $2,250**

Spillane, Mickey. *I, The Jury.*
New York: Dutton, 1947. And judge and just about whatever you want if you find this.
NF/F: $4,000   **G/VG: $1,800**

Stout, Rex. *Too Many Cooks.*
New York: Farrar & Rinehart, 1938. Includes recipe section so you can hire your own cook.
NF/F: $5,000   **G/VG: $1,600**

Raymond Chandler.

Ellery Queen.

PRICE GUIDE

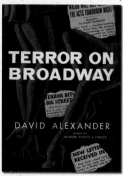

David Alexander.

Margery Allingham.

Margery Allingham.

Abbot, Anthony. *About The Murder of the Night Club Lady.*
First Edition: New York: Covici-Friede, 1931.
NF/F: $35   G/VG: $10

Adams, Cleve F. *Sabotage.*
First Edition: New York: E.P. Dutton & Co., 1940.
NF/F: $45   G/VG: $12

Adams, Samuel Hopkins. *Average Jones.*
First Edition: Indianapolis: Bobbs-Merrill, 1911.
NF/F: $350   G/VG: $120

Aird, Catherine. *Henrietta Who?*
First U.S. Edition: Garden City, NY: Doubleday/Crime Club, 1968.
NF/F: $100   G/VG: $25

Alexander, David. *Terror on Broadway.*
First Edition: New York: Random House, 1954.
NF/F: $65   G/VG: $25

Allen, Grant. *An African Millionaire. Episodes in the Life of the Illustrious Colonel Clay.*
First Edition: London: Grant Richards Ltd, 1897.
NF/F: $1,375   G/VG: $600

Allingham, Margery. Albert Campion Series:

_____. *The Crime at Black Dudley.*
First Edition: London: Heinemann, 1929.
NF/F: $850   G/VG: $375
First U.S. Edition as *The Black Dudley Murder*: Garden City, NY: Doubleday (Crime Club), 1929.
NF/F: $600   G/VG: $225

_____. *Mystery Mile.*
First Edition: London: Heinemann, 1930.
NF/F: $350   G/VG: $125

_____. *Look to the Lady.*
First Edition: London: Heinemann, 1931.
NF/F: $250   G/VG: $95
First U.S. Edition as *The Gyrth Chalice Mystery*: Garden City, NY: Doubleday Doran, 1931.
NF/F: $100   G/VG: $40

_____. *Sweet Danger.*
First Edition: London: Heinemann, 1934.
NF/F: $350   G/VG: $100

_____. *Death of a Ghost.*
First Edition: London: Heinemann, 1934.
NF/F: $250   G/VG: $95

_____. *Flowers for the Judge.*
First Edition: London: Heinemann, 1936.
NF/F: $200   G/VG: $75

_____. *The Case of the Late Pig.*
First Edition: Hodder and Stroughton, 1937.
NF/F: $300   G/VG: $100

_____. *The Fashion in Shrouds.*
First Edition: London: Heinemann, 1938.
NF/F: $500   G/VG: $200

_____. *Traitor's Purse.*
First Edition: London: Heinemann, 1941.
NF/F: $600   G/VG: $250

_____. *Coroner's Pidgin.*
First Edition: London: Heinemann, 1945.
NF/F: $150   G/VG: $55
First U.S. Edition as *Pearls Before Swine*: Garden City, NY: Doubleday Doran, 1945.
NF/F: $125   G/VG: $35

_____. *More Work for the Undertaker.*
First Edition: London: Heinemann, 1948.
NF/F: $100   G/VG: $35

_____. *The Tiger in the Smoke.*
First Edition: London: Chatto &
Windus, 1952.
NF/F: $100   **G/VG: $25**

_____. *The Beckoning Lady.*
First Edition: London: Chatto &
Windus, 1955.
NF/F: $55   **G/VG: $20**

_____. *Hide My Eyes.*
First Edition: London: Chatto &
Windus, 1958.
NF/F: $100   **G/VG: $35**

_____. *The China Governess.*
First Edition: London: Chatto &
Windus, 1963.
NF/F: $60   **G/VG: $25**

_____. *The Mind Readers.*
First Edition: London: Chatto &
Windus, 1965.
NF/F: $65   **G/VG: $25**

**Allingham, Margery and Youngman
Carter.** *Cargo of Eagles.*
First Edition: London: Chatto &
Windus, 1968.
NF/F: $85   **G/VG: $30**

_____. *Mr. Campion and Others.*
First Edition: London: Heinemann, 1939.
NF/F: $300   **G/VG: $155**

_____. *The Allingham Case-Book.*
First Edition: London: Chatto &
Windus, 1969.
NF/F: $75   **G/VG: $20**

_____. *The Allingham Minibus.*
First Edition: London: Chatto &
Windus, 1973.
NF/F: $75   **G/VG: $20**

_____. *The Return of Mr. Campion.*
First Edition: London: Hodder &
Stoughton, 1989.
NF/F: $25   **G/VG: $10**
(See: Carter, Youngman)

Ambler, Eric. *The Mask of Dimitrios.*
First Edition: London: Hodder &
Stoughton Ltd, 1939.
NF/F: $12,250   **G/VG: $1,000**
First U.S. Edition as *A Coffin for Dimitrios*:
New York: Alfred A. Knopf, 1939.
NF/F: $2,200   **G/VG: $650**

Ames, Delano. *The Body on Page One.*
First Edition: New York: Rinehart &
Co., 1951.
NF/F: $300   **G/VG: $85**

Anderson, Frederick Irving.
Adventures of the Infallible Godahl.
First Edition: New York: Thomas Y.
Crowell, 1914.
NF/F: $3,000   **G/VG: $600**

Anderson, Poul. *Perish by the Sword.*
First Edition: New York: Macmillan,
1959.
NF/F: $225   **G/VG: $50**

Anthony, Evelyn. *The Assassin.*
First Edition: London: Hutchinson,
1970.
NF/F: $40   **G/VG: $15**
First U.S. Edition: New York: Coward-
McCann, 1970.
NF/F: $25   **G/VG: $8**

Antony, Peter. *How Doth the Little
Crocodile.*
First Edition: London: Evans Brothers,
1952.
NF/F: $500   **G/VG: $100**
First U.S. Edition: New York:
Macmillan, 1957.
NF/F: $200   **G/VG: $85**

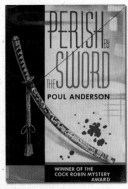

Poul Anderson.

Evelyn Anthony.

Peter Antony.

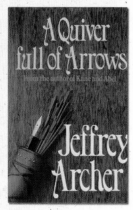

Jeffrey Archer.

Michael Avallone.

John Ball.

Archer, Jeffrey. *A Quiver Full of Arrows.*
First Edition: London: Hodder &
Stoughton, 1980.
NF/F: $65   **G/VG: $15**
First U.S. Edition: New York: Linden
Press/Simon & Schuster, 1982.
NF/F: $30   **G/VG: $10**

Ard, William. *A Private Party.*
First Edition: New York: Rinehart &
Co., 1953.
NF/F: $55   **G/VG: $15**

Arden, William. *A Dark Power.*
First Edition: New York: Dodd, Mead/
Red Badge, 1968.
NF/F: $55   **G/VG: $15**

Armstrong, Charlotte. *The
Unsuspected.*
First Edition: New York: Coward-
McCann, 1946.
NF/F: $165   **G/VG: $50**

Arrighi, Mel. *Freak-Out.*
First Edition: New York: G. P. Putnam,
1968.
NF/F: $45   **G/VG: $10**

Ashdown, Clifford. *The Further
Adventures of Romney Pringle.*
First Edition: London: Cassell, 1903.
NF/F: $400   **G/VG: $150**

Ashford, Jeffrey. *The D. I.*
First Edition: New York: Harper &
Brothers, 1961.
NF/F: $25   **G/VG: $10**

Atkey, Bertram. *Smiler Brun
Gentleman Crook.*
First Edition: London: George Newnes,
Ltd, 1923.
NF/F: $80   **G/VG: $25**

Avallone, Michael. *The Case of the
Violent Virgin.*
First Edition: London: W.H. Allen, 1960.
NF/F: $95   **G/VG: $30**

Bagby, George. *Here Comes the Corpse.*
First Edition: Garden City, NY:
Doubleday, Doran/ Crime Club, 1941.
NF/F: $125   **G/VG: $35**

Ball, John. *The Last Plane Out.*
First Edition: Boston: Little Brown,
1970.
NF/F: $35   **G/VG: $10**

_____. *Virgil Tibbs Series:*

_____. *In the Heat of the Night.*
First Edition: New York: Harper &
Row, 1965.
NF/F: $850   **G/VG: $325**

_____. *Cool Cottontail.*
First Edition: New York: Harper &
Row, 1966.
NF/F: $80   **G/VG: $30**

_____. *Johnny Get Your Gun.*
First Edition: Boston: Little Brown,
1969.
NF/F: $50   **G/VG: $15**

_____. *Five Pieces of Jade.*
First Edition: Boston: Little Brown,
1972.
NF/F: $50   **G/VG: $15**

_____. *The Eyes of Buddha.*
First Edition: Boston: Little Brown, 1976.
NF/F: $45   **G/VG: $15**

_____. *Then Came Violence.*
First Edition: Garden City, NY:
Doubleday, 1980.
NF/F: $60   **G/VG: $20**

_____. *Singapore.*
First Edition: New York: Dodd Mead, 1986.
NF/F: $30   **G/VG: $8**

Bellairs, George. *The Tormentors.*
First Edition: London: John Gifford Ltd, 1962.
NF/F: $30   **G/VG: $10**

Benson, Ben. *The Ninth Hour.*
First Edition: New York: M. S. Mill Company and William Morrow & Company, 1956.
NF/F: $45   **G/VG: $15**

Benson, Raymond. James Bond Series:

_____. *Zero Minus Ten.*
First Edition: London: Hodder & Stoughton, 1997.
NF/F: $90   **G/VG: $35**

_____. *Tomorrow Never Dies.*
First Edition: London: Hodder & Stoughton, 1997.
NF/F: $375   **G/VG: $135**

_____. *The Facts of Death.*
First Edition: London: Hodder & Stoughton, 1998.
NF/F: $65   **G/VG: $25**

_____. *The World is Not Enough.*
First Edition: London: Hodder & Stoughton, 1999.
NF/F: $225   **G/VG: $95**

_____. *High Time to Kill.*
First Edition: London: Hodder & Stoughton, 1999.
NF/F: $120   **G/VG: $50**

_____. *Doubleshot.*
First Edition: London: Hodder & Stoughton, 2000.
NF/F: $150   **G/VG: $60**

_____. *Never Dream of Dying.*
First Edition: London: Hodder & Stoughton, 2001.
NF/F: $65   **G/VG: $25**

_____. *The Man with the Red Tattoo.*
First Edition: London: Hodder & Stoughton, 2002.
NF/F: $200   **G/VG: $85**

_____. *Die Another Day.*
First Edition: London: Hodder & Stoughton, 2002.
NF/F: $120   **G/VG: $55**
(See Also: Ian Fleming, Robert Markham, John Gardner, Sebastian Faulks)

Bentley, E. C. *Trent Intervenes.*
First Edition: London: Thomas Nelson, 1938.
NF/F: $650   **G/VG: $200**
First U.S. Edition: New York: Alfred A. Knopf, 1938.
NF/F: $450   **G/VG: $100**

Berkeley, Anthony. *The Poisoned Chocolates Case.*
First Edition: Garden City, New York: Doubleday, Doran & Co., 1929.
NF/F: $850   **G/VG: $275**

_____. *Trial and Error.*
First Edition: Garden City, NY: Doubleday Doran, 1937.
NF/F: $710   **G/VG: $200**

George Bellairs.

Raymond Benson.

Anthony Berkeley.

Earl Derr Biggers.

Nicholas Blake.

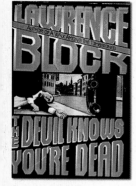

Lawrence Block.

Biggers, Earl Derr. Charlie Chan Series*:

_____. *The House Without a Key.*
First Edition: New York: Bobbs-Merrill, 1925.
NF/F: $350   **G/VG: $150**

_____. *The Chinese Parrot.*
First Edition: New York: Bobbs-Merrill, 1926.
NF/F: $225   **G/VG: $95**

_____. *Behind That Curtain.*
First Edition: New York: Bobbs-Merrill, 1928.
NF/F: $1,650   **G/VG: $600**

_____. *The Black Camel.*
First Edition: New York: Bobbs-Merrill, 1929.
NF/F: $900   **G/VG: $350**

_____. *Charlie Chan Carries On.*
First Edition: Indianapolis: Bobbs-Merrill, 1930.
NF/F: $1,500   **G/VG: $600**

_____. *Keeper of the Keys.*
First Edition: New York: Bobbs-Merrill, 1932.
NF/F: $450   **G/VG: $125**

Blake, Nicholas *The Beast Must Die.*
First Edition: London: Collins/Crime Club, 1938.
NF/F: $2,000   **G/VG: $800**
First U.S. Edition: New York: Harpers, 1938.
NF/F: $800   **G/VG: $300**

Blochman, Lawrence G. *Diagnosis: Homicide.*
First Edition: Philadelphia: Lippincott, 1950.
NF/F: $200   **G/VG: $65**

Block, Lawrence. *The Devil Knows You're Dead.*
First Edition: New York: William Morrow, 1993.
NF/F: $30   **G/VG: $10**

_____. The Bernie Rhodenbarr Series:

_____. *Burglars Can't be Choosers.*
First Edition: New York: Random House, 1977.
NF/F: $75   **G/VG: $30**

_____. *The Burglar in the Closet.*
First Edition: New York: Random House, 1978.
NF/F: $325   **G/VG: $125**

_____. *Burglar Who Liked to Quote Kipling.*
First Edition: New York: Random House, 1979.
NF/F: $85   **G/VG: $30**

_____. *Burglar Who Studied Spinoza.*
First Edition: New York: Random House, 1980.
NF/F: $75   **G/VG: $25**

_____. *Burglar Who Painted Like Mondrian.*
First Edition: New York: Arbor House, 1983.
NF/F: $25   **G/VG: $10**

_____. *Burglar Who Traded Ted Williams.*
First Edition: New York: E. P. Dutton, 1994.
NF/F: $15   **G/VG: $7**

_____. *Burglar Who Thought He Was Bogart.*
Limited Edition 650 signed copies: New York: E. P. Dutton, 1995.
NF/F: $30   **G/VG: $12**
First Edition: New York: E. P. Dutton, 1995.
NF/F: $15   **G/VG: $7**

_____. *Burglar in the Library.*
First Edition: np (Britain): No Exit Press, 1997.
NF/F: $300   **G/VG: $125**
First U.S. Edition: New York: E. P. Dutton, 1997.
NF/F: $10   **G/VG: $6**

_____. *Burglar in the Rye.*
First Edition: New York: E. P. Dutton, 1999.
NF/F: $20   **G/VG: $7**

_____. *Burglar on the Prowl.*
First Edition: New York: William Morrow, 2004.
NF/F: $15   **G/VG: $7**

Bodkin, McDonnell. *The Quests of Paul Beck.*
First Edition: Boston: Little Brown, 1910.
NF/F: $850   **G/VG: $200**

Boucher, Anthony. *The Case of the Seven of Calvary.*
First Edition: New York: Simon & Schuster, 1937.
NF/F: $650   **G/VG: $200**

Box, Edgar. *Death in the Fifth Position.*
First Edition: New York: E.P. Dutton, 1952.
NF/F: $450   **G/VG: $125**

Bradbury, Ray. *Death is a Lonely Business.*
First Edition (Limited & Signed): Franklin Center, PA: Franklin Library, 1985.
NF/F: $150   **G/VG: $45**
Note: A trade edition signed and inscribed by Bradbbury is about $300 double fine.
First Edition (trade): New York: Alfred A. Knopf, 1985.
NF/F: $45   **G/VG: $15**

Bramah, Ernest. *The Eyes of Max Carrados.*
First Edition: London: Grant Richards, 1923.
NF/F: $3,500   **G/VG: $2,000**
First U.S. Edition: New York: George H. Doran, 1924.
NF/F: $1,450   **G/VG: $600**

Brand, Christianna. *Green for Danger.*
First Edition: London: John Lane The Bodley Head, 1945.
NF/F: $400   **G/VG: $125**

Branson, H.C. *The Pricking Thumb.*
First Edition: New York: Simon & Schuster, 1942.
NF/F: $70   **G/VG: $20**

Braun, Lilian Jackson. *The Cat Who Went into the Closet.*
First Edition: New York: G.P. Putnam, 1993.
NF/F: $40   **G/VG: $12**

Brean, Herbert. *The Darker the Night.*
First Edition: New York: William Morrow & Co., 1949.
NF/F: $60   **G/VG: $20**

Broun, Daniel. *The Subject of Harry Egypt.*
First Edition: New York: Holt, Rhinehart and Winston, 1963.
NF/F: $25   **G/VG: $8**
First U.K. Edition: London: Victor Gollancz, 1963
NF/F: $10   **G/VG: $5**

Brown, Fredric. *The Dead Ringer.*
First Edition: New York: E.P. Dutton & Co., 1948.
NF/F: $650   **G/VG: $160**

Browne, Douglas G. *Too Many Cousins.*
First Edition: New York: Macmillan, 1953.
NF/F: $35   **G/VG: $12**

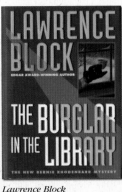
Lawrence Block

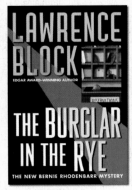
Lawrence Block.

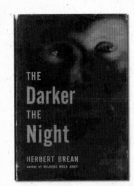
Herbert Brean.

James Lee Burke.

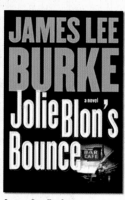

James Lee Burke.

James Lee Burke.

Bruce, Leo. *Cold Blood.*
First Edition: London: Victor Gollancz
Ltd, 1952.
NF/F: $65　　　　　　　　**G/VG: $30**
First U.S. Edition: Chicago: Academy, 1980.
NF/F: $30　　　　　　　　**G/VG: $15**

Buchan, John. *The Thirty-Nine Steps.*
First Edition: London & Edinburgh:
William Blackwood and Sons, 1915.
NF/F: $2,800　　　　　　**G/VG: $800**

Burke, James Lee. Dave Robicheaux
Series:

_____. *The Neon Rain.*
First Edition: New York: Henry Holt,
1987.
NF/F: $400　　　　　　　**G/VG: $175**

_____. *Heaven's Prisoners.*
First Edition: New York: Henry Holt,
1988.
NF/F: $175　　　　　　　　**G/VG: $70**

_____. *Black Cherry Blues.*
First Edition: Boston: Little, Brown,
1989.
NF/F: $140　　　　　　　　**G/VG: $50**

_____. *A Morning for Flamingos.*
First Edition: Boston: Little, Brown,
1990.
NF/F: $55　　　　　　　　**G/VG: $20**

_____. *A Stained White Radiance.*
First Edition: New York: Hyperion,
1992.
NF/F: $35　　　　　　　　**G/VG: $10**

_____. *In the Electric Mist with
Confederate Dead.* (150 copies).
Limited Edition: New Orleans: B. F.
Trice, 1993.
NF/F: $300　　　　　　**G/VG: Not Seen**
First Edition: New York: Hyperion, 1993.
NF/F: $25　　　　　　　　**G/VG: $10**

_____. *Dixie City Jam.*
First Limited Edition: New York:
Hyperion, 1994 (1,525 copies).
NF/F: $125　　　　　　　**Not Seen**
First Trade Edition: New York:
Hyperion, 1994.
NF/F: $20　　　　　　　　**G/VG: $8**

_____. *Burning Angel.*
Limited Edition: New Orleans: B. F.
Trice, 1995 (150 copies).
NF/F: $350　　　　　**G/VG: Not Seen**
First Edition: New York: Hyperion, 1995.
NF/F: $20　　　　　　　　**G/VG: $10**

_____. *Cadillac Jukebox.*
Limited Edition: New Orleans: B. F. Trice,
1996 (26 lettered, 175 numbered copies).
NF/F: $325　　　　　**G/VG: Not Seen**
First Edition: New York: Hyperion, 1996.
NF/F: $20　　　　　　　　**G/VG: $10**

_____. *Sunset Limited.*
First Edition: Garden City, NY:
Doubleday, 1998.
NF/F: $30　　　　　　　　**G/VG: $10**

_____. *Purple Cane Road.*
Limited Edition: New Orleans: B. F.
Trice, 2000 (150 copies).
NF/F: $150　　　　　**G/VG: Not Seen**
First Trade Edition: Garden City, NY:
Doubleday, 1998.
NF/F: $25　　　　　　　　**G/VG: $10**

_____. *Jolie Blon's Bounce.*
(26 lettered, 150 numbered copies.)
Limited Edition: New Orleans: B. F.
Trice, 2002.
NF/F: $250　　　　　**G/VG: Not Seen**
First Edition: New York: Hyperion, 1993.
NF/F: $20　　　　　　　　**G/VG: $8**

_____. *Last Car to the Elysian Fields.*
First Edition: New York: Simon &
Schuster, 2003.
NF/F: $20　　　　　　　　**G/VG: $8**

_____. *Crusader's Cross.*
First Edition: New York: Simon &
Schuster, 2005.
NF/F: $15   **G/VG: $6**

_____. *Pegasus Descending.*
Limited Edition: Gladestry: Scorpion
Press, 2006 (80 copies).
NF/F: $200   **G/VG: Not Seen**
First Edition: New York: Simon &
Schuster, 2006.
NF/F: $15   **G/VG: $6**

_____. *The Tin Roof Blowdown.*
Limited Edition: Gladestry: Scorpion
Press, 2007 (80 copies).
NF/F: $450   **G/VG: Not Seen**
First Edition: New York: Simon &
Schuster, 2007.
NF/F: $15   **G/VG: $6**

_____. *Swan Peak.*
Limited Edition: Gladestry: Scorpion
Press, 2008 (80 copies).
NF/F: $175   **G/VG: Not Seen**
First Edition: New York: Simon &
Schuster, 2008.
NF/F: $15   **G/VG: $6**

Burnett, W.R. *Little Caesar.*
First Edition: New York: Dial, 1929.
NF/F: $900   **G/VG: $250**

Burton, Miles. *Early Morning Murder.*
First Edition: London: Collins/Crime
Club, 1945.
NF/F: $280   **G/VG: $100**
First U.S. Edition as *Accidents Do
Happen*: Garden City, NY: Doubleday/
Crime Club, 1946.
NF/F: $85   **G/VG: $15**

Bush, Christopher. *The Perfect
Murder Case.*
First Edition: London: Heinemann, 1929.
NF/F: $250   **G/VG: $120**

First Edition: Garden City, NY:
Doubleday/Crime Club, 1929.
NF/F: $500   **G/VG: $185**

Butler, Ellis Parker. *Philo Gubb
Correspondence School Detective.*
First Edition: Boston: Houghton
Mifflin, 1918.
NF/F: $2,500   **G/VG: $1,000**

Cain, James M. *The Magician's Wife.*
First Edition: New York: Dial, 1965.
NF/F: $175   **G/VG: $55**

_____. *Past All Dishonor.*
First Edition: New York: Alfred A.
Knopf, 1946.
NF/F: $325   **G/VG: $100**

Cannell, Stephen J. *King Con.*
First Edition: New York: William
Morrow, 1997.
NF/F: $35   **G/VG: $10**

Canning, Victor. *The Satan Sampler.*
First Edition: New York: William
Morrow, 1980.
NF/F: $30   **G/VG: $10**

Carnac, Carol. *Upstairs and Downstairs.*
First Edition: Garden City, N.Y.:
Doubleday/Crime Club, 1950.
NF/F: $95   **G/VG: $25**

Carr, Caleb. *The Alienist.*
First Edition (Limited & Signed): Franklin
Center, PA: Franklin Library, 1985.
NF/F: $250   **G/VG: $85**
First Edition (trade): New York:
Random House, 1994.
NF/F: $75   **G/VG: $30**

Carr, John Dickson. *The Dead Sleep
Lightly.*
First Edition: Garden City, NY:
Doubleday, 1983.
NF/F: $50   **G/VG: $20**

James M. Cain.

Victor Canning.

Carol Carnac.

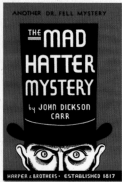

John Dickson Carr.

John Dickson Carr.

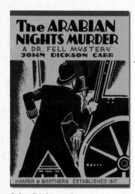

John Dickson Carr.

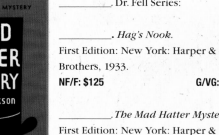

_____. Dr. Fell Series:

_____. *Hag's Nook.*
First Edition: New York: Harper & Brothers, 1933.
NF/F: $125   **G/VG: $45**

_____. *The Mad Hatter Mystery.*
First Edition: New York: Harper & Brothers, 1933.
NF/F: $500   **G/VG: $100**

_____. *The Eight of Swords.*
First Edition: New York: Harper & Brothers, 1934.
NF/F: $120   **G/VG: $45**

_____. *The Blind Barber.*
First Edition: New York: Harper & Brothers, 1934.
NF/F: $175   **G/VG: $75**

_____. *Death Watch.*
First Edition: New York: Harper & Brothers, 1935.
NF/F: $275   **G/VG: $100**

_____. *The Three Coffins.*
First Edition: New York: Harper & Brothers, 1935.
NF/F: $325   **G/VG: $125**

_____. *The Arabian Nights Murder.*
First Edition: New York: Harper & Brothers, 1936.
NF/F: $1,200   **G/VG: $300**

_____. *To Wake the Dead.*
First Edition: New York: Harper & Brothers, 1937.
NF/F: $200   **G/VG: $75**

_____. *The Crooked Hinge.*
First Edition: New York: Harper & Brothers, 1938.
NF/F: $1,000   **G/VG: $350**

_____. *The Problem of the Green Capsule.*
First Edition: New York: Harper & Brothers, 1939.
NF/F: $450   **G/VG: $175**

_____. *The Problem of the Wire Cage.*
First Edition: New York: Harper & Brothers, 1939.
NF/F: $200   **G/VG: $85**

_____. *The Man Who Could Not Shudder.*
First Edition: New York: Harper & Brothers, 1940.
NF/F: $500   **G/VG: $175**

_____. *The Case of the Constant Suicides.*
First Edition: New York: Harper & Brothers, 1941.
NF/F: $500   **G/VG: $200**

_____. *Death Turns the Tables.*
First Edition: New York: Harper & Brothers, 1941.
NF/F: $300   **G/VG: $100**

_____. *Till Death Do Us Part.*
First Edition: New York: Harper & Brothers, 1944.
NF/F: $120   **G/VG: $55**

_____. *He Who Whispers.*
First Edition: New York: Harper & Brothers, 1946.
NF/F: $150   **G/VG: $60**

_____. *The Sleeping Sphinx.*
First Edition: New York: Harper & Brothers, 1947.
NF/F: $75   **G/VG: $30**

_____. *Below Suspicion.*
First Edition: New York: Harper &
Brothers, 1949.
NF/F: $120   **G/VG: $55**

_____. *The Dead Man's Knock.*
First Edition: New York: Harper &
Brothers, 1958.
NF/F: $125   **G/VG: $45**

_____. *In Spite of Thunder.*
First Edition: New York: Harper &
Brothers, 1960.
NF/F: $200   **G/VG: $85**

_____. *The House at Satan's
Elbow.*
First Edition: New York: Harper &
Row, 1965.
NF/F: $65   **G/VG: $20**

_____. *Panic in Box C.*
First Edition: New York: Harper &
Row, 1966.
NF/F: $70   **G/VG: $20**

_____. *Dark of the Moon.*
First Edition: New York: Harper &
Row, 1967.
NF/F: $35   **G/VG: $10**

Carter, Youngman. *Albert Campion
Series:*

_____. *Mr. Campion's Farthing.*
First Edition: London: Heinemann,
1969.
NF/F: $40   **G/VG: $15**

_____. *Mr. Campion's Falcon.*
First Edition: London: Heinemann,
1970.
NF/F: $40   **G/VG: $15**
(See: Allingham, Margery)

Carvic, Heron. *Miss Seeton Sings.*
First Edition: New York: Harper &
Row, 1973.
NF/F: $45   **G/VG: $15**

Caunitz, William J. *One Police Plaza.*
First Edition: New York: Crown
Publishers, Inc., 1984.
NF/F: $40   **G/VG: $10**

Chandler, Raymond. *Philip Marlowe
Series:*

_____. *The Big Sleep.*
First Edition: New York: Alfred A.
Knopf, 1939.
NF/F: $21,500   **G/VG: $7,500**

_____. *Farewell, My Lovely.*
First Edition: New York: Alfred A.
Knopf, 1940.
NF/F: $5,000   **G/VG: $1,800**

_____. *The High Window.*
First Edition: New York: Alfred A.
Knopf, 1942.
NF/F: $5,500   **G/VG: $2,000**

_____. *The Lady in the Lake.*
First Edition: New York: Alfred A.
Knopf, 1943.
NF/F: $4,500   **G/VG: $1,700**

_____. *The Little Sister.*
First Edition: London: Hamish
Hamilton, 1949.
NF/F: $2,750   **G/VG: $1,200**
Points of Issue: First Issue is red cloth
with gilt lettering.
First U.S. Edition: Boston: Houghton
Mifflin, 1949.
NF/F: $2,100   **G/VG: $800**

_____. *The Simple Art of Murder.*
First Edition: Boston: Houghton
Mifflin, 1950.
NF/F: $2,500   **G/VG: $1,000**

Heron Carvic.

Raymond Chandler.

Raymond Chandler.

Raymond Chandler.

Leslie Charteris.

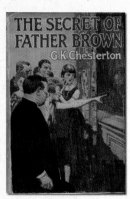

G.K. Chesterton.

_____. *The Long Good-Bye.*
First Edition: London: Hamish Hamilton, 1953.

NF/F: $2,100   **G/VG: $675**

Points of Issue: First Issue is gray cloth with orange lettering.
First U.S. Edition: Boston: Houghton Mifflin, 1954.

NF/F: $950   **G/VG: $200**

_____. *Playback.*
First Edition: London: Hamish Hamilton, 1958.

NF/F: $1,200   **G/VG: $350**

Points of Issue: First Issue is red cloth with silver lettering.
First U.S. Edition: Boston: Houghton Mifflin, 1958.

NF/F: $2,500   **G/VG: $800**

_____ **and Robert B. Parker.**
Poodle Springs.
Limited Edition: London: MacDonald, 1989 (250 copies).

NF/F: $150   **G/VG: Not Seen**

First U.S. Edition: Boston: Houghton Mifflin, 1954.

NF/F: $25   **G/VG: $10**

Charteris, Leslie. *The Ace Of Knaves.*
First Edition: London: Hodder & Stoughton, 1937.

NF/F: $1,600   **G/VG: $600**

First U.S. Edition: Garden City, NY: Doubleday, Doran/Crime Club, 1937.

NF/F: $700   **G/VG: $200**

_____. *Thieves' Picnic.*
First Edition: London: Hodder & Stoughton, 1937.

NF/F: $1,500   **G/VG: $500**

First U.S. Edition: Garden City, NY: Doubleday/Crime Club, 1937.

NF/F: $460   **G/VG: $100**

Chesterton, G.K. Father Brown Series*:

_____. *The Innocence of Father Brown.*
First Edition: London: Cassell, 1911.

NF/F: $1,500   **G/VG: $600**

First U.S. Edition: New York: John Lane, 1911.

NF/F: $250   **G/VG: $100**

_____. *The Wisdom of Father Brown.*
First Edition: London: Cassell, 1914.

NF/F: $200   **G/VG: $75**

First U.S. Edition: New York: John Lane, 1914.

NF/F: $100   **G/VG: $35**

_____. *The Incredulity of Father Brown.*
First Edition: London: Cassell, 1926.

NF/F: $2,800   **G/VG: $700**

First U.S. Edition: New York: Dodd Mead, 1926.

NF/F: $850   **G/VG: $250**

_____. *The Secret of Father Brown.*
First Edition: London: Cassell, 1927.

NF/F: $2,500   **G/VG: $650**

First U.S. Edition: New York: Harper, 1927.

NF/F: $200   **G/VG: $85**

_____. *The Scandal of Father Brown.*
First Edition: London: Cassell, 1935.
Points of Issue: Later Editions add the story "The Vampire of the Village."

NF/F: $1,450   **G/VG: $500**

First U.S. Edition: New York: Dodd Mead, 1943.

NF/F: $300   **G/VG: $100**

Christie, Agatha. *The Secret Adversary.*
First Edition: London: The Bodley Head, 1922.

NF/F: $4,200   **G/VG: $1,800**

First U.S. Edition: New York: Dodd, Mead, 1922.

NF/F: $800   **G/VG: $250**

_____. Hercule Poirot Series:

_____. *The Mysterious Affair at Styles.*
First Edition: New York: John Lane, 1920.
NF/F: $10,000 **G/VG: $3,500**
First U.K. Edition: London: The Bodley Head, 1921.
NF/F: $5,500 **G/VG: $2,500**

_____. *Murder on the Links.*
First Edition: New York: Dodd, Mead, 1923.
NF/F: $1,200 **G/VG: $475**
First U.K. Edition: London: The Bodley Head, 1921.
NF/F: $850 **G/VG: $250**

_____. *Poirot Investigates.*
First Edition: London: The Bodley Head, 1924.
NF/F: $2,200 **G/VG: $1,000**
First U.S. Edition: New York: Dodd, Mead, 1925.
NF/F: $1,200 **G/VG: $500**

_____. *The Murder of Roger Ackroyd.*
First Edition: London: Collins, 1926.
NF/F: $4,500 **G/VG: $2,000**
First U.S. Edition: New York: Dodd, Mead, 1926.
NF/F: $3,500 **G/VG: $1,500**

_____. *The Big Four.*
First Edition: London: Collins, 1927.
NF/F: $3,000 **G/VG: $1,200**
First U.S. Edition: New York: Dodd, Mead, 1926.
NF/F: $2,500 **G/VG: $925**

_____. *The Mystery of the Blue Train.*
First Edition: London: Collins, 1928.
NF/F: $4,500 **G/VG: $2,200**
First U.S. Edition: New York: Dodd, Mead, 1928.
NF/F: $3,000 **G/VG: $1,200**

_____. *Peril at End House.*
First Edition: New York: Dodd, Mead, 1932.
NF/F: $1,800 **G/VG: $550**
First U.K. Edition: London: Collins/Crime Club, 1932.
NF/F: $5,500 **G/VG: $1,950**

_____. *Lord Edgware Dies.*
First Edition: London: Collins/Crime Club, 1933.
NF/F: $3,300 **G/VG: $1,400**
First U.S. Edition as *Thirteen at Dinner*: New York: Dodd, Mead, 1933.
NF/F: $625 **G/VG: $250**

_____. *Murder on the Orient Express.*
First Edition: London: Collins/Crime Club, 1934.
NF/F: $3,000 **G/VG: $1,400**
First U.S. Edition as *Murder in the Calais Coach*: New York: Dodd, Mead, 1934.
NF/F: $3,000 **G/VG: $1,200**

_____. *Murder in Three Acts.*
First Edition: New York: Dodd, Mead, 1934.
NF/F: $2,500 **G/VG: $850**
First U.K. Edition as *Three Act Tragedy*: London: Collins/Crime Club, 1935.
NF/F: $1,500 **G/VG: $550**

_____. *Death in the Air.*
First Edition: New York: Dodd, Mead, 1935.
NF/F: $2,000 **G/VG: $650**
First U.K. Edition as *Death in the Clouds*: London: Collins/Crime Club, 1935.
NF/F: $3,500 **G/VG: $1,600**

Agatha Christie.

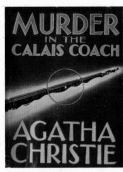

Agatha Christie.

Agatha Christie.

Agatha Christie.

Agatha Christie.

Agatha Christie.

_____. *The A. B. C. Murders.*
First Edition: London: Collins/Crime Club, 1936.
NF/F: $750   **G/VG: $300**
First U.S. Edition: New York: Dodd, Mead, 1936.
NF/F: $500   **G/VG: $200**

_____. *Murder in Mesopotamia.*
First Edition: London: Collins/Crime Club, 1936.
NF/F: $5,500   **G/VG: $2,000**
First U.S. Edition: New York: Dodd, Mead, 1936.
NF/F: $750   **G/VG: $275**

_____. *Cards on the Table.*
First Edition: London: Collins/Crime Club, 1936.
NF/F: $3,250   **G/VG: $1,200**
First U.S. Edition: New York: Dodd, Mead, 1937.
NF/F: $500   **G/VG: $175**

_____. *Dumb Witness.*
First Edition: London: Collins/Crime Club, 1937.
NF/F: $2,500   **G/VG: $800**
First U.S. Edition as *Poirot Loses a Client*: New York: Dodd, Mead, 1937.
NF/F: $700   **G/VG: $250**

_____. *Murder in the Mews.*
First Edition: London: Collins/Crime Club, 1937.
NF/F: $1,200   **G/VG: $500**
Points of Issue: First issue is blue boards with gilt lettering.
First U.S. Edition as *Dead Man's Mirror*: New York: Dodd, Mead, 1937.
NF/F: $500   **G/VG: $200**

_____. *Death on the Nile.*
First Edition: London: Collins/Crime Club, 1937.
NF/F: $7,500   **G/VG: $2,750**
Points of Issue: First issue is brown cloth with black lettering, original dust jacket price is 7s. 6d.
First Edition: New York: Dodd, Mead, 1938.
NF/F: $1,500   **G/VG: $650**

_____. *Appointment with Death.*
First Edition: London: Collins/Crime Club, 1938.
NF/F: $3,500   **G/VG: $1,650**
First U.S. Edition: New York: Dodd, Mead, 1938.
NF/F: $1,200   **G/VG: $500**

_____. *Hercule Poirot's Christmas.*
First Edition: London: Collins/Crime Club, 1938.
NF/F: $3,000   **G/VG: $1,400**
First U.S. Edition as *Murder for Christmas*: New York: Dodd, Mead, 1939.
NF/F: $250   **G/VG: $85**
Paperback Edition as *A Holiday for Murder*: New York: Avon, 1947.
NF/F: $35   **G/VG: $10**

_____. *The Regatta Mystery.*
First Edition: New York: Dodd, Mead, 1939.
NF/F: $300   **G/VG: $125**

_____. *Sad Cypress.*
First Edition: London: Collins/Crime Club, 1940.
NF/F: $1,200   **G/VG: $400**
First U.S. Edition: New York: Dodd, Mead, 1940.
NF/F: $750   **G/VG: $225**

_____. *One, Two Buckle My Shoe.*
First Edition: London: Collins/Crime Club, 1940.
NF/F: $1,000   **G/VG: $325**
First US Edition as *The Patriotic Murders*: New York: Dodd, Mead, 1941.
NF/F: $400   **G/VG: $125**
Paperback Edition as *An Overdose of Death*: New York: Dell, 1953.
NF/F: $20   **G/VG: $7**

_____. *Evil Under the Sun.*
First Edition: London: Collins/Crime Club, 1941.
NF/F: $1,450   **G/VG: $650**
First U.S. Edition: New York: Dodd, Mead, 1941.
NF/F: $850   **G/VG: $350**

_____. *Murder in Retrospect.*
First Edition: New York: Dodd, Mead, 1942.
NF/F: $550   **G/VG: $225**
First U.K. Edition as *Five Little Pigs*: London: Collins/Crime Club, 1942.
NF/F: $950   **G/VG: $400**

_____. *The Hollow.*
First Edition: New York: Dodd, Mead, 1946.
NF/F: $250   **G/VG: $75**
First U.K. Edition: London: Collins/Crime Club, 1946.
Points of Issue: First issue is red boards with black lettering on spine, original dust jacket price is 8s. 6d. net.
NF/F: $175   **G/VG: $65**
Paperback Edition as *Murder After Hours*: New York: Dell, 1954.
NF/F: $35   **G/VG: $10**

_____. *The Labors of Hercules.*
First Edition: New York: Dodd, Mead, 1947.
NF/F: $300   **G/VG: $95**
First U.K. Edition: London: Collins/Crime Club, 1947.
Points of Issue: First issue is orange cloth with black lettering on spine, original dust jacket price is 8s. 6d. Net.
NF/F: $155   **G/VG: $35**

_____. *There is a Tide.*
First Edition: New York: Dodd, Mead, 1948.
NF/F: $250   **G/VG: $100**
First U.K. Edition as *Taken at the Flood*: London: Collins/Crime Club, 1948.
NF/F: $500   **G/VG: $185**

_____. *Witness for the Prosecution and Other Stories.*
First Edition: New York: Dodd, Mead, 1948.
NF/F: $400   **G/VG: $175**

_____. *Three Blind Mice and Other Stories.*
First Edition: New York: Dodd, Mead, 1950.
NF/F: $200   **G/VG: $75**

_____. *The Underdog and Other Stories.*
First Edition: New York: Dodd, Mead, 1951.
NF/F: $150   **G/VG: $50**

_____. *Mrs McGinty's Dead.*
First Edition: New York: Dodd, Mead, 1952.
NF/F: $185   **G/VG: $55**
First U.K. Edition: London: Collins/Crime Club, 1952.
Points of Issue: First issue is red cloth with black lettering on spine.
NF/F: $550   **G/VG: $200**

Agatha Christie.

Agatha Christie.

Agatha Christie.

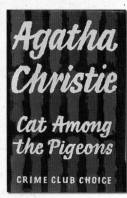

Agatha Christie.

Agatha Christie.

Agatha Christie.

_____. *Funerals Are Fatal.*
First Edition: New York: Dodd, Mead, 1953.
NF/F: $100   **G/VG: $35**
First U.K. Edition as *After the Funeral*:
London: Collins/Crime Club, 1953.
Points of Issue: First issue is green
boards with black lettering.
NF/F: $350   **G/VG: $145**
Paperback Edition as *Murder at the
Gallop*: London: Fontana Books, 1963.
NF/F: $50   **G/VG: $15**

_____. *Hickory, Dickory, Dock.*
First Edition: London: Collins/Crime
Club, 1955.
NF/F: $500   **G/VG: $185**
First U.S. Edition as *Hickory, Dickory,
Death*: New York: Dodd, Mead, 1956.
NF/F: $200   **G/VG: $75**

_____. *Dead Man's Folly.*
First Edition: New York: Dodd, Mead, 1956.
NF/F: $150   **G/VG: $65**
First U.K. Edition: London: Collins/
Crime Club, 1956.
NF/F: $100   **G/VG: $30**

_____. *Cat Among Pigeons.*
First Edition: London: Collins/Crime
Club, 1959.
NF/F: $200   **G/VG: $75**
First U.S. Edition: New York: Dodd,
Mead, 1960.
NF/F: $75   **G/VG: $25**

_____. *The Adventure of the
Christmas Pudding.*
First Edition: London: Collins/Crime
Club, 1960.
NF/F: $200   **G/VG: $60**

_____. *The Clocks.*
First Edition: London: Collins/Crime
Club, 1963.
Points of Issue: First issue is orange
boardsclocks with black lettering on spine.
NF/F: $185   **G/VG: $80**
First U.S. Edition: New York: Dodd,
Mead, 1964.
NF/F: $80   **G/VG: $25**

_____. *Third Girl.*
First Edition: London: Collins/Crime
Club, 1966.
NF/F: $95   **G/VG: $25**
First U.S. Edition: New York: Dodd,
Mead, 1967.
NF/F: $65   **G/VG: $25**

_____. *Hallowe'en Party.*
First Edition: London: Collins/Crime
Club, 1969.
NF/F: $135   **G/VG: $55**
First U.S. Edition: New York: Dodd,
Mead, 1969.
NF/F: $35   **G/VG: $15**

_____. *Elephants Can
Remember.*
First Edition: London: Collins/Crime
Club, 1972.
NF/F: $150   **G/VG: $65**
First U.S. Edition: New York: Dodd,
Mead, 1972.
NF/F: $120   **G/VG: $45**

_____. *Poirot's Early Cases.*
First Edition: London: Collins/Crime
Club, 1974.
NF/F: $95   **G/VG: $35**

_____. *Curtain.*
First Edition: London: Collins/Crime
Club, 1975.
NF/F: $100   **G/VG: $25**
First U.S. Edition: New York: Dodd,
Mead, 1975.
NF/F: $100   **G/VG: $15**

_____. Miss Marple Series:

_____. *Murder at the Vicarage.*
First Edition: London: Collins/Crime
Club, 1930.
NF/F: $2,500 **G/VG: $750**
First U.S. Edition: New York: Dodd,
Mead, 1952.
NF/F: $1,850 **G/VG: $650**

_____. *The Body in the Library.*
First Edition: London: Collins/Crime
Club, 1942.
NF/F: $1,850 **G/VG: $550**
First U.S. Edition: New York: Dodd,
Mead, 1942.
NF/F: $350 **G/VG: $150**

_____. *The Moving Finger.*
First U.K. Edition: London: Collins/
Crime Club, 1943.
NF/F: $755 **G/VG: $300**
First Edition: New York: Dodd, Mead, 1942.
NF/F: $650 **G/VG: $200**

_____. *A Murder is Announced.*
First Edition: London: Collins/Crime
Club, 1950.
NF/F: $425 **G/VG: $150**
First U.S. Edition: New York: Dodd,
Mead, 1950.
NF/F: $250 **G/VG: $95**

_____. *They Do It with Mirrors.*
First Edition: London: Collins/Crime
Club, 1951.
NF/F: $375 **G/VG: $120**
First U.S. Edition as *Murder With
Mirrors*: New York: Dodd, Mead, 1952.
NF/F: $180 **G/VG: $60**

_____. *A Pocket Full of Rye.*
First Edition: London: Collins/Crime
Club, 1953.
NF/F: $400 **G/VG: $150**
First U.S. Edition: New York: Dodd, Mead, 1953.
NF/F: $50 **G/VG: $20**

_____. *4:50 from Paddington.*
First Edition: London: Collins/Crime
Club, 1957.
Points of Issue: First issue is red cloth
with black lettering on spine.
NF/F: $225 **G/VG: $85**
First U.S. Edition as: *What Mrs.
McGillicuddy Saw!*: New York: Dodd,
Mead, 1957.
NF/F: $75 **G/VG: $35**

_____. *The Mirror Crack'd from
Side to Side.*
First Edition: London: Collins/Crime
Club, 1962.
NF/F: $135 **G/VG: $60**
First U.S. Edition as: *The Mirror
Crack'd:* New York: Dodd, Mead, 1962.
NF/F: $25 **G/VG: $10**

_____. *A Caribbean Mystery.*
First Edition: London: Collins/Crime
Club, 1964.
Points of Issue: First issue is red cloth
with gilt lettering on a bright red spine.
NF/F: $125 **G/VG: $60**
First U.S. Edition: New York: Dodd,
Mead, 1964.
NF/F: $50 **G/VG: $15**

_____. *At Bertram's Hotel.*
First Edition: London: Collins/Crime
Club, 1965.
NF/F: $95 **G/VG: $35**
First U.S. Edition: New York: Dodd,
Mead, 1966.
NF/F: $35 **G/VG: $15**

_____. *Nemesis.*
First Edition: London: Collins/Crime
Club, 1971.
Points of Issue: First issue is red cloth
with gilt Nemesis lettering on spine.
NF/F: $85 **G/VG: $35**
First U.S. Edition: New York: Dodd,
Mead, 1971.
NF/F: $60 **G/VG: $20**

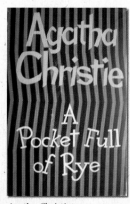

Agatha Christie.

Agatha Christie.

Tucker Coe.

Manning Coles.

Patricia Cornwell.

_____. *Sleeping Murder.*
First Edition: London: Collins/Crime Club, 1976.
NF/F: $50   **G/VG: $20**
First U.S. Edition: New York: Dodd, Mead, 1976.
NF/F: $25   **G/VG: $10**

_____. *The Thirteen Problems.*
First Edition: London: Collins/Crime Club, 1932.
NF/F: $250   **G/VG: $95**

_____. *Miss Marple's Final Cases and Two Other Stories.*
First Edition: London: Collins/Crime Club, 1979.
NF/F: $45   **G/VG: $20**

Clark, Douglas. *Premedicated Murder.*
First Edition: London: Victor Gollancz, 1975.
NF/F: $150   **G/VG: $60**
First Edition: New York: Scribners, 1975.
NF/F: $35   **G/VG: $10**

Clason, Clyde B. *Dragon's Cave.*
First Edition: Garden City, NY: Doubleday/Crime Club, 1939.
NF/F: $400   **G/VG: $130**

Coe, Tucker. *Murder Among Children.*
First Edition: New York: Random House, 1967.
NF/F: $135   **G/VG: $30**

Cohen, Octavus Roy. *Dangerous Lady.*
First Edition: New York: Macmillan, 1946.
NF/F: $65   **G/VG: $15**

Coles, Manning. *Now or Never.*
First Edition: Garden City, NY: Doubleday/Crime Club, 1951.
NF/F: $65   **G/VG: $25**
First U.K. Edition: London: Hodder and Stoughton, 1951.
NF/F: $45   **G/VG: $15**

_____. *Drink to Yesterday.*
First Edition: New York: Alfred A. Knopf, 1941.
NF/F: $400   **G/VG: $100**

Collins, Michael. *The Brass Rainbow.*
First Edition: New York: Dodd, Mead, 1969.
NF/F: $45   **G/VG: $15**

Connington, J. J. *The Case With Nine Solutions.*
First Edition: Boston: Little Brown, 1929.
NF/F: $400   **G/VG: $100**

Cornwell, Patricia. Kay Scarpetta Series:

_____. *Postmortem.*
First Edition: New York: Scribner's, 1990.
NF/F: $2,200   **G/VG: $800**

_____. *Body of Evidence.*
First Edition: New York: Scribner's, 1991.
NF/F: $250   **G/VG: $100**

_____. *All That Remains.*
First Edition: New York: Scribner's, 1992.
NF/F: $75   **G/VG: $30**

_____. *Cruel and Unusual.*
First Edition: New York: Scribner's, 1993.
NF/F: $65   **G/VG: $25**

_____. *The Body Farm.*
First Edition: New York: Scribner's, 1994.
NF/F: $35   **G/VG: $15**

_____. *From Potter's Field.*
First Edition: New York: Scribner's, 1995.
NF/F: $20   **G/VG: $8**

_____. *Cause of Death.*
Limited Edition: New York: Putnam's, 1996 (185 numbered copies).
NF/F: $200   **G/VG: Not Seen**
First Edition: New York: Putnam's, 1996.
NF/F: $20   **G/VG: $8**

_____. *Unnatural Exposure.*
Limited Edition: New York: Putnam's,
1997 (175 numbered copies).
NF/F: $275   **G/VG: Not Seen**
First Edition: New York: Putnam's, 1997.
NF/F: $20   **G/VG: $8**

_____. *Point of Origin.*
Limited Edition: New York: Putnam's,
1998 (500 numbered copies).
NF/F: $100   **G/VG: Not Seen**
First Edition: New York: Putnam's, 1998.
NF/F: $20   **G/VG: $8**

_____. *Black Notice.*
Limited Edition: New York: Putnam's,
1999 (200 numbered copies).
NF/F: $175   **G/VG: Not Seen**
First Edition: New York: Putnam's, 1999.
NF/F: $20   **G/VG: $8**

_____. *The Last Precinct.*
Limited Edition: New York: Putnam's,
2000 (175 numbered copies).
NF/F: $200   **G/VG: Not Seen**
First Edition: New York: Putnam's,
1999.
NF/F: $20   **G/VG: $8**

_____. *Blow Fly.*
First Edition: New York: Putnam's, 2003.
NF/F: $20   **G/VG: $8**

_____. *Trace.*
First Edition: New York: Putnam's, 2004.
NF/F: $20   **G/VG: $8**

_____. *Predator.*
First Edition: New York: Scribner's, 2005.
NF/F: $20   **G/VG: $8**

Coxe, George Harmon. *Lady Killer.*
First Edition: New York: Alfred A.
Knopf, 1949.
NF/F: $75   **G/VG: $20**

Crane, Francis. *The Cinnamon
Murder.*
First Edition: New York: Random
House, 1946.
NF/F: $60   **G/VG: $15**

Creasey, John. *The Toff and the Spider.*
First Edition: London: Hodder &
Stoughton, 1965.
NF/F: $45   **G/VG: $15**
First U.S. Edition: New York: Walker &
Company, 1965.
NF/F: $35   **G/VG: $10**

_____. *The Depths.*
First Edition: London: Hodder &
Stoughton, 1963.
NF/F: $55   **G/VG: $20**
First Edition: New York: Walker, 1967.
NF/F: $20   **G/VG: $8**

Crispin, Edmund. *The Long Divorce.*
First Edition: London: Victor Gollancz,
1951.
NF/F: $180   **G/VG: $55**
First U.S. Edition: New York: Dodd
Mead, 1951.
NF/F: $55   **G/VG: $20**

Crofts, Freeman Wills. *Man Overboard.*
First Edition: London: Collins/ Crime
Club, 1936.
NF/F: $1,200   **G/VG: $300**
First U.S. Edition: New York: Dodd,
Mead, 1936.
NF/F: $225   **G/VG: $65**

Cumberland, Marten. *And Then
Came Fear.*
First Edition: Garden City, NY:
Doubleday/Crime Club, 1948.
NF/F: $85   **G/VG: $40**

Cunningham, A.B. *Murder at Deer Lick.*
First Edition: New York: Dutton, 1939.
NF/F: $325   **G/VG: $100**

John Creasey.

Freeman Wills Crofts.

A.B. Cunngingham.

Lillian De La Torre.

Thomas B. Dewey.

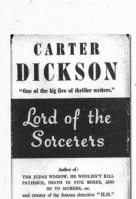

Carter Dickson.

Daly, Elizabeth. *Deadly Nightshade.*
First Edition: New York: Farrar &
Rinehart, 1940.
NF/F: $400   **G/VG: $100**

Dean, Spencer. *The Merchant of
Murder.*
First Edition: Garden City, NY:
Doubleday, 1959.
NF/F: $45   **G/VG: $10**

Deighton, Len. Unnamed Hero (Harry
Palmer) Series:

_____. *The Ipcress File.*
First Edition: London: Hodder &
Stoughton, 1962.
NF/F: $1,500   **G/VG: $700**
First U.S. Edition: New York: Simon
and Schuster, 1963.
NF/F: $250   **G/VG: $85**

_____. *Horse Under Water.*
First Edition: London: Jonathon Cape,
1963.
NF/F: $350   **G/VG: $100**

_____. *Funeral in Berlin.*
First Edition: London: Jonathon Cape,
1964.
NF/F: $225   **G/VG: $100**

_____. *The Billion-Dollar Brain.*
First Edition: London: Jonathon Cape,
1966.
NF/F: $125   **G/VG: $45**

_____. *An Expensive Place to Die.*
First Edition: London: Jonathon Cape,
1967.
NF/F: $200   **G/VG: $70**

_____. *Spy Story.*
First Edition: London: Jonathon Cape,
1974.
NF/F: $100   **G/VG: $35**

_____. *Yesterday's Spy.*
First Edition: London: Jonathon Cape,
1975.
NF/F: $65   **G/VG: $25**

_____. *Twinkle, Twinkle Little Spy.*
First Edition: London: Jonathon Cape,
1976.
NF/F: $85   **G/VG: $25**

De La Torre, Lillian. *Dr. Sam
Johnson, Detector.*
First Edition: New York: Alfred A.
Knopf, 1946.
NF/F: $200   **G/VG: $55**

Derleth, August. *Three Problems for
Solar Pons.*
First Edition: Sauk City, WI: Mycroft &
Moran, 1952.
NF/F: $500   **G/VG: $125**

Dewey, Thomas B. *The Brave Bad
Girls.*
First Edition: New York: Simon &
Schuster/Inner Sanctum, 1956.
NF/F: $45   **G/VG: $15**

Dickson, Carter. *Lord of the
Sorcerers.*
First Edition: London: William
Heinemann, 1946.
NF/F: $300   **G/VG: $75**

Diehl, William. *Sharky's Machine.*
First Edition: New York: Delacorte,
1978.
NF/F: $95   **G/VG: $20**

Disney, Doris Miles. *Room For
Murder.*
First Edition: Garden City, NY
Doubleday, 1955.
NF/F: $40   **G/VG: $10**
First U.K. Edition: London: W.
Foulsham & Co., 1959.
NF/F: $25   **G/VG: $10**

Doyle, Sir Arthur Conan. *Sherlock Holmes Series:*

_____. *A Study in Scarlet.*
First Edition: London: Ward Locke, 1888.
NF/F: $25,500   **G/VG: $9,000**
First U.S. Edition: Philadelphia: J. B. Lippincott, 1890.
NF/F: $5,000   **G/VG: $1,800**

_____. *The Sign of the Four.*
First Edition: London: Spencer Blackett, 1890.
NF/F: $15,500   **G/VG: $4,000**

_____. *The Adventures Of Sherlock Holmes.*
First Edition: London: George Newnes, 1892.
Points of Issue: The first issue has a blank street sign on the front cover.
NF/F: $4,500   **G/VG: $2,800**
First Edition: New York: Harper & Brothers, 1892.
NF/F: $900   **G/VG: $300**

_____. *The Memoirs Of Sherlock Holmes.*
First Edition: London: George Newnes, 1894. Points of Issue: Blue beveled boards lettered in gilt decorated in black.
NF/F: $3,500   **G/VG: $1,500**
First Edition: New York: Harper & Brothers, 1894. Points of Issue: 6 pages of ads follow text block in first issue.
NF/F: $600   **G/VG: $175**

_____. *The Hound of the Baskervilles.*
First Edition: London: Georges Newnes, 1902. Points of Issue: The first issue lacks a publication date on the verso.
NF/F: $7,500   **G/VG: $2,500**

_____. *The Return Of Sherlock Holmes.*
First Edition: London: Georges Newnes, 1905.
Points of Issue: "you" on page 3 line 3 in first issue.
NF/F: $4,000   **G/VG: $1,700**

_____. *The Valley of Fear.*
First Edition: New York: George H. Doran, 1915.
NF/F: $18,000   **G/VG: $8,500**
First U.K. Edition: London: Smith Elder, 1915.
NF/F: $2,000   **G/VG: $800**

_____. *His Last Bow.*
First Edition: London: John Murray, 1917.
NF/F: $3,000   **G/VG: $950**
First U.S. Edition: New York: George H. Doran, 1917.
NF/F: $2,600   **G/VG: $1,000**

_____. *The Case-Book Of Sherlock Holmes.*
First Edition: London: John Murray, 1927.
NF/F: $9,500   **G/VG: $3,800**
First Edition: New York: George H. Doran, 1927.
NF/F: $2,200   **G/VG: $900**

DuBois, Theodora. *Death Is Late to Lunch.*
First Edition: Boston: Houghton Mifflin, 1941.
NF/F: $75   **G/VG: $35**

Dunning, John. Cliff Janeway Series:

_____. *Booked to Die.*
First Edition: New York: Charles Scribners, 1992.
NF/F: $1,450   **G/VG: $550**

_____. *The Bookman's Wake.*
First Edition: New York: Charles Scribners, 1995.
NF/F: $45   **G/VG: $15**

Sir Arthur Conan Doyle.

John Dunning.

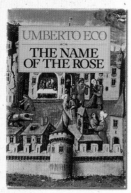

Umberto Eco.

James Ellroy.

A.A. Fair.

_____. *The Bookman's Promise.*
First Edition: New York: Charles
Scribners, 2004.
NF/F: $25   **G/VG: $10**

_____. *The Sign of the Book.*
First Edition: New York: Charles
Scribners, 2005.
NF/F: $30   **G/VG: $12**

_____. *The Bookwoman's Last Fling.*
First Edition: New York: Charles
Scribners, 2006.
NF/F: $20   **G/VG: $8**

Eco, Umberto. *The Name of the Rose.*
First Edition in English: London:
Secker & Warburg, 1983.
NF/F: $500   **G/VG: $125**
First U.S. Edition: New York: Harcourt
Brace, 1983.
NF/F: $225   **G/VG: $65**

Egan, Lesley. *My Name Is Death.*
First Edition: New York: Harper, 1964.
NF/F: $25   **G/VG: $10**

Ellroy, James. *White Jazz.*
First Edition: New York: Alfred A.
Knopf, 1992.
NF/F: $150   **G/VG: $30**

Erskine, Margaret. *Case With Three
Husbands.*
First Edition: Garden City, NY:
Doubleday/Crime Club, 1967.
NF/F: $55   **G/VG: $15**
First U.K. Edition: London: Hodder and
Stoughton, 1967.
NF/F: $35   **G/VG: $10**

Fair, A.A. Donald Cool/Bertha Lam Series:

_____. *The Bigger They Come.*
First Edition: New York: William
Morrow, 1939.
NF/F: Not Seen   **G/VG: $55**

_____. *Turn on the Heat.*
First Edition: New York: William
Morrow, 1940.
NF/F: $600   **G/VG: $145**

_____. *Gold Comes in Bricks.*
First Edition: New York: William
Morrow, 1940.
NF/F: $1,000   **G/VG: $550**

_____. *Spill the Jackpot.*
First Edition: New York: William
Morrow, 1941.
NF/F: $75   **G/VG: $30**

_____. *Double or Quits.*
First Edition: New York: William
Morrow, 1941.
NF/F: $725   **G/VG: $125**

_____. *Owls Don't Blink.*
First Edition: New York: William
Morrow, 1942.
NF/F: $500   **G/VG: $75**

_____. *Bats Fly at Dusk.*
First Edition: New York: William
Morrow, 1942.
NF/F: $325   **G/VG: $70**

_____. *Cats Prowl at Night.*
First Edition: New York: William
Morrow, 1943.
NF/F: $275   **G/VG: $85**

_____. *Give 'em the Ax.*
First Edition: New York: William
Morrow, 1944.
NF/F: $425   **G/VG: $50**

_____. *Crows Can't Count.*
First Edition: New York: William
Morrow, 1946.
NF/F: $85   **G/VG: $20**

_____. *Fools Die on Friday.*
First Edition: New York: William Morrow, 1947.
NF/F: $275   **G/VG: $80**

_____. *Bedrooms Have Windows.*
First Edition: New York: William Morrow, 1949.
NF/F: $85   **G/VG: $30**

_____. *Top of the Heap.*
First Edition: New York: William Morrow, 1952.
NF/F: $75   **G/VG: $30**

_____. *Some Women Won't Wait.*
First Edition: New York: William Morrow, 1953.
NF/F: $85   **G/VG: $35**

_____. *Beware the Curves.*
First Edition: New York: William Morrow, 1956.
NF/F: $75   **G/VG: $30**

_____. *You Can Die Laughing.*
First Edition: New York: William Morrow, 1957.
NF/F: $95   **G/VG: $50**

_____. *Some Slips Don't Show.*
First Edition: New York: William Morrow, 1957.
NF/F: $75   **G/VG: $25**

_____. *The Count of Nine.*
First Edition: New York: William Morrow, 1958.
NF/F: $65   **G/VG: $25**

_____. *Pass the Gravy.*
First Edition: New York: William Morrow, 1959.
NF/F: $55   **G/VG: $20**

_____. *Kept Women Can't Quit.*
First Edition: New York: William Morrow, 1960.
NF/F: $95   **G/VG: $30**

_____. *Bachelors Get Lonely.*
First Edition: New York: William Morrow, 1961.
NF/F: $85   **G/VG: $35**

_____. *Shills Can't Cash Chips.*
First Edition: New York: William Morrow, 1961.
NF/F: $75   **G/VG: $35**

_____. *Try Anything Once.*
First Edition: New York: William Morrow, 1962.
NF/F: $65   **G/VG: $25**

_____. *Fish or Cut Bait.*
First Edition: New York: William Morrow, 1963.
NF/F: $55   **G/VG: $20**

_____. *Up for Grabs.*
First Edition: New York: William Morrow, 1964.
NF/F: $55   **G/VG: $20**

_____. *Cut Thin to Win.*
First Edition: New York: William Morrow, 1965.
NF/F: $50   **G/VG: $15**

_____. *Widows Wear Weeds.*
First Edition: New York: William Morrow, 1966.
NF/F: $45   **G/VG: $15**

_____. *Traps Need Fresh Bait.*
First Edition: New York: William Morrow, 1967.
NF/F: $65   **G/VG: $15**

A.A. Fair.

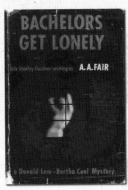

A.A. Fair.

A.A. Fair.

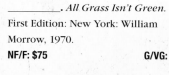

Sebastian Faulks.

Gerard Fisher.

Ian Fleming.

_____. *All Grass Isn't Green.*
First Edition: New York: William
Morrow, 1970.
NF/F: $75　　　　　　　**G/VG: $20**

Faulkner, William. *Intruder in the Dust.*
First Edition: New York: Random
House, 1948.
NF/F: $1,450　　　　　**G/VG: $450**

Faulks, Sebastian. James Bond Series:

_____. *Devil May Care.*
Limited Edition: New York/London:
Random House/Doubleday, 2008 (300
copies).
NF/F: $2,500　　　**G/VG: Not Seen**
Limited Edition: London: Penguin,
2008 (500 copies).
NF/F: $850　　　　**G/VG: Not Seen**
First Trade Edition: London: Penguin,
2008
NF/F: $35　　　　　**G/VG: Not Seen**
(See Also: Ian Fleming, Robert
Markham, John Gardner, Raymond
Benson).

Ferrigno, Robert. *Dead Man's Dance.*
First Edition: New York: G.P. Putnam,
1995.
NF/F: $20　　　　　　　**G/VG: $5**

Fickling, G. G. *Blood and Honey.*
First Edition: New York: Pyramid
Books, 1961. Points of Issue:
Paperback Original Pyramid #G-623.
NF/F: $45　　　　　　　**G/VG: $10**

Fish, Robert L. *The Fugitive.*
First Edition: New York: Simon and
Schuster, 1962.
NF/F: $155　　　　　　**G/VG: $30**

_____. *The Murder League.*
First Edition: New York: Simon &
Schuster, 1968.
NF/F: $40　　　　　　　**G/VG: $15**

Fisher, Gerard. *Hospitality for
Murder.*
First Edition: New York: Washburn/
Chantecler, 1959.
NF/F: $25　　　　　　　**G/VG: $10**

Fleming, Ian. James Bond Series:

_____. *Casino Royale.*
First Edition: London: Jonathan Cape,
1953. Points of Issue: Black cloth with
red heart vignette on upper cover and
titles on the spine, in gun metal gray.
NF/F: $30,000　　　　**G/VG: $12,500**
First U.S. Edition: New York:
Macmillan, 1954.
NF/F: $1,650　　　　　**G/VG: $725**

_____. *Live and Let Die.*
First Edition: London, Jonathan Cape,
1954.
NF/F: $22,000　　　　**G/VG: $9,750**
First U.S. Edition: New York: Viking
Press, 1955.
NF/F: $1,400　　　　　**G/VG: $625**

_____. *Moonraker.*
First Edition: London: Jonathan
Cape, 1955. Points of Issue: Page ten
misprints shoot as "shoo" on page ten
in the first state.
NF/F: $18,500　　　　**G/VG: $7,775**
First U.S. Edition: New York:
Macmillan, 1955.
NF/F: $2,000　　　　　**G/VG: $900**

_____. *Diamonds are Forever.*
First Edition: London, Jonathan Cape,
1956.
NF/F: $7,000　　　　　**G/VG: $3,000**
First U.S. Edition: New York: Viking
Press, 1956.
NF/F: $800　　　　　　**G/VG: $325**

_____. *From Russia with Love.*
First Edition: London: Jonathan Cape, 1957.
NF/F: $7,500   **G/VG: $2,500**
First U.S. Edition: New York:
Macmillan, 1957.
NF/F: $145   **G/VG: $45**

_____. *Dr. No.*
First Edition: London: Jonathan Cape, 1958.
NF/F: $8,500   **G/VG: $3,250**
First U.S. Edition: New York:
Macmillan, 1958.
NF/F: $350   **G/VG: $100**

_____. *Goldfinger.*
First Edition: London: Jonathan Cape, 1959.
NF/F: $8,000   **G/VG: $3,000**
First U.S. Edition: New York:
Macmillan, 1959.
NF/F: $550   **G/VG: $225**

_____. *For Your Eyes Only.*
First Edition: London: Jonathan Cape,
1960.
NF/F: $4,500   **G/VG: $2,000**
First U.S. Edition: New York: Viking
Press, 1960.
NF/F: $450   **G/VG: $200**

_____. *Thunderball.*
First Edition: London: Jonathan Cape,
1961.
NF/F: $3,500   **G/VG: $1,200**
First U.S. Edition: New York: Viking
Press, 1961.
NF/F: $475   **G/VG: $200**

_____. *The Spy Who Loved Me.*
First Edition: London: Jonathan
Cape, 1962. Points of Issue: The first
state has a line between e and m in
"Fleming" on the title page.
NF/F: $1,450   **G/VG: $625**
First U.S. Edition: New York: Viking
Press, 1962.
NF/F: $145   **G/VG: $45**

_____. *On Her Majesty's Secret
Service.*
Limited Edition: London: Jonathan
Cape, 1963 (250 numbered copies).
NF/F: $27,000   **G/VG: $10,000**
First Edition: London: Jonathan Cape,
1963.
NF/F: $1,100   **G/VG: $550**
First U.S. Edition: New York: New
American Library, 1963.
NF/F: $100   **G/VG: $40**

_____. *You Only Live Twice.*
First Edition: London: Jonathan Cape,
1964.
NF/F: $550   **G/VG: $200**
First U.S. Edition: New York: New
American Library, 1964.
NF/F: $75   **G/VG: $35**

_____. *The Man with the Golden
Gun.*
First Edition: London: Jonathan Cape,
1965.
NF/F: $155   **G/VG: $65**
First U.S. Edition: New York: New
American Library, 1965.
NF/F: $150   **G/VG: $45**

_____. *Octopussy and The
Living Daylights.*
First Edition: London: Jonathan Cape,
1966.
NF/F: $275   **G/VG: $75**
First U.S. Edition: New York:
Macmillan, 1957.
NF/F: $100   **G/VG: $35**
(See Also: Robert Markham, John Gardner,
Raymond Benson, Sebastian Faulks).

Fletcher, Lucille. *A novelization from
the screen play by Alan Ullmann.
Sorry, Wrong Number.*
First Edition: New York: Random
House, 1948.
NF/F: $95   **G/VG: $25**

Ian Fleming.

Ian Fleming.

Ian Fleming.

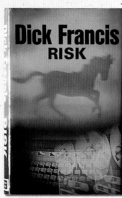

Dick Francis.

Dick Francis.

R. Austin Freeman.

Foley, Rae. *Wake the Sleeping Wolf.*
First Edition: New York: Dodd, Mead,
1952.
NF/F: $160   **G/VG: $45**

Ford, Leslie. *The Woman in Black.*
First Edition: New York: Charles
Scribner's, 1947.
NF/F: $95   **G/VG: $20**

Francis, Dick. *Risk.*
First Edition: London: Michael Joseph,
1977.
NF/F: $135   **G/VG: $45**
First U.S. Edition: New York: Harper &
Row, 1977.
NF/F: $85   **G/VG: $25**

_____. *Twice Shy.*
First Edition: London: Michael Joseph,
1981.
NF/F: $85   **G/VG: $40**
First U.S. Edition: .New York: G.P.
Putnam's, 1982.
NF/F: $40   **G/VG: $15**

Freeling, Nicolas. *Because of the
Cats.*
First Edition: London: Victor Gollancz,
1963.
NF/F: $85   **G/VG: $25**
First Edition: New York: Harper &
Row, 1964.
NF/F: $25   **G/VG: $10**

Freeman, R. Austin. Dr. Thorndyke
Series:

_____. *The Red Thumb Mark.*
First Edition: London: Hodder &
Stoughton, 1907.
NF/F: $1,450   **G/VG: $575**
First U.S. Edition: New York: Donald
W. Newton, 1911.
NF/F: $595   **G/VG: $300**

_____. *John Thorndyke's Cases.*
First Edition: London: Hodder &
Stoughton, 1909.
NF/F: $1,100   **G/VG: $425**

_____. *The Eye of Osiris.*
First Edition: London: Hodder &
Stoughton, 1911.
NF/F: $550   **G/VG: $200**
First U.S. Edition: New York: P. F.
Collier, 1911.
NF/F: $300   **G/VG: $95**

_____. *The Mystery of 31 New Inn.*
First Edition: London: Hodder &
Stoughton, 1912.
NF/F: $900   **G/VG: $375**
First U.S. Edition: Philadelphia: John C.
Winston, 1913.
NF/F: $850   **G/VG: $325**

_____. *The Singing Bone.*
First Edition: London: Hodder &
Stoughton, 1912. Points of Issue: A first
issue has: p. 3, risen space before 'THE'
in running title; p. 4, antepenultimate
line, 't' in 'train' broken; p. 19, risen
furniture after last line; p. 46, last line,
extra full-stop after 'head'; p. 170, l.1,
broken 'n' in 'man'; p. 184, l.7, broken
'm' in 'mother'; p. 226, l.23, 'his' for
'he'; p. 231, l.5, question mark after
'that' instead of an exclamation mark; p.
235, l.5, 'know' for 'now.
NF/F: $650   **G/VG: $300**

_____. *A Silent Witness.*
First Edition: London: Hodder &
Stoughton, 1914.
NF/F: $575   **G/VG: $225**

_____. *Helen Vardon's
Confession.*
First Edition: London: Hodder &
Stoughton, 1922.
NF/F: $850   **G/VG: $475**

_____. *The Cat's Eye.*
First Edition: London: Hodder &
Stoughton, 1923.
NF/F: $375   **G/VG: $150**

_____. *Dr. Thorndyke's
Casebook.*
First Edition: London: Hodder &
Stoughton, 1923.
NF/F: $550   **G/VG: $175**
First U.S. Edition as: *The Blue Scarab*:
New York: Dodd Mead, 1924.
NF/F: $125   **G/VG: $55**

_____. *The Mystery of Angelina
Frood.*
First Edition: London: Hodder &
Stoughton, 1924.
NF/F: $400   **G/VG: $155**
First U.S. Edition: New York: Dodd
Mead, 1925.
NF/F: $125   **G/VG: $45**

_____. *The Shadow of the Wolf.*
First Edition: London: Hodder &
Stoughton, 1925.
NF/F: $250   **G/VG: $100**
First U.S. Edition: New York: Dodd
Mead, 1925.
NF/F: $145   **G/VG: $55**

_____. *The Puzzle Lock.*
First Edition: London: Hodder &
Stoughton, 1925.
NF/F: $750   **G/VG: $325**
First U.S. Edition: New York: Dodd
Mead, 1926.
NF/F: $250   **G/VG: $95**

_____. *The D'arblay Mystery.*
First Edition: London: Hodder &
Stoughton, 1926.
NF/F: $275   **G/VG: $100**
First U.S. Edition: New York: Dodd
Mead, 1926.
NF/F: $100   **G/VG: $40**

_____. *A Certain Dr. Thorndyke.*
First Edition: London: Hodder &
Stoughton, 1927.
NF/F: $350   **G/VG: $125**
First U.S. Edition: New York: Dodd
Mead, 1928.
NF/F: $125   **G/VG: $50**

_____. *The Magic Casket.*
First Edition: London: Hodder &
Stoughton, 1927.
NF/F: $600   **G/VG: $225**
First U.S. Edition: New York: Dodd
Mead, 1927.
NF/F: $250   **G/VG: $85**

_____. *As a Thief in the Night.*
First Edition: London: Hodder &
Stoughton, 1928.
NF/F: $225   **G/VG: $85**
First U.S. Edition: New York: Dodd
Mead, 1928.
NF/F: $350   **G/VG: $100**

_____. *The Famous Cases of Dr.
Thorndyke.*
First Edition: London: Hodder &
Stoughton, 1929.
NF/F: $250   **G/VG: $95**

_____. *Mr. Pottermack's
Oversight.*
First Edition: London: Hodder &
Stoughton, 1930.
NF/F: $850   **G/VG: $350**
First U.S. Edition: New York: Dodd
Mead, 1930.
NF/F: $350   **G/VG: $125**

_____. *Pontifex, Son and
Thorndyke.*
First Edition: London: Hodder &
Stoughton, 1931.
NF/F: $925   **G/VG: $400**
First Edition: New York: Dodd Mead, 1931.
NF/F: $450   **G/VG: $200**

R. Austin Freeman.

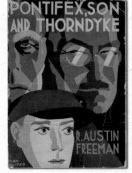

R. Austin Freeman.

R. Austin Freeman.

David Frome.

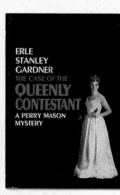

Erle Stanley Gardner.

_____. *When Rogues Fall Out.*
First Edition: London: Hodder &
Stoughton, 1931.
NF/F: $850　　　　　**G/VG: $375**
First Edition: New York: Dodd Mead, 1931.
NF/F: $250　　　　　**G/VG: $75**

_____. *Dr. Thorndyke
Intervenes.*
First Edition: London: Hodder &
Stoughton, 1933.
NF/F: $400　　　　　**G/VG: $175**
First U.S. Edition: New York: Dodd
Mead, 1933.
NF/F: $200　　　　　**G/VG: $75**

_____. *For the Defense: Dr.
Thorndyke.*
First Edition: London: Hodder &
Stoughton, 1934.
NF/F: $350　　　　　**G/VG: $125**
First U.S. Edition: New York: Dodd
Mead, 1936.
NF/F: $250　　　　　**G/VG: $95**

_____. *The Penrose Mystery.*
First Edition: London: Hodder &
Stoughton, 1936.
NF/F: $400　　　　　**G/VG: $150**
First U.S. Edition: New York: Dodd
Mead, 1936.
NF/F: $275　　　　　**G/VG: $125**

_____. *Felo de Se?*
First Edition: London: Hodder &
Stoughton, 1937.
NF/F: $500　　　　　**G/VG: $225**

_____. *The Stoneware Monkey.*
First Edition: London: Hodder &
Stoughton, 1938.
NF/F: $875　　　　　**G/VG: $400**

_____. *Mr. Polton Explains.*
First Edition: London: Hodder &
Stoughton, 1940.
NF/F: $650　　　　　**G/VG: $275**

_____. *Dr. Thorndyke's Crime File.*
First Edition: New York: Dodd Mead,
1941.
NF/F: $85　　　　　**G/VG: $25**

_____. *The Jacob Street Witness.*
First Edition: London: Hodder &
Stoughton, 1942.
NF/F: $350　　　　　**G/VG: $100**
First U.S. Edition as: *The Unconscious
Witness*: New York: Dodd Mead, 1942.
NF/F: $200　　　　　**G/VG: $85**

Frome, David. *Mr. Pinkerton Has the
Clue.*
First Edition: New York: Farrar &
Rinehart, 1936.
NF/F: $175　　　　　**G/VG: $65**

Gardner, Erle Stanley. *The Case of
the Queenly Contestant.*
First Edition: New York: William
Morrow, 1967.
NF/F: $85　　　　　**G/VG: $25**

_____. *The Case of the Troubled
Trustee.*
First Edition: New York: William
Morrow, 1965.
NF/F: $80　　　　　**G/VG: $25**

Gardner, John. James Bond Series:

_____. *License Renewed.*
First Edition: London: Jonathan Cape,
1981.
NF/F: $65　　　　　**G/VG: $25**
First U.S. Edition: New York: Richard
Marek, 1981.
NF/F: $50　　　　　**G/VG: $20**

_____. *For Special Services.*
First Edition: London: Jonathan Cape, 1982.
NF/F: $85　　　　　**G/VG: $40**
First U.S. Edition: New York: Coward,
McCann and Geoghegan, 1982.
NF/F: $65　　　　　**G/VG: $25**

_____. *Icebreaker.*
First Edition: London: Jonathan Cape, 1983.
NF/F: $100   **G/VG: $45**
First U.S. Edition: New York: Putnam, 1983.
NF/F: $25   **G/VG: $10**

_____. *Role of Honour.*
First Edition: London: Jonathan Cape, 1984.
NF/F: $65   **G/VG: $25**
First U.S. Edition: New York: Putnam, 1984.
NF/F: $145   **G/VG: $35**

_____. *Nobody Lives Forever.*
First Edition: London: Jonathan Cape, 1986.
NF/F: $100   **G/VG: $35**
First U.S. Edition: New York: Putnam, 1986.
NF/F: $145   **G/VG: $35**

_____. *No Deals, Mr. Bond.*
First Edition: London: Jonathan Cape, 1987.
NF/F: $60   **G/VG: $25**
First U.S. Edition: New York: Putnam, 1987.
NF/F: $35   **G/VG: $15**

_____. *Scorpius.*
First Edition: London: Hodder & Stoughton, 1988.
NF/F: $60   **G/VG: $20**
First U.S. Edition: New York: Putnam, 1988.
NF/F: $45   **G/VG: $20**

_____. *Win, Lose or Die.*
First Edition: London: Hodder & Stoughton, 1989.
NF/F: $75   **G/VG: $30**
First U.S. Edition: New York: Putnam, 1989.
NF/F: $35   **G/VG: $15**

_____. *License to Kill* (novelization of screenplay).
First Edition: New York: Armchair Detective Library, 1990. There Three Limited States one of 26 lettered copies, one of 100 numbered copies and an unknown group signed in slipcase, bound in blue. Only seen in Fine condition for $2,000.
NF/F: $125   **G/VG: $50**

_____. *Brokenclaw.*
First Edition: London: Hodder & Stoughton, 1990.
NF/F: $100   **G/VG: $40**
First U.S. Edition: New York: Putnam, 1990.
NF/F: $30   **G/VG: $10**

_____. *The Man from Barbarossa.*
First Edition: London: Hodder & Stoughton, 1991.
NF/F: $100   **G/VG: $45**
First U.S. Edition: New York: Putnam, 1991.
NF/F: $25   **G/VG: $8**

_____. *Death is Forever.*
First Edition: London: Hodder & Stoughton, 1992.
NF/F: $70   **G/VG: $30**
First U.S. Edition: New York: Putnam, 1992.
NF/F: $35   **G/VG: $15**

_____. *Never Send Flowers.*
First Edition: London: Hodder & Stoughton, 1993.
NF/F: $75   **G/VG: $30**
First U.S. Edition: New York: Putnam, 1993.
NF/F: $45   **G/VG: $15**

_____. *Sea Fire.*
First Edition: London: Hodder & Stoughton, 1994.
NF/F: $70   **G/VG: $30**
First U.S. Edition: New York: Putnam, 1994.
NF/F: $35   **G/VG: $15**

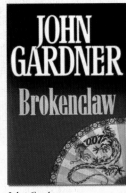

Erle Stanley Gardner.

John Gardner.

William Campbell Gault.

Anthony Gilbert.

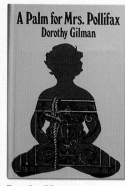

Dorothy Gilman.

_____. *Golden Eye.*
First Edition: London: Hodder & Stoughton, 1996. Note: Preceded by London: Coronet, 1995, paperback only seen as new, $1,500.
NF/F: $320   **G/VG: $140**

_____. *COLD.*
First Edition: London: Hodder & Stoughton, 1996.
NF/F: $400   **G/VG: $150**
First U.S. Edition: New York: Putnam, 1996.
NF/F: $50   **G/VG: $55**
(See Also: Ian Fleming, Robert Markham, Raymond Benson, Sebastian Faulks).

Garnet, A. H. *The Santa Claus Killer.*
First Edition: New Haven: Ticknor & Fields, 1981.
NF/F: $45   **G/VG: $10**

Garve, Andrew. *The Narrow Search.*
First Edition: London: Collins /Crime Club, 1957.
NF/F: $40   **G/VG: $10**
First U.S. Edition: New York: Harper & Brothers, 1957.
NF/F: $25   **G/VG: $10**

Gault, William Campbell. *The Hundred-Dollar Girl.*
First Edition: New York: E. P. Dutton, 1961.
NF/F: $185   **G/VG: $45**

Gilbert, Anthony. *Murder by Experts.*
First Edition: New York: Dial Press, Inc., 1937.
NF/F: $125   **G/VG: $50**

Gilbert, Michael. *Fear to Tread.*
First Edition: London: Hodder and Stoughton, 1953.
NF/F: $185   **G/VG: $55**
First U.S. Edition: New York: Harper & Brothers, 1953.
NF/F: $50   **G/VG: $10**

Gilman, Dorothy. Mrs. Pollifax Series:

_____. *The Unexpected Mrs. Pollifax.*
First Edition: Garden City, NY: Doubleday, 1966.
NF/F: $50   **G/VG: $15**

_____. *The Amazing Mrs. Pollifax.*
First Edition: Garden City, NY: Doubleday, 1970.
NF/F: $65   **G/VG: $20**

_____. *The Elusive Mrs. Pollifax.*
First Edition: Garden City, NY: Doubleday, 1971.
NF/F: $70   **G/VG: $30**

_____. *A Palm for Mrs. Pollifax.*
First Edition: Garden City, NY: Doubleday, 1973.
NF/F: $50   **G/VG: $15**

_____. *Mrs. Pollifax on Safari.*
First Edition: Garden City, NY: Doubleday, 1976.
NF/F: $25   **G/VG: $10**

_____. *Mrs. Pollifax on the China Station.*
First Edition: Garden City, NY: Doubleday, 1983.
NF/F: $40   **G/VG: $15**

_____. *Mrs. Pollifax and the Hong Kong Buddha.*
First Edition: Garden City, NY: Doubleday, 1985.
NF/F: $35   **G/VG: $10**

_____. *Mrs. Pollifax and the Golden Triangle.*
First Edition: Garden City, NY: Doubleday, 1973.
NF/F: $50   **G/VG: $15**

_____. *Mrs. Pollifax and the Whirling Dervish.*
First Edition: Garden City, NY: Doubleday, 1990.
NF/F: $45　　　　　**G/VG: $15**

_____. *Mrs. Pollifax and the Second Thief.*
First Edition: Garden City, NY: Doubleday, 1993.
NF/F: $25　　　　　**G/VG: $8**

_____. *Mrs. Pollifax Pursued.*
First Edition: Westminster, MD: Fawcett Books, 1995.
NF/F: $20　　　　　**G/VG: $8**

_____. *Mrs. Pollifax and the Lion Killer.*
First Edition: Westminster, MD: Fawcett Books, 1996.
NF/F: $40　　　　　**G/VG: $10**

_____. *Mrs. Pollifax, Innocent Tourist.*
First Edition: New York: Fawcett Columbine, 1997.
NF/F: $60　　　　　**G/VG: $20**

_____. *Mrs. Pollifax Unveiled.*
First Edition: New York: Ballantine Books, 2000.
NF/F: $35　　　　　**G/VG: $12**

The Gordons. *Case File: FBI.*
First Edition: Garden City, NY: Doubleday/Crime Club, 1953.
NF/F: $35　　　　　**G/VG: $10**
First U.K. Edition: London: Macdonald, 1954.
NF/F: $20　　　　　**G/VG: $8**

Grafton, Sue. Kinsey Milhone Series:

_____. *A is for Alibi.*
First Edition: New York: Holt, Rinehart and Winston, 1982.
NF/F: $750　　　　　**G/VG: $250**

_____. *B is for Burglar.*
First Edition: New York: Holt, Rinehart and Winston, 1985.
NF/F: $550　　　　　**G/VG: $145**

_____. *C is for Corpse.*
First Edition: New York: Henry Holt, 1986.
NF/F: $650　　　　　**G/VG: $150**

_____. *D is for Deadbeat.*
First Edition: New York: Henry Holt, 1987.
NF/F: $250　　　　　**G/VG: $85**

_____. *E is for Evidence.*
First Edition: New York: Henry Holt, 1988.
NF/F: $165　　　　　**G/VG: $55**

_____. *F Is For Fugitive.*
First Edition: New York: Henry Holt, 1989.
NF/F: $95　　　　　**G/VG: $25**

_____. *G is for Gumshoe.*
First Edition: New York: Henry Holt, 1990.
NF/F: $65　　　　　**G/VG: $20**

_____. *H is for Homicide.*
First Edition: New York: Henry Holt, 1991.
NF/F: $55　　　　　**G/VG: $20**

_____. *I is for Innocent.*
First Edition: New York: Henry Holt, 1992.
NF/F: $45　　　　　**G/VG: $15**

_____. *J is for Judgment.*
First Edition: New York: Henry Holt, 1993.
NF/F: $25　　　　　**G/VG: $10**

Sue Grafton.

Sue Grafton.

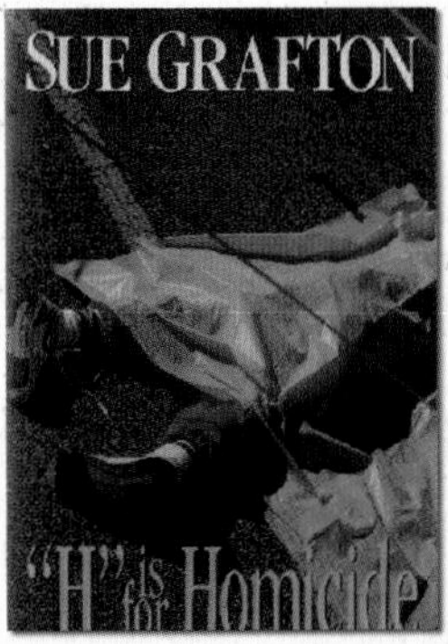

Sue Grafton.

John Grisham.

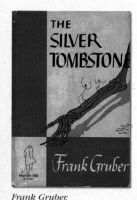

Frank Gruber.

Brett Halliday.

_____. *K is for Killer.*
First Edition: New York: Henry Holt,
1994.
NF/F: $25   **G/VG: $10**

_____. *L is for Lawless.*
First Edition: New York: Henry Holt,
1995.
NF/F: $25   **G/VG: $10**

_____. *M is for Malice.*
First Edition: New York: Henry Holt,
1996.
NF/F: $25   **G/VG: $10**

_____. *N is for Noose.*
First Edition: New York: Henry Holt,
1998.
NF/F: $25   **G/VG: $10**

_____. *O is for Outlaw.*
First Edition: New York: Henry Holt,
1999.
NF/F: $25   **G/VG: $10**

_____. *P is for Peril.*
First Edition: New York: Henry Holt,
2001.
NF/F: $25   **G/VG: $10**

_____. *Q is for Quarry.*
First Edition: New York: Henry Holt,
2002.
NF/F: $25   **G/VG: $10**

_____. *R is for Ricochet.*
First Edition: New York: Henry Holt,
2004.
NF/F: $25   **G/VG: $10**

_____. *S is for Silence.*
First Ed: New York: Henry Holt, 2005.
NF/F: $25   **G/VG: $10**

_____. *T is for Trespass.*
First Edition: New York: Henry Holt, 2007.
NF/F: $25   **G/VG: $10**

Green, Anna-Katherine. *The Filigree
Ball.*
First Edition: Indianapolis: Bobbs-
Merrill, 1903.
NF/F: $130   **G/VG: $30**

Greene, Graham. *The Captain and
the Enemy.*
First Edition: Toronto: Lester & Orpen
Dennys, 1988.
NF/F: $85   **G/VG: $35**
First U.K. Edition: London: Reinhardt
Books/Viking, 1988.
NF/F: $75   **G/VG: $30**
First U.S. Edition: New York: Viking,
1988.
NF/F: $30   **G/VG: $10**

Grisham, John. *The Firm.*
Limited Edition: New York: Doubleday,
1991 (350 copies).
NF/F: $1,250   **G/VG: Not Seen**
First Edition: New York: Doubleday,
1991.
NF/F: $275   **G/VG: $65**

Gruber, Frank. *The Silver Tombstone.*
First Edition: New York: Farrar &
Rinehart, 1945.
NF/F: $115   **G/VG: $30**

Haggard, William. *The Arena.*
First Edition: London: Cassell & Co., 1961.
NF/F: $45   **G/VG: $15**
First U.S. Edition: New York: Ives
Washburn, 1961.
NF/F: $25   **G/VG: $10**

Halliday, Brett. *Marked for Murder.*
First Edition: New York: Dodd Mead,
1945.
NF/F: $125   **G/VG: $40**

_____. *Framed in Blood.*
First Edition: New York: Dodd, Mead,
1951.
NF/F: $65   **G/VG: $20**

Hammett, Dashiell. *The Dain Curse.*
First Edition: New York: Alfred A.
Knopf, 1929.
NF/F: $25,000   **G/VG: $9,000**

_____. *The Thin Man.*
First Edition: New York: Alfred A.
Knopf, 1934.
NF/F: $8,000   **G/VG: $1,800**

Hare, Cyril. *That Yew Tree's Shade.*
First Edition: London: Faber & Faber,
1954.
NF/F: $100   **G/VG: $35**
First U.S. Edition: as: *Death Walks The
Woods.* Boston: Little, Brown, 1954.
NF/F: $50   **G/VG: $10**

Hart, Frances Noyes. *The Bellamy Trial.*
First Edition: New York: Doubleday,
Page, 1927.
NF/F: $1,250   **G/VG: $250**

Harvester, Simon. *Red Road.*
First Edition: London: Jarrolds, 1963.
NF/F: $35   **G/VG: $10**
First U.S. Edition: New York: Walker,
1964.
NF/F: $25   **G/VG: $8**

Hastings, Macdonald. *Cork in the
Doghouse.*
First Edition: London: Michael Joseph,
1957.
NF/F: $65   **G/VG: $20**
First U.S. Edition: New York: Alfred A.
Knopf, 1958.
NF/F: $60   **G/VG: $10**

Head, Matthew. *The Devil in the Bush.*
First Edition: New York: Simon and
Schuster, 1945.
NF/F: $75   **G/VG: $20**

Heard, H.F. *A Taste for Honey.*
First Ed: New York: Vanguard, 1941.
NF/F: $120   **G/VG: $25**

Heberden, M.V. *The Case of the Eight
Brothers.*
First Edition: Garden City, NY:
Doubleday/Crime Club, 1948.
NF/F: $75   **G/VG: $25**

Higgins, George V. *Friends of Eddie
Coyle.*
First Edition: New York: Alfred A.
Knopf, 1972.
NF/F: $175   **G/VG: $25**

Highsmith, Patricia. Ripley Series:

_____. *The Talented Mr. Ripley.*
First Edition: New York: Coward-
McCann, 1955.
NF/F: $3,600   **G/VG: $1,250**

_____. *Ripley Under Ground.*
First Edition: Garden City, NY:
Doubleday, 1970.
NF/F: $800   **G/VG: $375**

_____. *Ripley's Game.*
First Edition: New York: Alfred A.
Knopf, 1974.
NF/F: $300   **G/VG: $125**

_____. *The Boy Who Followed
Ripley.*
First Edition: New York: Lippencott &
Crowell, 1980.
NF/F: $100   **G/VG: $30**

_____. *Ripley Under Water.*
First Edition: London: Limited
Editions, 1991.
NF/F: $300   **G/VG: $165**
First U.S. Edition: New York: Alfred A.
Knopf, 1992.
NF/F: $200   **G/VG: $80**

Hillerman, Tony. *Fly on the Wall.*
First Edition: New York: Harper &
Row, 1971.
NF/F: $1,500   **G/VG: $400**

George V. Higgins.

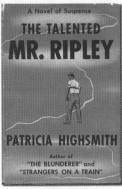
Patricia Highsmith.

Tony Hillerman.

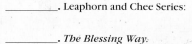

Tony Hillerman.

_____. Leaphorn and Chee Series:

_____. *The Blessing Way.*
First Edition: New York: Harper & Row, 1970.
NF/F: $2,700   G/VG: $1,200

_____. *Dance Hall of the Dead.*
First Edition: New York: Harper & Row, 1973.
NF/F: $1,800   G/VG: $800

_____. *Listening Woman.*
First Edition: New York: Harper & Row, 1978.
NF/F: $750   G/VG: $325

_____. *People of Darkness.*
First Edition: New York: Harper & Row, 1980.
NF/F: $400   G/VG: $125

_____. *The Dark Wind.*
First Edition: New York: Harper & Row, 1982.
NF/F: $300   G/VG: $100

Tony Hillerman.

_____. *The Ghostway.*
Limited Edition: San Diego: Dennis McMillan, 1984 (300 copies).
NF/F: $750   G/VG: Not Seen
First Edition: New York: Harper & Row, 1984.
NF/F: $200   G/VG: $75

_____. *Skinwalkers.*
First Edition: New York: Harper & Row, 1986.
NF/F: $100   G/VG: $35

_____. *A Thief of Time.*
First Edition: New York: Harper & Row, 1988.
NF/F: $35   G/VG: $15

_____. *Talking God.*
First Edition: New York: Harper & Row, 1989.
NF/F: $35   G/VG: $15

Tony Hillerman.

_____. *Coyote Waits.*
First Edition: New York: Harper & Row, 1990.
NF/F: $35   G/VG: $15

_____. *Sacred Clowns.*
First Edition: New York: Harper Collins, 1993.
NF/F: $30   G/VG: $10

_____. *The Fallen Man.*
First Edition: New York: Harper Collins, 1996.
NF/F: $30   G/VG: $10

_____. *The First Eagle.*
First Edition: New York: Harper Collins, 1998.
NF/F: $25   G/VG: $10

_____. *Hunting Badger.*
First Edition: New York: Harper Collins, 1999.
NF/F: $25   G/VG: $10

_____. *The Wailing Wind.*
First Edition: New York: Harper Collins, 2002.
NF/F: $25   G/VG: $10

_____. *The Sinister Pig.*
First Edition: New York: Harper Collins, 2003.
NF/F: $20   G/VG: $8

_____. *Skeleton Man.*
First Edition: New York: Harper Collins, 2004.
NF/F: $20   G/VG: $8

_____. *The Shape Shifter.*
First Edition: New York: Harper Collins, 2006.
NF/F: $20   G/VG: $8

Hirschberg, Cornelius. *Florentine Finish.*
First Edition: New York: Harper & Row, 1963.
NF/F: $55   **G/VG: $15**

Hoch, Edward D. *The Thefts of Nick Velvet.*
Limited Edition: New York: Mysterious Press, 1978 (250 copies).
NF/F: $145   **G/VG: $55**
First Edition (Trade): New York: Mysterious Press, 1978.
NF/F: $45   **G/VG: $15**

Holmes, H.H. *Rocket To The Morgue.*
First Edition: New York: Duell, Sloan & Pearce, 1942.
NF/F: $650   **G/VG: $130**

Holton, Leonard. *A Problem in Angels.*
First Edition: New York: Dodd Mead, 1970.
NF/F: $30   **G/VG: $10**

Homes, Geoffrey. *The Doctor Died at Dusk.*
First Edition: New York: William Morrow, 1936.
NF/F: $200   **G/VG: $50**

Hornung, E.W. Raffles Series:

_____. *The Amateur Cracksman.*
First Edition: London: Methuen, 1899.
NF/F: $750   **G/VG: $225**
First U.S. Edition: New York: Scribners, 1899.
NF/F: $125   **G/VG: $45**

_____. *The Black Mask.*
First Edition: London: Grant Richards, 1901.
NF/F: $550   **G/VG: $175**

_____. *A Thief in the Night.*
First Edition: London: Chatto & Windus, 1905.
NF/F: $550   **G/VG: $150**

_____. *Mr. Justice Raffles.*
First Edition: London: Smith, Elder & Co, 1909.
NF/F: $350   **G/VG: $125**
First U.S. Edition: New York: Scribners, 1909.
NF/F: $75   **G/VG: $25**

Hunter, Alan. *Gently With The Painters.*
First Edition: London: Cassell, 1960.
NF/F: $100   **G/VG: $30**
First U.S. Edition: New York: Macmillan, 1976.
NF/F: $25   **G/VG: $10**

Iles, Francis. *Malice Aforethought. The Story of a Commonplace Crime.*
First Edition: London: Mundanus [Victor Gollancz], 1931.
NF/F: $1,050   **G/VG: $450**

Innes, Michael. *Appleby's End.*
First Edition: London: Victor Gollancz, 1945.
NF/F: $155   **G/VG: $45**
First Edition: New York: Dodd, Mead, 1945.
NF/F: $50   **G/VG: $25**

Irish, William. *Phantom Lady.*
First Edition: Philadelphia: Lippincott, 1942.
NF/F: $1,250   **G/VG: $250**

_____. *I Wouldn't Be in Your Shoes.*
First Edition: Philadelphia: Lippincott, 1943.
NF/F: $750   **G/VG: $95**

James, P. D. *Shroud for a Nightingale.*
First Edition: London: Faber and Faber, 1971.
NF/F: $350   **G/VG: $100**
First U.S. Edition: New York Scribners, 1971.
NF/F: $165   **G/VG: $65**

Kane, Henry. *Armchair in Hell.*
First Edition: New York: Simon & Schuster, 1948.
NF/F: $45   **G/VG: $10**

Alan Hunter.

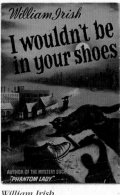
William Irish.

Henry Kane.

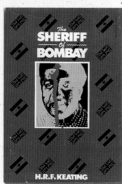

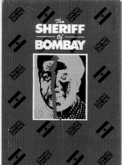

H.R.F. Keating.

Baynard Kendrick.

Karen Kijewski.

Keating, H.R.F. *The Sheriff of Bombay.*
First Edition: London: Collins, 1984.
NF/F: $45   **G/VG: $12**
First U.S. Edition: Garden City, NY:
Doubleday/Crime Club, 1984.
NF/F: $25   **G/VG: $10**

Keeler, Harry Stephen. *The Mysterious Mr. I.*
First Edition: New York: E. P. Dutton, 1938.
NF/F: $350   **G/VG: $100**

Keith, Carlton. *Crayfish Dinner.*
First Edition: Garden City, NY:
Doubleday/Crime Club, 1966.
NF/F: $65   **G/VG: $15**

Kellerman, Faye. *Sacred and Profane.*
First Edition: New York: Arbor House, 1987.
NF/F: $35   **G/VG: $10**

Kellerman, Jonathan. *The Clinic.*
First Edition: New York: Bantam Books, 1997.
NF/F: $15   **G/VG: $5**

Kemelman, Harry. *Saturday the Rabbi Went Hungry.*
First Edition: New York: Crown, 1966.
NF/F: $80   **G/VG: $25**

Kendrick, Baynard. *Blind Man's Bluff.*
First Edition: Boston: Little, Brown, 1943.
NF/F: $85   **G/VG: $20**

Kijewski, Karen. Kat Colorado Series:

_____. *Katwalk.*
First Edition: New York: St. Martin's Press, 1989.
NF/F: $300   **G/VG: $125**

_____. *Katapult.*
First Edition: New York: St. Martin's Press, 1990.
NF/F: $150   **G/VG: $55**

_____. *Kat's Cradle.*
First Edition: Garden City, NY:
Doubleday, 1992.
NF/F: $200   **G/VG: $75**

_____. *Copy Kat.*
First Edition: New York: St. Martin's Press, 1989.
NF/F: $45   **G/VG: $15**

_____. *Wild Kat.*
Limited Edition: Huntington Beach:
CA: Cahill Publishing, 1994 (150 copies).
NF/F: $125   **G/VG: Not Seen**
First Edition: Garden City, NY:
Doubleday, 1994.
NF/F: $25   **G/VG: $10**

_____. *Alley Kat Blues.*
First Edition: Garden City, NY:
Doubleday, 1994.
NF/F: $20   **G/VG: $8**

_____. *Honky Tonk Kat.*
First Edition: New York: Putnam, 1996.
NF/F: $20   **G/VG: $8**

_____. *Kat Scratch Fever.*
First Edition: New York: Putnam, 1996.
NF/F: $20   **G/VG: $8**

_____. *Stray Kat Waltz.*
First Edition: New York: Putnam, 1996.
NF/F: $20   **G/VG: $8**

King, Rufus. *Museum Piece No. 13.*
First Edition: Garden City, NY:
Doubleday/Crime Club, 1946.
NF/F: $125   **G/VG: $40**

Klinger, Henry. *Lust For Murder.*
First Edition: New York: Trident Press, 1966.
NF/F: $35   **G/VG: $10**

Lacy, Ed. *Room to Swing.*
First Edition: New York: Harper & Brothers, 1957.
NF/F: $225   **G/VG: $55**

Lathen, Emma. *Murder Without Icing.*
First Edition: New York: Simon and
Schuster, 1972.
NF/F: $50   **G/VG: $10**

Latimer, Jonathan. *Red Gardenias.*
First Edition: Garden City, NY:
Doubleday Doran/Crime Club, 1939.
NF/F: $650   **G/VG: $225**

Leblanc, Maurice. *The Woman of Mystery.*
First Edition in English: New York:
Macauley Company, 1916.
NF/F: $450   **G/VG: $85**

LeCarre, John. *The Looking-Glass War.*
First Edition: London: William
Heinemann, 1965.
NF/F: $255   **G/VG: $60**
First Edition: New York: Coward -
McCann, Inc., 1965.
NF/F: $25   **G/VG: $10**

Leonard, Charles L. *Sinister Shelter.*
First Edition: Garden City, NY:
Doubleday/Crime Club, 1949.
NF/F: $85   **G/VG: $20**
First Edition: New York: Delacorte
Press, 1974.
NF/F: $650   **G/VG: $200**

Leonard, Elmore. *Fifty-Two Pickup.*
First Edition: New York: Delacorte Press, 1974.
NF/F: $650   **G/VG: $200**

Linington, Elizabeth. *Date with Death.*
First Edition: New York: Harper &
Row, 1966.
NF/F: $45   **G/VG: $15**

Lockridge, Frances & Richard. *The Norths Meet Murder.*
First Edition: Cleveland: World, 1946.
NF/F: $55   **G/VG: $15**

Lorac, E.C.R. *Relative to Poison.*
First Edition: London: Collins/Crime
Club, 1947.
NF/F: $125   **G/VG: $50**
First U.S. Edition: Garden City, NY:
Doubleday/Crime Club, 1948.
NF/F: $60   **G/VG: $20**

MacDonald, John D. Travis McGee Series:

_____. *The Deep Blue Good-by.*
First Edition: Greenwich, CT: Fawcett
Publications, Inc., 1964.
Points of Issue: Paperback original
Fawcett Gold Medal k1405.
NF/F: $45   **G/VG: $12**
First Hardcover Edition: London:
Robert Hale, 1965.
NF/F: $1,500   **G/VG: $650**
First U.S. Hardcover Edition: New
York: Lippincott, 1975
NF/F: $500   **G/VG: $150**

_____. *Nightmare in Pink.*
First Edition: Greenwich, CT: Fawcett
Publications, Inc., 1964.
Points of Issue: Paperback original
Fawcett Gold Medal k1406.
NF/F: $75   **G/VG: $20**
First Hardcover Edition: New York:
Lippincott, 1976.
NF/F: $600   **G/VG: $200**

_____. *A Purple Place for Dying.*
First Edition: Greenwich, CT: Fawcett
Publications, Inc., 1964.
Points of Issue: Paperback original
Fawcett Gold Medal k1417.
NF/F: $55   **G/VG: $18**
First Hardcover Edition: New York:
Lippincott, 1976.
NF/F: $425   **G/VG: $150**

Henry Klinger.

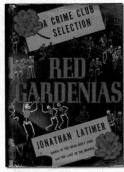

Jonathan Latimer.

Charles L. Leonard.

John D. MacDonald.

John D. MacDonald.

John D. MacDonald.

_____. *The Quick Red Fox.*
First Edition: Greenwich, CT: Fawcett
Publications, Inc., 1964.
Points of Issue: Paperback original
Fawcett Gold Medal k1464.
NF/F: $45   **G/VG: $18**
First Hardcover Edition: New York:
Lippincott, 1974.
NF/F: $525   **G/VG: $200**

_____. *A Deadly Shade of Gold.*
First Edition: Greenwich, CT: Fawcett
Publications, Inc., 1965.
Points of Issue: Paperback original
Fawcett Gold Medal d1499.
NF/F: $40   **G/VG: $18**
First Hardcover Edition: New York:
Lippincott, 1974.
NF/F: $325   **G/VG: $100**

_____. *Bright Orange for the
Shroud.*
First Edition: Greenwich, CT: Fawcett
Publications, Inc., 1965.
Points of Issue: Paperback original
Fawcett Gold Medal d1573.
NF/F: $35   **G/VG: $15**
First Hardcover Edition: New York:
Lippincott, 1972.
NF/F: $2,500   **G/VG: $500**

_____. *Darker than Amber.*
First Edition: Greenwich, CT: Fawcett
Publications, Inc., 1966.
Points of Issue: Paperback original
Fawcett Gold Medal d1674.
NF/F: $55   **G/VG: $20**
First Hardcover Edition: New York:
Lippincott, 1970.
NF/F: $625   **G/VG: $200**

_____. *One Fearful Yellow Eye.*
First Edition: Greenwich, CT: Fawcett
Publications, Inc., 1966.
Points of Issue: Paperback original
Fawcett Gold Medal d1759.
NF/F: $85   **G/VG: $30**
First Hardcover Edition: New York:
Lippincott, 1977.
NF/F: $425   **G/VG: $200**

_____. *Pale Gray for Guilt.*
First Edition: Greenwich, CT: Fawcett
Publications, Inc., 1968.
Points of Issue: Paperback original
Fawcett Gold Medal d1893.
NF/F: $40   **G/VG: $18**
First Hardcover Edition: London:
Robert Hale, 1969.
NF/F: $1000   **G/VG: $450**
First US Hardcover Edition: New York:
Lippincott, 1971.
NF/F: $325   **G/VG: $100**

_____. *The Girl in the Plain
Brown Wrapper.*
First Edition: Greenwich, CT: Fawcett
Publications, Inc., 1968.
Points of Issue: Paperback original
Fawcett Gold Medal t2023.
NF/F: $40   **G/VG: $15**
First Hardcover Edition: New York:
Lippincott, 1973.
NF/F: $375   **G/VG: $150**

_____. *Dress Her in Indigo.*
First Edition: Greenwich, CT: Fawcett
Publications, Inc., 1969.
Points of Issue: Paperback original
Fawcett Gold Medal t2127.
NF/F: $50   **G/VG: $20**
First Hardcover Edition: London:
Robert Hale, 1971.
NF/F: $325   **G/VG: $120**
First US Hardcover Edition: New York:
Lippincott, 1977.
NF/F: $600   **G/VG: $200**

_____. *The Long Lavender Look.*
First Edition: Greenwich, CT: Fawcett
Publications, Inc., 1969.
Points of Issue: Paperback original
Fawcett Gold Medal m2325.
NF/F: $65   **G/VG: $25**
First Hardcover Edition: New York:
Lippincott, 1972.
NF/F: $650   **G/VG: $275**

_____. *A Tan and Shady Silence.*
First Edition: Greenwich, CT: Fawcett
Publications, Inc., 1972.
Points of Issue: Paperback original
Fawcett Gold Medal m2513.
NF/F: $40   **G/VG: $18**
First Hardcover Edition: London:
Robert Hale, 1973.
NF/F: $250   **G/VG: $85**
First US Hardcover Edition: New York:
Lippincott, 1979.
NF/F: $400   **G/VG: $100**

_____. *The Scarlet Ruse.*
First Edition: Greenwich, CT: Fawcett
Publications, Inc., 1973.
Points of Issue: Paperback original
Fawcett Gold Medal p2744.
NF/F: $25   **G/VG: $10**
First Hardcover Edition: London:
Robert Hale, 1973.
NF/F: $250   **G/VG: $75**
First Hardcover Edition: New York:
Lippincott, 1980.
NF/F: $300   **G/VG: $75**

_____. *The Turquoise Lament.*
First Edition: New York: Lippincott, 1973.
NF/F: $200   **G/VG: $65**

_____. *The Dreadful Lemon Sky.*
First Edition: New York: Lippincott, 1974.
NF/F: $125   **G/VG: $50**

_____. *The Empty Copper Sea.*
First Edition: New York: Lippincott, 1978.
NF/F: $85   **G/VG: $35**

_____. *The Green Ripper.*
First Edition: New York: Lippincott, 1979.
NF/F: $75   **G/VG: $25**

_____. *Free Fall in Crimson.*
First Edition: New York: Harper and
Row, 1981.
NF/F: $65   **G/VG: $20**

_____. *Cinnamon Skin.*
First Edition: New York: Harper and
Row, 1982.
NF/F: $75   **G/VG: $15**

_____. *The Lonely Silver Rain.*
First Edition: New York: Alfred A.
Knopf, 1985.
NF/F: $50   **G/VG: $10**

MacDonald, Philip. *Something To Hide.*
First Edition: Garden City: Doubleday/
Crime Club, 1952.
NF/F: $300   **G/VG: $125**

MacDonald, Ross. Lew Archer Series:

As: MacDonald, John. *The Moving
Target.*
First Edition: New York: Alfred A.
Knopf, 1949.
NF/F: $5,100   **G/VG: $2,200**

As: MacDonald, John Ross. *The
Drowning Pool.*
First Edition: New York: Alfred A.
Knopf, 1950.
NF/F: $1,850   **G/VG: $750**

_____. *The Way Some People Die.*
First Edition: New York: Alfred A.
Knopf, 1951.
NF/F: $1,450   **G/VG: $550**

_____. *The Ivory Grin.*
First Edition: New York: Alfred A.
Knopf, 1952.
NF/F: $1,250   **G/VG: $500**

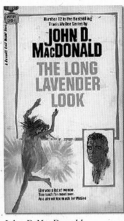

John D. MacDonald.

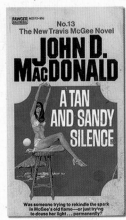

John D. MacDonald.

John D. MacDonald.

John Ross MacDonald.

Ross MacDonald.

_____. *Find a Victim.*
First Edition: New York: Alfred A.
Knopf, 1954.
NF/F: $1,800   **G/VG: $750**

_____. *The Barbarous Coast.*
First Edition: New York: Alfred A.
Knopf, 1956.
NF/F: $1,850   **G/VG: $750**

As: MacDonald, Ross. *The Doomsters.*
First Edition: New York: Alfred A.
Knopf, 1958.
NF/F: $1,600   **G/VG: $600**

_____. *The Galton Case.*
First Edition: New York: Alfred A.
Knopf, 1959.
NF/F: $500   **G/VG: $175**

_____. *The Wycherly Woman.*
First Edition: New York: Alfred A.
Knopf, 1961.
NF/F: $375   **G/VG: $125**

_____. *The Zebra-Striped Hearse.*
First Edition: New York: Alfred A.
Knopf, 1962.
NF/F: $225   **G/VG: $100**

_____. *The Chill.*
First Edition: New York: Alfred A.
Knopf, 1964.
NF/F: $500   **G/VG: $200**

_____. *The Far Side of the Dollar.*
First Edition: New York: Alfred A.
Knopf, 1965.
NF/F: $350   **G/VG: $125**

_____. *Black Money.*
First Edition: New York: Alfred A.
Knopf, 1966.
NF/F: $300   **G/VG: $100**

_____. *The Instant Enemy.*
First Edition: New York: Alfred A.
Knopf, 1968.
NF/F: $245   **G/VG: $85**

_____. *The Goodbye Look.*
First Edition: New York: Alfred A.
Knopf, 1969.
NF/F: $150   **G/VG: $65**

Markham, Robert. James Bond Series:

_____. *Colonel Sun.*
First Edition: London: Jonathan Cape,
1968.
NF/F: $325   **G/VG: $145**
First U.S. Edition: New York: Harper &
Row, 1968.
NF/F: $75   **G/VG: $25**
(See Also: Ian Fleming, John Gardner,
Raymond Benson, Sebastian Faulks).

Marric, J. J. *Gideon's Night.*
First Edition: London & Edinburgh:
Hodder and Stoughton, 1957.
NF/F: $35   **G/VG: $10**
First U.S. Edition: New York: Harper &
Brothers, 1957.
NF/F: $20   **G/VG: $8**

Marquand, John P. Mr. Moto Series:

_____. *Your Turn, Mr. Moto.*
First Edition: Boston: Little Brown Co,
1935.
NF/F: $125   **G/VG: $45**

_____. *Thank You, Mr. Moto.*
First Edition: Boston: Little Brown Co,
1936.
NF/F: $85   **G/VG: $35**

Robert Markham.

_____. *Think Fast, Mr. Moto.*
First Edition: Boston: Little Brown Co, 1937.
NF/F: $150   **G/VG: $65**

_____. *Mr. Moto is So Sorry.*
First Edition: Boston: Little Brown Co, 1938.
NF/F: $350   **G/VG: $125**

_____. *Last Laugh, Mr. Moto.*
First Edition: Boston: Little Brown Co, 1942.
NF/F: $300   **G/VG: $95**

_____. *Stopover: Tokyo.*
First Edition: Boston: Little Brown Co, 1957.
NF/F: $75   **G/VG: $25**

Marsh, Ngaio. *Died in the Wool.*
First Edition: London: Collins/Crime Club, 1945.
NF/F: $450   **G/VG: $100**
First U.S. Edition: Boston: Little, Brown and Company, 1945.
NF/F: $185   **G/VG: $50**

_____. *False Scent.*
First Edition: London: Collins/Crime Club, 1960.
NF/F: $70   **G/VG: $25**
First U.S. Edition: Boston: Little Brown, 1959.
NF/F: $30   **G/VG: $10**

Martini, Steve. *Prime Witness.*
First Edition: New York: G. P. Putnam, 1993.
NF/F: $15   **G/VG: $5**

Mason, A.E. W. *The House of the Arrow.*
First Edition: London & Edinburgh: Hodder and Stoughton, 1924.
NF/F: $600   **G/VG: $200**
First U.S. Edition: New York: George H. Doran, 1924.
NF/F: $350   **G/VG: $85**

Masterson, Whit. *The Gravy Train.*
First Edition: New York: Dodd, Mead, 1971.
NF/F: $35   **G/VG: $10**

Maugham, W. Somerset. *Ashenden: or The British Agent.*
First Edition: London: William Heinemann, 1928.
NF/F: $5,200   **G/VG: $750**
First U.S. Edition: Garden City, NY: Doubleday Doran, 1928.
NF/F: $200   **G/VG: $65**

McBain, Ed. *So Long as You Both Shall Live.*
First Edition: New York: Random House, 1976.
NF/F: $45   **G/VG: $10**

_____. Matthew Hope Series:

_____. *Goldilocks.*
First Edition: NY: Arbor House, 1977.
NF/F: $65   **G/VG: $25**

_____. *Rumpelstiltskin.*
First Edition: NY; Viking Press, 1981.
NF/F: $45   **G/VG: $20**

_____. *Beauty and the Beast.*
First Edition: London: Hamish Hamilton, 1982.
NF/F: $60   **G/VG: $20**
First U.S. Edition: NY: Holt Rinehart & Winston, 1982.
NF/F: $25   **G/VG: $10**

Ngaio Marsh.

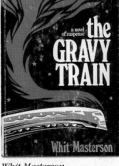

Whit Masterson.

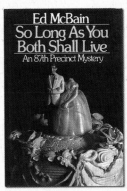

Ed McBain.

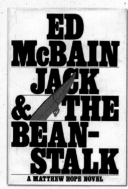

Ed McBain.

Wade Miller.

_____. *Jack and the Beanstalk.*
First Edition: NY: Holt Rinehart &
Winston, 1984.
NF/F: $45　　　　　　　**G/VG: $12**

_____. *Snow White & Rose Red.*
First Edition: NY: Holt Rinehart &
Winston, 1985.
NF/F: $45　　　　　　　**G/VG: $15**

_____. *Cinderella.*
First Edition: NY: Holt Rinehart &
Winston, 1986.
NF/F: $35　　　　　　　**G/VG: $10**

_____. *Puss in Boots.*
First Edition: NY: Holt Rinehart &
Winston, 1987.
NF/F: $25　　　　　　　**G/VG: $10**

_____. *The House that Jack
Built.*
First Edition: NY: Holt Rinehart &
Winston, 1988.
NF/F: $20　　　　　　　**G/VG: $8**

_____. *Three Blind Mice.*
First Edition: NY: Arcade, 1990.
NF/F: $35　　　　　　　**G/VG: $15**

_____. *Mary, Mary.*
First Edition: NY: Warner Books, 1992.
NF/F: $20　　　　　　　**G/VG: $8**

_____. *There Was a Little Girl.*
First Edition: NY: Warner Books, 1994.
NF/F: $20　　　　　　　**G/VG: $8**

_____. *Gladly the Cross-eyed
Bear.*
First Edition: NY: Warner Books, 1996.
NF/F: $20　　　　　　　**G/VG: $8**

_____. *The Last Best Hope.*
First Edition: NY: Warner Books, 1998.
NF/F: $20　　　　　　　**G/VG: $8**

McCloy, Helen. *The Imposter.*
First Edition: New York: Dodd, Mead,
1977.
NF/F: $35　　　　　　　**G/VG: $10**

McCutcheon, George Barr. *Anderson
Crow Detective.*
First Edition: New York: Dodd Mead, 1920.
NF/F: $100　　　　　　　**G/VG: $25**

McDougald, Roman. *Purgatory Street.*
First Edition: New York: Simon &
Schuster, 1946.
NF/F: $55　　　　　　　**G/VG: $15**

Millar, Margaret. *The Devil Loves Me.*
First Edition: Garden City, NY:
Doubleday, Doran/Crime Club, 1942.
NF/F: $650　　　　　　　**G/VG: $185**

Miller, Wade. *Shoot to Kill.*
First Edition: New York: Farrar, Strauss
& Young, 1948.
NF/F: $85　　　　　　　**G/VG: $20**

Mitchell, Gladys. *Spotted Hemlock.*
First Edition: London: Michael Joseph,
1958.
NF/F: $150　　　　　　　**G/VG: $50**
First Edition: New York: St. Martin's
Press 1985.
NF/F: $15　　　　　　　**G/VG: $8**

Morland, Nigel. *The Dear Dead Girls.*
First Edition: London: Cassell, 1961.
NF/F: $95　　　　　　　**G/VG: $25**

Morrison, Arthur. *The Hole in the Wall.*
First Edition: London: Methuen, 1902.
NF/F: $600　　　　　　　**G/VG: $150**

Morton, Anthony. *A Case for the Baron.*
First Edition: London: Sampson Low, 1945.
NF/F: $100　　　　　　　**G/VG: $45**
First U.S. Edition: New York: Duell,
Sloan and Pearce, 1949.
NF/F: $45　　　　　　　**G/VG: $15**

Nigel Morland.

Mosley, Walter. Easy Rawlins Series*:

_____. *Devil in a Blue Dress.*
First Edition: New York: Norton, 1990.
NF/F: $275   **G/VG: $110**

_____. *A Red Death.*
First Edition: New York: Norton, 1991.
NF/F: $95   **G/VG: $35**

_____. *White Butterfly.*
First Edition: New York: Norton, 1992.
NF/F: $80   **G/VG: $20**

_____. *Black Betty.*
First Edition: New York: Norton, 1994.
NF/F: $25   **G/VG: $12**

_____. *A Little Yellow Dog.*
First Edition: New York: Norton, 1996.
NF/F: $15   **G/VG: $6**

_____. *Gone Fishin'.*
First Edition: Baltimore: Black Classic
Press, 1997.
NF/F: $25   **G/VG: $10**

_____. *Bad Boy Brawly Brown.*
First Edition: Boston: Little Brown,
2002.
NF/F: $15   **G/VG: $6**

_____. *Six Easy Pieces.*
First Edition: New York: Atria, 2003.
NF/F: $15   **G/VG: $6**

_____. *Little Scarlet.*
First Edition: Boston: Little Brown,
2004.
NF/F: $15   **G/VG: $6**

_____. *Cinnamon Kiss.*
First Edition: Boston: Little Brown,
2005.
NF/F: $15   **G/VG: $6**

_____. *Blond Faith.*
First Edition: Boston: Little Brown,
2007.
NF/F: $15   **G/VG: $6**

Moyes, Patricia. *Dead Men Don't Ski.*
First Edition: London: Collins,
1959.
NF/F: $300   **G/VG: $85**
First U.S. Edition: New York: Rinehart,
1959.
NF/F: $75   **G/VG: $30**

Muller, Marcia. *Till The Butchers Cut Him Down.*
First Edition: New York: Mysterious
Press, 1994.
NF/F: $45   **G/VG: $15**

Nolan, William F. *Death Is For Losers.*
First Edition: Los Angeles: Sherbourne
Press, 1968.
NF/F: $35   **G/VG: $12**

Offord, Lenore Glen. *The Nine Dark Hours.*
First Edition: New York: Duell, Sloan
and Pearce, 1941.
NF/F: $75   **G/VG: $20**

O'Hanlon, James. *As Good as Murdered.*
First Edition: New York: Random
House, 1940.
NF/F: $45   **G/VG: $10**

Olsen, D.B. *Death Walks on Cat Feet.*
First Edition: Garden City, NY:
Doubleday/Crime Club, 1956.
NF/F: $40   **G/VG: $15**

Walter Mosley.

Patricia Moyes.

Marcia Muller.

Baroness Orczy.

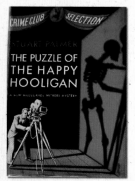

Stuart Palmer.

Stuart Palmer and Craig Rice.

Orczy, Baroness. *The Old Man in the Corner.*
First Edition: London: Greening & Co., 1909.
NF/F: $4,400   **G/VG: $1,600**

Palmer, Stuart. Hildegarde Withers Series:

_____. *The Penguin Pool Murder.*
First Edition: New York: Brentano's, 1931.
NF/F: $1,500   **G/VG: $650**

_____. *Murder on the Blackboard.*
First Edition: New York: Brentano's, 1932.
NF/F: $1,000   **G/VG: $450**

_____. *The Puzzle of the Pepper Tree.*
First Edition: Garden City, NY: Doubleday Doran, 1933.
NF/F: $600   **G/VG: $250**

_____. *The Puzzle of the Silver Persian.*
First Edition: Garden City, NY: The Crime Club/Doubleday, Doran, 1934.
NF/F: $475   **G/VG: $200**

_____. *The Puzzle of the Red Stallion.*
First Edition: Garden City, NY: The Crime Club/Doubleday, Doran, 1936.
NF/F: $250   **G/VG: $95**

_____. *The Puzzle of the Blue Banderilla.*
First Edition: Garden City, NY: The Crime Club/Doubleday, Doran, 1937.
NF/F: $600   **G/VG: $275**

_____. *Miss Withers Regrets.*
First Edition: Garden City, NY: The Crime Club/Doubleday, 1941.
NF/F: $275   **G/VG: $85**

_____. *The Puzzle of Happy Hooligan.*
First Edition: Garden City, NY: The Crime Club/Doubleday, 1941.
NF/F: $325   **G/VG: $100**

_____. *The Riddles of Hildegarde Withers.*
First Edition: New York: Jonathan Press/Lawrence E. Spivak, 1947. Points of Issue: Paperback original.
NF/F: Not Seen   **G/VG: $100**

_____. *Four Lost Ladies.*
First Edition: New York: M. S. Mill and William Morrow, 1949.
NF/F: $100   **G/VG: $45**

_____. *The Green Ace.*
First Edition: New York: M. S. Mill and William Morrow, 1950.
NF/F: $75   **G/VG: $25**

_____. *The Monkey Murder.*
First Edition: NY: Bestseller Mystery, 1950. Points of Issue: Paperback original, B128.
NF/F: Not Seen   **G/VG: $200**

_____. *Nipped in the Bud.*
First Edition: New York: M. S. Mill and William Morrow, 1951.
NF/F: $250   **G/VG: $100**

_____. *Cold Poison.*
First Edition: New York: M. S. Mill and William Morrow, 1954.
NF/F: $200   **G/VG: $75**

Palmer, Stuart & Craig Rice. *People Vs. Withers & Malone.*
First Edition: New York: Simon & Schuster, 1963.
NF/F: $135   **G/VG: $45**

Palmer, Stuart & Fletcher Flora.
Hildegarde Withers Makes the Scene.
First Edition: New York: Random
House, 1969.
NF/F: $60   **G/VG: $20**

Paretsky, Sara. V. I. Warshawski Series:

_____. *Indemnity Only.*
First Edition: New York: Dial Press, 1982.
NF/F: $350   **G/VG: $135**

_____. *Deadlock.*
First Edition: Garden City, NY: The
Dial Press, Doubleday, 1984.
NF/F: $300   **G/VG: $135**

_____. *Killing Orders.*
First Edition: New York: William
Morrow, 1985.
NF/F: $125   **G/VG: $45**

_____. *Bitter Medicine.*
First Edition: New York: William
Morrow, 1987.
NF/F: $75   **G/VG: $30**

_____. *Blood Shot.*
First Edition: New York: Delacorte, 1988.
NF/F: $85   **G/VG: $30**

_____. *Burn Marks.*
First Edition: New York: Delacorte, 1990.
NF/F: $65   **G/VG: $25**

_____. *Guardian Angel.*
Limited Edition: Bristol, UK: Scorpion
Press, 1992 (99 copies).
NF/F: $150   **G/VG: Not Seen**
First Edition: New York: Delacorte,
1992.
NF/F: $25   **G/VG: $10**

_____. *Tunnel Vision.*
First Edition: New York: Delacorte,
1994.
NF/F: $30   **G/VG: $12**

_____. *Windy City Blues.*
First Edition: New York: Delacorte,
1995.
NF/F: $25   **G/VG: $10**

_____. *Hard Time.*
First Edition: New York: Delacorte,
1999.
NF/F: $20   **G/VG: $8**

_____. *Total Recall.*
First Edition: New York: Delacorte,
2001.
NF/F: $20   **G/VG: $8**

_____. *Blacklist.*
First Edition: New York: Putnam, 2003.
NF/F: $20   **G/VG: $8**

_____. *Fire Sale.*
First Edition: New York: Putnam, 2005.
NF/F: $20   **G/VG: $8**

Parker, Robert B. *Ceremony.*
First Edition: New York: Delacorte
Press, 1982.
NF/F: $55   **G/VG: $20**

_____. *Valediction.*
First Edition: New York: Delacorte,
1984.
NF/F: $45   **G/VG: $15**

_____. Jesse Stone Series:

_____. *Night Passage.*
First Edition: New York: Putnam, 1997.
NF/F: $25   **G/VG: $12**

_____. *Trouble in Paradise.*
First Edition: New York: Putnam, 1998.
NF/F: $30   **G/VG: $10**

_____. *Death in Paradise.*
First Edition: New York: Putnam, 2001.
NF/F: $20   **G/VG: $8**

Sara Paretsky.

Robert B. Parker.

Robert B. Parker.

Parker, Robert B.

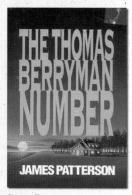

James Patterson.

James Patterson.

Elliot Paul.

_____. *Stone Cold.*
First Edition: New York: Putnam, 2003.
NF/F: $20   **G/VG: $8**

_____. *Sea Change.*
First Edition: New York: Putnam, 2005.
NF/F: $15   **G/VG: $6**

_____. *High Profile.*
First Edition: New York: Putnam, 2007.
NF/F: $15   **G/VG: $6**

_____. *Stranger In Paradise.*
First Edition: New York: Putnam, 2008.
NF/F: $15   **G/VG: $6**

Patterson, James. *The Thomas Berryman Number.*
First Edition: Boston: Little Brown, 1976.
NF/F: $425   **G/VG: $200**

_____. Alex Cross Series:

_____. *Along Came a Spider.*
First Edition: Boston: Little Brown, 1993.
NF/F: $65   **G/VG: $25**

_____. *Kiss the Girls.*
First Edition: Boston: Little Brown, 1995.
NF/F: $125   **G/VG: $45**

_____. *Jack and Jill.*
First Edition: Boston: Little Brown, 1996.
NF/F: $25   **G/VG: $10**

_____. *Cat and Mouse.*
First Edition: Boston: Little Brown, 1997.
NF/F: $25   **G/VG: $10**

_____. *Pop Goes the Weasel.*
First Edition: Boston: Little Brown, 1999.
NF/F: $35   **G/VG: $12**

_____. *Roses are Red.*
First Edition: Boston: Little Brown, 2000.
NF/F: $30   **G/VG: $10**

_____. *Violets are Blue.*
First Edition: Boston: Little Brown, 2001.
NF/F: $20   **G/VG: $8**

_____. *Four Blind Mice.*
First Edition: Boston: Little Brown, 2002.
NF/F: $25   **G/VG: $10**

_____. *The Big Bad Wolf.*
First Edition: Boston: Little Brown, 2003.
NF/F: $25   **G/VG: $10**

_____. *London Bridges.*
First Edition: Boston: Little Brown, 2004.
NF/F: $15   **G/VG: $6**

_____. *Mary, Mary.*
First Edition: Boston: Little Brown, 2005.
NF/F: $15   **G/VG: $6**

_____. *Cross.*
First Edition: Boston: Little Brown, 2006.
NF/F: $15   **G/VG: $6**

_____. *Double Cross.*
First Edition: Boston: Little Brown, 2007.
NF/F: $15   **G/VG: $6**

_____. *Cross Country.*
First Edition: Boston: Little Brown, 2008.
NF/F: $15   **G/VG: $6**

Patterson, Richard North. *The Lasko Tangent.*
First Edition: New York: W. W. Norton, 1979.
NF/F: $550   **G/VG: $165**

Paul, Elliot. *Hugger-Mugger in the Louvre.*
First Edition: New York: Random House, 1940.
NF/F: $135   **G/VG: $45**

Pentacost, Hugh. *The Campagne Killer.*
First Edition: New York: Dodd, Mead, 1972.
NF/F: $15   **G/VG: $8**

Perowne, Barry. *The Return of Raffles: Further Adventures of the Amateur Cracksman.*
First Edition: New York: John Day Co., 1933.
NF/F: $185   **G/VG: $55**

Peters, Ellis. Brother Cadfael Series*:

_____. *A Morbid Taste for Bones.*
First Edition: London: Macmillan, 1977.
NF/F: $1,500   **G/VG: $550**
First U.S. Edition: New York: Morrow, 1978.
NF/F: $550   **G/VG: $200**

_____. *One Corpse Too Many.*
First Edition: London: Macmillan, 1979.
NF/F: $1,000   **G/VG: $400**
First U.S. Edition: New York: Morrow, 1980.
NF/F: $300   **G/VG: $125**

_____. *Monk's Hood.*
First Edition: London: Macmillan, 1980.
NF/F: $650   **G/VG: $250**
First U.S. Edition: New York: Morrow, 1981.
NF/F: $250   **G/VG: $95**

_____. *Saint Peter's Fair.*
First Edition: London: Macmillan, 1981.
NF/F: $200   **G/VG: $85**
First U.S. Edition: New York: Morrow, 1981.
NF/F: $100   **G/VG: $35**

_____. *The Leper of Saint Giles.*
First Edition: London: Macmillan, 1981.
NF/F: $300   **G/VG: $100**
First U.S. Edition: New York: Morrow, 1982.
NF/F: $100   **G/VG: $40**

_____. *The Virgin in Ice.*
First Edition: London: Macmillan, 1982.
NF/F: $200   **G/VG: $85**
First U.S. Edition: New York: Morrow, 1983.
NF/F: $100   **G/VG: $35**

_____. *The Sanctuary Sparrow.*
First Edition: London: Macmillan, 1983.
NF/F: $300   **G/VG: $250**
First U.S. Edition: New York: Morrow, 1983.
NF/F: $85   **G/VG: $35**

_____. *The Devil's Novice.*
First Edition: London: Macmillan, 1983.
NF/F: $225   **G/VG: $75**
First U.S. Edition: New York: Morrow, 1984.
NF/F: $95   **G/VG: $25**

_____. *Dead Man's Ransom.*
First Edition: London: Macmillan, 1984.
NF/F: $85   **G/VG: $25**
First U.S. Edition: New York: Morrow, 1984.
NF/F: $45   **G/VG: $15**

_____. *The Pilgrim of Hate.*
First Edition: London: Macmillan, 1984.
NF/F: $150   **G/VG: $65**
First U.S. Edition: New York: Morrow, 1984.
NF/F: $70   **G/VG: $25**

_____. *An Excellent Mystery.*
First Edition: London: Macmillan, 1985.
NF/F: $175   **G/VG: $70**
First U.S. Edition: New York: Morrow, 1986.
NF/F: $100   **G/VG: $35**

Barry Perowne.

Ellis Peters.

Ellis Peters.

Ellis Peters.

Ellis Peters.

Joyce Porter.

_____. *The Raven in the Foregate.*
First Edition: London: Macmillan, 1986.
NF/F: $150   **G/VG: $45**
First U.S. Edition: New York: Morrow, 1986.
NF/F: $85   **G/VG: $25**

_____. *The Rose Rent.*
First Edition: London: Macmillan, 1986.
NF/F: $85   **G/VG: $25**
First U.S. Edition: New York: Morrow, 1986.
NF/F: $45   **G/VG: $15**

_____. *The Hermit of Eyton Forest.*
First Edition: London: Headline Press, 1986.
NF/F: $200   **G/VG: $95**
First U.S. Edition: New York: Mysterious Press, 1988.
NF/F: $75   **G/VG: $25**

_____. *The Confession of Brother Haluin.*
First Edition: London: Headline Press, 1988.
NF/F: $100   **G/VG: $35**
First U.S. Edition: New York: Mysterious Press, 1988.
NF/F: $85   **G/VG: $25**

_____. *The Heretic's Apprentice.*
First Edition: London: Headline Press, 1989.
NF/F: $75   **G/VG: $20**
First U.S. Edition: New York: Mysterious Press, 1990.
NF/F: $55   **G/VG: $15**

_____. *The Potter's Field.*
First Edition: London: Headline Press, 1989.
NF/F: $60   **G/VG: $20**
First U.S. Edition: New York: Mysterious Press, 1990.
NF/F: $35   **G/VG: $15**

_____. *The Summer of the Danes.*
First Edition: London: Headline Press, 1991.
NF/F: $80   **G/VG: $20**
First U.S. Edition: New York: Mysterious Press, 1991.
NF/F: $35   **G/VG: $15**

_____. *The Holy Thief.*
First Edition: London: Headline Press, 1992.
NF/F: $65   **G/VG: $15**
First U.S. Edition: New York: Mysterious Press, 1992.
NF/F: $35   **G/VG: $15**

_____. *Brother Cadfael's Penance.*
First Edition: London: Headline Press, 1994.
NF/F: $55   **G/VG: $15**
First U.S. Edition: New York: Mysterious Press, 1992.
NF/F: $25   **G/VG: $10**

Peters, Elizabeth. *Lion in the Valley.*
First Edition: New York: Atheneum, 1986.
NF/F: $375   **G/VG: $95**

Philips, Judson. *Murder as the Curtain Rises.*
First Edition: New York: Dodd Mead, 1981.
NF/F: $30   **G/VG: $10**

Porter, Joyce. *Dover One.*
First Edition: London: Jonathan Cape, 1964.
NF/F: $125   **G/VG: $55**
First U.S. Edition: New York: Scribner's, 1964.
NF/F: $55   **G/VG: $15**

Post, Melville Davisson. *Uncle Abner: Master of Mysteries.*
First Edition: New York & London: D. Appleton & Co, 1918.
NF/F: $6,500   **G/VG: $1,600**

Postgate, Raymond. *Verdict of Twelve.*
First Edition: Garden City, NY:
Doubleday Doran/Crime Club, 1940.
NF/F: $500   **G/VG: $225**

Prather, Richard S. *Kill The Clown.*
First Edition: Greenwich, CT: Fawcett,
1962.
Points of Issue: Paperback original
Fawcett Gold Medal #s1208.
NF/F: $25   **G/VG: $10**
First UK and Hardcover Edition:
London: Hammond & Hammond, 1967.
NF/F: $40   **G/VG: $15**

Proctor Maurice. *Devils Due.*
First Edition: New York: Harper
Brothers, 1960.
NF/F: $35   **G/VG: $15**

Propper, Milton M. *The Strange
Disappearance of Mary Young.*
First Edition: New York: Harper &
Brothers, 1929.
NF/F: $350   **G/VG: $125**

Punshon, E.R. *Night's Cloak.*
First Edition: New York: Macmillan,
1944.
NF/F: $65   **G/VG: $20**

Puzo, Mario. *The Godfather.*
First Edition: New York: G.P. Putnams,
1969.
NF/F: $2,500   **G/VG: $450**

Queen, Ellery. *The Roman Hat
Mystery.*
First Edition: New York: Fredrick
Stokes, 1929.
NF/F: $2,000   **G/VG: $750**

_____. *There Was An Old
Woman.*
First Edition: Boston: Little Brown,
1943.
NF/F: $255   **G/VG: $55**

Quentin, Patrick. *My Son, the
Murderer.*
First Edition: New York: Simon &
Schuster, 1954.
NF/F: $45   **G/VG: $10**

Rawson, Clayton. *The Footprints on
the Ceiling.*
First Edition: New York: Putnam, 1939.
NF/F: $1,250   **G/VG: $450**

Reeve, Arthur B. *Pandora.*
First Edition: New York: Harper, 1926.
NF/F: $550   **G/VG: $225**

Reichs, Kathy. *Deja Dead.*
First Edition: New York: Scribners,
1997.
NF/F: $95   **G/VG: $25**

Reilly, Helen. *Death Demands an
Audience.*
First Edition: Garden City, NY:
Doubleday Doran/Crime Club, 1940.
NF/F: $200   **G/VG: $60**

Rendell, Ruth. *The Secret House Of
Death.*
First Edition: London: John Long, 1968.
NF/F: $1,200   **G/VG: $375**
First Edition: New York: Doubleday/
Crime Club, 1968.
NF/F: $120   **G/VG: $45**

Rhode, John. *Hendon's First Case.*
First Edition: New York: Dodd, Mead,
1935.
NF/F: $650   **G/VG: $75**

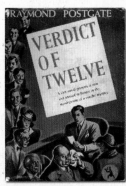
Raymond Postgate.

Ellery Queen.

Arthur B. Reeve.

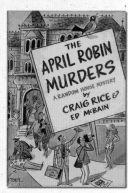

Craig Rice and Ed McBain.

Mary Roberts Rinehart.

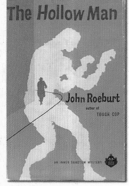

John Roeburt.

Rice, Craig & Ed McBain. *The April Robin Murders.*
First Edition: New York: Random House, 1958.
NF/F: $420   G/VG: $100

Rinehart, Mary Roberts. *Tish.*
First Edition: Boston: Houghton Mifflin, 1916.
NF/F: $375   G/VG: $100

Roeburt, John. *The Hollow Man.*
First Edition: New York: Simon & Schuster, 1954.
NF/F: $45   G/VG: $12

Rohmer, Sax. *Bimbashi Baruk of Egypt.*
First Edition: New York: Robert M. McBride Co., 1944.
NF/F: $325   G/VG: $100

_____. Fu Manchu Series:

_____. *The Mystery Of Dr. Fu Manchu.*
First Edition: London: Methuen, 1913.
NF/F: $2,400   G/VG: $950
First U.S. Edition: as: *The Insidious Dr. Fu Manchu.* New York: McBride, Nast, 1913.
NF/F: $1,250   G/VG: $475

_____. *The Return Of Dr. Fu Manchu.*
First Edition: New York: McBride, 1916.
NF/F: $1,550   G/VG: $750
First U.K. Edition: as: *The Devil Doctor.* London: Methuen, 1913.
NF/F: $850   G/VG: $300

_____. *The Si-Fan Mysteries.*
First Edition: London: Methuen, 1917.
NF/F: $750   G/VG: $250
First U.S. Edition: as: *The Hand Fu Manchu:* New York: McBride, 1917.
NF/F: $550   G/VG: $150

_____. *The Daughter Of Fu Manchu.*
First Edition: Garden City, NY: Doubleday Doran/Crime Club, 1931.
NF/F: $1,200   G/VG: $450
First U.K. Edition: London: Cassell, 1931.
NF/F: $1,000   G/VG: $300

_____. *The Mask Of Fu Manchu.*
First Edition: Garden City, NY: Doubleday Doran/Crime Club, 1932.
NF/F: $650   G/VG: $200
First U.K. Edition: London: Cassell, 1933.
NF/F: $450   G/VG: $100

_____. *Fu Manchu's Bride.*
First Edition: Garden City, NY: Doubleday Doran/Crime Club, 1933.
NF/F: $550   G/VG: $150
First U.K. Edition: as: *The Bride of Fu Manchu:* London: Cassell, 1933.
NF/F: $550   G/VG: $100

_____. *The Trail Of Fu Manchu.*
First Edition: Garden City, NY: Doubleday Doran/Crime Club, 1934.
NF/F: $350   G/VG: $75
First U.K. Edition: London: Cassell, 1934.
NF/F: $150   G/VG: $50

_____. *President Fu Manchu.*
First Edition: Garden City, NY: Doubleday Doran/Crime Club, 1936.
NF/F: $450   G/VG: $100
First U.K. Edition: London: Cassell, 1936.
NF/F: $250   G/VG: $30

_____. *The Drums Of Fu Manchu.*
First Edition: Garden City, NY: Doubleday Doran/Crime Club, 1936.
NF/F: $300   G/VG: $100
First U.K. Edition: London: Cassell, 1936.
NF/F: $250   G/VG: $100

_____. *The Island Of Fu Manchu.*
First Edition: London: Cassell, 1941.
NF/F: $550   **G/VG: $150**
First U.S. Edition: Garden City, NY:
Doubleday Doran/ Crime Club, 1941.
NF/F: $250   **G/VG: $75**

_____. *Shadow Of Fu Manchu.*
First Edition: Garden City, NY:
Doubleday Doran/Crime Club, 1948.
NF/F: $350   **G/VG: $150**
First U.K. Edition: London: Herbert
Jenkins, 1949.
NF/F: $300   **G/VG: $100**

_____. *Re-Enter Fu Manchu.*
First Edition: Greenwich, Conn.:
Fawcett, 1957 (paperback original).
NF/F: $50   **G/VG: $10**
First U.K. Edition: as: *Re-Enter Dr. Fu
Manchu.* London: Herbert Jenkins,
1957.
NF/F: $450   **G/VG: $150**

_____. *Emperor Fu Manchu.*
First Edition: London: Herbert Jenkins,
1959.
NF/F: $400   **G/VG: $100**
First U.S. Edition: Greenwich, Conn.:
Fawcett, 1959 (paperback original).
NF/F: $35   **G/VG: $10**

Roos, Kelley. *Grave Danger.*
First Edition: New York: Dodd, Mead,
1965.
NF/F: $35   **G/VG: $10**

Ross, Barnaby. Drury Lane Series:

_____. *The Tragedy of X.*
First Edition: New York: Viking, 1932.
NF/F: $175   **G/VG: $75**

_____. *The Tragedy of Y.*
First Edition: New York: Viking, 1932.
NF/F: $125   **G/VG: $60**

_____. *The Tragedy of Z.*
First Edition: New York: Viking, 1933.
NF/F: $85   **G/VG: $30**

_____. *Drury Lane's Last Case.*
First Edition: New York: Viking, 1933.
NF/F: $85   **G/VG: $35**

Sanders, Lawrence. *The Anderson
Tapes.*
First Edition: New York: G. P.
Putnam's, 1970.
NF/F: $125   **G/VG: $45**

Sandford, John. *Rules of Prey.*
First Edition: New York: G.P. Putnams,
1989.
NF/F: $200   **G/VG: $80**

Sapper. *Tiny Carteret.*
First Edition: London: Hodder &
Stoughton, no date [1930].
NF/F: $350   **G/VG: $115**

Sayers, Dorothy L. Lord Peter
Whimsey Series:

_____. *Whose Body?*
First Edition: New York: Boni and
Liveright, 1923.
NF/F: $2,500   **G/VG: $1,000**
First U.K. Edition: London: T Fisher
Unwin, 1923.
NF/F: $1,400   **G/VG: $600**

_____. *Clouds of Witness.*
First Edition: London: T Fisher Unwin,
1926.
NF/F: $1,200   **G/VG: $500**
First U.S. Edition: New York: Dial Press
- Lincoln Mac Veagh, 1927.
NF/F: $500   **G/VG: $200**

Sax Rohmer.

Sax Rohmer.

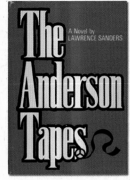
Lawrence Sanders.

Dorothy L. Sayers.

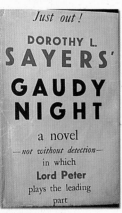

Dorothy L. Sayers.

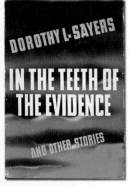

Dorothy L. Sayers.

_____. *Unnatural Death.*
First Edition: London: Ernest Benn, 1927.
NF/F: $1,500   **G/VG: $500**
First U.S. Edition as *The Dawson Pedigree*: New York: Dial Press - Lincoln Mac Veagh, 1928.
NF/F: $400   **G/VG: $175**

_____. *The Unpleasantness at the Bellona Club.*
First Edition: London: Ernest Benn, 1928.
NF/F: $1,300   **G/VG: $550**
First U.S. Edition: New York: Payson & Clarke, 1928.
NF/F: $600   **G/VG: $250**

_____. *Lord Peter Views the Body.*
First Edition: London: Victor Gollancz Ltd, 1928.
NF/F: $1,000   **G/VG: $450**
First U.S. Edition: New York: Brewer and Warren, 1928.
NF/F: $500   **G/VG: $200**

_____. *Strong Poison.*
First Edition: London: Victor Gollancz Ltd, 1930.
NF/F: $750   **G/VG: $250**
First U.S. Edition: New York: Brewer and Warren, 1930.
NF/F: $300   **G/VG: $100**

_____. *Five Red Herrings.*
First Edition: London: Victor Gollancz Ltd, 1931.
NF/F: $500   **G/VG: $225**
First U.S. Edition as *Suspicious Characters*: New York: Brewer and Putnam, 1931.
NF/F: $300   **G/VG: $100**

_____. *Have His Carcase.*
First Edition: London: Victor Gollancz Ltd, 1932.
NF/F: $500   **G/VG: $225**
First U.S. Edition: New York: Brewer, Warren and Putnam, 1932.
NF/F: $350   **G/VG: $125**

_____. *Hangman's Holiday.*
First Edition: London: Victor Gollancz Ltd, 1933.
NF/F: $4,500   **G/VG: $2,250**
First U.S. Edition: New York: Harcourt, Brace, 1933.
NF/F: $600   **G/VG: $275**

_____. *Murder Must Advertise.*
First Edition: London: Victor Gollancz Ltd, 1933.
NF/F: $1,200   **G/VG: $350**
First U.S. Edition: New York: Harcourt, Brace, 1933.
NF/F: $800   **G/VG: $325**

_____. *The Nine Tailors.*
First U.K. Edition: London: Victor Gollancz Ltd, 1934.
NF/F: $1,650   **G/VG: $450**
First Edition: New York: Harcourt, Brace, 1934.
NF/F: $1,200   **G/VG: $475**

_____. *Gaudy Night.*
First Edition: London: Victor Gollancz Ltd, 1935.
NF/F: $900   **G/VG: $350**
First U.S. Edition: New York: Harcourt, Brace, 1936.
NF/F: $500   **G/VG: $175**

_____. *Busman's Honeymoon.*
First Edition: London: Victor Gollancz Ltd, 1937.
NF/F: $800   **G/VG: $350**
First U.S. Edition: New York: Harcourt, Brace, 1937.
NF/F: $300   **G/VG: $100**

_____. *In the Teeth of Evidence.*
First Edition: London: Victor Gollancz Ltd, 1939.
NF/F: $1,100   **G/VG: $450**
First U.S. Edition: New York: Harcourt, Brace, 1940.
NF/F: $500   **G/VG: $225**

_____. and Jill Paton Walsh.
Thrones, Dominations.
First Edition: London: Hodder &
Stoughton, 1998.
NF/F: $50   **G/VG: $20**
First Edition: New York: St. Martin's, 1998.
NF/F: $35   **G/VG: $10**

Scherf, Margaret. *The Elk and the
Evidence.*
First Edition: Garden City, NY:
Doubleday/Crime Club, 1952.
NF/F: $125   **G/VG: $45**

Scoppettone, Sandra. *Playing Murder.*
First Edition: New York: Harper &
Row, 1985.
NF/F: $50   **G/VG: $15**

Shannon, Dell. *Coffin Corner: A Luis
Mendoza Mystery.*
First Edition: New York: William
Morrow & Co., 1966.
NF/F: $40   **G/VG: $10**

Simenon, Georges. *Shadow Falls.*
First Edition in English: London:
George Routledge and Sons Ltd., 1945.
NF/F: $275   **G/VG: $50**
First U.S. Edition: New York: Harcourt
Brace, 1945.
NF/F: $350   **G/VG: $65**

Smith, Martin Cruz. *Gorky Park.*
First Edition: New York: Random
House, 1981.
NF/F: $95   **G/VG: $25**
First U.K. Edition: London: Collins,
1981.
NF/F: $55   **G/VG: $20**

Spillane, Mickey. *The Erection Set.*
First Edition: New York: E. P. Dutton,
1972.
NF/F: $250   **G/VG: $85**

_____. *The Last Cop Out.*
First Edition: New York: E.P. Dutton,
1973.
NF/F: $95   **G/VG: $30**

_____. Mike Hammer Series:

_____. *I, the Jury.*
First Edition: New York: E.P. Dutton,
1947.
NF/F: $4,000   **G/VG: $1,800**

_____. *My Gun is Quick.*
First Edition: New York: E.P. Dutton,
1950.
NF/F: $2,500   **G/VG: $1,250**

_____. *Vengeance is Mine*
First Edition: New York: E.P. Dutton,
1950.
NF/F: $2,500   **G/VG: $950**

_____. *The Big Kill.*
First Edition: New York: E.P. Dutton,
1951.
NF/F: $350   **G/VG: $125**

_____. *Kiss Me, Deadly.*
First Edition: New York: E.P. Dutton,
1952.
NF/F: $700   **G/VG: $25**

_____. *The Girl Hunters.*
First Edition: New York: E.P. Dutton,
1962.
NF/F: $125   **G/VG: $55**

_____. *The Snake.*
First Edition: New York: E.P. Dutton,
1964.
NF/F: $95   **G/VG: $25**

_____. *The Twisted Thing.*
First Edition: New York: E.P. Dutton,
1966.
NF/F: $85   **G/VG: $25**

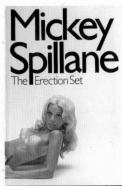

Mickey Spillane.

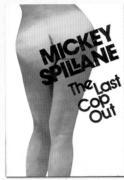

Mickey Spillane.

Mickey Spillane.

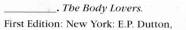

Mickey Spillane.

Rex Stout.

Rex Stout.

_____. *The Body Lovers.*
First Edition: New York: E.P. Dutton, 1967.
NF/F: $95   **G/VG: $35**

_____. *Survival...Zero!*
First Edition: New York: E.P. Dutton, 1970.
NF/F: $60   **G/VG: $20**

_____. *The Killing Man.*
First Edition: Franklin Center, PA: Franklin Library, 1989.
NF/F: $125   **G/VG: $55**
First Trade Edition: New York: E.P. Dutton, 1989.
NF/F: $75   **G/VG: $25**

_____. *Black Alley.*
First Edition: New York: E.P. Dutton, 1996.
NF/F: $35   **G/VG: $10**

_____ **with Max Allan Collins.**
The Goliath Bone.
First Edition: New York: Harcourt, 2008.
NF/F: $25   **G/VG: $8**

Stout, Rex. Nero Wolfe Series:

_____. *Fer-De-Lance.*
First Edition: New York: Farrar & Rinehart, 1934.
NF/F: $18,000   **G/VG: $7,500**

_____. *The League of Frightened Men.*
First Edition: New York: Farrar & Rinehart, 1935.
NF/F: $1,800   **G/VG: $600**

_____. *The Rubber Band.*
First Edition: New York: Farrar & Rinehart, 1936.
NF/F: $850   **G/VG: $300**

_____. *The Red Box.*
First Edition: New York: Farrar & Rinehart, 1937.
NF/F: $650   **G/VG: $275**

_____. *Too Many Cooks.*
First Edition: New York: Farrar & Rinehart, 1938.
NF/F: $5,000   **G/VG: $1,600**

_____. *Some Buried Caesar.*
First Edition: New York: Farrar & Rinehart, 1939.
NF/F: $925   **G/VG: $375**

_____. *Over My Dead Body.*
First Edition: New York: Farrar & Rinehart, 1940.
NF/F: $2,500   **G/VG: $825**

_____. *Where There's a Will.*
First Edition: New York: Farrar & Rinehart, 1940.
NF/F: $1,250   **G/VG: $550**

_____. *Black Orchids.*
First Edition: New York: Farrar & Rinehart, 1942.
NF/F: $1,750   **G/VG: $700**

_____. *Not Quite Dead Enough.*
First Edition: New York: Farrar & Rinehart, 1944.
NF/F: $950   **G/VG: $325**

_____. *The Silent Speaker.*
First Edition: New York: Viking, 1946.
NF/F: $500   **G/VG: $225**

_____. *Too Many Women.*
First Edition: New York: Viking, 1947.
NF/F: $400　　　　　　　　**G/VG: $150**

_____. *And Be a Villain.*
First Edition: New York: Viking, 1948.
NF/F: $275　　　　　　　　**G/VG: $125**

_____. *Trouble in Triplicate.*
First Edition: New York: Viking, 1949.
NF/F: $550　　　　　　　　**G/VG: $200**

_____. *The Second Confession.*
First Edition: New York: Viking, 1949.
NF/F: $325　　　　　　　　**G/VG: $135**

_____. *Three Doors to Death.*
First Edition: New York: Viking, 1950.
NF/F: $95　　　　　　　　**G/VG: $35**

_____. *In the Best Families.*
First Edition: New York: Viking, 1950.
NF/F: $225　　　　　　　　**G/VG: $85**

_____. *Curtains for Three.*
First Edition: New York: Viking, 1951.
NF/F: $300　　　　　　　　**G/VG: $120**

_____. *Murder by the Book.*
First Edition: New York: Viking, 1951.
NF/F: $275　　　　　　　　**G/VG: $125**

_____. *Triple Jeopardy.*
First Edition: New York: Viking, 1952.
NF/F: $200　　　　　　　　**G/VG: $75**

_____. *Prisoner's Base.*
First Edition: New York: Viking, 1952.
NF/F: $100　　　　　　　　**G/VG: $35**

_____. *The Golden Spiders.*
First Edition: New York: Viking, 1953.
NF/F: $125　　　　　　　　**G/VG: $50**

_____. *Three Men Out.*
First Edition: New York: Viking, 1954.
NF/F: $150　　　　　　　　**G/VG: $65**

_____. *The Black Mountain.*
First Edition: New York: Viking, 1954.
NF/F: $250　　　　　　　　**G/VG: $100**

_____. *Before Midnight.*
First Edition: New York: Viking, 1955.
NF/F: $200　　　　　　　　**G/VG: $80**

_____. *Three Witnesses.*
First Edition: New York: Viking, 1956.
NF/F: $135　　　　　　　　**G/VG: $60**

_____. *Might as Well Be Dead.*
First Edition: New York: Viking, 1956.
NF/F: $125　　　　　　　　**G/VG: $45**

_____. *Three for the Chair.*
First Edition: New York: Viking, 1957.
NF/F: $200　　　　　　　　**G/VG: $80**

_____. *If Death Ever Slept.*
First Edition: New York: Viking, 1957.
NF/F: $115　　　　　　　　**G/VG: $40**

_____. *And Four to Go.*
First Edition: New York: Viking, 1958.
NF/F: $200　　　　　　　　**G/VG: $75**

_____. *Champagne for One.*
First Edition: New York: Viking, 1958.
NF/F: $175　　　　　　　　**G/VG: $75**

_____. *Plot It Yourself.*
First Edition: New York: Viking, 1959.
NF/F: $125　　　　　　　　**G/VG: $55**

_____. *Three at Wolfe's Door.*
First Edition: New York: Viking, 1960.
NF/F: $65　　　　　　　　**G/VG: $25**

Rex Stout.

Rex Stout.

Rex Stout.

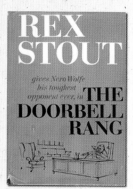

Rex Stout.

Phoebe Atwood Taylor.

Alice Tilton.

_____. *Too Many Clients.*
First Edition: New York: Viking, 1960.
NF/F: $200   G/VG: $95

_____. *The Final Deduction.*
First Edition: New York: Viking, 1961.
NF/F: $85   G/VG: $30

_____. *Homicide Trinity.*
First Edition: New York: Viking, 1962.
NF/F: $150   G/VG: $65

_____. *Gambit.*
First Edition: New York: Viking, 1962.
NF/F: $100   G/VG: $40

_____. *The Mother Hunt.*
First Edition: New York: Viking, 1963.
NF/F: $115   G/VG: $40

_____. *Trio for Blunt Instruments.*
First Edition: New York: Viking, 1964.
NF/F: $100   G/VG: $35

_____. *A Right to Die.*
First Edition: New York: Viking, 1964.
NF/F: $100   G/VG: $30

_____. *The Doorbell Rang.*
First Edition: New York: Viking, 1965.
NF/F: $150   G/VG: $65

_____. *Death of a Doxy.*
First Edition: New York: Viking, 1966.
NF/F: $150   G/VG: $60

_____. *The Father Hunt.*
First Edition: New York: Viking, 1968.
NF/F: $100   G/VG: $35

_____. *Death of a Dude.*
First Edition: New York: Viking, 1969.
NF/F: $125   G/VG: $45

_____. *Please Pass the Guilt.*
First Edition: New York: Viking, 1973.
NF/F: $75   G/VG: $30

_____. *A Family Affair.*
First Edition: New York: Viking, 1975.
NF/F: $85   G/VG: $20

_____. *Death Times Three.*
First Edition: New York: Bantam, 1985.
NF/F: $65   G/VG: $10

Symonds, Julian. *The Killing of Francie Lake.*
First Edition: London: Collins, 1962.
NF/F: $30   G/VG: $10

Taylor, Phoebe Atwood. *The Perennial Boarder.*
First Edition: New York: W.W. Norton & Co., 1941.
NF/F: $195   G/VG: $65

Tey, Josephine. *Miss Pym Disposes.*
First Edition: New York: The Macmillan Co., 1947.
NF/F: $150   G/VG: $40

Thayer, Lee. *Guilt Edged.*
First Edition: New York: Dodd Mead, 1951.
NF/F: $45   G/VG: $15

Thorp, Roderick. *Nothing Lasts Forever.*
First Edition: New York: W.W. Norton, 1979.
NF/F: $125   G/VG: $55

Tilton, Alice. *Dead Ernest.*
First Edition: New York: W. W. Norton, 1944.
NF/F: $180   G/VG: $30

Train, Arthur. *No Matter Where.*
First Edition: New York: Scribners, 1933.
NF/F: $115   **G/VG: $45**

_____. *Page Mr. Tutt.*
First Edition: New York: Charles Scribners, 1926.
NF/F: $275   **G/VG: $95**

Traver, Robert. *Anatomy of a Murder.*
First Edition: New York: St. Martins, 1958.
NF/F: $400   **G/VG: $125**
First U.K. Edition: London Faber & Faber, 1958.
NF/F: $80   **G/VG: $20**

Tucker, Wilson. *Red Herring.*
First Edition: New York: Rinehart, 1951.
NF/F: $55   **G/VG: $20**
First Edition: London: Cassell & Co, 1953.
NF/F: $35   **G/VG: $15**

Uhnak, Dorothy. *The Investigation.*
First Edition: New York: Simon and Schuster, 1977.
NF/F: $40   **G/VG: $12**

Upfield, Arthur. *Death of a Swagman.*
First Edition: Garden City, NY: Doubleday/Crime Club, 1945.
NF/F: $350   **G/VG: $120**
First U.K. Edition: London: Francis Aldor, 1946.
NF/F: $275   **G/VG: $75**
First Australian Edition: Sydney: Angus & Robertson, 1947.
NF/F: $500   **G/VG: $185**

Vandercook, John W. *Murder in Haiti.*
First Edition: New York: Macmillan, 1956.
NF/F: $95   **G/VG: $25**
First Edition: London: Eyre & Spottiswoode, 1956.
NF/F: $45   **G/VG: $12**

Van Dine, S.S. Philo Vance Series*:

_____. *The Benson Murder Case.*
First Edition: New York: Charles Scribners, 1926.
NF/F: $950   **G/VG: $425**

_____. *The Canary Murder Case.*
First Edition: New York: Scribners, 1927.
NF/F: $300   **G/VG: $125**

_____. *The Greene Murder Case.*
First Edition: New York: Charles Scribners, 1928.
Points of Issue: Roman numerals on title page (MCMXXVIII) and "copyright 1928" on copyright page with Scribner's seal.
NF/F: $1,450   **G/VG: $625**

_____. *The Bishop Murder Case.*
First Edition: New York: Scribners, 1929.
NF/F: $600   **G/VG: $225**

_____. *The Scarab Murder Case.*
First Edition: New York: Charles Scribners, 1930.
NF/F: $550   **G/VG: $175**

Arthur Train.

Arthur Train.

Arthur Upfield.

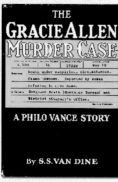

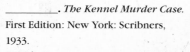

S.S. Van Dine.

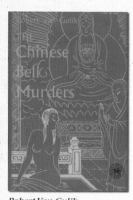

Robert Van Gulik.

Robert Van Gulik.

_____. *The Kennel Murder Case.*
First Edition: New York: Scribners, 1933.
NF/F: $500   **G/VG: $200**

_____. *The Dragon Murder Case.*
First Edition: New York: Charles Scribners, 1933.
NF/F: $450   **G/VG: $125**

_____. *The Casino Murder Case.*
First Edition: New York: Scribners, 1934.
NF/F: $800   **G/VG: $350**

_____. *The Garden Murder Case.*
First Edition: New York: Charles Scribners, 1935.
NF/F: $650   **G/VG: $175**

_____. . *The Kidnap Murder Case.*
First Edition: New York: Scribners, 1936.
NF/F: $350   **G/VG: $100**

_____. *The Gracie Allen Murder Case.*
First Edition: New York: Charles Scribners, 1938.
NF/F: $550   **G/VG: $225**

_____. *The Winter Murder Case.*
First Edition: New York: Scribners, 1933.
NF/F: $300   **G/VG: $100**

Van Gulik, Robert. Judge Dee Series*:

_____. *The Chinese Maze Murders.*
First Edition in English: The Hague and Bandung: W. Van Hoeve Ltd., 1956.
NF/F: $1,000   **G/VG: $400**
First U.K. Edition: London: Michael Joseph, 1962.
NF/F: $250   **G/VG: $85**

_____. *The Chinese Bell Murders.*
First Edition in English: London: Michael Joseph, 1958.
NF/F: $450   **G/VG: $175**
First U.S. Edition: New York: Harper & Brothers, 1958.
NF/F: $95   **G/VG: $25**

_____. *The Chinese Lake Murders.*
First Edition in English: London: Michael Joseph, 1960.
NF/F: $200   **G/VG: $85**
First U.S. Edition: New York: Harper & Brothers, 1960.
NF/F: $75   **G/VG: $25**

_____. *The Chinese Gold Murders.*
First Edition in English: London: Michael Joseph, 1959.
NF/F: $350   **G/VG: $125**
First U.S. Edition: New York: Harper & Brothers, 1959.
NF/F: $125   **G/VG: $55**

_____. *The Chinese Nail Murders.*
First Edition in English: London: Michael Joseph, 1961.
NF/F: $375   **G/VG: $165**
First U.S. Edition: New York: Harper & Row, 1962.
NF/F: $250   **G/VG: $85**

_____. *The Haunted Monastery.*
First Edition in English: Kuala Lumpur: Art Printing Works, 1961.
NF/F: $600   **G/VG: $250**
First U.K. Edition: London: Heinneman, 1963.
NF/F: $125   **G/VG: $55**
First U.S. Edition: New York: Charles Scribner's Sons, 1969.
NF/F: $100   **G/VG: $35**

_____. *The Emperor's Pearl.*
First Edition in English: London: Heinemann, 1963.
NF/F: $300   **G/VG: $100**
First U.S. Edition: New York: Charles Scribner's Sons, 1963.
NF/F: $85   **G/VG: $25**

_____. *The Lacquer Screen.*
First Edition in English: Kuala Lumpur: Art Printing Works, 1962.
NF/F: $600   **G/VG: $250**
First U.K. Edition: London: Heinneman, 1964.
NF/F: $100   **G/VG: $40**
First U.S. Edition: New York: Charles Scribner's Sons, 1969.
NF/F: $75   **G/VG: $25**

_____. *The Red Pavillion.*
First Edition in English: London: Heinemann, 1964.
NF/F: $100   **G/VG: $40**
First U.S. Edition: New York: Charles Scribner's Sons, 1968.
NF/F: $75   **G/VG: $30**

_____. *The Monkey and the Tiger.*
First Edition in English: London: Heinemann, 1965.
NF/F: $150   **G/VG: $65**
First U.S. Edition: New York: Charles Scribner's Sons, 1968.
NF/F: $125   **G/VG: $50**

_____. *The Willow Pattern.*
First Edition in English: London: Heinemann, 1965.
NF/F: $135   **G/VG: $60**
First U.S. Edition: New York: Charles Scribner's Sons, 1965.
NF/F: $100   **G/VG: $35**

_____. *Murder in Canton.*
First Edition in English: London: Heinemann, 1967.
NF/F: $75   **G/VG: $25**
First U.S. Edition: New York: Charles Scribner's Sons, 1967.
NF/F: $65   **G/VG: $25**

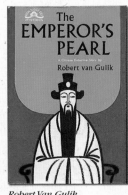

Robert Van Gulik.

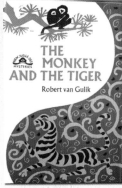

Robert Van Gulik.

R.A.J. Walling.

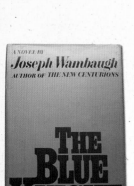

Joseph Wambaugh.

_____. *The Phantom of the Temple.*
First Edition in English: London: Heinemann, 1966.
NF/F: $75   **G/VG: $25**
First U.S. Edition: New York: Charles Scribner's Sons, 1966.
NF/F: $75   **G/VG: $25**

_____. *Judge Dee at Work.*
First Edition in English: London: Heinemann, 1967.
NF/F: $200   **G/VG: $80**
First U.S. Edition: New York: Charles Scribner's Sons, 1967.
NF/F: $150   **G/VG: $40**

_____. *Necklace and Calabash.*
First Edition in English: London: Heinemann, 1967.
NF/F: $275   **G/VG: $135**
First U.S. Edition: New York: Charles Scribner's Sons, 1967.
NF/F: $95   **G/VG: $35**

_____. *Poets and Murder.*
First Edition in English: London: Heinemann, 1968.
NF/F: $150   **G/VG: $60**
First U.S. Edition: New York: Charles Scribner's Sons, 1972.
NF/F: $85   **G/VG: $30**

Vickers, Roy. *The Department of Dead Ends.*
First Edition: London: Faber & Faber, 1949.
NF/F: $450   **G/VG: $125**

Wade, Henry. *The Litmore Snatch.*
First Edition: New York: Macmillan, 1957.
NF/F: $65   **G/VG: $15**

Wallace, Edgar. *Jack O'Judgment.*
First Edition: London: Ward, Lock, and Co., 1920.
NF/F: $600   **G/VG: $200**

_____. *Murder Book of J. G. Reeder.*
First Edition: Garden City, NY: Doubleday, Doran/Crime Club, 1929.
NF/F: $400   **G/VG: $150**

Walling R.A.J. *Stroke of One.*
First Edition: New York: William Morrow, 1931.
NF/F: $195   **G/VG: $85**
First U.K. Edition: London: Methuen & Co., 1931.
NF/F: $75   **G/VG: $20**

Wambaugh, Joseph. *The Blue Knight.*
First Edition: Boston: Atlantic/Little, Brown, 1972.
NF/F: $100   **G/VG: $35**

Waugh, Hillary. *The Girl Who Cried Wolf.*
First Edition: Garden City, NY: Doubleday/Crime Club, 1958.
NF/F: $75   **G/VG: $30**

Webb, Jack. *One For My Dame.*
First Edition: New York: Holt, Rinehart, and Winston, 1961.
NF/F: $85   **G/VG: $25**

Wells, Carolyn. *Sleeping Dogs.*
First Edition: Garden City, N.Y.: Doubleday, Doran/ Crime Club, 1929.
NF/F: $250   **G/VG: $100**

Wentworth, Patricia. *Eternity Ring.*
First Edition: Philadelphia & New York: Lippincott, 1948.
NF/F: $125   **G/VG: $45**

Wilde, Percival. *P. Moran, Operative.*
First Edition: New York: Random House, 1947.
NF/F: $125   **G/VG: $35**

Williams, Valentine. *The Curiosity of Mr. Treadgold.*
First Edition: Boston: Houghton Mifflin, 1937.
NF/F: $125   **G/VG: $30**

Woods, Sara. *Serpent's Tooth.*
First Edition: London: Collins/Crime Club, 1971.
NF/F: $80   **G/VG: $25**
First U.S. Edition: New York: Holt Rinehart Winston, 1971.
NF/F: $45   **G/VG: $10**

Yaffe, James. *Mom Among The Liars.*
First Edition: New York: St. Martins Press, 1992.
NF/F: $30   **G/VG: $10**

Percival Wilde.

Valentine Williams.

OCCULT AND PARANORMAL

A few years ago, on a bet, a mathematician analyzed the predictions of the psychics in a supermarket tabloid and statistically compared them to the weather reports on a major New York City television station. A direct confrontation of the scientific with the occult.

The meteorologist, a scientist backed by years of study, using computers, radar, and all the other accoutrements of the modern age, versus the psychic who, somehow, sees, feels, or dreams what the future will be. Who came out on top? Who predicted the future with more accuracy? Actually it wasn't even close. The psychics outdid the scientists almost two to one. How? The entire fascination with the literature of the hidden and the unexplained is really a search for that answer.

The field is a broad one and a confusing one. Bookstores label it in different ways, and divide it into different categories. Astrology, numerology, divination, prophesy, magic, magick, occult, unexplained, witchcraft, UFO, metaphysics, secret societies, psychic, herbology, and New Age are all labels one can find on used bookstore shelves. A writer like Immanuel Velikovsky could end up in the Science section, while another, like Manly Palmer Hall, could be in Philosophy. That is a lot of the fun and the challenge in collecting it, it's hidden, like the name says- "Occult."

Some categories are obvious. Astrology, for example, is always going to fit in and get grouped together. Other categories are not so out front, however. Herbs, naturopathic, homeopathic medicine and related areas can end up with Dr. Atkin's diet books in "Health and Nutrition."

Books in this are rarely on any best seller list, and those that do make it, such as Jay Anson's *Amityville Horror* or Van Daniken's *Chariots of the Gods*, tend to be a bit on the sensational and controversial side. Many books, however, tend to remain in print much longer than in other genres. The 19th and early 20th century occult writers, such as Aleister Crowley, Manly P. Hall, Dion Fortune, A. E. Waite and Helena Blavatsky, are all in print, while their contemporaries in other genres are only available in the out-of-print market.

All of this tends to compress the market a bit. While the more expensive end of the spectrum is considerably lower in price than genres, the bottom tends toward higher prices. New books and more recent used books are a little more expensive than the normal run of trade publications. Perhaps that's because authors like H. P. Blavatsky and Aleister Crowley aren't really welcome at the book of the month club.

Like illustration and the philosophy/religion genres, many, if not most, occult books are collected as "First Thus" rather than true firsts. With a genre that is as old as this one, the true first may well be a stone tablet, which makes it a bit difficult to put it on a wooden bookcase or display on a glass-topped table.

Ancient knowledge and modern speculation, things that really do go bump in the night and everything we can't explain. A collection of "curious and long-forgotten lore" as Poe once termed it. It can be rewarding, very interesting and, who knows, it may allow you to turn that annoying neighbor into a frog.

TEN CLASSIC RARITIES

Blavatsky, Helena Petrovna. *Isis Unveiled.*
New York: Theosophical Society, 1877. 1,000 copies of the first printing sold in a week. Three printings in 1877 are indistinguishable.
NF/F: $15,000   **G/VG: $10,000**

Budge, E.A. Wallis. *The Book of the Dead: Facsimiles of the Papyri of Hunefer, Anhai, Karasher and Netchemet with Supplementary text from the papyrus of Nu, with transcripts, translations, etc.*
London, British Museum, 1899. Find it and know what to do after your funeral.
NF/F: $2,000   **G/VG: $950**

Crowley, Aleister. *777 Vel Prolegomena Symbolica Ad Systemam Sceptico-Mysticae Viae Explicandae, Fundamentum Hieroglyphicum Sanctissimorum Scientiae Summae (Liber DCCLXXVII).*
London & Felling-on-Tyne, 1909. You won't need magick to profit from this one.
NF/F: $3,600   **G/VG: $2,000**

Frazer, Sir James George. *The Golden Bough. A Study in Magic & Religion.*
London, 1911. 13 volumes bound in leather.
NF/F: $3,300   **G/VG: $1,500**

Hall, Manly P. *An Encyclopedic Outline of Masonic Hermetic Qabbalistic and Rosicrucian Symbolical Philosophy.*
San Francisco: H. S. Crocker, 1928. The Fifth printing, a limited edition of 800 bound in vellum with a slipcase.
NF/F: $1,200   **G/VG: $875**

Kawaguchi, Ekai. *Three Years in Tibet- With the original Japanese illustrations.*
Adyar, India: The Theosophical Office, 1909. One of the prettier publications of the Theosophical Press.
NF/F: $1,600   **G/VG: $900**

Ouspensky, P. D. *The Symbolism of the Tarot (Philosophy of occultism in pictures and numbers. Pen-pictures of the twenty two tarot).*
St. Petersburg (Russia): The Trood Printing and Publishing Co., 1913. Most of the English Translation was shipped to the U.S.
NF/F: $1,200   **G/VG: $550**

Saint-Germain, Comte De. *La Tres Sainte Trinosophie: a Parallel French and English Text.*
Los Angeles: The Phoenix Press, 1933.
NF/F: $2,500   **G/VG: $1,100**

Scott, Walter. *Letters on Demonology and Witchcraft, Addressed to J.G. Lockhart, Esq.*
London : John Murray, 1830. The First Edition is illustrated by George Cruikshank.
NF/F: $1,600   **G/VG: $800**

Waite, A. E. *Saint-Martin the French Mystic and the Story of Modern Martinism.*
London: William Rider and Son Ltd., 1922. A revised but definitive edition of original 1901 publication.
NF/F: $1,200   **G/VG: $650**

P.D. Outpensky.

PRICE GUIDE

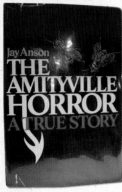

Jay Anson.

THE SOUL
AND ITS MECHANISM
THE PROBLEM OF PSYCHOLOGY

Alice A. Bailey.

Achad, Frater. *Q.B.L. or, The Bride's Reception.*
First Edition: Chicago, IL: Privately
Printed for the Author Collegium Ad
Spiritum Sanctum, 1922.
NF/F: $400   **G/VG: $140**

_____. *Thirty One Hymns to the
Star Goddess.*
First Edition: Chicago: Will Ransom, 1923.
NF/F: $375   **G/VG: $200**

Agrippa, Henry Cornelius. *Occult
Philosophy or Magic Book One
Natural Magic.*
First Edition Thus: Chicago: Hahn &
Whitehead, 1897.
NF/F: $250   **G/VG: $95**

_____. *On the Superiority of
Woman Over Man.*
First Edition in English: New York:
American News Company, 1873.
NF/F: $250   **G/VG: $100**

_____. *The Philosophy Of
Natural Magic.*
First Edition Thus: Chicago de
Laurence Scott, 1913.
NF/F: $185   **G/VG: $70**

Albertus, Frater. *The Seven Rays of
the Q.B.L.*
First Edition: Salt Lake City, UT:
Paracelsus Research Society, 1968.
NF/F: $125   **G/VG: $55**

_____. *Gently I Answered And Said.*
First Edition: Salt Lake City, UT:
Paracelsus Research Society, 1978.
NF/F: $185   **G/VG: $65**

Alder, Vera Stanley. *When Humanity
Comes of Age.*
First Edition: London: Andrew Dakans, 1950.
NF/F: $100   **G/VG: $30**

Andrews, George C. *Extra-
Terrestrials Among Us.*
First Edition: St. Paul, MN: Llewellyn
Publications, 1986.
NF/F: $45   **G/VG: $12**

Anson, Jay. *The Amityville Horror.*
First Edition: Englewood Cliffs, N.J.:
Prentice Hall, 1977.
NF/F: $100   **G/VG: $35**

Arundale, George S. *Nirvana.*
First Edition: Adyar: Theosophical
Publishing House, 1926.
NF/F: $85   **G/VG: $20**

Ashpole, Edward. *The Search for
Extra - Terrestrial Intelligence.*
First Edition: London: Blandford Press,
1989.
NF/F: $25   **G/VG: $8**

Bailey, Alice A. *Letters on Occult
Meditation.*
First Edition: New York: Lucis
Publishing Co, 1922.
NF/F: $80   **G/VG: $20**

_____. *From Bethlehem to
Calvary - The Initiations of Jesus.*
First Edition: New York: Lucis
Publishing Company, 1937.
NF/F: $75   **G/VG: $15**

_____. *Education in the New
Age.*
First Edition: New York: Lucis
Publishing Company, 1954.
NF/F: $85   **G/VG: $25**

_____. *The Soul and Its Mechanism.*
First Edition: New York: Lucis
Publishing Company, 1930.
NF/F: $100   **G/VG: $40**

Baker, Alan. *The Encyclopaedia of Alien Encounters.*
First Edition: London: Virgin, 1999.
NF/F: $35   **G/VG: $12**

Barrett, Francis. *The Magus. A Complete System of Occult Philosophy.*
First Edition: London: Lackington, Allen and Co., 1801. Only two examined; one at $24,500 and one at $25,000. Facsimile of 1801 Edition First Thus: New York: University Books, 1967.
NF/F: $145   **G/VG: $55**

Baskin, Wade. *The Sorcerer's Handbook.*
First Edition: New York: Philosophical Library, 1974.
NF/F: $45   **G/VG: $15**

_____. *A Dictionary of Satanism.*
First Edition: New York: Philosophical Library, 1972.
NF/F: $45   **G/VG: $15**

Bayless, Raymond. *Experiences Of A Psychical Researcher.*
First Edition: New Hyde Park, NY: University Books, 1972.
NF/F: $25   **G/VG: $10**

_____. *The Enigma of the Poltergeist.*
First Edition: West Nyack, NY: Parker, 1967.
NF/F: $45   **G/VG: $15**

Bergier, Jacques & Pauwels, Louis.
The Dawn of Magic.
First Edition in English: London: Anthony Goggs & Phillips, 1963.
NF/F: $200   **G/VG: $65**
First U.S. Edition as *Morning of the Magicians*: New York: Stein & Day, 1964.
NF/F: $95   **G/VG: $25**

_____. *Impossible Possibilities.*
First U.S. Edition: New York: Stein & Day, 1971.
NF/F: $35   **G/VG: $10**

Bergier, Jacques & the Editors of INFO. *Extraterrestrial Intervention.*
First Edition Thus: Chicago: Henry Regnery, 1974.
NF/F: $35   **G/VG: $12**

Bergier, Jacques. *Secret Doors Of The Earth.*
First U.S. Edition: Chicago: Henry Regnery, 1975.
NF/F: $80   **G/VG: $20**

Berlitz, Charles & William L. Moore. *The Roswell Incident.*
First Edition: New York: Grosset & Dunlap, 1980.
NF/F: $85   **G/VG: $15**

Berlitz, Charles. *The Mystery of Atlantis.*
First Edition: New York: Grosset & Dunlap, 1971.
NF/F: $50   **G/VG: $15**

_____. *The Bermuda Triangle.*
First Edition: Garden City, NY: Doubleday, 1974.
NF/F: $45   **G/VG: $10**

Bernstein, Morey. *The Search for Bridey Murphy.*
First Edition: Garden City, NY: Doubleday, 1956.
NF/F: $95   **G/VG: $25**

Besant, Annie. *The Building of the Kosmos and Other Lectures.*
First Edition: London: Theosophical Publishing Society, 1894.
NF/F: $325   **G/VG: $125**

_____. *The Ideals of Theosophy.*
First Edition: Madras, India: The Theosophist Office, 1912.
NF/F: $300   **G/VG: $125**

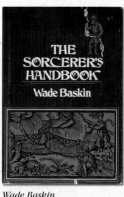
Wade Baskin.

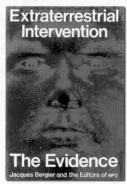
Jacques Bergier and the editors of INFO.

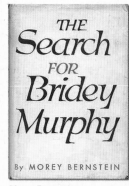
Morey Bernstein.

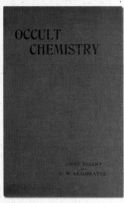

Annie Besant and C.W. Leadbeater.

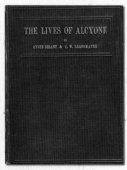

Annie Besant and C.W. Leadbeater.

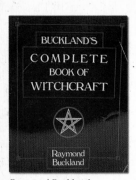

Raymond Buckland.

_____. *Evolution and Occultism.*
First Edition: London: The
Theosophical Publishing Society, 1913.
NF/F: $275   **G/VG: $115**

Besant, Annie & C. W. Leadbeater.
Occult Chemistry.
First Edition: London: Theosophical
Publishing Society, 1908.
NF/F: $465   **G/VG: $225**

_____. *The Lives of Alcyone.*
(Two Volumes).
First Edition: Adyar, Madras:
Theosophical Publishing House, 1924.
NF/F: $500   **G/VG: $200**

Blavatsky, Helena Petrovna. *The
Secret Doctrine.* (Six Volumes).
First Edition Thus, Fourth Edition:
Adyar: Theosophical Publishing
House, 1938.
NF/F: $200   **G/VG: $80**

_____. *Nightmare Tales.*
First Edition: London: Theosophical
Publishing Society, 1892.
NF/F: $600   **G/VG: $200**

_____. *The Theosophical
Glossary.*
First Edition: London: Theosophical
Publishing Co., 1892.
NF/F: $450   **G/VG: $200**

_____. *The Voice of the Silence
and Other Chosen Fragments.*
First Edition: New York: Elliott B. Page
& Co., 1899.
NF/F: $85   **G/VG: $25**

_____. *A Modern Panarion: A
Collection Of Fugitive Fragments.*
First Edition: London: The
Theosophical Publishing Society, 1895.
NF/F: $100   **G/VG: $35**

Blum, Howard. *Out There The
Government's Secret Quest for
Extraterrestrials.*
First Edition: New York: Simon and
Schuster, 1990.
NF/F: $35   **G/VG: $10**

Blum, Ralph H. *The Serenity Runes-
Five Keys to the Serenity Prayer.*
First Edition: New York: St. Martin
Press, 1998.
NF/F: $45   **G/VG: $10**

Boehme, Jacob. *Mysterium Magnum
or an Exposition of the First Book of
Moses.*
First Edition Thus: London: John M.
Watkins, 1924.
NF/F: $1,000   **G/VG: $325**

_____. *Concerning The Three
Principles of The Divine Essence.*
First Edition Thus: London: John M.
Watkins, 1910.
NF/F: $285   **G/VG: $125**

_____. *The Confessions of Jacob
Boehme.*
First U.S. Edition: New York: Alfred A.
Knopf, 1920.
NF/F: $175   **G/VG: $80**

Bonewitz, Ra. *The Crystal Heart a
Practical Guide to Healing the Heart
Centre with Crystals.*
First Edition: London: Aquarian Press,
1989.
NF/F: $20   **G/VG: $8**

Brennan, J.H. *Occult Reich.*
First Edition: London: Futura Books,
1974. Points of Issue: Paperback
Original.
NF/F: $55   **G/VG: $15**

Briffault, Robert. *Psyche's Lamp: a Revaluation of Psychological Principals as Foundation of All Thought.*
First Edition: London: Allen & Unwin, 1921.
NF/F: $50　　　　　**G/VG: $12**

Buckland, Raymond. *The Magick Of Chant-O-Matics.*
First Edition: Englewood Cliffs, NJ: Prentice Hall, 1977.
NF/F: $85　　　　　**G/VG: $25**

_____. *Buckland's Complete Book of Witchcraft.* Points of Issue: Paperback Original.
First Edition: St. Paul, MN: Llewellyn, 1995.
NF/F: $45　　　　　**G/VG: $10**

Budge, E. A. Wallis. *The Gods of the Egyptians.*
First Edition: London: Methuen & Co., 1904.
NF/F: $1,500　　　　　**G/VG: $800**

_____. *Egyptian Magic.*
First Edition: London: Kegan Paul, Trench, Trübner/New York: Henry Frowde, Oxford University Press, 1899.
NF/F: $350　　　　　**G/VG: $100**

Bulwer-Lytton, Edward. *Zanoni.* (Two Volumes).
First U.S. Edition: New York: Harper & Brothers, 1842.
NF/F: $650　　　　　**G/VG: $200**
First Edition Thus: Philadelphia: J. B. Lippincott Company, 1867.
NF/F: $150　　　　　**G/VG: $65**

Caddy, Eileen. *Spirit of Findhorn.*
First Edition: New York: Harper & Row, 1976.
NF/F: $85　　　　　**G/VG: $30**

Carrington, Hereward. *Modern Psychial Phenomena.* Recent Researches and Speculations.
First Edition: New York: Dodd Mead, 1919.
NF/F: $95　　　　　**G/VG: $35**

_____. *The Problems of Psychical Research.*
First Edition: New York: W. Rickey & Co., 1914.
NF/F: $250　　　　　**G/VG: $85**
First U.K. Edition: London: William Rider, 1914.
NF/F: $75　　　　　**G/VG: $30**

Castaneda, Carlos. Don Juan Series:

_____. *The Teachings of Don Juan. A Yaqui Way of Knowledge.*
First Edition: Berkeley: University of California Press, 1968.
NF/F: $1,100　　　　　**G/VG: $500**

_____. *A Separate Reality.*
First Edition: New York: Simon & Schuster, 1971.
NF/F: $700　　　　　**G/VG: $225**

_____. *Journey to Ixtlan: the Lessons of Don Juan.*
First Edition: New York: Simon & Schuster, 1972.
NF/F: $125　　　　　**G/VG: $45**

_____. *Tales of Power.*
First Edition: New York: Simon & Schuster, 1974.
NF/F: $125　　　　　**G/VG: $35**

_____. *The Second Ring of Power.*
First Edition: New York: Simon & Schuster, 1977.
NF/F: $100　　　　　**G/VG: $35**

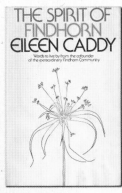
Eileen Caddy.

Carlos Castaneda.

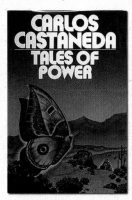
Carlos Castaneda.

James Churchward.

Daniel Cohen.

_____. *The Eagle's Gift.*
First Edition: New York: Simon &
Schuster, 1981.
NF/F: $35   **G/VG: $15**

_____. *The Fire From Within.*
First Edition: New York: Simon &
Schuster, 1984.
NF/F: $35   **G/VG: $15**
First U.K. Edition: London: Century,
1985.
NF/F: $50   **G/VG: $20**

_____. *The Power of Silence.*
First Edition: New York: Simon &
Schuster, 1987.
NF/F: $65   **G/VG: $25**

_____. *The Art of Dreaming.*
First Edition: Scranton, PA: Harper
Collins, 1993.
NF/F: $40   **G/VG: $15**

_____. *Magical Passes.*
First Edition: Scranton, PA: Harper
Collins, 1998.
NF/F: $85   **G/VG: $25**

_____. *The Wheel of Time.*
First Edition: Los Angeles: LA Eidolona
Press, 1998.
NF/F: $20   **G/VG: $10**

_____. *The Active Side of
Infinity.*
First Edition: Scranton, PA:
HarperCollins, 1999.
NF/F: $30   **G/VG: $10**

Cayce, Edgar Evans. *Edgar Cayce on
Atlantis.*
First Edition: New York: Hawthorn
Books, 1968.
NF/F: $60   **G/VG: $15**

**Cayce, Edgar Evans and Hugh Lynn
Cayce.** *The Outer Limits of Edgar
Cayce's Power.*
First Edition: New York: Harper &
Row, Publishers, 1971.
NF/F: $85   **G/VG: $20**

_____. *Faces of Fear.*
First Edition: San Francisco: Harper &
Row, 1980.
NF/F: $25   **G/VG: $10**

Cavendish, Richard. *The Black Arts.*
First Edition: London: Routledge &
Kegan Paul, 1967.
NF/F: $65   **G/VG: $25**

Cerminara, Gina. *Many Mansions.*
First Edition: New York: William
Sloane, 1950.
NF/F: $75   **G/VG: $20**

Churchward, James. MU Series:

_____. *Cosmic Forces; As They
Were Taught in Mu The Ancient Tale
that Religion and Science are Twin
Sisters.*
First Edition: Mount Vernon, NY:
Published by the Author, 1934.
NF/F: $225   **G/VG: $75**

_____. *Cosmic Forces: As They
Were Taught in Mu Relating to the
Earth.*
First Edition: Mount Vernon, NY:
Published by the author, 1935.
NF/F: $250   **G/VG: $85**

_____. *The Lost Continent of Mu
The Motherland of Man.*
First Edition: New York: William
Edwin Rudge, 1926.
NF/F: $300   **G/VG: $145**

Clymer, R. Swinburne. *A Compendium of Occult Laws.*
First Edition: Quakertown, PA: The Philosophical Publishing Company, 1938.
NF/F: $225   **G/VG: $90**

_____. *Christisis. Higher Soul Culture.*
First Edition: Allentown, PA: The Philosophical Publishing Company, 1911.
NF/F: $95   **G/VG: $35**

Cohen, Daniel. *Monsters, Giants and Little Men from Mars.*
First Edition: Garden City, NY: Doubleday, 1975.
NF/F: $55   **G/VG: $15**

Conway, David. *Secret Wisdom: The Occult Universe Explored.*
First Edition: London: Jonathan Cape, 1985.
NF/F: $55   **G/VG: $20**

Crowley, Aleister. *Magick.*
First Edition Thus: New York: Samuel Weiser, 1974.
NF/F: $115   **G/VG: $35**

_____. *Magick in Theory and Practice.*
First Edition: Paris: Lecram Press, 1929. Points of Issue: "Published for Subscribers Only," with a dust jacket and a colored plate of the sigil of "Master Theron."
NF/F: $2,900   **G/VG: $1,200**

_____. *Moonchild.*
First Edition: London: The Mandrake Press, 1929. Points of Issue: First issue is green cloth with gilt lettering on spine.
NF/F: $3,200   **G/VG: $1,100**

_____. *The Magical Record of the Beast 666.*
Limited Edition: London: Duckworth, 1972 (250 copies).
NF/F: $750   **G/VG: Not Seen**
First Edition: London: Duckworth, 1972.
NF/F: $250   **G/VG: $85**

_____. *The Vision and the Voice.*
First Edition Thus: Dallas, TX: Sangreal, 1972.
NF/F: $130   **G/VG: $50**

_____. *White Stains.*
First Edition: Amsterdam: Leonard Smithers, 1898.
NF/F: $8,500   **G/VG: $3,800**

_____. *The Winged Beetle.*
First Edition: London: "Privately Printed," 1910.
NF/F: $8,500   **G/VG: $3,800**

Crowley, Aleister as by Master Therion. *Liber Aleph: The Book of Wisdom and Folly.*
First Edition Thus: West Point, CA: Thelema Publishing Co., 1962.
NF/F: $625   **G/VG: $300**

Crowley, Aleister as by Khaled Khan. *The Heart of the Master.*
First Edition: London: O.T.O., 1938.
NF/F: $1,500   **G/VG: $600**

Dass, Baba Ram. *Doing Your Own Being.*
First Edition: London: Neville Spearman, 1973.
NF/F: $45   **G/VG: $20**

Davies, Rodney. *Supernatural Disappearances.*
First Edition: London: Robert Hale, 1995.
NF/F: $85   **G/VG: $20**

David Conway.

Aleister Crowley.

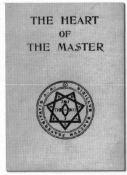

Aleister Crowley as by Khaled Khan.

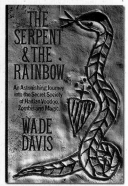

Wade Davis.

Martin Ebon.

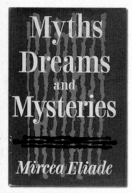

Mircea Eliade.

Davis, Wade. *The Serpent & The Rainbow.*
First Edition: New York: Simon & Schuster, 1985.
NF/F: $80   G/VG: $20
First U.K. Edition: London: Collins, 1986.
NF/F: $110   G/VG: $30

Day, Harvey. *Occult Illustrated Dictionary.*
First Edition: New York: Oxford University Press, 1976.
NF/F: $65   G/VG: $20

de Plancy, Colin. *Dictionary of Demonology.*
First Edition of Wade Baskin Translation: London: Peter Owen, 1965.
NF/F: $75   G/VG: $30

Dixon, Jean. *My Life and Prophecies.*
First Edition: New York: William Morrow, 1969.
NF/F: $15   G/VG: $5

Doyle, Sir Arthur Conan. *The History of Spiritualism.* (Two Volumes)
First Edition: London: Cassell, 1926.
NF/F: $1800   G/VG: $800

_____. *The Coming of the Fairies.*
First Edition: London: Hodder and Stoughton, 1922.
NF/F: $850   G/VG: $365
First Edition: New York: George H. Doran Co., 1922.
NF/F: $1,600   G/VG: $700

Ebon, Martin. *The Devil's Bride: Exorcism: Past and Present.*
First Edition: New York: Harper & Row, 1974.
NF/F: $50   G/VG: $15

_____. *Beyond Space and Time: An ESP Casebook.*
First Edition: New York: The New American Library, 1967.
NF/F: $50   G/VG: $15

Eliade, Mircea. *Myths, Dreams and Mysteries: The Encounter Between Contemporary Faiths and Archaic Realities.*
First Edition in English: London: Harvill Press, 1960.
NF/F: $125   G/VG: $40
First U.S. Edition: New York: Harper & Row, 1960.
NF/F: $75   G/VG: $25

Ellis, Peter Berresford. *The Druids.*
First Edition: London: Constable, 1994.
NF/F: $75   G/VG: $20
First U.S. Edition: Grand Rapids, MI: Eerdman, 1994.
NF/F: $65   G/VG: $25

Evans, Christopher. *Cults of Unreason.*
First Edition: London: Harrap, 1973.
NF/F: $45   G/VG: $10

Ferro, Robert and Michael Grumley. *Atlantis-The Autobiography of a Search.*
First Edition: Garden City, NY: Doubleday, 1970.
NF/F: $30   G/VG: $10

Fort, Charles. *Book of the Damned.*
First Edition: New York: Boni & Liveright, 1919.
NF/F: $900   G/VG: $550

_____. *New Lands.*
First Edition: New York: Boni and Liveright, 1923.
NF/F: $120   G/VG: $40

_____. *Lo!*
First Edition: New York: Claude Kendall, 1931.
NF/F: $200   G/VG: $85

_____. *Wild Talents.*
First Edition: New York: Claude
Kendall, 1931.
NF/F: $100　　　　　　　　**G/VG: $30**

Fortune, Dion. *Goat - Foot God.*
First Edition: London: Williams and
Norgate, 1936.
NF/F: $750　　　　　　　　**G/VG: $325**

_____. *The Cosmic Doctrine.*
First Edition: London: The Society of
the Inner Light, 1949.
NF/F: $175　　　　　　　　**G/VG: $60**

_____. *Practical Occultism in
Daily Life.*
First Edition: London: Williams and
Norgate, 1935.
NF/F: $125　　　　　　　　**G/VG: $45**

_____. *Moon Magic Being The
Memoirs of a Mistress of that Art.*
First Edition: London: The Aquarian
Press, 1956.
NF/F: $115　　　　　　　　**G/VG: $35**

Fowler, Raymond. *The Andreasson
Affair.*
First Edition: Englewood Cliffs, NJ:
Prentice-Hall, 1979.
NF/F: $45　　　　　　　　**G/VG: $10**

Frost, Gavin and Yvonne. *Power
Secrets from a Sorcerer's Private
Magnum Arcanum.*
First Edition: West Nyack, NJ: Parker
Publishing. 1980.
NF/F: $65　　　　　　　　**G/VG: $25**

Fox, Oliver. *Astral Projection.
A Record of Out of the Body
Experiences.*
First Edition: New Hyde Park, NY:
University Books, 1962.
NF/F: $85　　　　　　　　**G/VG: $20**

Friedman, Stanton T. *Top Secret/
Majic.*
First Edition: New York: Marlowe, 1996.
NF/F: $50　　　　　　　　**G/VG: $12**

Gardner, G. B. as by Scire. *High
Magic's Aid.*
First Edition: London: Michael
Houghton, 1949.
NF/F: $650　　　　　　　　**G/VG: $215**
First U.S. Edition: Boston: Houghton
Mifflin, 1949.
NF/F: $275　　　　　　　　**G/VG: $100**

Gardner, G. B. *The Meaning of
Witchcraft.*
First Edition: London: The Aquarian
Press, 1959.
NF/F: $100　　　　　　　　**G/VG: $35**
First Edition Thus: London & New
York: Aquarian Press/Samuel Weiser,
1971.
NF/F: $80　　　　　　　　**G/VG: $20**

George, Llewellyn. *A to Z Horoscope
Maker and Delineator.*
First Edition: Los Angeles Llewellyn,
1928.
NF/F: $265　　　　　　　　**G/VG: $125**

_____. *Planetary Hour Book.*
First Edition: Los Angeles, CA:
Astrological Bulletin, 1929.
NF/F: $260　　　　　　　　**G/VG: $100**

Gibson, Walter B. and Litzka R. *The
Complete Illustrated Book of the
Psychic Sciences.*
First Edition: Garden City, NY:
Doubleday, 1966.
NF/F: $65　　　　　　　　**G/VG: $20**

_____. *Complete Illustrated
Book of Divination and Prophecy.*
First Edition: Garden City, NY:
Doubleday, 1973.
NF/F: $25　　　　　　　　**G/VG: $8**

Dion Fortune.

Raymond Fowler.

Stanton T. Friedman.

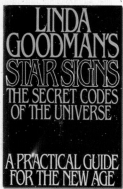

Linda Goodman.

Kenneth Grant.

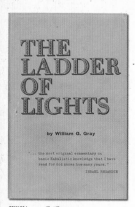
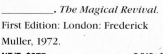

William G. Gray.

Goodman, Linda. *Linda Goodman's Sun Signs.*
First Edition: New York: Taplinger, 1968.
NF/F: $95 G/VG: $30

_____. *Star Signs : Secret Codes Of The Universe.*
First Edition: New York: St. Martin's Press, 1987.
NF/F: $55 G/VG: $15

Grant, Kenneth. *Outside The Circles Of Time.*
First Edition: London: Frederick Muller, 1980.
NF/F: $550 G/VG: $200

_____. *The Magical Revival.*
First Edition: London: Frederick Muller, 1972.
NF/F: $375 G/VG: $130
First U.S. Edition: New York: Samuel Weiser, 1973.
NF/F: $250 G/VG: $95

Gray, William G. *The Ladder Of Lights (or Qabalah Renovata).*
First Edition: Toddington, UK: Helios Books, 1975.
NF/F: $100 G/VG: $40

_____. *The Talking Tree.*
First U.S. Edition: New York: Samuel Weiser, Inc., 1977.
NF/F: $140 G/VG: $50

Gurdjieff, G. *Meetings with Remarkable Men.*
First Edition as Rencontres Avec Des Hommes Remarquables: Paris: Juillard, 1960.
NF/F: $675 G/VG: $200
First Edition in English: London: Routledge & Kegan Paul, 1963.
NF/F: $450 G/VG: $125
First U.S. Edition: New York: E. P. Dutton, 1963.
NF/F: $225 G/VG: $65

_____. *All and Everything. An Objective Impartial Criticism of the Life of Man, or Beelzebub's Tales to his Grandson.*
First U.S. Edition: New York: Harcourt Brace, 1950.
NF/F: $325 G/VG: $125

_____. *Life is Real Only Then, When "I am."*
First U.S. Edition: New York: E.P Dutton, 1981.
NF/F: $85 G/VG: $30

Hall, Manly P. *Shadow Forms.*
First Edition: Los Angeles: Hall Publishing Co., 1925.
NF/F: $155 G/VG: $65

_____. *Lectures on Ancient Philosophy.*
First Edition: Los Angeles, CA: The Hall Publishing Company, 1929.
NF/F: $175 G/VG: $65

_____. *Codex Rosae Crucis.*
First Edition: Los Angeles: The Philosophers Press, 1938.
NF/F: $450 G/VG: $125

_____. *Initiates of the Flame.*
First Edition: Los Angeles: The Phoenix Press, 1922.
NF/F: $325 G/VG: $145

Hartmann, Franz. *Among The Gnomes. An Occult Tale of Adventure in the Untersberg.*
First Edition in English: London: T. Fisher Unwin, 1895.
NF/F: $350 G/VG: $165
First U.S. Edition: Boston: Occult Publishing Company, 1896.
NF/F: $200 G/VG: $85

_____. *Magic, White and Black, or the Science of Finite and Infinite Life, Containing Practical Hints for Students of Occultism.*
Third Edition: London: George Redway, 1888.
NF/F: $225   **G/VG: $85**

_____. *With the Adepts: An Adventure Among The Rosicrucians.*
First U.S. Edition: Boston: Occult Publishing Company, 1893.
NF/F: $165   **G/VG: $75**

_____. *Cosmology, Or Cabala. Universal Science. Alchemy. Containing The Mysteries Of The Universe Regarding God Nature Man. The Macrocosm and Microcosm, Eternity and Time Explained According To The Religion Of Christ, By Means Of The Secret Symbols Of The Rosicrucians Of The Sixteenth And Seventeenth Centuries. Copied And Translated From An Old German Manuscript, And Provided With A Dictionary Of Occult Terms.*
First U.S. Edition: Boston: Occult Publishing Co., 1888.
NF/F: $2,300   **G/VG: $1,000**

Hatch, D. P. *Some More Philosophy of the Hermetics.*
First U.S. Edition: Los Angeles: R. R. Baumgardt, 1898.
NF/F: $95   **G/VG: $40**

_____. *Some Philosophy Of The Hermetics.*
First U.K. Edition: London: Kegan, Paul, Trench, 1898.
NF/F: $150   **G/VG: $55**

Heindel, Max. *Rosicrucian Cosmo-Conception.*
First Edition: Seattle, WA: Rosicrucian Fellowship, 1909.
NF/F: $90   **G/VG: $35**

_____. *Ancient and Modern Initiation.*
First Edition: Oceanside, CA: Rosicrucian Fellowship, 1931.
NF/F: $45   **G/VG: $15**

_____. *Occult Principles of Health and Healing.*
First Edition: Oceanside, CA: Rosicrucian Fellowship, 1938.
NF/F: $95   **G/VG: $30**

_____. *Teachings of an Initiate.*
First Edition: Oceanside, CA: Rosicrucian Fellowship, 1927.
NF/F: $55   **G/VG: $25**

Hitching, Francis. *Earth Magic.*
First Edition: New York: William Morrow, 1977.
NF/F: $55   **G/VG: $20**

Holmes, Ronald. *Witchcraft in British History.*
First Edition: London: Frederick Muller, 1974.
NF/F: $140   **G/VG: $60**

Holroyd, Stuart. *Minds without Boundaries.*
First Edition: n.p.: Danbury Press, 1975.
NF/F: $30   **G/VG: $10**

Holzer, Hans. *Psychic Photography. Threshold of a New Science?*
First Edition: New York: McGraw-Hill. 1969.
NF/F: $125   **G/VG: $45**

_____. *The Aquarian Age Is There intelligent Life on Earth?*
First Edition: Indianapolis, IN: Bobbs-Merrill, 1971.
NF/F: $35   **G/VG: $10**

Manly P. Hall.

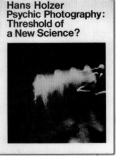

Hans Holzer.

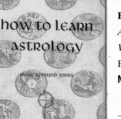

Hans Holzer.

_____. *The Truth about Witchcraft.*
First Edition: Garden City, NY: Doubleday, 1969.
NF/F: $55   **G/VG: $15**

Howe, Ellic. *The Magicians Of The Golden Dawn: A Documentary History Of A Magical Order 1887-1923.*
First Edition: London: Routledge & Kegan Paul, 1972.
NF/F: $145   **G/VG: $75**

_____. *Urania's Children. The Strange World of the Astrologers.*
First Edition: London: William Kimber, 1967.
NF/F: $95   **G/VG: $45**

Huson, Paul. *Mastering Witchcraft. A Practical Guide for Witches, Warlocks, and Covens.*
First Edition: New York: Putnams, 1970.
NF/F: $125   **G/VG: $30**

_____. *Mastering Herbalism.*
First Edition: New York: Stein & Day, 1974.
NF/F: $85   **G/VG: $20**

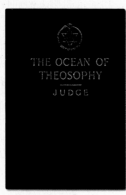

Marc Edmund Jones.

Jones, Marc Edmund. *How to Learn Astrology.*
First Edition: Philadelphia, PA: David McKay, 1941.
NF/F: $65   **G/VG: $15**

_____. *Key Truths of Occult Philosophy. An Introduction to the Codex Occultus.*
First Edition: Los Angeles, CA: J.F. Rowny Press, 1925.
NF/F: $65   **G/VG: $20**

Judge, William Q. *The Ocean of Theosophy.*
First Edition: New York and London: The Path & The Theosophical Publishing Society, 1893.
NF/F: $145   **G/VG: $55**

_____. *Practical Occultism.*
First Edition: Pasadena, CA: Theosophical University Press, 1951.
NF/F: $45   **G/VG: $15**

Kardec, Allan. *Spiritualist's Philosophy. The Spirit's Book.*
First Edition in English: London: Trubner & Co., 1875.
NF/F: $400   **G/VG: $155**

_____. *Experimental Spiritism: Book On Mediums; Guide For Mediums And Invocators.*
First Edition Thus: Colby and Rich, Publishers, 1874.
NF/F: $525   **G/VG: $200**

Kautz, William H and Melanie Branon; with foreword and forecast by Kevin Ryerson. *Channeling: The Intuitive Connection.*
First Edition: San Francisco: Harper & Row, 1987.
NF/F: $25   **G/VG: $8**

Khei. F.:R.:C.: 0-X. *Rosicrucian Symbology: a treatise wherein the Discerning Ones will find the Elements of Constructive Symbology and Certain Other Things.*
First Illustrated Edition: New York: Macoy Publishing & Masonic Supply Company, 1916.
NF/F: $250   **G/VG: $100**

Khei X. *Rosicrucian Fundamentals. A Synthesis of Religion, Science and Philosophy.*
First Edition: New York: Societas Rosicruciana In America, 1920.
NF/F: $300   **G/VG: $125**

King, Basil. *The Abolishing Of Death.*
First Edition: New York: Cosmopolitan Book Corp., 1919.
NF/F: $55   **G/VG: $20**

King, Francis. *Sexuality, Magic and Perversion.*
First Edition: Secaucus, NJ: The Citadel Press, 1972.
NF/F: $175　　　　　　**G/VG: $85**

_____. *The Magical World Of Aleister Crowley.*
First U.S. Edition: New York: Coward, McCann & Geoghegan, 1978.
NF/F: $100　　　　　　**G/VG: $40**

_____. *The Secret Rituals of the O.T.O.*
First Edition: London: C.W. Daniel, 1973.
NF/F: $550　　　　　　**G/VG: $250**

King, Godfre Ray. *The "I AM" Discourses.*
First Edition: Schaumburg, IL: Saint Germain Press, 1935.
NF/F: $150　　　　　　**G/VG: $75**

Kingsford, Anna & Edward Maitland. *The Virgin Of The World.*
First Edition: Madras: P. Kailasam Bros., 1885.
NF/F: $300　　　　　　**G/VG: $145**

Knight, Gareth. *Practical Guide to Qabalistic Symbolism.* (Two Volumes).
First Edition: Cheltenham: Helios, 1976.
NF/F: $100　　　　　　**G/VG: $45**

_____. *The Practice of Ritual Magic.*
First Edition: Cheltenham: Helios, 1969.
NF/F: $60　　　　　　**G/VG: $20**

Lamb, Geoffrey. *Magic, Witchcraft and the Occult.*
First Edition: London: David & Charles, 1997.
NF/F: $50　　　　　　**G/VG: $12**

LaVey, Anton Szandor. *The Satanic Rituals.*
First Edition: Secaucus, NJ: University Books, Inc., 1972.
NF/F: $300　　　　　　**G/VG: $100**

_____. *The Compleat Witch or What to do When the Virtue Fails.*
First Edition: New York: Dodd, Mead, 1971.
NF/F: $200　　　　　　**G/VG: $75**

Leadbeater, C. W. *The Perfume of Egypt and Other Weird Stories.*
First Edition: Adyar, Madras, India: The Theosophist Office, 1911.
NF/F: $125　　　　　　**G/VG: $55**

_____. *The Other Side of Death.*
First U.K. Edition: London: Theosophical Publishing Society, 1904.
NF/F: $165　　　　　　**G/VG: $65**

_____. *Some Glimpses Of Occultism. Ancient And Modern.*
First U.S. Edition: Chicago: Theosophical Book Concern, 1903.
NF/F: $100　　　　　　**G/VG: $35**

Leek, Sybil. *ESP: The Magic Within You.*
First Edition: London: Abelard-Schuman, 1971.
NF/F: $100　　　　　　**G/VG: $35**

_____. *Diary of a Witch.*
First Edition: Englewood Cliffs, NJ: Prentice-Hall, 1968.
NF/F: $125　　　　　　**G/VG: $50**

Levi, Eliphas. *Transcendental Magic.*
First Edition of translation by Arthur Edward Waite : London: George Redway, 1896.
NF/F: $650　　　　　　**G/VG: $275**

_____. *The Magical Ritual of the Sanctum Regnum.*
First Edition of translation by W. Wynn Westcott: London: George Redway, 1896.
NF/F: $475　　　　　　**G/VG: $200**

Francis King.

Anton Szandor LaVey.

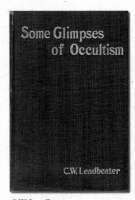

C.W. Leadbeater.

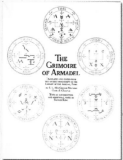

THE
GRAIL
FROM
CELTIC MYTH
TO
CHRISTIAN
SYMBOL

Roger Sherman Loomis

Roger Sherman Loomis.

Mathers S. L. MacGregor.

Lewi, Grant. *Astrology for the Millions.*
First Edition: New York: Doubleday, Doran & Co., 1940.
NF/F: $75   G/VG: $20

Lewis, H. Spencer. *Essays of a Modern Mystic.*
First Edition: San Jose: Supreme Grand Lodge of AMORC, 1962.
NF/F: $45   G/VG: $15

_____. *The Mystical Life of Jesus.*
First Edition: San Jose, CA: The Rosicrucian Press, 1929.
NF/F: $65   G/VG: $25

_____. *Mansions of the Soul: The Cosmic Conception.*
First Edition: San Jose, CA: The Rosicrucian Press, 1930.
NF/F: $55   G/VG: $15

Lodge, Oliver J. *Christopher: A Study in Human Personality.*
First Edition: London: Cassell, 1918.
NF/F: $60   G/VG: $20
First U.S. Edition: New York: George H. Doran, 1919.
NF/F: $35   G/VG: $10

_____. *Why I Believe in Personal Immortality.*
First Edition: London: Cassell, 1928.
NF/F: $250   G/VG: $100

_____. *The Immortality of the Soul.*
First Edition: Boston: The Ball Publishing Co., 1908.
NF/F: $200   G/VG: $85

Long, Max Freedom. *Recovering the Ancient Magic.*
First Edition: London: Rider & Co., 1936.
NF/F: $525   G/VG: $200

_____. *The Secret Science Behind Miracles.*
First Edition: Los Angeles, CA: Kosmon Press, 1948.
NF/F: $155   G/VG: $55

_____. *Growing into Light.*
First Edition: Vista, CA: Huna Research, 1955.
NF/F: $75   G/VG: $20

Loomis, Roger Sherman. *The Grail from Celtic Myth to Christian Symbol.*
First Edition: Cardiff, University of Wales Press, 1963.
NF/F: $200   G/VG: $75
First U.S. Edition: New York: Columbia University Press, 1963.
NF/F: $100   G/VG: $40

Maple, Eric. *The Dark World of Witches.*
First Edition: London: Robert Hale, 1962.
NF/F: $65   G/VG: $20

_____. *The Domain of Devils.*
First Edition: London: Robert Hale, 1966.
NF/F: $65   G/VG: $20

_____. *Witchcraft The story of man's search for supernatural power.*
First Edition: London: Octopus Books, 1973.
NF/F: $60   G/VG: $20

MacGregor-Mathers, S. L. (trans.). *The Book of The Sacred Magic of Abra-Melin, The Mage.*
First Edition: London: John M. Walkins, 1900.
NF/F: $2300   G/VG: $925
Second US Edition: Chicago: De Laurence Co., 1932.
NF/F: $250   G/VG: $200

_____. *The Grimoire of Armadel.*
First Edition Thus: New York: Samuel Weiser, 1980.
NF/F: $100   G/VG: $45

MacNeice, Louis. *Astrology.*
First U.S. Edition: Garden City, NY:
Doubleday, 1964.
NF/F: $75   **G/VG: $25**

Mead, G.R.S. *Thrice-Greatest Hermes.*
(Three Volumes)
First Edition: London and Benares: The
Theosophical Publishing Society, 1906.
NF/F: $850   **G/VG: $250**

_____. *Fragments of a Faith
Forgotten.*
First Edition: London: The Theosophical
Publishing Society, 1900.
NF/F: $300   **G/VG: $125**

_____. *Quests Old And New.*
First Edition: London: G. Bell & Sons,
1913.
NF/F: $200   **G/VG: $85**

_____. *Some Mystical Adventures.*
First Edition: London: John M.
Watkins, 1910.
NF/F: $180   **G/VG: $65**

Michell, John. *The View Over
Atlantis.*
Limited Edition: London: Sago Press,
1969 (150 copies).
NF/F: $250   **G/VG: Not Seen**
First Edition: London: Garnstone Press,
1969.
NF/F: $45   **G/VG: $20**

Muldoon, Sylvan. *The Case for Astral
Projection.*
First Edition: Chicago: The Aries Press,
1936.
NF/F: $80   **G/VG: $25**

_____. *Psychic Experiences of
Famous People.*
First Edition: Chicago: The Aries Press,
1947.
NF/F: $60   **G/VG: $20**

Murray, Margaret Alice. *The Witch-
Cult in Western Europe.*
First Edition: Oxford: Clarendon Press, 1921.
NF/F: $225   **G/VG: $95**

Nauman, St. Elmo. *Exorcism
Through the Ages.*
First Edition: New York: Philosophical
Library, 1974.
NF/F: $45   **G/VG: $10**

Norvell, Anthony. *How To Develop
Your Psychic Powers For Health,
Wealth, and Security.*
First Edition: West Nyack, NY: Parker
Publishing Company, 1969.
NF/F: $35   **G/VG: $10**

_____. *Mind Cosmology: How
to Translate Your Inner Dreams Into
The Outer Reality You Desire!*
First Edition: West Nyack, N.Y.: Parker
Publishing Company, 1971.
NF/F: $45   **G/VG: $12**

Olcott, Henry Steel. *Old Diary
Leaves: The True Story of The
Theosophical Society.*
First Trade Edition: New York:
Putnams, 1895.
NF/F: $175   **G/VG: $65**

Ophiel. *The Oracle of Fortuna.*
First Edition: St. Paul, MN: Peach
Publishing, 1969.
NF/F: $155   **G/VG: $50**

_____. *The Art and Practice of the Occult.*
First Edition: St. Paul, MN: Peach
Publishing, 1968.
NF/F: $225   **G/VG: $90**

_____. *The Art and Practice of
Clairvoyance.*
First Edition: St. Paul, MN: Peach
Publishing, 1969.
NF/F: $150   **G/VG: $55**

G.R.S. Mead.

Sylvan Muldoon.

Ophiel.

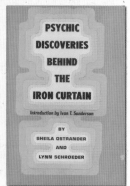

Sheila Ostrander and Lynn Schroeder.

P.D. Ouspensky.

Derek and Julia Parker.

Oesterreich, T. K. *Possession, Demoniacal and Other, among Primitive Races, in Antiquity, The Middle Ages, and Modern Times.*
First Edition in English: London: Kegan, Paul & Trench, 1930.
NF/F: $275   **G/VG: $80**
First U.S. Edition as: *Obsession and Possession by Spirits Both Good and Evil.*: Chicago: The de Laurence Company, 1935.
NF/F: $245   **G/VG: $65**

Ostrander, Sheila & Lynn Schroeder. *Psychic Discoveries Behind the Iron Curtain.*
First Edition: Englewood Cliffs, NJ: Prentice-Hall, 1970.
NF/F: $40   **G/VG: $15**

Ouspensky, P.D. *Strange Life of Ivan Osokin.*
First Edition in English (Limited): London: Stourton Press, 1947 (326 copies).
NF/F: $425   **G/VG: $145**
First Edition (Trade): London: Faber & Faber, 1948.
NF/F: $95   **G/VG: $35**

_____. *In Search of the Miraculous.*
First Edition: New York: Harcourt, Brace, 1949.
NF/F: $100   **G/VG: $35**

_____. *The Fourth Way. A Record of Talks and Answers to Questions based in the teachings of G.I. Gurdjieff.*
First Edition: New York: Alfred A. Knopf, 1957.
NF/F: $85   **G/VG: $30**

_____. *Talks With A Devil.*
First Edition: New York: Alfred A. Knopf, 1973.
NF/F: $95   **G/VG: $25**

Panchadasi, Swami. *The Astral World: Its Scenes, Dwellers, and Phenomena.*
First Edition: Chicago: Advanced Thought Publishing Co., 1915.
NF/F: $55   **G/VG: $20**

_____. *Clairvoyance and Occult Powers.*
First Edition: Chicago: Advanced Thought Publishing Co., 1916.
NF/F: $45   **G/VG: $15**

Papus. *The Tarot Of The Bohemians.*
First U.K. Edition: London: Chapman & Hall, 1892.
NF/F: $275   **G/VG: $135**

_____. *The Qabalah - Secret Tradition of the West.*
First Edition Thus: New York: Samuel Weiser, 1977.
NF/F: $65   **G/VG: $25**

Parker, Derek and Julia. *The Compleat Astrologer.*
First Edition: New York: McGraw-Hill, 1971.
NF/F: $85   **G/VG: $25**

Perriman, A.E. *Broadcasting from Beyond.*
First Edition: London: Spiritualist Press, 1952.
NF/F: $25   **G/VG: $10**

Phylos the Thibetan. *A Dweller on Two Planets or The Dividing of the Way.*
First Edition Thus: Los Angeles: Borden Publishing, 1952.
NF/F: $150   **G/VG: $55**

_____. *An Earth Dwellers Return.*
First Edition: Milwaukee, WI: Lemurian Press, 1940.
NF/F: $95   **G/VG: $30**

Price, Harry. *Rudi Schneider. a Scientific Examination of His Mediumship.*
First Edition: London: Methuen & Co., 1930.
NF/F: $250   **G/VG: $85**

_____. *Confessions of a Ghost Hunter.*
First Edition: London: Putnams, 1936.
NF/F: $95   **G/VG: $35**

_____. *Leaves from a Psychist's Case-Book.*
First Edition: London: Gollancz, 1933.
NF/F: $65   **G/VG: $25**

Rampa, T. Lobsang. Third Eye Series:

_____. *The Third Eye: The Autobiography of a Tibetan Lama.*
First Edition: London: Seker & Warburg, 1956.
NF/F: $85   **G/VG: $30**
First U.S. Edition: Garden City, NY: Doubleday, 1957.
NF/F: $75   **G/VG: $30**

_____. *My Visit to Venus.*
First Edition: Clarksburg, WV: Saucerian Books, 1966.
NF/F: $60   **G/VG: $20**

_____. *Doctor from Lhasa.*
First Edition: London: Souvenir Press, 1959.
NF/F: $35   **G/VG: $15**

_____. *The Rampa Story.*
First Edition: London: Souvenir Press, 1960.
NF/F: $75   **G/VG: $30**

_____. *Cave of the Ancients.*
First Edition: London: Souvenir Press, 1963.
NF/F: $35   **G/VG: $15**

_____. *Living with the Lama.*
First Edition: London: Transworld Publishers, 1964.
NF/F: $65   **G/VG: $25**

_____. *You Forever.*
First Edition: New York: Pageant Press, 1966.
NF/F: $135   **G/VG: $60**

_____. *Wisdom of the Ancients.*
First Edition: London: Corgi, 1965.
NF/F: $35   **G/VG: $15**

_____. *The Saffron Robe.*
First Edition: New York: Pageant Press, 1966.
NF/F: $125   **G/VG: $55**

_____. *Chapters of Life.*
First Edition: London: Corgi, 1967.
NF/F: $18   **G/VG: $6**

_____. *Beyond the Tenth.*
First Edition: London: Corgi, 1969.
NF/F: $25   **G/VG: $10**

_____. *Feeding the Flame.*
First Edition: London: Corgi, 1971.
NF/F: $25   **G/VG: $10**

_____. *The Hermit.*
First Edition: London: Corgi, 1971.
NF/F: $35   **G/VG: $15**

_____. *The Thirteenth Candle.*
First Edition: London: Corgi, 1972.
NF/F: $25   **G/VG: $12**

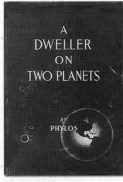
Phylos the Thibetan.

Harry Price.

T. Lobsang Rampa.

T. Lobsang Rampa.

Rossell Hope Robbins.

Jane Roberts.

_____. *Candlelight.*
First Edition: London: Corgi, 1973.
NF/F: $30   **G/VG: $15**

_____. *Twilight.*
First Edition: London: Corgi, 1975.
NF/F: $40   **G/VG: $15**

_____. *As It Was!*
First Edition: London: Corgi, 1976.
NF/F: $40   **G/VG: $15**

_____. *I Believe.*
First Edition: London: Corgi, 1976.
NF/F: $50   **G/VG: $20**

_____. *Three Lives.*
First Edition: London: Corgi, 1977.
NF/F: $75   **G/VG: $30**

_____. *Tibetan Sage.*
First Edition: London: Corgi, 1980.
NF/F: $65   **G/VG: $25**

Redpath, Ian. *Messages from the Stars: Communication and Contact with Extraterrestrial Life.*
First Edition: New York: Harper & Row, 1978.
NF/F: $35   **G/VG: $15**

Regardie, Israel. *Golden Dawn, VOLS 1-4, "An Account of the Teachings, Rites and Ceremonies of the Order of the Golden Dawn."*
First Edition: Chicago: The Aries Press, 1937-1940.
NF/F: $650   **G/VG: $350**

_____. *The Tree of Life: A Study in Magic.*
First Edition: London: Rider & Co., 1932.
NF/F: $165   **G/VG: $65**

_____. *The Middle Pillar: A Co-Relation of the Principles of Analytical Psychology and the Elementary Techniques of Magic.*
First Edition: Chicago: Aries Press, 1938.
NF/F: $185   **G/VG: $100**

Robbins, Rossell Hope. *The Encyclopedia of Witchcraft and Demonology.*
First Edition: New York: Crown, 1959.
NF/F: $65   **G/VG: $25**

Roberts, Jane. Seth Series:

_____. *Seth Speaks The Eternal Validity of the Soul.*
First Edition: Englewood Cliffs, NJ: Prentice-Hall, 1972.
NF/F: $70   **G/VG: $20**

_____. *The Nature of Personal Reality: A Seth Book.*
First Edition: Englewood Cliffs, NJ: Prentice-Hall, 1974.
NF/F: $95   **G/VG: $30**

_____. *The Unknown Reality, Volume I & II.*
First Edition: Englewood Cliffs, NJ: Prentice-Hall, 1977.
NF/F: $75   **G/VG: $25**

_____. *The Nature of the Psyche: Its Human Expression.*
First Edition: Englewood Cliffs, NJ: Prentice-Hall, 1979.
NF/F: $55   **G/VG: $15**

_____. *Dreams, "Evolution," And Value Fulfillment Volume I & II.*
First Edition: Englewood Cliffs, NJ: Prentice-Hall, 1986.
NF/F: $45   **G/VG: $15**

_____. *The Magical Approach.*
First Edition: np (U.S.): Amber-Allen Publ., New World Library, 1995.
NF/F: $15   **G/VG: $5**

_____. *The Way Toward Health.*
First Edition: np (U.S.): Amber-Allen
Publ., New World Library, 1997.
NF/F: $20   **G/VG: $10**

Roberts, Susan. *The Magician of the Golden
Dawn The Story of Aleister Crowley.*
First Edition: Chicago: Contemporary
Books, 1978.
NF/F: $60   **G/VG: $20**

Rohmer, Sax. *The Romance of
Sorcery.* First U.S. Edition: New York:
E. P. Dutton, 1915.
NF/F: $350   **G/VG: $135**

Saint-Germain, Comte C. De. *Practical
Astrology: Scholarly, Simple, Complete
Simple Method of Casting Horoscopes.* First
U.S. Edition: Chicago: Laird & Lee, 1901.
NF/F: $155   **G/VG: $65**

_____. *Study Of Palmistry For
Professional Purposes And Advanced
Students.*
First U.S. Edition: Chicago: Laird & Lee,
1900.
NF/F: $100   **G/VG: $45**

Sepharial. *The Numbers Book.*
First Edition: Slough Bucks, England:
W. Foulsham, 1957.
NF/F: $75   **G/VG: $20**

_____. *The World Horoscope
Hebrew Astrology.*
First Edition: London: W. Foulsham, 1965.
NF/F: $35   **G/VG: $15**

_____. *New Dictionary of
Astrology.*
First Edition: New York: Galahad, 1963.
NF/F: $55   **G/VG: $15**

Seth, Ronald. *In The Name of the Devil.*
First Edition: New York: Walker, 1969.
NF/F: $30   **G/VG: $12**

Sinnett, A. P. *Incidents in the Life of
Madame Blavatsky.*
First Edition: London: George Redway, 1886.
NF/F: $65   **G/VG: $25**

_____. *Growth of the Soul.*
First U.K. Edition: London:
Theosophical Publishing Society, 1896.
NF/F: $255   **G/VG: $115**

Sladek, John. *The New Apocrypha: A
Guide to Strange Science and Occult Beliefs.*
First Edition: London: Hart-Davis,
MacGibbon, 1973.
NF/F: $200   **G/VG: $85**

Spence, Lewis. *The Mysteries of
Britain, or the Secret Rites and
Traditions of Ancient Britain Restored.*
First Edition: London: Rider & Co, nd.
NF/F: $225   **G/VG: $100**

_____. *The Fairy Tradition In Britain.*
First Edition: London: Rider & Co., 1948.
NF/F: $200   **G/VG: $85**

_____. *The Magic Arts in Celtic
Britain.*
First Edition: London: Rider & Co, nd.
NF/F: $275   **G/VG: $115**

St. Clair, David. *Watseka: America's
Most Extraordinary Case of
Possession and Exorcism.*
First Edition: Chicago: Playboy Press, 1977.
NF/F: $200   **G/VG: $95**

Stearn, Jess. *Edgar Cayce: The
Sleeping Prophet.*
First Edition: Garden City, NY:
Doubleday, 1967.
NF/F: $70   **G/VG: $25**

_____. *Soul Mates.*
First Edition: New York: Bantam
Books, 1984.
NF/F: $25   **G/VG: $10**

Ronald Seth.

John Sladek.

Lewis Spence.

John Symonds.

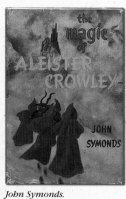

John Symonds.

Paul Tabori.

_____. *The Search for the Girl With the Blue Eyes.*
First Edition: Garden City, NY: Doubleday, 1968.
NF/F: $45   G/VG: $15

Steiner, Rudolf. *Christianity as Mystical Fact.*
Third Edition in English: London: Rudolf Steiner Publishing Company, 1938.
NF/F: $55   G/VG: $20
First Edition Thus: West Nyack, NY: Rudolph Steiner Publications, Inc, 1961.
NF/F: $35   G/VG: $15

_____. *The Gates of Knowledge.*
First Edition in English: New York: Putnams, 1912.
NF/F: $200   G/VG: $90

_____. *Anthroposophy: An Introduction.*
First U.K. Edition: London: H. Collison, 1931.
NF/F: $65   G/VG: $15

_____. *Cosmic Workings in Earth and Man.*
First Edition in English: London: Rudolf Steiner Publishing Company, 1952.
NF/F: $75   G/VG: $30

St. George, E.A. *The Casebook of a Working Occultist.*
First Edition: London: Rigel Press, 1972.
NF/F: $35   G/VG: $10

Summers, Montague. *The Vampire: His Kith and Kin.*
First Edition: London: Kegan, Paul, Trench, Trubner, 1928.
NF/F: $245   G/VG: $135

_____. *The Vampire In Europe.*
First Edition: London: Kegan, Paul, Trench, Trubner, 1929.
NF/F: $425   G/VG: $150

_____. *The Werewolf.*
First Edition: London: Kegan, Paul, Trench, Trubner, 1933.
NF/F: $325   G/VG: $100

_____. *A Popular History of Witchcraft.*
First Edition: London: Kegan, Paul, Trench, Trubner, 1937.
NF/F: $175   G/VG: $65

Swedenborg, Emmanuel. *A Treatise Concerning Heaven And Hell, And Of The Wonderful Things Therein.*
First U.S. Edition: Baltimore, MD: Anthony Miltenberger, 1812.
NF/F: $800   G/VG: $300

_____. *Arcana Coelestia.*
(Thirteen Volumes).
First Edition Thus: New York: Swedenborg Foundation, 1965.
NF/F: $150   G/VG: $100

_____. *The Doctrine of Life for the New Jerusalem.*
First Edition Thus: London, the Swedenborg Society, 1913.
NF/F: $85   G/VG: $35

Symonds, John. *The Great Beast.*
First Edition: London, New York, Melbourne, Sydney, Cape Town: Rider and Company, 1951.
NF/F: $450   G/VG: $200

_____. *The Magic Of Aleister Crowley.*
First Edition: London: Frederick Muller Ltd, 1958.
NF/F: $175   G/VG: $65

Tabori, Paul. *Companions of the Unseen.*
First Edition: New Hyde Park, NY: University Books, 1968.
NF/F: $45   G/VG: $12

Tart, Charles. *Altered States of Consciousness.*
First Edition: New York: John Wiley, 1969.
NF/F: $60   **G/VG: $25**

_____. *Waking Up: Overcoming the Obstacles to Human Potential.*
First Edition: Boston: Shambhala, 1986.
NF/F: $45   **G/VG: $10**

Thomas, Eugene E. *Brotherhood of Mt. Shasta.*
First Edition: Los Angeles, CA: DeVorss, 1946.
NF/F: $75   **G/VG: $35**

Torrens, R. G. *Golden Dawn : Its Inner Teachings.*
First Edition: London: Neville Spearman Ltd., 1969.
NF/F: $100   **G/VG: $40**

_____. *The Secret Rituals of the Golden Dawn.*
First U.S. Edition: New York: Samuel Weiser, 1973.
NF/F: $250   **G/VG: $95**

Valentine, Tom. *Psychic Surgery.*
First Edition: Chicago, IL: Regnery, 1973.
NF/F: $75   **G/VG: $25**

Von Daniken, Erich. Chariots of the Gods? Series:

_____. *Chariots of the Gods?*
First U.S. Edition: New York: Putnams, 1968.
NF/F: $100   **G/VG: $45**

_____. *Return to the Stars.*
First Edition in English: London: Souvenir Press, 1970.
NF/F: $65   **G/VG: $20**

_____. *The Gold of the Gods.*
First Edition in English: London: Souvenir Press, 1972.
NF/F: $65   **G/VG: $15**
First U.S. Edition: New York: Putnams, 1973.
NF/F: $35   **G/VG: $10**

_____. *In Search of Ancient Gods.*
First U.S. Edition: New York: Putnams, 1973.
NF/F: $40   **G/VG: $10**
First U.K. Edition: London: Souvenir Press, 1974.
NF/F: $45   **G/VG: $15**

_____. *Miracles of the Gods.*
First U.S. Edition: New York: Delacorte Press, 1975.
NF/F: $65   **G/VG: $25**

_____. *According to the Evidence.*
First Edition in English: London: Souvenir Press, 1977.
NF/F: $35   **G/VG: $12**

_____. *Signs of the Gods.*
First U.S. Edition: New York: Putnams, 1980.
NF/F: $45   **G/VG: $15**
First U.K. Edition: London: Souvenir Press, 1980.
NF/F: $30   **G/VG: $12**

_____. *Pathways to the Gods.*
First U.S. Edition: New York: Putnams, 1982.
NF/F: $35   **G/VG: $10**

_____. *The Gods and Their Grand Design.*
First U.S. Edition: New York: Putnams, 1984.
NF/F: $50   **G/VG: $20**

_____. *The Eyes of the Sphinx.*
First U.S. Edition: New York: Berkeley, 1996.
NF/F: $40   **G/VG: $15**

R. G. Torrens.

Erich Von Daniken.

Erich Von Daniken.

Von Daniken, Erich

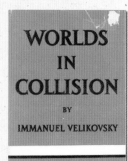

Immanuel Velikowsky.

Immanuel Velikowsky.

Paul Robert Walker.

_____. *The Return of the Gods.*
First Edition in English: Shaftesbury,
Dorset: Element, 1997.
NF/F: $20   **G/VG: $10**

_____. *Odyssey of the Gods.*
First Edition in English: Shaftesbury,
Dorset: Element, 2000.
NF/F: $25   **G/VG: $10**

_____. *The Gods Were Astronauts.*
First Edition in English: London: Vega,
2002.
NF/F: $80   **G/VG: $20**

Velikovsky, Immanuel. *Worlds in Collision.*
First Edition: New York: The
Macmillan Co., 1950.
NF/F: $300   **G/VG: $125**

_____. Ages In Chaos Series*:

_____. *Ages In Chaos.*
First Edition: Garden City, NY:
Doubleday, 1952.
NF/F: $300   **G/VG: $125**

_____. *Oedipus and Akhnaton.*
First Edition: Garden City, NY:
Doubleday, 1960.
NF/F: $80   **G/VG: $35**

_____. *Ramses II and His Time.*
First Edition: Garden City, NY:
Doubleday, 1978.
NF/F: $65   **G/VG: $20**

_____. *Peoples of the Sea.*
First Edition: Garden City, NY:
Doubleday, 1977.
NF/F: $65   **G/VG: $25**

Waite, Arthur Edward. *The
Brotherhood of the Rosy Cross.*
First Edition: London: William Rider &
Son. 1924.
NF/F: $600   **G/VG: $225**

_____. *The Book of Black Magic
and Pacts.*
First Edition: London: George Redway,
1898.
NF/F: $2,200   **G/VG: $1,050**

_____. *The Holy Kabbalah A
Study of the Secret Tradition in Israel.*
First Edition: London: Williams and
Norgate, 1929.
NF/F: $950   **G/VG: $500**

_____. *The Secret Tradition
in Goetia. The Book of Ceremonial
Magic. Including the Rites and
Mysteries of Goetic Theurgy, Sorcery
And Infernal Necromancy.*
First Edition: London: William Rider &
Son, 1911.
NF/F: $750   **G/VG: $400**

_____. *The Quest of the Golden
Stairs.*
First Edition: London: Theosophical
Publishing House, 1927.
NF/F: $200   **G/VG: $95**

Walker, Benjamin. *Encyclopedia of
Metaphysical Medicine.*
First Edition: London: Routledge &
Kegan Paul, 1978.
NF/F: $75   **G/VG: $20**

_____. *Tantrism: Its Secret
Principles and Practices.*
First Edition: Wellingborough, UK:
Aquarian Press, 1982.
NF/F: $85   **G/VG: $25**

_____. *Beyond the Body: The
Human Double and the Astral Plane.*
First Edition: London: Routledge &
Kegan Paul, 1974.
NF/F: $60   **G/VG: $20**

Walker, Paul Robert. *Bigfoot and Other Legendary Creatures.*
First Edition: New York: Harcourt Brace, 1992.
NF/F: $65   **G/VG: $20**

Watson, Lyall. *Gifts of Unknown Things.*
First U.S. Edition: New York: Simon and Schuster, 1976.
NF/F: $45   **G/VG: $15**

Watts, Alan W. *The Way of Zen.*
First Edition: New York: Pantheon, 1957.
NF/F: $250   **G/VG: $75**

_____. *Nature, Man and Woman.*
First Edition: New York: Pantheon, 1958.
NF/F: $150   **G/VG: $65**

_____. *In My Own Way An Autobiography.*
First Edition: New York: Pantheon Books, 1972.
NF/F: $110   **G/VG: $40**

Wellesley, Gordon. *Sex And The Occult.*
First Edition: London: Souvenir Press Ltd., 1973.
NF/F: $50   **G/VG: $18**

W. Wynn Westcott (trans). *Isiac Tablet or the Bembine Table of Isis.*
Facsimile of 1887.
First Edition: Los Angeles: Philosophical Research Society, nd.
NF/F: $95   **G/VG: $35**

Webb, James. *The Occult Establishment.*
First Edition: Glasgow, Scotland: Richard Drew Publishing, 1981.
NF/F: $110   **G/VG: $35**

_____. *The Occult Underground.*
First Edition: La Salle, IL: Open Court Publishing Company, 1974.
NF/F: $100   **G/VG: $40**

White, Stewart Edward. *The Unobstructed Universe.*
First Edition: New York: Dutton, 1940.
NF/F: $145   **G/VG: $55**

Wilcox, John. *An Occult Guide to South America.*
First Edition: New York: Laurel Tape and Film, Inc., 1976.
NF/F: $20   **G/VG: $6**

Wilson, Colin. *The Occult.*
First Edition: London: Hodder and Stoughton, 1971.
NF/F: $125   **G/VG: $40**

_____. *Beyond the Occult: Twenty Years' Research Into the Paranormal.*
First Edition: London: Bantam Press, 1988.
NF/F: $95   **G/VG: $30**

_____. *Men of Mystery: A Celebration Of the Occult.*
First Edition: London: W.H. Allen, 1977.
NF/F: $70   **G/VG: $25**

Yates, Frances A. *The Occult Philosophy in the Elizabethan Age.*
First Edition: London: Routledge & Kegan Paul, 1979.
NF/F: $110   **G/VG: $45**

_____. *The Rosicrucian Enlightenment.*
First Edition: London & Boston: Routledge & Kegan Paul, 1972.
NF/F: $235   **G/VG: $100**

Zolar. *The History of Astrology.*
First Edition: New York: Arco, 1972.
NF/F: $35   **G/VG: $12**

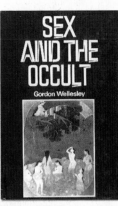

Gordon Wellesley.

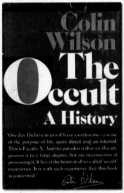

Colin Wilson.

Frances A. Yates.

PHILOSOPHY AND RELIGION

Like the occult, this is a very old area featuring books that were originally handwritten, or even chiseled in stone. Although it is, perhaps, a little more volatile for the collector.

Advances in philosophy or religion usually take time to become noticed or recognized. Who was the leading living theologian, or leading philosopher at the turn of the twentieth century? The fact is that we don't know yet. That is a lot of the enjoyment in collecting it. The hunt for the future in either field.

Much of this genre is collected as First Thus. It crosses cultural barriers, withstands the passage of time and transcends language. Few people today could read Plato in his original form, most people in the Western world would be lost in the ideograms of Confucius' first editions, and don't even think about Zoroaster.

I have always enjoyed reading in this area. Speculations, reasonings, conclusions about man, God and the universe are things that I find to be utterly fascinating. The more I read, the more I notice how right Socrates was all those centuries ago. Told he was the wisest man in Athens, he replied that he knew nothing, but that he was the only man in Athens who knew that he knew nothing. Collecting and reading all these nothings have given me hour upon hour of pleasure. Selling and dealing in them has been both profitable and rewarding.

It is a field full of small and obscure publishers, writers and thinkers, full of both tomorrow and the stuff of landfills. The successful collector will have both, and not only profit materially, but mentally and spiritually as well. Perhaps that is one of the best deals going.

Note on Bibles

The Bible is, at least in the Western world, the commonest book. I have seen numerous copies of it from the 1700s in yard sales in older communities. In Europe, it is not uncommon to find earlier copies. I have also seen and helped collectors build collections of the Bible in all its variations. Despite being old, however, few copies of the Bible are worth much. Rare and important Bibles are extremely rare and most are the property of libraries and museums. The *Gutenberg Bible* was also the first printed book and very valuable. The first Bible in any language, such as The *Mentelin Bible* in German printed in 1460, is usually valuable. Oddities and misprints, such as the Devil's Bible which left a "not" or two out of the 10 commandments, are also desirable. Some Bibles, such as that illustrated by Gustave Dore, are valuable for the illustrations. The average Bible, however, even those 200 or more years old, are not worth much in the used book market.

One other facet of Bible collecting has to do with the practice of keeping family history on the blank pages. A bible owned by a prominent family, or showing the birth of a prominent person, might bring a good deal due to its historical value.

TEN CLASSIC RARITIES

Emerson, Ralph Waldo. *Nature.*
Boston: James Munroe and Company, 1836.
First Edition, first state, has P. 94 misnumbered 92.
NF/F: $6,500   **G/VG: $3,000**

Glover, Mary Baker. *Science and Health.*
Boston: Christian Scientist Publishing Company, 1875. Note the name of the author, reprints are as by Mary Baker Eddy, the first issue contains an errata slip.
NF/F: $5,000   **G/VG: $2,200**

Holmes, Oliver Wendell. *The Common Law.*
Boston: Little, Brown, and Company, 1881. Original is bound in russet cloth.
NF/F: $3,500   **G/VG: $1,600**

Hurston, Zora Neale. *Moses Man of the Mountain.*
Philadelphia: J.B. Lippincott Co., 1939. A study of Moses from an African-American folklore standpoint -- as the great "Voodoo Man" of the Bible.
NF/F: $3,500   **G/VG: $1,500**

Kyoka, Izumi. *The Tale Of The Wandering Monk.*
New York: The Limited Editions Club, 1995.
First U.S. Edition bound in white silk.
NF/F: $2,600   **G/VG: $1,400**

Lewis, C.S. *The Screwtape Letters.*
London: Geoffrey Bles, 1942.
Instructions from the Devil, find this and buy him out.
NF/F: $4,500   **G/VG: $2,100**

Merton, Thomas. *The Tower of Babel.*
Hamburg, Germany: Printed for James Laughlin, 1957. A limited edition of 250 copies signed by Merton and the artist G. Marcks.
NF/F: $2,800   **G/VG: $1,600**

Rand, Ayn. *Capitalism: The Unknown Ideal.*
New York: The New American Library, 1966. Limited to 700 copies signed by Rand.
NF/F: $3,700   **G/VG: $2,400**

Russell, Bertrand. *German Social Democracy: Six Lectures.*
London: Longmans Green & Co. 1896. There are four variant bindings, 1,000 copies total in First Edition.
NF/F: $2,500   **G/VG: $1,100**

Thoreau, Henry David. *Walden: or, Life in the Woods.*
Boston: Ticknor and Fields, 1854.
Simplify your life by finding this.
NF/F: $35,000   **G/VG: $12,000**

Zora Neale Hurston.

C.S. Lewis.

Ayn Rand.

PRICE GUIDE

Mortimer J. Adler.

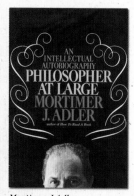

Mortimer J. Adler.

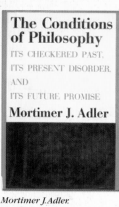

Mortimer J. Adler.

Abbott, Lyman. *My Four Anchors.*
First Edition: Boston: The Pilgrim
Press, 1911.
NF/F: $30   **G/VG: $10**

_____. *The Christian Ministry.*
First Edition: Boston: Houghton
Mifflin, 1905.
NF/F: $125   **G/VG: $35**

Adams, Hannah. *The History of
the Jews from The Destruction of
Jerusalem to the Present Time.*
First Edition: London: A. Macintosh, 1818.
NF/F: $385   **G/VG: $150**

_____. *Truth and Excellence of
the Christian Religion Exhibited.*
First Edition: Boston: John West, 1804.
NF/F: $500   **G/VG: $130**

_____. *A Narrative Of The
Controversy Between The Rev.
Jedidiah Morse, Dd, And The Author.*
First Edition: Boston: Cummings &
Hilliard, 1814.
NF/F: $250   **G/VG: $95**

Addams, Jane. *Newer Ideals of Peace.*
First Edition: New York: Macmillan, 1907.
NF/F: $750   **G/VG: $285**

Adler, Mortimer J. *What Man
has Made of Man. A Study of the
Consequences of Platonism and
Positivism in Psychology.*
First Edition: New York: Longmans,
Green and Co., 1937.
NF/F: $65   **G/VG: $30**

_____. *The Time of Our Lives:
The Ethics of Common Sense.*
First Edition: New York: Holt, Rinehart
& Winston, 1970.
NF/F: $50   **G/VG: $20**

_____. *Philosopher at Large.*
First Edition: New York: Macmillan, 1977.
NF/F: $80   **G/VG: $20**

_____. *The Conditions of
Philosophy: Its Checkered Past, Its
Present Disorder, and Its Future
Promise.*
First Edition: New York: Atheneum, 1965.
NF/F: $60   **G/VG: $25**

Alcott, Amos Bronson. *Tablets.*
First Edition: Boston: Roberts Brothers,
1868.
NF/F: $275   **G/VG: $125**

Andrews, Stephen Pearl. *Discoveries
in Chinese or the Symbolism of the
Primitive Characters of the Chinese
System of Writing.*
First Edition: New York: Charles B.
Norton, 1854.
NF/F: $475   **G/VG: $150**

Appleyard, Brian. *Understanding
The Present: Science and The Soul of
Modern Man.*
First Edition: London: Picador, 1992.
NF/F: $30   **G/VG: $10**

Arendt, Hannah. *The Origins of
Totalitarianism.*
First Edition: New York: Harcourt
Brace, 1951.
NF/F: $700   **G/VG: $235**

_____. *The Human Condition.*
First Edition: Chicago: University of
Chicago Press, 1958.
NF/F: $265   **G/VG: $115**

_____. *Eichmann in Jerusalem.
A Report on the Banality of Evil.*
First Edition: London: Faber and Faber,
1963.
NF/F: $275   **G/VG: $75**
First U.S. Edition: New York: Viking, 1963.
NF/F: $185   **G/VG: $55**

_____. *The Burden of Our Time.*
First Edition: London: Secker &
Warburg, 1951.
NF/F: $75   **G/VG: $25**

Arnold, Matthew. *God & The Bible.*
First Edition: London: Smith, Elder, 1875.
NF/F: $160   **G/VG: $65**

_____. *Literature and Dogma: An Essay Towards a Better Apprehension of the Bible.*
First Edition: London: Smith, Elder, 1873.
NF/F: $150   **G/VG: $55**

_____. *Culture and Anarchy. An Essay in Political and Social Criticism.*
First Edition: London: Smith, Elder, 1869.
NF/F: $450   **G/VG: $195**

Arthur, Timothy Shay. *Ten Nights In A Barroom and What I Saw There.*
First Edition: Philadelphia: Lippincott, Grambo & Co., 1855.
NF/F: $125   **G/VG: $45**

Aurobindo, Sri. *Lights on Yoga.*
First Edition: Howrah, Calcutta: N Goswami, 1935.
NF/F: $145   **G/VG: $65**

_____. *The Human Cycle.*
First Edition: Pondicherry: Sri Aurobindo Ashram, 1949.
NF/F: $125   **G/VG: $35**

_____. *The Human Cycle - The Ideal of Human Unity - War and Self-Determination.*
First Edition: Pondicherry: Sri Aurobindo Ashram, 1962.
NF/F: $85   **G/VG: $25**

_____. *Ilion. An Epic in Quanitative Hexameters.*
First Edition: Pondicherry: Sri Aurobindo Ashram, 1957.
NF/F: $65   **G/VG: $25**

Ayer, A. J. *Language Truth And Logic.*
First Edition: London: Gollancz, 1936.
NF/F: $1,000   **G/VG: $450**

_____. *Philosophical Essays.*
First Edition: London: Macmillan, 1954.
NF/F: $200   **G/VG: $85**

_____. *The Problem of Knowledge.*
First Edition: London: Macmillan, 1956.
NF/F: $125   **G/VG: $45**

_____. *The Origins of Pragmatism.*
First Edition: London: Macmillan, 1968.
NF/F: $115   **G/VG: $35**

Babbitt, Irving. *The Dhammapada.*
First U.S. Edition: New York: James Laughlin, 1936.
NF/F: $40   **G/VG: $10**

Bain, Alexander. *Senses and the Intellect.*
First Edition: London: John W. Parker and Son, 1855.
NF/F: $500   **G/VG: $210**

_____. *The Emotions and the Will.*
First Edition: London: John W. Parker and Son, 1859.
NF/F: $550   **G/VG: $235**

_____. *Mental & Moral Science. A Compendium of Psychology & Ethics.*
First Edition: London: Longmans, 1868.
NF/F: $235   **G/VG: $100**

Ballou, Adin. *Practical Christian Socialism.*
First Edition: Hopewell & New York: The author & Fowlers and Wells, 1854.
NF/F: $1,600   **G/VG: $650**

Baker, Herschel. *The Dignity of Man Studies in the Persistence of an Idea.*
First Edition: Cambridge, MA: Harvard University Press, 1947.
NF/F: $95   **G/VG: $30**

_____. *The Wars Of Truth.*
First Edition: Cambridge, MA: Harvard University Press, 1952.
NF/F: $65   **G/VG: $20**

Barzun, Jacques. *The Culture We Deserve.*
First Edition: Middletown, CT: Wesleyan University Press, 1989.
NF/F: $75   **G/VG: $25**

Sri Aurobindo

A. J. Ayer.

Philosophical Essays

A J Ayer

A. J. Ayer.

Borna Bebek.

Ernest Becker.

Ernest Becker.

Bebek, Borna. *The Third City: Philosophy At War With Positivism.*
First Edition: London: Routledge & Kegan Paul, 1982.
NF/F: $40   **G/VG: $15**

_____. *Santhana: One Man's Road to the East.*
First Edition: London: Bodley Head, 1980.
NF/F: $45   **G/VG: $15**

Becker, Ernest. *Zen: A Rational Critique.*
First Edition: New York: Norton, 1961.
NF/F: $125   **G/VG: $45**

_____. *Escape from Evil.*
First Edition: New York: Free Press, 1975.
NF/F: $45   **G/VG: $1**

Beecher, Henry Ward. *Royal Truths.*
First Edition: Boston: Tichnor and Fields, 1866.
NF/F: $550   **G/VG: $60**

_____. *Lectures to Young Men on Various Important Subjects.*
First Edition: New York: Derby and Jackson, 1857.
NF/F: $150   **G/VG: $45**

_____. *Freedom and War.*
First Edition: Boston: Ticknor & Fields 1863.
NF/F: $110   **G/VG: $35**

Belloc, Hilaire. *On Nothing & Kindred Subjects.*
First Edition: London: Methuen, 1908.
NF/F: $125   **G/VG: $40**

_____. *On Something.*
First Edition: London: Methuen & Co., 1910.
NF/F: $115   **G/VG: $35**

_____. *On Everything.*
First Edition: London: Methuen & Co., 1909.
NF/F: $135   **G/VG: $45**

Bergson, Henri. *Creative Evolution.*
First U.K. Edition: London: St. Martin's, 1911.
NF/F: $550   **G/VG: $200**
First U.S. Edition: New York: Henry Holt, 1911.
NF/F: $435   **G/VG: $125**

_____. *Time and Free Will. An Essay on the Immediate Data of Consciousness.*
First U.K. Edition: London: Swan Sonnenschein, 1910.
NF/F: $260   **G/VG: $95**
First U.S. Edition: New York: Macmillan, 1910.
NF/F: $180   **G/VG: $65**

_____. *Two Sources of Morality and Religion.*
First Edition in English: New York: Henry Holt, 1935.
NF/F: $125   **G/VG: $50**

_____. *Creative Mind.*
First Edition Thus: New York: Philosophical Library, 1946.
NF/F: $100   **G/VG: $40**

Berkeley, George. *The Works. To which is added, An Account of his Life, and Several of his Letters to Thomas Prior, Dean Gervais, and Mr. Pope. (Two Volumes).*
First Edition: London: Printed for G. Robinson, 1784.
NF/F: $7,500   **G/VG: $3,700**

_____. *Alciphron, or the Minute Philosopher. In Seven Dialogues. Containing an Apology for the Christian Religion, against those who are called Freethinkers.*
First Edition: London: J. Tonson, 1732.
NF/F: $3,200   **G/VG: $1,200**

Berrigan, Daniel. *The Bow in the Clouds. Man's Covenant with God.*
First Edition: New York: Coward-McCann, 1961.
NF/F: $75   **G/VG: $25**

_____. *The Bride.* Essays in the Church.
First Edition: New York: Macmillan, 1959.
NF/F: $85   **G/VG: $30**

_____. *America Is Hard To Find.*
First Edition: Garden City, NY: Doubleday, 1972.
NF/F: $85   **G/VG: $35**

Berrigan, Philip. *Widen the Prison Gates Writing from Jails April 1970 - December 1972.*
First Edition: New York: Simon and Schuster, 1973.
NF/F: $45   **G/VG: $20**

_____. *A Punishment for Peace.*
First Edition: New York: Macmillan, 1969.
NF/F: $55   **G/VG: $20**

Blood, Benjamin. *Optimism, The Lesson of Ages. A Compendium of Democratic Theology, Designed to Illustrate Necessities Whereby All Things are as They are, and to Reconcile Discontents of Men with the Perfect Love and Power of Ever-Present God.*
First Edition: Boston: Bela Marsh, 1860.
NF/F: $1,000   **G/VG: $350**

Bonhoeffer, Dietrich. *Act and Being.*
First U.S. Edition: New York: Harper & Brothers, 1961.
NF/F: $75   **G/VG: $25**
First U.K. Edition: London: Collins, 1962.
NF/F: $55   **G/VG: $20**

_____. *Sanctorum Communio.*
First Edition: London: Collins, 1963.
NF/F: $85   **G/VG: $30**

Bosanquet, Bernard. *A History of Aesthetic.*
First Edition: London: Swan Sonnenschein, 1892.
NF/F: $500   **G/VG: $100**

_____. *The Meeting of Extremes in Contemporary Philosophy.*
First Edition: London, Macmillan, 1921.
NF/F: $285   **G/VG: $125**

_____. *Implication and Linear Inference.*
First Edition: London: Macmillan, 1920.
NF/F: $45   **G/VG: $20**

Boteach, Shmuel. *Wrestling With The Devine: A Jewish Response to Suffering.*
First Edition: Northvale, New Jersey: Jason Aronson Inc., 1995.
NF/F: $65   **G/VG: $20**

Blondel, Maurice. *The Letter On Apologetics and History and Dogma.*
First U.S. Edition: New York: Holt, Rinehart and Winston, 1964.
NF/F: $60   **G/VG: $20**

Bradley, Francis Herbert. *Appearance and Reality.*
First Edition: London: Swan Sonnenschein, 1893.
NF/F: $375   **G/VG: $125**

Daniel Berrigan.

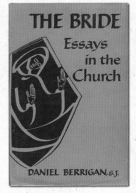

Daniel Berrigan.

Daniel Berrigan.

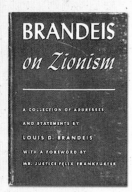

Louis D. Brandeis.

Louis D. Brandeis.

Brandeis, Louis D. *Other People's Money.*
First Edition: New York: Frederick A. Stokes, 1914.
NF/F: $550   **G/VG: $200**

_____. *Brandeis on Zionism.*
A Collection of Addresses and Statements by Louis D. Brandeis.
First Edition: Washington, D.C.: Zionist Organization of America, 1942.
NF/F: $115   **G/VG: $35**

Brisbane, Albert. *Social Destiny of Man: or, Association and Reorganization of Industry.*
First Edition: Philadelphia: C. F. Stollmeyer, 1840.
NF/F: $285   **G/VG: $125**

Brownson, Orestes A. *An Oration on the Scholar's Mission.*
Points of Issue: Paperback Original.
First Edition: Boston: Benjamin H. Green, 1843.
NF/F: $165   **G/VG: $70**

Burke, Kenneth. *Permanence and Change: An Anatomy of Purpose.*
First Edition: New York: New Republic, Inc., 1935.
NF/F: $350   **G/VG: $75**

_____. *The Rhetoric Of Religion Studies In Logology.*
First Edition: Boston: Beacon Press, 1961.
NF/F: $50   **G/VG: $20**

_____. *The Philosophy of Literary Form: Studies in Symbolic Action.*
First Edition: Baton Rouge, LA: Louisiana State University, 1941.
NF/F: $265   **G/VG: $90**

Bushnell, Horace. *Nature and the Supernatural.*
First Edition: New York: Scribner, 1858.
NF/F: $185   **G/VG: $60**

_____. *Views Of Christian Nurture, And Of Subjects Adjacent Thereto.*
First Edition: Hartford, CT: Edwin Hunt, 1847.
NF/F: $100   **G/VG: $45**

_____. *Moral Uses of Dark Things.*
First Edition: New York: Scribners, 1868.
NF/F: $65   **G/VG: $25**

Butler, Nicholas Murray. *The Meaning of Education and Other Essays and Addresses.*
First Edition: New York: Macmillan, 1898.
NF/F: $65   **G/VG: $25**

_____. *The International Mind.*
First Edition: New York: Scribers, 1912.
NF/F: $75   **G/VG: $30**

Carnap, Rudolf. *Unity of Science.*
First Edition in English: London: Kegan, Paul Trench, Trubner, 1934.
NF/F: $600   **G/VG: $180**

_____. *The Logical Syntax of Language.*
First Edition in English: London: Kegan Paul, Trench, Trubner, 1937.
NF/F: $350   **G/VG: $145**

Cassirer, Ernest. *The Myth of the State.*
First Edition: New Haven, CT: Yale University Press, 1946.
NF/F: $150   **G/VG: $40**

Channing, William Ellery. *Duties Of Children. A Sermon, Delivered On The Lord's Day, April 12, 1807, To The Religious Society In Federal-Street.*
Points of Issue: Paperback original in marbled wraps.
First Edition: Boston: Manning & Loring, 1807.
NF/F: $550   **G/VG: $225**

_____. *Slavery.*
First Edition: Boston: James Munroe, 1835.
NF/F: $400   **G/VG: $165**

_____. *Conversations in Rome: Between an Artist, A Catholic, and a Critic.*
First Edition: Boston: W. Crosby and H. P. Nichols, 1847.
NF/F: $275   **G/VG: $100**

Chardin, Pierre Teilhard de. *The Future of Man.*
First U.S. Edition: New York: Harper & Row, 1964.
NF/F: $85   **G/VG: $30**
First U.K. Edition: London: Collins, 1964.
NF/F: $45   **G/VG: $20**

_____. *Science and Christ.*
First U.S. Edition: New York: Harper & Row, 1965.
NF/F: $65   **G/VG: $15**

Chatterji, Mohini M. *The Bhagavad Gita or The Lord's Lay.*
First U.S. Edition: Boston: Ticknor, 1887.
NF/F: $115   **G/VG: $55**

Chesterton, G.K. *What's Wrong with the World.*
First Edition: London: Cassell, 1910.
NF/F: $135   **G/VG: $60**
First U.S. Edition: New York: Dodd, Mead, 1910.
NF/F: $80   **G/VG: $35**

_____. *The Resurrection of Rome.*
First Edition: London: Hodder and Stoughton, 1930.
NF/F: $450   **G/VG: $95**
First U.S. Edition: New York: Dodd, Mead, 1930.
NF/F: $125   **G/VG: $40**

_____. *The Catholic Church and Conversion.*
First Edition: London: Burnes, Oates & Washbourne Ltd, 1927.
NF/F: $135   **G/VG: $40**

_____. *The Thing: Why I am a Catholic.*
First U.S. Edition: New York: Dodd, Mead, 1930.
NF/F: $110   **G/VG: $35**

Chetwood, Thomas B. *God and Creation.*
First Edition: New York, Benziger Brothers, 1928.
NF/F: $50   **G/VG: $15**

_____. *A Handbook of Newman.*
First Edition: New York: Schwartz, Kirwin and Fauss, 1927.
NF/F: $35   **G/VG: $10**

Clarke, James Freeman. *Ten Great Religions.*
First Edition: Boston: James R. Osgood and Company, 1871.
NF/F: $225   **G/VG: $85**

_____. *Modern Unitarianism.*
First Edition: Philadelphia: Lippincott, 1886.
NF/F: $185   **G/VG: $55**

_____. *Nineteenth Century Questions.*
First Edition: Boston: Houghton Mifflin, 1897.
NF/F: $75   **G/VG: $30**

Clifford, William Kingdon. *The Common Sense of the Exact Sciences.*
First U.S. Edition: New York: D. Appleton, 1885.
NF/F: $235   **G/VG: $130**

_____. *Mathematical Papers.*
First Edition: London: Macmillan, 1882.
NF/F: $675   **G/VG: $225**

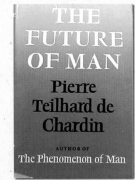

Pierre Teilhard de Chardin..

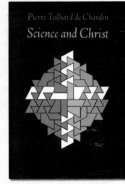

Pierre Teilhard de Chardin.

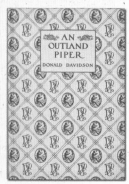

Donald Davidson.

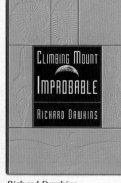

Richard Dawkins.

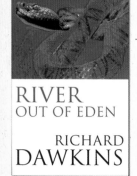

Richard Dawkins.

_____. *Lectures and Essays.*
First Edition: London: Macmillan,
1879.
NF/F: $375   **G/VG: $150**

Cobbe, Frances Power. *Religious Duty.*
First Edition: Boston: William V.
Spencer, 1865.
NF/F: $135   **G/VG: $60**

Cohen, Morris. *The Faith of a Liberal.*
First Edition: New York: Henry Holt,
1946.
NF/F: $95   **G/VG: $35**

_____. *The Meaning of Human History.*
First Edition: LaSalle, IL: Open Court,
1947.
NF/F: $90   **G/VG: $25**

Collingwood, Robin George.
Speculum Mentis or the Map of Knowledge.
First Edition: Oxford: At the Clarendon
Press, 1924.
NF/F: $125   **G/VG: $65**

_____. *Essay on Metaphysics.*
First Edition: Oxford: At the Clarendon
Press, 1940.
NF/F: $175   **G/VG: $65**

_____. *The Principles of Art.*
First Edition: Oxford: At the Clarendon
Press, 1940.
NF/F: $285   **G/VG: $100**

Conant, James Bryant. *General Education in a Free Society.*
First Edition: Cambridge, MA: Harvard
University Press, 1945.
NF/F: $200   **G/VG: $90**

_____. *Our Fighting Faith.*
First Edition: Cambridge, MA: Harvard
University Press, 1942.
NF/F: $70   **G/VG: $25**

Constant, Benjamin. *Adolphe and The Red Note-Book.*
First Edition: London: Hamish
Hamilton, 1948.
NF/F: $65   **G/VG: $20**
First U.S. Edition: Indianapolis, IN:
Bobbs Merrill, 1959.
NF/F: $35   **G/VG: $15**

Dalberg-Acton, John Emerich Edward. *The History of Freedom and Other Essays.*
First Edition: London: Macmillan, 1907.
NF/F: $125   **G/VG: $40**

_____. *Lectures On Modern History.*
First Edition: London: Macmillan, 1906.
NF/F: $120   **G/VG: $45**

Davidson, Donald. *An Outland Piper.*
First Edition: Boston: Houghton
Mifflin, 1924.
NF/F: $750   **G/VG: $260**

_____. *The Attack on Leviathan.*
First Edition: Chapel Hill, NC:
University of North Carolina, 1938.
NF/F: $650   **G/VG: $100**

Davidson, Thomas. *Rousseau and Education According to Nature.*
First Edition: New York: Scribners,
1898.
NF/F: $135   **G/VG: $40**

Dawkins, Richard. *Climbing Mount Improbable.*
First Edition: New York: Norton, 1996.
NF/F: $55   **G/VG: $10**

_____. *River Out of Eden.*
First Edition: London: Weidenfeld &
Nicholson, 1995.
NF/F: $100   **G/VG: $35**

Debs, Eugene V. *Labor and Freedom.*
First Edition: St. Louis, MO: Phil
Wagner, 1916.
NF/F: $185   **G/VG: $75**

_____. *Walls and Bars.*
First Edition: Chicago: Socialist Party, 1927.
NF/F: $125   **G/VG: $45**

Deleuze, Gilles & Felix Guattari.
Anti-Oedipus: Capitalism and Schizophrenia.
First Edition: New York: Viking, 1977.
NF/F: $195   **G/VG: $75**

Deleuze, Gilles & Felix Guattari.
What is Philosophy?
First Edition: New York: Columbia Univ., 1994.
NF/F: $45   **G/VG: $15**

Deloria, Vine. *The Metaphysics of Modern Existence.*
First Edition: New York: Harper & Row, 1979.
NF/F: $150   **G/VG: $65**

Dewey, John. *Studies in Logical Theory.*
First Edition: Chicago: University of Chicago Press, 1903.
NF/F: $350   **G/VG: $165**

_____. *The Quest for Certainty: A Study of the Relation of Knowledge and Action.*
First Edition: New York: Minton Balch, 1929.
NF/F: $195   **G/VG: $80**

_____. *The Study of Ethics: A Syllabus.*
First Edition: Ann Arbor: The Inland Press, 1897.
NF/F: $160   **G/VG: $75**

Dresser, Horatio W. *Health and the Inner Life.*
First Edition: New York: G.P. Putnams, 1906.
NF/F: $65   **G/VG: $20**

_____. *A Physician to the Soul.*
First Edition: New York: G.P. Putnams, 1908.
NF/F: $95   **G/VG: $30**

Dummett, Michael. *Origins of Analytic Philosophy.*
First Edition: London: Duckworth, 1993.
NF/F: $75   **G/VG: $35**

_____. *The Interpretation of Frege's Philosophy.*
First Edition: London: Duckworth, 1981.
NF/F: $160   **G/VG: $50**

_____. *The Game of Tarot.*
First Edition: London: Duckworth, 1980.
NF/F: $400   **G/VG: $130**

Durant, Will. *Philosophy and the Social Problem.*
First Edition: New York: Macmillan, 1917.
NF/F: $150   **G/VG: $65**

_____. *The Mansions of Philosophy; A Survey of Human Life and Destiny.*
First Edition: New York: Simon & Schuster, 1929.
NF/F: $50   **G/VG: $20**

Eddy, Mary Baker. *Pulpit and Press.*
First Edition: Concord, NH: Republican Press Association, 1895.
NF/F: $700   **G/VG: $280**

_____. *Unity of Good.*
First Edition: Boston, by the Author, 1888.
NF/F: $195   **G/VG: $85**

_____. *Christian Healing and The People's Idea of God: Sermons Delivered at Boston.*
First Edition: Boston: Allison Stewart, 1909.
NF/F: $75   **G/VG: $35**

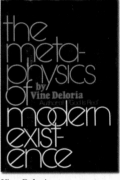

Gilles Deleuze and Felix Guattari.

Vine Deloria.

Michael Dummett.

The Immense Journey

An imaginative naturalist explores the mysteries of man and nature

LOREN EISLEY

Loren Eisley.

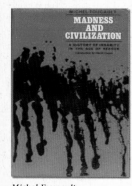

TOBACCO AND ALCOHOL

John Fiske.

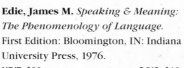

MICHEL FOUCAULT'S
MADNESS AND CIVILIZATION

A HISTORY OF INSANITY IN THE AGE OF REASON

Michel Foucault.

Eddy, Sherwood. *A Pilgrimage of Ideas: The Re-Education of Sherwood Eddy.* First Edition: New York.: Farrar & Rinehart, 1934.
NF/F: $85   **G/VG: $35**

_____. *The Kingdom of God and the American Dream.* The Religious and Secular Ideals of American History. First Edition: New York: Harper & Brothers, 1941.
NF/F: $60   **G/VG: $25**

_____. *God In History.* First Edition: New York: Association Press, 1947.
NF/F: $35   **G/VG: $12**

Edie, James M. *Speaking & Meaning: The Phenomenology of Language.* First Edition: Bloomington, IN: Indiana University Press, 1976.
NF/F: $30   **G/VG: $10**

Eiseley, Loren. *The Immense Journey.* First Edition: New York: Random House, 1957.
NF/F: $150   **G/VG: $60**

_____. *The Mind as Nature.* First Edition: New York: Harper & Row, 1962.
NF/F: $90   **G/VG: $35**

_____. *The Innocent Assassins.* First Edition: New York: Scribners, 1973.
NF/F: $250   **G/VG: $85**

_____. *Darwin and the Mysterious Mr. X: New Light on the Evolutionists.* First Edition: New York: E. P. Dutton, 1979.
NF/F: $150   **G/VG: $55**

Emerson, Ralph Waldo. *The Method of Nature. An Oration delivered before the Society of the Adelphi, in Waterville.* First Edition: Boston: Samuel Simkins, 1841.
NF/F: $700   **G/VG: $275**

_____. *English Traits.* First Edition: Boston: Phillips, Sampson, and Company, 1856.
NF/F: $450   **G/VG: $200**

_____. *Society and Solitude.* First Edition: Boston: Fields, Osgood & Co., 1870.
NF/F: $500   **G/VG: $200**

Farber, Marvin. *The Foundation of Phenomenology Edmund Husserl and the Quest for a Rigorous Science of Philosophy.* First Edition: Cambridge, MA: Harvard University Press, 1943.
NF/F: $85   **G/VG: $35**

_____. *Naturalism and Subjectivism.* First Edition: Albany, NY: Charles C Thomas, 1959.
NF/F: $65   **G/VG: $25**

Fiske, John. *Tobacco and Alcohol.* First Edition: New York: Leypoldt and Holt, 1869.
NF/F: $250   **G/VG: $100**

_____. *A Century of Science And Other Essays.* First Edition: Boston: Houghton Mifflin, 1899.
NF/F: $145   **G/VG: $60**

_____. *Myths and Myth-Makers: Old Tales and Superstitions interpreted by Comparative Mythology.* First Edition: Boston: James R. Osgood and Company, 1874.
NF/F: $195   **G/VG: $70**

Foucault, Michel. *Madness and Civilization.* First U.K. Edition: London: Tavistock, 1967.
NF/F: $320   **G/VG: $110**

_____. *Death and the Labyrinth.*
First U.S. Edition: Garden City, NY:
Doubleday, 1986.
NF/F: $150   **G/VG: $65**

_____. *The Use of Pleasure.*
First U.S. Edition: New York: Pantheon,
1985.
NF/F: $165   **G/VG: $70**

_____. *Discipline and Punish.*
First U.S. Edition: New York: Pantheon,
1977.
NF/F: $100   **G/VG: $35**

Frege, Gottlob. *The Foundations
of Arithmetic. A logico-mathematic
enquiry into the concept of number.*
First U.K. Edition: Oxford: Basil
Blackwell, 1950.
NF/F: $250   **G/VG: $100**

Frothingham, Octavius Brooks.
Transcendentalism in New England.
First Edition: New York: G.P. Putnams,
1876.
NF/F: $135   **G/VG: $85**

_____. *The Cradle of the Christ.
a Study in Primitive Christianity.*
First Edition: New York: G.P. Putnams,
1877.
NF/F: $185   **G/VG: $80**

_____. *Recollections and
Impressions, 1822-1890.*
First Edition: New York: G.P. Putnams,
1891.
NF/F: $95   **G/VG: $45**

Fuller, R. Buckminster. *Nine Chains
to the Moon.*
First Edition: Philadelphia: Lippincott,
1938.
NF/F: $300   **G/VG: $120**

Gass, William. *On Being Blue: A
Philosophical Inquiry...Critical Path.*
First Edition: New York: St. Martin's, 1981.
NF/F: $130   **G/VG: $40**

Gass, William. *On Being Blue: A
Philosophical Inquiry.*
First Edition: Boston: David R. Godine,
1975.
NF/F: $45   **G/VG: $15**

George, Henry. *Progress and
Poverty.*
First Edition: San Francisco: by the
Author, 1879.
NF/F: $3,500   **G/VG: $2,100**
First Trade Edition: New York: D.
Appleton, 1880.
NF/F: $500   **G/VG: $185**

Goldman, Emma. *The Social
Significance of Modern Drama.*
First Edition: Boston: Richard G.
Badger, 1914.
NF/F: $125   **G/VG: $50**

Graham, Billy. *Peace with God.*
First Edition: Garden City, NY:
Doubleday, 1953.
NF/F: $55   **G/VG: $15**

_____. *Angels: God's Secret
Agents.*
First Edition: Garden City, NY:
Doubleday, 1975.
NF/F: $45   **G/VG: $15**

Hall, G. Stanley. *Senescence. The Last
Half of Life.*
First Edition: New York: D. Appleton,
1922.
NF/F: $65   **G/VG: $30**

_____. *Life and Confessions of a
Psychologist.*
First Edition: New York & London: D.
Appleton, 1923.
NF/F: $75   **G/VG: $30**

_____. *Founders of Modern
Psychology.*
First Edition: New York: D. Appleton,
1912.
NF/F: $95   **G/VG: $30**

R. Buckminster Fuller.

Henry George.

Billy Graham.

William Ernest Hocking.

Douglas R. Hofstadter.

Harris, Thomas Lake. *The New Republic A Discourse of the Prospects, Dangers, Duties and Safeties of the Times.* First Edition: Santa Rosa, CA: Fountaingrove Press, 1891.
NF/F: $600   **G/VG: $325**

_____. *The Breath of God with Man. An Essay On The Grounds And Evidences Of Universal Religion.* First Edition: New York: Brotherhood Of New Life, 1867.
NF/F: $375   **G/VG: $150**

Hedge, Frederic Henry. *The Sick Woman. A Sermon for the Time.* First Edition: Boston: Prentiss and Deland, 1863.
NF/F: $75   **G/VG: $35**

_____. *The Primeval World Of Hebrew Tradition.* First Edition: Boston: Roberts Brothers, 1870.
NF/F: $120   **G/VG: $30**

Hegel, Georg Wilhelm Friedrich. *Hegel's Science of Logic.* (2 Volumes). First U.K. Edition: London: George Allen & Unwin, 1929.
NF/F: $625   **G/VG: $250**

_____. *Lectures on the Philosophy of Religion.* First U.K. Edition: London, Kegan Paul, 1895.
NF/F: $585   **G/VG: $260**

_____. *The Phenomenology of Mind.* First U.K. Edition: London: Swan Sonnenschein, 1910.
NF/F: $450   **G/VG: $125**

Heidegger, Martin. *Existence and Being.* First Edition in English: London: Vision Press, 1949.
NF/F: $350   **G/VG: $135**

_____. *Being and Time.* First Edition in English: London: SCM Press, 1962.
NF/F: $600   **G/VG: $275**

_____. *Introduction to Metaphysics.* First U.S. Edition: New Haven: Yale University Press, 1959.
NF/F: $275   **G/VG: $95**

Hicks, Granville. *Eight Ways of Looking at Christianity.* First Edition: New York: The Macmillan Company, 1926.
NF/F: $200   **G/VG: $75**

Hocking, William Ernest. *The Lasting Elements of Individualism.* First Edition: New Haven: Yale University Press, 1937.
NF/F: $55   **G/VG: $20**

_____. *Man and the State.* First Edition: New Haven: Yale University Press, 1926.
NF/F: $95   **G/VG: $35**

_____. *Thoughts on Death and Life.* First Edition: New York: Harper and Brothers, 1937.
NF/F: $50   **G/VG: $20**

Hofstadter, Douglas R. *Godel, Escher, Bach.* First Edition: New York: Basic Books, 1979.
NF/F: $350   **G/VG: $125**

Hook, Sydney. *The Metaphysics of Pragmatism.* First Edition: Chicago & London: The Open Court Publishing Company, 1927.
NF/F: $300   **G/VG: $35**

_____. *Pragmatism and the Tragic Sense of Life.* First Edition: New York: Basic Books, 1974.
NF/F: $95   **G/VG: $35**

_____. *The Paradoxes of Freedom.*
First Edition: Berkeley: University of
California, 1962.
NF/F: $55   **G/VG: $15**

_____. *The Hero In History: A
Study in Limitation and Possibility.*
First Edition: New York: John Day, 1943.
NF/F: $75   **G/VG: $30**

Hopkins, Mark. *Lectures on Moral
Science.*
First Edition: New York: Sheldon, 1862.
NF/F: $125   **G/VG: $70**

_____. *Miscellaneous Essays and
Discourses.*
First Edition: Boston: T. R. Marvin,
1847.
NF/F: $95   **G/VG: $40**

_____. *The Scriptural Idea of
Man.*
First Edition: New York: Scribners, 1883.
NF/F: $55   **G/VG: $20**

Howe, Julia Ward. *From the Oak to
The Olive.*
First Edition: Boston: Lee and Shepard,
1868.
NF/F: $275   **G/VG: $125**

_____. *Is Polite Society Polite?
And Other Essays.*
First Edition: Boston & New York:
Lamson, Wolfe, & Company, 1895.
NF/F: $300   **G/VG: $165**

Hume, David. *An Enquiry
Concerning The Principles Of Morals.*
First Edition: London: Printed for A.
Millar; 1751.
NF/F: $7,000   **G/VG: $4,200**

James, Henry, Sr. *The Nature of Evil.*
First Edition: New York: D. Appleton,
1855.
NF/F: $275   **G/VG: $125**

James, William. *The Will to Believe
and Other Essays in Popular
Philosophy.*
First Edition: New York: Longmans
Green, 1897.
NF/F: $400   **G/VG: $225**

_____. *A Pluralistic Universe.*
First Edition: New York: Longmans
Green, 1909.
NF/F: $250   **G/VG: $120**

_____. *Pragmatism, A New
Name for Some Old Ways of Thinking.*
First Edition: New York: Longmans
Green, 1907.
NF/F: $2,600   **G/VG: $750**

Jaspers, Karl. *Philosophy.* (Three
Volumes).
First U.S. Edition: Chicago: University
of Chicago Press, 1969-71.
NF/F: $295   **G/VG: $115**

_____. *Truth and Symbol.*
First Edition in English: London: Vision
Press, 1959.
NF/F: $85   **G/VG: $25**

_____. *Man in the Modern Age.*
First Edition: New York: Henry Holt,
1933.
NF/F: $160   **G/VG: $55**

Jeans, Sir James Hopwood.
Astronomy and Cosmogony.
First Edition: Cambridge: University
Press, 1928.
NF/F: $145   **G/VG: $55**

Jung, C.G. *Memories, Dreams,
Reflections.*
First Edition: London: Collins, 1963.
NF/F: $185   **G/VG: $70**

Keynes, John Maynard. *How to Pay
for the War.*
First Edition: London: Macmillan,
1940.
NF/F: $265   **G/VG: $110**

Sidney Hook

John Maynard Keynes.

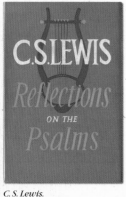

Max Lerner.

C. S. Lewis.

Kojeve, Alexandre. *Introduction to the Reading of Hegel.*
First U.S. Edition: New York: Basic Books, 1969.
NF/F: $95   **G/VG: $35**

Lang, Graham A. *Towards Technocracy.*
First Edition: Los Angeles: The Angelus Press, 1933.
NF/F: $65   **G/VG: $20**

Lerner, Max. *Actions and Passions Notes on the Multiple Revolution of Our Time.*
First Edition: New York: Simon and Schuster, 1949.
NF/F: $75   **G/VG: $20**

_____. *America as a Civilization Life and Thought in the United States Today.*
First Edition: New York: Simon and Schuster, 1957.
NF/F: $85   **G/VG: $25**

_____. *The Age of Overkill.*
First Edition: New York: Simon & Schuster, 1962.
NF/F: $65   **G/VG: $20**

Lewis, Clarence Irving. *The Ground & Nature Of The Right.*
First Edition: New York: Columbia University Press, 1955.
NF/F: $45   **G/VG: $20**

_____. *Mind and the World Order.*
First Edition: New York: Scribners, 1929.
NF/F: $85   **G/VG: $45**

_____. *Values and Imperatives: Studies in Ethics.*
First Edition: Palo Alto, CA: Stanford University Press, 1969.
NF/F: $35   **G/VG: $15**

Lewis, C.S. *Reflections on the Psalms.*
First Edition: London: Geoffrey Bles, 1958.
NF/F: $250   **G/VG: $85**

_____. *Great Divorce: A Dream.*
First Edition: London: Geoffrey Bles / The Centenary Press, 1945.
NF/F: $240   **G/VG: $125**
First U.S. Edition: New York: Macmillan, 1946.
NF/F: $200   **G/VG: $100**

Lieber, Francis. *Letters to a Gentleman in Germany.*
First Edition: Philadelphia: Carey, Lea and Blanchard, 1834.
NF/F: $300   **G/VG: $130**

_____. *Stranger in America.*
First Edition: Philadelphia: Carey, Lea and Blanchard, 1835.
NF/F: $275   **G/VG: $125**

Lynd, Robert S. and Helen Merrell. *Middletown, A Study in American Culture.*
First Edition: New York, Harcourt, Brace and Company, 1929.
NF/F: $125   **G/VG: $65**

_____. *Middletown In Transition: A Study of Cultural Conflicts.*
First Edition: New York, Harcourt, Brace and Company, 1937.
NF/F: $100   **G/VG: $45**

Lyotard, Jean-Francois. *Political Writings.*
First Edition: Minneapolis, MN: University of Minnesota Press, 1993.
NF/F: $175   **G/VG: $55**

_____. *The Differend.*
First Edition: Minneapolis, MN: University of Minnesota Press, 1988.
NF/F: $150   **G/VG: $50**

Marcuse, Herbert. *Eros and Civilization.*
First Edition in English: Boston: Beacon, 1955.
NF/F: $280   **G/VG: $95**

_____. *Studies in Critical Philosophy.*
First U.S. Edition: Boston: Beacon
Press, 1972.
NF/F: $100   **G/VG: $35**

_____. *Counter-Revolution and Revolt.*
First U.S. Edition: Boston: Beacon
Press, 1972.
NF/F: $85   **G/VG: $35**

Maritain, Jacques. *Creative Intuition In Art And Poetry.*
First Edition: New York: Pantheon
Books, 1953.
NF/F: $225   **G/VG: $95**

_____. *France My Country. Through the Disaster.*
First Edition: New York: Longmans,
Green, 1941.
NF/F: $280   **G/VG: $115**

_____. *Man's Approach to God.*
First U.S. Edition: Latrobe, PA:
Archabbey Press, 1960.
NF/F: $95   **G/VG: $55**

_____. *The Dream of Descartes.*
First U.S. Edition: New York:
Philosophical Library, 1944.
NF/F: $450   **G/VG: $185**

May, Rollo. *The Art of Counseling.*
First Edition: Nashville, TN: Abingdon
Press, 1939.
NF/F: $250   **G/VG: $75**

_____. *Love & Will.*
First Edition: New York: W.W. Norton, 1969.
NF/F: $75   **G/VG: $20**

_____. *Power and Innocence.*
First Edition: New York: W.W. Norton, 1972.
NF/F: $40   **G/VG: $10**

Mead, George Herbert. *Philosophy of the Present.*
First Edition: Chicago: Open Court, 1932.
NF/F: $140   **G/VG: $60**

Mencken, H.L. Prejudices Series:

_____. *Prejudices First Series.*
First Edition: New York: Alfred A.
Knopf, 1919.
NF/F: $250   **G/VG: $100**

_____. *Prejudices Second Series.*
First Edition: New York: Alfred A.
Knopf, 1920.
NF/F: $3,000   **G/VG: $125**

_____. *Prejudices Third Series.*
First Edition: New York: Alfred A.
Knopf, 1922.
NF/F: $750   **G/VG: $300**

_____. *Prejudices Fourth Series.*
Limited Edition: New York: Alfred A.
Knopf, 1924 (110 copies).
NF/F: $1,650   **G/VG: $750**
First Edition: New York: Alfred A.
Knopf, 1919.
NF/F: $350   **G/VG: $100**

_____. *Prejudices Fifth Series.*
Limited Edition: New York: Alfred A.
Knopf, 1924 (192 copies).
NF/F: $700   **G/VG: $300**
First Edition: New York: Alfred A.
Knopf, 1924.
NF/F: $225   **G/VG: $100**

_____. *Prejudices Sixth Series.*
Limited Edition: New York: Alfred
A. Knopf, 1927 (50 copies on Japan
vellum).
NF/F: $2,500   **G/VG: Not Seen**
Limited Edition: New York: Alfred A.
Knopf, 1927 (140 copies on rag).
NF/F: $500   **G/VG: $225**
First Edition: New York: Alfred A.
Knopf, 1927.
NF/F: $175   **G/VG: $65**

_____. *Selected Prejudices.*
First Edition: New York: Alfred A.
Knopf, 1919.
NF/F: $200   **G/VG: $75**

Herbert Marcuse.

Jacques Maritain.

Rollo May.

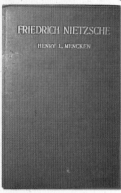

H. L. Mencken.

Thomas Merton

Maurice Merleau-Ponty.

_____. *The Philosophy Of Friedrich Nietzsche.*
First Edition: Boston: Luce and Company, 1908.
Points of Issue: Spine reads "Philosophy of Neitzsche" in first issue.
NF/F: $350   **G/VG: $120**
First U.K. Edition: London: T. Fisher Unwin, 1908.
NF/F: $250   **G/VG: $100**

Merton, Thomas. *Original Child Bomb.*
Limited Edition: Norfolk, CT: New Directions, 1962 (500 copies).
NF/F: $935   **G/VG: $500**
First Edition (Trade): Norfolk, CT: New Directions, 1962.
NF/F: $75   **G/VG: $30**

_____. *The Ascent of Truth.*
First Edition: New York: Harcourt, Brace, 1951.
NF/F: $115   **G/VG: $55**

_____. *The Seven Storey Mountain.*
First Edition: New York: Harcourt, Brace, 1948.
NF/F: $1,750   **G/VG: $650**

_____. *Seeds of Contemplation.*
First Edition: Norfolk, CT: New Directions, 1949.
NF/F: $800   **G/VG: $200**

Merleau-Ponty, Maurice. *Sense and Non-Sense.*
First U.S. Edition: Evanston, IL: Northwestern University, 1964.
NF/F: $70   **G/VG: $25**

_____. *The Structure of Behavior.*
First U.S. Edition: Boston: Beacon Press, 1963.
NF/F: $55   **G/VG: $25**

_____. *Humanism and Terror.*
First U.S. Edition: Boston: Beacon Press. 1969.
NF/F: $125   **G/VG: $45**

Meyerson, Emile. *Identity and Reality.*
First U.K. Edition: London: George Allen & Unwin, 1930.
NF/F: $255   **G/VG: $90**

Newman, John Henry. *Apologia Pro Vita Sua.*
First Edition: London; Longman, Roberts and Green. 1864.
NF/F: $5,075   **G/VG: $2,000**

_____. *Lyra Apostolica.*
First Edition: Derby: Henry Mozley and Sons, 1836.
NF/F: $700   **G/VG: $200**

_____. *An Essay on the Development of Christian Doctrine.*
First Edition: London: James Toovey, 1845.
NF/F: $520   **G/VG: $155**

Niebuhr, Reinhold. *The Structure Of Nations And Empires.*
First Edition: New York: Scribners, 1959.
NF/F: $65   **G/VG: $25**

_____. *Pious and Secular America.*
First Edition: New York: Scribners, 1958.
NF/F: $45   **G/VG: $15**

Nietzsche, Friedrich. *Thus Spake Zarathustra.*
First Edition in English: New York: Macmillan, 1896.
NF/F: $5,500   **G/VG: $2,500**

_____. *Dawn of Day.*
First U.S. Edition: New York: Macmillan, 1903.
NF/F: $1,400   **G/VG: $650**
First U.K. Edition: London: T. Fischer Unwin, 1903.
NF/F: $1,250   **G/VG: $700**

_____. *Beyond Good and Evil.*
First U.S. Edition: New York: Macmillan, 1907.
NF/F: $1,250   **G/VG: $525**

Palmer, Ray. *Hymns and Sacred Pieces.*
First Edition: New York: Anson D. F. Randolph, 1865.
NF/F: $225   **G/VG: $125**

Peirce, Charles Sanders. *Collected Papers.* (Six Volumes).
First Edition: Cambridge, MA: Harvard University Press, 1931-1935.
NF/F: $1,650   **G/VG: $825**

Porter, Noah. *Elements of Intellectual Science.*
First Edition: New York: Scribners, 1887.
NF/F: $145   **G/VG: $50**

Rand, Ayn. *Capitalism: The Unknown Ideal.*
First Edition (Trade): New York: The New American Library, 1966.
NF/F: $125   **G/VG: $35**

_____. *For the New Intellectual.*
First Edition: New York: Random House, 1961.
NF/F: $250   **G/VG: $120**

_____. *The Virtue of Selfishness a New Concept of Egoism.*
First Edition: New York: New American Library, 1964.
NF/F: $225   **G/VG: $75**

Rauschenbusch, Walter. *For God and the People: Prayers of the Social Awakening.*
First Edition: Boston: Pilgrim Press, 1910.
NF/F: $80   **G/VG: $35**

_____. *The Social Principles of Jesus.*
First Edition: New York: Methodist Book Concern, 1916.
NF/F: $65   **G/VG: $25**

_____. *Christianity and the Social Crisis.*
First Edition: Boston: Pilgrim Press, 1915.
NF/F: $85   **G/VG: $30**

Reed, Sampson. *Observations on the Growth of the Mind.*
First Edition: Boston: Cummings, Hilliard, 1826.
NF/F: $275   **G/VG: $165**

_____. *A Biographical Sketch Of Thomas Worcester, DD, For Nearly Fifty Years The Pastor of the Boston Society of the New Jerusalem, with Some Account of the Origin and Rise of That Society.*
First Edition: Boston: New Church Union, 1880.
NF/F: $95   **G/VG: $35**

Reichenbach, Hans. *Atom And Cosmos.*
First U.S. Edition: New York: Macmillan, 1933.
NF/F: $135   **G/VG: $40**

_____. *The Rise of Scientific Philosophy.*
First U.S. Edition: Berkeley and Los Angeles: University Of California Press, 1951.
NF/F: $245   **G/VG: $85**

Friedrich Nietzsche.

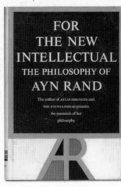
Ayn Rand.

Richard Rorty.

Bertrand Russell.

Bertrand Russell.

_____. *Experience and Prediction. An Analysis of the Foundations and the Structure of Knowledge.*
First Edition: Chicago: University Of Chicago Press, 1938.
NF/F: $160　　　　　**G/VG: $70**

Riley, Woodbridge. *Men and Morals: The Story of Ethics.*
First Edition: Garden City, NY: Doubleday, 1929.
NF/F: $75　　　　　**G/VG: $30**

_____. *The Founder of Mormonism.*
First Edition: New York: Dodd, Mead, 1902.
NF/F: $175　　　　　**G/VG: $85**

Ripley, George. *The Latest Form of Infidelity" Examined. A Letter to Mr. Andrews Norton, Occasioned by His "Discourse Before the Association of the Alumni of the Cambridge Theological School," On the 19th of July, 1839. By an Alumnus of that School.*
Points of Issue: Paperback Original.
First Edition: Boston: James Munroe, 1839.
NF/F: $625　　　　　**G/VG: $175**

Rorty, Richard. *Philosophy and the Mirror of Nature.*
First Edition: Princeton, NJ: Princeton University Press, 1979.
NF/F: $600　　　　　**G/VG: $155**

_____. *Consequences of Pragmatism, (Essays: 1972- 1980).*
First Edition: Minneapolis, MN: University of Minnesota Press, 1982.
NF/F: $135　　　　　**G/VG: $50**

_____. *Achieving Our Country, Leftist Thought in Twentieth-Century America.*
First Edition: Cambridge, MA: Harvard University Press, 1998.
NF/F: $75　　　　　**G/VG: $25**

Runes, Dagobert D. *On the Nature of Man: An Essay in Primitive Philosophy.*
First Edition: New York: Philosophical Library, 1956.
NF/F: $45　　　　　**G/VG: $20**

_____. *A Book of Contemplation.*
First Edition: New York: Philosophical Library, 1957.
NF/F: $30　　　　　**G/VG: $15**

_____. *Classics In Logic: Readings in Epistemology Theory of Knowledge and Dialectics.*
First Edition: New York: Philosophical Library, 1962.
NF/F: $35　　　　　**G/VG: $25**

Russell, Bertrand. *Philosophy.*
First U.S. Edition: New York: W.W. Norton, 1927.
NF/F: $265　　　　　**G/VG: $115**

_____. *Mysticism and Logic.*
First Edition: London: Longmans, Green, 1918.
NF/F: $200　　　　　**G/VG: $110**
First U.S. Edition: New York: W.W. Norton, 1929.
NF/F: $200　　　　　**G/VG: $80**

_____. *Introduction To Mathematical Philosophy.*
First Edition: London; Allen & Unwin; 1919.
NF/F: $850　　　　　**G/VG: $200**

Russell, Charles Taze. *Millennial Dawn.* (Three Volumes).
First Edition: Allegheny, PA: Watch Tower Bible And Tract Society, 1886-1891.
NF/F: $1,500　　　　　**G/VG: $275**

_____. *Pastor Russell's Sermons.*
First Edition: Brooklyn, NY: Peoples Pulpit Association, 1917.
NF/F: $325　　　　　**G/VG: $145**

_____. *The Divine Plan of the Ages.*
First Edition: Brooklyn, NY: Watch
Tower Bible And Tract Society, 1915.
NF/F: $350   **G/VG: $175**

Russell, George William. (as by A.E.)
The Candle of Vision.
First Edition: London: Macmillan, 1919.
NF/F: $125   **G/VG: $55**

_____. *Imaginations and
Reveries.*
First Edition: Dublin and London:
Maunsel, 1915.
NF/F: $100   **G/VG: $45**

_____. *The Living Torch.*
First Edition: London: Macmillan, 1937.
NF/F: $50   **G/VG: $25**

Ryle, Gilbert. *Concept of Mind.*
First Edition: London: Hutchinson
House, 1949.
NF/F: $500   **G/VG: $275**
First U.S. Edition: New York: Barnes &
Noble, 1949.
NF/F: $200   **G/VG: $75**

_____. *Dilemmas.*
First Edition: Cambridge: Cambridge
University Press, 1954.
NF/F: $300   **G/VG: $125**

_____. *On Thinking.*
First Edition: London: Basil Blackwell, 1979.
NF/F: $145   **G/VG: $45**

Santayana, George. *The Sense
of Beauty Being the Outlines of
Aesthetic Theory.*
First U.K. Edition: London: Adam and
Charles Black, 1896.
NF/F: $225   **G/VG: $65**
First U.S. Edition: New York: Scribners,
1896.
NF/F: $180   **G/VG: $50**

_____. *Interpretations of Poetry
and Religion.*
First Edition: New York: Scribners, 1900.
NF/F: $300   **G/VG: $100**

_____. Realms of Being Series:

_____. *The Realm of Essence.*
First Edition: New York: Charles
Scribner's Sons, 1927.
NF/F: $240   **G/VG: $110**

_____. *The Realm of Matter.*
First Edition: New York: Charles
Scribner's Sons, 1923.
NF/F: $220   **G/VG: $85**

_____. *The Realm of Truth.*
First Edition: London: Constable, 1937.
NF/F: $180   **G/VG: $65**
First U.S. Edition: New York: Charles
Scribner's Sons, 1938.
NF/F: $130   **G/VG: $40**

_____. *The Realm of Spirit.*
First Edition: New York: Charles
Scribner's Sons, 1940.
NF/F: $250   **G/VG: $100**

Sartre, Jean-Paul. *Being and
Nothingness.*
First Edition In English: New York:
Philosophical Library, 1956.
NF/F: $300   **G/VG: $130**

_____. *Existentialism.*
First U.S. Edition: New York:
Philosophical Library, 1947.
NF/F: $150   **G/VG: $85**

_____. *Two Plays.*
First U.K. Edition: New York:
Philosophical Library, 1947.
NF/F: $150   **G/VG: $85**

_____. *The Emotions, Outline Of
A Theory.*
First U.S. Edition: London: Hamish
Hamilton, 1946.
NF/F: $200   **G/VG: $65**

Schuller, Robert H. *Reach Out for
New Life.*
First Edition: New York: Hawthorn
Books, 1977.
NF/F: $15   **G/VG: $6**

George Santayana.

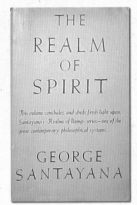

George Santayana.

Jean-Paul Sartre.

Schuller, Robert H.

Ninian Smart.

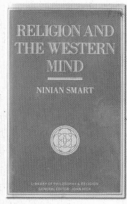

Ninian Smart.

_____. *The Peak to Peek Principle.*
First Edition: Garden City, NY:
Doubleday, 1980.
NF/F: $45   **G/VG: $15**

Sheen, Fulton J. *The Moral Universe.*
First Edition: Milwaukee: Bruce
Publishing, 1936.
NF/F: $200   **G/VG: $85**

_____. *The Seven Last Words.*
First Edition: New York & London:
Century Co., 1933.
NF/F: $95   **G/VG: $35**

_____. *The Mystical Body Of Christ.*
First Edition: New York: Sheed &
Ward, 1935.
NF/F: $85   **G/VG: $30**

Smart, Ninian. *The Religious
Experience of Mankind.*
First Edition: New York: Scribners, 1969.
NF/F: $75   **G/VG: $25**

_____. *Worldviews:
Crosscultural Explorations of Human
Beliefs.*
First Edition: New York: Scribners,
1983.
NF/F: $65   **G/VG: $20**

_____. *Religion and the Western
Mind.*
First Edition: Albany, NY: State
University of New York, 1987.
NF/F: $145   **G/VG: $50**

Smith, Joseph W. *Gleanings from
the Sea: Showing the Pleasures, Pains
and Penalties of Life Afloat, with
Contingemcies Ashore.*
First Edition: Andover, Massachusetts:
Joseph W. Smith, 1887.
NF/F: $350   **G/VG: $200**

Spencer, Herbert. *A System of
Synthetic Philosophy.* (Six Volumes).
First Edition: London: Williams and
Norgate, 1898.
NF/F: $800   **G/VG: $350**

_____. *Education Intellectual
Moral And Physical.*
First Edition: London: G. Mainwaring,
1861.
NF/F: $555   **G/VG: $195**

Thompson Francis. *Health &
Holiness.*
First Edition: London: J. Masters, 1905.
NF/F: $145   **G/VG: $55**

Thoreau, Henry David. *Excursions.*
First Edition: Boston: Ticknor and
Fields, 1863.
NF/F: $1,950   **G/VG: $900**

_____. *Maine Woods.*
First Edition: Boston: Ticknor & Fields,
1864.
NF/F: $2,350   **G/VG: $850**

Trench, Richard Chenevix.
*The Fitness of Holy Scripture for
Unfolding the Spiritual Life of Men.*
First Edition: London: Macmillan,
Barclay and Macmillan, John W.
Parker, 1845.
NF/F: $95   **G/VG: $35**

Trine, Ralph Waldo. *The Man Who
Knew.*
First Edition: London: G. Bell, 1936.
NF/F: $165   **G/VG: $65**

_____. *In The Fire Of The Heart.*
First Edition: New York: McClure,
Phillips, 1906.
NF/F: $85   **G/VG: $35**

_____. *In Tune with the Infinite.*
First Edition: New York: Thomas Y.
Crowell & Co., 1897.
NF/F: $100   **G/VG: $35**

Veblen, Thorstein. *The Theory of the
Leisure Class.*
First Edition: New York, Macmillan,
1899.
NF/F: $7,000   **G/VG: $3,700**

_____. *Absentee Ownership And Business Enterprise In Recent Times.*
First Edition: New York: Huebsch, 1923.
NF/F: $675   **G/VG: $300**

_____. *The Place of Science in Modern Civilization.*
First Edition: New York: Huebsch, 1919.
NF/F: $350   **G/VG: $175**

Von Hugel, Baron Frederick. *Essays and Addresses on the Philosophy of Religion.*
First Edition: London: Dent, 1928.
NF/F: $50   **G/VG: $15**

Wallace, Alfred Russel. *Studies Scientific and Social.* (Two Volumes).
First Edition: London: Macmillan, 1900.
NF/F: $850   **G/VG: $345**

_____. *Bad Times.*
First Edition: London: Macmillan, 1885.
NF/F: $650   **G/VG: $400**

Ward, William George. *Essays on the Philosophy of Theism.* (Two Volumes).
First Edition: London: Kegan Paul, Trench, 1884.
NF/F: $185   **G/VG: $80**

_____. *Essays on the Church's Doctrinal Authority.*
First Edition: London: Burnes, Oates & Washbourne, 1889.
NF/F: $75   **G/VG: $30**

Whitefield, George. *The Christian's Companion.*
First Edition: London: by the booksellers, 1738.
NF/F: $900   **G/VG: $400**

_____. *Fifteen Sermons Preached on Various Important Subjects, Carefully Corrected and Revised According to the Best London Edition.*
First U.S. Edition: Philadelphia: Mathew Carey, 1794.
NF/F: $500   **G/VG: $200**

Whitehead, Alfred North. *Process and Reality.*
First Edition: New York & London: Macmillan, 1929.
NF/F: $950   **G/VG: $325**

_____. *The Concept of Nature.*
First Edition: Cambridge: at the University Press, 1920.
NF/F: $250   **G/VG: $95**

_____. *Symbolism Its Meaning and Effect.*
First Edition: Cambridge: Cambridge University Press, 1928.
NF/F: $200   **G/VG: $80**

Wittgenstein, Ludwig. *Tractatus Logico-Philosophicus.*
First U.K. Edition: London: Kegan, Paul, Trench, Trubner, 1922.
NF/F: $2,500   **G/VG: $1,050**
First U.S. Edition: New York: Harcourt, Brace, 1922.
NF/F: $2,000   **G/VG: $850**

_____. *Philosophical Investigations.*
First Edition in English: Oxford: Basil Blackwell, 1953.
NF/F: $800   **G/VG: $350**

_____. *Remarks on the Foundations of Mathematics.*
First Edition in English: New York: Macmillan, 1956.
NF/F: $650   **G/VG: $220**

Wojtyla, Karl (Pope John Paul II).
Sources of Renewal, The Implementation of the Second Vatican Council.
First U.K. Edition: New York: Harper & Row, 1981.
NF/F: $120   **G/VG: $40**

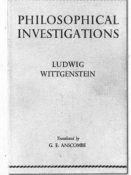

Ludwig Wittgenstein.

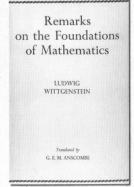

Ludwig Wittgenstein.

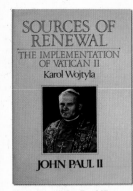

Karl (Pope John Paul II) Wojtyla.

POETRY AND BELLES LETTRES

Belles lettres, to write for the sake of beauty alone. Literature is, after all is said and done, an art form.

The well-turned phrase, the beautiful description, the poem that makes your heart a dancer, these are belles lettres. It is writing simply for the sake of art, exploring the limits of what the soul can draw from rearrangements of the dictionary.

The format can be almost anything. It can be a book of poetry, a collection of essays or stories, or even a novel. The telling factor is the beauty, the novelty, the art of it. Perhaps it can be called painting with words.

Arthur Machen found it to be the perfect, sublime combination of terror and beauty. The dividing line for me has always been whether it appeals to my mind or to my emotions. If it makes me feel, it's belles lettres.

It is a field that holds a lot more small press and vanity publications than other genres. While novelists might get a healthy advance for their first book, poets, for about the last two centuries or more, seem to be expected to prove themselves through small or vanity presses. Auden, Poe, Wordsworth, Coleridge, Machen, Dylan Thomas and Paul Lawrence Dunbar all self- or subsidy published their introductions to the world of publication.

Small presses are a major factor in the genre. Black Sun, Sylvia Beach's Shakespeare and Co., Harriet Weaver's Egoist Press, Lawrence Ferlinghetti's City Lights, California's Black Sparrow Press have all brought out classics of belles lettres. The field is a specialized one as the most sought after books are extremely rare and hence rather expensive. This is the champagne area in the collector's market, the high end.

It often crosses over into the illustration area, books that are a collaborative effort aimed at producing a multimedia experience. The artistic "marriage" of William Morris and Edward Bourne-Jones at Kelmscott Press is a prime example. More modern examples might be the LEC publication of Arthur Rimbaud's *A Season in Hell*, illustrated by Robert Mapplethorp, and the University of California's publication of Alain Robbe-Grillet's *La Belle Captive*, illustrated by Rene Magritte. Sometimes the collaboration of a literary and a graphic artist produces something so wondrous that it is a pleasure just to hold it in your hands.

This is an area that can be extremely personal. If it touches you. If you find, while reading, that you reach up to wipe a tear from your cheek, or if you are laughing so hard that you have to put the book down, well, then you've found a book that belongs in your collection of belles lettres.

These are the books that never grow old. The books that open new worlds, new thoughts, new interpretations every time they are opened; every time they are read from the first reading to readings extending to June 1st of never. They are as wondrous and beautiful as any work of art can be, for that is what they are - works of art.

There are no other areas of art, so accessible, so easily attainable, by the average man as belles lettres. To hold the first edition, the very first appearance in the world of a book that touches you, that reaches you, is equivalent to owning the Mona Lisa, and no man in the world today is rich enough to afford that.

TEN CLASSIC RARITIES

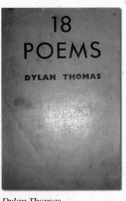

Dylan Thomas.

Auden, W.H. *Poems.*
(Privately printed) S[tephen].
H[arold]. S[pender]. n.p. [Frognal,
Hampstead] 1928.
**$50,000 in almost any condition, probably
higher.**

Bridges, Robert. *The Testament of
Beauty (privately printed for the
author) n.p.*
[Oxford] n.d. [1927-9]. Five volumes in
unprinted wrappers.
NF/F: $5,000   **G/VG: $2,300**

cummings, e.e. *The Enormous
Room.*
Boni and Liveright: New York, 1922.
First issue, the word "shit" intact in the
last line of page 219. In later issues the
word was blocked out.
NF/F: $5,000   **G/VG: $2,400**

Dunbar, Paul Lawrence. *Majors and
Minors.*
Toledo, Ohio: Hadley & Hadley,
Printers and Binders, 1895. Dunbar's
second book, published at his own
expense.
NF/F: $3,000   **G/VG: $1,400**

Eliot, T.S. *The Wasteland.*
New York. Boni and Liveright. 1922.
"Mountain" correctly spelled on page
41.
NF/F: $12,500   **G/VG: $6,000 .**

Hughes, Langston. *Weary Blues.*
New York: Alfred A. Knopf, 1926.
Finding it cures the blues.
NF/F: $11,000   **G/VG: $6,000**

Pound, Ezra. *Imaginary Letters
Paris: Black Sun Press, 1930.*
Printed on Japan Vellum. Finding this
pays in real banknotes.
NF/F: $3,600   **G/VG: $2,500**

Stein, Gertrude. *Dix Portraits.*
Paris: Editions de la Montagne, 1930.
Trade Edition, one of 400 copies on
Alpha Paper, numbered from 101 to
500.
NF/F: $2,500   **G/VG: $1,200**

Thomas, Dylan. *18 Poems.*
London: The Sunday Referee and The
Parton Bookshop, 1934. Price per
poem is hefty.
NF/F: $16,000   **G/VG: $7,200**

Yeats, W.B. *The Wanderings of Oisin.*
London: Kegan Paul, Trench, 1889.
Dark blue cloth with black endpapers.
NF/F: $3,100   **G/VG: $1,400**

PRICE GUIDE

W. H. Auden.

W. H. Auden.

Joseph Auslander.

Adams, Leonie. *Those Not Elect.*
First Edition: New York: Robert M.
McBride, 1925.
NF/F: $650   **G/VG: $200**

Agee, James. *Permit Me Voyage.*
First Edition: New Haven: Yale
University Press, 1934.
NF/F: $1,200   **G/VG: $375**

Aiken, Conrad. *The Charnel Rose.*
First Edition: Boston: The Four Seas
Company, 1918.
NF/F: $900   **G/VG: $400**

_____. *Priapus and The Pool.*
First Edition: Cambridge: Dunster
House, 1922.
NF/F: $400   **G/VG: $175**

_____. *The Pilgrimage of Festus.*
First Edition: New York: Alfred A.
Knopf, 1923.
NF/F: $125   **G/VG: $55**

Akers, Elizabeth. *The Silver Bridge.*
First Edition: Boston: Houghton
Mifflin, 1886.
NF/F: $155   **G/VG: $65**

**Antoninus, Brother (William
Everson).** *San Joaquin.*
First Edition: Los Angeles: Ritchie,
1939.
NF/F: $2,500   **G/VG: $1,400**

_____. *The Last Crusade.*
First Edition: Berkeley: Oyez, 1969.
NF/F: $300   **G/VG: $165**

_____. *The Crooked Lines of
God: Poems 1949-1954.*
First Edition: Detroit: University of
Detroit Press, 1959.
NF/F: $375   **G/VG: $155**

Auden, W.H. *Poems.*
First Ed: London: Faber & Faber, 1930.
NF/F: $3,200   **G/VG: $900**

_____. *The Dance of Death.*
First Edition: London: Faber & Faber, 1933.
NF/F: $1,000   **G/VG: $600**

_____. *Collected Shorter Poems
1927-1957.*
First U.S. Edition: New York: Random
House, 1966.
NF/F: $300   **G/VG: $115**
First U.K. Edition: London: Faber &
Faber, 1966.
NF/F: $175   **G/VG: $65**

_____. *The Double Man.*
First Edition: New York: Random
House, 1941.
NF/F: $350   **G/VG: $110**

Auslander, Joseph. *Riders at the Gate.*
First Edition: New York: The
Macmillan Company, 1938.
NF/F: $75   **G/VG: $25**

Bacon, Leonard. *The Legend of Quincibald.*
Limited Edition: New York: Harper &
Brothers, 1928 (50 specified copies,
some unnumbered copies unspecified).
Points of Issue: Issued in a slipcase.
NF/F: $125   **G/VG: $65**
First Edition (trade): New York Harper
& Brothers, 1928.
NF/F: $35   **G/VG: $10**

_____. *Lost Buffalo and other
poems.*
Limited Edition: New York: Harper &
Brothers, 1930 (50 copies).
NF/F: $80   **G/VG: $35**
First Edition (trade): New York: Harper
& Brothers, 1930.
NF/F: $35   **G/VG: $10**

Barnes, Djuna. *Ryder.*
First Edition: New York: Horace
Liveright, 1928. Points of Issue: The first
printing states "limited to 3,000 copies."
NF/F: $500   **G/VG: $200**

_____. *The Book of Repulsive
Women.* Points of Issue: A stapled
chapbook.
First Edition: New York: Guido Bruno,
1915.
NF/F: $1,400   **G/VG: $575**

_____. *A Book.*
First Edition: New York: Boni and
Liveright, 1923.
NF/F: $1,500   **G/VG: $450**

Benet, Stephen Vincent. *John
Brown's Body.*
Limited Edition: Garden City, NY:
Doubleday, Doran, 1928 (201 copies).
NF/F: $650   **G/VG: $220**
First Edition: Garden City, NY:
Doubleday, Doran, 1928.
NF/F: $250   **G/VG: $95**

_____. *Five Men and Pompey.*
First Edition: Boston: Four Seas
Company, 1915.
NF/F: $600   **G/VG: $225**

_____. *Heavens and Earth.*
First Edition: New York: Henry Holt
and Company, 1920.
NF/F: $400   **G/VG: $140**

Benet, William Rose. *Starry Harness.*
First Edition: New Haven, CT: Duffield
and Green, 1933.
NF/F: $100   **G/VG: $45**

_____. *Wild Goslings: A
Selection of Fugitive Pieces.*
First Edition: New York: George H.
Doran Company, 1927.
NF/F: $85   **G/VG: $30**

_____. *The Falconer of God.*
First Edition: New Haven, CT: Yale
University Press, 1914.
NF/F: $150   **G/VG: $70**

Berryman, John. *77 Dream Songs.*
First Edition: New York: Farrar, Straus,
1964.
NF/F: $850   **G/VG: $300**

Betjeman, John. *Continual Dew: A
Little Book of Bourgeois Verse.*
First Edition: London: John Murray,
1937.
NF/F: $500   **G/VG: $185**

_____. *First and Last Loves.*
First Edition: London: John Murray, 1952.
NF/F: $245   **G/VG: $110**

Bishop, Elizabeth. *North & South.*
First Edition: Boston: Houghton Mifflin
Company, 1946. Points of Issue:
The first was printed in an issue of
1,000 copies, a 1955 re-issue is often
designated a first edition, be wary.
NF/F: $2,500   **G/VG: $900**

Blanding, Don. *The Virgin of Waikiki.*
First Trade Edition: New York: Henry
M. Snyder, 1933.
NF/F: $100   **G/VG: $35**

_____. *Floridays.*
First Edition: New York: Dodd, Mead,
1941.
NF/F: $50   **G/VG: $20**

_____. *The Rest of the Road.*
First Edition: New York: Dodd, Mead,
1937.
NF/F: $75   **G/VG: $25**

Bogan, Louise. *Dark Summer.*
First Edition: New York: Charles
Scribner's Sons, 1929.
NF/F: $775   **G/VG: $250**

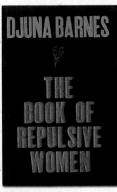

Djuna Barnes.

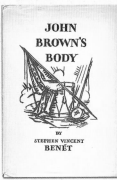

Stephen Vincent Benet.

William Rose Benet.

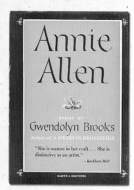

Gwendolyn Brooks.

Charles Bukowski.

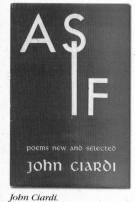

John Ciardi.

_____. *Body of This Death.*
First Edition: New York: Robert M.
McBride & Company, 1923.
NF/F: $750   **G/VG: $265**

Branch, Anna Hempstead. *Sonnets
from a Lock Box.*
First Edition: Boston; Houghton
Mifflin, 1929.
NF/F: $120   **G/VG: $35**

Brooks, Gwendolyn. *Annie Allen.*
First Edition: New York: Harper &
Brothers, 1949.
NF/F: $1,050   **G/VG: $400**

_____. *A Street in Bronzeville.*
First Edition: New York: Harper &
Brothers, 1945.
NF/F: $1,250   **G/VG: $500**

Bukowski, Charles. *Days Run Away
Like Wild Horses Over the Hills.*
Limited Edition: Los Angeles: Black
Sparrow, 1969 (50 numbered copies +
250 copies).
NF/F: $2,200   **G/VG: $900**
First Trade Edition (softcover): Los
Angeles: Black Sparrow, 1969.
NF/F: $55   **G/VG: $20**

_____. *Horsemeat.* Limited
Edition: Santa Barbara: Black Sparrow,
1982 (125 copies).
NF/F: $2,500   **G/VG: $1,400**

_____. *Ham on Rye.*
(26 lettered copies + 100 numbered
copies). Limited Edition: Santa
Barbara: Black Sparrow Press, 1982.
NF/F: $3,000   **G/VG: $1,100**

Brinnin, John Malcolm. *The Garden
is Political.*
First Edition: New York: Macmillan,
1942.
NF/F: $55   **G/VG: $20**

Bynner, Witter. *Indian Earth.*
First Edition: New York: Alfred A.
Knopf, 1929.
NF/F: $75   **G/VG: $35**

Carlton, Will. *Farm Festivals.*
First Edition: New York: Harper &
Brothers, 1881.
NF/F: $25   **G/VG: $10**

_____. *City Ballads.*
First Edition: New York: Harper &
Brothers, 1886.
NF/F: $40   **G/VG: $20**

Carmen, Bliss. *By the Aurelian Wall
and Other Elegies.*
First U.S. Edition: Boston: Lamson,
Wolffe and Company, 1898.
NF/F: $75   **G/VG: $30**

_____. *The Friendship Of Art.*
First Edition: Boston: L. C. Page, 1904.
NF/F: $65   **G/VG: $35**

Ciardi, John. *As If.*
First Edition: New Brunswick: Rutgers
University Press, 1955.
NF/F: $125   **G/VG: $45**

_____. *Homeward to America.*
First Edition: New York: Henry Holt,
1939.
NF/F: $150   **G/VG: $65**

Coatsworth, Elizabeth. *Mouse
Musings.*
First Edition: Hingham, MA:
Peuterschein, 1954. Points of Issue:
Japanese folded book.
NF/F: $250   **G/VG: $100**

_____. *The Cat Who Went to
Heaven.*
First Edition: New York: Macmillan,
1930.
NF/F: $350   **G/VG: $130**

Coffin, Robert P. Tristram. *Strange Holiness.*
First Edition: New York: Macmillan, 1935.
NF/F: $95　　　　　　　**G/VG: $40**

Conkling, Grace Hazard. *Ship's Log and Other Poems.*
First Edition: New York: Alfred A. Knopf, 1924.
NF/F: $45　　　　　　　**G/VG: $15**

_____. *Witch and Other Poems.*
First Edition: New York: Alfred Knopf, 1929.
NF/F: $45　　　　　　　**G/VG: $20**

Cooke, Rose Terry. *Huckleberries Gathered from New England Hills.*
First Edition: Boston: Houghton, Mifflin, 1892.
NF/F: $125　　　　　　　**G/VG: $40**

Corso, Gregory. *Gasoline.*
Points of Issue: Paperback Original Pocket Poets Series #8.
First Edition: San Francisco: City Lights Books, 1958.
NF/F: $300　　　　　　　**G/VG: $135**

Corwin, Norman. *On a Note of Triumph.*
First Edition: New York: Simon and Schuster, 1945.
NF/F: $95　　　　　　　**G/VG: $30**

Crane, Hart. *The Bridge. A Poem.*
First Trade Edition: New York: Horace Liveright, 1930.
NF/F: $650　　　　　　　**G/VG: $235**

_____. *White Buildings.*
First Edition: New York: Boni & Liveright, 1926. Points of Issue: Allen Tate's name incorrectly on title page.
NF/F: $3,300　　　　　　**G/VG: $1,450**

_____. *Collected Poems of Hart Crane.*
Limited Edition: New York: Liveright, 1933 (50 copies).
NF/F: $2,030　　　　　　**G/VG: Not Seen**
First Edition: New York: Liveright, 1933.
Points of Issue: The first state lacks a period following "Inc" on the title page.
NF/F: $850　　　　　　　**G/VG: $345**

Crane, Nathalia. *The Janitor's Boy and Other Poems.*
First Edition: New York: Thomas Seltzer, 1924.
NF/F: $155　　　　　　　**G/VG: $50**

_____. *Lava Lane and Other Poems.*
First Edition: New York: Thomas Seltzer, 1925.
NF/F: $135　　　　　　　**G/VG: $40**

Cummings, E.E. *Eimi.*
First Edition: New York: Covici-Friede, 1933.
NF/F: $1,500　　　　　　**G/VG: $400**

_____. *Tulips And Chimneys.*
Limited Edition: New York: Thomas Seltzer, 1922 (1,381 copies).
NF/F: $1,650　　　　　　**G/VG: $700**

_____. *Santa Claus: A Morality.*
Limited Edition: New York: Henry Holt, 1946 (250 copies).
NF/F: $750　　　　　　　**G/VG: $300**
First Trade Edition: New York: Henry Holt, 1946.
NF/F: $300　　　　　　　**G/VG: $135**

Day-Lewis, Cecil. *Noah and the Waters.*
Limited Edition: London: Leonard and Virginia Woolf at the Hogarth Press, 1936 (100 copies).
NF/F: $680　　　　　　　**G/VG: Not Seen**
First Edition: London: Leonard and Virginia Woolf at the Hogarth Press, 1936.
NF/F: $180　　　　　　　**G/VG: $80**

Grace Hazard Conkling.

E. E. Cummings.

James Dickey.

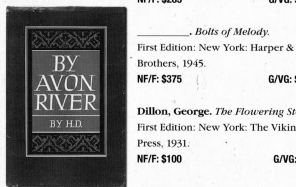

Emily Dickinson.

Hilda Doolittle.

_____. *The Magnetic Mountain.*
First Edition: London: Leonard and
Virginia Woolf at the Hogarth Press,
1933.
NF/F: $450   **G/VG: $250**

_____. *Country Comets.*
First Edition: London: Martin
Hopkinson & Company Ltd., 1928.
NF/F: $295   **G/VG: $115**

Dickey, James. *Drowning With*
Others.
First Edition: Middletown, CT:
Wesleyan University Press, 1962.
NF/F: $450   **G/VG: $165**

_____. *Buckdancer's Choice.*
First Edition: Middletown, CT:
Wesleyan University Press, 1965.
NF/F: $250   **G/VG: $95**

_____. *Helmets.*
First Edition: Middletown, CT:
Wesleyan University Press, 1964.
NF/F: $200   **G/VG: $75**

Dickinson, Emily. *Further Poems*
of Emily Dickinson: Withheld from
Publication by her Sister Lavinia.
First Edition: Boston: Little Brown, 1929.
NF/F: $285   **G/VG: $125**

_____. *Bolts of Melody.*
First Edition: New York: Harper &
Brothers, 1945.
NF/F: $375   **G/VG: $135**

Dillon, George. *The Flowering Stone.*
First Edition: New York: The Viking
Press, 1931.
NF/F: $100   **G/VG: $35**

_____. *Boy in the Wind.*
First Edition: New York: The Viking
Press, 1927.
NF/F: $155   **G/VG: $55**

Doolittle, Hilda (as by H.D.). *By*
Avon River.
First Edition: New York: Macmillan,
1949.
NF/F: $200   **G/VG: $85**

_____. *Red Roses for Bronze.*
First Edition: London: Chatto &
Windus, 1931.
NF/F: $235   **G/VG: $95**

_____. *Hedylus.*
First Edition: London and Boston: Basil
Blackwell and Houghton, Mifflin, 1928.
NF/F: $300   **G/VG: $125**

Dugan, Alan. *Poems.*
First Edition: New Haven, CT: Yale
University Press, 1961.
NF/F: $245   **G/VG: $95**

_____. *Poems 2.*
First Edition: New Haven, CT: Yale
University Press, 1963.
NF/F: $75   **G/VG: $25**

Dunbar, Paul Lawrence. *The Heart of*
Happy Hollow.
First Edition: New York: Dodd, Mead,
1904.
NF/F: $800   **G/VG: $325**

_____. *Poems of the Cabin and Field.*
First Edition: New York: Dodd, Mead,
1899.
NF/F: $375   **G/VG: $165**

_____. *When Malindy Sings.*
First Edition: New York: Dodd, Mead,
1903.
NF/F: $350   **G/VG: $160**

Eberhart, Richard. *A Bravery of*
Earth. Points of Issue: First State
contains an errata slip.
First Edition: London: Cape, 1930.
NF/F: $400   **G/VG: $185**

_____. *An Herb Basket.*
Limited Edition: Cummington, MA:
Cummington Press, 1950 (155 copies).
NF/F: $375   **G/VG: $200**

Eliot, T. S. *The Cocktail Party.*
Point of Issue: Misprint "here" for
"her" on Page 29.
First Edition: London: Faber and Faber,
1950.
NF/F: $1,950   **G/VG: $1,000**

_____. *Poems.*
First Edition: New York: Alfred A.
Knopf, 1920.
NF/F: $3,500   **G/VG: $1,250**

_____. *Old Possum's Book Of
Practical Cats.*
First Edition: London: Faber and Faber,
1939.
NF/F: $4,000   **G/VG: $1,800**

_____. *The Sacred Wood.*
First Edition: London: Methuen, 1920.
NF/F: $2,500   **G/VG: $1,100**

Engle, Paul. *Worn Earth.*
First Edition: New Haven: Yale
University Press, 1932.
NF/F: $150   **G/VG: $50**

_____. *Always The Land.*
First Edition: New York: Random
House, 1941.
NF/F: $100   **G/VG: $35**

Fearing, Kenneth. *Poems.*
First Edition: New York: Dynamo, 1935.
NF/F: $285   **G/VG: $115**

_____. *Stranger at Coney Island
and Other Poems.*
First Edition: New York: Harcourt,
Brace, 1948.
NF/F: $85   **G/VG: $35**

Ferlinghetti, Lawrence. *A Coney
Island Of The Mind.*
First Edition: Norfolk, CT: New
Directions, 1958.
NF/F: $450   **G/VG: $180**

_____. *The Old Italians Dying.*
Limited Edition: San Francisco: City
Lights Books, 1976 (50 copies).
NF/F: $300   **G/VG: $125**

Field, Eugene. *Poems of Childhood.*
Points of Issue: Illustrated with color
plates by Maxfield Parrish.
First Edition: New York: Charles
Scribners, 1904.
NF/F: $1,400   **G/VG: $650**

_____. *The Symbol and the Saint.*
First Edition: Mt. Vernon, NY: William
Edwin Rudge, 1924.
NF/F: $275   **G/VG: $110**

_____. *The Love Affairs of A
Bibliomaniac.*
First Edition: New York: Scribners, 1896.
NF/F: $250   **G/VG: $115**

Fletcher, John Gould. *South Star.*
First Edition: New York: Macmillan, 1941.
NF/F: $95   **G/VG: $40**

_____. *Fire and Wine.*
First Edition: London: Grant Richards,
1913.
NF/F: $250   **G/VG: $100**

_____. *Selected Poems.*
First Edition: New York: Farrar &
Rinehart, 1938.
NF/F: $75   **G/VG: $25**

Ford, Charles Henri. *Sleep In A Nest
Of Flames.*
First Edition: Norfolk, CT: New
Directions, 1949.
NF/F: $125   **G/VG: $40**

T. S. Eliot.

Kenneth Fearing.

Lawrence Ferlinghetti.

George Garrett.

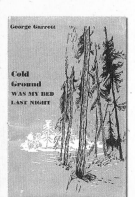

George Garrett.

Paul Goodman.

Frost, Robert. *A Boy's Will.*
First Edition: London: David Nutt, 1913.
Points of Issue: Four binding states, possibly
more Nutt's bankruptcy scattered cut and
gathered copies, most ending up with
Dunster House Bookshop in Cambridge,
Mass. Bronze Pebbled and White Linen
bindings are the most common.
NF/F: $5,000   **G/VG: $2,250**
First U.S. Edition: New York: Henry
Holt, 1915. Points of Issue: "Aind" at
last line of p. 14.
NF/F: $3,500   **G/VG: $1,100**

_____. *Mountain Interval.*
First Edition: New York: Henry Holt, 1916. Points
of Issue: Lines 6 and 7 repeated on p. 88, and
with "come" for "gone" on p. 93 in the first state.
NF/F: $4,500   **G/VG: $1,250**

_____. *New Hampshire.*
Limited Edition: New York: Henry
Holt, 1923 (350 copies).
NF/F: $2,500   **G/VG: $1,250**
First Trade Edition: New York: Henry
Holt, 1923.
NF/F: $1,000   **G/VG: $300**

_____. *A Further Range.*
Limited Edition: New York: Henry
Holt, 1936 (803 copies).
NF/F: $650   **G/VG: $275**
First Trade Edition: New York: Henry
Holt, 1936.
NF/F: $135   **G/VG: $60**

Garrett, George. *The Sleeping Gypsy
and Other Poems.*
First Edition: Austin, TX: University of
Texas Press, 1958.
NF/F: $100   **G/VG: $40**

_____. *Cold Ground Was My Bed
Last Night.*
First Edition: Columbia, MO:
University of Missouri Press, 1964.
NF/F: $85   **G/VG: $35**

Garrique, Jean. *Selected Poems.*
First Edition: Urbana, IL: University of
Illinois Press, 1992.
NF/F: $25   **G/VG: $10**

Ginsberg, Allen. *Reality Sandwiches.*
First Edition: San Francisco: City Lights
Books, 1963. Points of Issue: Softcover,
Number 18 in the Pocket Poets.
NF/F: $200   **G/VG: $70**

_____. *T.V. Baby Poems.*
Limited Edition: London: Cape Goliard
Press, 1967 (1,500 copies).
NF/F: $650   **G/VG: $200**
First Trade Edition: London: Cape
Goliard Press, 1967.
NF/F: $125   **G/VG: $50**

_____. *Kaddish and Other Poems
1958-1960.*
Points of Issue: Softcover, Number 14
in the Pocket Poets.
First Edition: San Francisco: City
Lights Books, 1961. Publisher's ten-line
statement on rear cover replaced by
a twenty-three line statement in later
printings.
NF/F: $425   **G/VG: $125**

Goodman, Paul. *North Percy.*
Limited Edition: Los Angeles: Black
Sparrow Press, 1968 (250 copies).
NF/F: $125   **G/VG: $45**
First Edition (Softcover-Trade): Los
Angeles: Black Sparrow Press, 1968.
NF/F: $35   **G/VG: $15**

Guest, Edgar A. *Over Here.*
First Edition: Chicago: Reilly and
Britton, 1918.
NF/F: $75   **G/VG: $35**

_____. *Passing Throng.*
First Edition: Chicago: Reilly & Lee, 1923.
NF/F: $50   **G/VG: $15**

_____. *A Heap O' Livin'.*
First Edition: Chicago: Reilly & Lee, 1916.
NF/F: $95   **G/VG: $30**

Guiney, Louise Imogen. *Happy Ending, The Collected Lyrics of Louise Imogen Guiney.*
First Edition: Boston & NY: Houghton Mifflin, 1909.
NF/F: $300   **G/VG: $125**

Guiterman, Arthur. *Death and General Putnam.*
First Edition: New York: Dutton, 1935.
NF/F: $45   **G/VG: $15**

_____. *Ballads of Old New York.*
First Edition: New York: Harper & Brothers, 1920.
NF/F: $65   **G/VG: $25**

Heyward, Dubose. *Skylines and Horizons.*
First Edition: New York: Macmillan, 1924.
NF/F: $400   **G/VG: $175**

Hecht, Anthony. *A Summoning Of Stones.*
First Edition: New York: Macmillan, 1954.
NF/F: $200   **G/VG: $80**

_____. *The Venetian Vespers.*
Limited Edition: Boston: David R. Godine, 1979 (165 copies).
NF/F: $450   **G/VG: $225**
First Edition (Trade): New York: Atheneum, 1979.
NF/F: $85   **G/VG: $35**

Hillyer, Robert. *The Death Of Captain Nemo.*
First Edition: New York: Alfred A. Knopf, 1949.
NF/F: $125   **G/VG: $45**

_____. *The Relic and Other Poems.*
First Edition: New York: Alfred A. Knopf, 1957.
NF/F: $125   **G/VG: $50**

Howe, M.A. De Wolfe. *Shadows.*
First Edition: Boston: Copeland and Day, 1897.
NF/F: $135   **G/VG: $55**

Hubbard, Elbert. *One Day; a Tale of the Prairies.*
First Edition: Boston: Arena, 1893.
NF/F: $900   **G/VG: $350**

_____. *This Then is a William Morris Book: Being A Little Journey By Elbert Hubbard, & Some Letters, Heretofore Unpublished, Written To His Friend & Fellow Worker, Robert Thomson, All Throwing A Side-Light, More or Less, On The Man and His Times.*
Limited Edition: East Aurora, New York: The Roycrofters, 1907 (203 copies).
NF/F: $575   **G/VG: $65**

Hughes, Langston. *The Ways of White Folks.*
First Edition: New York: Alfred A. Knopf, 1934.
NF/F: $575   **G/VG: $250**

_____. *Tambourines to Glory.*
First Edition: New York: John Day, 1958.
NF/F: $350   **G/VG: $135**

_____. *Simple Speaks His Mind.*
First Edition: New York: Simon & Schuster, 1950.
NF/F: $550   **G/VG: $225**

Edgar A. Guest.

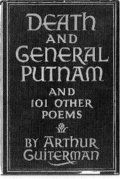

Arthur Guiterman.

Robert Hillyer.

Ted Hughes.

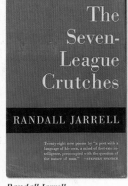

Randall Jarrell.

Randall Jarrell.

Hughes, Langston and Roy DeCarava. *The Sweet Flypaper of Life.*
First Edition: New York: Simon & Schuster, 1955.
NF/F: $800   **G/VG: $375**

Hughes, Ted. *Crow.*
First Edition: London: Faber and Faber, 1970.
NF/F: $1,100   **G/VG: $365**
First U.S. Edition: New York: Harper and Row, 1970.
NF/F: $125   **G/VG: $45**
Limited Edition: London: Faber and Faber, 1973 (400 copies). Points of Issue: Illustrated by Leonard Baskin, signed by Hughes and Baskin.
NF/F: $1,250   **G/VG: $500**

_____. *The Hawk in the Rain.*
First Edition: London: Faber and Faber, 1957.
NF/F: $750   **G/VG: $265**
First U.S. Edition: NY: Harper & Brothers, 1957.
NF/F: $400   **G/VG: $185**

_____. *Gaudette.*
First Edition: London: Faber & Faber, 1977.
NF/F: $125   **G/VG: $45**
First U.S. Edition: New York: Harper & Row, 1977.
NF/F: $75   **G/VG: $30**

Jarrell, Randall. *The Lost World.*
First Edition: New York: Macmillan, 1965.
NF/F: $85   **G/VG: $30**

_____. *A Sad Heart at the Supermarket. Essays & Fables.*
First Edition: New York: Atheneum, 1962.
NF/F: $245   **G/VG: $100**

_____. *The Seven League Crutches.*
First Edition: New York: Harcourt Brace, 1951.
NF/F: $500   **G/VG: $185**

Jeffers, Robinson. *Dear Judas.*
Limited Edition: New York: Horace Liveright, 1929 (375 copies).
NF/F: $700   **G/VG: $325**
First Edition: New York: Horace Liveright, 1929.
NF/F: $450   **G/VG: $195**

_____. *Thurso's Landing and Other Poems.*
First Edition: : New York: Horace Liveright, 1932.
NF/F: $450   **G/VG: $195**

_____. *The Women at Point Sur.*
Limited Edition: New York: Boni & Liveright, Inc., 1927 (265 copies).
NF/F: $725   **G/VG: $300**
First Edition: New York: Boni & Liveright, Inc., 1927.
NF/F: $265   **G/VG: $125**

Kemp, Harry. *The Passing God.*
First Edition: New York: Brentano's, 1919.
NF/F: $35   **G/VG: $15**

Kerouac, Jack. *Scattered Poems.*
First Edition: San Francisco: City Lights Books, 1971.
Points of Issue: Pocket Poets # 28
NF/F: $85   **G/VG: $35**

Kilmer, Joyce. *Trees and Other Poems.*
First Edition: New York: George H. Doran, 1914. Points of Issue: Lacks "Printed in the U.S.A." on the verso, used in later printings.
NF/F: $750   **G/VG: $285**

_____. *Main Street and Other Poems.*
First Edition: New York: George H. Doran, 1917.
NF/F: $250   **G/VG: $80**

Kipling, Rudyard. *Departmental Ditties, Barrack-Room Ballads and Other Verses.*
First U.S. Edition: New York: United States Book Company, successors to John W. Lovell Company, 1890 (Pirated Edition).
NF/F: $450   **G/VG: $190**

Kreymborg Alfred. *Scarlet and Mellow.*
First Edition: New York: Boni & Liveright, 1926.
NF/F: $165   **G/VG: $65**

_____. *Manhattan Men.*
First Edition: New York: Coward-McCann, 1929.
NF/F: $55   **G/VG: $25**

Kunitz, Stanley. *Intellectual Things.*
First Edition: Garden City, NY: Doubleday Doran, 1930.
NF/F: $550   **G/VG: $175**

Lanier, Sidney. *Poems.*
First Edition: Philadelphia: J. B. Lippincott, 1877.
NF/F: $200   **G/VG: $95**

Lazarus, Emma. *Admetus and Other Poems.*
First Edition: New York: Hurd And Houghton, 1871.
NF/F: $725   **G/VG: $275**

Le Gallienne, Richard. *The Religion of a Literary Man.*
First Edition: London: Elkin Matthews & John Lane, 1893.
NF/F: $260   **G/VG: $100**

_____. *Painted Shadows.*
First U.S. Edition: Boston: Little, Brown, 1904.
NF/F: $200   **G/VG: $75**

Lindsay, Vachel. *The Congo and Other Poems.*
First Edition: New York: Macmillan, 1914.
NF/F: $1,200   **G/VG: $450**

_____. *General William Booth Enters Heaven and Other Poems.*
First Edition: New York: Mitchell Kennerly, 1913.
NF/F: $900   **G/VG: $400**

_____. *Every Soul is a Circus.*
First Edition: New York: Macmillan, 1929.
NF/F: $475   **G/VG: $150**

_____. *The Golden Whales of California and Other Rhymes in the American Language.*
First Edition: New York: Macmillan, 1920.
NF/F: $275   **G/VG: $125**

Lowell, Amy. *Men, Women And Ghosts.*
First Edition: New York: Macmillan, 1916.
NF/F: $200   **G/VG: $75**

_____. *Pictures of the Floating World.*
First Edition: New York: Macmillan, 1919.
NF/F: $300   **G/VG: $135**

_____. *Can Grande's Castle.*
First Edition: New York: Macmillan, 1918.
NF/F: $195   **G/VG: $75**

Lowell, Robert. *Land of Unlikeness.*
Limited Edition: Cummington, MA: Cummington Press, 1944 (250 copies).
NF/F: $7,500   **G/VG: $1,250**

_____. *Lord Weary's Castle.*
First Edition: New York: Harcourt, Brace, 1946.
NF/F: $500   **G/VG: $175**

_____. *Near the Ocean.*
First Edition: New York, Farrar, Straus and Giroux, 1967.
NF/F: $225   **G/VG: $85**

Alfred Kreymborg.

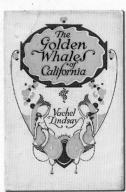

Vachel Lindsay.

Amy Lowell.

Archibald MacLeish.

Edgar Lee Masters.

McCrae, John. *In Flanders Fields.*
First Edition: Toronto: William Briggs,
1919.
NF/F: $225   **G/VG: $85**
First U.K. Edition: London: Hodder &
Stoughton, 1919.
NF/F: $275   **G/VG: $90**
First U.S. Edition: New York: Putnams,
1919.
NF/F: $150   **G/VG: $75**

McGinley, Phyllis. *A Short Walk from
the Station.*
First Edition: New York: Viking, 1951.
NF/F: $65   **G/VG: $20**

_____. *The Plain Princess.*
First Edition: Philadelphia: J. B.
Lippincott, 1945.
NF/F: $85   **G/VG: $35**

Machen, Arthur. *Ornaments in Jade.*
First Edition: New York: Alfred A.
Knopf, 1924.
NF/F: $325   **G/VG: $160**

_____. *Strange Roads With the
Gods in Spring.*
Limited Edition: London: The Classic
Press, 1924 (300 copies).
NF/F: $300   **G/VG: $175**
First Edition (Trade): London: The
Classic Press, 1924.
NF/F: $95   **G/VG: $40**

MacLeish, Archibald. *Tower of Ivory.*
First Edition: New Haven: Yale
University Press, 1917.
NF/F: $275   **G/VG: $115**

_____. *The Pot of Earth.*
First Edition: Boston: Houghton
Mifflin, 1925.
NF/F: $150   **G/VG: $50**

_____. *The Happy Marriage and
Other Poems.*
First Edition: Boston: Houghton
Mifflin, 1924.
NF/F: $150   **G/VG: $45**

March, Joseph Moncure. *The Wild Party.*
Limited Edition: Chicago: Pascal
Covici, 1928 (750 copies).
NF/F: $385   **G/VG: $140**

_____. *The Set-Up.*
Limited Edition: New York: Covici-
Friede, 1928 (275 copies).
NF/F: $350   **G/VG: $125**

Markham, Edwin. *The Man With The
Hoe.*
First Edition: San Francisco, CA: A. M.
Robertson, 1899.
NF/F: $575   **G/VG: $225**

_____. *Gates of Paradise and
other Poems.*
First Edition: Garden City, NY:
Doubleday Page, 1920.
NF/F: $110   **G/VG: $35**

Masefield, John. *Salt-Water Ballads.*
First Edition: London: Grant Richards, 1902.
NF/F: $1,200   **G/VG: $525**
First U.S. Edition: New York:
Macmillan, 1913.
NF/F: $250   **G/VG: $100**

_____. *The Midnight Folk.*
First Edition: London: Heinemann, 1927.
NF/F: $375   **G/VG: $115**

_____. *Right Royal.*
First Edition: London: Heinemann, 1920.
NF/F: $150   **G/VG: $60**

Masters, Edgar Lee. *Spoon River
Anthology.*
First Edition: New York: Macmillan, 1915.
NF/F: $4,500   **G/VG: $1,800**

_____. *Starved Rock.*
First Edition: New York: Macmillan, 1919.
NF/F: $75   G/VG: $30

Merwin, W.S. *A Mask For Janus.*
First Edition: New Haven: Yale University Press, 1952. Points of Issue: Errata slip tipped-in at page 34.
NF/F: $1,100   G/VG: $375

Miles, Josephine. *Lines At Intersection.*
First Edition: New York: Macmillan, 1939.
NF/F: $65   G/VG: $30

Millay, Edna St. Vincent. *Renascence and Other Poems.*
Points of Issue: Watermarked Paper.
First Edition: New York: Mitchell Kennerley, 1917.
NF/F: $2500   G/VG: $950

_____. *Buck in the Snow and Other Poems.*
First Edition: New York: Harper and Brothers, 1928.
NF/F: $250   G/VG: $65

_____. *Wine from These Grapes.*
First Edition: New York: Harper & Brothers, 1934.
NF/F: $300   G/VG: $115

_____. *Make Bright the Arrows.*
First Edition: New York: Harper & Brothers, 1940.
NF/F: $105   G/VG: $40

Miller, Joaquin. *In Classic Shades and Other Poems.*
First Edition: Chicago: Belford - Clarke, 1890.
NF/F: $300   G/VG: $55

Moore, Marianne. *Observations.*
First Edition: New York: Dial Press, 1924.
NF/F: $2,800   G/VG: $1,200

_____. *O To Be A Dragon.*
First Edition: New York: Viking, 1959.
NF/F: $325   G/VG: $125

Moore, Merrill M. *One Thousand Autobiographical Sonnets.*
First Edition: New York: Harcourt, Brace, 1938.
NF/F: $275   G/VG: $100

Nash, Ogden. *Hard Lines.*
First Edition: New York: Simon and Schuster, 1931.
NF/F: $250   G/VG: $100

_____. *The Face is Familiar.*
First Edition: Boston: Little, Brown, 1940.
NF/F: $100   G/VG: $35

_____. *Free Wheeling.*
First Edition: New York: Simon & Schuster, 1931.
NF/F: $165   G/VG: $50

Nathan, Robert. *Youth Grows Old.*
First Edition: New York: Robert M. McBride, 1922.
NF/F: $150   G/VG: $65

_____. *Morning in Iowa.*
First Edition: New York: Alfred A. Knopf, 1944.
NF/F: $80   G/VG: $30

_____. *A Cedar Box.*
Limited Edition: Indianapolis: Bobbs-Merrill, 1929 (1,500 copies).
NF/F: $135   G/VG: $55

Edna St.Vincent Millay.

Marianne Moore.

Robert Nathan.

Dorothy Parker.

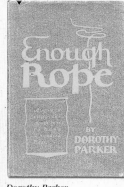

Dorothy Parker.

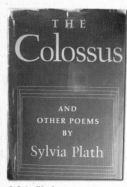

Sylvia Plath.

Noguchi, Yone. *Seen and Unseen.*
First Edition: New York: Orientalia, 1920.
NF/F: $450   **G/VG: $200**

O'Sheel, Shaemas. *Jealous of Dead Leaves.*
First Edition: New York: Boni & Liveright, 1928.
NF/F: $75   **G/VG: $25**

Parker, Dorothy. *Sunset Gun.*
Limited Edition: New York: Boni & Liveright, 1928 (275 copies).
NF/F: $650   **G/VG: $300**
First Edition (Trade): New York: Boni & Liveright, 1928.
NF/F: $135   **G/VG: $40**

_____. *Enough Rope.*
First Edition: New York: Boni & Liveright, 1926.
NF/F: $775   **G/VG: $260**

Patchen, Kenneth. *Red Wine and Yellow Hair.*
First Edition: New York: New Directions, 1949.
NF/F: $650   **G/VG: $125**

_____. *First Will & Testament.*
First Edition: Norfolk, CT: New Directions, 1939.
NF/F: $750   **G/VG: $250**

_____. *The Famous Boating Party.*
First Edition: New York: New Directions, 1954.
NF/F: $350   **G/VG: $100**

Plath, Sylvia. *The Colossus.*
First Edition: London: Heinemann, 1960.
NF/F: $2,250   **G/VG: $800**

Pound, Ezra. *Lustra.*
Limited Edition: London: Elkin Mathews, 1916 (200 copies).
NF/F: $3,500   **G/VG: $1,100**
First Edition (Trade-Abridged): London: Elkin Mathews, 1916.
NF/F: $475   **G/VG: $170**

_____. *Personae.*
First Edition: London: Elkin Mathews, 1909.
NF/F: $1,000   **G/VG: $350**

_____. *Pavannes and Divisions.*
First Edition: New York: Alfred A. Knopf, 1918. Points of Issue: The first issue is bound in dark blue cloth blindstamped with gilt on the spine.
NF/F: $1,800   **G/VG: $550**

_____. *ABC of Reading.*
First U.S. Edition: New Haven: Yale University, 1934.
NF/F: $195   **G/VG: $55**

Ransom, John Crowe. *Two Gentlemen In Bonds.*
First Edition: New York: Alfred A. Knopf, 1927.
NF/F: $650   **G/VG: $225**

Reese, Lizette Woodworth. *A Branch of May.*
First Edition: Baltimore: Cushings & Bailey, 1887.
NF/F: $475   **G/VG: $180**

Rexroth, Kenneth. *In Defense of the Earth.*
First Edition: New York: New Directions, 1956.
NF/F: $200   **G/VG: $70**

_____. *In What Hour.*
Point of Issue: Contains errata slip.
First Edition: New York: Macmillan,
1940.
NF/F: $325   **G/VG: $145**

_____. *The Signature of All
Things.*
First Edition: New York: New
Directions, 1949.
NF/F: $225   **G/VG: $85**

Rich, Adrienne Cecile. *A Change of
World.*
First Edition: New Haven, CT: Yale
University Press, 1951.
NF/F: $1,500   **G/VG: $650**

_____. *The Diamond Cutters
And Other Poems.*
First Edition: New York: Harper
& Brothers, 1955. Points of Issue:
Harper's code "H – E" on verso.
NF/F: $700   **G/VG: $235**

Riding, Laura. *The Life Of The Dead.*
Limited Edition: London: Arthur
Barker, 1933 (200 copies).
NF/F: $850   **G/VG: $400**

Riley, James Whitcomb. *Child-World.*
Limited Edition: Indianapolis, Bowen-
Merrill, 1897 (100 copies).
NF/F: $550   **G/VG: $200**
First Trade Edition: Indianapolis,
Bowen-Merrill, 1897. Points of Issue:
First Issue has a misprint on page ix
"Proem."
NF/F: $180   **G/VG: $50**

_____. *An Old Sweetheart of
Mine.*
First Illustrated Edition (Howard
Chandler Christy): Indianapolis, IN:
Bobbs-Merrill, 1902.
NF/F: $530   **G/VG: $195**

_____. *Rubaiyat of Doc Sifers.*
First Edition: New York: Century, 1897.
NF/F: $275   **G/VG: $145**

Robinson, Edwin Arlington. *King
Jasper.*
First Edition: New York: Macmillan,
1935.
NF/F: $350   **G/VG: $100**

_____. *The Children of the Night.*
First Edition: Boston: Richard G.
Badger, 1897.
NF/F: $550   **G/VG: $225**

_____. *Tristram.*
First Edition: New York: Macmillan,
1927. Point of Issue: first issue has
"rocks" for "rooks" on p 86.
NF/F: $100   **G/VG: $35**

_____. *Cavender's House.*
First Edition: New York: Macmillan,
1929.
NF/F: $125   **G/VG: $45**

Roethke, Theodore. *Open House.*
Limited Edition: New York: Alfred A.
Knopf, 1941 (1,000 copies).
NF/F: $1,500   **G/VG: $150**

Rukeyser, Muriel. *Wake Island.*
First Edition: Garden City, NY:
Doubleday Doran, 1942.
NF/F: $1,000   **G/VG: $385**

Kenneth Rexroth.

James Whitcomb Riley.

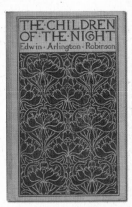
Edwin Arlington Robinson.

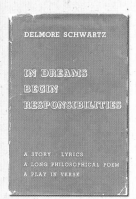

Delmore Schwartz.

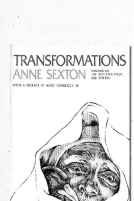

Anne Sexton.

Karl Shapiro.

Sandburg, Carl. *Cornhuskers.*
First Edition: New York: Henry Holt and Co., 1918. Points of Issue: In the first issue the price for Chicago Poems in the list opposite the title page is "$130."
NF/F: $1,000   G/VG: $425

_____. *Chicago Poems.*
First Edition: New York: Henry Holt, 1916.
NF/F: $1,750   G/VG: $685

_____. *Potato Face.*
First Edition: New York: Harcourt Brace, 1930.
NF/F: $500   G/VG: $195

Sarton, May. *Encounter in April.*
First Edition: Boston: Houghton Mifflin. 1937.
NF/F: $700   G/VG: $300

_____. *Inner Landscape.*
First Edition: Boston: Houghton Mifflin, 1939.
NF/F: $325   G/VG: $115

Schwartz, Delmore. *In Dreams Begin Responsibilities.*
First Edition: Norfolk, CT: New Directions, 1938.
NF/F: $650   G/VG: $200

_____. *Vaudeville For a Princess and Other Poems.*
First Edition: Norfolk, CT: New Directions, 1950.
NF/F: $275   G/VG: $100

Sexton, Anne. *The Book of Folly.*
Limited Edition: Boston: Houghton Mifflin, 1972 (500 copies).
NF/F: $600   G/VG: $275
First Edition (Trade): Boston: Houghton Mifflin, 1972.
NF/F: $75   G/VG: $25

_____. *Transformations.*
First Edition (Trade): Boston: Houghton Mifflin, 1971.
NF/F: $85   G/VG: $35

Shapiro, Karl. *Trial of a Poet.*
Limited Edition: New York: Reynal & Hitchcock, 1947 (250 copies).
NF/F: $400   G/VG: $60
First Edition (Trade): New York: Reynal & Hitchcock, 1947.
NF/F: $55   G/VG: $20

_____. *In Defense of Ignorance.*
First Edition: New York: Random House, 1960.
NF/F: $125   G/VG: $35

Simpson, Louis. *Caviare at the Funeral.*
First Edition: New York: Franklin Watts, 1980.
NF/F: $45   G/VG: $15

Snodgrass, W.D. *Heart's Needle.*
First Edition: New York: Alfred A. Knopf, 1959.
NF/F: $450   G/VG: $175

Snow, Wilbert. *Down East.*
First Edition: New York: Gotham House, 1932.
NF/F: $85   G/VG: $25

Snyder, Gary. *A Range of Poems.*
First Edition: London: Fulcrum Press, 1967.
NF/F: $850   G/VG: $300

_____. *The Back Country.*
First Edition: New York: New Directions, 1968.
NF/F: $250   G/VG: $95

_____. *Earth House Hold.*
First Edition: New York: New Directions, 1969.
NF/F: $325   G/VG: $135

Speyer, Leonora. *Slow Wall: Poems New and Selected.*
First Edition: New York: Alfred A. Knopf, 1939.
NF/F: $65   **G/VG: $25**

_____. *Fiddler's Farewell.*
First Edition: New York: Alfred A. Knopf, 1926.
NF/F: $95   **G/VG: $30**

Stein, Gertrude. *Two Poems.*
First Edition: Paulet, VT: The Banyan Press, 1948.
NF/F: $250   **G/VG: $100**

_____. *Rose Is A Rose Is A Rose Is A Rose.*
First Edition: New York: William R. Scott, 1939.
NF/F: $325   **G/VG: $150**

Stevens, Wallace. *Harmonium.*
First Edition: New York: Alfred A. Knopf, 1923. Points of Issue: The first issue is bound in red, yellow, blue and white checkered boards.
NF/F: $12,500   **G/VG: $4,800**

_____. *The Man With The Blue Guitar & Other Poems.*
First Edition: New York: Alfred A. Knopf, 1937. Points of Issue: The first state dust jacket has "conjunctioning" on the front flap.
NF/F: $1,600   **G/VG: $625**

_____. *The Auroras of Autumn.*
First Edition: New York: Alfred A. Knopf, 1950.
NF/F: $700   **G/VG: $255**

_____. *Parts Of A World.*
First Edition: New York: Alfred A. Knopf, 1942.
NF/F: $950   **G/VG: $350**

Stoddard, Charles Warren. *South Sea Idyls.*
First Edition: Boston: James R. Osgood, 1873.
NF/F: $450   **G/VG: $125**

_____. *A Troubled Heart and How it was Comforted at Last.*
First Edition: Notre Dame, IN: Joseph A. Lyons, 1885.
NF/F: $200   **G/VG: $100**

Taylor, Bayard. *The Masque of the Gods.*
First Edition: Boston: James R. Osgood and Company, 1872.
NF/F: $100   **G/VG: $30**

Teasdale, Sara. *Rivers to the Sea.*
First Edition: New York: Macmillan, 1915.
NF/F: $500   **G/VG: $225**

_____. *Flame and Shadow.*
First Edition: New York: Macmillan, 1920.
NF/F: $500   **G/VG: $200**

_____. *Sonnets to Duse and other Poems.*
First Edition: Boston: The Poet Lore Company Publishers, 1907.
NF/F: $2,500   **G/VG: $1,100**

Thomas, Dylan. *Deaths and Entrances.*
First Edition: London: J.M. Dent, 1946.
NF/F: $1,000   **G/VG: $475**
Limited Edition: Gwasg Greynog: Powys, 1984 (250 copies).
NF/F: $2,000   **G/VG: Not Seen**

_____. *In Country Sleep.*
Limited Edition: New York: New Directions, 1952 (100 copies).
NF/F: $5,000   **G/VG: $2,200**
First Edition (Trade): New York: New Directions, 1952.
NF/F: $500   **G/VG: $150**

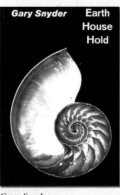
Gary Snyder.

Leonora Speyer.

Dylan Thomas.

Henry Van Dyke.

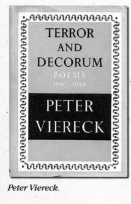

Peter Viereck.

Robert Penn Warren.

_____. *Under The Milkwood.*
First Edition: London: J.M. Dent, 1954.
NF/F: $350   **G/VG: $100**
First U.S. Edition: New York: New
Directions, 1954.
NF/F: $190   **G/VG: $100**

Untermeyer, Louis. *Challenge.*
First Edition: New York: The Century
Co., 1914.
NF/F: $100   **G/VG: $40**

_____. *First Love: A Lyric
Sequence.*
First Edition: Boston: Sherman French,
1911.
NF/F: $150   **G/VG: $55**

Van Doren, Mark. *The Country Year.*
First Edition: New York: William
Sloane Associates, 1946.
NF/F: $100   **G/VG: $35**

_____. *Now the Sky & Other
Poems.*
First Edition: New York: Albert &
Charles Boni, 1928.
NF/F: $250   **G/VG: $85**

Van Dyke, Henry. *The Golden Key.*
First Edition: New York: Scribners,
1926.
NF/F: $225   **G/VG: $95**

_____. *The Blue Flower.*
First Edition: NY: Scribners, 1902.
NF/F: $120   **G/VG: $55**

Viereck, Peter. *Terror and Decorum
Poems 1940-1948.*
First Edition: New York: Scribners,
1948.
NF/F: $90   **G/VG: $35**

_____. *The Tree Witch.*
First Edition: New York: Scribners,
1961.
NF/F: $85   **G/VG: $30**

Warren, Robert Penn. *Promises:
Poems 1954-1956.*
First Edition: New York: Random
House, 1957.
NF/F: $350   **G/VG: $100**

_____. *Now And Then: Poems
1976-1978.*
First Edition: New York: Random
House, 1978.
NF/F: $250   **G/VG: $90**

_____. *Or Else: Poems, 1968-
1973.*
Limited Edition: New York: Random
House, 1974 (300 copies).
NF/F: $165   **G/VG: $75**
First Edition (Trade): New York:
Random House, 1974.
NF/F: $30   **G/VG: $10**

Widdemer Margaret. *The Singing
Wood.*
First Edition: New York: Adelphi
Company, 1926.
NF/F: $225   **G/VG: $90**

_____. *The Road to Downderry
and Other Poems.*
First Edition: New York: Farrar &
Rinehart, 1932.
NF/F: $110   **G/VG: $50**

Wilbur, Richard. *The Beautiful
Changes and other Poems.*
First Edition: New York: Renal &
Hitchcock, 1947.
NF/F: $350   **G/VG: $100**

_____. *Things of This World.*
First Edition: New York: Harcourt
Brace, 1956.
NF/F: $400   **G/VG: $145**

**Wilcox, Ella Wheeler (As by Ella
Wheeler).** *Maurine.*
First Edition: Milwaukee: Cramer,
Aikens & Cramer, 1876.
NF/F: $385   **G/VG: $200**

_____. *Poems of Experience.*
First Edition: London: Gay and
Handcock, 1910.
NF/F: $100   **G/VG: $45**

_____. *Poems of Passion.*
First Edition: Chicago: Belford, Clarke
& Co, 1883.
NF/F: $180   **G/VG: $55**

_____. *An Erring Woman's Love.*
First Edition: Chicago: W.B. Conkey,
1892.
NF/F: $75   **G/VG: $25**

Williams, William Carlos. *Journey
to Love.*
First Edition: New York: Random
House, 1955.
NF/F: $300   **G/VG: $120**

_____. *The Broken Span.*
First Edition: Norfolk, CT: New
Directions, 1941.
NF/F: $750   **G/VG: $300**

_____. *The Desert Music.*
Limited Edition: New York: Random
House, 1954 (111 copies).
NF/F: $2,500   **G/VG: $1,000**
First Edition (Trade): New York:
Random House, 1954.
NF/F: $100   **G/VG: $35**

Winters, Yvor. *The Bare Hills: A
Book of Poems.*
First Edition: Boston: Four Seas
Company, 1927.
NF/F: $275   **G/VG: $125**

_____. *The Proof.*
First Edition: New York: Coward-
McCann, 1930.
NF/F: $195   **G/VG: $75**

Wurdemann, Audrey. *House of Silk.*
First Edition: New York: Harold Vinal,
1927.
NF/F: $165   **G/VG: $55**

_____. *The Seven Sins.*
First Edition: New York: Harper and
Brothers, 1935.
NF/F: $75   **G/VG: $25**

Wylie, Elinor. *Nets to Catch the Wind.*
First Edition: New York: Harcourt
Brace, 1921.
NF/F: $225   **G/VG: $95**

_____. *Black Armour.*
First Edition: New York: George H.
Doran, 1923.
NF/F: $175   **G/VG: $60**

Zaturenska, Marya. *Threshold and
Hearth.*
First Edition: New York: Macmillan,
1934.
NF/F: $75   **G/VG: $30**

Ella Wheeler Wilcox.

Elinor Wylie.

Elinor Wylie.

VANITY AND SMALL PRESS

There are a lot of reasons for a book, just as there is for any work of art. The author wants to communicate; the publisher, however, usually has other motives. For some, money is not it. Some do it for the love of creating a beautiful thing.

Book publishing is a big business and giant corporations control it. And, whenever this happens to anything, the focus becomes money. And as the song says: "… you can't mix love with money. 'Cause if you do, it's gonna hurt somebody." It has currently reached the point where it is hurting nearly everyone.

At the end of the Second World War, war and depression having scattered the energy of book publishing, there was a truly creative couple decades in literature. Small presses made an impact. Henry Miller and Frank Harris with Obelisk; James Joyce with Shakespeare and Company; and Ernest Hemingway with Three Mountains, opened the doors in the twenties and thirties. The war was over and literature was ready to go to the stars. And the fifties and sixties started to answer.

Allen Ginsberg, Gregory Corso, Jack Kerouac, William S. Burroughs "howled" their "angel-headed hipster" ideas into the public consciousness. A whole new idea about literature, a whole new way to put words together, and get it all across. It found its voice through small presses, and was a major force in the art before a "major" publisher deigned to publish any of it.

Over on the other side of the Atlantic, some Frenchmen (and women) also decided that literature needed some new ideas and forms. Michel Butor, Alaine Robbe-Grillet, Natalie Serrault, Robert Pinget and others started pushing the envelope. The "major" publishers in America disregarded them until 1985 when one of their number, Claude Simon, won the Nobel Prize.

Literature, in America, is currently stuck in a rut that started about 1970 and it just gets deeper. Getting a book published isn't a matter of ability, or creativity, it's a matter of politics and suede shoe salesmen. And the books show it. Most of the production of the major publishers in literature, isn't. It's hack-written retreads by connected people, sold by agents who chose their clients as if they were functional illiterates. Ask a major publisher to publish a book, the answer you'll get is that you need to find a good enough suede shoe salesman. Major publishers have lost the author-publisher connection, the most vital connection in all of the art of literature.

To heighten the idiocy, books get "edited" before they get published. If the book is literature it is analogous to a painting, the publisher is the gallery. Now tell me, what you think Picasso might have said if a gallery owner told him he wouldn't exhibit his painting until the gallery's assistants touched it up a bit.

I ran into something recently that showed me the state of literature in America. A client of mine wanted to find, as he put it: "A self-published songbook by James D. Macdonald, it was done in 1975." Now I know James D. Macdonald as a laughably bad sci-fi writer whose books, when I get them in a lot, are part of my yearly donation to the VNSA book drive here in Arizona. In any case, looking for a copy led me to his campaign against Publish America.

Seems James has a mad on for this publisher who will actually publish your book asking nothing from you. Yes they're looking for you to buck the sales machines of the major publishers, but as far as I can see, little else. However, James is on a tear. He has a dictum: "Money follows the writer." Well, maybe if he is an ad copywriter. I've made more money selling the work of Percy Shelley, John Keats, Arthur Machen, H. P. Lovecraft, Iris Owens (Harriet Daimler), and a hundred other noteworthy authors than they ever made from it. If you write for money, you're a hack, a prostitute, and we'd all be better off if you used your talents elsewhere.

And then there's his "literary hoax" Atlanta Nights. Chapters written by (marginally) published writers, writing badly (which comes naturally I suspect). He said that Publish America accepted it. Of course they did. This is what a bunch of writers did in 1969 with Lyle Stuart: Penelope Ashe. *Naked Came the Stranger*. New York: Lyle Stuart, 1969; a best seller and it'll set you back a pretty penny as a collectible; I got five hundred for a double fine copy. About the best way to describe this "hoax" is in the words of Salvador Dali: "The first man to compare the cheeks of a young woman to a rose was obviously a poet; the first to repeat it was possibly an idiot." This idiot is so fixated on ripping off other people's work that he hasn't any of his own. Try one of his books. The planets and characters have their names changed, great sci-fi. Hell, I never found his self-published book, but if it showed literary talent I guess I feel sorry for him. He lost the vision and chose to be a hack writer and hit man for the corporate establishment.

If he has no talent, then I guess he's doing the best he can. If he does, he must feel the pain of his hypocrisy, and I wouldn't wish that on any artist.

Thank God I'm a bookseller. I know that literature is alive and well. It's alive in the author who goes to a vanity press, or self-publishes his work. It's alive in small publishers, whose object is beauty, literary beauty. So what I really want you to do is to read the below as an essay. These are the books that were published out of love for the art, the gambles, the hopes, the dreams, the things that make it all worthwhile. And I guess I want it to be taken seriously because I really need someone, somewhere, somehow, to scramble every idea I ever held about what a book is, and I need it bad.

Literature doesn't depend on the publisher, only the writer. A book is a book, and it being published by a major publisher, a vanity press, a small press or by the author is an irrelevancy to a book collector. About the only conclusion to be drawn in today's world is that if it is published by a major publisher, chances are it isn't really all that good, and that's a shame. However, the path to publication has become so politicized that better work cannot slip through the net anymore and the only literature of any worth is coming out of small and vanity presses. As such they are the premier target of opportunity for the book collector.

TEN CLASSIC RARITIES

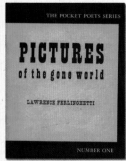

Lawrence Ferlinghetti.

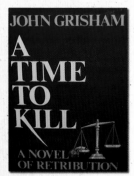

John Grisham.

Bukowski, Charles. *Run With the Hunted.*
Chicago: Midwest Poetry Chapbooks, 1962. Only 300 copies of this, but it's not the only one of Bukowski's early works that pays well; most are in four figures.
NF/F: $3,500   **G/VG: $2,800**

Conroy, Pat. *The Boo.*
Verona, VA: McClure Press, 1970. A bit more common than most self-published books.
NF/F: $6,000   **G/VG: $2,250**

Fast, Howard. *Spartacus.*
New York: By the Author, 1952. Blocked from publication by membership in the Communist party, Fast published this classic on his own hook.
NF/F: $1,800   **G/VG: $400**

Ferlinghetti, Lawrence. *Pictures of a Gone World.*
San Francisco: City Lights Pocket Bookshop, 1955. Whence City Lights, one of America's most influential small presses.
NF/F: $2,500   **G/VG: $900**

Grey, Zane. *Betty Zane.*
New York: Charles Francis Press, 1903. A pure unadulterated vanity press production with a vanity press publisher.
NF/F: $3,800   **G/VG: $1,200**

Grisham, John. *A Time to Kill.*
New York, Wynwood Press, 1989. A small-press production Grisham sold from the trunk of his car, call it sweat-subsidy publishing.
NF/F: $2,500   **G/VG: $1,000**

Hubbard, L. Ron. *Dianetics.*
Phoenix: Hubbard Dianetic Research Foundation, 1955. Founding a religion is a tough business, but it might help to have this.
NF/F: $1,000   **G/VG: $400**

Paolini, Christopher. *Eragon.*
Livingston, Montana: Paolini International LLC, 2002. This one caught on fast , so to get a Fine original, expect to pay five figures.
NF/F: $12,500   **G/VG: $2,500**

Robinson, Edwin Arlington. *The Torrent and the Night Before.*
Maine: Robinson, Gardiner, 1896. Like *Betty Zane*, a pure vanity production that led to one of the most celebrated careers in American literature.
NF/F: $6,500   **G/VG: $2,200**

Rombauer, Irma von Starkloff. *The Joy of Cooking.*
St. Louis: A.C. Clayton, 1931. A widow self-publishing her recipes became an American classic.
NF/F: $4,800   **G/VG: $2,100**

PRICE GUIDE

Adair, Cecil (Evelyn Everett Green).
Shimmering Waters.
First U.S. Edition: Philadelphia:
Dorrance, nd (1928).
NF/F: $175   **G/VG: $70**

Alhazred, Abdul. *AL AZIF (The
Necronomicon).*
Limited Edition: Philadelphia:
Owlswick Press, 1973 (348 copies).
NF/F: $750   **G/VG: $300**

Aldington, Richard. *Images (1910-1915).*
First Edition: London: The Poetry
Bookshop, 1915.
NF/F: $420   **G/VG: $140**

Allen, James Egert. *The Negro in
New York.*
First Edition: New York: Exposition
Press, 1964.
NF/F: $90   **G/VG: $40**

Amis, Kingsley. *Bright November:
Collected Poems.*
First Edition: London: The Fortune
Press, 1943.
NF/F: $3,600   **G/VG: $2,100**

Applegate, John S. "Bud." *Thy
Kingdom Come; Tales of a Small
Town Lawyer.*
First Edition: New York: Vantage Press,
1991.
NF/F: $50   **G/VG: $12**

Appelhof, Mary. *Worms Eat My Garbage.*
First Edition: Kalamazoo, MI: Flower
Press, 1982.
NF/F: $200   **G/VG: $35**

Arias, Arturo. *After the Bombs.*
First Edition: Willimantic, CT:
Curbstone Press, 1990.
NF/F: $150   **G/VG: $35**

Arnovitz, Erwin. *Of Blood and Oil.*
First Edition: New York: Exposition
Press, 1951.
NF/F: $95   **G/VG: $30**

Atwood, Margaret. *Double
Persephone.*
First Edition: Ontario, Canada:
Hawkshead Press, 1961.
NF/F: $550   **G/VG: $135**

Ault, Louise. *Artist in Woodstock;
George Ault: The Independent Years.*
First Edition: Philadelphia: Dorrance,
1978.
NF/F: $300   **G/VG: $115**

Auster, Paul. *The Art of Hunger.*
First Edition: London: Menard Press,
1982.
NF/F: $500   **G/VG: $150**

Austin, Edward O. *The Black
Challenge.*
First Edition: New York: Vantage Press,
1958.
NF/F: $135   **G/VG: $45**

Babcock, Joe. *The Tragedy of Miss
Geneva Flowers.*
First Edition: np: Closet Case Books,
2002.
NF/F: $65   **G/VG: $15**

Badger, Clark. *Sun and Saddle
Leather.*
First Edition: Boston: Richard G.
Badger, 1915.
NF/F: $650   **G/VG: $155**

Bailey-Williams, Nicole. *A Little Piece
of Sky.*
First Edition: Philadelphia: Sugarene's
Press, 2000.
NF/F: $65   **G/VG: $20**

Richard Aldington.

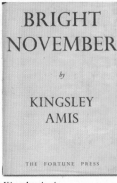
Kingsley Amis.

Joe Babcock.

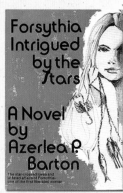

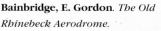

Bainbridge, E. Gordon. *The Old Rhinebeck Aerodrome.*
First Edition: New York: Exposition Press, 1977.
NF/F: $100   **G/VG: $30**

Baisden, Michael. *Men Cry in the Dark.*
First Edition: Irving, TX: Legacy Publishing, 1997.
NF/F: $145   **G/VG: $40**

Azerlea P. Barton.

Banks, Russell. *Searching for Survivors.*
First Edition: New York: Fiction Collective, 1975.
NF/F: $345   **G/VG: $80**

Barnes, Peter W & Cheryl Shaw Barnes. *Nat, Nat, the Nantucket Cat.*
First Edition: Alexandria, VA: Vacation Spot Publishing, 1993.
NF/F: $50   **G/VG: $15**

Barton, Azerlea P. *Forsythia Intrigued by the Stars.*
First Edition: Hicksville, NY: Exposition Press, 1976.
NF/F: $65   **G/VG: $20**

Cleo Lund Berger.

Bass, Rick. *Brown Dog of the Yaak.*
First Edition: Minneapolis, MN: Milkweed Editions, 1999.
NF/F: $500   **G/VG: $25**

Batista, Fulgencio. *Cuba Betrayed.*
First Edition: New York: Vantage, 1962.
NF/F: $400   **G/VG: $135**

Bayliss, Jonathan. *Prologos.*
First Edition: Ashburnham, MA: Basilicum Press, 1999.
NF/F: $75   **G/VG: $20**

August J. Bock.

Beckett, Samuel. *Poems in English.*
First Edition: London: John Calder/ Riverrun, 1961.
NF/F: $1250   **G/VG: Not Seen**

Berg, Stephen. *Shaving.*
First Edition: Marshfield, MA: Four Way Books, 1998.
NF/F: $125   **G/VG: $20**

Berger, Cleo Lund. *Detour: A Novel of Life in a CCC-Camp During the Depression Era.*
First Edition: New York: Exposition Press, 1959.
NF/F: $175   **G/VG: $65**

Blackstock, Graham Belcher. *Sojurn in Occupied Japan.*
First Edition: New York: Vantage Press, 1979.
NF/F: $65   **G/VG: $30**

Blanding, Don. *The Virgin of Waikiki.*
First Edition: Los Angeles: Privately Printed, 1926.
NF/F: $250   **G/VG: $150**

Bock, August J. *Knight of the Napkin.*
First Edition: New York: Exposition Press, 1951.
NF/F: $75   **G/VG: $25**

Bodenheim, Maxwell. *Minna and Myself.*
First Edition: New York: Pagan Publishing, 1918. Points of Issue: Page 67, line 35 "Posner."
NF/F: $350   **G/VG: $85**

Borgnis, Mervin E. *We Had A Shore Fast Line.*
First Edition: New York: Exposition Press, 1979.
NF/F: $500   **G/VG: $225**

Bourde, Danielle. *White Candles, Sex and Michelle Dubois.*
First Edition: Hicksville, NY: Exposition Press, 1975.
NF/F: $275   G/VG: $95

Brent, Lynton Wright. *The Bird Cage.*
First Edition: Philadelphia: Dorrance, 1945.
NF/F: $180   G/VG: $55

Brey, Jane W. T. *A Quaker Saga: The Watsons of Strawberryhowe, The Wildmans and Other Allied Families from Englands' North Counties and Lower Bucks County in Pennsylvania.*
First Edition: Philadelphia: Dorrance, 1967.
NF/F: $335   G/VG: $80

Blumenthal, John. *What's Wrong With Dorfman: A Novel.*
First Edition: Thousand Oaks, CA: Farmer Street Press, 2000.
NF/F: $60   G/VG: $20

Brauer, Jeff. *Sexy New York, 2000.*
First Edition: Brooklyn, NY: On Your Own Publications, 1999.
NF/F: $60   G/VG: $15

Bryant, Dorothy. *Killing Wonder.*
First Edition: Berkeley, CA: Ata Books, 1981.
NF/F: $100   G/VG: $15

Bures, Jen. *The House of Chaos.*
First Edition: New York: Vantage Press, 1958.
NF/F: $50   G/VG: $10

Butler, Octavia E. *Parable of the Sower.*
First Edition: New York: Four Walls Eight Windows, 1993.
NF/F: $200   G/VG: $70

Callenbach, Ernest. *Ecotopia. The Notebooks and Reports of William Weston.*
First Edition: Berkeley, CA: Banyan Tree Books, 1975.
NF/F: $100   G/VG: $30

Callender, Signe. *Gems of Thought - Poems and Aphorisms.*
New York: Exposition Press, 1966.
NF/F: $200   G/VG: $80

Campbell, Morris L. *The Bulldogger: A Western Novel of Love and Adventure.*
New York: Exposition Press, 1959.
NF/F: $150   G/VG: $45

Carter, Frederick. *Gold Like Glass - A Tale.*
Limited Edition: London: The Twyn Barlwm Press, 1932 (200 copies).
NF/F: $330   G/VG: Not Seen

Cave, Hugh B. *Murgunstrumm and Others.*
First Edition: Chapel Hill, NC: Carcosa, 1977.
NF/F: $300   G/VG: $110

Chambers, Ruth Coe. *The Chinaberry Album.*
First Edition: San Francisco: Mercury House, 1988.
NF/F: $125   G/VG: $15

Childish, Billy. *Conversations with Doctor X.*
First Edition: Rochester, NY: Hangman Books, 1987.
NF/F: $325   G/VG: $130

Chomsky, Noam. *Terrorizing the Neighborhood: American Foreign Policy in the Post Cold War Era.*
First Edition: Oakland, CA: AK Press, 1991.
NF/F: $110   G/VG: $30

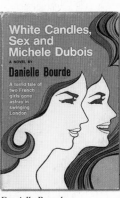
Danielle Bourde.

Lynton Wright Brent.

Marris L. Campbell.

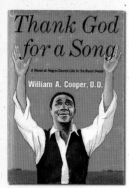

William A. Cooper.

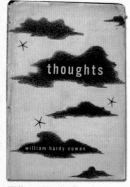

Gregory Corso.

Coe, Jacques. *Fame, Fraud, and Fortune.*
First Edition: Smithtown, NY: Exposition Press, 1982.
NF/F: $125   **G/VG: $50**

Cooper, William A., D.D. *Thank God for a Song: A Novel of Negro Church Life in the South.*
First Edition: New York: Exposition Press, 1962.
NF/F: $175   **G/VG: $60**

Corn, Laura. *101 Nights of Grrreat Sex.*
First Edition: Np: Park Avenue Publishers, 1995.
NF/F: $100   **G/VG: $40**

_____. *101 Nights of Grrreat Romance.*
First Edition: Np: Park Avenue Publishers, 1996.
NF/F: $90   **G/VG: $35**

Corso, Gregory. *The Mutation of the Spirit: A Shuffle Poem.*
Points of Issue: printed as separate sheets to be reordered to form new poems.
First Edition: New York: Death Press, 1964.
NF/F: $650   **G/VG: $300**

_____. *Vestal Lady On Brattle A Collection of Poems Written In Cambridge Massachusetts. 1954-1955.*
Point of Issue: Paperback Original.
First Edition: Cambridge, MA: Richard Brukenfeld, 1955.
NF/F: $400   **G/VG: $225**

Corriveau, M. Louise. *Quints To Queens.*
First Edition: New York: Vantage Press, 1976.
NF/F: $175   **G/VG: $35**

Cotton, Ella Earls. *A Spark for My People.*
First Edition: New York: Exposition Press, 1954.
NF/F: $90   **G/VG: $40**

Cotton, Joseph. *Vanity Will Get You Somewhere.*
First Edition: San Francisco: Mercury House, 1987.
NF/F: $150   **G/VG: $45**

Covey, Cyclone. *THE WOW BOYS: The Story of Stanford's Historic 1940 Football Season, Game by Game.*
First Edition: New York: Exposition Press, 1957.
NF/F: $300   **G/VG: $200**

_____. *Calalus: a Roman Jewish Colony in America from the Time of Charlemagne Through Alfred the Great.*
First Edition: New York: Vantage Press, 1975.
NF/F: $120   **G/VG: $25**

Cowen, James. *Saga of a Security Guard.*
First Edition: New York: Vantage Press, 1969.
NF/F: $50   **G/VG: $20**

Cowen, William Hardy. *Thoughts.*
First Edition: New York: Exposition Press, 1950.
NF/F: $350   **G/VG: $140**

Crane, Hart. *The Bridge. A Poem.*
Limited Edition: Paris: The Black Sun Press, 1930 (200 copies).
NF/F: $5,500   **G/VG: $2,600**

Creeley, Robert. *The Whip.*
First Edition: Palma de Mallorca:
Migrant Press, 1957 (100 copies).
Points of Issue: Hardcover.
NF/F: $850   **G/VG: $550**
First Edition: Palma de Mallorca:
Migrant Press, 1957 (500 copies).
Points of Issue: Bound in wraps.
NF/F: $225   **G/VG: $30**

Crevel, Réne; Max Ernst. *Mr. Knife and Mrs. Fork.*
First Edition: Paris: The Black Sun
Press, 1929.
NF/F: $35,000   **G/VG: $20,000**

Crumb, Robert. *The Story of My Life.*
First Trade Edition: Santa Barbara:
Ginko Press, 1992.
NF/F: $80   **G/VG: $35**
Limited Edition: Santa Rosa: Black
Sparrow Press, 1990 (26 Copies).
NF/F: $750   **Not Seen**

Cummings, Jeane. *Look Here, J.B.!*
First Edition: Philadelphia: Dorrance,
1957.
NF/F: $100   **G/VG: $35**

Curley, Edmund C. *Crispus Attucks – The First to Die.*
First Edition: Philadelphia: Dorrance, 1973.
NF/F: $50   **G/VG: $15**

Daniel, Lee. *Dragon Mountain.*
First Edition: New York: Vantage Press, 1985.
NF/F: $300   **G/VG: $125**

Danticat, Edwidge. *Breath, Eyes, Memory.*
New York: Soho Press, 1994.
NF/F: $300   **G/VG: $50**

Danner, Craig Joseph. *Himalayan Dhaba.*
First Edition: Hood River, Oregon:
Crispin/Hammer Publishing Co., 2001.
NF/F: $70   **G/VG: $20**

De Monte, Alpha. *In Return For.*
First Edition: Smithtown, NY:
Exposition Press, 1983.
NF/F: $150   **G/VG: $65**

Denning, Ruth Miller. *Micko, In the Land of Far-Away.*
First Edition: New York: Exposition
Press, 1956.
NF/F: $85   **G/VG: $30**

Di Filippo, Paul. *Ciphers: A Post-Shannon Rock 'N' Roll Mystery.*
First Edition: San Francisco: Permeable
Press, 1997.
NF/F: $45   **G/VG: $20**

Doner, Mary Frances. *Cleavenger vs. Castle. A case of breach of promise and seduction.*
First Edition: Philadelphia: Dorrance,
1968.
NF/F: $100   **G/VG: $40**

Donovan, Truly. *Chandler's Daughter: A Lexy Connor Mystery.*
First Edition: Aurora, CO: Write Way,
2000.
NF/F: $60   **G/VG: $10**

Dorfman, Ariel. *Terapia.*
First Edition: New York: Seven Stories
Press, 2001.
NF/F: $65   **G/VG: $20**

Doyle, Edard F. *Forty Years a Fan.*
First Edition: Philadelphia: Dorrance,
1972.
NF/F: $150   **G/VG: $60**

Dusart, Jay. *The North American Cowboy: A Portrait.*
First Edition: Prescott, AZ: The
Consortium Press, 1983.
NF/F: $105   **G/VG: $50**

Jeane Cummings.

Alpha De Monte.

Ruth Miller Denning.

John R. Erickson.

F. Scott Fitzgerald.

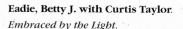

V. Ray Foster.

Eadie, Betty J. with Curtis Taylor.
Embraced by the Light.
First Edition: Placerville, CA: Gold Leaf
Press, 1992.
NF/F: $75   G/VG: $30

Eaves, Louise Ruland. *Turmoil.*
First Edition: Philadelphia: Dorrance,
1973.
NF/F: $130   G/VG: $75

Eisley, Loren. *The Brown Wasps:
a Collection of Three Essays in
Autobiography.*
Limited Edition: Mt. Horeb, WI: The
Perishable Press Limited, 1969 (241
Copies).
NF/F: $2,500   G/VG: Not Seen

Eliot, T.S. *Prufrock And Other
Observations.*
First Edition: London: The Egoist
Press: 1917.
NF/F: $45,000   G/VG: $22,000

Ennis, Willie Jr. *Poetically Speaking.*
First Edition: New York: Exposition
Press, 1957.
NF/F: $150   G/VG: $60

Erb, Russell C. *Poisoning the Public.*
First Edition: Philadelphia: Dorrance,
1937.
NF/F: $55   G/VG: $25

Erickson, John R. *Hank the Cowdog
and The Case of the One-eyed Killer
Stud Horse.*
First Edition: Perryton, TX: Maverick
Books, Inc., 1987.
NF/F: $550   G/VG: $70

Faggett, Harry Lee. *Lines to a Little
Lady.*
First Edition: Philadelphia: Dorrance,
1977.
NF/F: $150   G/VG: $65

Falconer, Lois C. *To Kim with Love.*
First Edition: Pittsburgh: Dorrance,
1983.
NF/F: $50   G/VG: $10

Filanowski, Deborah. *...and Guppies
Eat Their Young.*
First Edition: Philadelphia: Plan B
Press, 2004.
NF/F: $45   G/VG: $15

Finlay, Ian Hamilton. *The Dancers
Inherit the Party.*
First Edition: Worcester, England/
Ventura, CA: The Migrant Press, 1960.
NF/F: $575   G/VG: $75

Firbank, Arthur Annesley Ronald.
*Odette d'Antrevernes and A study in
temperament.*
First Edition: London: Elkin Mathews.
1905.
NF/F: $825   G/VG: $75

Fitzgerald, F. Scott. *Borrowed Time.*
First Edition: London: The Grey Walls
Press, 1951.
NF/F: $680   G/VG: $65

Floyd, E. Randall. *Deep in the Heart.*
First Edition: Augusta, GA: Harbor
House Publishers, 1998.
NF/F: $55   G/VG: $15

Ford, Charles Henri. *The Overturned
Lake.*
First Edition: Cincinnati, OH: Little
Man Press, 1941.
NF/F: $200   G/VG: $85

Foster, V. Ray. *Rebel Blood.*
First Edition: New York: Exposition
Press, 1954.
NF/F: $150   G/VG: $55

Fox, Donald S. *The White Fox of Andhra.*
First Edition: Philadelphia: Dorrance, 1977.
NF/F: $150　　　　**G/VG: $65**

Frances, Mary Lee. *The Tray Upstairs.*
First Edition: Hicksville, NY: Exposition Press, 1983.
NF/F: $150　　　　**G/VG: $65**

Francisco, Timothy and Patricia Weaver. *Village Without Mirrors.*
First Editions: Minneapolis: Milkweed Editions, 1989.
NF/F: $125　　　　**G/VG: $55**

Frank, Peter. *Something Else Press: An Annotated Bibliography.*
First Edition: Kingston, NY: McPherson & Co., 1983.
NF/F: $250　　　　**G/VG: $100**

Fries, Roy E. *Patriotic Thoughts of a Marine.*
First Edition: Philadelphia: Dorrance, 1943.
NF/F: $100　　　　**G/VG: $30**

Frisch, Larry. *The Dream-Boaters.*
First Edition: New York: Exposition Press, 1953.
NF/F: $120　　　　**G/VG: $45**

Frost, Gavin and Yvonne. *THE WITCH'S BIBLE. How to Practice the Oldest Religion.*
First Edition: St. Louis, MO: Al-Jon Press, 1986.
NF/F: $170　　　　**G/VG: $40**

Gardner, Benjamin F. *A Black Man Speaks of Hate.*
First Edition: Philadelphia: Dorrance, 1969.
NF/F: $70　　　　**G/VG: $15**

Gawsworth, John. *Mishka and Madeleine.*
Limited Edition: London: The Twyn Barlwm Press, 1932 (225 copies).
NF/F: $170　　　　**G/VG: $50**

Giancol, Anthony. *The Three Racketeers.*
First Edition: New York: Vantage Press, 1955.
NF/F: $200　　　　**G/VG: $60**

Ginsberg, Allen. *Ankor Wat.*
First Edition: London: Fulcrum Press, 1968.
NF/F: $1,500　　　　**G/VG: $240**

_____. *Illuminated Poems.*
First Edition: New York and London: Four Walls Eight Windows, 1996.
NF/F: $650　　　　**G/VG: $75**

_____. *Honorable Courtship: From the Author's Journals, January 1-15, 1955.*
Limited Edition: Minneapolis, MN: Coffee House Press, 1993 (200 copies). Points of Issue: Five engravings laid in.
NF/F: $450　　　　**G/VG: Not Seen**

Giovanni, Nikki. *Black Feeling Black Talk.*
First Edition: Detroit, MI: privately printed, 1968.
NF/F: $400　　　　**G/VG: $270**

Gish, Mark F. *Pretty Things.*
First Edition: New York: Vantage Press, 1983.
NF/F: $150　　　　**G/VG: $25**

Glick, Peter Jr. *The Aftermath.*
First Edition: New York: Vantage Press, 1965.
NF/F: $120　　　　**G/VG: $20**

Donald S. Fox.

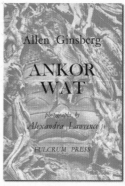
Larry Frisch.

Allen Ginsberg.

ANKOR WAT

photographs by
Alexandra Lawrence

FULCRUM PRESS

Allen Ginsberg.

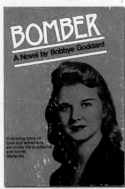

Bobbye Goddard.

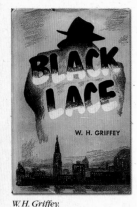

W. H. Griffey.

Jay Hall.

Goddard, Bobbye. *Bomber.*
First Edition: Hicksville, New York:
Exposition Press, 1979.
NF/F: $150　　　　　　**G/VG: $50**

Golas, Thaddeus. *The Lazy Man's Guide to Enlightenment.*
First Edition: Palo Alto, CA: Seed
Center 1972.
NF/F: $200　　　　　　**G/VG: $95**

Goldin, Hyman E. *The Case of the Nazarene Reopened.*
First Edition: New York: Exposition
Press, 1948.
NF/F: $225　　　　　　**G/VG: $100**

Goodman, Paul. *The Dead of Spring.*
Point of Issue: Spiral bound.
First Edition: Glen Gardner, NJ:
Libertarian Press, 1950.
NF/F: $225　　　　　　**G/VG: $75**

_____. *Parents Day.*
First Edition: Saugatuck, CT: The 5x8
Press, 1951.
NF/F: $110　　　　　　**G/VG: $45**

Gorcey, Leo B. *An Original Dead End Kid Presents Dead End Yells, Wedding Bells, Cockle Shells and Dizzy Spells.*
First Edition: New York: Vantage Press,
1967.
NF/F: $785　　　　　　**G/VG: $275**

Graves, Robert. *Over the Brazier.*
First Edition: London: The Poetry
Bookshop, 1916.
NF/F: $2,000　　　　　**G/VG: $1,000**

_____. *To Whom Else?*
Limited Edition: Deya, Majorca: The
Seizin Press, 1931 (200 copies).
NF/F: $850　　　　　　**G/VG: $250**

Griffey, W. H. *Black Lace.*
First Edition: New York: Vantage Press,
1952.
NF/F: $145　　　　　　**G/VG: $35**

Guirdham, Arthur. *Paradise Found.*
First Edition: Winnipeg: Turnstone
Press, 1980.
NF/F: $200　　　　　　**G/VG: $65**

Gunner, Frank. *Crumbling Precipice.*
First Edition: New York: Vantage Press,
1958.
NF/F: $225　　　　　　**G/VG: $70**

Hall, Jay. *Evidently Murdered.*
First Edition: Philadelphia: Dorrance,
1943.
NF/F: $200　　　　　　**G/VG: $75**

Hall, Manly P. *The Lost Keys of Masonry: The Legend of Hiram Abiff.*
First Edition: Los Angeles: privately
published by the author, 1923.
NF/F: $100　　　　　　**G/VG: $35**

Harris, E. Lynn. *Invisible Life.*
First Edition: Atlanta: Consortium
Press, 1991.
NF/F: $200　　　　　　**G/VG: $75**

Harris, Thomas Lake. *Star-Flowers, a Poem of the Woman's Mystery.* (First
Canto).
First Edition: Fountaingrove, CA:
privately printed, 1886.
NF/F: $550　　　　　　**G/VG: $300**

Hass, Robert. *Winter Morning in Charlottesville.*
Limited Edition: Knotting, The Sceptre
Press, 1977 (150 copies).
NF/F: $350　　　　　　**G/VG: $200**

Hatem, J. S. *We Called Them Gods.*
First Edition: New York: Vantage Press, 1976.
NF/F: $225   **G/VG: $90**

Hemingway, Ernest. *In Our Time.*
Limited Edition: Paris: Three
Mountains Press, 1924 (170 copies).
NF/F: $150,000   **G/VG: $50,000**

Hido, Todd. *Outskirts.*
First Edition: Tucson, AZ: Nazraeli
Press, 2002.
NF/F: $1,000   **G/VG: $450**

Holgren, Beryl. *Frank Baney: Forty
Years a Montana Law Enforcer.*
First Edition: New York: Vantage Press, 1965.
NF/F: $75   **G/VG: $36**

Holmes, John Clellon. *The Bowling
Green Poems.*
First Edition: California, PA: Arthur &
Kit Knight, 1977.
NF/F: $125   **G/VG: $55**

Horner, Roland. *Errant Caprice.*
First Edition: New York: Vantage Press, 1955.
NF/F: $100   **G/VG: $25**

Howard, Robert E. *Always Comes
Evening.*
First Edition: Sauk City, WI: Arkham
House, 1957. Points of Issue: Compiled by
Glenn Lord. Published by Arkham House,
subsidized by Lord; 636 copies printed:
the first 536 copies were imprinted on the
spine with the lettering running bottom
to top, European style, the final 100 copies
were imprinted top to bottom, American
style. Both states are about equal.
NF/F: $2,800   **G/VG: $1,250**

Hughes, Ted. *A Solstice.*
Limited Edition: Knotting, The Sceptre
Press, 1978 (350 copies).
NF/F: $350   **G/VG: $50**

Hummel, Leonard C. *An Experience
in Listening to the Dead: The Perils of
Nationalism.*
First Edition: New York: Exposition
Press, 1970.
NF/F: $300   **G/VG: $110**

Humphrey, Lillie Muse. *Aggie.*
First Edition: New York: Vantage Press,
1955.
NF/F: $125   **G/VG: $35**

Ilonka. *Sex Cage.*
First Edition: New York: Vantage Press,
1969.
NF/F: $225   **G/VG: $75**

Jacocha-Ernst, Chris. *A Cthulhu
Mythos Bibliography and
Concordance.*
First Edition: Seattle, WA: Tynes
Cowan, 1997.
NF/F: $50   **G/VG: $30**

Jarry, Hawke. *Black School-Master.*
First Edition: New York: Exposition
Press, 1970.
NF/F: $150   **G/VG: $65**

Jarvis, Antoine J. *The Virgin Islands
and their People.*
First Edition: Philadelphia: Dorrance,
1944.
NF/F: $80   **G/VG: $25**

Jeffers, Robinson. *Stars.*
First Edition: The Flame Press:
Pasadena, 1930. Points of Issue: Bound
in black paper boards. All but six
copies were destroyed prices below
are simply the two I found for sale.
NF/F: $12,500   **G/VG: $2,850**
Second Issue: The Flame Press:
Pasadena, 1930 (110 copies). Points of
Issue: Bound in blue wraps.
NF/F: $750   **G/VG: $200**

Robert E. Howard.

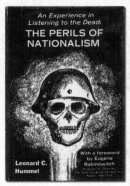

Leonard C. Hummel.

Ilonka.

Latifa Johnson.

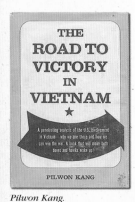

Pilwon Kang.

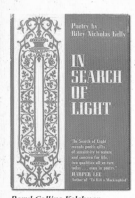

Beryl Collins Kelchner.

Johnson, Dewayne B. & Kenn Thomas. *Flying Saucers Over Los Angeles.* First Edition: Kempton, IL: Adventures Unlimited Press, 1998.
NF/F: $75   **G/VG: $15**

Johnson, G. P. *I Was Fighting for Peace, But, Lord, There Was Much More.* First Edition: Hicksville, NY: Exposition Press, 1979.
NF/F: $200   **G/VG: $45**

Johnson, Latifa. *Sheila Goes to Reno.* First Edition: New York: Vantage Press, 1952.
NF/F: $120   **G/VG: $45**

Johnson, Robert Leland. *The American Heritage of James Norman Hall.* First Edition: Philadelphia: Dorrance, 1969.
NF/F: $140   **G/VG: $55**

Kang, Pilwon. *The Road to Victory in Vietnam.* First Edition: New York: Exposition Press, 1970.
NF/F: $95   **G/VG: $30**

Kenney, Elna E. *Under the Saucer's Shadow.* First Edition: New York: Vantage Press, 1974.
NF/F: $225   **G/VG: $50**

Kelchner, Beryl Collins. *In Search of Light.* First Edition: New York: Exposition Press, 1969.
NF/F: $45   **G/VG: $10**

Kelly, Riley Nicholas. *Overtones of Time.* First Edition: New York: Exposition Press, 1953.
NF/F: $350   **G/VG: $100**

Kemp, Raymond. *Love, Sex, and Marriage.* First Edition: New York: Vantage Press, 1968.
NF/F: $150   **G/VG: $50**

Kennedy, B.F. Jr. *Buried Treasure of Casco Bay.* First Edition: New York: Vantage Press, 1963.
NF/F: $125   **G/VG: $40**

Kerouac, Jack. *Book of Dreams.* First Edition: San Francisco: City Lights Books, 1961. Points of Issue: The First State has dark blue wraps.
NF/F: $475   **G/VG: $175**

King, Robert B. *Ferguson's Castle.* First Edition: Hicksville, NY: Exposition Press, 1978.
NF/F: $75   **G/VG: $25**

Kinsella, W. P. *The Alligator Report.* First Edition: Minneapolis, MN: Coffee House Press, 1985.
NF/F: $60   **G/VG: $20**

_____. *The First and Last Annual Six Towns Area Old Timers' Baseball Game.* Limited Edition: Minneapolis, MN: Coffee House Press, 1991 (150 copies). Points of Issue: Five loose engravings laid in.
NF/F: $500   **G/VG: Not Seen**

Knight, Angela. *The Forever Kiss.* First Edition: Seminole, FL: Red Sage Publishing, 2004.
NF/F: $60   **G/VG: $10**

Kunitz, Stanley. *The Wellfleet Whale.* First Edition: New York: Sheep Meadow Press, 1983.
NF/F: $80   **G/VG: $20**

L'Amour, Louis. *Smoke From This Altar.*
First Edition: Oklahoma City: Lusk Publishing Company, 1939.
NF/F: $5,000　　　　**G/VG: $875**

LaCroix, Ernest O. *Banking is Serious Business (Don't You Believe It!).*
First Edition: Hicksville, New York: Exposition Press, 1979.
NF/F: $95　　　　**G/VG: $30**

Lasner, Robert. *For Fucks Sake.*
First Edition: Brooklyn, NY: Ig publishing, 2002.
NF/F: $95　　　　**G/VG: $30**

Lawrence, D.H. *The Paintings of D.H. Lawrence.*
Limited Edition: London: The Mandrake Press, 1929 (510 copies).
NF/F: $1,200　　　　**G/VG: $400**

Levi, Primo. *Shema: Collected Poems of Primo Levi.*
First Edition: London: Menard Press, 1976.
NF/F: $120　　　　**G/VG: $35**

Levy, Burt S. *The Last Open Road: A Novel.*
First Edition: Oak Park, Illinois, U.S.A.: Think Fast Ink, 1994.
NF/F: $60　　　　**G/VG: $20**

Lewis, Janet. *The Wheel in Midsummer.* Points of Issue: Paperback Original.
First Edition: Lynn: The Lone Gull, 1927.
NF/F: $385　　　　**G/VG: $200**

_____. *The Wife of Martin Guerre.*
First Edition: San Francisco: Colt Press, 1941.
NF/F: $325　　　　**G/VG: $150**

Leyner, Mark. *I Smell Esther Williams & Other Stories.*
First Edition: Tallahassee, FL: Fiction Collective Two, 1983.
NF/F: $250　　　　**G/VG: $75**

Liggett, William. *My Seventy-five Years Along the Mexican Border.*
First Edition: New York: Exposition Press, 1964.
NF/F: $250　　　　**G/VG: $100**

Lindsay, Vachel. *The Tree of Laughing Bells.*
First Edition: n.p.: by the Author, 1905.
NF/F: $3,000　　　　**G/VG: $1,400**

_____. *Rhymes To Be Traded For Bread.* Points of Issue: Staple bound on newsprint stock.
First Edition: Springfield, IL: by the Author, 1912.
NF/F: $850　　　　**G/VG: $400**

Lord, Eric Meredith. *The Wayward Angel: A Comedy-Fantasy in Three Acts.*
First Edition: Exposition Press: New York, 1965.
NF/F: $100　　　　**G/VG: $75**

Lowell, Susan. *Ganado Red.*
First Edition: Minneapolis: Milkweed Editions, 1988.
NF/F: $170　　　　**G/VG: $20**

Machen, Arthur. *Chapters Five and Six of The Secret Glory.*
First Edition: Leyburn, UK: Tartarus Press, 1991.
NF/F: $150　　　　**G/VG: $60**

Mackey, James Dean. *Us Fellers.*
First Edition: Philadelphia: Dorrance, 1953.
NF/F: $175　　　　**G/VG: $55**

Ernest O. LaCroix.

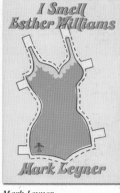
Mark Leyner.

James Dean Mackey.

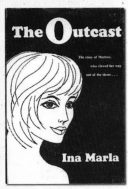

Ina Marla.

Joseph A. Marshal.

Joan M. Mercier.

Macnee, Patrick. *Blind in One Ear: the Avenger Returns.*
First Edition: San Francisco: Mercury House, 1992.
NF/F: $100   **G/VG: $25**

MacRae, Kevin. *Nikki.*
First Edition: New York: Vantage Press, 1955.
NF/F: $110   **G/VG: $30**

Madelin, Richard. *Careful!*
First Edition: Brooklyn. NY: Ig Publishing, 2004.
NF/F: $70   **G/VG: $8**

Manno, Martha. *Sundays at Sarah's: An Anthology of Women's Writing.*
First Edition: Seekonk, MA: Little Pear Press, 2003.
NF/F: $35   **G/VG: $10**

Marla, Ina. *Outcast.*
First Edition: New York: Exposition Press, 1954.
NF/F: $125   **G/VG: $40**

Marshal, Joseph A. *Leather Lungs.*
First Edition: Philadelphia: Dorrance, 1974.
NF/F: $200   **G/VG: $85**

Martinez, Soraida. *Verdadism.*
First Edition: Lindenwold, NJ: Soraida Books, 1999.
NF/F: $75   **G/VG: $30**

Maximoff, Nicholas. *Afanassiev is Dead.*
First Edition: New York: Exposition Press, 1965.
NF/F: $85   **G/VG: $50**

McCaffrey, Anne. *A Time When.*
Limited Edition: Boston: NESFA Press, 1975 (800 copies).
NF/F: $800   **G/VG: $200**

McConnell, Jean S. *The Round Tower.*
First Edition: Philadelphia: Dorrance, 1966.
NF/F: $125   **G/VG: $25**

McGee, Bob. *Three Dozen Sonnets.*
First Edition: Montreal: Vehicule Press, 1973.
NF/F: $100   **G/VG: $20**

McGowan, William N. *Put Something There To Touch.*
First Edition: New York: Vantage Press, 1999.
NF/F: $50   **G/VG: $15**

McGuiness, Ryan. *flatnessisgod.*
First Edition: New York: Soft Skull Press, 1973.
NF/F: $105   **G/VG: $40**

Mercier, Joan M. *The Mystery of the Disappearing Pets.*
First Edition: New York: Vantage Press, 1965.
NF/F: $100   **G/VG: $40**

Miller, Henry. *Remember to Remember.*
London: Grey Walls Press, 1952.
NF/F: $600   **G/VG: $100**

_____. *Of By & About Henry Miller: A Collection of Pieces.*
First Edition: Yonkers, NY: Alicat Bookshop Press, 1947.
NF/F: $750   **G/VG: $200**

Miller, Virgil E. *Splinters from Hollywood Tripods: Memoirs of a Cameraman.*
First Edition: New York: Exposition Press, 1964.
NF/F: $350   **G/VG: $75**

Minty, Judith. *Letters to My Daughters.*
First Edition: Ann Arbor, MI: Mayapple Press, 1980.
NF/F: $45   **G/VG: $10**

Misrach, Richard. *Telegraph 3 A.M. : the street people of Telegraph Avenue, Berkeley, California : photographs/by Richard Misrach.*
First Edition: Berkeley, CA: Cornucopia Press, 1974.
NF/F: $835   **G/VG: $300**

Mo, Timothy. *Brownout on Breadfruit Boulevard.*
First Edition: London, Paddleless Press, 1995.
NF/F: $75   **G/VG: $30**

Molnar, E. F. *The Slave of Ea: A Sumerian Legend.*
First Edition: Philadelphia: Dorrance, 1934.
NF/F: $350   **G/VG: $120**

Moore, Allen H., M. D. *Mustard Plaster's And Printer's Ink. A Kaleidoscope Of A Country Doctor's Observations About People, Places And Things.*
First Edition: New York: Exposition Press, 1959.
NF/F: $195   **G/VG: $30**

Morse, A. Hastings. *Blondes Prefer Gentlemen.*
First Edition: Philadelphia: Dorrance, 1938.
NF/F: $250   **G/VG: $100**

Murphy, James M. *The Gabby Hartnett Story: From a Mill Town to Cooperstown.*
First Edition: Smithtown, NY: Exposition Press, 1983.
NF/F: $350   **G/VG: $135**

Nelson, C. M. *The Fortunate Years.*
First Edition: New York: Vantage Press, 1983.
NF/F: $250   **G/VG: $70**

Neuberg, Victor. *Swift Wings: Songs of Sussex.*
Limited Edition: Steyning: The Vine Press, 1921 (590 copies).
NF/F: $220   **G/VG: $175**

Newman, Judith Sternberg. *In the Hell of Auschwitz.*
First Edition: New York: Exposition Press, 1963.
NF/F: $80   **G/VG: $35**

Nin, Anais. *Winter of Artifice.*
Limited Edition: New York: Gemor Press, nd (1942) (500 copies).
NF/F: $2,200   **G/VG: $300**

Oden, Gloria. *Naked Frame - Love Poems By.*
First Edition: New York: Exposition Press, 1952.
NF/F: $130   **G/VG: $40**

Oe, Kenzaburo. *Nip the Buds, Shoot the Kids.*
First Edition: London and New York: Marion Boyers, 1995.
NF/F: $200   **G/VG: $60**

O'Hara, Frank. *Lunch Poems.*
First Edition: San Francisco: City Lights Books, 1964. Points of Issue: $125 price on the cover.
NF/F: $1,000   **G/VG: $150**

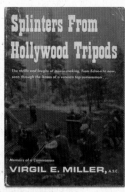

Virgil E. Miller.

E. F. Molnar.

A. Hastings Morse.

Michael Ondaatje.

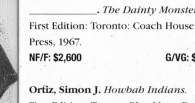

Olga Park.

Kenneth Patchen.

Oldenburg, Claes, and Emmett Williams. *Store Days: Documents from the Store and Ray Gun Theater.*
First Edition: New York: Something Else Press, 1967.
NF/F: $1,000   **G/VG: $180**

Ondaatje, Michael. *Rat Jelly.*
First Edition: Toronto: Coach House Press, 1973.
NF/F: $1,500   **G/VG: $175**

_____. *Claude Glass.*
First Edition: Toronto: Coach House Press, 1979.
NF/F: $250   **G/VG: $90**

_____. *The Dainty Monsters.*
First Edition: Toronto: Coach House Press, 1967.
NF/F: $2,600   **G/VG: $90**

Ortiz, Simon J. *Howbah Indians.*
First Edition: Tucson: Blue Moon Press. 1978.
NF/F: $175   **G/VG: $45**

O'Sheel, Shaemas. *The Blossomy Bough: Poems.*
First Edition: New York: published by the author through The Franklin Press, 1911.
NF/F: $125   **G/VG: $45**

Park, Olga. *Between Time & Eternity.*
First Edition: New York: Vantage Press, 1960.
NF/F: $85   **G/VG: $40**

Patchen, Kenneth. *Outlaw of the Lowest Planet.*
First Edition: London: The Grey Walls Press, 1946.
NF/F: $500   **G/VG: $45**

_____. *The Journal of Albion Moonlight.*
First Edition: Mount Vernon, NY: By the Author, 1941. Points of Issue: An edition of 50 followed by an edition of 265, generally treated as a single issue.
NF/F: $750   **G/VG: $250**

_____. *To Say If You Love Someone.*
First Edition: Prairie City, IL: The Decker Press, 1948.
NF/F: $3,500   **G/VG: $1,200**

Paul, Doris A. *The Navajo Code Talkers.*
First Edition: Philadelphia: Dorrance, 1973.
NF/F: $875   **G/VG: $95**

Pearce, Michael. *The Snake Catcher's Daughter.*
First Edition: Scottsdale, AZ: Poisoned Pen Press, 2000.
NF/F: $100   **G/VG: $30**

Pickens, Vinton Liddell. *Serendipity.*
First Edition: New York: Vantage Press, 1964.
NF/F: $100   **G/VG: $25**

Pickering, Lucy. *Birds of Sorrow.*
First Edition: New York: Vantage Press, 1978.
NF/F: $80   **G/VG: $40**

Plath, Sylvia. *Wreath for a Bridal.*
Limited Edition: Farnham: The Sceptre Press, 1970 (100 copies).
NF/F: $330   **G/VG: $180**

Plexus, Paul P. *Realism.*
First Edition: New York: Vantage Press, 1978.
NF/F: $50   **G/VG: $10**

Popoff, Irmis B. *GURDJIEFF: His Work on Myself, With Others, For the Work.*
First Edition: New York: Vantage Press, 1969.
NF/F: $200   **G/VG: $70**

Potter, Beatrix. *The Adventures of Peter Rabbit.*
London: Privately printed for the author by Strangeways, London, 1901.
Points of Issue: The first print run was 250 copies designated by the 1901 date, the second run was 1902.
NF/F: $85,000   **G/VG: $45,000**

Pound, Ezra. *A Draft of XXX Cantos.*
Limited Edition: Paris: Hours Press, 1930 (200 copies).
NF/F: $8,700   **G/VG: $1,500**

_____. *Indiscretions.*
Limited Edition: Paris: Three Mountains Press, 1923 (300 copies).
NF/F: $1,600   **G/VG: $600**

_____. *Imaginary Letters.*
First Edition: Paris: Black Sun Press, 1930. Points of Issue: Printed on Navarre Paper.
NF/F: $3,000   **G/VG: $1,450**

Powers, Tim. *An Epitaph in Rust.*
Limited Edition: Boston: NESFA Press, 1989 (1,000 copies).
NF/F: $250   **G/VG: $80**

Pratt, Sherman W. *Decisive Battles of the Korean War.*
First Edition: New York: Vantage Press, 1992.
NF/F: $200   **G/VG: $65**

Redfield, James. *The Celestine Prophecy.*
First Edition: Hoover, Alabama: Satori Publishing, 1993.
NF/F: $2,500   **G/VG: $475**

Reed, Lynnel. *Lynnel Be Not Afraid; Biography of Madame Rider-Kelsey.*
First Edition: New York: Vantage Press, 1955.
NF/F: $70   **G/VG: $45**

Reed, Mary and Eric Mayer. *Two for Joy.*
First Edition: Scottsdale, AZ: Poisoned Pen Press, 2000.
NF/F: $170   **G/VG: $25**

Reid, Forest. *Notes and Impressions.*
First Edition: Newcastle, The Mourne Press, 1942.
NF/F: $300   **G/VG: $95**

Rember, Winthrop Allen. *Eighteen Visits To Mars.*
First Editions: New York: Vantage Press, 1956.
NF/F: $500   **G/VG: $210**

Rexroth, Kenneth. *The Art of Worldly Wisdom.*
First Edition: Prairie City, IL: Decker Press, 1949.
NF/F: $450   **G/VG: $150**

Rhodes, Eugene Manlove. *Little World Waddies.*
First Edition: Chico, CA: Carl Hertzog, Printer, 1946.
NF/F: $500   **G/VG: $200**

Riding, Laura. *Four Unposted Letters to Catherine.*
First Edition: Paris: Hours Press, 1930 (200 copies).
NF/F: $1,000   **G/VG: $275**

Roberts, Glen. *Prometheus Outnumbered.*
First Edition: Philadelphia: Dorrance, 1969.
NF/F: $80   **G/VG: $15**

Robinson, Emily Parker. *Blacks in the Deep South.*
First Edition: New York: Vantage Press, 1974.
NF/F: $160   **G/VG: $45**

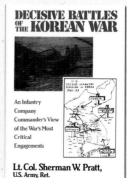

Sherman W. Pratt.

Emily Parker Robinson.

Henry Marco Ross.

Harry G. Scott.

Mitzi Shodo.

Rodman, Julius Scammon. *The Kahuna Sorcerers of Hawaii, Past and Present with a Glossary of Ancient Religious Terms and the Books of the Hawaiian Royal Dead.* First Edition: Smithtown, NY: Exposition Press, 1979.
NF/F: $350   **G/VG: $100**

Ross, Henry Marco. *That Fatal Year and Selected Stories.*
First Edition: New York: Exposition Press, 1968.
NF/F: $70   **G/VG: $15**

Roth, Dieter. *246 Little Clouds.*
First Edition: New York: Something Else Press, 1967.
NF/F: $1,000   **G/VG: $225**

Rountree, Moses. *Strangers in the Land.*
First Edition: Philadelphia: Dorrance, 1969.
NF/F: $90   **G/VG: $60**

Rowley, Richard. *Fifty Sonnets for Felicity.* Newcastle, The Mourne Press, 1942.
NF/F: $120   **G/VG: $80**

Rukeyser, Muriel. *Orpheus.*
First Edition: San Francisco: Centaur Press, 1949.
NF/F: $125   **G/VG: $50**

Sallis, James. *Limits of the Sensible World.*
First Edition: Austin, TX: Host Publications, 1994.
NF/F: $75   **G/VG: $15**

Schumacher, George. *Maurice Thompson Archer and Author.*
First Edition: New York: Vantage Press, 1968.
NF/F: $125   **G/VG: $45**

Scott, Harry G. (Intro by Grantland Rice.) *Jock Sutherland.*
First Edition: New York: Exposition Press, 1954.
NF/F: $75   **G/VG: $35**

Seers, Stan. *UFOs - The Case for Scientific Myopia.*
First Edition: New York: Vantage Press, 1983.
NF/F: $200   **G/VG: $65**

Shapiro, Eddie. *Peddlers of the Flesh.*
First Edition: New York: Vantage Press, 1959.
NF/F: $150   **G/VG: $50**

Shepard, Sam. *Motel Chronicles.*
San Francisco: City Lights Books, 1982.
NF/F: $450   **G/VG: $50**

Shijachki, Milan D. *The Red Mata Hari.*
First Edition: New York: Exposition Press, 1957.
NF/F: $75   **G/VG: $30**

Shodo, Mitzi. *The Juice of the Lemon is Sour.*
First Edition: New York: Vantage Press, 1970.
NF/F: $260   **G/VG: $85**

Sholl, Anna McClure. *The Unclaimed Letter.*
First Edition: Philadelphia: Dorrance, 1921.
NF/F: $80   **G/VG: $20**

Simic, Charles. *Nine Poems. A Childhood Story.*
First Edition: Cambridge: Exact Change, 1989 (25 signed copies, 500 total copies. Unsigned priced).
NF/F: $200   **G/VG: $50**

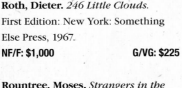

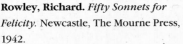

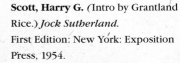

Sinclair, Iain. *Suicide Bridge.*
First Edition: London: Albion Village
Press, 1979.
NF/F: $95   **G/VG: $40**

_____. *The Kodak Mantra
Diaries October 1966 to June 1971.*
First Edition: London: Albion Village
Press, 1971. Points of Issue: Spiral
Bound elephant folio.
NF/F: $210   **G/VG: $100**

_____. *Lud Heat.*
First Edition: London: Albion Village
Press, 1975.
NF/F: $140   **G/VG: $100**

Sinclair, Upton. *Oil!*
First Edition: Pasadena, CA: By the
Author, 1927.
NF/F: $3,750   **G/VG: $750**

_____. *The Goose Step.*
First Edition: Pasadena, CA: By the
Author, 1923.
NF/F: $800   **G/VG: $85**

Smith, Evelyn Charlotte. *The Twisted
Strands of Fate and Other Stories.*
First Edition: New York: Vantage Press,
1990.
NF/F: $50   **G/VG: $20**

Smyth, Robert. *Broken Arrows.*
First Edition: Cambridge, MA: Yellow
Moon Press, 1982.
NF/F: $40   **G/VG: $20**

Snyder, Earl. *General Leemy's Circus:
A Navigator's Story of the 20th Air
Force in World War II.*
First Edition: New York: Exposition
Press, 1955.
NF/F: $140   **G/VG: $30**

Snyder, Gary. *Riprap.*
First Edition: Ashland, MA: Origin
Press, 1959.
NF/F: $2,000   **G/VG: $950**

_____. *Six Sections From
Mountains And Rivers Without End.*
First Edition: San Francisco: Four
Seasons Foundation, 1965.
NF/F: $275   **G/VG: $95**

Sondergard, Sid. *The Smile of
Blazing Wings and Other Plays.*
Hicksville, NY: Exposition Press, 1978.
NF/F: $55   **G/VG: $15**

Spencer, Camika C. *When All Hell
Breaks Loose.*
First Edition: Dallas, TX: Akimac
Publishing, 1997.
NF/F: $55   **G/VG: $15**

Spencer Magee, Grace. *Ten Angels in
A Pontiac.*
First Edition: New York: Exposition
Press, 1965.
NF/F: $125   **G/VG: $40**

Stamey, DeKeller. *The Spirit of the
Belfry.*
First Edition: Philadelphia: Dorrance,
1935.
NF/F: $55   **G/VG: $15**

Starker, Terry. *Red Sky in Mourning.*
First Edition: Baltimore, MD:
PublishAmerica, 2005.
NF/F: $85   **G/VG: $25**

Stein, Gertrude. *An Acquaintance
With Description.*
Limited Edition: London, The Seizin
Press, 1929 (225 copies).
NF/F: $2,250   **G/VG: $750**

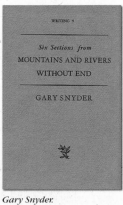

WRITING 9

Six Sections from
MOUNTAINS AND RIVERS
WITHOUT END

GARY SNYDER

Gary Snyder.

THE SPIRIT
OF THE
BELFRY

DeKELLER STAMEY

DeKeller Stamey.

Leonard Christopher Swan.

Christy Thomas.

Stevens, Wallace. *Selected Poems.*
First Edition: London: The Fortune
Press, 1952.
NF/F: $550   **G/VG: $200**

Stewart, Rosemary. *Checkmate.*
First Edition: New York: Vantage Press,
1991.
NF/F: $120   **G/VG: $25**

Stimson, Edward W. *Renewal in
Christ.*
First Edition: New York: Vantage Press,
1979.
NF/F: $125   **G/VG: $75**

Stoddard, William O. *Lincoln's Third
Secretary The Memoirs of William O.
Stoddard.*
First Edition: New York: Exposition
Press, 1955.
NF/F: $60   **G/VG: $25**

_____. *Anything Goes: Origins
of the Cult of Scientific Irrationalism.*
First Edition: Sydney: Macleay Press,
1998.
NF/F: $200   **G/VG: $40**

Swan, Leonard Christopher. *Hello
Doctor! I've Got a Dog.*
First Edition: New York: Exposition
Press, 1974.
NF/F: $90   **G/VG: $20**

Stove, David. *Scientific Irrationalism.*
First Edition: Sydney: Macleay Press,
1998.
NF/F: $800   **G/VG: $135**

Tassi, Dan. *The Mind and Time and
Space.*
First Edition: Philadelphia: Dorrance,
1962.
NF/F: $75   **G/VG: $25**

Taylor, Albert. *Soul Traveler: a Guide
to Out of Body Experiences and the
Wonders Beyond.*
First Edition: Covina, CA: Verity Press,
1996.
NF/F: $280   **G/VG: $125**

Taylor, Marie. *The Last Laugh.*
First Edition: New York: Vantage Press,
1992.
NF/F: $60   **G/VG: $20**

Thomas, Christy. *Newshawk.*
First Edition: New York: Exposition
Press, 1962.
NF/F: $75   **G/VG: $25**

Thoreau, Henry David. *A Week On
The Concord And Merrimac Rivers.*
First Edition: Boston and Cambridge:
James Munroe, 1849. Points of Issue:
Basically vanity published, Thoreau
got most of the first printing cut and
gathered binding as they sold over
a number of years so the bindings
vary widely.
NF/F: $19,500   **G/VG: $7,000**

Toplitsky, Tania. *It Happened in a
Rooming House.*
First Edition: New York: Vantage Press,
1970.
NF/F: $55   **G/VG: $20**

Tucker, Joe. *Steelers' Victory After Forty.*
First Edition: Hicksville, NY: Exposition Press, 1973.
NF/F: $170   **G/VG: $65**

Twilight, Astrella. *Crown of Flame: Book 1: The First Kindling.*
First Edition: Baltimore: PublishAmerica, 2008.
NF/F: $60   **G/VG: $20**

Tyrrell, Patricia Anne. *The Bones in the Womb.*
First Edition: Newquay, Cornwall: Sixforty Press, 2002.
NF/F: $90   **G/VG: $25**

Upfield, Arthur W. *The House of Cain.*
First Edition: Philadelphia: Dorrance, 1929.
NF/F: $3,500   **G/VG: $1,550**

Vaiol, Jane. *Becky's Little World.*
First Edition: New York: Exposition Press, 1957.
NF/F: $60   **G/VG: $25**

Van Liere, Edward J. *A Doctor Enjoys Sherlock Holmes.*
First Edition: New York: Vantage Press, 1969.
NF/F: $200   **G/VG: $40**

Varma, Devendra P. *The Evergreen Tree of Diabolical Knowledge.*
First Edition: Washington, DC: Consortium Press, 1972.
NF/F: $385   **G/VG: $100**

Vassilatos, Gerry. *Secrets of Cold War Technology: Project HAARP and Beyond.*
First Edition: Kempton, IL: Adventures Unlimited Press, 2000.
NF/F: $315   **G/VG: $150**

_____. *Lost Science.*
First Edition: Kempton, IL: Adventures Unlimited Press, 2000.
NF/F: $170   **G/VG: $50**

Vaucher, Gee. *Crass Art and Other Pre Post-Modernist Monsters.*
First Edition: Oakland, CA: AK Press, 1999.
NF/F: $300   **G/VG: $100**

Vicari, Justin. *In a Garden of Eden.*
First Edition: Philadelphia: Plan B Press, 2004.
NF/F: $80   **G/VG: $15**

Vidal, Gore. *A Thirsty Evil: Seven Short Stories.*
First Edition: New York: The Zero Press, 1956.
NF/F: $330   **G/VG: $100**

Virg, Leo. *Twenty Trillion Light-Years Through Space.*
First Edition: New York: Vantage Press, 1958.
NF/F: $50   **G/VG: $15**

Vitto, Frank. *To Know You Care....*
First Edition: New York: Vantage Press, 1974.
NF/F: $60   **G/VG: $15**

Arthur W. Upfield.

Gerry Vassilatos.

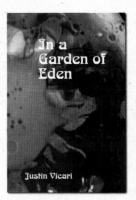
Justin Vicari.

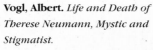

Rocky Whitely.

G.T. Whitson.

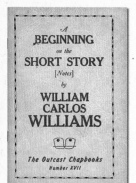

William Carlos Williams.

Vogl, Albert. *Life and Death of Therese Neumann, Mystic and Stigmatist.*
First Edition: New York: Vantage Press, 1978.
NF/F: $100   **G/VG: $35**

Wade, Horace. *Tales of the Turf.*
First Edition: New York: Vantage Press, 1956.
NF/F: $60   **G/VG: $10**

Wadsworth, Edward. *The Black Country.*
First Edition: London: The Ovid Press, 1920.
NF/F: $670   **G/VG: $250**

Waldman, Anne. *Nice to See You. Homage to Ted Berrigan.*
First Edition: Minneapolis, MN: Coffee House Press, 1991.
NF/F: $100   **G/VG: $40**

Walker, Jennie (Charles Boyle). *24 for 3.*
London: CB Editions, 2007.
NF/F: $110   **G/VG: $60**

West, Nathaniel. *The Dream Life Of Balso Snell.*
First Edition: Paris: Contact Editions, 1931.
NF/F: $4,250   **G/VG: $2,100**

Wheelock, Gertrude Mercia. *A Fairy Story for Little Girls.*
First Edition: Philadelphia: Dorrance, 1922.
NF/F: $125   **G/VG: $45**

White, 'Ceil. *Tomorrow Is Another Day.*
First Edition: Philadelphia: Dorrance, 1941.
NF/F: $125   **G/VG: $50**

Whitely, Rocky. *Crazy Charlie's Crew.*
First Edition: Hicksville, New York: Exposition Press, 1977.
NF/F: $125   **G/VG: $50**

Whitson, G.T. *Roaring Wheels.*
First Edition: Philadelphia: Dorrance, 1947.
NF/F: $450   **G/VG: $170**

Willeford, Charles. *Proletarian Laughter. Poems.*
First Edition: Yonkers, NY: The Alicat Bookshop Press, 1948.
NF/F: $575   **G/VG: $125**

Williams, William Carlos. *A Beginning on the Short Story.*
First Edition: Yonkers, NY: The Alicat Bookshop Press, 1950. Points of Issue: Known to go beyond stated 750 copy limit, binding varies, cream and tan, priority unknown.
NF/F: $275   **G/VG: $50**

_____. *The Knife of the Times and Other Stories.*
First Edition: Ithaca, NY: The Dragon Press, 1932.
NF/F: $1,500   **G/VG: $275**

_____. *An Early Martyr.*
First Edition: New York: The Alcestis
Press, 1935.
NF/F: $3,200   **G/VG: $1,600**

_____. *Kora in Hell:
Improvisations.*
First Edition: Boston: The Four Seas
Company, 1920.
NF/F: $750   **G/VG: $350**

Williamson, Hugh P. *South of the
Middle Border.*
First Edition: Philadelphia: Dorrance,
1946.
NF/F: $120   **G/VG: $40**

Wilson, T. P. Cameron. *Magpies in
Picardy.*
First Edition: London: The Poetry
Bookshop, 1919.
NF/F: $125   **G/VG: $70**

Wolfe, Gene. *Planet Engineering.*
Limited Edition: Boston: NESFA Press,
1984 (1,000 copies).
NF/F: $85   **G/VG: $30**

Wood, Bentley. *Wildlife Ripoff - Texas
Style - A Game Warden's Expose.*
First Edition: Hicksville, New York:
Exposition Press, 1975.
NF/F: $150   **G/VG: $60**

Wright, Bruce. *The Ghost of North
America: The Story of the Eastern
Panther.*
First Edition: New York: Vantage Press,
1959.
NF/F: $120   **G/VG: $35**

Zoline, Pamela. *The Heat Death of
the Universe.*
First Edition: Kingston, NY:
McPherson & Co., 1988. Points of
Issue: Issued in blue boards in a mylar
dust jacket.
NF/F: $175   **G/VG: $90**

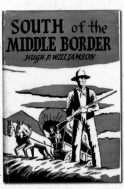

Hugh P. Williamson.

VINTAGE FICTION

A box of old books has a certain smell. I've never been able to describe it. It's not quite musty, though I suppose that's as good a word for it as any. There are elements of tobacco and leather, and fine wine; elements of sunshine, and dark closed places. I first encountered it in my grandmother's attic on Long Island and I guess you could say it clung to me.

If we view the craft of fiction, which is really being a very good, professional liar, by the conventions of the craft rather than a calendar, modern fiction began to develop in the nineteen twenties. Several eras preceded it. The odor I remember so well is how they smell in my mind when I find some of them.

A little more than a century ago, fiction writing was almost a language onto itself. Called "purple prose," the fiction of the 19th century featured overblown, poetic descriptions, and sentences that filled a page or two without stopping for a breath. Fascinating, wonderful stuff to read. Its masters were Edward Bulwer-Lytton, Prime Minister Benjamin Disraeli and the man from the Isle of Man, Hall Caine. For many years, the literary controversy over the finest novel centered on two books, *Pelham* by Bulwer-Lytton and *Vivian Grey* by Disraeli. The curious fact is that this era of overblown description, twisty allegory and symbolic prose produced what is still considered the best, or certainly one of the best, novels ever written, Herman Melville's *Moby Dick, or The Whale*.

The 18th century produced many wonderful books as well. Some of these have become enduring classics, and abridged for children and young readers. *Robinson Crusoe* and *Gulliver's Travels* top the list of great 18th century fiction commonly abridged to introduce children to literature.

As the 19th century wound down, young writers began writing in a "conversational" style. Their books came out like a story told before a roaring fire on a winter's night. Arthur Conan Doyle, James M. Barrie, Henry Rider Haggard and others began telling stories as if some old man was sitting with his grandchildren to remember the past. Some figures crossed over the lines between "purple prose" era and the conversational style. Arthur Machen's unique prose, for example, would be exploited by horror and other writers right on to the best seller list today, a prime example being Stephen King.

For the collector, these old books can be a wonderful area to play about in. A lot of the books were best sellers in their day, and still are relatively common as well as relatively inexpensive.

Vintage fiction is wonderful to read and fascinating to collect. The smell lingers in your mind and the thoughts stay on the tip of your brain.

TEN CLASSIC RARITIES

Bierce, Ambrose. *Can Such Things Be?* New York: Cassell, 1893. In this case, obviously.
NF/F: $6,500   **G/VG: $3,750**

Collins, Wilkie. *The Woman In White.* (Three Volumes).
London: Sampson Low, Son & Co, 1860. No mystery to making out on this.
NF/F: $16,000   **G/VG: $7,500**

Crane, Stephen (as by Johnston Smith). *Maggie a Girl of the Streets.* New York: Self-Published, 1893. Should keep you off the streets.
NF/F: $30,000   **G/VG: $12,000**

Eliot, George. *The Mill on the Floss.* (Three-volume set).
Edinburgh and London: William Blackwood, 1860. Two Bindings A) original orange-brown cloth, with 16 pages of ads in volume three. No ad leaf in the front of volume one. B) light brown cloth with blindstamped covers and gilt titles to the spine.
NF/F: $5,200   **G/VG: $2,100**

Hawthorne, Nathaniel. *The Scarlet Letter.*
Boston: Ticknor, Reed & Fields, 1850. First State has a misprint "reduplicate" for "repudiate" at line 20 page 21.
NF/F: $13,500   **G/VG: $5,500**

James, Henry. *Daisy Miller: A Comedy In Three Acts.*
Boston: James R Osgood & Co, 1883. First hardcover issue binding with James R. Osgood colophon on spine.
NF/F: $1,200   **G/VG: $600**

Melville, Herman. *Moby-Dick; or, The Whale.*
New York: Harper & Brothers, 1851. First American edition, first unexpurgated edition. Most were destroyed in a fire, those left are red hot collectibles.
NF/F: $101,000   **G/VG: $62,500**

Morris, William. *The Life and Death of Jason.*
Hammersmith: Kelmscott Press, 1895. Printed in red and black, with two full-page illustrations by Edward Burne-Jones and initials and decorations by Morris. Bound in limp vellum with ribbon ties.
NF/F: $15,000   **G/VG: $6,200**

Trollope, Anthony. *Prime Minister.*
London: Chapman & Hall, 1876. First Edition in the eight monthly parts: brown cloth-cased with original printed wrappers bound in.
NF/F: $7,000   **G/VG: $2,500**

Twain, Mark. *The Adventures of Tom Sawyer.*
London: Chatto and Windus, [June] 1876. The true first edition of the American classic.
NF/F: $28,000   **G/VG: $9,500**

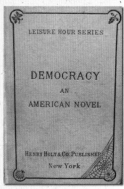

Henry Adams.

PRICE GUIDE

Adams, Henry. *Democracy: An American Novel.*
First Edition: New York: Henry Holt and Company, 1880.
NF/F: $600   **G/VG: $175**

Adams, John Turvill. *Knight of the Golden Melice.*
First Edition: New York: Derby & Jackson, 1857.
NF/F: $100   **G/VG: $40**

_____. *The Lost Hunter: A Tale of Early Times.*
First Edition: New York: Derby & Jackson, 1856.
NF/F: $175   **G/VG: $85**

_____. *The White Chief Among Red Men.*
First Edition: New York: Derby & Jackson, 1856.
NF/F: $145   **G/VG: $65**

Aimard, Gustave. *The Last of the Incas, A Romance of the Pampas.*
First Edition: London: Ward Lock, 1862.
NF/F: $300   **G/VG: $165**

_____. *The Gold Seekers.*
First Edition: London: Ward & Lock, 1862.
NF/F: $200   **G/VG: $85**

_____. *The Indian Scout.*
First Edition: London: Ward & Lock, 1861.
NF/F: $600   **G/VG: $265**

Ainsworth, William Harrison. *Leaguer of Lathom.*
First Edition: London: Tinsley Brothers, 1876.
NF/F: $600   **G/VG: $225**

_____. *Rookwood.*
First Edition: London, Richard Bentley, 1834.
NF/F: $1,000   **G/VG: $400**

_____. *The Tower of London: A Historical Romance.*
First Edition: London: Richard Bentley, 1840.
NF/F: $800   **G/VG: $355**

Aldrich, Thomas Bailey. *Story Of A Bad Boy.*
Points of Issue: First state with p. 14, line 20, reading "scattered" for "scatters," and p. 197, line 10, "abroad" for "aboard."
First Edition: Boston: Fields, Osgood, & Co, 1870.
NF/F: $800   **G/VG: $255**

_____. *The Course of True Love Never Did Run Smooth.*
First Edition: New York: Rudd and Carleton, 1858.
NF/F: $450   **G/VG: $165**

Alger, Jr., *Horatio.* Luck and Pluck; or John Oakley's Inheritance.
First Edition: Boston: Loring, 1869.
NF/F: $2,100   **G/VG: $1,200**

_____. *Boy's Fortune, or, The Strange Adventures of Ben Baker.*
First Edition: Philadelphia: Henry T. Coates & Co., 1882.
NF/F: $800   **G/VG: $265**

Anstey, F. *Vice Versa; Or A Lesson To Fathers.*
First Edition: London: Smith, Elder and Co, 1882.
NF/F: $750   **G/VG: $245**

_____. *The Brass Bottle.*
First Edition: London: Smith, Elder & Co., 1900.
NF/F: $235   **G/VG: $85**
First U.S. Edition: New York: D. Appleton, 1900.
NF/F: $65   **G/VG: $30**

_____. *Mr. Punch's Pocket Ibsen: A Collection of Some of the Master's Best-Known Dramas Condensed, Revised, and Slightly Rearranged.*
First Edition: London: William Heinemann, 1893.
NF/F: $260   **G/VG: $115**

Bangs, John Kendrick. *A House-Boat on the Styx.*
First Edition: New York: Harper and Brothers, 1896.
NF/F: $550   **G/VG: $125**

_____. *The Pursuit of the House-Boat.*
First Edition: New York: Harper & Brothers Pubs., 1897.
NF/F: $375   **G/VG: $140**

_____. *Toppleton's Client Or, A Spirit in Exile.*
First Edition: New York: Charles L. Webster & Company, 1893.
NF/F: $285   **G/VG: $125**

Baring-Gould, Sabine. *Domitia.*
First Edition: London: Methuen, 1898.
NF/F: $125   **G/VG: $60**

_____. *Richard Cable. The Lightshipman.* (Three Volumes)
First Ed: London: Smith Elder, 1888.
NF/F: $195   **G/VG: $80**

_____. *Cheap Jack Zita.* (3 Vols)
First Edition: London: Methuen, 1893.
NF/F: $450   **G/VG: $195**

Barrie, James M. *When a Man's Single. A Tale of Literary Life.*
First Ed: London: Hodder & Stoughton, 1888. Points of Issue: The first issue has two pages of ads after the text.
NF/F: $500   **G/VG: $220**

_____. *A Tillyloss Scandal.*
Points of Issue: This is an American Pirate, cobbled together from magazine pieces. The first edition carries the address: "43, 45 and 47 East Tenth Street" and was issued in buff-colored wraps.
First Edition: New York: Lovell Coryell, 1893.
NF/F: $345   **G/VG: $160**

_____. *The Thrums Series:*

_____. *Auld Licht Idyls.*
First Edition: London: Hodder & Stoughton, 1888. Points of Issue: The first issue has two pages of ads after the text.
NF/F: $550   **G/VG: $175**

_____. *A Window in Thrums.*
First Edition: London: Hodder & Stoughton, 1889.
NF/F: $200   **G/VG: $75**

_____. *The Little Minister.*
(Three Volumes).
First Edition: London: Cassell & Co., 1891. Points of Issue: The text runs to the last page in all three volumes and the end of Volume One carries 16 pages of ads.
NF/F: $750   **G/VG: $300**

_____. *Sentimental Tommy.*
First Edition: London: Cassell & Co., 1896. Points of Issue: The date code on the advertising is "6G-896."
NF/F: $350   **G/VG: $100**

_____. *Tommy and Grizel.*
First Edition: London: Cassell & Co., 1900.
NF/F: $95   **G/VG: $40**

Barr, Amelia E. *Beads of Tasmer.*
First Edition: New York: James Clarke, 1893.
NF/F: $250   **G/VG: $95**

John Kendrick Bangs.

Amelia E. Barr.

Edward Bellamy.

Edward Bellamy.

_____. *Jan Vedder's Wife.*
First Edition: New York: Dodd Mead, 1885.
NF/F: $150   **G/VG: $50**

_____. *The Bow of Orange Ribbons.*
First Edition: New York: Dodd, Mead, & Co, 1886.
NF/F: $65   **G/VG: $20**

_____. *Remember the Alamo.*
First Edition: New York: Dodd Mead, 1888.
NF/F: $100   **G/VG: $35**

Bates, Arlo. *The Diary of a Saint.*
First Edition: Boston: Houghton Mifflin, 1902.
NF/F: $60   **G/VG: $25**

_____. *The Puritans.*
First Edition: Boston: Houghton Mifflin, 1899.
NF/F: $125   **G/VG: $40**

Bellamy, Edward. *Looking Backward 2000-1887.*
First Edition: Boston: Ticknor and Company, 1888. Points of Issue: "Press of J. J. Arakelyan" on verso in first printing.
NF/F: $825   **G/VG: $300**

_____. *Equality.*
First Edition: New York: D. Appleton & Co., 1897.
NF/F: $700   **G/VG: $300**

_____. *The Blindman's World.*
First Edition: Boston: Houghton Mifflin, 1898.
NF/F: $250   **G/VG: $85**

Bennett, Emerson. *Clara Moreland; or, Adventures in the Far South-West.*
First Edition: Philadelphia: T. B. Peterson, 1853.
NF/F: $155   **G/VG: $70**

Besant, Walter. *Beyond the Dreams of Avarice.*
First Edition: London: Chatto & Windus, 1895.
NF/F: $145   **G/VG: $65**

_____. *The World Went Very Well Then.* (Three Volumes).
First Edition: London: Chatto & Windus, 1887.
NF/F: $400   **G/VG: $160**

_____. *St. Katherine's By the Tower.* (Three Volumes).
First Edition: London: Chatto & Windus, 1891.
NF/F: $625   **G/VG: $260**

Bierce, Ambrose. *Black Beetles in Amber.*
First Edition: San Francisco and New York: Western Authors Publishing Co., 1892.
NF/F: $625   **G/VG: $275**

_____. *Shapes of Clay.*
First Edition: San Francisco: W.E. Wood, 1903. Points of Issue: Page 71 lines and 6 read: "We've nothing better here than bliss. Walk in. But I must tell you this:".
NF/F: $1,425   **G/VG: $450**

_____. *Tales of Soldiers and Civilians.*
First Edition: San Francisco: E.L.G. Steele, 1891.
NF/F: $1,400   **G/VG: $525**

Blackmore, Richard Doddridge. *Cripps, the Carrier. A Woodland Tale.* (Three Volumes).
First Edition: London: Sampson Low, 1876.
NF/F: $185   **G/VG: $90**

Borrow, George. *Lavengro: The Scholar - The Gypsy - The Priest.* (Three Volumes).
First Edition: London: John Murray, 1851.
NF/F: $750   **G/VG: $285**

Ambrose Bierce.

_____. *The Romany Rye; a Sequel to "Lavengro."*
First Edition: London: John Murray, 1857.
NF/F: $440   **G/VG: $200**

Bronte, Charlotte (as by Currer Bell). *Jane Eyre.* An Autobiography.
First Edition: London: Smith, Elder & Co., 1847 (Three Volumes).
NF/F: $58,500   **G/VG: $24,000**
First U.S. Edition: New York: Harper & Brothers, 1848.
NF/F: $3,200   **G/VG: $950**

_____. *Shirley, A Tale.*
First Edition: London: Smith, Elder & Co, 1849.
NF/F: $4,000   **G/VG: $1,700**

_____. *Villette.*
First Edition: London: Smith, Elder & Co, 1853.
NF/F: $8,500   **G/VG: $3,400**
First U.S. Edition: New York: Harper And Brothers, 1853.
NF/F: $7,050   **G/VG: $2,100**

Bronte, Emily (as by Ellis Bell). *Wuthering Heights.*
First U.S. Edition: New York: Harper & Brothers Publishers, 1848.
NF/F: $28,000   **G/VG: $9,500**

Bunner, H. C. "Short Sixes" Stories to be Read While the Candle Burns.
First Edition: New York: Puck, Keppler & Schwarzmann, 1891
NF/F: $255   **G/VG: $95**

_____. *More "Short Sixes."*
First Edition: New York: Puck, Keppler & Schwarzmann, 1894.
NF/F: $150   **G/VG: $65**

_____. *A Woman of Honor.*
First Edition: Boston: James R. Osgood, 1883.
NF/F: $220   **G/VG: $100**

Burnett, Francis Hodgson. *Little Lord Fauntleroy.*
Points of Issue: First State has Devinne Press seal on Page 201.
First Edition: New York: Scribners, 1886.
NF/F: $1,700   **G/VG: $800**
First U.K. Edition: London: Frederick, Warne and Co., 1886.
NF/F: $500   **G/VG: $195**

_____. *A Lady of Quality.*
First Edition: New York: Scribners, 1896
NF/F: $300   **G/VG: $85**

_____. *Louisiana.*
First Edition: New York: Scribners, 1880.
NF/F: $95   **G/VG: $40**

Butler, Samuel. *The Way of All Flesh.*
First Edition: London: Grant Richards, 1903.
NF/F: $1,050   **G/VG: $455**
First U.S. Edition: New York: E. P. Dutton, 1910.
NF/F: $370   **G/VG: $165**

Bynner, Edwin Lassetter. *Damen's Ghost.*
First Edition: Boston: Houghton Mifflin/James R. Osgood, 1881.
NF/F: $95   **G/VG: $40**

_____. *Agnes Surriage.*
First Edition: Boston: Ticknor And Company, 1887.
NF/F: $85   **G/VG: $40**

H. C. Bunner.

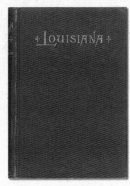

Francis Hodgson Burnett.

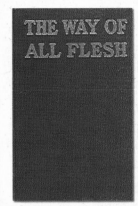

Samuel Butler.

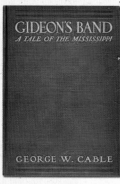

George Washington Cable.

Hall Caine.

Lewis Carroll.

Cable, George Washington. *The Grandissimes: A Story of Creole Life.* First Edition: New York: Scribners, 1880.
NF/F: $265   G/VG: $70

_____. *Gideon's Band: A Tale of the Mississippi.* First Edition: New York: Scribner's, 1914.
NF/F: $325   G/VG: $125

_____. *The Cavalier.* First Edition: New York: Charles Scribner's, 1901.
NF/F: $245   G/VG: $90

Caine, Hall. *A Son of Hagar: A Romance of Our Time.* First Edition: London: Chatto and Windus, 1887.
NF/F: $500   G/VG: $245

_____. *The Scapegoat: A Romance.* First Edition: London: William Heinemann, 1891.
NF/F: $375   G/VG: $190

Caine, Hall (as by W. Ralph Hall Caine). *Isle of Man.* First Edition: London: Adam and Charles Black, 1909.
NF/F: $185   G/VG: $75

Carroll, Lewis. *Alice's Adventures in Wonderland.* First Edition: London: Macmillan, 1866.
Points of Issue: An issue of 1856 was suppressed and destroyed 500 copies are thought to survive.
NF/F: $52,500   G/VG: $25,000
First U.S. Edition: New York: D. Appleton, 1866.
NF/F: $22,000   G/VG: $12,000

_____. *The Hunting of the Snark.* Limited Edition: London: Macmillan, 1876 (20 in dark blue, 20 in white and 100 in rd for presentation.)
NF/F: $17,000   G/VG: $10,000
First Edition: London: Macmillan, 1876.
Points of Issue: Issued in buff cloth with black endpapers.
NF/F: $3,000   G/VG: $1,100

_____. *Though the Looking Glass.* First Edition: London, Macmillan, 1872.
NF/F: $14,000   G/VG: $7500

Caruthers, William Alexander. *The Cavaliers of Virginia, or The Recluse of Jamestown.* An Historical Romance of the Old Domonion. (Two Volumes). First Edition: New York: Harper & Brothers, 1834-1835.
NF/F: $550   G/VG: $235

Catherwood, Mary. *The Queen of the Swamp, and Other Plain Americans.* First Edition: Boston: Houghton, Mifflin, 1899.
NF/F: $85   G/VG: $30

_____. *The White Islander.* First Edition: New York: The Century Co., 1893.
NF/F: $50   G/VG: $30

Chopin, Kate. *A Night in Acadie.* First Edition: Chicago: Way & Williams, 1897.
NF/F: $2,850   G/VG: $1,050

_____. *Bayou Folk.* First Edition: Boston: Houghton Mifflin, 1894.
NF/F: $750   G/VG: $300

_____. *The Awakening.*
First Edition: Chicago: Herbert S. Stone, 1899.
NF/F: $8,200   **G/VG: $3,500**

Cobb, Sylvanus. *The Gunmaker of Moscow or Vladimir the Monk.*
First Edition: New York: Robert Bonner's Sons, 1888.
NF/F: $150   **G/VG: $55**

_____. *Karmel the Scout or The Rebel of the Jerseys.*
First Edition: Philadelphia: Henry T. Coates, 1896.
NF/F: $75   **G/VG: $30**

Collins, Wilkie. *The Queen of Hearts.* (Three Volumes).
First Edition: London: Hurst and Blackett, 1859.
NF/F: $4,100   **G/VG: $1,800**

_____. *After Dark.* (Two Volumes).
First Edition: London: Smith, Elder, 1856.
NF/F: $14,000   **G/VG: $5,300**

_____. *The Moonstone.* (Three Volumes).
First Edition: London: Tinsley Brothers, 1868.
NF/F: $9,500   **G/VG: $4,600**

Conrad, Joseph. *Almayer's Folly: The Story of an Eastern River.*
First Edition: London: T. Fisher Unwin, 1895.
NF/F: $3,800   **G/VG: $1,800**

_____. *Lord Jim.*
First Edition: Edinburgh and London: Blackwood, 1900.
NF/F: $6,500   **G/VG: $2,600**

Cooper James Fenimore.
Leatherstocking Tales:

_____. *The Deerslayer: or, The First War-Path. A Tale.*
First Edition: Philadelphia: Lea & Blanchard, 1841.
NF/F: $2,700   **G/VG: $1,400**

_____. *Last of the Mohicans A Narrative of 1757.*
First Edition: Philadelphia: H.C. Carey & I. Lea, 1826.
NF/F: $37,500   **G/VG: $16,000**

_____. *Pathfinder; or, The Inland Sea.* (Two Volumes).
First Edition: Philadelphia: Lea & Blanchard, 1840. Points of Issue: Second volume lacks a copyright notice in the first issue.
NF/F: $3,100   **G/VG: $1,500**

_____. *Pioneers, or the Sources of the Susquehanna; A Descriptive Tale.*
First Edition: New-York: Charles Wiley, 1823.
NF/F: $2,200   **G/VG: $900**

_____. *The Prairie: A Tale.*
First Edition: Philadelphia: H.C. Carey & I. Lea, 1827.
NF/F: $2,500   **G/VG: $1,000**

Crane, Stephen. *Maggie a Girl of the Streets.*
First Edition (Trade): New York: D. Appleton, 1896.
NF/F: $6,500   **G/VG: $2,800**

_____. *Red Badge of Courage.*
First Edition: New York: D. Appleton and Company, 1895. Points of Issue: In the first state, page 225 has "congratulated" in unbroken type.
NF/F: $7,500   **G/VG: $3,100**

Kate Chopin.

Stephen Crane.

Stephen Crane.

Richard Harding Davis.

Richard Harding Davis.

Charles Dickens.

_____. *The Open Boat and Other Tales of Adventure.*
First Edition: New York: Doubleday McClure, 1898.
NF/F: $1,000   **G/VG: $460**

Crawford, Francis Marion. *Via Crucis; a Romance of the Second Crusade.*
First Edition: New York: Macmillan, 1899.
NF/F: $200   **G/VG: $65**

_____. *The Ralstons.* (Two Volumes).
First Edition: New York: Macmillan, 1895.
NF/F: $145   **G/VG: $65**

Davis, Rebecca Harding. *Kent Hampden.*
First Edition: New York: Scribners, 1892.
NF/F: $185   **G/VG: $80**

Davis, Richard Harding. *Van Bibber and Others.*
First Edition: New York: Harper & Brothers, 1892. Points of Issue: The first issue lacks any ad pages at the rear.
NF/F: $200   **G/VG: $90**

_____. *In the Fog.*
First Ed: New York: R. H. Russell, 1901.
NF/F: $245   **G/VG: $110**

_____. *Gallegher and Other Stories.*
First Edition: New York: Scribners, 1891. Points of Issue: The first issue lacks an ad for "Famous Women of the French Court."
NF/F: $175   **G/VG: $65**

De Forest, John William. *Overland: A Novel.*
First Edition: New York: Sheldon and Co., 1871.
NF/F: $100   **G/VG: $45**

Dickens, Charles. *Great Expectations.* (Three Volumes)
First Edition: London: Chapman and Hall, 1861.
NF/F: $36,000   **G/VG: $16,400**

_____. *A Christmas Carol.*
First Edition: London: Chapman and Hall, 1843.
NF/F: $37,500   **G/VG: $18,000**

Dickens, Charles (as by Boz). *Oliver Twist.* (Three Volumes.)
First Edition: London: Richard Bentley, 1838.
NF/F: $18,500   **G/VG: $8,500**

Disraeli, Benjamin. *Vivian Grey.* (Five Volumes.)
First Edition: London: Henry Colburn, 1826-27.
NF/F: $2,500   **G/VG: $1,000**

_____. *Henrietta Temple, A Love Story.* (Three Volumes.)
First Edition: London: Henry Colburn, 1837.
NF/F: $925   **G/VG: $360**
First U.S. Edition: Philadelphia: Carey and Hart, 1837.
NF/F: $470   **G/VG: $225**

_____. *Endymion.* (Three volumes.)
First Edition: London: Longmans, Green, 1880.
NF/F: $650   **G/VG: $260**

Dodge, Mary Mapes. *Hans Brinker or the Silver Skates.*
First Edition: New York: James O'Kane, 1866.
NF/F: $1,800   **G/VG: $800**

_____. *When Life Is Young.*
First Edition: New York: Century, 1894.
NF/F: $165   **G/VG: $55**

Dostoevsky, Fyodor. *Poor Folk.*
First Edition of Lena Milman
Translation: London: Elkin Mathews,
1894.
NF/F: $500   **G/VG: $225**

Doyle, Arthur Conan. *The White Company.* (Three volumes.)
First Edition: London; Smith, Elder,
1891.
NF/F: $12,500   **G/VG: $6,400**

_____. *The Refugees.* (Three
volumes.)
First Edition: London: Longmans
Green, 1893.
NF/F: $4,000   **G/VG: $1,800**
First U.S. Edition: New York: Harper &
Brothers, 1893.
NF/F: $550   **G/VG: $245**

_____. *A Duet With An
Occasional Chorus.*
First Edition: London: Grant Richards,
1899.
NF/F: $285   **G/VG: $135**
First U.S. Edition: New York: D.
Appleton, 1899.
NF/F: $95   **G/VG: $35**

DuMaurier, George. *The Martian.*
Limited Edition: London and New
York: Harper & Brothers, 1897 (250
copies).
NF/F: $200   **G/VG: $75**
First Edition: London and New York:
Harper & Brothers, 1897.
NF/F: $75   **G/VG: $30**

_____. *Trilby, A Novel.*
First Edition: London: Osgood,
McIlvaine, 1895.
NF/F: $320   **G/VG: $150**
First U.S. Edition: New York: Harper &
Brothers, 1894.
NF/F: $80   **G/VG: $30**

_____. *Peter Ibbetson.*
First Edition: New York: Harper &
Brothers, 1891.
NF/F: $185   **G/VG: $75**
First U.K. Edition: London: Osgood,
McIlvaine, 1892 (two volumes).
NF/F: $350   **G/VG: $135**

Eliot, George. *Romola*
Limited Edition: London: Smith, Elder,
1880 (1,000 copies, two volumes).
NF/F: $3,400   **G/VG: $1,600**
First Edition (Trade): London: Smith,
Elder, 1863 (three volumes).
NF/F: $1,400   **G/VG: $555**

_____. *Silas Marner The Weaver
of Raveloe.*
First Edition: Edinburgh and London:
William Blackwood and Sons, 1861.
NF/F: $5,000   **G/VG: $2,200**

_____. *Daniel Deronda.* (Four
Volumes.)
First Edition: Edinburgh and London:
William Blackwood, 1876.
NF/F: $2,800   **G/VG: $1,200**

Evans, Augusta Jane. *Beulah.*
First Edition: New York: Derby &
Jackson, 1859.
NF/F: $150   **G/VG: $80**

_____. *Inez: A Tale of the Alamo.*
First Edition: New York: W. L. Pooley,
1864.
NF/F: $225   **G/VG: $90**

Flaubert, Gustave. *Madame Bovary.*
First Edition of Eleanor Marx-Aveling
translation: London: Vizetelly & Co.,
1886.
NF/F: $9,500   **G/VG: $3,600**

Arthur Conan Doyle.

George DuMaurier.

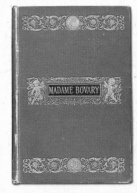

Gustave Flaubert.

John Fox.

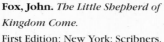

Henry B. Fuller.

Henry B. Fuller.

Foote, Mary Hallock. *The Desert and the Sown.*
First Edition: Boston: Houghton Mifflin, 1902.
NF/F: $75   **G/VG: $35**

_____. *A Touch of Sun and Other Stories.*
First Edition: Boston: Houghton Mifflin, 1903.
NF/F: $170   **G/VG: $65**

Ford, Paul Leicester. *A Warning To Lovers.*
First Edition: New York: Dodd, Mead, 1906.
NF/F: $250   **G/VG: $100**

_____. *Love Finds the Way.*
First Edition: New York: Dodd Mead, 1904.
NF/F: $260   **G/VG: $135**

_____. *Wanted - A Matchmaker.*
First Edition: New York: Dodd Mead, 1900.
NF/F: $275   **G/VG: $105**

Fox, John. *The Little Shepherd of Kingdom Come.*
First Edition: New York: Scribners, 1903. Points of issue: The first State has "laugh" for lap page 61, line 14.
NF/F: $165   **G/VG: $70**
First Edition Thus: New York: Scribners, 1931. Illustrated by N.C. Wyeth.
NF/F: $400   **G/VG: $175**
Limited Edition: New York: Scribners, 1931. Illustrated by N.C. Wyeth (500 copies).
NF/F: $3,000   **G/VG: $850**

_____. *The Trail of the Lonesome Pine.*
First Edition: New York: Charles Scribner's Sons, 1908. Points of Issue: First Issue has a Scribner's seal on the verso.
NF/F: $165   **G/VG: $75**

_____. *"Hell fer Sartain": And Other Stories.*
First Edition: New York: Harper & Brothers, 1897.
NF/F: $125   **G/VG: $45**

Fuller, Henry B. *The Puppet-Booth.*
First Edition: New York: Century Co., 1896.
NF/F: $700   **G/VG: $200**

_____. *The Cliff-Dwellers.*
First Edition: New York: Harper & Brothers, 1893.
NF/F: $185   **G/VG: $95**

_____. *The Chatelaine of La Trinite.*
First Edition: New York: The Century Co., 1892.
NF/F: $225   **G/VG: $75**

Gaskell, Elizabeth (as by Mrs. Gaskell). *Wives and Daughters.*
First Edition: London: Smith, Elder, 1866 (two volumes).
NF/F: $1,000   **G/VG: $425**
First U.S. Edition: New York: Harper & Brothers, 1866.
NF/F: $680   **G/VG: $325**

Gautier, Theophile. *One of Cleopatra's Nights.*
First Edition of Lafcadio Hearn Translation: New York: R. Worthington, 1882.
NF/F: $575   **G/VG: $200**

_____. *Clarimonde.*
First Edition of Lafcadio Hearn Translation: New York: Brentano's, 1899.
NF/F: $525   **G/VG: $250**

Gissing, George (as by Anonymous). *Demos.*
First Edition: London: Smith, Elder, 1886 (three volumes).
NF/F: $2,000   **G/VG: $875**

Gissing, George. *Denzil Quarrier. A Novel.*
First Edition: London: Lawrence & Bullen, 1892.
NF/F: $525   **G/VG: $275**

_____. *The Private Papers of Henry Ryecroft.*
First Edition: Westminster: Archibald Constable & Co., 1903. Points of Issue: The first issue has three pages of ads following text.
NF/F: $600   **G/VG: $215**
Limited Edition: Portland, Maine: Thomas B. Mosher, 1921 (700 copies).
NF/F: $100   **G/VG: $60**

Gogol, Nikolai. *Dead Souls.*
First Edition in English: London: T. Fisher Unwin, 1893. Points of Issue: Copies from a withdrawn issue by Vizetelly 1887 may exist, I have not seen a copy.
NF/F: $750   **G/VG: $300**
Limited Edition: New York: Limited Editions Club, 1944 (1,500 copies in two volumes).
NF/F: $150   **G/VG: $80**

_____. *The Inspector-General.*
First Edition of Arthur Sykes translation: London: Walter Scott, 1892. Points of Issue: First State includes an errata slip.
NF/F: $420   **G/VG: $195**

Gould, Nat. *Who Did it?*
First Edition: Manchester: George Routledge and Sons, 1896.
NF/F: $95   **G/VG: $30**

_____. *The Old Mare's Foal.*
First Edition: London: George Routledge and Sons, 1899.
NF/F: $95   **G/VG: $45**

Habberton, John. *The Worst Boy in Town.*
First Edition: New York: Putnam, 1880.
NF/F: $135   **G/VG: $75**

_____. *Helen's Babies.*
First Edition: Boston: Loring, 1876.
NF/F: $400   **G/VG: $190**

_____. *Other People's Children.*
First Edition: New York: Putnam, 1877.
NF/F: $150   **G/VG: $65**

Haggard, H. Rider. *Dawn.*
First Edition: London: Hurst and Blackett, 1884 (three volumes).
NF/F: $9,100   **G/VG: $5,000**

_____. *The Wizard.*
First Edition: Bristol & London: J. W. Arrowsmith & Simpkin, Marshall, Hamilton, Kent, n.d.
NF/F: $950   **G/VG: $380**
First U.S. Edition: New York Longmans, Green, and Co., 1896. Points of Issue: Issued with an (now) extremely rare dust jacket, unlike newer books this is priced without a jacket due to the fact that most books of this era had no jacket.
NF/F: $275   **G/VG: $100**

_____. *Mr. Meeson's Will.*
First Edition: London: Spencer Blackett, 1888.
NF/F: $700   **G/VG: $340**

Hale, Edward Everett. *Man Without a Country.*
Points of Issue: Softcover in mauve wraps.
First Edition: Boston: Ticknor & Fields, 1865.
NF/F: $1,500   **G/VG: $725**

_____. *The Fortunes of Rachel.*
First Edition: New York: Funk & Wagnalls, 1884.
NF/F: $175   **G/VG: $65**

George Gissing.

H. Rider Haggard.

H. Rider Haggard.

Joel Chandler Harris.

Joel Chandler Harris.

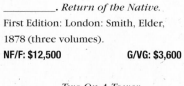

Bret Harte.

_____. *Philip Nolan's Friends, A Story Of The Change Of Western Empire.*
First Edition: New York: Scribner, Armstrong, & Co., 1877.
NF/F: $110   **G/VG: $45**

Hardy, Thomas. *Tess of the d'Urbervilles: A Pure Woman Faithfully Presented.*
First Edition: London: James R. Osgood, McIlvaine, 1891 (three volumes). Points of Issue: Chapter XXV for 'Chapter XXXV' on page 199 of volume 2.
NF/F: $17,500   **G/VG: $8,800**

_____. *Return of the Native.*
First Edition: London: Smith, Elder, 1878 (three volumes).
NF/F: $12,500   **G/VG: $3,600**

_____. *Two On A Tower.*
First Edition: London: Sampson Low, Marston, Searle and Rivington, 1882 (three volumes).
NF/F: $9,500   **G/VG: $3,800**

Harris, Joel Chandler. *Uncle Remus His Songs & His Sayings.*
First Edition: New York : D. Appleton, 1881. Points of Issue: The last line on page 9 "presumptive."
NF/F: $15,000   **G/VG: $6,800**

_____. *Sister Jane.*
First Edition: Boston: Houghton Mifflin, 1896.
NF/F: $310   **G/VG: $135**

_____. *The Story of Aaron (so named) the Son of Ben Ali.*
First Edition: Boston & New York: Houghton Mifflin, 1896.
NF/F: $885   **G/VG: $300**

Harrison, Constance Cary (as by Mrs. Burton). *The Merry Maid of Arcady, His Lordship and Other Stories.*
First Edition: Boston, London, New York: Lamson Wolffe, 1897.
NF/F: $85   **G/VG: $40**

Harte, Bret. *The Lost Galleon and Other Tales.*
First Edition: San Francisco: Towne and Bacon, 1867.
NF/F: $800   **G/VG: $310**

_____. *Barker's Luck and Other Stories.*
First Edition: Boston: Houghton, Mifflin and Company, 1896.
NF/F: $150   **G/VG: $60**

_____. *A Sappho of Green Springs and Other Tales.*
First Edition: London: Chatto & Windus, 1891.
NF/F: $175   **G/VG: $75**
First U.S. Edition: Boston & New York: Houghton Mifflin, 1891.
NF/F: $65   **G/VG: $30**

Hawthorne, Nathaniel. *Mosses from an Old Manse.*
First Edition: New York: Wiley & Putnam, 1846 (two volumes).
NF/F: $6,000   **G/VG: $2,700**

_____. *Twice-Told Tales.*
First Edition: Boston: American Stationers Co. John B. Russell, 1837.
NF/F: $6,500   **G/VG: $2,800**

_____. *The House of the Seven Gables.*
First Edition: Boston: Ticknor, Reed & Fields, 1851.
NF/F: $5,200   **G/VG: $2,500**

Hearn, Lafcadio. *Shadowings.*
First Edition: Boston: Little, Brown and
Company, 1900.
NF/F: $1,000   G/VG: $400

_____. *Stray Leaves from
Strange Literature.*
First Edition: Boston: James R. Osgood,
1884.
NF/F: $1,000   G/VG: $450

_____. *Youma. The Story of a
West-Indian Slave.*
First Edition: New York: Harper &
Brothers, 1890.
NF/F: $350   G/VG: $145

Hemon, Louis. *Monsieur Ripois and
Nemesis.*
First Edition of William Aspenwall
Bradley translation: New York:
Macmillan, 1925.
NF/F: $150   G/VG: $50

Henry, O. *Strictly Business.*
First Edition: Garden City, NY:
Doubleday Page, 1910.
NF/F: $2,500   G/VG: $1,000

_____. *Cabbages and Kings.*
First Edition: New York: McClure
Phillips, 1904.
NF/F: $775   G/VG: $300

_____. *Heart of the West.*
First Edition: New York: The McClure
Company, 1907.
NF/F: $550   G/VG: $235

Henty, G.A. *Under Drake's Flag: Tale
of the Spanish Main.*
First Edition: London: Blackie & Son,
1883.
NF/F: $325   G/VG: $100

_____. *A Knight of the White
Cross.*
First Edition: London: Blackie & Son,
1886.
NF/F: $325   G/VG: $140

_____. *A March on London,
Being the Story of Wat Tyler's
Insurrection.*
First Edition: New York: Scribners,
1897.
NF/F: $375   G/VG: $125
First U.K. Edition: London: Blackie &
Son, 1898.
NF/F: $350   G/VG: $110

Holland, J.G. *Nicholas Minturn.*
First Edition: New York: Scribner
Armstrong, 1877.
NF/F: $65   G/VG: $25

**Holley, Marietta (as by Josiah
Allen's Wife).** Samantha Series:

_____. *Josiah Allen's Wife as a
P.A. and P.I.*
First Edition: Hartford, Conn.:
American Publishing Company, 1877.
NF/F: $125   G/VG: $45

_____. *The Lament of the
Mormon Wife.*
First Edition: Hartford, Conn.:
American Publishing Company, 1880.
NF/F: $325   G/VG: $145

_____. *My Wayward Partner.*
First Edition: Hartford, Conn.:
American Publishing Company, 1880.
NF/F: $325   G/VG: $150

**Holley, Marietta (as by Josiah
Allen's Wife).** *Sweet Cicely: Josiah
Allen as a Politician.*
First Edition: New York: Funk and
Wagnalls, 1885.
NF/F: $125   G/VG: $50

Lafcadio. Hearn.

G.A. Henty.

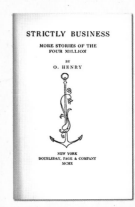
O Henry.

Marietta Holley.

Marietta Holley.

Marietta Holley.

_____. *Samantha at Saratoga: Or, "Flirtin' With Fashion."*
First Edition: Philadelphia: Hubbard Brothers, 1887.
NF/F: $95   **G/VG: $30**

_____. *Samantha Among the Brethren.*
First Edition: New York & London: Funk & Wagnalls, 1890.
NF/F: $100   **G/VG: $35**

_____.*Samantha on the Race Problem.*
First Edition: Boston: Union Publishing/Dodd Mead, 1892.
NF/F: $150   **G/VG: $60**

_____. *Samantha at The World's Fair.*
First Edition: New York & London: Funk & Wagnalls, 1893.
NF/F: $75   **G/VG: $30**

_____. *Josiah's Alarm and Abel Perry's Funeral.*
First Edition: Philadelphia: Lippincott, 1895.
NF/F: $225   **G/VG: $85**

_____. *Samantha in Europe.*
First Edition: New York: Funk & Wagnalls, 1895.
NF/F: $135   **G/VG: $60**

Holley, Marietta (as by Josiah Allen's Wife). *Samantha at the St. Louis Exposition.*
First Edition: New York: G. W. Dillingham, 1904.
NF/F: $130   **G/VG: $50**

_____. *Around the World With Josiah Allen's Wife.*
First Edition: New York: G. W. Dillingham, 1904.
NF/F: $95   **G/VG: $35**

_____. *Samantha Vs. Josiah: Being the Story of the Borrowed Automobile and What Became of It.*
First Edition: New York: Funk & Wagnalls, 1906.
NF/F: $175   **G/VG: $75**

_____.*Samantha on Children's Rights.*
First Edition: New York: G. W. Dillingham, 1909.
NF/F: $135   **G/VG: $40**

_____. *Josiah's Secret.*
First Edition: New York: Hungerford-Holbrook, 1910.
NF/F: $95   **G/VG: $35**

_____. *Samantha at Coney Island and a Thousand Other Islands.*
First Edition: New York: Christian Herald, 1911.
NF/F: $120   **G/VG: $50**

Holley, Marietta (as by Josiah Allen's Wife). *Samantha on the Woman Question.*
First Edition: New York: Fleming H. Revell, 1913.
NF/F: $150   **G/VG: $40**

_____. *Josiah Allen on the Woman Question.*
First Edition: New York: Fleming H. Revell, 1914.
NF/F: $85   **G/VG: $30**

Howard, Blanche Willis. *The Garden of Eden.*
First Edition: New York: Scribners, 1900.
NF/F: $115   **G/VG: $45**

_____. *Aunt Serena.*
First Edition: Boston: James R. Osgood, 1881.
NF/F: $60   **G/VG: $25**

Howells, W. D. *The Rise of Silas Lapham.*
First Edition: Boston: Ticknor & Co., 1885. Points of Issue: Word "sojurner" unbroken on page 16 in first state.
NF/F: $400   **G/VG: $170**

_____. *The Lady of the Aroostook.*
First Edition: Cambridge, MA: Houghton, Osgood and Co., 1879.
NF/F: $165   **G/VG: $65**

_____. *Mouse-Trap and Other Farces.*
First Edition: New York: Harper & Brothers, 1889.
NF/F: $95   **G/VG: $40**

Ingraham, Col. Prentiss. *Buffalo Bill and the White Queen or, The Shadow of the Aztecs.*
Points of Issue: Paperback Original.
First Edition: New York: Street & Smith, 1911.
NF/F: $75   **G/VG: $30**

_____. *The Corsair Queen; or, the Gipsies of the Sea.*
Points of Issue: Paperback Original first is Beadle's Dime Library, Vol. XII, No. 155.
First Edition: New York: Beadle & Adams, 1881.
NF/F: $80   **G/VG: $35**

_____. *Buffalo Bill in the Land of Dread or, The Quest of the Unknown.* Points of Issue: Paperback Original.

First Edition: New York; Street & Smith Corp; 1915.
NF/F: $75   **G/VG: $30**

James, Henry. *Passionate Pilgrim and other Tales.*
First Edition: Boston: James R. Osgood, 1875.
NF/F: $4,000   **G/VG: $1,900**

_____. *Watch and Ward.*
First Edition: Boston: Houghton, Osgood and Company, 1878.
NF/F: $1,450   **G/VG: $625**

_____. *Better Sort.*
First U.S. Edition: New York: Scribners, 1903.
NF/F: $325   **G/VG: $100**
First U.K. Edition: London: Methuen, 1903.
NF/F: $250   **G/VG: $100**

Janvier, Thomas A. *The Aztec Treasure-House.*
First Edition: New York: Harper & Brothers, 1890.
NF/F: $250   **G/VG: $85**

_____. *The Uncle of a Angel and Other Stories.*
First Edition: New York: Harper and Brothers, 1891.
NF/F: $85   **G/VG: $30**

Jewett, Sarah Orne. *A Native of Winby and Other Tales.*
First Edition: Boston: Houghton Mifflin, 1893.
NF/F: $265   **G/VG: $125**

Blanche Willis Howard.

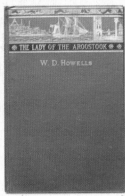

W. D. Howells.

Thomas A. Janvier.

Sarah Orne Jewett.

Jack London.

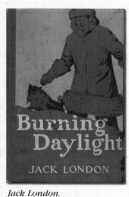

Jack London.

_____. *The Country of the Pointed Firs.*
First Edition: Boston: Houghton Mifflin, 1896.
NF/F: $650   **G/VG: $285**

_____. *Country Doctor.*
First Edition: Boston: Houghton Mifflin, 1884.
NF/F: $460   **G/VG: $215**

Jones, John Beauchamp. *Rival Belles.* Or, *Life in Washington.*
First Edition: Philadelphia: T.B. Peterson & Bros., 1864.
NF/F: $80   **G/VG: $35**

_____. *The Winkles.* Or, *The Merry Monomaniacs.*
First Edition: New York: D. Appleton, 1855.
NF/F: $85   **G/VG: $40**

Judson, Edward Zane Carroll (as by Ned Buntline). *Matanzas; or A Brother's Revenge. A Tale of Florida.*
Points of Issue: Paperback Original.
First Edition: Boston: George H. Williams, 1848.
NF/F: $950   **G/VG: $425**

_____. *The White Wizard or, The Great Prophet of the Seminoles. A Tale of Mystery in the South and North.*
Points of Issue: Paperback Original.
First Edition: New York: Frederic A. Brady. n.d.
NF/F: $900   **G/VG: $400**

Kaler, James Otis. *Jenny Wren's Boarding House - A Story of Newsboy Life in New York.*
First Edition: Boston: Estes & Lauriat, 1893.
NF/F: $150   **G/VG: $85**

Kaler, James Otis (as by James Otis). *Toby Tyler, or Ten Weeks With a Circus.*
First Edition: New York: Harper & Brothers, 1881.
NF/F: $360   **G/VG: $140**

_____. *The Boy Captain.*
First Edition: Boston: Estes and Lauriat, 1896.
NF/F: $150   **G/VG: $55**

Lawrence, George Alfred. *Silverland.*
First Edition: London: Chapman And Hall, 1873.
NF/F: $365   **G/VG: $175**

_____. *Barren Honour.*
First Edition: London: Parker, Son, and Bourn, 1862 (two volumes).
NF/F: $525   **G/VG: $225**

Lippard, George. *New York: Its Upper Ten And Lower Million.*
First Edition: Cincinnati, OH: H. M. Rulison, 1853.
NF/F: $700   **G/VG: $250**

London, Jack. *Night-Born.*
First Edition: New York: The Century Co., 1913.
NF/F: $1,600   **G/VG: $600**

_____. *The Call of the Wild.*
First Edition: New York: Macmillan, 1903.
NF/F: $9,500   **G/VG: $4,000**

_____. *Burning Daylight.*
First Edition: New York: Macmillan, 1910. Points of Issue: "The/MacMillan/Company" on the spine in first issue.
NF/F: $8,000   **G/VG: $3,300**

Loti, Pierre. *The Book of Pity and of Death.*
First Edition in English: London, Paris and Melbourne: Cassell, 1892.
NF/F: $180   **G/VG: $65**

_____. *Madame Chrysantheme.*
First Edition in English: London: George Routledge and Sons, 1897.
NF/F: $235   **G/VG: $80**

_____. *Ramuntcho.*
First U.S. Edition: New York: R. F. Fenno, 1897.
NF/F: $90   **G/VG: $35**

Lytton, Edward Bulwer. *Pelham; or, The Adventures of a Gentleman.*
First Edition: London: Henry Colburn, 1828 (three volumes).
NF/F: $925   **G/VG: $400**

_____. *The Last Days of Pompeii.*
First Edition: London: Richard Bentley, 1834 (three volumes).
NF/F: $1,550   **G/VG: $600**
First U.S. Edition: New York: Harper & Brothers, 1834 (two volumes).
NF/F: $400   **G/VG: $185**

_____. *Lucretia or the Children of the Night.*
First Edition: London: Saunders and Otley, 1846 (three volumes).
NF/F: $750   **G/VG: $300**

Major, Charles. *Dorothy Vernon of Haddon Hall.*
First Edition: NY: Macmillan, 1902.
NF/F: $150   **G/VG: $45**

Marvel, Ik. *Dream Life: A Fable of the Seasons.*
First Edition: New York: Charles Scribner, 1851.
NF/F: $175   **G/VG: $60**

_____. *Seven Stories, with Basement and Attic.*
First Edition: New York: Charles Scribner, 1865.
NF/F: $80   **G/VG: $25**

Melville, Herman. *The Piazza Tales.*
First Edition: New York and London: Dix & Edwards and Sampson Low, 1856.
NF/F: $5,950   **G/VG: $2,200**

_____. *Pierre; or The Ambiguities.*
First Edition: New York: Harper & Brothers, 1852.
NF/F: $2,500   **G/VG: $1,500**

_____. *Mardi: and a Voyage Thither.*
First Edition: London: Richard Bentley, 1849 (three volumes).
NF/F: $6,800   **G/VG: $2,800**
First U.S. Edition: New York: Harper & Brothers, 1849.
NF/F: $7,000   **G/VG: $3,100**

Mitchell, S. Weir. *Hugh Wynne Free Quaker.*
First Edition: New York : Century Co., 1897.
NF/F: $850   **G/VG: $350**

_____. *Constance Trescot. A Novel.*
First Edition: New York: Century Co., 1905.
NF/F: $85   **G/VG: $25**

Nesbit, Edith. *The Story of the Amulet.*
First Edition: London: T. Fisher Unwin. 1906.
NF/F: $400   **G/VG: $135**

Charles Major.

S. Weir Mitchell.

Frank Norris.

Thomas Nelson Page.

Pansy.

Norris, Frank. *Yvernelle: A Legend of Feudal France.*
First Edition: Philadelphia: J. B. Lippincott, 1892.
NF/F: $3,700   **G/VG: $1,500**

_____. *McTeague, A Story of San Francisco.*
Points of Issue: first state has "moment" as last word on page 106.
First Edition: Garden City, NY: Doubleday & McClure, 1899.
NF/F: $1,800   **G/VG: $650**

_____. *The Octopus: A Story of California. The Epic of Wheat.*
First Edition: Garden City, NY: Doubleday, Page, 1901.
NF/F: $350   **G/VG: $145**

Optic, Oliver. *A Victorious Union: The Blue and the Gray Afloat.*
First Edition: Boston: Lothrop, Lee & Shepard, 1893.
NF/F: $500   **G/VG: $265**

_____. *The Boat Club.*
First Edition: Boston: Brown, Bazin, 1855.
NF/F: $225   **G/VG: $85**

_____. *Marrying a Beggar or the Angel in Disguise and Other Tales.*
First Edition: Boston: Wentworth, Hewes, 1859.
NF/F: $200   **G/VG: $85**

Ouida. *La Strega and Other Stories.*
First Edition: London, Sampson Low, Marston, 1899.
NF/F: $220   **G/VG: $80**

_____. *Ariadnê, The Story of a Dream.*
First Edition: London: Chatto & Windus, 1877 (three volumes).
NF/F: $440   **G/VG: $215**
First U.S. Edition: Philadelphia: J.B. Lippincott, 1877.
NF/F: $100   **G/VG: $45**

_____. *The Waters of Edera.*
First Edition: London: T. Fisher Unwin, 1900.
NF/F: $150   **G/VG: $65**

Page, Thomas Nelson. *In Ole Virginia.*
First Edition: New York: Scribners, 1887.
NF/F: $400   **G/VG: $15**

_____. *Two Prisoners.*
First Edition: New York: R. H. Russell, 1898.
NF/F: $175   **G/VG: $65**

_____. *Red Rock. A Chronicle of Reconstruction.*
First Edition: New York: Scribners, 1898.
NF/F: $200   **G/VG: $90**

Pansy. *Making Fate.*
First Edition: Boston: Lothrop Publishing Company, 1895.
NF/F: $75   **G/VG: $35**

_____. *A New Graft on the Family Tree.*
First Edition: Boston: Lothrop Publishing Company, 1880.
NF/F: $100   **G/VG: $40**

Pater, Walter. *Imaginary Portraits.*
First Edition: London: Macmillan and Co., 1887.
NF/F: $775   **G/VG: $280**

_____. *Marius the Epicurean.*
First Edition: London: Macmillan, 1885
(two volumes).
NF/F: $400   **G/VG: $195**

Peck, George W. *Peck's Bad Boy and
His Pa.*
First Edition: Chicago: Bedford, Clarke,
1883.
NF/F: $450   **G/VG: $145**

_____. *The Grocery Man and
Peck's Bad Boy.*
First Edition: Chicago: Bellford, Clarke
& Co. 1883.
NF/F: $15   **G/VG: $75**

**Peterson, Charles Jacobs (as by J.
Thornton Randolph).** *The Cabin
and Parlor; Or, Slaves and Masters.*
First Edition: Philadelphia: T. B.
Peterson, 1852.
NF/F: $725   **G/VG: $325**

Poe, Edgar Allen. *Manuscript Found
in a Bottle in The Gift: A Christmas
and New Year's Present for 1836.*
First Edition: Philadelphia: E.L. Carey
& A. Hart, 1835.
NF/F: $1,400   **G/VG: $650**

Porter, Jane. *The Scottish Chiefs.*
First Edition: London: Printed for
Longman, Hurst, Rees, and Orme, 1810
(five volumes).
NF/F: $3,600   **G/VG: $1,700**

Pyle, Howard. *Yankee Doodle, an
Old Friend in a New Dress.*
First Edition: New York: Dodd, Mead,
1881.
NF/F: $2,300   **G/VG: $900**

_____. *The Merry Adventures
of Robin Hood of Great Renown, in
Nottinghamshire.*
First Edition: New York: Scribners,
1883.
NF/F: $1,250   **G/VG: $700**

_____. *Otto of the Silver Hand.*
First Edition: New York: Scribners,
1888.
NF/F: $550   **G/VG: $200**

Quiller-Couch, Arthur. *Dead Man's
Rock.*
First Edition: London: Cassell, 1887.
NF/F: $425   **G/VG: $200**

Quiller-Couch, Arthur (as by Q).
*Noughts and Crosses Stories, Studies
and Sketches.*
First Edition: London: Cassell, 1891.
NF/F: $200   **G/VG: $35**
First U.S. Edition: New York: Scribners,
1898.
NF/F: $95   **G/VG: $35**

_____. *The Blue Pavilions.*
First Edition: London: Cassell, 1891.
NF/F: $80   **G/VG: $30**

Radcliffe, Ann. *The Mysteries of
Udolpho, a Romance; Interspersed
with Some Pieces of Poetry.*
First Edition: London: G.G. & J.
Robinson, 1794 (four volumes).
NF/F: $7,000   **G/VG: $2,800**

_____. *Italian: Or the
Confessional of the Black Penitents: A
Romance.* (Three volumes.)
First Edition: London: T. Cadell Jun
And W. Davies, 1797.
NF/F: $3,500   **G/VG: $1,400**

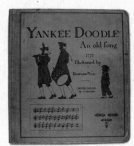
George W. Peck.

Howard Pyle.

Howard Pyle.

Opie Read.

Read, Opie. *Judge Elbridge.*
First Edition: New York: Rand, McNally
& Co, 1899.
NF/F: $275   **G/VG: $95**

_____. *A Kentucky Colonel.*
First Edition: Chicago: F.J. Sculte, 1890.
NF/F: $100   **G/VG: $35**

_____. *Bolanyo.*
First Edition: Chicago: Way & Williams, 1897.
NF/F: $385   **G/VG: $175**

Reade, Charles. *The Cloister and the
Hearth. A Tale of the Middle Ages.*
First Edition: London: W. Clowes for
Trubner & Co, 1861
NF/F: $8,200   **G/VG: $4,500**

_____. *White Lies: A Story.*
First Edition: London: Trubner & Co.,
1857 (three volumes).
NF/F: $800   **G/VG: $395**

Reid, Captain Mayne. *The White
Chief: A Legend of North Mexico.*
First Edition: London: David Bogue,
1855 (three volumes).
NF/F: $1,500   **G/VG: $650**
First U.S. Edition: New York: DeWitt
and Davenport, 1857.
NF/F: $175   **G/VG: $55**

Rives, Amelie. *World's-End.*
First Edition: New York: Frederick A.
Stokes, 1914.
NF/F: $65   **G/VG: $20**

Roe, E. P. *Opening a Chestnut Burr.*
First Edition: New York: Dodd Mead, 1874.
NF/F: $40   **G/VG: $15**

**Rolfe, Frederick William (as by
Baron Corvo).** *Hadrian The Seventh.*
First Edition: London: Chatto &
Windus, 1904.
NF/F: $5,700   **G/VG: $3,000**

_____. *Don Tarquinio. A
Kataleptic Phantasmatic Romance.*
First Edition: London: Chatto &
Windus, 1905.
NF/F: $3,400   **G/VG: $1,600**

_____. *Stories Toto Told Me.*
Points of Issue: Paperback Original,
green/gray wraps printed by John
Wilson & Son at the University Press,
Cambridge, Mass.
First Edition: London: John Lane, The
Bodley Head, 1898.
NF/F: $700   **G/VG: $300**

Russell, William Clark. *A Strange
Voyage.*
First Edition: London: Sampson Low,
Marston, Searle & Rivington, 1885.
NF/F: $250   **G/VG: $100**

_____. *List Ye Landsmen! A
Romance of Incident.*
First Edition: London & New York:
Cassell, 1892.
NF/F: $75   **G/VG: $30**

Saltus, Edgar. *Mr. Incoul's
Misadventure.*
First Edition: New York: Benjamin &
Bell, 1887.
NF/F: $125   **G/VG: $45**

_____. *Imperial Purple.*
First Edition: Chicago: Morrill,
Higgins, 1892.
NF/F: $95   **G/VG: $30**

_____. *A Transient Guest and
Other Episodes.*
First Edition: Chicago, New York
and San Francisco: Belford, Clarke;
London: Henry J. Drane, 1889.
NF/F: $135   **G/VG: $50**

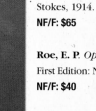

E. P. Roe.

Edgar Saltus.

Shaw, Henry Wheeler (as by Josh Billings). *Josh Billings on Ice.*
First Edition: New York: G.W. Carleton, 1868.
NF/F: $195   **G/VG: $45**

_____. *Old Probability : Perhaps Rain - Perhaps Not.*
First Edition: New York G.W. Carleton 1879.
NF/F: $125   **G/VG: $50**

_____. *Everybody's Friend.*
First Edition: Hartford, CT: American Publishing, 1874.
NF/F: $100   **G/VG: $30**

Smith, Elizabeth Oakes. *Bertha and the Lily.*
First Edition: Boston: Cinn Derby, 1854.
NF/F: $350   **G/VG: $100**

Southworth, Emma D.E.N. *The Bridal Eve.* Points of Issue: Paperback Original.
First Edition: New York: Street & Smith, 1901.
NF/F: $35   **G/VG: $10**

_____. *The Gipsy's Prophecy. A Tale of Real Life.*
First Edition: Philadelphia: T.B. Peterson & Brothers, 1861.
NF/F: $185   **G/VG: $65**

Spofford, Harriet Prescott. *The Thief in the Night.*
First Edition: Boston: Roberts Brothers, 1872.
NF/F: $275   **G/VG: $125**

_____. *The Maid He Married.*
First Edition: Chicago: Herbert S. Stone, 1899.
NF/F: $200   **G/VG: $85**

Stephens, Ann Sophia. *Fashion and Famine: A Tale.*
First Edition: London: W. Kent/Ward & Lock, 1854.
NF/F: $125   **G/VG: $45**

Stevenson, Robert Louis. *David Balfour: Being Memoirs of His Adventure at Home and Abroad.*
First Edition: London: Cassell, 1893. Points of Issue: First Issue has the following points: page 40, line 11 "business"; page 64, line 1 "nine o'clock"; page 101, line 10 "Islands"; as well as the rear ads dated "5G.486" and "5B.486."
NF/F: $350   **G/VG: $110**
First U.S. Edition: New York: Scribners, 1893.
NF/F: $85   **G/VG: $25**

_____. *The Wrecker.*
First Edition: London: Cassell, 1892.
NF/F: $285   **G/VG: $100**

_____. *The Master of Ballantrae.*
First Edition: London: Cassell & Co, 1889.
NF/F: $195   **G/VG: $70**
First U.S. Edition: New York: Scribners, 1889.
NF/F: $165   **G/VG: $65**

Stockton, Frank R. *The Casting Away of Mrs. Lecks and Mrs. Aleshine.*
First Edition: New York: Century Co., 1886. Points of issue: The signatures are numbered on P. 9, 25, 49, 57, 73, 81, 97, 105, 121 and 125 in the first issue.
NF/F: $200   **G/VG: $60**

_____. *Ting-A-Ling.*
First Edition: New York: Hurd and Houghton, 1870.
NF/F: $800   **G/VG: $310**

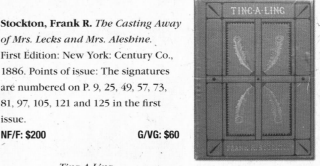

Robert Louis Stevenson.

Frank R. Stockton.

Frank R. Stockton.

Ruth McEnery Stuart.

Albion Winegar Tourgee.

Anthony Trollope.

_____. *The Lady, or the Tiger? and Other Stories.*
First Edition: New York: Scribers, 1884.
NF/F: $1,200   **G/VG: $500**

Stowe, Harriet Beecher. *Uncle Tom's Cabin.*
First Edition: Boston & Cleveland, OH: John P. Jewett & Co. & Jewett, Proctor and Worthington, 1852 (two volumes). Points of Issue: The second printing carries "ten thousand" on the title page.
NF/F: $32,000   **G/VG: $15,000**

_____. *Dred: A Tale of the Great Dismal Swamp.*
First Edition: Boston: Phillips, Sampson, 1856 (two volumes).
NF/F: $1,250   **G/VG: $600**

_____. *Oldtown Folks.*
First Edition: London: Sampson Low, Son, and Marston, 1869 (three volumes).
NF/F: $850   **G/VG: $325**
First U.S. Edition: Boston: Fields, Osgood, 1869.
NF/F: $270   **G/VG: $120**

Stuart, Ruth McEnery. *In Simpkinsville.*
First Edition: New York: Harper & Brothers, 1897.
NF/F: $100   **G/VG: $40**

_____. *The River's Children.*
First Edition: New York: Phelps Publishing Company, 1904.
NF/F: $665   **G/VG: $300**

Terhune, Mary Virginia (as by Marion Harland). *The Royal Road or Taking Him at His Word.*
First Edition: New York: Anson D. F. Randolph and Company, 1894.
NF/F: $85   **G/VG: $25**

Thomas, Frederick William. *East and West. A Novel.*
First Edition: Philadelphia: Carey, Lea & Blanchard, 1836.
NF/F: $400   **G/VG: $165**

Tolstoy, Leo N (Tolstoi, Lyof N). *Anna Karenina.*
First Edition in English: New York: Thomas Y. Crowell and Co., 1886.
NF/F: $2,800   **G/VG: $1,250**

_____. *War and Peace.*
First U.S. Edition: New York, William S. Gottsberger, 1886.
NF/F: $21,500   **G/VG: $10,000**

Tourgee, Albion Winegar. *A Fool's Errand.*
First Edition: New York: Fords, Howard & Hulbert, 1879.
NF/F: $275   **G/VG: $95**

Townsend, Mary Ashley. *Distaff and Spindle.*
First Edition: Philadelphia: J. B. Lippincott, 1895.
NF/F: $140   **G/VG: $55**

Trollope, Anthony. *Lady Anna.*
First Edition: London: Chapman and Hall, 1874.
NF/F: $3,100   **G/VG: $1,200**

_____. *Barchester Towers.*
First Edition: London: Longman,
Brown, Green, Longmans, & Roberts.
1857 (three volumes).
NF/F: $9,500   **G/VG: $4,000**

Turgeniev, Ivan Sergheievitch.
Fathers and Sons.
First Edition in English: New York:
Leypoldt & Holt, 1867.
NF/F: $6,500   **G/VG: $2,800**

Twain, Mark. *The Celebrated*
Jumping Frog of Calaveras County.
First Edition: New York: C. H. Webb,
1867. Points of Issue: Ads precede title
page in first issue "life" is unbroken
in the last line of page 66 and "this" is
unbroken in the last line on page 198.
NF/F: $30,000   **G/VG: $8,500**

_____. *The Prince and the*
Pauper.
First Edition: Boston: James R. Osgood,
1882. Points of Issue: "Franklin Press"
on the verso.
NF/F: $8,200   **G/VG: $3,000**

_____. *Punch, Brothers, Punch!*
And Other Sketches.
First Edition: New York: Slote,
Woodman, 1878. Points of Issue: The
title page of the first issue had "Mark
Twain" in roman type.
NF/F: $1,800   **G/VG: $650**

Wallace, Lew. *Ben-Hur. A Tale of the*
Christ.
First Edition: New York: Harper &
Brothers, 1880. Points of Issue: The first
issue has a misprint on page 11 line 37
"be-became" and a two-line dedication
"To/The Wife of My Youth," changed
to "To/The Wife of My Youth/Who Still
Abides with Me" in later editions.
NF/F: $1,800   **G/VG: $600**

_____. *The Prince of India.*
First Edition: New York: Harper
& Brothers Publishers, 1893 (two
volumes).
NF/F: $175   **G/VG: $55**

Woolson, Constance Fenimore. *For*
the Major.
First Edition: New York: Harper &
Brothers, 1883.
NF/F: $135   **G/VG: $50**

_____. *Horace Chase.*
First Edition: New York: Harper &
Brothers, 1894.
NF/F: $85   **G/VG: $30**

Mark Twain.

Mark Twain.

FIRST EDITION IDENTIFIER

What is a First Edition?

A general definition for a first edition is the first time that a written work appears in a separate cover. This is an elastic definition and can create some disagreement. To take an example:

Paso Por Aqui by Eugene Manlove Rhodes is one of the most famous and sought after Western novels. Its first appearance was in the *Saturday Evening Post* in February of 1927. It was published as the second novel in *Once in the Saddle* by Houghton Mifflin shortly thereafter. It was republished by Houghton Mifflin in 1949 in *The Best Novels and Short Stories of Eugene Manlove Rhodes*. The first edition of *Paso Por Aqui*, by the definition here, is by the University of Oklahoma, in 1973. However, if you can find *Once in the Saddle* in the first printing, you have a book worth, depending on condition, from $500 to $1,000. The University of Oklahoma "first" is worth from $25 to $50.

So, when you say, "first edition" you are basically talking about the first appearance of a piece of writing in book form. Ideally, you want the first printing, the first state, complete as it was issued (with errata slips, dust jacket, etc.) This is important to the collector in the same way an original painting is important to an art collector. It represents the first appearance in the real world of the piece of writing.

While it can be said each publisher has a unique way of marking first editions, there are some basic methods:

METHOD 1
The date on the title page matches the copyright date, and no additional printings are listed on the verso (copyright page).

METHOD 2
The verso does not list additional printings.

METHOD 3
"First Edition," "First Printing," "First Impression," "First Issue" or a variation of these printed on the title page or verso.

METHOD 4
"First Published (date)" or "Published (date)" on the verso.

METHOD 5
A colophon (publisher's logo) printed on the title page, verso or at the end of the book.

METHOD 6
A printer's code, basically a line of numbers or letters printed on the verso, showing a "1" or an A at one end or the other, with certain variations (explanation follows the chart.) If the book has an ISBN number, check this first.

There are also unique methods which are exclusive to a single publisher or only two or three publishers (explanation and list follows the chart.)

METHOD 1

A.A. Wyn, Inc.
A & C Black LTD, Before 1947
Alan Swallow, Publisher
Albert and Charles Boni
Albert Whitman
Alfred A, Knopf Inc.
Alliance Book Corporation
American Publishing
   Company
Arcadia House
Arco Publishing Co. Inc
Argus Books
Arizona Silhouettes
Ashmolean Museum
Atlantic Monthly Press
   (After 1925)
Beacon Press
Ben Abramson
Boni & Gaer Inc.
Books West Southwest
Brentano's, Before 1927
Brewer & Warren
Brewer, Warren and Putnam
Bridge, + Code 1-10
Bruce Humphries, Inc.
Cameron Associates
Century Company (US), Fitfully
Charles Scribner's
   Sons (Before 1929),
   Before 1929
Chaterson Limited
Columbia University
Creative Press
Crown Publishers
David McKay Co. Inc.
Deseret
Dial Press (Lincoln MacVeagh)
Dietz Press
Dodd Mead & Co.
Duffield & Co.
Duffield & Green
Duke University
Dunster House Bookshop
Edward J. Clode Inc.
Elliot Stock
Equinox Cooperative Press
Ernest Benn

Falmouth Publishing
   House, Inc.
Forest Press
Four Seas Company
Frances P. Harper
Frederick Stokes & Co.
G. Howard Watt
G.P.Putnam's Sons
G.W.Carleton
George W. Stewart
   Publisher Inc.
Greenberg, Publisher, Inc.
H.C. Kinsey & Company Inc.
H.W.Wilson Company
Harrison Smith &
   Robert Haas Inc.
Harrison Smith Inc.
Harvard University Press
Hastings House
   Publishers, Inc.
Henry Holt & Co. Inc.
Henry Schumann Inc.
Hill & Wang
Hillman-Curl, Inc.
Hogarth Press
Holt Rinehart & Winston Inc.
Horace Liveright Inc.
Horizon Press
Howell Soskin Publishers
Indiana University
   Press, Before 1974
Iowa State University Press
IT Publications
Ives Washburn Inc.
James Pott
Janus Press
Jewish Publication Society
John C.Winston Co.
John Murray, Before 1982
John W. Luce & Company
Johns Hopkins
   University Press
Julian Messner
Lantern Press, Inc.
Liveright Publishing Corp.
Loring & Mussey, Inc.
Lothrop Publishing Company

Lothrop, Lee &
   Shepard Co. Inc.
Louisiana State
   University Press
Marshall Jones Company
Martin Hopkinson
McDowell Obolensky
McGraw Hill Book Company
McNally & Loftin, Publishers
Minnesota Historical
   Society (After 1940)
Museum of New Mexico,
   Before 1981
Museum Press
Ohio State University Press
Ohio University Press
Oxford University Press
Pantheon Books, Inc.
Payson & Clarke Ltd.
Pelligrini and Cudahy
Penn Publishing Company
Peter Smith
Princeton University Press
R.R.Bowker
Rae D. Henkle Co. Inc.
Rand McNally & Company
Reilly & Britton Co.
Reilly & Lee Co. Inc.
Reynal and Hitchcock Inc.
Richard R. Smith
Roy Publishers Inc.
Rupert Hart-Davis
Rutgers University Press
Sagamore Press
Sage Books
Sears Publishing Company
Sheridan House Inc.
Simon & Schuster
Something Else Press
Southern Illinois
   University Press
Stackpole Books
Stanford University Press
State Historical Society
   of Wisconsin
Stein & Day Publishers
Stephen Daye Press

Superior Publishing Company
Suttonhouse
Syracuse University Press
Talbot Press Ltd.
Thomas Y. Crowell
Ticknor & Fields
Ticknor and Company
Trident Press
Twayne Publishers Inc.
University of Alabama Press
University of Arizona Press
University of California Press
University of Chicago Press
University of Colorado Press
University of Illinois Press
University of Kentucky Press
University of Miami Press
University of Michigan Press
University of
   Minnesota Press
University of Nebraska Press
University of North
   Carolina Press
University of
   Pennsylvania Press
University of
   Pittsburgh Press
University of
   Tennessee Press
University of Texas Press
University of
   Washington Press
University of Wisconsin
   Press, Before 1970
Vanguard Press
W.A.Wilde Company
Western Reserve University
Westernlore
Weybright and Talley Inc.
Whittlesey House
Willet, Clarke and Company
William-Fredrick Press
William Godwin
William Penn Publishing
   Company
Yale University Press
Ziff-Davis Publishing

METHOD 2

101 Productions
A.H. & A. W. Reed
A. Kroch & Son
A.S.Barnes & Co. Inc.
A. R. Mowbray
Abington Press
Academic Press
Academy Chicago
Ace/Putnam
Acropolis Books
ACS
Adam Hilger
Adirondack Mountain Club
Advocado Press
Ashanta Press
Alan Wolfsy
Alaska Northwest
Alan R. Liss
Albert & Charles Boni
Alfred Publishing
Alfred A, Knopf Inc.
ALICEJAMES Books
Allen A. Knoll
Allen D. Bragdon.
Allen Publishing
Alpha Beat Press
Amber Lane Press
American Bar Foundation
American Catholic Press
American Library
    Association
American Publishing
    Company
Amphoto
Anchorage.Press
Anvil Press
Appletree Press
Applezaba Press
Architectual Book
    Publishing
Archway Press
Arden Press
Argus Book Shop
Arion Press
Arkham House
Arlington House
Art Institute of Chicago

Arthur H. Clark
Asher-Gallant
Ashmolean Museum
Ashton Scholastic
Aspen Publishers
Associated University
    Presses
Asylum Arts
Ave Maria Press
B.W.Dodge & Company
B.W.Huebach
Bailey Bros. & Swinfin
Baker & Taylor
Baker House
Bancroft-Sage
Banyan Books
Barnard & Westwood
Barre Publishing
    Company Inc.
Bartholomew Books
Basil Blackwell
Battery Press
Baylor University
Beechhurst Press
Beehive Press
Behrman House
Being Publications
Bergh Publishing
Bess Press
Bicycle Books
Blackie & (and) Son,
    Before 1957
Blackwell Scientific
Bloch Publishing
Blue Wind Press
Bolchazy-Carducci
Boni & Gaer Inc.
Boni & Liveright
The Book Guild Limited
Bottom Dog Press
Boxwood Press
The Branden Press
Brewer & Warren
Brewer, Warren and Putnam
British Academy
Brockhampton Press
Brompton Books

Bronx County Historical
    Society
Brooke House
Brookings Institute
Brooklyn Botanic Garden
Bruce Publishing
    (Milwaukee, WI)
Bull Run of Vermont
Burning Cities
Burning Deck
Burns & Mac Eachern
Butterworth & Co.
Butterworths PTY
C.M.Clarke Publishing Co.
C. V. Mosby
Caddo Gap
California Institute of
    Public Affairs
California State
    University Press
Camino E.E. & Book Co.
Canada Law Book
Capra
Caratzas Brothers
Carolina Academic Press
Carolina Wren Press
Carolrhoda Books
Carstens
Cassell & Co., Before 1976
Castalia Bookmakers
Castle Books
Catholic University
    Press of America
Cave Books
Caxton Printers
Centaur Press LTD
Center for Japanese Studies
Chapman & Hall
Charles L. Webster
    and Company
Charles Scribner's
    Sons (Before 1929),
    Before 1929
Charles Press
Charles River
Charles T. Branford
Charleton Press

Chatto & Windus
Chester R. Heck
Chilton
China Books
Christian Focus
Christopher Helm
    Publishing LTD
Christopher Publishing
    House
Chronicle Books
Cicerone Press
Citadel Press, Before
    1949 & After 1988
City Lights
Clarity Press
Clarity Press
Clearwater Publishing
Cloud, Inc
Cloudcap
Coffee House
Colonial Williamsburg
    Foundation
Columbia University
Commonwealth Press
Concordia
Conservatory of
    American Letters
Copeland and Day
Copper Beech
Copper Canyon
Cornell Maritime Press
Cornell University Press
Cornerstone
Cosmopolitan Book
    Corporation
Cottage Publications
Council for British
    Archeology
Countryman Press
Covici-Friede
Coward, McCann and
    Geohegan
Coward-McCann Inc.
Creative Age Press Inc.
Crossing Press
Crossroad/Continuum
Crown Publishers

Currency Press
Dana-Estes
Dartmouth Publications
Darnell Corporation
David & Charles LTD
David & Charles PLC
Davis-Poynter
Dembner Books
Denlinger's
DeVorss
Dharma
Dial Press (Lincoln
   MacVeagh)
Diana Press
Diane Publishing
Didier
Dillon Press
Discovery
Disney
Dodd Mead & Co.
Dolphin
Doral
Dorling Kidersley
Doubleday Page & Company
Dreenan Press
Duffield & Co.
Duffield & Green
Dumbarton Oaks
Dunster House Bookshop
E. M. Hale
E.P.Dutton & Co. Inc.
Eastern Press
Eaton & Mains
Eclipse
Eden Publishing
Edmund Ward
Edward Arnold
Edward J. Clode Inc.
Elkin Matthews
Ellicott Press
Elliot Right Way
Emerson Books
Empty Bowl
Ensign Press
Enterprise Publications
Eric Partridge LTD
Eric Partridge LTD
Essex Institute
ETC Publications
Evanston

F.Tennyson Neeley
Fabian Society
Fairchild Books
Famedram
Fields, Osgood & Co.
The Figures
Fithian Press
Fleming H. Revell Company
Flyleaf Press
Fordham University
Forum
Forward Movement
Frances P. Harper
Franciscan University Press
Frank Maurice
Franklin Publishing
Franklin Watts Inc.
Frederick Stokes & Co.
Frederick Ungar
Free Spirit
Freedom Press
G.P.Putnam's Sons
G.W.Carleton
G.W. Dillingham Company
G W Graphics
Gambling Times
Garamond Press
Gaslight
Gay & Hancock
Genealogical Publishing
George Newnes
George Routledge & Sons
George Routledge &
   Sons, Kegan Paul,
   Trench,Trubner
George Weidenfeld
   & Nicholson
Geographical Association
Gill and Macmillan
Golden West
Goose Lane
Gower
Grafton
Granada
Grant Richards
Graphic Arts Center
Gray's
Great Western
Greenberg, Publisher, Inc.
Greenlawn Press

Gresham Press
Grey Fox
Grey Walls
Grindstone Press
Grossman
Gulf Publishing
H.C. Kinsey & Company Inc.
H.W.Wilson Company
Hale, Cushman & Flint
Hammond, Hammond & Co.
Hampshire Bookshop
Hancock House
Hanging Loose Press
Harrison Smith &
   Robert Haas Inc.
Harrison Smith Inc.
Harry Cuff
Harvard Business School
Harvard University Press
Harvey Miller
Hastings House Publishers,
   Inc., letterpress
Haynes
Heath Cranton
Hellman, Williams
Hendrick-Long
Henkle-Yewdale
Henry Altemus
Henry E. Huntington Library
Henry Schumann Inc.
Herald Press
Herbert Jenkins,
   Before 1948
Herbert S. Stone & Co.
Hermitage
Hobby Horse
Hoffman Press
Hogarth Press
Holiday House, Inc.,
   Before 1988
Holmes and Meier
Homestead, guide-books
Hoover Institution
Hope Publishing House
Horn Book
Horwitz Grahame
House of Anansi
Howard University
Howe Brothers
Howell-North

Hull University
Humanities Press
Huntington Library
Hyperion
I. E. Clark
Ian Henry
Icarus Press
Ignatius Press
Illuminated Way
Images Australia PTY
Impact
Indiana Historical Society
Indiana University
   Press , After 1974
Inform
Inner Traditions
Institute of Jesuit
   Sources, Before 1993
Institute of Psychological
   Research
Institute Chemical
   Engineers (UK)
Institute of Electrical
   Engineers (UK)
Intermedia Press
International
   Universities Press
IOP Publishing
Irish Academic Press
Islamic Foundation
Island Press (Australia)
Island Press Cooperative
Ives Washburn Inc.
J.A.Allen & Co.
J. M. Dent & Sons,
   Before 1936
J. Michael Pearson
J. Whittaker & Sons
Jacaranda Press
James M. Heineman
James Nisbet
James R. Osgood and Company
Jargon
Jarolds. After 1948
John Day, After 1937
John Hamilton
John Knox Press
John Lane Company
John Lane The Bodley
   Head LTD, Before 1928

John Long
John Murray, After 1982
John W. Luce & Company
John Wiley & Sons
Johns Hopkins
    University Press
Jonathon Cape and
    Robert Ballou
Jordan (s)
Judson Press
Julian Messner
Juniper Press
Kalmbach
Kayak
KC Publications
Kegan Paul, Trench,
    Trubner & Co., LTD
Kelsey St.
Kindred
King's Crown Press
Lacis
Lantern Press, Inc.
Lawrence and Wishart
Lawrence J. Gomme
Lea
Lea & Febiger
Lee and Shepard
Legacy
Lennard Associates
Lerner Publications
Leyland
Liberty Fund
Lightning Tree
Lillian Barber Press
Little Brown and Company
Little Hills Press PTY LTD
Liveright Publishing Corp.
Liverpool University Press
Livingston
Log House
Longmans Green & Co.
Longstreet House
Lothrop Publishing
    Company
Louise Corteau, Editrice
Louisiana State
    University Press
Lynne Rienner
M. S. Mill
Macaulay

MacFarland, Walter & Ross
Macmillan Inc.
Macy-Masius
Marion Boyars
    Publishers, Inc.
Martin Hopkinson
Maryland State Archives
Maurice Fridberg
Maxwell Droke
McClelland and Stewart
McClure Phillips & Co.
McGraw Hill Ryerson
Medici Society, Child & Art
Memphis State University
Mercer University Press
Mercier Press
Meridian Books
Meridonal
Merlin Press, Inc.
Metropolitan Museum of Art
Michell Kennerly
Michigan State
    University Press
Minton Balch & Co,
Missouri Archaelogical Press
MIT Press
MMB Music
Modern Language
    Association
Modern Age Books
Mojave
Montana Historical Society
Moody Press, After 1960
Morehouse
Morehouse-Barlow
Morehouse-Graham
Morgan & Lester
Morgan & Morgan
Mosaic
Mosby Yearbook
Mountain Press
Moutin de Gruyter
Murray & McGee
Museum of Modern Art
Museum of New Mexico,
    After 1981
Mycroft & Moran
Mystery House
National Foundation Press
National Library of Australia

National Museums
    of Scotland
National Museum of
    Women in the Arts
Nautical and Aviation
Naylor
Neale Publishing Company
Nelson-Hall
Netherlandic Press
New Directions, After 1976
New Harbinger
New Poets Series
New Republic
New South
New South Wales
    University Press
New View
Nine Muses
Nonesuch
North Atlantic
North Point Press,
    Before 1988
North Star
Northwestern
    University Press
Northwoods Press
Noyes, Platt & Company
Oak Knoll
Oakwood Press
O'Hara
Ohio University Press
Oliver Durrell
On Stream
Open Court
Orbis
Oregon Historical Press
Oregon State
    University Press
Oriel Press
O'Reilly and Associates
Otago
Outrider Press
Outrigger
Oxmoor House
Oyez
P & R
Pacific Books
Padre Productions,
    Before 1994
Para Publishing

Paraclete Press
Pascal Covici
Passport Press
Paternoster
Pathway Press
Patrice Press
Paul Elek
Paul S. Eriksson
Payson & Clarke Ltd.
Pelican Publishing
Penn Publishing Company
Pennsyvania State
    University Press
Pennyworth Press
Peregrine Smith
Permanent Press, 1988-1993
Perry & North
Peter Halban
Phaidon Press
Philosophical Library
Phoenix Book Shop
Philip Allan & Co.
Philip C. Duschnes
Pickering & Inglis LTD
Picton Press
Pictorial Histories
Plenum
Plough Publishing House
Poet's Press
Poetry Bookshop
Polygonal
Poolbeg Press
Post-Apollo
Potomac Books
Prentice-Hall
Prentice-Hall Australia
Preservation Press
Press Porcepic
Primavera Press
Princeton University Press
Prism Press
Puckerbush
Pudding House
Pulp Press
Pulse-Finger Press
Purdue University Press
Purchase Press
Pygmy Forest Press
Quadrangle
Quail Street

Quixote
R & E
R.H.Russell
R.R.Bowker
Rabeth Publishing,
    Before 1995
Ragweed Press
Rainbow Books
Reed Books PTY
Reference Publications
Regnery Gateway
Regular Baptist Press
Reilly & Britton Co.
Reilly & Lee Co. Inc.
Renaissance House
Resources for the Future
Riba
Richard G. Badger
Richard Marek
Richard R. Smith
Richards Press
Robert Hale
Robert R. Knapp
Robert Welch
Roberts Brothers
Rocky Mountain Books
Rosendale Press
Royal Society
Royal Society of Chemistry
Running Press
Russell-Sage
Rutgers University Press
S. Evelyn Thomas
Sage Books
St. Botolph
St. James Press
St. Martin's Press, Inc.
Salem House
Samuel Curl
San Diego State
    University Press
Sand Dollar
Sandhill Crane Press
Scarlet Press
Schoken
Scottish Academic Press
Sea Horse
Sears Publishing Company
Second Coming
Sepher-Hermon Press

Seren Books
Servant Publications
Sheed & Ward Inc.
Shengold
Sheridan House Inc.
Sherman French & Company
Shire
Shoal Creek
Sidgwick & Jackson LTD
Silver Burdett Company
Sixteenth Century Journal
Skeffington & Son
Skelton Robinson
Small Maynard and
    Company
Smith Settle
Society for Promoting
    Christian Knowledge
Soho Book Company
Som Publishing
Something Else Press
Sono Nis Press
SOS Publications
Southbound Press
Southern Illinois
    University Press
Southern Methodist
    University Press
Southwest Press
Sphere Books
Stackpole Sons
Stanton and Lee
Stanwix House
State University Of
    New York Press
Stream Press
Stein & Day Publishers
Stephen Daye Press
Stephen Greene
Sterling
Stone and Kimball
Stobart & Sons
Stobart Davies Ltd.
Storm
Stormline Press
Strawberry Hill
Studio Limited
Studio Publications
Sulzberger & Graham
Suttonhouse

Swallow Press (Ohio
    University)
T & T Clark Limited
T. S. Denison
Tabb House
Talisman House
Talon Books
Tamaroack Books
Tandem Press (U. S.)
Tatsch
Temple University Press
Texas Christian
    University Press
Texas Western Press
Thames and Hudson Ltd.
Thames and Hudson Pty.
Thistledown Press
Thomas Jefferson University
Thomas Seltzer
Thomas Y. Crowell,
    After 1926
Thunder's Mouth,
    Before 1993
Tia Chucha
Ticknor & Fields
Ticknor and Company
Transaction Books
Trend House
Trident Press
Trout Creek
TSG
Tundra Books of Montreal
Tundra Books of
    Northern New York
Turner Co.
Turner Publishing
Turtle Island
Turton & Armstrong PTY
Twayne Publishers Inc.
Twentieth Century Fund
Twenty-Third Publications
Universe Books
University Books
University Classics
University of Arizona Press
University of Arkansas Press
University of British
    Columbia Press
University of Calgary Press
University of California Press

University of Chicago Press
University of Georgia Press
University of Hull Press
University of Illinois
    Press, Before 1985
University of Kansas
    Museum of Natural
    History
University of
    Massachusetts Press
University of Missouri Press
University of New
    South Wales
University of North
    Carolina Press
University of
    Pennsylvania Press
University of
    Queensland Press
University of
    Rochester Press
University of Utah Press
University of Wales Press
University Press of America
University Press of Colorado
University Press of Florida
University Press of Hawaii
University Press of Kansas
University Press of
    Mississippi
University Press of
    New England
University Press of Virginia
University Presses of Florida
University Society
Unwin, Hyman, Inc.
Urizen Books
Van Nostrand Reinhold
Van Petten
Vandamere
Vedanta
Vestal Press
Victor Gollancz
Viet Nam Generation
Viking Penguin
Viking Press
Vixen
W.A.Wilde Company
W. D. Hoard
W. H. Freeman

W. Heffer & Sons
Wm. B. Eerdmans
Wadsworth Publishing
Walter Neale
Warren H. Green
Wartburg Press
Watermark Press
Watson-Guptill
Way and Williams
Wayne State
  University Press
Webb Research
Westcott Cove
West Coast Poetry Review

Western Producer
  Prairie Books
Westernlore
Westland
Westminster Press,
  After 1977
Westview
White Cockade
White Pine
Whitehorse Press
Wilderness Press
Wilfred Funk
Willet, Clarke and Company
William Blackwood & Sons

William Carey Library
William Collins & Son
William Edward Rudge
William Heinemann,
  Before 1920
William L. Bauhan
William Morrow & Co.
  Inc., After 1976
Williams & Wilkins
Winchester Press
Windswept House
Windward House
Windward Publishing
Wingbow Press, Before 1981

Winston-Derek
Wishart, After 1935
Wolfhound Press
Wood Lake
Woodbridge Press
World Leisure
World Resources
World Scientific
Yachting
Yale Center for British Art
Ziff-Davis Publishing
  Company
Ziggurat Press
Zondervan

METHOD 3

A & C Black LTD, After 1947
Adam and Charles Black
Ace
Aivia Press
Alabatross Books
Aletheia Publishing
Alfred A, Knopf Inc.
Altamount Press
Alyson Publications
Ancient City Press
Andrews and McMeel
Antique Collector's Club
Antonson Publishing
Aperture
Ariel Press
Artabras
Atheneum Publishers
Atlantic Monthly Press
  (After 1925)
Avon
Baachus Press
Barlenmir House
Barricade Books
Beach Holme
Beautiful America
Berkshire House
Bern Potter
Bernard Geis Associates
Better Homes and Gardens
Bhaktivedanta Book Trust
Big Sky
Big Table

Birch Brook Press
Black Swan
Black Tie Press
Blue Dove Press
Boa Editions
Bobbs-Merrill Company
Boni & Liveright, fitfully
The Borgo Press
Bradt Publications,
  Before 1989
Brentano's , After 1927
Brick Row
Broadside Press
Brown, Son & Ferguson
Bruccoli Clark Layman
Bulfinch Press
Burgess & Wickizer
Burns, Oates & Washbourne,
  After 1937
Bush Press
Cadmus Editions
Calder Publications
Cambridge University
  Press (UK & Australia)
Camden House
Camelot
Captain Fiddle
Cardoza
Carnegie Mellon
Carpenter Press
Causeway Press Limited
Cecil Palmer

Cedar Bay Press
Celestial Arts
Center for Afro-
  American Studies
Center for Western Studies
Centerstream
Chariot
Chatham Press
Cheever
Chelsea Green
Chicago Review
Christopher-Gordon
Christopher Helm
Citadel Press
Clarkson N. Potter Inc.
Claude Kendall &
  Willoughby Sharp
Claude Kendall Inc.
Cliffhanger Press
Coldwater Press
Collier
Conari Press
Cosmopolitan Book
  Corporation, After 1927
Cottage Press
Covici-Friede
Covici-McGee
Coward, McCann and
  Geohegan
Coward-McCann Inc.
Crossway Books (UK)
Culinary Arts

Curbstone
Cypress Press
Dalkey Archive
David R. Godine
DAW Books
Dawn Horse Press
Delacorte Press
Depth Charge
Dial Press
Dimi Press
Dodge Publishing Company
Dog Ear Press
Donning
Dorial
Dorrance & Co.
Dorsey Press
Doubleday & Co.
Doubleday Doran & Company
Doubleday Page & Company
Douglas West
Down Home
Duell, Sloan and Pearce
Duffield & Co., Fitfully
Duffield & Green
Dustbooks
E.P.Dutton & Co. Inc.
Eagle's View
Eakin Press
Earth Magic
East Woods Press
Ecco Press
Eden Press

Edgar Rice Burroughs
Educational Technology
Eighth Mountain
Entwhistle Books
EPM Publications
Epworth Press
Eric Partridge LTD
Europa
F. S. Crofts
Fantasy Publishing
Far Corner
Farrar & Rinehart Inc.
Farrar Straus & Cudahy
Farrar Straus and Giroux
Farrar Straus
Feminist Press
Feral House
Fiction Collective
Fjord Press
Follet Publishing Company
Fordham University
Four Walls Eight Windows
Franciscan Press
Franklin Watts Inc.
Frederic C. Beil
Fromm International
Gaff Press
Gambit
Ganley
Gannet
Garber
Gaslight
George Braziller Inc.
George H. Doran & Co.
George Newnes
George Shumway
Gibbs Smith
Girl Scouts of America
Glade House
GLB Publishers
Gleniffer Press
Globe Pequot
Globe Press
Gnome Press
Gnomon Press, After 1991
Gold Eagle
Golden West Historical
   Publications
Gollehon, After 1995
Great Ocean

Grebner Books
Green Books
Greenfield Review
Greenwillow
Greystone Press
Grove Press
Gryphon
Gumbs & Thomas
Harcourt Brace etc.
Harper & Row
Harper Collins
Harpswell
Harrison Smith &
   Robert Haas Inc.
Harrison Smith Inc.
Hawthorn
Haynes
Heat Press
Heimburger House
Henry Holt & Co. Inc.
Herbert Jenkins, After 1948
Hermes Publications
Hermitage House
High-Lonesome Books
Historic New Orleans
Holiday House, Inc.,
   After 1988
Holt Rinehart & Winston Inc.
Homestead
Horace Liveright Inc.
Howell Press
Hudson Hills
Humanics Publishing
IDE House
Industrial Press
Info Devil
Institute of Jesuit
   Sources, After 1993
International Publishers
Ivor Nicholson & Watson
J.B.Lippencott
James Nisbet
Jane's Information Group
Jewish Publication Society
John F. Blair
John Calder
John Muir
Jonathon David
Joseph J. Binns
Junius-Vaughn

Kalimat Press
Kanchenjunga
Kensington
Kent State University Press
Kitchen Sink
Kivaki Press
Know Inc.
Kodansha International
L.C.Page & Co.
Ladan
Lahontian Images
Lane Publishing
Lapis Press
Larin
Lawrence Hill
Lerner Publications
Levite of Apache
Leyland
Liberty Bell Press
Libra Press
Library of America,
   Complilations
Lightning Tree, Sporatic
Liguori, After 1994
Limelight
Little Brown and Company
Llewellyn
Longmans Green & Co.
Lord John Press
Loring & Mussey, Inc.
M.Barrows & Company
MacLay & Associates
Macmillan Inc.
Macrae-Smith Company
Mark Zieseng
Masquerade Books
Maupin House
May Davenport
McGraw Hill Book Company
McPherson
Meredith Books
Meriwether
Merriam-Webster
Michael Haag
Michael Kesend
Middle Atlantic Press
Mockingbird Books
Moffat Yard and Company
Monad Press
Moon Publications

Morton
Mountaineers Books
Multimedia Publishing
Mysterious Press
Mystic Seaport Museum
Nags Head Art
Naiad Press
National Woodlands
Nelson, Foster & Scott
New Amsterdam
New Dawn
New Directions, After 1970
New England Cartographics
New England Press,
   After 1986
New Native Press
New Star
New York Culture Review
New York Graphic Society
New York Zoetrope
Noonday
Northland, After 1972
Oakhill Press
Oberlin College Press
Ocean View
Odyssey Press
O'Laughlin
Oliver & Boyd
Open Hand
Overlook Press
Oxford University Press
Oxmoor House, Art Books
Padre Productions,
   After 1994
Panjandrum
Paragon House
Parnassus
Pascal Covici, Fitful
Pathfinder
Paul A. Struck
Pegasus Publishing
Pen Rose
Penmaen Press
Penzler Books
Pequot Press
Pergamon Press Inc.
Permanent Press, After 1993
Persea Books
Peter Marcan
Philosophical Research

Pineapple Press, After 1985
Plan B
Playwrights Canada
Plympton Press
Pocahontas Press
Pressworks Publishing
Price/Stern/Sloan
Pruett
Purple Finch Press
Purple Mountain Press
Pushcart Press
Pyne Press
Quail Ridge Press
Quest (Theosophical Society)
Quill & Brush
Quill Driver
Rabeth Publishing,
    After 1995
Ram
Ramparts Press
Random House Inc.
Ranger International
Ravian Press
Rawson, Wade
Raymond Flatteau
Reader's Digest, Anthologies
Real Comet Press
Red Crane
Redbird Press
Regent House
Reilly & Lee Co. Inc.,
    After 1937
Release Press
Reynal and Hitchcock Inc.
Rice University Press
Rich & Cowan
Rider
Rising Tide Press
Rivercross
Rizzoli International

Robert M. McBride
Robert Speller
Rockbridge
Rockport Press
Rough Guides LTD
Roundwood Press
Royal House
Safari Press
Saint Bede's
St. Herman of Alaska
    Brotherhood
St. Paul's House
Saltire House
Seaver
Self-Counsel Press
Seven Star
Seymour Lawrence
Shambhala
Sheffield Academic Press
Simon & Schuster
Sleepy Hollow Restorations
The Smith
Sohnen-Moe
Soho Press
Sphinx
Spoon River
Spring Publications
Stackpole Books
Station Hill
Stemmer House
Stephen-Paul
Steve Davis
Still Waters Press
Stone Wall Press
Stonehill
Strether and Swann
Summit
Sun & Moon Press
Sun Publishing, After 1981
Sunnyside

Sunset Publishing
Suttonhouse, After 1937
Swallow Press
Tafford
Talon Books, After 1994
Tamarack Press
Taplinger Publishing Co. Inc.
Taunton Press
Texas A & M University Press
Texas Monthly Press
Texas Tech University Press
Theater Arts
Theosophical Publishing
    House (Wheaton)
Theosophical
    University Press
Thunder's Mouth, After 1993
Tilbury House
Times Books
TOR
Tory Corner Editions
Trail's End Publishing Inc.
Transatlantic Arts
Treehaus
Triumph
Troubador
Two Bytes
Underwood-Miller
University of Alaska Press
University of Illinois
    Press, After 1985
University of New
    Mexico Press
University of Oklahoma Press
University of South
    Carolina Press
University of
    Tennessee Press
University of Wisconsin
    Press, After 1970

Urban Institute
Ure Smith
U. S. Games Systems
Viking UK
Villard
Vision Books
W. H. & O.
W & R Chambers
W. W. Norton, Before 1976
Wake-Brook House
Washington Researchers
Washington State
    University Press
Water Row Press
Waterfront
Watson-Guptill
Weatherhill
Webb Publishing
Wesleyan University Press
Westminster/John Knox
Whitson
William Morrow & Co.
    Inc., Before 1976
William Sloane
    Associates Inc.
Wilfred Funk
Wingbow Press, After 1981
Wisconsin House
Witherby
Woman's Press
World Bank
World Publishing Company
Yankee
Yellow Hook
Zephyr Press
Zephyrus Press
Zero Press
Zoland Books

METHOD 4

A & C Black Limited
A.C.McClurg & Co.
ABC (All Books for Children)
Abelard-Schuman, Ltd.
Airlife Publishing
Alan Sutton
Alan Swallow, Publisher
Albyn Press
Allan Wingate
Allen Publishing
Amber Lane Press
Anderson Press
Andrew Dakers
Andre Deutsch
Angus and Robertson
Antique Collector's Club
Aquarian Press
Architectual Press
Arlen House
Art and Education Publishers
Arthur Baker
Ashgrove Press
Auckland University Press
Avalon Press
B.T.Batsford
Background Books
Banner of Truth Trust
Barn Owl Books
Basil Blackwell and Mott
    (Basil Blackwell Limited)
BBC Books
Bergin & Garvey
Bernard's LTD
Black Lace
Blackie & (and) Son,
    After 1957
Blanford Press
Bloodaxe Books
The Bodley Head
The Book Guild Limited
Boydell & Brewer
Boydell Press
Bradt Publications,
    After 1989
Brick Row
British Library
British Museum

British Museum Press
Burke Publishing
Burns, Oates & Washbourne,
    Before 1937
Butterworth-Heinemann
Butterworth Scientific
Butterworths
C. & J. Temple
C. W. Daniel
Cambridge University
    Press (North America)
Canterbury University Press
Carcanet New Press
Cassell & Co., After 1976
Cassell LTD
Cassell Publishers/ PLC
Castle Books
Century (UK)
Century Benham
Century Hutchinson
Charles Knight
Cherrytree Press
Christian Classics
Christopher Johnson
Cleaver-Hume
Colin Smythe
Constable & Company
Co-Operative Union LTD
Cork University Press
Country Life LTD
Cressrelles
D. S. Brewer
Darton, Longman & Todd
Dee-Jay Publications
Dennis Dobson
Department of Primary
    Industries
Downlander
Ebury Press
Edinburgh University Press
Eldon Press
ELM Publications
Ernest Benn
Evans Brothers
Eveleigh Nash and Grayson
Eyre & Spottiswoode
Faber & Faber

Faber & Gwyer
Fairchild Books
Falcon Pres
Far Corner
Fernhurst
Firebird Books
Focal Press
Frances Lincoln, After 1988
Frank Cass
Frederic C. Beil
Frederick Fell Publishers
Frederick Muller
Funk & Wagnells Inc.
G. Bell & Sons
G.W.Dillingham Company
Geoffrey Bles
Geoffrey Chapman
George Allen & Unwin
George Harrap
Gerald Duckworth
Gerald Howe
Gordon Fraser Gallery
Grafton
Granada
Granta
Grayson & Grayson
Graywolf
Greenwood
Greville Press
Grey Seal
Guiness
Halcyon Press
Hamish Hamilton
Hannibal Books
Harcourt Brace etc.
Harper Collins PTY (Aust.)
Harper Collins LTD (N.Z.)
Harrap Ltd
Harrap Publishing
Harvester Press
Heinemann New Zealand
Henry Holt & Co. Inc.
Henry T. Coates & Co.
Her Majesty's
    Stationary Office
Herbert Press
Hill of Content

H. Karnac LTD
Hodder & Stroughton
Hollis and Carter
Holt Rinehart & Winston Inc.
Houghton Mifflin Australia
Houghton Mifflin Company
Hugh Evelyn
Humanities Press
    International
Hurst & Blackett
Hutchinson
Institute of Education
Intellect
IPD Enterprises
Italica Press
J.B.Lippencott
J. Garnet Miller
J. M. Dent & Sons, After 1936
Jacaranda Wiley
James & James
James Duffy
Jarolds, Before 1948
John Day, Before 1937
John Lane The Bodley
    Head LTD, After 1928
John Westhouse
Jonathon Cape
Jonathon Cape and Robert
    Ballou, fitfully
Jonathon Cape &
    Harrison Smith
Journeyman Press
Kevin Weldon &
    Associates PTY
L.C.Page & Co.
Lansdowne Press
Latimer House
Leicester University Press
Leo Cooper
Lewis Copeland Company
Lindsay Drummond
Lone Eagle
Longman, Inc.
Longman Cheshire PTY
Lothrop, Lee &
    Shepard Co. Inc.
Lovatt Dickson

Luman Christi
Lund Humphries
Lutterworth
MacDonald
Macy-Masius
Mansell
Marion Boyars
   Publishers. LTD
Martin Brian & O'Keefe LTD
Martin Secker & Warburg,
   After 1976
McClure Phillips & Co.
McPhee Gribble PTY
Medici Society
Melbourne University Press
Mercat Press
Merlin Books LTD
Methuen
Michael Joseph
Milestone
Mills & Boon
Motorbooks
National Library of Scotland
Neville-Spearman
New American Library
New English Library
New Woman's Press
Noel Douglas
Oasis Books
O'Brien
Old VicarageOMF
   International
Open University Press
Orion
Pan, Antholog-ies
Pan Macmillan PTY

Patrick Stephens Ltd.
Pegasus Press
Penguin (Australia)
Perivale Press
Peter Davies
Peter Owen
Pleiades Books
Porpoise Press
Prager
Prentice-Hall UK
Price Milburn
Proscenium
Quota Press
R.Cobden-Sanderson
Rand McNally & Company
Reed Publishing LTD
Reinhardt Books
Rex Collings
Riccardi Press
Richard W. Baron
Rigby LTD
Riverrun
Robert M. McBride
Roland Harvey
Routledge
Routledge, Chapman,
   and Hall
Roulege & Kegan Paul
Royal College of General
   Practitioners
Rupert Hart-Davis
S. B. Publications
Sage Publications LTD
Saint Andrews Press
St. Martin's Press (Australia)
Saltire House

Samuel Weiser
Scarthin Books
SCM Press LTD
Search Press
Selwyn & Blount
Serpent's Tail
Sheldon Press
Shepheard-Walwyn
Sidgwick & Jackson
   (Australia)
Sigma Books
Silver Link
Sinclair-Stevenson
Skoob
Smith Gryphon
Spindlewood
Spinifex Press
SR Books
Stephen Greene, After 1984
Street & Massey
Sunflower
T & A D Poyser
T. N. Foulis
T. Werner Laurie
Tandem Press (New Zealand)
Thames and Hudson Inc.
Thomas Nelson & Sons

Thomas Telford
Thornton Butterworth
Thorson's
Tolley Publishing
Town House and
   Country House
Transportation Trails
Trigon Press

Turnstone
UCL Press
Unicorn Press
University College of
   Cape Breton Press
University of Montana
   Linguistics Laboratory
University Of Otago Press
University of Western
   Australia Press
Unwin, Hyman Limited
Ure Smith
Veloce
Victoria University Press
Viking Press
Virago Press
Virgin
W. Heinemann
Walker and Co.
Walter McVitty
Ward Lock
Weidenfeld & Nicholson
Wheat Forders
Whitney Library of Design
Widescope International PTY
William Collins PTY
William Heinemann,
   After 1920
William Kimber
William R. Scott
Williams & Northgate
Windrush Press
Winslow
Wishart, Before 1935
Yale University Press
Ziff-Davis Limited

METHOD 5

Adastra Press
Bobbs-Merrill Company,
   Before 1936
Brewin Books

Bruce Humphries, Inc.
Carriage House
Coward-McCann Inc.,
   Before 1936

Farrar & Rinehart Inc.
Farrar Straus & Cudahy
Farrar Straus and Giroux
Farrar Straus

Frederick Stokes & Co.
George H. Doran & Co.
Rinehart
Wilde & Johnson

METHOD 6

A. L. Burt
Abington Press
Altermus
Avenel
Black's Reader's Service
Blakiston
Blue Ribbon Books
Blue Star
Bracken Books

Collier, Before 1989
Cupples & Leon
Dover
Eland Books
Fiction Library
Goldsmith
Greenwich House
Grosset & Dunlap
Hurst

J. Walter Black
Library of America
Literary Guild
Little Blue Books
Modern Library
New Classics
Pan
Reader's Digest
Rio Grande Press

Saalfield
Street and Smith
Sun Dial
Thorndike Press
Tower
Triangle
Ye Galleon

ENGLISH LANGUAGE PUBLISHERS USING UNIQUE OR SEMI-UNIQUE METHODS

D.Appleton & Co. Appleton-Century Crofts*: The print run is at the end of the text, (1) being a First Edition.

Arcadia House: No date on Title page, "1" on the verso.

Arkham House: Carried a colophon page with edition noted at the end of the text.

Black Sparrow: Edition and Printing noted on colophon page in the rear and the title page printed in color.

Bruce Publishing (St. Paul, MN): The printing is indicated in the lower left corner of the last page.

Carrick & Evans Inc.: First Editions have an "A" on the verso.

Cokesbury Press: First Editions have a "C" at the foot of the verso.

Coward-McCann: To 1936 put a colophon on verso, a colophon with a torch signified a first edition.

Thomas Y. Crowell Company Inc.: The First Edition has a "1" at the foot of the verso.

Jonathon David: A number "1" above the date on the verso indicates a first edition.

Stanley Gibbons: The Edition number is carried on the title page.

Golden Cockerell: A limited edition publisher, exceptions to exclusive first editions in their line (reprints) are: *Adam & Eve & Pinch Me* (1921), *Rummy* (1932), and *Tapster's Tapestry* (1938) by A. E. Coppard; *Tersichore & Other Poems* (1921) by H.T. Wade-Gery; *The Puppet Show* (1922) by Matin Armstrong; *Consequences* (1932) and *Anthology; The Hansom Cab* and the *Pigeons* (1935) by L. A. G. Strong; *The Epicure's Anthology* (1936) edited by Nancy Quennell; *The Tale of the Golden Cockerell* (1936) by A. S. Pushkin; *Chanticleer* (1936) *a Bibliography; Ana the Runner* (1937) by Patrick Miller; *Here's Flowers* (1937) *An Anthology* Edited by Joan Ritter; *Mr. Chambers and Persephone* (1937), and *The Lady from Yesterday* (1939) by Christopher Whitfield; *Goat Green* (1937) by T. F. Pwys; *The White Llama* (1938) *Being the La Venganza del Condor of V. G. Calderon; Brief Candles* (1938) by Lawrence Binyon; and *The Wisdom of the Cymry* (1939) by Winifred Faraday.

Grune & Stratton: "A" on the last page of the index indicates a first printing.

Harcourt Brace, etc.*: No date on Title page, "1" on the verso. Also "First Edition" over a line of letters beginning with B.

Harper, etc.: Uses all methods except 5.

From 1912 to 1971 used a number code for Month and Year, month starting with A-January through M (excepting J) December followed by the year alphabetically beginning with M-1912, and returning to A in 1926, and 1951. Code corresponding to copyright date is a First. Thusly:

A-Jan	G-Jul
B-Feb	H-Aug
C-Mar	I-Sep
D-Apr	K-Oct
E-May	L-Nov
F-Jun	M-Dec

M-1912 A-1926 P-1940

N-1913 B-1927 Q-1941

O-1914 C-1928 R-1942

P-1915 D-1929 S-1943

Q-1916 E-1930 T-1944

R-1917 F-1931 U-1945

S-1918 G-1932 V-1946

T-1919 H-1933 W-1947

U-1920 I-1934 X-1948

V-1921 K-1935 Y-1949

W-1922 L-1936

X-1923 M-1937

Y-1924 N-1938

Z-1925 O-1939

Herald Press: Before 1993, carried the publication date below the publisher's imprint on the title page on first editions only.

IGI Publications: A number "1" next to the last page number signifies a first edition.

Wayne L. McNaughton: Three numbers seperated by . as 1.1.1. The first is the stock number, second, edition, third, print run

Mycroft & Moran: Carried a colophon page with edition noted at the end of the text.

Permanent Press: Carried a colophon page with edition noted at the end of the text.

Random House: "First Edition" stated over a number line beginning at 2.

Charles Scribner's Sons*-: Between 1929 and 1973 an "A" on the verso designated a First. A colophon accompanying the A was fitfully used at the foot of the verso.

Martin Secker: Bibliographic history on the verso.

Martin Secker & Warburg: Bibliographic history on the verso.

Sheed & Ward LTD: Bibliographic history on the verso.

Frederick Warne & Co. Inc.: A number 1 at the foot of the verso is a First.

Franklin Watts Inc.*: A number 1 at the foot of the verso is a First.

BOOKMAN'S GLOSSARY

Advance Reading Copy: Abbreviated ARC. A copy distributed to reviewers and/or the book trade previous to publication (See also: Uncorrected Proof).

Association copy: A book given to an acquaintance prominent person by the author, signed or unsigned.

Back matter: Pages following text.

Bands: 1) Cords on which a book is sewn, 2) ridges across the spine of a leather-bound book.

Belles lettres: Literature written for purposes of art, usually poetry, essays and the like.

Beveled boards: Books bound on boards with slanting (beveled) edges.

Bibliography: 1) The technique of describing books academically, 2) the science of books, 3) a book containing and cataloguing other books by author, subject, publisher, etc.

Blind stamp: Embossed impression on a book cover without ink or gilt.

Boards: Hardbound book covers.

Bookplate: Ownership label in a book.

Book sizes:
atlas folio ....16" X 25"
elephant folio .... 14" X 23"
folio ....12" X 15"
4to (quarto)..................9" X 12"
8vo (octavo) ....6" X 9"
12mo (duodecimo)...... 5" X 7 ½"
16mo (Sextodecimo) ....
..................................4¼" X 6 ¾"
18mo (Vicesimo-quarto)............
..................................4" X 6 ¼"
24 mo (Tricesimo) .... 3½" X 6"

Bosses: Metal ornamentations on a book cover.

Broadside: Printed on one side only.

Buckram: Heavy cloth used in book binding.

Cancels: Any part of the book that has been replaced for the original printing, usually to replace defective leaves.

Chapbook: Small format, cheaply made book.

Codex: Manuscript book, or book printed from a hand-written manuscript.

Colophon: A device used by printers and publishers to identify themselves, like a crest. Used by some publishers to designate a first edition.

Copyright: Literally the right to copy or publish.

Copyright page: Reverse of the title page, also called the "verso."

Curiosa: Books of unusual subject matter generally used for occult books and sometimes as a euphemism for erotica.

Dedication: Honorary inscription by an author printed with a literary work.

Deposit copy: Copy of the book deposited in the national library to secure copyright.

Detent: Blind stamp used on rear board to designate a book club edition.

Endpapers: Papers preceding and following the front matter, text and back matter of a book.

Erotica: Books dealing with sexual matters.

Ex-library/ex libris: A book formerly in a library/books formerly owned usually followed by the owner's or former owner's name.

Facsimile: Exact copy or reproduction.

First edition: First appearance of a work, for the most part, independently, between its own covers.

First impression: Synonymous with "First Edition."

First issue: Synonymous with "First Edition."

First printing: Product of the initial print run of a work; is either a "First Edition," or "First Thus."

Flexible binding: 1) A binding of limp material, usually leather, 2) a binding technique that allows a new book to lie flat while open.

Foreword: Same as introduction.

Format: Basically the number of times the printed original is folded: Folio - once. Quarto - twice. Octavo - thrice. Duodecimo - four times. Sextodecimo - five times. Vicesimo-quarto - six times. Tricesimo - seven times.

Foxing: Age darkening of paper, also called "age toning."

Free end paper: Blank page(s) between endpaper and front and back matter.

Front matter: Pages preceding text.

Half-binding: Usually used with leather as "half-leather" or cloth as "half cloth." Spine and corners are in leather or cloth.

Head band: 1) Small band of cloth inside the back of the spine of a book, 2) decorative illustration or photo at the head of a page or chapter.

Imprimatur: A license to publish where censorship exists.

Imprint: 1) Publisher's name, 2) printer's name.

In print: Book is available new.

Incunabula: Books produced before 1501.

Interleaved: Blank pages added to book for notes, etc.

Introduction: Preliminary text, also called foreword.

Jacket: Printed or unprinted paper wrapped around a book, also called dust jacket or dust wrapper.

Leaves: Single pages of a bound book.

Library binding: Endpapers as well as first and last signatures reinforced and smythe sewn.

Limited edition: A single edition for which only a limited number of copies are printed before the printing plates are destroyed.

Marginalia: Notes printed in the margin.

N.d. (no date): Indicates the book has no date of publication or copyright.

N.p. (no place): Indicates a book has no printed place of publication.

Nihil obstat: Indicates a book has the sanction of the Roman Catholic Church.

O.p. (Out of print): Book is no longer available new.

Pirate(d) edition: Book issued without the consent of the copyright holder, usually in another country.

Plate: Illustration printed on special paper and bound with the book.

Points: Additions, deletions or errors that result in identifying points.

Posthumous: Published after the author's death.

Private press: Publisher, usually small and specialized.

Pseudonym: Pen name or false name used by an author.

Quarter binding: Spine covered in cloth or leather.

Reback: Quarter bind over original binding.

Rebind: A book rebound from the original.

Recto: Right hand page, usually used to refer to the title page.

Remainder: Publisher's overstock sold cheaply.

Remainder mark: Any marking used to identify a remaindered book.

Reprint: All printings after the first.

Review copy: Gratis copy of a book sent out for review.

Rubricated: Printed in red and black.

Signature: A folded printed sheet ready for sewing and binding, 2) a letter or number placed on the first page of a signature as a binding guide.

Slip-case: A box manufactured to hold a particular book.

State: A change that occurs during a print run, such as the correction of a typo, or a change in the binding or dust jacket.

Tip in: A leaf added on a single page, or glued to a blank page.

Title page: Page which gives the title, author, publisher, etc., referred to as the "recto."

Unauthorized edition: Same as pirate edition.

Uncorrected proof: Book issued before the final edit, usually used as an advance reading copy or review copy.

Uncut: Leaves that have not been machine cut.

Unopened: Folded edges that have not been cut.

Vanity press: A publisher subsidized by the author.

Variant: Points or states without a known priority.

Verso: Left hand page identified with the copyright page.

Woodcut: Engraving printed from a carved block of wood.

Wormed: Insect damaged.

Wrapper: Separate jacket, or the covers of a paperbound book.

Dig Deeper into Your Collecting

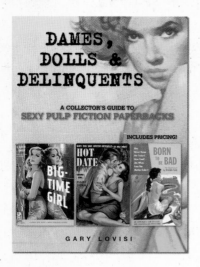
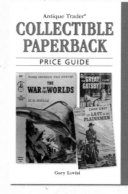